Behold the Antichrist

Behold the Antichrist

Bentham on Religion

Delos B. McKown

Prometheus Books

59 John Glenn Drive
Amherst, New York 14228-2197

Published 2004 by Prometheus Books

Inquiries should be addressed to
Prometheus Books
59 John Glenn Drive
Amherst, New York 14228–2197
VOICE: 716–691–0133, ext. 207
FAX: 716–564–2711
WWW.PROMETHEUSBOOKS.COM

08 07 06 05 04   5 4 3 2 1

Library of Congress Cataloging-in-Publication Data

McKown, Delos Banning.
    Behold the Antichrist : Bentham on religion / Delos B. McKown.
        p. cm.
    Includes bibliographical references and index.
    ISBN 1–59102–116–2
    1. Bentham, Jeremy, 1748–1832—Religion. I. Title.

B1574.B34M38 2003
230'.092—dc22

                                                             2003024467

Printed in Canada on acid-free paper

To Laura Lee and Susan,

whose father

I am delighted to be.

Contents

Abbreviations

Primary Materials

AINR   *Analysis of the Influence of Natural Religion on the Temporal Happiness of Mankind*
CECE   *Church-of-England Catechism Examined*
CJB   *Correspondence of Jeremy Bentham*
NPBJ   *Not Paul, but Jesus*
WJB   *Works of Jeremy Bentham*

Bible Versions

IB   Interlinear Bible, translated by Jay Green
KJV   King James (or Authorized) Version
LB   Living Bible
MLB   Modern Language Bible
MTB   Moffatt Translation
NEB   New English Bible
NT   New Testament
NTIV   New Testament International Version

OT   Old Testament
RSV   Revised Standard Version
TBAT   The Bible, American Translation
WNT   Williams New Testament

DICTIONARIES, ENCYCLOPEDIAS, AND OTHER REFERENCE WORKS

CLD   *Classic Latin Dictionary*
DCR   *Dictionary of Comparative Religion*
DHI   *Dictionary of the History of Ideas*
DNB   *Dictionary of National Biography*
DP   *Dictionary of Philosophy*
DPR   *Dictionary of Philosophy and Religion*
DWO   *Dictionary of Word Origins*
EJ   *Encyclopedia Judaica*
EOR   *Encyclopedia of Religion*
EP   *Encyclopedia of Philosophy*
ERE   *Encyclopedia of Religion and Ethics*
ET   *Encyclopedia of Theology*
EU   *Encyclopedia of Unbelief*
GEL   *Greek-English Lexicon*
GELNT   *Greek-English Lexicon of the New Testament*
HBD   *Harper's Bible Dictionary*
IDB   *Interpreter's Dictionary of the Bible*
LEM   *Larousse Encyclopedia of Mythology*
NCE   *New Columbia Encyclopedia*
ODCC   *Oxford Dictionary of the Christian Church*
ODJR   *Oxford Dictionary of the Jewish Religion*
OED   *Oxford English Dictionary*
REP   *Routledge Encyclopedia of Philosophy*
TCE   *The Catholic Encyclopedia*

JOURNALS

AA   *American Anthropologist*
ABR   *Australian Biblical Review*
AO   *Archives of Ophthalmology*
AR   *American Rationalist*
AS   *American Scholar*
BJECS   *British Journal for Eighteenth-Century Studies*

BNL	Bentham Newsletter
BR	Bible Review
CJT	Canadian Journal of Theology
ER	Edinburgh Review
HJ	Hibbert Journal
HTR	Harvard Theological Review
IESS	International Encyclopedia of the Social Sciences
JBL	Journal of Biblical Literature
JEH	Journal of Ecclesiastical History
JHI	Journal of the History of Ideas
JR	Journal of Religion
JSSR	Journal for the Scientific Study of Religion
KY	Kenyon Review
Mn	Mind
MNL	Mill Newsletter
Na	Nature
NTS	New Testament Studies
Nu	Numen: International Review for the History of Religion
PAAPA	Proceedings and Address of the American Philosophical Association
PC	Problems of Communism
RH	Religious Humanism
RS	Religious Studies
SHR	Southern Humanities Review
SJP	Southern Journal of Philosophy
TAL	The Alabama Lawyer
TRHS	Transactions of the Royal Historical Society
Ut	Utilitas

Magazines

AR	The American Rationalist
CS	Church & State
FI	Free Inquiry
FTh	The Free Thinker
NYTM	New York Times Magazine
Om	Omni Magazine
Pa	Parade Magazine
SA	Scientific American
THu	The Humanist

BULLETINS, NEWSLETTERS, REVIEWS

NS   *New Scientist*
NYRB   *New York Review of Books*
RNCSE   *Reports of the National Center for Science Education*
RW   *Religion Watch*
SHB   *Secular Humanist Bulletin*

NEWSPAPERS

AJC   *Atlanta Journal-Constitution*
BN   *Birmingham News*
BPH   *Birmingham Post-Herald*
KS   *Knoxville Sentinel*
MA   *Montgomery Advertiser*
NYRB   *New York Review of Books*
NYT   *New York Times*
OAN   *Opelika-Auburn News*
SS   *Stars and Stripes*

Preface

At the eleventh hour before the publication of *The Encyclopedia of Unbelief* in 1985, I received a phone call from its editor, Gordon Stein. He wondered whether or not I would do the entries on Jeremy Bentham and John Stuart Mill. Someone, it seems, had failed to deliver. I readily agreed to do the entry on Mill but confessed total ignorance of Bentham on religion. Anticipating my ignorance, Gordon assured me that he would send photocopies of the most important primary materials. True to his word, there quickly arrived three works by Bentham (or by his immediate disciples): *Analysis of the Influence of Natural Religion on the Temporal Happiness of Mankind; Not Paul, but Jesus;* and *Church-of-England Catechism Examined.* To say that I was surprised and excited by what I read in these works is putting it mildly.

With the deadline looming for the submission of the entries on Bentham and Mill, I busied myself and completed these in the nick of time, but at the cost of too little opportunity to become familiar with the more important secondary works on Bentham on religion. Once the entries were finished, I turned again, of necessity, to my routine of administration, teaching, and research at Auburn University, where I was the head professor of the philosophy department. I could not, however, forget Bentham and knew that I must return to him one day to try to do justice to his powerful attacks on religion. It seemed to me that on this topic he had been unfairly overlooked by academics and unbelievers alike.

But, alas, I was dilatory in resuming my work on Bentham. Other demands on my time and energy, an astonishing variety of distractions and diversions, and no small measure of sloth kept me from getting this book finished with dispatch. I continue to pay an emotional price for this, for the essential condition of my book and its chief cheerleader have both ceased to be without ever seeing a word of it. The essential condition was, of course, Gordon Stein, an astonishing polymath and major collector of free-thought literature. Without his request, I am sure I would never have known anything of Bentham on religion. Gordon died prematurely, in 1996, when I was less than two-thirds finished with the work that follows.

If Gordon was the essential condition of this book, then Joseph Fletcher, the founding father of biomedical ethics, was its chief cheerleader. During much of his life, Joe was a theologian of the Episcopal Church, but then, as he said to me in a private conversation, "I went as a visiting scholar to the medical school of the University of Virginia and got *biologized.*" Thereafter, still identifying himself puckishly as a theologian, he shed all vestiges of Christian theology. Joe's cheerleading took two forms, one unconscious, the other conscious. Richard Taylor (himself a distinguished philosopher) once wrote of Fletcher, "He seems to have read everything, and to have analyzed everything he has read."[1] Knowing this, I rejoiced to learn that Joe was as profoundly ignorant of Bentham on religion as I had been and as excited as I was at the treasures that lie in his trenchant analyses thereof. Joe's conscious act of cheerleading consisted in urging me on with all deliberate speed, lest someone beat me to it. Although Joe was rich in years when he died, in 1991, I had scarcely put pen to paper by that time. Imagining today how much Gordon Stein and Joseph Fletcher would have reveled in this book is but a faint shadow of the pleasure I would have enjoyed, putting copies of it into their hands.

In the pages that follow, several nuts and bolts of composition need to be addressed. Since each of the major sections that follows is built around a collection of Bentham's writings, and since each of these sections is lengthy, I have decided to call them parts rather than chapters. Within each part, however, the same pattern of subdivisions appears: (1) a brief intro-duction to the work at issue, followed by a distillation of it plus commen-tary, (2) a defense of it against its critics, and (3) criticisms of mine, showing where Bentham's mistakes really lie. Notes for each part are con-inuously numbered but are found immediately after the chapter to which they refer. Since *Analysis of the Influence of Natural Religion on the Temporal Happiness of Mankind, Not Paul, but Jesus,* and *Church-of-England Catechism Examined* are all about religion in general and Christianity in particular, there is some commonality, but, though all are logically consistent with one another, none is presupposed by any other, nor is any a logical conse-quence of any other. The order in which I have taken them up is arbitrary and could be altered without gain or loss. Accordingly, the reader may read parts 1, 2, and 3 in any order without gain or loss.

Except in direct quotations, I have not accompanied dates with B.C. and A.D. but have adopted the newer symbolism of B.C.E. (Before the Common Era) and C.E. (Common Era). Moreover, I have dispensed with C.E. as unnecessary, since B.C.E. will always be shown when appropriate.

Another matter of style has to do with single quotes. In addition to using single quotes around quotations within quotations, I have used these whenever doing what logicians call *mentioning* a term, rather than *using* that term. For example, in the sentence *the proper tools are essential to getting a job done right*, the word *tools* is being *used* to refer to various implements. In the sentence *'Tools' is a word of five alphabetic characters*, 'tools' is being *mentioned*. Here 'tools' is to be read as the word (term, or symbol) *tools*, the reference being to the word itself and not to anything named by it. Double quotation marks will be used in normal ways: (1) to enclose directed quotations; (2) to name shorter works such as essays, articles, poems, etc.; and (3) to mean "so-called." Being able to distinguish between the use of a term and the mention of a term will be crucial in understanding part 3, wherein Bentham's philosophy of language is featured.

I have routinely used the King James (or Authorized) Version of the Bible, when quoting biblical texts, except when some other translation seems to fix the meaning in question more adequately. I have made this choice for two reasons: (1) Bentham used the King James, except when doing his own translating, and (2) using it fends off carping critics who seem to think that any departure from it puts the reader in danger of accepting satanically inspired mistranslations and consequent misinterpretations. The King James Version, however, is not always the most accurate translation available.

In several direct quotations, the reader will come upon a perplexing mode of reference looking like "UC" or "UCL," followed by Arabic numerals, or by lowercase Roman numerals, or both. These refer to unpublished papers of Bentham, housed at the University of London. My knowledge of these materials, I regret to say, is secondhand, coming as it does through the research of professors James Steintrager and James E. Crimmins, each of whom is quoted on numerous occasions in the pages that follow. While this book awaited publication, Prometheus Books published (in 2003) a reprint of *Analysis of the Influence of Natural Religion on the Temporal Happiness of Mankind*. Numbers in parentheses in the distillation in part 1 refer to page numbers in the reprint. Numbers in parentheses in the distillations of *Not Paul, but Jesus* and of *Church-of-England Catechism Examined* are to pages in the original, primary materials I used. Readers who wish to see these pages will need to be both diligent in their search and lucky, as these pages are currently hard to acquire.

In addition to the primary materials on religion sent to me by Gordon Stein, I have relied on the *Works of Jeremy Bentham*, edited by John Bowring,

Bentham's literary executor. The shortcomings of the Bowring edition have long been known and are now being rectified (as time, money, and effort become available) by the Bentham Project at University College, London. Under the aegis of this project, eleven volumes of Bentham's correspondence have now been published, with volumes 12, 13, and 14 in progress. Other works by the project have either appeared or are in progress, but none is of especial interest to religion except for a forthcoming work on Bentham's *Church of Englandism*, under the editorship to Professor James E. Crimmins of Huron College, London, Ontario. Should my tome inspire any of its readers to want to know more about the Bentham Project and *The Collected Works of Jeremy Bentham* (in progress), they have but to use the following Internet address: www.ucl.ac.uk/Bentham-Project/.

It is incumbent on me to mention the kindness of several people who have contributed to this work. First, I wish to thank Mary Beth Evans, who, while still an undergraduate at Auburn University, reduced the *Analysis of the Influence of Natural Religion on the Temporal Happiness of Mankind* to a series of formal arguments. I also wish to thank my former colleagues, associate professors Stephen White, PhD, and Jan Wojcik, PhD, for reading various parts of the manuscript. Professor Peter Harzem, PhD, Hudson Professor of Psychology, deserves double thanks for reading parts of the manuscript and for a number of illuminating conversations about Bentham. Professor Harzem has seen the auto-icon (i.e., the waxen head and clothed skeleton) of Jeremy Bentham at the University of London. Finally, I wish to express my appreciation to the eminent Bentham scholar, Professor James E. Crimmins, for providing me with offprints of three of his very valuable articles and for setting me straight on two erroneous judgments on related issues I had once entertained about Bentham. Since I have taken advice from none of these worthies, it follows that none is responsible for any mistakes I may have made.

NOTE

1. Richard Taylor, "Joseph Fletcher: Father of Biomedical Ethics," *Free Inquiry* 4, no. 2 (1984): 17.

Part I

Analysis of the Influence of Natural Religion on the Temporal Happiness of Mankind: How Bentham Upended Deism

Chapter 1

Introduction and Distillation
with Commentary

In England, in 1822, there appeared a small book of 140 pages that bore the splendidly descriptive title *Analysis of the Influence of Natural Religion on the Temporal Happiness of Mankind* (hereafter referred to as *AINR*). According to the title page, the book was written by one Philip Beauchamp, but no matter how many Philip Beauchamps the world contained at the time, no one of them wrote this book. The man who actually put it to paper, as we now have it, was George Grote (1794–1871), best known to scholars as a historian of Greece and to the history of universities as a founder, president, and vice-chancellor of the University of London.[1] James Mill, the father of John Stuart Mill, introduced Grote to Jeremy Bentham in 1817 or thereabout. Grote, involved at the time in his father's banking business, quickly adopted Bentham and the elder Mill as his mentors, becoming well-acquainted with utilitarianism straight away. From a "mass of written material committed to him by Bentham," Grote proceeded to stitch together the *AINR*.[2] Neither Bentham nor Grote, however, publicly acknowledged any part in its creation. Both were prudent men, and Grote was not above artful concealment when anything smacking of atheism could be traced to his pen.[3]

Bentham, who was seventy-four years old in 1822, had outlined the work a decade earlier and had commenced to flesh it out in 1815, but only episodically. As was the case with many of his projects, he left it unfinished.[4] Having no literary ambitions as such, Bentham did not mind turning his manuscripts over to a trusted hand to complete. Sir John Bowring, literary executor and editor of the *Works of Jeremy Bentham* (in eleven volumes), chose not to include the *AINR*, thus leaving it as little known to posterity as it was to contemporaries upon its publication. Bowring, a pious Unitarian and author of the well-known hymn "In the Cross of Christ I Glory," thought Bentham's writings on religion too "bold and adventurous for publication."[5] Perhaps so, for they were once characterized as constituting "the most stringent attack made on theism between d'Holbach and Feuerbach."[6]

Opinions vary as to how much Grote contributed to the *AINR*. Historian of ideas Elie Halévy, in listing it among Bentham's works, identified Grote as merely its editor.[7] James Steintrager, a major Bentham scholar, believed that although Grote surely wrote the *AINR*, it was clearly based on Bentham's manuscripts—manuscripts that could have supported a more extensive treatment of natural religion than the *AINR*, as it now stands.[8] Historian of ideas David Berman, however, sees it as a collaborative effort with Grote as the major partner and Bentham the minor;[9] and Bentham scholar G. Croom Robertson, to complete the spectrum, took it to be mostly the work of Grote, though dependent somewhat on Bentham's thought.[10] Since the two are always linked in its production, since Bentham offered to look it over for improvements he might make,[11] and since there is no hint of any friction between the two over its contents, one can be quite confident that herein the mind of Bentham can be seen in the hand of Grote. This, in any case, is how I shall treat it. The *AINR* was published, fittingly, by the freethinker Richard Carlile.[12]

As Bentham saw it, the world was rife with the idea that even though religious doctrines were false, "it would be salutary to deceive mankind into a belief of their truth" (p. 20). In the reigning view, so important was religion to "the rectitude and consolation" of humankind that religious doctrines (though clearly perfidious) ought "to have been invented and inculcated" (p. 19). Bentham sought to upend the religious worldview by suggesting that even though religious doctrines were true, belief in them might nonetheless be pernicious to human happiness in this life. Since it was his stated intention merely to examine the influence of natural religion on the temporal happiness of people, he determined not to touch on issues of truth and falsity in religious doctrines. Thus epistemology and theology yielded to psychology and to the philosophy of utility in his analysis of natural religion. Furthermore, Bentham refused to denominate as superstition the various pagan religions of the world while retaining "religion" as an honorific synonym for Christianity.

The alternation above between religion and natural religion is significant. By natural religion Bentham meant "all religious belief not specifically determined and settled by some revelation [or reputed revelation] from the Being to whom the belief relates" (p. 20). Religion not based on revelation was to him fundamental to all religions based on revelation, because "if it be discovered that Religion, unassisted by revelation, is the foe and not the benefactor of mankind, we can then ascertain whether the good effects [if any] engrafted upon her by an alleged revelation are sufficient to neutralize the bitterness of her natural fruit" (ibid.). Put differently, Bentham took a kind of minimal religious theism (often called deism in England) to be fundamental to such theological elaborations on a common theme as one finds in Judaism, Christianity, and Islam. 'Minimal religious theism' may seem to many a curious term, but it will become clearer later when its meaning is distinguished from absolutely minimal theism.

To Bentham, religion meant "belief in the existence of an almighty Being, by whom pains and pleasures are dispensed to mankind during an infinite and future state of existence" (p. 30). This is a singularly lean definition. Thus, he avoided the conundrums spawned by ordinary notions of omnipotence. It was sufficient (for him) that the almighty Being mentioned above exercises such overwhelming power that human beings can never resist or modify it. For all anyone can ascertain from his definition, natural religion does not require that this everlasting Being be the "Maker of Heaven and Earth," only that the Being at issue is in a position to dispense pains and pleasures to humans in an infinite and future state of existence. This, of course, requires that humans survive death and retain consciousness in the endless state posited in the definition. The principal difference between religion à la Bentham and the deism of his time is that nothing in the definition above logically requires that the "almighty Being" be well disposed by nature toward human beings—nor does anything in empirical experience.

Bentham's object was to analyze whether such beliefs were productive of "happiness or misery in the present life" (p. 31). If on the whole natural religion produced happiness, then to him it could be called useful; if on the whole, misery, then it could be called abuseful. Since we humans cannot know whether postmortem pains and pleasures are dependent on present beliefs and behaviors or are independent of these, as would be implied by predestinarian theology, the posthumous future for Bentham's natural religionist must logically be a source of great anxiety, "replete with impending pain and misery" (p. 32). In the case of the predestinarian, the horror of helplessness necessarily accompanies the anxiety of ignorance. The situation of the natural religionist who rejects predestinarianism is not, however, greatly to be preferred.

Bentham wrote, "Pain is a far stronger, more pungent, and more distinct sensation than pleasure; it is more various in its shapes, more definite and impressive upon the memory, and lays hold of the imagination with greater mastery and permanence. Pain, therefore, is far more likely to obtrude itself upon the conceptions, where there exists no positive evidence to circumscribe their range, than pleasure" (p. 34). Such is the situation of all natural religionists, who, in total ignorance of what is to come after death, must be filled with dread over what may befall them. Those, of course, who look to a blissful afterlife know no such dread, but whence their confidence? The unbeliever, on the contrary, has no fear of death, only of the pains of dying and the loss of life's pleasures. Of natural religion it must be concluded that instead of "soothing apprehensions which cannot wholly be dispelled, it would superadd fresh grounds of uneasiness, wrapped up in an uncertainty which only renders them more painful and depressing" (p. 36).

It might be thought that natural religion is *useful* to humans in providing rules of conduct for individuals, obedience to which rules conduces to public happiness. Alas, natural religion (as Bentham defined it) is implicit with no such rules. Moreover, temporal experience "imparts no information on the subject" (p. 38). Thus, those who think that postmortem pains and pleasures are contingent upon present conduct are at a total loss as to which kinds of conduct. Nor do postmortem sanctions fare any better than present admonitions. "It seems, therefore," Bentham wrote, "almost unaccountable, that natural religion, how rich soever its promises, how terrible soever its threats, should exercise the least influence upon human conduct, since the conditions of its awards are altogether veiled from our sight" (p. 39). Although, logically, natural religion should exercise no influence on behavior, Bentham thought, nevertheless, that it did. How? Why?

Although natural religion itself provides no directive rules for human conduct, it is nevertheless associated with rules of conduct extraneous to it. "Natural religion," Bentham wrote, "merely implants . . . the expectation of a posthumous existence, involving awards of enjoyment and suffering apportioned by an invisible Being" (p. 41). Upon this basis, human fancy sets to work speculating as to the character and/or temper of the invisible Being. Put in more modern terms, it is one thing to take the universe to be artifactual in nature (thus presupposing an artificer) and something quite different, logically, to assume that human beings will survive death to reap weal or woe from the cosmic artificer postulated in natural religion.

Taking the major premise of natural religion for granted, assuming that humans will have postmortem experiences, and being ever aware that certain kinds of conduct here and now conduce to pains and others to pleasures, it is all but inevitable that human fancy should turn to the relationship, if any, between present conduct and postmortem experience. Lacking any empirical data that can shed light on the matter and dismissing for the moment, at least, any valid self-disclosure on the part of the cosmic artificer, we are, perforce, thrown back upon unbridled speculation about his character and/or temper. Said Bentham:

> If he is conceived to be perfectly beneficent—having no personal affections of his own, or none but such as are coincident with the happiness of mankind—patronising those actions alone which are useful, and exactly in the degree in which they are useful—detesting in a similar manner and proportion those which are hurtful—then the actions agreeable to him will be beneficial to mankind, and inducements to the performance of them will promote the happiness of mankind. If, on the other hand, he is depicted as unbeneficent—as having personal affections seldom coincident with human happiness, frequently injurious to it, and almost always frivolous and exactive, favouring actions which are not useful at all, or not in the degree in which they are useful—disapproving with the same caprice and without any reference to utility—then the course of action by which his favour is to be sought, will be more or less injurious to mankind, and inducements to pursue it will in the present life tend to the production of unhappiness. (p. 43)

Listening to the "epithets of eulogy and reverence" with which the votaries of natural religion refer to the almighty Being posited in their religion, one would think him exceedingly well disposed toward humankind. Natural religion, however, implies a Deity whose character is one of "caprice and tyranny." This discrepancy is not hard to explain. The only data supplied by natural religion from which the "temper and inclination" of the Deity can be inferred are a "power to which we can assign no limits—an agency which we are unable to comprehend or frustrate" (p. 44). Conceived in this way, the Deity of natural religion is clearly a tyrant and logically a source of terror. To the tyranny implied must be added the unknown and incomprehensible nature of divine agency. In human affairs, incomprehensible behavior in small matters is denominated caprice; in large, insanity. On its own terms, then, natural religion confronts its devotees with a divine despot, with one who rules alone (beholden to none) in unfathomable ways.

The foregoing does not, however, imply complete malevolence toward humankind. Complete malevolence plus limitless power would surely have resulted in a much worse (even if a more comprehensible, because predictable) universe than the one we inhabit. By the same token, a completely benevolent Deity plus limitless power could equally surely have produced a much better (and, perhaps, an equally comprehensible) world. Bentham upended Plato's doctrine of the demiurge, of the perfectly well-intentioned artificer, limited largely by the vagaries of matter, by asserting "the inherent goodness and incorruptible excellence of matter" as the only check on the machinations of a malevolent artificer. Bentham wrote, "I admit that there is not the smallest evidence for this, but it is just as well supported, and just as probable as the preceding theory of Plato" (pp. 46–47). Bentham concluded that the Deity of natural religion must be recognized as fluctuating in incomprehensible ways between good and evil, but on balance more an object of terror than of hope.

Despite the vagaries of a Deity who at best fluctuates between malevolence and benevolence toward human beings and who does so without apparent principle, that is, any comprehensible rules, the natural religionist persists in heaping terms of "reverence and eulogy" upon him. In order to get at the principle underlying this behavior, Bentham analyzed the language of praise and dispraise (or blame) as follows: "Each [i.e., praise and dispraise] is a species of sanction, vested in the hands of every individual, and employed by him for his own benefit; the former *remuneratory*, and destined to encourage the manifestation of kindness towards him; the latter *punitory*, and intended to prevent injurious treatment" (p. 48). Bentham noted that the human use of dispraise is in exact proportion to the power of the dispraiser, whereas praise is exactly proportional to the weakness of the praiser. The Deity of natural religion, for example, has no use for praise from human beings but can blame them as much as he likes. Human beings, contrariwise, are too weak in relation to this Deity to use blame but know no bounds in their praise of Him. Bentham wrote, "The vehemence of our praise is thus not measured by the extent of the kindness bestowed, but by the superiority of the donor to the receiver, and implies only the dependence and disparity of the latter" (p. 52). So, the capricious despot of natural theology receives the "largest and most prodigal encomiums" (ibid.). Since he has no real need of human praise, the efficacy of such flattery is suspect at best, even though psychologically comprehensible.

It is clear that to Bentham the Deity of natural religion is modeled upon "those earthly sovereigns in whom the most irresistible might resides" (p. 54). Although he was mistaken in thinking that this Deity would seek to *increase* his dominion, having all dominion already, he was right in thinking that this Deity would be able to engage in universal espionage upon the thoughts of human beings. The omniscience accorded him would guarantee that. Moreover, no increase in dominion or knowledge would be needed to implant in humans an "incessant feeling of helplessness, insecurity, and fear" (p. 56). Given such a Deity, what pleasure could he derive from the well-being of the human community?

The line of thought that likens the Deity of natural religion to the most puissant of human potentates implies that his darlings will be those who "disseminate his influence among men" and "are most effectively employed in rendering his name dread and reverenced" (p. 57). Such are priests, broadly conceived. By the same token, atheists will be most abominated. Second in divine approbation will be those who extol the Deity effusively and "depress themselves . . . by abstaining on his account from agreeable occupations, and performing ceremonies which can be ascribed to no other motive than the desire of pleasing him." Second in abomination will be those who "brave his power" or slight Him in some way or other through indifference or irreverence.

It should not be forgotten that Bentham took natural religion itself to provide (logically speaking) no directive rules for human conduct. Any rules associated with it were, in his terminology, extraneous. The source of the extraneous rules of conduct has now been disclosed: it lies in the analogy human beings are inclined to make between absolute monarchs (or tyrants) of a terrestrial sort and the almighty Being posited by natural religion. Rather than merely asserting that the universe is an artifact (necessitating an artificer) and then dropping further concern over the precise nature of the artificer, humankind proceed to model the presumed artificer upon those earthly sovereigns who rule alone, beholden to none. Once the egotistical disposition and character of such despots is established, the supreme Artificer of natural religion acquires the same characteristics. Moreover, the various ways human beings find to cope with terrestrial despots are transferred to their presumed relationships to the supreme Being of natural religion. Having established, to his satisfaction, the imaginative link between despotism and deity, Bentham's question remained the same, namely, does natural religion conduce to the temporal happiness of humankind? "It seems clear . . . that the posthumous hopes and fears held out by natural religion must produce the effect of encouraging actions useless and pernicious to mankind" (p. 61).

Bentham bolstered his line of reasoning above with four subsidiary arguments. First, he wondered what would happen if pagans, for example, were to lose faith in their Deity or in a future state (or both). Would they not dismiss the (presumed) injunctions of the natural religion hitherto undergirding their heathenish beliefs? Cetainly, but how would this change their behavior? The physical and social sources of pain and pleasure would remain the same. Put in more modern terms, the contingencies of behavior would persist as before. Whatever had been useful or abuseful would remain so, and there would still remain "ample motive to behaviour beneficial to society—ample motive against conduct injurious to it" (p. 63). The loss of religious belief would not conduce to (or be equal to) any loss of motive for "conduct really useful to mankind." Bentham wrote, "If the practices enjoined by natural religion would expire without its support, this must be because there is no motive left to perform them. But to say that there is no such motive, proves that the practices produce no temporal benefit whatever: E converso, therefore, he who would maintain that pious works are temporally beneficial, must also affirm, that there would be motive enough to perform them, supposing our earthly existence to terminate in annihilation" (pp. 63–64).

Believers commonly laud natural religion as crucial in motivating people to behave in ways conducive to temporal benefit and deplore unbelief as providing no such motivation. Unbelievers, however, are as motivated to acquire temporal benefit as believers. Religious motivation to temporal benefit is therefore useless.

Second, each religion is distinguished from all others by its unique set of (theological or metaphysical) beliefs and ceremonial practices. Here Bentham did not resort to his normal bifurcation of religion into natural and revealed. It is enough to recognize that Jains and Sikhs, for example, belong to different religions. To continue, being told that there are such people as Lamaist, Shintoist, and Shaktist priests allows one to assume that each espouses different religious beliefs and ceremonial practices but does not allow any assumptions as to the moral tenor of their lives, as to whether or not their characteristic behavior is beneficial or noxious. They may, for all one knows, be parasitic on their respective societies. If on the other hand, one were assured that the priests in question were men of "justice, veracity, or prudence," virtues known throughout the world to conduce to public benefit, their religious beliefs and modes of piety or ceremonial practice would be trivial or of no consequence whatsoever. Said Bentham, "If therefore piety consisted of a collection of qualities calculated to produce temporal benefit, you would discover the same identity between Pagan and Christian piety, as there is between Pagan and Christian justice or veracity" (p. 64). That this is not the case indicates how little a given religion may contribute to human well-being or, worse, how pernicious it may be.

Third, at its best, religion merely reinforces law with supernatural sanctions. "If the injunctions of piety," Bentham wrote, "inculcated performance or abstinence merely according as the action specified was beneficial or injurious in the present life, religion would be precisely coincident with human laws" (p. 65). Bentham, if pressed, would probably had added the following qualifications: provided that the laws were wise, well drawn, and properly focused on human benefit. Religion here is portrayed as a follower, not as a leader. Its principal task, it would seem, is to reinforce the positive (i.e., the existing) morality and/or law of a given time and place, not to open new vistas nor to inspire better laws. Religion, however, is not always (or even often) at its best: "Throughout the globe, under every various system, we observe the most innocuous of human pleasures criminated and interdicted by piety; pleasures such as the worst of human legislators never forbad, and never could discover any pretence for forbidding. We observe a peculiar path of merit and demerit traced out exclusively by religion—embracing numerous actions which the law has left unnoticed, and which we may therefore infer, are not recognized as deserving either reward or punishment with reference to the present life" (p. 66). The end in view of religious mandates cannot be the same as that of (secular) legislators. The extent to which the latter aim at human well-being is the extent to which the former (except when coincident) diverge from that end. At its worst, religion may aim at ends which the modern, tolerant, secular state may have to curb.

Fourth, the injunctions of religion, touching on one's proper relationships to others, can be classified as two: duty to the Deity and duty to other humans. However beneficial duty to other humans may be, duty to the Deity can never produce any temporal happiness, because, by definition, it involves "a rule restrictive on our conduct on those occasions when the interests of other men are not at all concerned" (p. 67). Said Bentham, "[H]e who whips himself every night, or prefaces every mouthful with a devotional formula, can hardly be supposed to have contemplated even the smallest temporal profit, or to have had any other end in view, than that of pleasing the Deity" (p. 58). Surely, such behavior profits the human species not one whit.

Granted that superhuman inducements to behave in this (good) way and not to behave in that (bad) way are associated with (if not dictated by) natural religion, questions still arise as to their extent and efficiency. To make headway in answering such questions, superhuman inducements must be isolated and abstracted from the crowd of perfectly natural human motives with which they intermingle—no easy task. Assuming for the moment that superhuman inducements are purely beneficial, "what," Bentham wondered, "is the number and importance of those cases in which human inducements would be inapplicable and inoperative but in which posthumous expectations alone would efficiently supply the defect?" (p. 70). He thought that such cases were (and would be) few and generally unimportant.

Only when a crime is known and the criminal unknown, leaving human inducements and expectations inoperative, might superhuman inducements "be vindicated as indispensably necessary for the maintenance of good conduct" (p. 72). Social reliance on superhuman sanctions need not, however, be great. "For," Bentham wrote, "wherever the legislator can distinguish what actions it is desirable either to encourage or to prevent, he can always annex to them a measure of temporal reward or punishment commensurate to the purpose" (p. 70). Given good laws, clear definition of what is criminal, efficient detection, and just courts, the temporal punishments, if quick and commensurate to the purpose, are sufficient and enable societies to dispense with supernatural or posthumous sanctions.

The line of reasoning immediately above is predicated on the notion that superhuman inducements are purely beneficial. Bentham, on the contrary, thought them more productive of evil than of good. "We should not," he wrote, "desire to introduce instruments for multiplying and protracting human torture," certainly not from a "foreign" (in this case, a superhuman) source. With respect to the good and evil that superhuman inducements produce, questions of efficiency and inefficiency arise. By way of introducing this subject, Bentham said, "All inducements are expectations either of pleasure or pain. The force with which all expectations act upon the human bosom varies according as they differ in 1. Intensity,—2. Duration,—3. Certainty,—4. Propinquity. These are the four elements of *value* which constitute and measure the comparative strength of all human motives" (p. 74; emphasis added). To gauge the efficiency or inefficiency of posthumous expectations, one has only to consider them in relation to the four values named above.

Respecting propinquity, postmortem inducements are, in most cases, exceedingly weak and thus inefficient. Bentham was well aware of the fact that a small amount of pain speedily delivered is more efficient in controlling or modifying human behavior than the threat of great pain long delayed. Posthumous inducements are also defective in certainty and thus inefficient for a second reason. To compensate for these weaknesses, believers in posthumous inducements magnify their intensity and duration, but, alas, can do so only in imagination. Actual experiences of heavenly bliss and of hellish torture are not to be had in this world. Moreover, to take the fancied horrors of hell really seriously would be tantamount to madness, as Bentham saw it. Indeed, "human comfort" in this life requires that posthumous threats be inefficient. Respecting this inefficiency in repressing crime, Bentham wrote, "To this purpose it has been shewn that they are wholly inadequate; for during the influence of temptation, the only season in which a man commits crime, they find no place in the mind, and therefore can interpose no barrier. On the other hand, they act with the highest effect at a period when they cannot by possibility produce any temporal benefit—that is, at the close of life: and the extent of their influence is always in an inverse ratio to the demand for it" (p. 80).

Despite the real inefficiency of posthumous inducements, their "dominion in human affairs" appears to be extensive. To Bentham this contrariety between appearance and reality lay in a "misconception regarding the actual motives of mankind." The God of natural religion is routinely portrayed as "delighting in the contemplation of his own superiority, in demanding human acknowledgement thereof, and in the debasement, the privation, and the misery of mankind" entailed by any disobedience (p. 82). Although each person may wish to avoid the full cost of such obedience, there is no strong motivation to help others avoid it. On the contrary, each person may be happy to help the Deity exact from others the last full measure of obedience that (allegedly) pleases him, because in that way one may seem at least to be on the Lord's side and may enjoy whichever benisons such partisanship affords. Since others will be motivated similarly, the end result is that each person falls under the surveillance of the rest. Said Bentham, "A strong public antipathy is pointed against impious conduct; the decided approbation of the popular voice is secured in favour of religious acts. The praise or blame of his earthly companions, will thus become the real actuating motive to religious observances on the part of each individual. By an opposite conduct it is not merely the divine denunciations that he provokes, but also the hostility of innumerable crusaders, who long to expiate their own debts by implacable warfare against the recusant" (p. 83).

So, it is the "esteem and censure of one's fellows" and/or the expectations thereof that really induce people to act as they do, relative to divinity, not posthumous threats or blandishments—which are little more than epiphenomenal. Nevertheless, there will be a strong motive to make it seem otherwise. Religious acts that are explained away as just a requirement of social life will lose their uniquely religious character and will stand nobody in good stead with the Deity. It simply will not do religiously to say, I have served Thee faithfully, O Lord, because of the approbation and disapprobation of my peers. Nor will it do to say to those in the neighborhood, Because of your praise and blame, I have served our God in all things. Bentham wrote, "No individual, therefore, will be able to steer clear of the public enmity, unless he not only renders those pious acts of homage, but also succeeds in convincing others that he is actuated in rendering them entirely by the fear of God" (p. 84). It is, then, the popular sanction that bids individuals to bow and scrape before the unseen presence. It remains only for individuals to deceive themselves, as well as others, for the charade to be complete.

There is little mystery as to how superhuman (or posthumous or religious) inducements, though weak in themselves, become strong. Quite simply, they "enlist in their service the irresistible arm of public opinion" all the while pretending that it is not so (ibid.). Religion, in short, uses "the very same engines as morality" (p. 85). Bentham thought that moral conduct sprang from "the mutual wants and interests" of humankind. Among other goals, each person wants his or her neighbors to be virtuous. Virtuous behavior can, of course, be known. It is that behavior that excites social approval or avoids disapproval. Religious acts, though ineffectual in themselves, gain social approval just as secular acts gain social approval, in the process becoming moral. It appears to the popular mind, at least, that it is in the interest of each person that his neighbor be religious as well as moral. The same social sanctions used to gain the neighbor's moral behavior are used to gain the neighbor's religious observance. In this way, there is a (perceived) cooperation "with the views of God, which may have the [additional] effect of partially discharging, or at least of lightening" each person's social obligations. Hence the imperative to establish orthodoxy and to proscribe heterodoxy and unbelief.

Although (to Bentham) there were no significant, objectifiable benefits of a temporal sort that sprang from religion, whereas there were many from morality, the two, religion and morality, enter into a close association, as explained above. Once an orthodoxy has been established, it burdens believers with common privations, taxes them (or extorts monetary contributions), and exacts services from them. Little wonder, then, that the orthodox envy the unorthodox who evade the common privations, taxes, and services required of the faithful. Little wonder that the orthodox want the unorthodox to conform and that they feel exonerated when this occurs. Little wonder that the orthodox incriminate the unorthodox when they refuse to conform. Bentham wrote, "All these principles conspire to sharpen my acrimony against my non-conforming neighbour, and render me doubly dissatisfied with that state of respite and impunity in which Omnipotence still permits him to live. In this condition of mind, nothing can be more gratifying than the self-assumed task of executing the divine wrath upon his predestined head" (p. 86).

Having done with his critique of the weaknesses and inefficiencies of superhuman inducements, Bentham next fixed his gaze on instances of their total disregard. To do this he turned from natural religion (as he had hypothesized it) to revealed religion. By revealed religion, it must be remembered, he meant nothing more than any religion whose precepts (presumably disclosed by some deity or other) are written down, become fixed, and remain independent of subsequent alterations in "national feeling." Put differently, a society or believing community may come to diverge from the precepts on which it *presumes* it is based but which it has forgotten (in part at least) or simply ignores. Examining how this happens provides the best illustration of the almighty influence of public opinion against the puny force of superhuman inducements. To make his point Bentham used as examples dueling, fornication, simony, and perjury. In biblical religion, dueling is obviously contrary to divine law, because it involves the possibility (at least) of killing without just cause, which must therefore be classified as murder. Yet in Bentham's day dueling was common among socioeconomic classes well prepared through literacy for being able to know what Scripture forbids. Moreover, in the case of dueling, the command of Scripture and the counsel of common sense (against unnecessary pain, hazard, and loss—to others as well as to oneself) are concurrent. Despite all, men will, nevertheless, murder one another, if public opinion views the refusal to duel as contemptible and withdraws credit from all who will not accept challenges to defend their honor. A rich bounty of divine credit for such men is nothing compared to the withdrawal of *human* credit from them if they are perceived to be cowardly and dishonorable. So much for the efficacy of superhuman inducements when they run counter to public opinion!

Of fornication little needs to be said. Though clearly forbidden by Scripture, a given society (fancying itself built on biblical injunctions) may be quite lenient toward it, regarding boys as the kind of creatures who will be boys, and girls as the kind of creatures who, if not simply weak, are willing to aid boys in fulfilling their imperative. Unless the society in question is puritanical, the divine admonition is left to operate unsupported. Said Bentham, "To what extent it operates thus singlehanded the state of all great cities notoriously attests" (p. 89). Obviously, where the toleration of prostitution is high, regard for the Deity's displeasure is low. Of simony, even less needs to be said. Bentham merely noted that the frequency of its practice was equal to the strictness with which it was forbidden.

Bentham lavished more attention on perjury than on any of the foregoing examples. Since perjury involves oaths, he turned his attention thereto, saying, "The person who takes an oath solemnly calls down upon himself the largest measure of divine vengeance, if he commits a particular act. In this imprecation it is implied, that he firmly anticipates the infliction of these penalties, if he becomes guilty of this self-condemned behaviour" (ibid.).

Then, remembering his own days at Oxford, no doubt, he remarked on how having taken there the oath (stemming from Archbishop Laud), students—including the most scrupulous religionists—proceeded to forget or ignore these whenever they occasioned even the slightest inconvenience. The reason for this blithe attitude was simple. Times had changed, the regulations at issue had come to be seen as silly or useless, and there was no longer any human sanction upholding them. The oath that all had taken, however, did not involve human sanctions but *divine* sanctions of the most trenchant sort. Presumably the strength of the posthumous fears, involved in the oath, remained unaltered (despite human alteration), but, quite clearly, the absence of any popular sanction left the divine sanction debilitated and decrepit.

Another confirmation of Bentham's point could be found in the conduct of jurors. When called upon to administer a law that they and popular opinion had come to view as "sanguinary and impolitic," they completely forgot or ignored their oath. Said Bentham, "Public opinion gave, and public opinion has taken away; and all the sway, which super-human expectations possess over human behaviour is surreptitiously procured, from their coincidence with this omnipotent sanction" (p. 91).

Despite the relationships Bentham believed he had discovered between public opinion and superhuman sanctions, he knew that there were some people who marched to their own drummers, spurning ordinary social sanctions and even welcoming obloquy. Some of these people were (and are) quite simply insane, but what about the rest? Bentham applied a theory of associationism to explain the rest. He wrote, "For when the associations of credit have once linked themselves with any course of behaviour . . . an individual will not unfrequently persevere in it, though the harvest which he reaps may not actually gratify and realize the association." By associations of credit, he meant the esteem individuals gain from behaving as they do: "A similar anxiety for veneration and influence over the sentiments of others, possesses the religionist," he wrote. How else could zeal for religious proselytizing be explained, he wondered?

In the second section of the *AINR*, Bentham, still eschewing the subject of revealed religion, noted how variable natural religion is around the globe. Despite this variability, a common "motive," he said, "pervades all its votaries" (p. 97). All who wish to give proof of their attachment to the Deity must inflict pain upon themselves for His sake, with no thought of any independent reward for doing so. This excluded all suffering whose result might benefit other people and from whom praise might flow. "Mankind," Bentham noted, "will measure your devotion to God by the amount and intensity of the pain which you thus gratuitously inflict upon yourself" (p. 98). Those whose perfervid piety does not reach such a pitch may settle for lesser but useless privations including

- Fasting
- Celibacy
- Absence from repose
- Abstinence from cleanliness, personal decoration, and innocent comforts
- Abstinence from social enjoyments and mirth
- Abstinence from remedies for disease
- Gratuitous surrender of property, time, and labor
- Surrender of dignity and honors (p. 99)

Less agonizing than "stripes and mutilation," which characterize relatively few, the aggregate of suffering stemming from the eight privations above is doubtless far greater and has the tendency to lay "whole societies under contribution." Bentham wrote, "For public opinion, which merely encourages and provokes, by excess admiration, the voluntary tortures of the enthusiast, acts as a compulsory force in extorting self-denial and asceticism" (p. 100).

Believing himself in the first part of the *AINR* to have elucidated the psychology underlying such religious acts, Bentham summarized his position as follows:

The reason why the privations are thus required by the popular voice, while the self-inflictions are left optional, is because the earliest and most natural mode which occurs for conciliating the unseen misanthrope, is to consign to his use some gratifying and valuable possession. A man despoils himself of some piece of property and bestows it to satisfy the wants of his Deity: The Ostiak, according to Pallas, takes a quantity of meat and places it between the lips of his idol—other nations present drink to the Gods by throwing it out of the cup upon the ground; that is, by rendering it useless to any human being. It is these donatives, or acts of privation, which are originally conceived as recommending the performer to divine favour. Sacrifices of other sorts are subsequently super-added— and abstinences from certain enjoyments, on the plea of consecrating them to the Deity. Hence the public opinion is at the outset warmly enlisted in exacting self-denying performances for his benefit. (p. 100)

In addition to unprofitable sufferings and useless privations, Bentham perceived in natural religion yet a third mischief, namely, that of engendering undefined terrors. In particular, upon those who are ill, enfeebled, or despondent and upon such folk as nuns suffering the melancholy of confinement and an almost professional preoccupation with sin, religion adds yet another level of anxiety—the posthumous flames and torments of hell. Less intense but more pervasive is a fourth mischief—that of guilt exacted as a tax on forbidden but innocuous pleasures, pleasures so seductive that nearly all participate in them but believe themselves to have sinned in doing so.

The four mischiefs of natural religion detailed above afflict the individual believer alone. Other religious mischiefs, however, have social ramifications. The first of these is the creation of "factitious antipathy" between people. Factitious antipathy would exist even if religion did not, but wherever religion appears it adds substance to the "predisposing causes" endemic to the human species. Bentham called those antipathies that are uniquely religious artificial. Three of these deserve close attention:

- Unbelief in the existence of the Deity
- Nonobservance of His will
- Malobservance of His will

Of all antipathies, Bentham opined, the most unqualified and universal is that which believers (in God) feel toward unbelievers. This is not, however, a symmetrical relationship, unbelievers not so much feeling hatred toward believers as contempt for them for their credulity and lack of critical acumen, that is, for their silliness in being so easily duped or misled. This is extremely vexatious to believers, leading as it does to ridicule and potential loss of standing in the eyes of others. The mere fact of unbelief imputes error, incompetence, and lack of persuasive power to those who fancy that their faith is as solid as the Rock of Gibraltar and equally as obvious. Being challenged in this particular way at once diminishes the reliability and influence of believers and threatens the social credit that they would have continued enjoying but for the challenge. Furthermore, vociferous asseveration of orthodox views on behalf of the Deity proves to be an inexpensive way of staying in His good graces among those who do not relish privations on His behalf and who have no stomach for serving Him through self-inflicted stripes and mutilation.

Observant believers feel some, but much less, antipathy toward unobservant believers than toward unbelievers. The reasons are fairly obvious. Unobservant believers present no serious theological challenges to believers which only superior reason can put down, something observant believers can seldom, if ever, muster. Nor do observant believers fear ridicule from that quarter. Quite the contrary—unobservant believers may be entirely orthodox in theory, as it were, and may even praise observant believers for their punctilious and exacting performance of the appropriate ceremonies and creedal avowals. Ascetic believers, however, find much in the nonobservant to disparage, for the latter in their dismissal of even the ordinary observances call into sharp question the efficacy of the extraordinary privations that ascetics assume over and above the ordinary. To think that these might be for nothing is disquieting, to say the least.

"Mal-observance, like unbelief, includes non-observance," wrote Bentham (p. 110). It engenders degrees of antipathy toward others midway between those reserved for unbelievers at the one extreme and those reserved for nonobservant believers at the other. The greater the stress a particular religion places on pious practices, the greater the abhorrence its practitioners feel toward those undertaking contrary rituals. It is unfortunate that natural religion cannot resolve such disputes, for it permits no rational inference to be drawn respecting the aptness of any particular set of pious practices. Accordingly, the practices that actually exist, annexed to this dogmatical system of religion or to that, are clearly deficient in reason. Believers may claim *authority*, in lieu of rationality, for their favorite rituals or liturgies but will find it very difficult to support these, logically, in the face of dissent. Herein the seeds of bitter antipathy are sown. From the standpoint of the votaries of a given faith, dissenters slight the one true God and worship false ones, a disgusting situation indeed. Bentham wrote, "It is not easy to estimate the total sum of evil introduced by this means— but when we contemplate the universal prevalence of religious hatred, and its daily and hourly interference with the life of human conduct—creating factitious motives for inflicting mutual evil, or withholding assistance—we shall be authorized in placing to its account no inconsiderable portion of the misery that pervades human society" (p. 111).

In addition to creating factitious antipathies, religion compounds its mischief by sanctioning the same. In so doing, it perverts popular opinion, corrupts moral sentiments, and inhibits social improvement. The temporal happiness of a nation (society or community) depends on having an operative majority of citizens who know what truly conduces thereto and what does not. To measures that are productive of well-being, positive social sanctions can and should be added; to measures that are not, negative sanctions can and should be annexed. In this way virtue can be recognized and vice decried, "Now the efficacy of public hate, considered as a restraint upon mis-deeds, depends upon its being constantly and exclusively allied with the real injury of the public—upon its being uniformly called forth whenever their happiness is endangered, and never upon any mistaken or imaginary alarms" (pp. 112–13). The creation of imaginary alarms, however, is one of religion's bitter fruits. In focusing on another (imaginary) world, it causes men to hate, here and now, certain ideas or objects that do not really harm them. In so doing it distorts public opinion, misdirects moral sentiment, and dissipates the forces of censure, some being drained away from deterring individuals whose behavior poses real threats to restraining those whose behavior does not.

Animosity toward anyone becomes "unredeemed malignity" unless it is put in the service of societal happiness through the proper functioning of negative sanctions aimed at real evils. Religion, more focused on the happiness of its feigned kingdom hereafter than on the happiness of actual kingdoms here and now, unleashes pointless animosities. Said Bentham, "It is by exciting and keeping alive this malignity, that religion enforces her causeless prohibitions; and, therefore her influence is injurious, not only by obstructing an innocuous gratification, but by all the malice and animosity which she plants in the human bosom in order to effect her purpose. A pernicious restriction is thus completed by still more pernicious means" (p. 114).

That which is true of religious misdirection and misapplication of negative sanctions is also true of its mischievous utilization of positive sanctions. It is imperative for a society (a nation or community) to know wherein its temporal well-being lies and crucial for it to reinforce behaviors that conduce thereto. Religion appropriates exactly the same mechanisms of reinforcement but directs them to individual well-being in an imagined posthumous state. In so doing it "draws off a portion of the popular favour from its legitimate task of encouraging acts conducive to human felicity" (ibid.). In this manner religion cheats the public. Bentham wrote the stinging indictment that follows: "The popular sanction, thus mis-applied both in its encouraging and restrictive branches, may become the unconscious instrument of evil to almost any extent. It may criminate and interdict any number of innocent enjoyments, like the eating of pork—or any acts however extensively useful, like loans of money upon interest. And it may heap profuse veneration on monastic stripes and self-denial, or ratify the cruelty which persecution inflicts upon the unhappy dissenter" (ibid.). Religion, in short, "introduces a false apprehension of what is praiseworthy and what is blameworthy."

If religion induces people to call bad that which is innocent (the eating of pork, for example) and to call good that which is harmful to the individual and useless to society (the self-mutilation of an ascetic, for example), people will know neither when they are blaming the truly blameworthy nor when they are praising the truly praiseworthy. This confusion in the application of sanctions is allied to a further misapplication— a misapplication of moral terms. The Deity of natural religion has been shown, logically, to be a capricious tyrant, yet he is described habitually in "epithets of the most superlative and unmingled praise." Whatever he likes (even human sacrifice) is denominated good; whatever he dislikes (such as eating pork) is denominated vicious, however nutritious or useful it may be. Since the likings and the dislikings of the Deity are quixotic (i.e., can be reduced to no clear principle), profound confusion reigns in morality. As Bentham wrote, "Hence the same misdirection of eulogy and censure, by which mankind have been deluded into favouring those who did not harm them and persecuting their benefactors, has given birth besides to another unhappy effect. The science of morality has become so doubtful and embarrassed, so destitute of all centre and foundation, as to lose all authority, and to be incapable either of rectifying current mistakes, or guarding against future ones" (p. 116).

Moralists who can specify no means or principle (such as utility) whereby they can test, try, or warrant what pass for moral pronouncements degrade ethics into a mere "catalogue of reigning sentiments." Should all citizens in a given community, society, or nation (or an effective majority thereof) agree in approving certain practices and in disapproving others, the depraved moralist will appeal to their agreements "as an invincible testimony to the justice of their feeling[s]" (ibid.). It is but a short step from this to the notion that nature herself speaks with a uniform voice respecting moral approbation and disapprobation. Thus does one travel from nature to nature's God and on to nature's morality—made holy by its God. Two evils clearly ensue: (1) the notion that some kinds of behavior are unnatural and therefore immoral and (2) effective prohibitions against various kinds of social improvements, the achievement of which is perceived to go against nature.

Bentham expanded upon these evils as follows: "[T]he epithet *unnatural* indicates perhaps the most severe, aggravated, and relentless odium ever harboured in the human bosom. It is perfectly self-justifying, nor does the accused dare to call for any proof or testimony in support of the change [i.e., any overthrow of the "established" course of nature]: it is also quite irresistible, and no plea can be heard in mitigation of its effect" (p. 118). Once opinion has established a given status quo as natural, God-given, moral, and sanctified, any "augmentation of human happiness, by an improved knowledge of facts, is *unnatural*, or contrary to the laws of nature: that is, it is an impious counteraction to the designs of God" (pp. 118–19). Against anything perceived to be *unnatural*, the bitterest antipathies of religion are unleashed. To make his case concrete, Bentham had but to point to the discoveries of Galileo or to the Church's intolerant response to such physical and medicinal improvements as the emetic and (subsequent to Bentham's time) the introduction of anesthetic in childbirth and the like. Numerous contemporary, as well as historical, examples could be given of pious obstructionism in the face of potential improvements in the human condition.

Universally, human beings confront a world of "pains and wants." To allay the one and satisfy the other become major goals in life. Said Bentham, "If a man does not know the way to avoid or to remedy an impending pain, he will be compelled to suffer it: If he does not know the way to procure any particular pleasure, the pleasure will not seek him of its own accord, and he will, therefore, be obliged to forego it" (p. 121). The avoidance of pain and the pursuit of pleasure are not, it should be noted, the carefree fruits of happenstance but of knowledge. When properly rooted in experience, instrumental knowledge (his term) consists in believing in facts rather than in fictions. Only then is knowledge truly useful. To distinguish the one from the other, intelligence must put action(s) to the test. In short, the consequences of behavior must become known. Given a conformity of belief with experience, human beings can make genuine progress in exempting themselves from pains and in enjoying the pleasant fruits of intelligence. "And conversely," wrote Bentham, "whatever tends to disjoin belief from experience must be regarded as crippling . . . and tending to disqualify our mental faculties for purposes of temporal happiness" (p. 122). A major force in human life *disjoining* belief from experience is religion. Their total divorce is, of course, insanity.

Consider the major premise of natural religion, namely, belief in the contention that there exists a Being "unseen, unheard, untouched, untasted, and unsmelt—his place of residence unknown—his shape and dimensions unknown—his original beginning undiscovered" (p. 124). The very terms 'invisible,' 'infinite,' and 'eternal,' with which he is customarily described, are all negatives and imply no possibility of our empirical experience of this putative Being. There is no need to espouse atheism to recognize that he has been rendered "extra-experimental" from the outset. Thus does the mental depravation enjoined by natural religion commence.

The belief that the Being mentioned above was the original creative power that designed the universe is unsupported by experience. There is no experience of the "commencement of things," and design, so important to natural theology, is known to us only in animals and in ourselves. In each case its effects are confined to the displacement of matter and the "admotion or amotion of its particles to and from each other" (p. 125). The concept of omnipotence is usually put forth to remedy the situation in the case of God, but once this idea enters the arena, it could as well apply to fire or water as to the divine mind or will. "When the fairy with her all-powerful wand has once been introduced, it is as easy to explain the sudden rise of a palace as of a cottage," Bentham observed (p. 120). So, once again, religion calls for the divorce of belief from experience, a most mischievous requirement.

Yet another mischief of religion is its inculcation of the notion that the Deity is an agent active in this world. Said Bentham, "You believe that the Deity interferes occasionally to modify the train of events in the present life. Your belief is avowedly unconformable to experience, for the very essence of the divine interposition is to be extrinsic and irreconcilable to the course of nature. But mark the further consequences: You dethrone and cancel the authority of experience in every instance whatever; and you thus place yourself out of condition to prove any one fact, or to disprove any other" (p. 126). To illustrate, suppose several witnesses, sane and sober, to see Smythe point a pistol at Browne and further to see Smythe pull its trigger. These witnesses hear the pistol's discharge and see Browne fall. Upon closer inspection they see a hole in Browne's head from which brain and blood ooze. Suppose further that upon ballistic examination, the ball in Browne's brain bears the markings characteristic of Smythe's pistol. Browne, it should be noted, lies dead, and the state accordingly indicts Smythe for murder. If God works miracles and had wanted Browne dead, why could he not have laid Browne low one nanosecond (or less) before Symthe's ball struck? How then could Smythe justly be convicted of murder? Smythe, in fact, may have intended to miss Browne, merely hoping to frighten him. Given miracles, God might have altered the trajectory of Smythe's bullet making it hit Browne, despite Smythe's intention to the contrary. The bullet, of course, might have lodged in a nonvital area of Browne's brain, yet he might have died anyway of a divine cause having nothing to do with his punctured brain and Smythe's antecedent actions. Indeed, Smythe may have fired a blank, the ball in Browne's head having been put there miraculously by God who could easily have scored it with the ballistic markings characteristic of Smythe's pistol. Bentham wrote, "Hence the belief of an unseen agent, infringing at pleasure the laws of nature, appears to be pregnant with the most destructive consequences. It discredits and renders inadmissible the lessons of experience: It vitiates irrevocably the processes both of proof and refutation, thereby making truth incapable of being established, and falsehood incapable of being detected" (p. 128).

Bentham noted that not many years had passed since witchcraft had been recognized and prohibited as a legal offense, numerous persons having been convicted of it and executed, others merely persecuted by their peers. According to this frame of mind, the divine despot of natural religion is not the only agent who interposes his will into the order of nature; demons and Satan, their prince, do the same. Given such imbecilic and pernicious beliefs on the part of people in general, a person accused of demonic possession might "have ridden an hundred miles through the air in as many seconds" (p. 129), rendering valid alibis useless, making facts impossible to explain, and evidence impossible to marshal. "To him who believes in the intervention of incomprehensible and unlimited Beings," said Bentham, "no story can appear incredible" (p. 130). Human minds at the mercy of such fictions are "cheated and overrun," eager in such a depraved state of mind to seek out diviners, to heed specious prophecies, to resort to magic, to seek convictions on trial by ordeal (amounting to fruitless torture), and to portray the Deity as pliant, partial, and without principle: "Expectations from the divine attribute of *pliability* have been and still continue to be universal. At least this is the foundation of the frequent prayers which are put up to Heaven for different species of relief—built, not upon the benevolence of God, for then his assistance would be extended to all the needy, whether silent or clamorous; but upon his yielding and accessible temper, which though indifferent if not addressed, becomes the warm and compliant partizan of every petitioner" (p. 133).

Bentham thought ill of supplicatory and intercessory prayers. When not associated with madness as in the case of those who ask for the moon, as it were, expecting to get it (and there are such people), prayer is either pernicious or useless. Bentham was especially offended by the idiotic proverb "God never sends a child but he sends food for it to eat," the natural inference from which is that one may marry and proceed to reproduce with no provisions whatsoever, nor the means for gaining any (pp. 134–35). One has but to ask the Deity for one's daily bread. However, in this world for aught experience teaches, people eat bread only by their own industry or by the industry of other people. Anything that lessens the use of intelligence in planning to achieve goals, anything that disjoins beliefs from experience, and anything that would lessen effort and industry is pernicious. When not pernicious, prayer, being mere words ritually mouthed and expected to have no real effect, is useless. Bentham asked and answered the following:

> Why should a man employ the slow and toilsome methods to which experience chains him down, when the pleasure which he seeks may be purchased by a simple act of prayer? Why should he plough, and sow, and walk his annual round of anxiety, when by the mere expression of a request, an omnipotent ally may be induced to place the mature produce

instantly within his grasp? No, it is replied—God will not assist him unless he employs all his own exertions: He will not favour the lazy. In this defence however it is implied, either that the individual is not to rely upon God at all, in which case there is no motive to offer up the prayer— or that he is to feel a reliance, and yet act as if he felt none whatever. It is implied, therefore, that the conduct of the individual is to be exactly the same as if he did not anticipate any super-human interference. By this defence, you do indeed exculpate the belief in supernatural agency from the charge of producing pernicious effects—because you reduce it to a mere non-entity, and make it produce no effects at all. (p. 134)

Prayer, Bentham decided, does not promote temporal happiness at all.

Another mischief of religion, of nation- or society-wide import, is the suborning and extortion of unwarranted belief. Religion accomplishes this by declaring that certain beliefs fall within the categories of "duty and merit" (p. 136). According to this, one ought to believe on authority what the religion teaches, without respect to evidence, for which one will then be rewarded. By the same token, disbelief in the favored dogmas is viewed as willful disobedience and lack of merit, deserving punishment. "So far as these threats and premiums are operative at all," said Bentham, "the effect must be, to make a man believe that which he would not naturally have believed, and disbelieve that which he would not naturally have disbelieved" (p. 137). To introduce rewards and punishments into the arenas of belief and disbelief is to introduce "lateral and extraneous forces" that pervert the process of making intelligent judgments. An analogy from common life would be that of bribing judges and threatening jurors. To introduce hope and fear, profit and loss into one's life as one weighs evidence pro and con for a particular belief is to distort rationality profoundly. Of the unsupported bribes of religion, Bentham wrote, "This sort of reward, indeed, operates as a direct bounty upon credulity—that is, upon belief unsupported by sufficient and self-convincing evidence. The weaker the evidence, the greater the merit in believing. This follows irresistibly. For if it is necessary to encourage belief by an artificial bounty, it would be useless to apply this stimulus to any doctrine which would of itself command the assent of mankind" (p. 138).

When assent to a particular proposition as true or dissent from it as false become questions of bribery and intimidation and not of unperturbed rationality, the individual brings into contempt "the guide whom he has deserted. . . . He accordingly speaks in the most degrading terms of the fallibility and weakness of human reason, and of her incapacity to grasp any very lofty or comprehensive subject. It thus becomes a positive merit to decide contrary to reason rather than with her" (p. 139). Such an outlook, so contrary to the achievement of profit and the avoidance of loss in this life, leads to "blindness and confusion." Bentham believed credulity to be the most fatal of mental conditions, leading as it does to "incessant disappointment and loss." "Error, when once implanted," he wrote, "uniformly and inevitably propagates its species" (ibid.).

In addition to creating factitious antipathies and perverting the intellect, natural religion causes yet another mischief—that of depraving the temper of the average believer. Bentham did not think that people who are made miserable by what they have been taught to believe of religion are particularly useful in promoting the general happiness. He stated as a general rule that "whatever curtails the personal comfort and happiness of any individual, disqualifies him to any equal extent from imparting happiness to his fellow creatures." Even those religionists who do not heap needless privations upon themselves exhibit a perpetual uneasiness and dissatisfaction with their lives. To Bentham there was (and is) a lack of consistency (and too great an element of happenstance) in the controls of religion over human behavior for it to create genuine mental calm in its devotees:

"The fitful and intermittent character of its inducements, incapable of keeping a steady purchase upon the mind, and daily overborne by urgent physical wants—the endless and almost impracticable compliances exacted in its code—the misty attributes of its legislator, who treats every attempt to inquire into his proceedings as the most unpardonable of insults—all these render it quite impossible for a religionist to preserve any thing like a satisfactory accordance between his beliefs and his practice" (p. 141). The result is a feeling of "inferiority and degradation . . . continually renovated" that "never ceases to vex the resolving and re-resolving sinner." Such is original (and persistent) sin! Said Bentham, "Dissatisfied with his own conduct, it is hardly possible that a man can be satisfied with that of others. We are told indeed that this consciousness of imperfection in ourselves ought to engender humility, and indulgence towards the defects of our brethren. But rarely indeed does it produce any such effect as this. Its general tendency is to sharpen the edge of envy—to make us more acute in hunting out and magnifying the faults of others, inasmuch as nearly the sole comfort remaining to us is, the view of others equally distant from the same goal" (ibid.).

The last great mischief that religion perpetuates is the creation of a "standing army" for the perpetration of all its other mischiefs, personal and social (p. 143). Those who constitute this army are the clergy, the practitioners of priestcraft. In the main, such people are "animated with an interest incurably and in every point hostile to human happiness" (p. 148). Those who would put themselves forward as temporal, terrestrial agents of the Deity and offer the services of their specialized ("aërial") knowledge to the laity depend on "human ignorance and incapacity." Once an area of concern is brought under the control of human competence, the Deity loses part of His previous domain, and His agents another bit of their influence. For those whose chief ally is ignorance, the goals are to disjoin the beliefs of people from their daily experience and to do so on a continual basis, and to magnify the importance of *"extra-experimental* belief." The clergy, of course, would have us believe that they are very learned in such knowledge. Those who do not comply with their goals have no need, no use whatsoever for clergy, because they do not regard the clergy as more capable in *any* way than they themselves. With nothing to offer, the practitioners of priestcraft lose their function—and their income.

The clergy would like the laity to regard them as the "licensed interpreters" of the divine will and its decrees. If and when these decrees are unavailable for intelligent scrutiny and possible criticism, the licensed law-interpreter rises to the majestic level of the grand and remote lawgiver—and establishes a monopoly. It is manifest that the interest of the monopolist, whether secular or sacred, lies in preserving the monopoly, in extending its wealth and power as much as circumstances will permit. "Now this," Bentham observed, "is irreconcilably at variance with that of society."

It is in the interest of religious monopolists to ensure an abundant and continuing supply of (presumed) offenses against the Deity. This can be achieved by prohibiting those acts "which there is the most frequent and powerful temptation to commit." Bentham wrote, "Now the temptation to perform any act is of course proportional to the magnitude of the pleasurable, and the smallness of the painful, consequences by which it is attended. Those deeds, therefore, which are the most delightful, and the most innoxious, will meet with the severest prohibitions in the religious code, and be represented as the most deeply offensive to the divine majesty. Because such deeds will be most frequently repeated and will accordingly create the amplest demand for the expiatory formula" (p. 152). Concomitantly priests will describe the Deity as irritable, vindictive, and capricious (i.e., his ways past discovery, but ever a source of anxiety). Even the episodic (but forgiven) sins of a short life merit *eternal* damnation, so profoundly offensive to the Deity are the sins in question represented to be. Having proscribed sins (even when innocuous) and having magnified the divine wrath out of all proportion, priests have but to throw themselves into the breach, to present themselves as possessing expiatory powers—available for hire, as it were. They who know the divine mind as nobody else knows it have efficacious prayers and ceremonies at the ready. Priests become, therefore, essential for the solace and succor of sinners.

The greater the "insecurity and helplessness" felt by people in their relation to the Deity, the better it is for His (self-appointed) representatives—the priests. For priests' security, it is also important that people in general perceive their sufferings and ill-fortune as just deserts and not as the unjust actions of the Supreme Despot. No matter how ruthless he may be toward humanity, he must be represented to be holy and beneficent. Should people begin to murmur against him, or to consider revolt, the priesthood would fall into the most precarious of positions. To avoid such a professional disaster and to extend their sway, priests and their hierarchies feed on "human ignorance, extra-experimental belief, appalling conceptions of the Deity, intense dread of his visitations, and a perversion of the terms of praise and censure on his behalf." None of this conduces to the genuine happiness of humanity in this life.

Despite the powerful engines at their disposal, the clergy by no means control all the contingencies of behavior: "For motives thus subject to fluctuation, the constant presence of a standing brotherhood is peculiarly requisite, in order to watch those periods when the mind is most vulnerable to their influence—to multiply and perpetuate, if possible, these temporary liabilities, and to secure the production of some permanent result during the continuance of the fit" (p. 155). So, the clergy are quick to strike in periods of "sickness—mental affliction—approaching death—childhood. . . ." Of these the approach of death is most productive. People about to depart this life can often be induced to ease their departure by alleviating their dread through gifts to the church, temple, mosque, or what have you. In this manner the sacerdotal class enriched, other potential beneficiaries defrauded—but the dead are not helped at all.

The clergy are in an enviable position, though not one that should delight the rest of us, once it is understood. Said Bentham of the clergy, "They are, ex-officio, both framers of the divine law, and vendors of the divine pardons for infringements of it. They have named the acts which require forgiveness as well as the price at which it should be purchased" (p. 157). If in earthly matters the lawmaker were also the agent "for the sale of licenses to elude it," terrestrial laws would be "inconceivably burdensome and exactive so that there should be no possibility of observing them" (p. 158). In short, the holy middlemen who serve the Deity have a vested interest in seeing his decrees broken. This serves neither the Deity nor the legitimate interests of humanity.

The clergy conduct their business in the coin of *"extra-experimental"* belief (as Bentham put it, p. 160), or what we would likely call nonempirical belief. Nothing that they say of a theological sort is (or can be) put to the test under controlled conditions. Rationalizations of the most exquisite sort are ever at their beck and call. Should an incomprehensible event occur, they will interpret it. Should it serve their purposes to distort "the physical links among phenomena," they will smuggle in "divine intentions." Should a useful (to them) coincidence occur, they will make of it a (holy) prodigy. Should a prediction accidentally come to pass, it will have been prophesied by a holy one who sees the future. Said Bentham, "Mendacity itself becomes consecrated, when employed in behalf of religion;

and the infinity of pious frauds, which may be cited from the pages of history, sufficiently attests the zeal and effect with which the sacerdotal class have laboured in the diffusion of this unreal currency" (ibid.). When systematized, this mendacity "lays claim to the title and honours of a separate science," the science of theology, a science of immaterial entities (whatever these may be) known in a nonempirical, nonexperimental way (however this may be done). This aërial science is "thickly and authoritatively" spread abroad. Its practitioners and professors, when skilled at their craft, reap all the credit that is ordinarily "annexed to superiority in any other department" (p. 161). Fraud of frauds!

The final variance between ordinary human interest in happiness and the specialized interests of the sacerdotal class lies in their conspiracy with the governing class. The clergy take it upon themselves to plant within the public mind "feelings which may neutralize all hatred of slavery, and facilitate the business of [economic] spoilation" (p. 162). Bentham wrote,

> By their influence over the moral sentiments, they place implicit submission among the first of all human duties. They infuse the deepest reverence for temporal power, by considering the existing authorities as established and consecrated by the immaterial Autocrat above, and as identified with his divine majesty. The duty of mankind towards the earthly government becomes the same as duty to God—that is, an unvarying 'prostration both of the understanding and will.' Besides this direct debasement of the moral faculties for the purpose of assuring non-resistance, the supernatural terrors, and the *extra-experimental* belief, which the priesthood are so industrious in diffusing, all tend to the very same result. (pp. 162–63)

The ruling class returns the favor by supplying the priesthood with physical protection and "compulsory tribute," i.e., church taxes. The symbiosis thus achieved is, of course, "sanctified by the holy name of religion" (p. 163). In such a system, "irreligion and heresy become crimes of the deepest dye, and the [priestly] class are thus secured in their task of working on the public mind, from all competition or contest." According to Bentham, the common ends of both the aristocracy and the clergy are the "prostration and plunder of the community" (p. 164), hardly ends compatible with human happiness and well-being in this world.

NOTES

1. *DNB*, s. v. "Grote."
2. Ibid.; see also introduction to *CJB*, vol. 10, p. xxiii.
3. David Berman, *A History of Atheism in Britain: From Hobbes to Russell* (London: Croom Helm, 1988), pp. 192–93.

4. James E. Crimmins, *Secular Utilitarianism: Social Science and the Critique of Religion in the Thought of Jeremy Bentham* (Oxford: Clarendon Press, 1990), p. 207.

5. Ibid., p. 4. For more on Bowring's piety, Unitarianism, and versifying, see R. K. Webb, "John Bowring and Unitarianism," *Ut* 4, no. 1 (1992): 43–79.

6. David Berman, "Jeremy Bentham's Analysis of Religion," *FTh* (Oct. 1982): 152.

7. Elie Halévy, *The Growth of Philosophical Radicalism* (London: Faber and Faber, 1928), p. 544.

8. James Steintrager, "Morality and Belief: The Origin and Purpose of Bentham's Writings on Religion," *MNL* 6 (spring 1971): 3, 14 n. 37.

9. Berman, *History of Atheism in Britain*, p. 192.

10. *DNB*, s. v. "Grote."

11. Berman, *History of Atheism in Britain*, p. 192.

12. *DNB* and *EU*, s. v. "Carlile, Richard."

Chapter 2

A Defense

The most common things in life are often the most difficult to encapsulate with words. Religion is no exception, being notoriously difficult to define to the satisfaction of all, or even of most, informed parties. The many attempted definitions of religion can, however, be categorized by type. J. Milton Yinger, a well-known sociologist of religion, has identified three of these, the valuative, the substantive, and the functional.[13] The valuative approach is quick to separate religion from what it takes to be superstition, magical practices, and any of its more "vulgar" manifestations. It attempts to identify the highest manifestations of religion with what religion really is. For example, the biblical book of Micah uses this approach when it says, "He hath taught thee, O man what is good; and what doth the LORD require of thee, but to do justly, and to love mercy, and to walk humbly with thy God" (Mic. 6:8). Selecting the ethical as the highest manifestation of religion, Micah ignores the formal institution of Judaism with its priesthood and holy places, its new moons and festivals, and its various cultic practices, including the ritual sacrifice of animals.[14] The valuative approach leads to the bifurcation of religious phenomena into true and false or higher and lower forms. It then spurns the false or the lower as superstitious. It always expresses the value system of the individual who is doing the evaluating and the bifurcating. It leads to the critical question: who says that what somebody or other takes to be the highest manifestation of religion is to be identified with the essence of religion? As we shall see, Bentham had no truck with this approach.

The substantive in the substantive definition refers to the approach to religion that puts primary emphasis on the content (or substance) of a belief or system of beliefs. Historically, belief in spirits, in supernatural beings, or in a supreme supernatural being has been taken to be both sufficient and necessary to make a given doctrine and the person(s) holding it religious. Émile Durkheim, however, identified a category he thought to be deeper and more fundamental than that of individualized spirits or supernatural beings—namely, the category of the sacred: "*A religion is a unified system of beliefs and practices relative to sacred things, that is to say, things set apart and forbidden—beliefs and practices which unite into one single moral community called a church all those who adhere to them.*"[15]

It must be recognized that the mere presence of belief in the putative object of the English word spelled with a G, an o, and a d (in that way and in that order) does not make the belief religious. Aristotle, for example, used the Greek *Theos* (i.e., "God") but did not mean thereby to refer to any Prime Mover or First Cause taken to be sacred and therefore to be feared, worshiped, propitiated, or prayed to. Moreover, Spinoza used the Latin *Deus* ("God") extensively but not in the traditional, reverential way. When, for example, he spoke of the will of God, he meant the laws of nature. Granted that 'God' may not necessarily imply that a statement containing it is ipso facto religious and granted that there may have been (or still are) primitive religions without personalized deities, still and all, throughout most of the history of the West, at least, statements of belief involving 'God' have been taken to entail the sacred (or the holy) and to be religious by that very fact. Clearly Bentham favored the substantive approach to religion by providing his own terse, substantive definition of it, italicized below.[16] He did not, however, dwell on the category of the sacred.

The functional approach to religion neither provides nor accepts any one valuative definition, nor does it place emphasis on any particular content of doctrines or system thereof. Rather, it asks the question, how does a religion function in the lives of those whose religion it is?[17] Put differently, what does religion do that nothing else does? To illustrate, if somebody were to ask for a definition of agriculture, we could all provide a clear functional definition. Agriculture is comprised of all those activities involved in planting, nurturing, and harvesting food and natural fibers. Similarly, one could ask, what is health care? The answer would be all those activities (especially the professional ones) involved in diagnosing and trying to cure diseases, in treating wounds, setting bones, and performing surgery, in prescribing medicines or various regimens for preventing ill health or for promoting good health, etc. Approached in this way, religion is cast in what for many is a new light, for the task now is to find what its unique functions are. Complications arise immediately, because religion, functionally speaking, overlaps with morality, with patriotism, and with aesthetics, at the very least. Moreover, it either is, or is a major manifestation of, what nowadays is called ideology. It is not imperative here to untangle this tangled skein of factors and features but simply to note the existence of the functionalist approach to religion.

Bentham was not altogether blind to this approach. He recognized, for example, a religious sanction that could operate in human affairs. To him a sanction was a "source of obligatory power" that could motivate individuals through the application of pains and pleasures. In the case of the religious sanction, the pains and pleasures at issue would, according to theology, emanate from the "immediate hand of a superior invisible being; either in the present life or in a future [one]." "The cultivation of religion," he wrote, "has two objects: to increase the force of this sanction; [and] to give this force a suitable direction." If the direction were supportive of utility, then religion would (to him) be benign. But, whether benign or malign, Bentham was clearly aware of at least some of the roles of religion in human life understood functionally.[18]

To summarize, Bentham did not approach any religious doctrine in the *AINR* as though it were true. His aim was to discover the implications of his basically substantive (but to some extent functional) definition of religion. He wanted to know what should follow logically in the way of temporal happiness and unhappiness, if individuals believed it were true that *there is an almighty being who dispenses pains and pleasures throughout an infinite and future time*. Accordingly, he did not separate religions into true and false varieties. Although he knew that religion might sometimes function in a useful way (as when bolstering a moral sanction for good behavior) and that it might on other occasions function in an abuseful way (as when distracting people from permissible pleasures here and now), he refused to call the latter 'superstition' while reserving 'religious' for honorific use in referring to the former. 'Religious' was not a term he used for something invariably good, while 'superstitious' was reserved exclusively for the presumed evils of false belief. In short, the distinction between the two was to him specious:

> The ordinary solution of this difficulty is to attribute all the good to *religion*, and all the evil to superstition. But this distinction, in this sense, is purely verbal. The thing itself is not changed, because the name is changed, and it is called religion in the one case, and superstition in the other. The motive which acts upon the mind, in both cases, is precisely the same: it is always the fear of evil and the hope of good from an Almighty Being, respecting whom different ideas have been formed. Hence, in speaking of the conduct of the same man on the same occasion, some will attribute it to religion, and others to superstition.[19]

Having discerned three different approaches to comprehending religion, each with its champions, it is now time to ask how good a definition Bentham created. To him, it must be remembered, religion means "belief in the existence of an almighty Being, by whom pleasures and pains are dispensed to mankind during an infinite and future state of existence."[20] By seizing on belief at the outset, he revealed his substantivist approach and rightly so. At least as far as the "religions of the book" are concerned in the cultures of the West (Jewish, Christian, and Islamic), that which distinguishes the religious person from the irreligious person usually lies in what is sincerely believed respecting the appropriate theological content.[21]

Throughout his writings Bentham used 'the Almighty', an 'almighty Being', and 'God' as synonyms, but he made no ontological commitment thereby.[22] Moreover, the theological question as to just how powerful a being would have to be to qualify for or merit the adjective 'almighty' never engaged him. Thus, he avoided the conundrums that arise when 'omnipotent', 'omniscient', and 'omnipresent' are used as adjectives modifying the noun-substantive 'God'.[23] To continue, it mattered not one whit to his definition of religion whether a being called the Almighty or God created the cosmos or not; out of nothing or out of something preexisting; at a certain time or in eternity, whatever any of this might mean. If one conceives of an absolutely minimal theism maintaining only that the universe is artifactual, thus necessitating an artificer, that and *nothing* more, it is dubious that religion would ever have arisen or become involved, functionally, in human belief. Such a belief would merely be explanatory of the universe at a certain level, a fact like any other fact, and interesting, perhaps, but irrelevant to human life, because vacuous. Such a spare deism as this has seldom, if ever, had many devotees. It is hard to feel much reverential awe for an artificer who has given up monarchical power over his artifact and departed the scene, refusing to answer prayers or to participate in any kind of redemption of the sort human beings crave.

The next component of Bentham's definition of religion concerns those activities of the almighty Being (believed in) that most please or pinch human beings. As far as the religions of the West are concerned, what the Almighty does with his power that really matters most is to dispense pleasures and pains. These, of course, are presumed to come in the forms of reward and punishment, either here or hereafter. At the level of natural sanctions, the occurrence of pleasures and pains is not necessarily in the form of rewards and punishments. The enjoyment of a fine meal, for example, may be the natural result of one's own achievements and not a reward at all. So, too, may the pains of climbing Mt. Everest be the natural result of the rigors required. At the moral and political levels, however, the sanctions of pleasure and pain most often, if not always, take the form of rewards and punishments. So, too, with religion, which Bentham saw as a kind of semisocial sanction.[24] Though there can be moral rules and secular laws without religion, should religion make its appearance, it will want people to behave as a given society (together with its culture) wants people to behave. In short, the celestial monarch of religion will back up the earthly king of some realm or other in the enforcement of commonly accepted morality and law.[25] Thus does religion function to control behavior; thus can it be manipulated by moral and political leaders.

The last part of Bentham's definition of religion involves the idea of an infinite and future time. As has been pointed out, an absolutely minimal theism would claim only that the universe is an artifact and that it therefore must have had an artificer at its inception, even though it may no longer be under the governance of that artificer. That this inferred being will dispense pains and pleasures to humans after their death is a signal addition to absolutely minimal theism, even though the two ideas have long been associated in the West. That such pains and pleasures will continue infinitely is an elaboration on the addition at issue. Granted that many miscreants die without justice having been done to them, why should they not live only as long after death as is necessary to receive their just deserts? Why should they live forevermore in punishment or reward? There is no logical connection between belief in life after death (whether brief, long, or endless) and the notion that the universe is an artifact. Nevertheless, these ideas have been taken to be essential to the dominant religion of the West for the past two thousand years.[26]

The question now arises, quite naturally, as to how good a definition of religion Bentham's is. Given the paucity of dependable ethnographic research and writing in his day, it is clear that he could not have known much about primitive religions in general (even if he had wanted to), nor could he have known in particular that "certain Australian tribes worship vomit."[27] He was also ignorant, at the other extreme, of the austere and highly refined meditative practices of Hinayana Buddhist monks in Sri Lanka[28] and of the sometimes agnostic speculations of the one(s) who wrote some of the verses constituting the Rig Veda and who are yet thought of, usually, as being religious.[29] The same was true of his ignorance of the theory and practice of Yoga in India and of Zen in Japan. In short, grist for religion's mill was and is much, much more varied than Bentham knew or could have known. Nevertheless, as far as the theological heart of Christianity and Islam, and to a lesser extent Judaism, are concerned, his definition is true as far as it goes.

Even before defining religion in the *AINR*, Bentham had bifurcated it into natural and revealed types. By revealed religion he meant any religion "settled by some revelation (or reputed revelation) from the Being to whom the belief relates." Revealed religion presupposes a divine revealer who discloses himself (or herself, as we would now add) to one or more humans in some fashion or other, the self-disclosure at issue taking the form of information that could not have been attained (or could not be attainable) by natural human powers. That the ancient Hebrews, their Israelite descendants, and, by extension, modern Jews are a chosen people is such a self-disclosure, or a reputed one. Deuteronomy 7:6 says, "For thou *art* an holy people unto the Lord thy God: the Lord thy God hath chosen thee to be a special people unto himself, above all people that *are* upon the face of the earth." This information could not have been (or could not be) attained by the use of pure reason or by any kind of human inquiry, scientific, historical, or otherwise. Respecting Christianity, we find in Galatians 1:11–12 St. Paul saying, "But I certify to you, brethren, that the gospel which was preached of me is not after [or from] man. For I neither received it of man, neither was I taught *it* but by the revelation of Jesus Christ." If St. Paul himself had not told us that his theology was true, because it was revealed uniquely to him, we should never have known it, or perhaps not even have guessed it. Respecting Islam, Bentham himself quoted its most famous creedal statement, *"La illah allah, Mohammed resoul allah"* (There is no god but Allah, and Mohammed is his messenger [or prophet]).[30] Such embroideries on basic theistic themes were far outside the logical limits of Bentham's analysis and interested him not one bit.

All other religion he called natural and believed that since it was based on reason (or reputedly on reason) rather than on revelation, it was fair game for his rational analysis. Since religion is broader in fact and in conception than is theology (which is merely its intellectual component), it would have been better if he had written of natural theology rather than of natural religion, but he did not. Nor did he refer to deism except on the rarest of occasions.[31] This is curious, since deism was the thinking person's theism in Bentham's time, especially in England, France, and the United States.[32]

Historians of England in general and students of Bentham in particular are aware that it would have been legally dangerous for him and his fellow freethinkers to have attacked Christianity directly or to have slighted the Established Church, so intertwined was it with the British Crown.[33] Bentham's fear lest he be accused of blasphemy or of seditious libel and his native prudence are often singled out as the reasons he attacked natural religion (i.e., deism) rather than revealed religion (in his case, Christianity).[34] Presumably he could get at revealed religion covertly by attacking natural religion overtly. There is doubtless some truth in this, but two points to the contrary need to be noticed. First, Christianity was itself, in his day, deeply involved in natural theology, nowadays often called philosophical theology.[35] The reason for this involvement is obvious. To predicate one's religion on faith and faith alone (as some Protestants have done and continue to do), is to invite the destructive question, If there are no good reasons for a particular faith, why adopt that faith and not some other one?[36] At least since the time of England's own St. Anselm (1033–1109) and his famous ontological argument for the existence of a being none greater than which can be conceived (an argument based on pure reason), Christian thinkers have explicitly busied themselves with philosophical (or natural) theology. The equally famous cosmological and teleological arguments of St. Thomas Aquinas (1225–1275) were proffered to prove logically that there must be a First Cause and Mover of all things (i.e., a necessary being) but not to establish such uniquely Christian doctrines as, for example, the Trinity and the Incarnation, doctrines beyond the efficacy of reason, doctrines that can be based only on revelation, presumably.[37] Theologians in the Church of England were no less assiduous in utilizing philosophical theology than were their Catholic counterparts. Thus, in analyzing natural religion, Bentham was analyzing the philosophical component of the dominant faith of his time and place, but without mentioning it by name.

Second, and more important, in attacking natural religion (or natural theology, as I prefer), Bentham was directly attacking the most advanced theology of his time, not simply using it as a sly way of attacking a more primitive revealed religion.[38] As British historian Basil Willey writes,

> This was the Golden Age of natural theology and deistical freethinking: The age of Spinoza and of Bayle, of the Cambridge Platonists, of Locke, Toland, Blount, Collins, Clarke, Wollaston, Shaftesbury, Tindal, and the rest. During the Christian centuries religion had rested upon revelation; now it rested largely upon "Nature," and even the orthodox, who retained the supernatural basis, felt that faith must be grounded firmly upon Nature before one had recourse to super-nature. "All the duties of Christian religion," says Archbishop Tillotson himself, "which respect God, are no other but what natural light prompts me to, excepting the two sacraments, and praying to God in the name and by the mediation of Christ."[39]

So, in the *AINR* Bentham chose to analyze deism in its full flower, the most advanced theology of the day. He was in fact quite explicit about this when he wrote, "For if it be discovered that Religion, unassisted by revelation, is the foe and not the benefactor of mankind, we can then ascertain whether the good effects engrafted upon her by any alleged revelation, are sufficient to neutralize the bitterness of her natural fruits." Put differently, one could ask, what can the species do to redeem the genus? Bentham, no doubt, thought that the species (i.e., Christianity) could do nothing to redeem the genus (natural religion), and herein he made his greatest mistake, but not for the reasons given by his critics. In due time, I intend to make all of this clear to the reader.

Having defined religion, having bifurcated it into natural and revealed types, and having selected the former as basic, Bentham proceeded to ignore revealed religion and any benign influence it might have, focusing instead on whether or not natural religion could be depended on to produce temporal happiness in its devotees. Happiness was (and is) to be understood as the balance of human pleasures over the debit of pains, especially of unnecessary pains. Unhappiness is, of course, the opposite. Benevolence in any being, human or superhuman, is to be measured by the will to produce human happiness; malevolence, the reverse.

In one of only a half-dozen footnotes appearing in the *AINR*, Bentham launched a body blow not only against Judeo-Christian theism but also against the best that religiously minimal theism could offer:

> Plato tells us that the Deity is perfectly and systematically well intentioned, but that he was prevented from realizing these designs, by the inherent badness and intractable qualities of matter. This supposition does indeed vindicate the intentions of the supreme Being, but only by grievously insulting his power and limiting his omnipotence. According to this theory, the Deity becomes a perfectly *comprehensible* person. . . . But at the same time that he becomes perfectly comprehensible, he becomes a dead letter with regard to all human desires and expectations. For by the supposition his power only extends to the production of the already existing amount of good. He can produce no more good—that is, he can be of no farther use to any one, and therefore it is vain to trouble ourselves about him.
>
> But what evidence is there for this doctrine of Plato? Not the shadow of an argument can be produced in its favor, and where nothing is set up as a defence, one cannot tell where to aim an attack. The only mode of assailing it is by constructing a similar phantom of one's own side, in order to expose the absurdity of the first by its resemblance to the second. Conformably to this rule, I affirm that the Deity is perfectly and systematically malevolent, and that he was only prevented from realising these designs by the inherent goodness and incorruptible excellence of matter. I admit that there is not the smallest evidence for this, but it is just as well supported, and just as probable as the preceding theory of Plato.[40]

Upon restoring honor to any deity that may exist by attributing omnipotence to his inferred being (as in Christianity and deism), two consequences manifest themselves. First, if there were an almighty benevolent deity, there would be a much greater balance of human pleasures over pains than is the case. Second, if there were an almighty malevolent deity, there would be a much greater balance of pains over pleasures than is the case. Experience clearly teaches (as Bentham saw it) that the relation between pains and pleasures in this life lies somewhere between these two extremes, tilting now in one direction, now in the other. By making the artificer (or demiurge in Plato's language) finite and defeasible by matter, to some extent at least, this inferred being is, as we have seen, rendered useless to humanity, having already done, through his artifice in contriving our world, all the good that he can do. However, by attributing all power to the artificer, while simultaneously experiencing the world as we do, he is, perforce, rendered incomprehensible, quixotic, and capricious. This point cannot be overemphasized.

How, then, can anyone who believes in life after death not face death with utmost fear, trembling, and dread? Moreover, how can such a belief together with belief in the deity of natural religion (just described) not blight the whole of life, the gloom impending at its end casting a pall over its beginning and all intervening years? The standard response is, no doubt, that in living a moral life one can recommend oneself to the presumed judge of the quick and the dead. But one can no more recommend oneself confidently to an almighty, quixotic, capricious being than one can extract moral rules from the artifact (i.e., the world) such a being is supposed to have contrived. Contrary to the stoics and others like them, Bentham denied that nature provides prescriptions for moral actions.[41] Such, of course, is human conceit in favor of itself that whatever is taken to be the highest in morality at a given time and place is conjectured to be precisely that which pleases most the presumed judge of the quick and the dead. Alas, there is no known way to please a being about whose character and temperament experience teaches nothing and concerning whom inferences drawn from the cosmos (taken as an artifact) yield only a capricious tyrant. Upon a moment's reflection, it is truly a fearful thing not just to fall into the hands of an angry god (à la Jonathan Edwards) but into the hands of a quixotic despot. Thus is Bentham's point made: even if the major premise of natural theology were true, it would be better in this life not to believe it.

If Bentham had not been so intent on undercutting confidence in a benevolent judge of the quick and the dead, and if he had not been so determined to show that natural religion is antithetical to secular utilitarianism, he would have been in an ideal position to contribute to a general theory of why human beings (alone among animals) are religious. To have done this, however, he would have had to be more empirical in outlook and less devoted to the use of logic alone in trying to establish what to him were the pernicious influences of religion. He could, for example, have prefigured Bergson in a more helpful way than he did by investigating as thoroughly as possible the various social functions resulting from society-wide belief in divine sanctions. Bergson explained thereby a very great deal of what he called static religion.[42] More important than this, Bentham could have contributed to an understanding of what I call the monarchical principle of religion (or a component thereof), a full understanding of which has become possible only recently and has yet to be completed. What this means will become clear in the paragraphs that follow.

At an elementary level Bentham knew of the identity of kings and gods.

He wrote, "*Gods* have their *attributes: kings and peers theirs. Kings* are 'Gods with us'—their representatives and images upon earth. Peers are creations of the crown."[43] Moreover, he knew that natural religionists (non-Christian as well as Christian), saddled in belief with a celestial but quixotic, capricious despot, proceed to deal with him very much as they deal with his "images" here below. The deity of natural religion, in short, is modeled upon "those earthly sovereigns in whom the most irresistible might resides." Conscious of human weakness in the (presumed) presence of almighty personal power, pious believers resort to the verbal sanction of flattery, heaping upon him the "largest and most prodigal encomiums." Moreover, the pious will attempt to find favor with their deity by doing what they take to be his will, forgetting that an almighty Being has no more need of help than of flattery. The logic involved here, of course, is the logic of human self-interest, not the logic of inquiry or of deductive consistency.

Desperate to curry favor with almighty personalized power, the pious are inclined to deny themselves innocuous pleasures and may even heap upon themselves extreme and useless pains and privations. In a more positive way, they will often go to great lengths, even endangering themselves, to glorify their deity and to proselytize in his name, will excoriate deviants from the "true way" (i.e., the heterodox), and will abominate unbelievers, perceived to be the enemies of the divine. To summarize, whatever works with a powerful mortal despot will be utilized with redoubled energy in dealing with an immortal and endlessly powerful one. The problem is that Bentham did not learn anything about human beings from this. What might he have learned or at least caught an inkling of?

From the ancient Greek thinker Euhemerus (c. 300 B.C.E.) to the contemporary American psychologist Julian Jaynes, there is a thread of thought holding that the gods were once men. Euhemerism maintained that popular, heroic, charismatic leaders (in distant antiquity) often became, after their deaths the gods that common people worshiped, and Jaynes in writing about the Natufian settlement at Eynon (c. 9000 B.C.E.) in what is now Israel identifies its dead king as the first god in history. He writes, "This was a paradigm of what was to happen in the next eight millennia. The king dead is a living god. The king's tomb is the god's house, the beginning of . . . temples."[44] So, though a king of England in Bentham's time was the image of the Christian God among contemporary Englishmen, historically the order was reversed, the human king coming first, then, in his image, the first god.[45] Although the Bible-god is most often referred to as the Lord, he is specifically called the King of Kings (Rev. 17:14), a Great King above all gods (Ps. 95:3), is taken to be one's personal God and King (Ps. 74:12), and the King of Zion (Ps. 149:2; Isa. 44:6). In the year that king Uzziah died, Isaiah claims to have seen the King, the Lord of hosts (Isa. 6:1–5). In one way or another, this monarchical theme is repeated over and over again in the Bible.

At a deeper level of theorizing than that required to explain how the consciousness of modern humans evolved from what Jaynes calls the bicameral mind of archaic humans (see footnote 163 below) lies the larger question of how modern humans as a biological species evolved from simian stock. A prominent theorist at this deeper, more comprehensive level is the British zoologist Desmond Morris, who has written that "in a behavioral sense, religious activities consist of the coming together of large groups of people to perform repeated and prolonged submissive displays to appease a dominant individual."[46] Anyone who has attended a worship service at which people close their eyes, bow their heads, clasp their hands in front of them, and kneel (or perhaps only genuflect) will know whereof he writes. Pictures of Chinese salaaming or kowtowing also make the point. At an even deeper level of theorizing than the ethological level of Morris and others lies the sociobiological level (including genetics) investigated by Edward O. Wilson. At one point Wilson, citing Peter Marin, notes the "masochistic relief that results from placing oneself into the hands of a *master* to whom omnipotence has been granted" (emphasis added).[47] Nothing in the foregoing is intended to suggest that the scholars in question have succeeded in resolving the whole riddle of human religiosity; the point, rather, is to substantiate what I call the monarchical principle of religion as we know it and as Bentham knew it.

Granted that the deity of natural religion is logically prior to more elaborated theisms (because simpler and more general), the etiology of the concept of deity in the West's favorite religion reverses this order. First came the Bible-god, maker of heaven and earth, father of humanity (or at least of a chosen people), king of all, judge of the quick and the dead, and executioner, as it were, or savior (through grace) of those whom he would punish or reward. Next, and much later, came the application to the Bible-god of the predicates of omnipotence, omniscience, omnipresence, etc., from the hands of philosophically trained converts to Pauline Christianity in the early centuries of our era. Finally came the simplifications of the natural theologians, who stripped what they took to be superstitious accretions (such as the Trinity) from the concept of deity.

Granted that any agent intelligent and creative enough to have made this world must be to humans awesomely powerful, still and all, does this require or merit the term 'omnipotence'? Is the meaning of any of the 'omni-' words above based on human experience or knowledge of any sort, or are these but terms of flattery, submissiveness, and obeisance, examples of the characteristic language (together with certain gestures and actions) of underlings in the presence of dominant monarchical authority? Clearly, the meaning of these terms is not based on experience or knowledge. Equally clearly, it is fully compatible with what underlings say and do in the presence of irresistible, potentially dangerous personal power.

To return to Bentham's stated object of examining natural religion relative to human happiness here and now, it is important to notice, I think, that omnipresence (whatever the origin of its application to deity) means that the possessor thereof is always looking over everybody's shoulder, that no act can go unnoticed and unsanctioned, positively or negatively. Moreover, granting omniscience to this presumed deity means that he engages in "universal espionage," as Bentham so aptly observed, even upon the most transient thought and on those intentions most quickly recanted, as well as in witnessing every human act. This goes far beyond what any earthly monarch, tyrant, or banana republic dictator can do. Logically, the result ought to be extreme anxiety to all who believe in such a deity, for such power denies all privacy to human beings. If to err is human (as to which most of us would agree), then a multitude of prospective punishments must occur in the imaginations of believers, if not in reality. How, then, can natural religion not be a hell on earth, so to speak?

In addition to confronting humans with an irresistibly powerful, but capricious and not uniformly benevolent, deity of despotic mien,[48] natural religion burdens its devotees with a second source of unhappiness: in varying degrees it cripples human intelligence in the pursuit of pleasure and in the avoidance of pain by disjoining, uncoupling, or detaching religious beliefs from empirical experiences. In short, natural religion turns the believer into a schizophrenic (etymologically speaking, a person whose mind is torn in two) gaining one sort of information about the world through sensation while being informed contrariwise through religious doctrines held on faith.

As though the frightful deity depicted above were not bad enough, the natural religionist is led to believe that this almighty Being is invisible, omnipresent, infinite, and eternal. These terms are so often mouthed reverentially in connection with references to the deity of natural religion (and to the Christianity deity too) that they seem to ascribe positive characteristics, but in point of fact they are all negative and as such render that to which they presumably apply "extra-experimental," to use Bentham's term. To be invisible means to be unseeable by any ocular means, not unseeable because too tiny (such as a virus) to be seen without a microscope or unseeable because too far away (such as a distant star) to be seen without a telescope but unseeable by nature, yet (presumably) real. In the classical Protagorean sense, however, it is through sensory experience that man is the *measurer* of all things: "of existing things, that they exist; of nonexistent things, that they do not exist."[49] Put differently, the human organisms that do this kind of measuring (deciding what is and what is not) use themselves (i.e., their own being) as the meter stick of reality, so to speak. To hypothesize a being invisible by nature is to commit oneself to one-knows-not-what and to being incapable of knowing the difference between the truly invisible and the nonexistent, sometimes a distinction of crucial importance.

At first sight 'omnipresent' seems to be the most positive of predicates, but from an empirical standpoint it means to be nowhere. As philosopher Thomas Vernon has written, "What is it that has no body, that cannot be seen or heard, that is completely immaterial, yet is present throughout the Universe? If you want an honest answer, go to Lucretius. Lucretius said it is 'the void,' nothingness in other words. God is nothing."[50] This point is perhaps made more clear by separating nothingness into no-thing-ness and saying that the Deity is no-thing.[51] To mean by divine omnipresence that a person might feel the prickings of conscience no matter where she is (or was) at the time of committing an immoral act or to feel that a divine eye, metaphorically speaking, is always looking over her shoulder (see Ps. 139:11–13) is one thing; it is something quite different to try to make "being-everywhere-at-once" an essential characteristic of a personal being such as is (supposed to be) the deity of natural religion. To imply the latter is to go beyond all possibility of sensuous experience and to cease to comprehend what is meant by 'being' in 'omnipresent being'.

'Infinite' also names a negative predicate. 'Infinite' means boundless. It is easy for human beings to illustrate the futility of seeking the boundless. They have but to look at attempts at reaching the largest possible number. Since a person can always add 1 to any number or can add any even, odd, or prime number thereto, the task is clearly hopeless. In the spirit of Bentham's philosophy of language it is interesting to note that even though 'largest possible number' can be spoken, spoken of, or written about, it can refer to nothing, for there is no such number. It is thus a fictitious term referring to a nonentity, the two together, in human imagination, feigning reality. Tricks of language of this sort, which are endemic in theology, must never be forgotten. To Bentham, such nouns as infinity, invisibility, and omnipresence are the names of fictitious entities.

'Eternal' has two sharply contrasted meanings. In common parlance it usually means everlasting time and refers to anything in endless process, without beginning or ending. At the metaphysical level, however, it means timeless and refers to that which always is as it is, never coming into being or ceasing to be. If we understand by time a requirement of any sort of activity and by the measure of time the use of one process to measure the advance or unfolding of another process, then the timeless is that which is inactive or changeless. Because the deity of natural theology is said to be changeless, he is called eternal. To Bentham, neither everlasting time nor timelessness is ever experienced (sensuously) by human beings. Thus the eternal as well as the infinite, the omnipresent, and the invisible are "extra-experimental."[52] How, then, can human beings speak of such matters reasonably, except in abstract domains such as those of mathematics and logic, and what, we must wonder, is the state of mind of natural religionists when they assert belief in a being "unseen, unheard, untouched, untasted, and unsmelt—his place of residence unknown—his shape and dimensions unknown—his original beginning undiscovered"?

Neither the distinguished natural theologians of the time, such as William Paley (born in 1743, only five years before Bentham), nor Bentham himself sought out the possibility of any psychosocial origin of the "divine attributes" mentioned above. For the most part the theologians in question relied on what to them was the self-evidence of analogical reasoning. As human beings stand in relation to the artifacts of their contrivance, so (the argument went and still goes) an almighty artificer stands to the universe. Since the cosmic artifact is immense and complicated, the artificer must be almighty (for all practical purposes at least). Since the artificer is never seen, it stands to reason that he must be invisible. Since one can go nowhere in the natural world without finding evidence of design, his intelligence, intentions, and influence at least, are omnipresent, if not his very person. Since neither beginning nor end were known (to natural theologians) to characterize the cosmos, its artificer must be eternal, etc. Bentham torpedoed the deists' analogical reasoning using a simple epistemological approach. He observed that human beings *know* design only in themselves and in animals. We know clearly, for example, that we design shelters with which to shelter ourselves and that we fabricate objects such as machines to work for us and thus to facilitate our lives. We also know that some animals, acting as agents, alter the environment for the ends of their respective species. Consider, for example, the comb of the honeybee, the cylindrical nurseries of the mud dauber, the nests of hornets and birds, and the dams and dwellings of beavers. Beyond the examples above (and their ilk) and a few instances of animals' using sticks as rudimentary tools we know nothing of other agents of design, of designing activities in nature, or of nature itself as designed.

It is not that the natural theologians Bentham had in mind reasoned from the microscope or the telescope to the human eye and thus from the fabricators of the former to a supreme fabricator of the latter; it is that from the outset (a priori) they viewed the universe (whether ordered, or disordered, or a mixture thereof) as a result, a product, an artifact. They were unwarranted in this interpretation, because it was (and is) based on no human sensory experience of the commencement of all things. Furthermore, respecting designs issuing from organisms, the effects thereof are confined to the alteration (but not to the creation) of preexisting materials, that is, to the "admotion or amotion of its particles to and from each other." The almighty being of natural theology, on the contrary, was (and is) usually supposed to have made the world out of nothingness, a proposition no human being was (or is) in a position to verify or even to think probable. Thus, analogical reasoning as used in natural theology rests on faith and faith alone. Such reasoning is nothing but rationalizing what is already believed.

While I write these words, there lies close at hand an issue of the magazine *Free Inquiry*.[53] Emblazoned across its cover are the words "Is Religion a Form of Insanity?" Bentham raised the same point in the *AINR*. To him, complete insanity was the total divorce of one's beliefs from one's empirical experiences, lesser degrees of separation paralleled by lesser degrees of insanity. Broadly speaking, Bentham took reason (or intelligence as is preferred nowadays) to be the sum of a human being's powers to distinguish truth from error. Thus, he was not thinking primarily of pure reason as it might be used, for example, in trying to prove Fermat's last theorem, but of memory, knowledge, insight, creativity, and reasoning prowess as *all* of these might be focused on the data of the senses in addressing the problems of daily life and in realizing one's goals. Paramount among human goals would have been to him the avoidance of unnecessary pains and the acquisition and enjoyment of as many socially sanctioned pleasures as possible. Seen in this way intelligence in distinguishing truth from error, fact from fiction, and reality from nonreality is crucially important to living a happy life. Those who cannot make such distinctions are in varying degrees crippled intellectually and doomed to make mistakes of judgment as to how to live, collectively as well as individually.

In view of the foregoing, let us take as an example a natural religionist (of the garden variety) and ask what chance this person has of living as happy a life as possible. By garden variety, I mean one whose deism is not of the bare-bones variety but is tinctured in no small degree by popular Christianity, as was in fact most deism. For maximum relevance, let us position this person in Bentham's England and for reasons of style let this person be treated now as male, now female. Let us also take him to be a gentleman of the sort educated (deplorably to Bentham) at Oxford or Cambridge. Here is a person who on the basis of nothing taught him by his senses anthropomorphizes his world as quick as a wink. Henceforth, it shall be viewed by him as an artifact, just because it is here, so to speak. The absence of any empirical evidence for the presence of its presumed artificer does not mean that this being died in the act of creation or succumbed later. No, he lives on and on endlessly, but is an invisible spirit. Nor is the artificer like an ever-living mud dauber or any other organism less than human. No, the artificer must be humanoid, but in a transcendent way, his creation, like a human artifact, only far more sublime, vast, and complicated.

But just how humanoid is one who is taken to have a mind but no brain; who sees and hears but has neither eyes nor ears; who speaks but has no vocal chords; who waxes hot and cold emotionally but has no heart (or as one might say nowadays, no limbic system); who is a person but was never socialized; who is moral but can never be held responsible for anything; who has a vast appetite for human praise but is incomparable and perfect; who is almighty and can do anything (not logically impossible and not out of keeping with this nature) but who needs human services here below; who is real but not physical; who is everywhere simultaneously but nowhere in particular except that he dwells in heaven; who knows everything but cannot know what it is like to learn anything, forget anything, change his mind, or put anything out of mind; who is eternal, having neither a past nor a future, but who acts in time implying both a before and an after relative to any act he may undertake; who knows the future of all individuals perfectly, in particular what each person intends to do or does that is evil but who causes no evil intentions or deeds? This list could go on but is already long enough to indicate that there is less in common between this allegedly humanoid but transcendent deity and human beings than there is between them and an almighty mud dauber.

To pursue a different tack for a time, so different are the perceptions our natural religionist has of her body (using her senses) when contrasted with the intuitions she has of what she calls her mind that she believes herself to be a dual creature, having both a physical body and a metaphysical something-or-other she variously calls her mind, soul, or spirit. Of the two she knows her body, though real, to be transient and believes that it is not to be identified with her living essence, whereas her (hypothesized) soul, once incarnated, is permanent and is to be identified with her true self. On grossly insufficient empirical grounds she believes that she (i.e., her soul) will live on forever after her body dies. She takes it as axiomatic that her peregrinations in the spirit world will not be aimless. On the contrary, she foresees a payoff in the world to come for a life well lived here and now. She believes strongly (but on the basis of no experience) that dread punishments await some people but not herself, for she has been a deist and has lived an upright life guided by reason. The empirical experiences she has had in this world of seeing the rain fall on the just and unjust alike, of seeing bad things happen to good people, and good things happen to bad people will not, she is confident, characterize the spirit world. On the contrary, even though lacking empirical evidence, she believes that justice will be done (or, paradoxically, mercy shown) once she has departed this world for the next one. She gives no credence to Bentham's inference that deists like herself should, on rational grounds, expect to fall into the hands of a quixotic despot in the kingdom of the dead.

For one thing, the natural religionist has (presumably) stayed on the right side of her deity by giving him glory, laud, and honor. She has said of her heavenly king everything that it is honorable to say of her earthly king, but has carried each eulogistic predicate to its supreme, open-ended degree. Whereas she has dutifully recognized the king (of England) here below to be powerful, she has most humbly recognized her heavenly king to be all-powerful. In fact she has gone so far in verbal praise that she no longer knows what she is talking about and cannot imagine that any of the excellent things she has had to say might be inconsistent or nonsensical. As far as she has thought things through, her omnipotent, omniscient deity, for example, ought to be able to put things from his mind if he wants to (and is omnipotent) but, alas, cannot do so, if he is also omniscient. It is monstrous to our theologian to think (as Bentham thought obvious) that the most certain infinity possessed by her deity is not infinite goodness, but limitless capriciousness.

How those paragons of reason, the deists of Bentham's day, could believe in such "extra-experimential" theological notions as theirs were and not be a bit mad went beyond his comprehension. Real insanity, of course, lay (and still lies) with the Christians. In addition to lodging their faith in all (or nearly all) of the predicates above when applied to their deity, they also contrive verbal conundrums that neither they nor anybody else can understand but which they accept as adorable mysteries to be taken on faith.[54] This is not a criticism but an admission on their part. The doctrine of the Trinity, and Christian commentary thereon, will make this point. Millions of believers on unnumbered occasions during the past fifteen centuries have mouthed 'Father', 'Son', and 'Holy Spirit' (or 'Ghost') reverentially, and have had the vague idea that they knew what they were saying, but not so. The doctrine of the Trinity illustrates this point perfectly (as expressed in Canon I of the Fourth Lateran Council in 1215):

> We firmly believe and openly confess that there is only one true God, eternal, beyond measure and unchangeable, incomprehensible, omnipotent and ineffable, the Father, the Son, and the Holy Spirit: Three persons but a single essence, substance, or nature that is wholly one; the Father proceeding from none, the Son proceeding from the Father alone, and the Holy Spirit from both in like manner; without beginning and having no end for ever: the Father begetting, the Son having been begotten, and the Holy Spirit proceeding; having the same substance, the same equality, the same omnipotence, and the same eternity. . . . This Holy Trinity, undivided in regard to its essence which is common to all, but distinct in regard to the attributes of the persons, gave the doctrine of salvation to the human race in due process of time.
>
> And finally the only begotten Son of God, Jesus Christ, made flesh by the Trinity in all its persons together, conceived of Mary, ever Virgin, with the cooperation of the Holy Spirit, made true man, composed of a rational soul and human flesh, one person in two natures, showed the way to life with greater clarity. . . . Though immortal and impassible in His divinity He yet became subject to suffering and death in His humanity; nay more, He suffered and died for the salvation of the human race on the wood of the cross, descended into hell, rose from the dead, and ascended into heaven. But He descended in the soul, and rose in the flesh, and ascended alike in both.[55]

The most important, but often overlooked, word in the preceding excerpt is 'ineffable', meaning incapable of being expressed in words. One can only marvel at the mental legerdemain of those who can express themselves at this length on an inexpressible topic.

The ineffable nature of the Trinity has not proved to be a drawback to Karl Rahner, a prominent Catholic theologian, who is as verbose as Canon I above:

> The Trinity is an absolute mystery which is not perspicuous to reason even after being revealed. . . . If there are any absolute mysteries, that of the Trinity is undoubtedly the most fundamental. Little explicit attention is given [by the Magisterium of the Catholic Church] to why and how the mystery remains meaningful for us. . . . The one God exists in three persons, subsistences, hypostases . . . who are the one divine nature (φύσις), essence, (οὐσία), substance (as distinguished from subsistence). . . . These persons are also (really) distinct from one another. . . . The Father has no principle of origin. . . . The Son is born of the substance of the Father . . . and only from the Father. . . . The Spirit is not begotten . . . but proceeds from the Father and the Son as from one principle . . . in a single spiration. . . . How this "begetting" and "breathing" are further distinguished is not explained by the Magisterium. The "relative" persons in God are not really distinguished from the essence of God . . . and hence do not form a quaternity. . . . In God all is one, except where an opposition of relationships exists. . . . Each of the divine persons is fully in the other . . . and each of them is the one true God. . . .[56]

It should go without saying that the three are coeval. How these things can be, "the human mind is unable to fathom." "Precisely how the procession of the Holy Ghost differs from the generation of the Son is . . . a mystery that we shall fathom only in heaven."[57]

That to which Christians refer when they mention the Incarnation is also a part of the "central mystery of Christianity," according to Karl Rahner.[58] Søren Kierkegaard, the eminent Protestant theologian, called this "mystery" a paradox and an absurdity: "What now is the absurd? The absurd is—that the eternal truth has come into Being in time, that God has come into being, has been born, has grown up, and so forth, precisely like any other individual human being, quite indistinguishable from other individuals.[59] Continuing in this vein, he added, "[Christianity] has proclaimed itself as the *Paradox*, and it has requested of the individual the inwardness of faith in relation to that which stamps itself as an offense to the Jews and a folly to the Greeks—and an absurdity to the understanding."[60]

Contrasted with this, the doctrines of the Immaculate Conception of Mary and the Virgin Birth of Jesus seem hardly mysterious at all but almost commonplace. St. Ephrem the Syrian (d. 373), the first poet of Mary and an adherent to what we would now call Eastern Orthodoxy, seemed not to have been overwhelmed in the slightest, either by paradox or absurdity. The following fragments of his work indicate how pellucid it all seemed to him:

> 16. Mary is the garden upon which descended from the Father the rain of benedictions. From that rain she herself sprinkled the face of Adam. Whereupon he returned to life, and arose from the sepulchre—he who had been buried by his foes in hell. . . .
>
> 20. Lo, a virgin is become a mother, preserving virginity with its seals unbroken. . . . She is made God's mother and is at the same time a servant, and the work of His wisdom.
>
> 21. The virgin, who gave birth to the Only-begotten, has nurtured God and man, has become Mother of the hidden Little One, who of the Father was born perfect and is made an Infant in her womb. . . .
>
> 45. Let the word of life be sent by Thy Majesty to the dwelling place of the dead, and say to Eve lying in the sepulchre: "Thy daughter with virginity unimpaired has brought forth the child who will pay thy debt."[61]

Since Mary is extolled here as the Mother of God it should follow (à la Bentham) that her mother (St. Anne) is the Grandmother of God and so on all the way back to Eve. That the one who was made from a rib of the first man should, in effect, be a great-grandmother (many times over) of the deity who made the first man is indeed a paradox worthy of hyperdulia.[62]

That a child (Jesus) of such parentage should have taken upon himself the sins of the world seems almost to be expected, a commonplace. Rahner, for example, feels no need to stress anything mysterious in describing the deliverance from sin (of the saved) effected by the sacrifice of Jesus, his death, burial, and descent into hell, his resurrection from the dead and his ascension into heaven, from whence he came. These items of faith, it would seem, are quite straightforward and free from paradox or absurdity.[63]

Whether the doctrines above are said to refer to absurdities, paradoxes, antinomies, or dialectical contradictions (depending on current theological fashions), they are all undergirded, overlaid, and buttressed around and about by miracles or, more precisely, by belief therein. These, presumably, guarantee the truth of each doctrine for the faithful no matter how patently absurd to the profane mind.[64] Thus do such doctrines evade (or seek to evade) the grasp of rational inquiry and criticism. The criteria for the miraculous, unfortunately, are never given at all convincingly. Hence, though unbelievers never know whether or not or when they are encountering a genuine miracle (as opposed to a rare, unexpected, but perfectly natural occurrence), believers always do know, or so it would seem.

To believe in magic and miracles, to trust in the efficacy of supplications addressed to an almighty being (of fire, water, spirit, or whatever), to change anything objective in the world, to abase (or even to torture) oneself before an invisible monarch in the skies, to fear a malevolent spirit (the devil) and his imps marauding on earth, to glory in admitted absurdities, and to profess belief in incomprehensible doctrines for the sake of saving one's soul (a dubious entity) was (and is) so greatly to divorce one's beliefs from one's experiences of the world as to be tantamount to madness as Bentham saw it. To him any mind that can entertain such absurd fictions has been and remains, quite literally, depraved. Such depravity prevents people from making rational choices in the search for the happiest life possible in this world, the only world of which we have any experiences, departure from which is departure from life.

The excursion above into the admitted paradoxes and absurdities of what Christians take to be revelations may seem to be a departure from Bentham's stated objective, namely, to assess natural, rather than revealed, religion; but not so. Very early in the *AINR*, he wrote, "[I]f it be discovered that Religion, unassisted by revelation is the foe and not the benefactor of mankind, we can then ascertain whether or not the good effects engrafted upon her by an alleged revelation are sufficient to neutralize the bitterness of her natural fruit." Three points, respecting Bentham, are crystal clear: (1) Natural religion (i.e., deism) yields bitter fruit; (2) alleged Christian revelations do not neutralize this bitterness; (3) they intensify it.

Before summarizing how or why (to Bentham) the fruit of revealed religion is far less palatable than that of deism, a puzzle needs to be addressed. On several occasions in the *AINR*, Bentham referred to the "ministers of natural religion" and in the Preface thereto he says pointedly that whenever the term 'sacerdotal class' is used it is to be understood as referring to the ministers in question. The puzzle is this: there were no such ministers, if we mean by this term pastors of like-minded congregations. I have been assured by an expert in English history that there was never an organized religious body in England composed of what Bentham thought of as natural religionists.[65] Such people, in a corporate sense, had no clergy, unlike various dissenting groups, nor was there ever a priesthood among deists or a hierarchy of deistical priests. The first thing that comes to mind is that Bentham was being disingenuous, that he used this ploy to throw sand in the eyes of his pious enemies. The second thing that comes to mind is that this was a way to extend the parallelism he had established between natural religion on the one hand and revealed religion on the other. Just as the latter had priests, so the former had ministers. Such ministers, if any, could merely have been the proponents of natural religion, that is, apologists for deism, not the *clergy* thereof. Or, perhaps he was thinking of the ministers of the minuscule flock of English Unitarians, chief among whom (for a time) was the eminent scientist, biblical scholar, and historian of religion Joseph Priestley. Priestley was antitrinitarian and progressively deistical in outlook as his ministry matured.[66] Finally, Bentham may have had in mind the most enlightened clergymen of the Established Church, also deistical in outlook but in ritual and good form stalwart representatives of Anglicanism.[67] Whatever the case, in the second half of the *AINR*, Bentham focused on the hocus-pocus of priests and to some extent on the (to him) useless antics of ascetics. Neither group, it should be noted, attracted natural religionists. In short, as the *AINR* progresses one can see the focus shift from rare, but unnamed, individuals such as a Priestley or a Tillotson to those blind guides who practice the priestcraft of a revealed religion, in this case Christianity. If Bentham could have remained alive in an Islamic state to write as he wrote in Christian England, he could have said almost the same unkind things about Islam that in fact he was saying about Christianity, and to a lesser extent he could have criticized Judaism in the same indirect, lightly veiled manner.

With deism flourishing among intellectuals and believed by some to be a religious rival to Christianity, with English Unitarianism mushrooming in various dissenting congregations, with men like Priestley evangelizing on its behalf and stoutly attacking the Christian "corruptions" of the original gospel, and with Anglicans like Tillotson boring from within, it is clear, then, that Bentham's "minister of natural religion" is more than a convenient creation with which to bludgeon Christians. The mischiefs of deism, however, were of an intellectual sort involving questionable assumptions, the misuse of analogical reasoning, and an unwarranted dismissal of empirical experience. To Bentham the result thereof ought logically to have been an increase in the pains of emotional distress over the pleasures of a tranquil mind in the life of the individual deist. Yet as the *AINR* progresses, the evils of revealed religion and the mischiefs of priestcraft are laid at the deists' doorstep. This is surely unfair, for the evils of deism were (and are) benign compared to the pernicious nature of Christianity.

Not content merely to proclaim marvels, miracles, and wonders for belief,[68] the Fathers of the Christian church contrived to offer absurdities, incomprehensibilites, and paradoxes.[69] In due time doctrines that nobody could understand were dogmatized, that is, made binding on the faithful, not on the basis of empirical fact or logic but on the authority of those who had promulgated the dogmas. 'Dogma' is a Greek word initially meaning "that which one thinks true, an opinion."[70] Progressively, it took on the meanings of "decree, ordinance, decision, command."[71] In the hands of the hierarchy that progressively took control of the Christian church, dogmas became sacred and thus slipped beyond inquiry or critics, their truth resting solely on the say-so of those whose dogmas they were. Then to the normal processes whereby people distinguish truth from error were added obligation, desert, threat, and punishment. One was obliged to believe what the hierarchy taught. If one did so, one was good, and great would be one's reward in heaven. Failure to do so implied guilt, the result of which could well be eternal damnation. In this manner, through the use of the holy carrot and the sacred stick, religion perverts the minds of all whom it touches. Bentham's fear was that such perversion in one area of life would spread inevitably to other areas, making it impossible for individuals to recognize where their own best interests and those of society lay.

Increasingly in control of the engines of education and thus of culture itself, the Christian hierarchy set about to see to it that every child had authoritative answers before he could ask any questions, that the metaphysical might intrude upon each life as forcefully as the physical, and that the supernatural might be made omnipresent before the natural could be grasped. Even more important, perhaps, every child had to learn that truth comes in two kinds, the sacred (or holy) and the profane. Holy truth, of course, is certain and easy to acquire (via sacerdotal pronouncement), whereas the latter is a sometime thing, hard to trust due to the distortions of the senses and the frailty of finite minds. In this way natural human powers are debased, making it difficult for such weak reeds to distinguish between "plain-believe" and make-believe, as it were.

Human nature being what it is, it is unlikely that all people at any time and place will be gullible in exactly the same way. So, it is axiomatic that those who hand down decrees will provoke dissent. Dissent aimed at holy decrees is, of course, not just error but wickedness. Thus the orthodox (those on the winning side) must rise up to smite the heterodox (those on the losing side). Being filled with pride (what they call principle), heretics must submit to correction or else! Since correction seldom comes easily to the heterodox (recalcitrant by nature if not demonically infested), the guardians of the one true faith (any one true faith) may have to resort to imprisonment, to implements of torture, or even to conflagrations. Better that a heretic burn for thirty minutes here, while repentance is still possible, than to burn forever in hell. To Bentham, people who thought in this way had minds that were, quite simply, depraved.

Assuming that uniformity in doctrine has been achieved (through whatever totalitarian techniques are needed), there still remains the unbelieving world outside the fold, peopled by the pagan, the heathen, and the infidel. Should these benighted folk bedevil the one true faith with their own true faith, the one true faith must defend itself. Intellectually, it does this through the manufacture of apologetics, that is, of learned rationalizations filled with every persuasive and halfway plausible fallacy known to human ingenuity. The effects on the brains of those exposed to this species of fraudulent reasoning are pernicious indeed. But, since the best defense is a good offense, the one true faith can and will send soldiers of the cross (sometimes masquerading as well-intentioned missionaries) to convert the unconverted in general and the would-be converters of other imperialistic religions in particular. Thus do two sets of theological absurdities combat one another, the one sometimes winning, sometimes the other. Upon winning, the winners honor their deity by brainwashing the losers, using the widest imaginable variety of techniques. Just as misery loves company, so faith rejoices in great numbers. Hence the enthusiasm for converts. Bentham, of course, was never deceived into thinking Christian dogmas true because Christian missionaries had been (and continue to be) astonishingly successful.

More disturbing to the hierarchy by far than skeptical children, dubious (but discreet) communicants, ranting heretics, and perfervid pagans are apostates, those who having once believed depart the faith.[72] This is especially true of those who were once in the clergy/ministry/priesthood/religious order of the one true faith, for in leaving the trade, as it were, they take all the trade secrets with them.[73] They know that the things they once thought sacred are not, that the words they once proclaimed to have come from their deity did not, that the rituals they performed have no independent efficacy apart from the credulous folk for whom the rituals were (or are) performed. They know that they know nothing that the laity cannot know. They know that the experiences people presume to confirm their faith are neither empirical nor logical but are psychosocial in nature. They know that those who look inward to see visions, who hear voices in their heads, and who tremble in worship as before a mighty king bear no evidence in support of their beliefs.[74] That theology masquerades as legitimate knowledge, but is not, is easy to see. If we compare a theologist with a biologist or a geologist, an obvious but rarely articulated difference appears. A professional biologist not only knows the literature of the field but has hands-on experience of living things, of cells, tissues, organisms, etc. The same is true of a geologist except that here the hands-on experience is of rock strata, upthrusts, mineral deposits, etc. The theologist (or more commonly, theologian) knows only what other theologians have thought, spoken, or written. The theologian has no hands-on experience of anything but tries to make it seem so by reference to emotional phenomena. Thus, the theologian is, more than anything else, like an untrained psychologist, practicing without a license. Theology may be called a sacred science, but it is neither sacred nor a science. Works of theology can display enormous erudition, to be sure, and the most finespun reasoning, but they are fraudulent, exhibiting no method worthy of the name and arriving at no truths whatsoever. Here again Bentham would see a flagrant example of mental depravation.

If he were alive today in the Christian West, Bentham would find nothing parallel to the intellectual atrocity heaped on Galileo by the Roman Catholic hierarchy, but he could find parallels in the Muslim world.[75] If he were to appear today in that part of the West known as the United States, he would find that the greatest intellectual fraud of the religiously inspired variety emanates primarily from Protestants.[76] A misnomer from the outset, it is called "scientific creationism" or "creationscience." He would find the people who believe in this nonsubject and who participate in its spread particularly imbecilic, because without any warrant for doing so (even without any biblical warrant), they have come to accept dogmatically the inane idea that the Bible is without error and have made this belief crucial to their (presumed) salvation. If the Bible is inerrent, then evolution cannot be factual (despite all the evidence for it) and Darwinism cannot be the proper explanation of its mechanism(s), because neither of the two creation stories in Genesis, chapters 1 and 2, says so. The "scientific creationists," as my American readers will know, want their favorite creation myth(s) taught as science on a par with contemporary views of evolution whenever the latter are brought up in the public schools. The mental "depravity" of the "scientific creationists" can be seen readily in the book *Of Pandas and People: The Central Question of Biological Origins.*[77]

The "scientific creationists" begin with the same unsupported assumption as the one assumed by Bentham's natural religionists—namely, that the universe is an artifact. Next they assume that the artificer still lives, as it were, to this day. This is followed by the assumption that the artificer is almighty and dispenses pleasures and pains to the "saved" and the "lost" respectively throughout the infinite future. Based on this illogical house of cards they proceed to use the same analogical reasoning Paley (b. 1743) used in Bentham's day and beg the same question thereby. This profound misuse of reason is compounded by two collateral absurdities, one spoken often and gladly, the other spoken only among friends. The first absurdity is to call the mishmash above scientific and to represent it as a rival to Darwinism or to any other *theory* of evolution.[78] The second absurdity is to take the Bible dogmatically to be without error in scientific subjects as well as in moral or religious ones.[79]

Respecting natural theology, Bentham's criticisms in the *AINR* are largely on target for the aforementioned reasons. The same is true of his notso-covert criticism of the revealed religion he knew best, that is, Christianity, including, most especially, its elaborate theology.[80] However, his criticisms of religion as a whole, whether natural or revealed, fall short of the mark.

NOTES

13. J. Milton Yinger, *Religion, Society, and the Individual* (New York: Macmillan, 1957), esp. pp. 6–17.

14. Isa. 1:10–15, taking much the same tack, mentions various religious activities typical of the Hebrew faith of the time that are pictured as being spurned by the Bible-god in favor of specifically ethical practices.

15. This is a very famous definition of religion that often appears in anthologies in both the sociology and the philosophy of religion. See *The Elementary Forms of the Religious Life*, trans. J. W. Swain (Glencoe, IL: Free Press, 1947), p. 47.

16. It would not be difficult to find more than one hundred definitions of religion. A classical source is James Leuba, appendix to *A Psychological Study of Religion: Its Origin, Function, and Future* (New York: AMS Press, 1965), pp. 339–61. Herein one finds forty-eight definitions not including Bentham's and not including some of the more recent ones such as Yinger's: "Religion . . . can be defined as a system of beliefs and practices by means of which a group of people struggles with these ultimate problems of human life. It is the refusal to capitulate to death, to give up in the face of frustration, to allow hostility to tear apart ones human associations" (*Religion, Society, and the Individual*, p. 9). Probably the most influential definition in contemporary America is that of Paul Tillich: "Being religious is being unconditionally [or ultimately] concerned" (*The Protestant Era*, trans. James Luther Adams [Chicago: University of Chicago Press, 1948], pp. xv, 58, 87, 273). Less popular, but also influential, is Clifford Geertz's definition, to wit: "(1) a system of symbols which acts to (2) establish powerful, pervasive, and long-lasting moods and motivations in men by (3) formulating conceptions of a general order to existence and (4) clothing these conceptions with such an aura of factuality that (5) the moods and motivations seem uniquely realistic" (*The Interpretation of Culture* [New York: Basic Books, 1973], p. 90). Anthony Wallace defines religion as "a set of rituals, rationalized by myth, which mobilize supernatural powers for the purpose of achieving or preventing transformations of state in man and nature" (*Religion: An Anthropological View* [New York: Random House, 1966], p. 107).

17. For more information on the functionalist approach to defining religion, see Yinger, *Religion, Society, and the Individual*, part 2, section 2.

18. See *An Introduction to the Principles of Morals and Legislation*, in *WJB*, 1:14; *Principles of Penal Law*, in *WJB*, 1:564; *General View of a Complete Code of Laws*, in *WJB*, 3:170; *An Introductory View of the Rationale of Evidence*, in *WJB*, 6:20–21, 261; and *Rationale of Judicial Evidence*, in *WJB*, 6:261.

19. See Bentham, *Penal Law*, in *WJB*, 1:566.

20. Bentham gave very nearly the same definition of religion elsewhere when he wrote,

> Religion is calculated to supply this deficiency of human power [in meting out rewards and punishments], by inculcating upon the minds of men the belief that there is a power engaged in supporting the same [moral and legal] ends, which is not subject to the same imperfections. It represents the Supreme Invisible Being as disposed to maintain the laws of society, and to reward and punish according to infallible rules, those actions which man has not the means of rewarding and punishing. Everything which serves to preserve and strengthen in the minds of men this fear of the Supreme Judge, may be comprehended under the general name of Religion. (*Complete Code of Laws*, 3:170)

21. Judaism, Christianity, and Islam are often referred to as "religions of the book" because of the centrality to each of writings taken to be sacred by their

respective devotees. These religions are often contrasted with the Eastern religions Hinduism and Buddhism, in which the written word plays a lesser role and meditative techniques play a greater role.

22. See *The Rationale of Reward*, in *WJB*, 2:261; *Swear Not At All*, in *WJB*, 5:191–92; *The Constitutional Code*, in *WJB*, 9:24. On one occasion at least he used the term 'all-powerful', writing," [F]or by Deity, what else does any man mean than the Being, whatever he be, by whom every thing is done?" (*Introduction to the Principles of Morals and Legislation*, in *WJB*, 1:58.

23. Among theologians, St. Augustine (354–430) had long since desisted from pushing the meaning of 'omnipotence' to its nth degree. Having elected to believe that his deity was both all-powerful and perfectly good, he was confronted with the questions of why and how evil, both natural and moral (i.e., sin), could be in the world. Respecting natural evil he contented himself with the belief that it was nothing positive in itself but was merely the lack of goodness. Since only his deity was perfectly good, it followed that every lesser being, created by that deity, would lack some of the divine goodness. Respecting sin he contented himself with the ideas that his omnipotent deity (though knowing all things) neither willed nor caused any sins but merely permitted their occurrence. Aside from the creation of all things, his omnipotence was, presumably, shown in two ways: (1) no sin, however great, nor all sins together, could thwart the divine plan, and (2) the deity in question could turn all sins against themselves and invariably bring forth good in accordance with his will. Many gallons of ink have been spilled over the problem of evil (and the resulting theodicies), even in our own time. Respecting omnipotence and omniscience, Professor Scott Hestevold of the University of Alabama has kindly called my attention to the question of whether or not a deity perfect in all ways could create a person who knows a secret unknown to that deity. Actually, a second, created person is not needed to make the point. One has only to ask whether or not an all-powerful deity could will to forget something that he, she, or it knows. If so, then there is something knowable that this deity no longer knows (fatal to omniscience); if not, then this inability is fatal to omnipotence, taken in the most literal sense. For an investigation of similar puzzles see Charles Hartshorne, *Omnipotence and Other Theological Mistakes* (Albany: State University of New York, 1984), esp. chap. 1. Bentham never allowed himself to be drawn into rationalizations over the implications of a priori, theological ideas. It was enough for his definition of religion in the *AINR* that the almighty Being of religion could dispense pleasures and pains at will in any degree at any time to anybody anywhere for any length of time, suffering neither restraint nor limitation. In the *AINR*, omnipotence never needs to mean more. For the aforementioned views of St. Augustine see his *Enchiridion*, trans. J. F. Shaw (Edinburgh: T. and T. Clark, 1892), book 9, esp. chaps. 94, and 100–104. The *Enchiridion* can also be found in *Basic Writings of Saint Augustine*, ed. Whitney J. Oates, vol. 1 (New York: Random House, 1948), esp. pp. 713–20.

24. In *Introduction to the Principles of Morals and Legislation*, in *WJB*, 1:56, Bentham took note that "the love of reputation, the desire of amity, and the motive of religion, may together be comprised under the division semi-social."

25. Among philosophers, Henri Bergson has written most brilliantly on the

function(s) of religion in society in chaps. 1 and 2 of *The Two Sources of Morality and Religion*, trans. Ashley Audra and Cloudesly Brereton (London: Macmillan, 1935).

26. Christianity is, of course, the dominant religion of the West, but what has just been said of it in the text above can also be said of Islam. Bentham, though never vitally interested in it, knew of Muhammad, of his religion, and of the Koran. See *Rationale of Judicial Evidence*, in *WJB*, 7:110, 158. He also, of course, knew of the religion of Moses. See *Introductory View of the Rationale of Evidence*, in *WJB*, 6:21. The association between an almighty creator (or artificer) of all things and life after death in a state of reward or of punishment is not, however, as straightforward in Judaism as it is in either Christianity or Islam. Prior to the third century B.C.E., Judaism viewed the postmortem condition of Israelites as one in which their shades descended into the earth to slumber in She'ol (a kind of dormitory of the dead) in a state neither of reward nor punishment. The Bible's most explicit (and perhaps first) mention of a resurrection of at least some of the dead to reward and punishment occurs in Dan. 12:2, a work of the intertestamental period, dated around 165 B.C.E. In the New Testament one of the distinctions given for separating Jews into Sadducees and Pharisees is that the former denied the resurrection whereas the latter accepted it (Acts 23:8). Following the New Testament period, notions of resurrection progressively dropped out of Judaism to be replaced by the idea of immortality. Respecting subsequent Judaism, including the modern varieties, it can be said that "generally some form of belief in immortality is essential," to meet the requirements of justice if nothing else. See Luther H. Harshbarger and John A. Mourant, *Judaism and Christianity: Perspectives and Traditions* (Boston: Allyn and Bacon, 1968), pp. 341–45. If one does not put too fine a point on distinctions between the resurrection of the dead (i.e., the revivification of their bodies) and their immortality (of the mind, soul, or spirit), then Bentham's definition of religion, as far as it goes, refers to beliefs shared by Jews, Christians, and Muslims.

27. See Clifford Geertz's contribution to *IESS*, s. v. "religion," esp. the anthropological study thereof.

28. Buddhism divides into two major schools, the Hinayana (or Theravada) and the Mahayana. The latter accepts a variety of manifestations of the Buddha who act as saviors. The former, although concerned with salvation, puts the burden of achieving it on the individual monk. This form of Buddhism is believed to be more ancient and more true to the initial practices of the historical Buddha than is the Mahayana, but he was for all practical purposes atheistic, or at the very least agnostic, rejecting "religious devotion as a way of salvation." See John B. Noss, *Man's Religions*, 4th ed. (London: Macmillan, 1969), part 2, chaps. 5 and 6. Whether or not Bentham could have seen original Buddhism as religious is an open question.

29. See "The Song of Creation," the 129th hymn of book 10 of the Rig Veda, in *Hindu Scriptures* (London: J. M. Dent and Sons, 1938), pp. 36–37.

30. Qtd. in *Rationale of Judicial Evidence*, in *WJB*, 7:111.

31. The only place of which I am aware in Bentham's published writings where he mentioned deism was in his letter to President John Quincy Adams of June 1, 1817, wherein he asked about religion, blasphemy, and prosecutions for libel in the United States. In the course of asking about the religion of Jesus, about Trinitarians, Unitarians, and Atheists he wondered whether or not belief in "Deism as contradis-

tinct to Unitarianism" would obstruct the temporal advancement of an individual. See *CJB*, 9:12–13. In the extensive index of *WJB*, vol. 11 (391 pages, each containing two columns of fine print) there is no entry for 'deism' and only two for 'natural religion' (one under the heading of 'natural' and the other under 'religion'), each referencing the same place in his writings. See *Justice and Codification Petitions*, in *WJB*, 5:458. It is not so surprising that there are no additional references to natural religion since Bowring, in his wisdom, chose to exclude Bentham's only work on the subject (the *AINR*) from the collected works.

32. In his *Dictionary* (of 1755) Samuel Johnson defined 'deist' as "a man who follows no particular religion but only acknowledges the existence of God, without any other article of faith." See Ernest C. Mossner, *EP*, s. v. "deism," esp. p. 327. This is identical with what I have called absolutely minimal theism. At this bare-bones level deism does not constitute religion. Indeed, it was sometimes perceived to be atheistic. See David Berman, *History of Atheism in Britain: From Hobbes to Russell* (London: Croom Helm, 1988), p. 76; Michael Hunter and David Wooten, *Atheism from the Reformation to the Enlightenment* (Oxford: Clarendon Press, 1992), pp. 233, 240. Even if deism did not teach explicit atheism, it could mean such things by 'God' as some "eternal inanimate matter, some Universal Nature, and Soul of the World," not at all what most theists had (or have) in mind. See the quote from Richard Bentley in Berman, *History of Atheism in Britain*, p. 104. According to Alfred William Benn, *The History of English Rationalism in the Nineteenth Century* (New York: Russell and Russell, 1962), 1:210, deism was perceived to be a rival religion to Christianity in the first half of the eighteenth century but became less hostile thereafter. In its fullest flower and closest to Christianity, deism consisted of the following beliefs:

> 1. One and only one God exists. 2. God has moral and intellectual virtues in perfection. 3. God's active powers are displayed in the world, created, sustained, and ordered by means of divinely sanctioned natural laws both moral and physical. 4. The ordering of events constitutes a general providence. 5. There is no special providence; no miracles or other divine interventions that violate the lawful natural order. 6. Men have been endowed with a rational nature which alone allows them to know truth and their duty when they think and choose in conformity with this nature. 7. The natural law requires the leading of a moral life, rendering to God, one's neighbor, and one's self what is due to each. 8. The purest form of worship and the chief religious obligation is to lead a moral life. 9. God has endowed men with immortal souls. 10. After death retributive justice is meted out to each man according to his acts. Those who fulfill the moral law and live according to nature are 'saved' to enjoy rewards; others are punished. 11. All other religious beliefs or practices conflicting with these tenets are to be regarded critically, as at best indifferent political institutions and beliefs, or as errors to be condemned and eradicated if it should be prudent to do so.

See Roger L. Emerson, *DHI*, s. v. "deism." In theological jargon, the deity of deism was an absconded (or absent) deity, transcendent over his universe but not immanent in it.

33. Benn wrote in his *History of English Rationalism*, "Sensible men . . . were not to publish books against revelation, nor even to obtrude their heterodox opinions in conversation" (1:210). He continued, "But the strongest motive of all for strict reticence was, no doubt, the fear of offending public opinion" (1:297). Yet attacking the Church of England is exactly what Bentham did in his *Church-of-Englandism*, published in 1818 and bearing his name rather than that of a disciple writing under a pseudonym. Part 3 of this volume focuses on Bentham's devastating critique of the Catechism of the Anglican Church.

34. Crimmins writes, "The charge of blasphemy was a frequent resort of government at this time, used to suppress literature deemed to be of a seditious or libelous nature as well as tracts aimed directly at the Church and Christian beliefs" (*Secular Utilitariansism: Social Science and the Critique of Religion in the Thought of Jeremy Bentham* [Oxford: Clarendon Press, 1990], pp. 129–30).

35. If one looks at *ET*, one will find under the general entry "natural theology" subsection B, titled, "natural theology and the theology of revelation." Each type of theology is of extreme importance to Catholic and Anglican forms of Christianity.

36. The well-known contemporary school of theology called Neo-Orthodoxy relies exclusively on faith and rejects natural theology totally as a valid source of theological knowledge. See Karl Barth, *Against the Stream: Shorter Post-War Writings*, ed. Ronald G. Smith (New York: Philosophical Library, 1954), pp. 210–16, and Emil Brunner, *The Christian Doctrine of God*, trans. Olive W. Lyon (Philadelphia: Westminster Press, 1950), pp. 132–36.

37. In his *Exposition of Boethius on the Trinity*, ed. B. Decker (Leiden: Brill, 1955), 1:4, c, Aquinas wrote, "That God is threefold and one is solely an item of belief and it can in no way be demonstrated, although some arguments can be given that are not necessarily convincing or even very probable except for a believer." In the same vein the Catholic theologian Karl Adam writes in *The Spirit of Catholicism* (Garden City, NY: Doubleday, 1954), pp. 49–50, "But natural reason leads me only so far, only to God as the principle and meaning of all things. . . . Thus the inner God, the whole God, the 'mystery which had been hidden from ages and generations (Col. 1:26)' is revealed to us men only by the supernatural way, only by the fact that He Himself speaks to us."

38. David Berman, "Jeremy Bentham's Analysis of Religion," *FTh* (1982): 152.

39. Basil Willey, *The Eighteenth Century Background: Studies in the Idea of Nature in the Thought of the Period* (New York: Columbia University Press, 1940), p. 3.

40. Bentham did not admire Plato, referring to him on one occasion as a "spoiled child of Socrates" (*Chrestomathia*, in *WJB*, 8:120).

41. Bentham called the notion of natural rights, twin brother of natural law, "nonsense upon stilts" (*Anarchical Fallacies*, in *WJB*, 2:501).

42. See n. 25 above.

43. *Bentham to Fellow-Citizens*, in *WJB*, 4:438.

44. It is impossible here to do justice to the rich and breathtaking theory that Jaynes has developed in *The Origin of Consciousness in the Breakdown of the Bicameral Mind* (Boston: Houghton Mifflin, 1976), pp. 141–43. See also the numerous index entries referring to God, Gods, God-kings, etc., p. 459. I shall have more to say about Jaynes, both in the text and in notes, toward the end of this chapter.

45. More than seven thousand years after the creation of history's first god, the

Bible-god is portrayed as an eminently human/kingly figure. This man of war (Exod. 15:3) is so earthbound that special precautions have to be undertaken lest he step in human feces while prowling the Hebrew military camp in the dark of night (Deut. 23:13–14). On one occasion this humanoid deity meets Moses at a lodging place and capriciously seeks to slay him (Exod. 4:24) but fails, indicating something less than omnipotence; on another occasion he allows Moses to look upon his backside (Exod. 33:23), a curious kind of spirit indeed. This selfsame deity claims all animal fat for himself, denying it to his people (the Hebrews) and enjoys, we are told (Exod. 29:15–18; Lev. 17:6) the scent of the smoke from the fat of fed beasts burning. Even more surprising we learn in Num. 31:32–40 that the Bible-god receives thirty-two virgins as his share of the booty taken from a particular rout of Midianites and that on one occasion at least he laid bare the secret parts of the daughters of Zion (Isa. 3:17). He appears not only to have been humanoid in general but also to have been exceedingly masculine in some of his interests.

The deity destined to become all-knowing in Western theology was anything but omniscient closer to his point of biblical origins. In the tale of the Tower of Babel (Gen. 11:1–9), the Bible-god, upon catching wind of human events, comes down from heaven to have a look-see. Surely an omniscient being would not have needed to bestir himself in this unseemly manner. Moreover, once on the scene, surveying the technological skills of Babel's builders, he observes (verse 6b) that henceforth anything that human beings could imagine they could achieve, a serious error in a deity omniscience bound. Nor is this all. In both the Old and New Testaments, the Bible-god is pictured as being on the defensive in the presence of human knowledge. In the Old Testament, Eve, the primal mother of humankind, is threatened with speedy death lest she should eat of the fruit of the tree of the knowledge of good and evil and become wise, having her eyes opened and knowing good and evil even as do the gods (Gen. 3:1–6). It is no accident that in the Old Testament the beginning of knowledge or wisdom is the fear of the Lord (Job 28:28; Prov. l:7). In the New Testament (1 Cor. 1:18–31, 3:18–20) St. Paul depicts the deity as one who had chosen to reveal himself through the moronic (or foolish), the weak, the lowly, and the despised in order to shame the literate, the learned, and the logical lest they should boast of their attainments. Paul never makes it clear why the Bible-god should have been so easily vexed by human arrogance of an intellectual sort. Even less should an omniscient deity take umbrage at human boastfulness (if such there be) over intellectual accomplishments, bound to be minuscule compared to his.

As for moral perfection, well, the Bible-god has more than a little for which to answer. In addition to his wholesale slaughter of human beings episodically (Gen. 7; Hosea 9:11–14) and his commands to the Israelites to exterminate their enemies root and branch (Deut. 20:16–17), he is also perfidious now and again. On one occasion he puts a lying spirit in the mouth of certain prophets (1 Kings 22:23). Indeed, says Ezek. 14:9, "And if the prophet be deceived when he hath spoken a thing, I the Lord have deceived that prophet." Nor does he lose this characteristic in the New Testament, for therein (2 Thess. 2:11) he is depicted as sending a strong delusion on certain people that they should be deceived, believing a lie.

46. Desmond Morris, *The Naked Ape* (New York: McGraw-Hill, 1967), p. 179. Morris believes that at one time and for a very long time our remote ancestors lived

in small, face-to-face groups similar to those of baboons, for example, living on the savannas of east-central Africa. In such groups leadership at any given time is lodged in a dominant male that in his prime is a veritable god-king to the other members of the group, settling squabbles and maintaining peace and order on the one hand and exercising leadership and providing protection against external dangers on the other. Hand-to-mouth life in a largely static social structure broke down when cooperative hunting began to replace gathering in the search for food. Such activity requires not only an element of obedience but also of individual initiative, the latter being antithetical to the unquestioned dominance of a single individual. The emotional need for such a god-king, however, persisted. Thus did our ancestors in imagination invent god(s) as a replacement for the real dominant male of the intimate social group (see esp. pp. 178–80). Morris also believes that as populations exploded, minor local deities gave way to super-gods, suitable to empires or to modern nation-states. All major groups of people nowadays, he notes, have a single super-god or an analog thereto. According to his book *The Human Zoo* (New York: McGraw-Hill, 1965), p. 31, aiding in the concept of the god as a father figure is the fact of human neoteny. In biology, neoteny refers to creatures that become sexually mature while still in the larval stage; applied to humans it means that we retain elements of juvenile plasticity throughout the whole of life. In short, we never grow up and continue even at an advanced age to need or to find solace in parental figures (Morris, *Manwatching: A Fieldguide to Human Behavior* [New York: Harry N. Abrams, 1977], p. 151). Sigmund Freud had long been aware of the analogical relationship between the child and the parent (especially the father) and the believer and his or her deity, but he could not go below the psychosocial level of explanation to the biological level, because at the time when he wrote *The Future of an Illusion* (1927), the biological concept of neoteny had yet to be applied to the human species. See *The Complete Psychological Works of Sigmund Freud*, ed. James Strachey (London: Hogarth Press, 1961), 21:17. Forgetting the rarefied deity of natural religion for a moment, the Bible-inspired god that Bentham confronted daily in his England was portrayed as the creator of all things, father of his people, king of heaven and earth, judge of all, and executioner or savior of whom he would. Given these divine roles, humans are, perforce, creatures, perpetual children, subjects of an absolute monarch, universally sinful defendants before the bar of divine justice, fallen beings deserving death, and, in some cases, recipients of grace, that is, of unmerited love, conducing to everlasting life. Many, many passages in both the *Old Testament* and the *New Testament* reveal this, and subsequent theology is replete with these themes. A number of puzzles in religious belief and behavior and what appear to be conundrums in theology can be clarified by understanding how much of religion is based on the model provided by the relationships of craven subjects to their tyrant. The following "Garland of Stalinisms," taken from *PC* 12 (March–April 1963): 87, will illustrate this point. *Pravda*, December 10, 1949, carried the following passage: "The heart of every Soviet citizen is warmed by his love of Stalin. In all languages of the world, humanity glorifies his name, the name of the promoter of popular happiness, of the head of working humanity." On the following day it outdid itself, to wit:

He is the friend of the sun
He will disarm all, his foes.
Your name is on our lips,
Your heart is in our hearts,
Your will in our deeds.
Stalin, the father, has sixteen daughters—
Sixteen loving Republics.

This, however, pales in comparison with *Pravda*'s achievement on August 28, 1936:

O Great Stalin. O Leader of the Peoples,
Thou who didst give birth to man,
Thou who didst make fertile the earth,
Thou who dost rejuvenate the centuries,
Thou who givest blossom to the spring. . . .

Further commentary hardly seems necessary.

47. Peter Marin, "The New Narcissism," *Harpers* (October 1975): 45–56, cited in Edward O. Wilson, *On Human Nature* (Cambridge: Harvard University Press, 1978), p. 185; also see the whole of chapter 8 on religion. Much of the same material appears in his *Sociobiology: The New Synthesis* (Cambridge: Harvard University Press, 1977), esp. pp. 559–62. In *On Human Nature*, Wilson makes what would have been an almost unbelievable statement just a generation earlier, to wit: "Most importantly, we have come to the crucial stage in the history of biology when religion itself is subject to the explanations of the natural sciences. As I have tried to show, sociobiology can account for the very origin of mythology by the principles of natural selection acting on the genetically evolving material structure of the human brain" (p. 192). The otherwise excellent book by J. Samuel Preuss, *Explaining Religion: Criticism and Theory from Bodin to Freud* (New Haven: Yale University Press, 1987) ends with no inkling of the possibility of deeper levels of explanation of religion than any hitherto reached. The simple fact is that religion is now being biologized, as it were. For example, see the Gifford Lectures for 1989 by Walter Burkert, published as *Creation of the Sacred: Tracks of Biology in Early Religions* (Cambridge: Harvard University Press, 1996). Also see Vernon Reynolds and R. E. S. Tanner, *The Biology of Religion* (London: Longman, 1983). Another straw in the biological winds is Mark Ridley's "Infected With Science," *NS* 25 (December 1993–January 1994): 22–24, wherein the author (who teaches anthropology and biology at Emory University) asks did the "cerebral circuits" of human beings evolve "to carry rational, even scientific thoughts about nature and society, or to mystify them with religious meanings?" He also raises the ominous point that in a Darwinian struggle for existence perhaps "religious enthusiasm can crowd out rationality." How religion evolved in the human species is not a "spiritual" question but a sociobiological one.

48. It must be remembered that if the deity of natural religion were truly benevolent toward human beings, then he would have made a far better world than he did, being almighty.

49. See Fragment 12.6 in John Mansley Robinson, *An Introduction to Early Greek Philosophy* (Boston: Houghton Mifflin, 1968), p. 245.

50. Vernon is professor emeritus of philosophy at the University of Arkansas. See his article "An Omnipotent God," *AR* 34 (September–October 1989): 39.

51. Paul Tillich, a philosophical (i.e., natural) theologian of high visibility during the mid-twentieth century, made much of the no-thing-ness of God. In addition to attacking popular "unspecified" theism and criticizing biblical theism (too anthropological and personalistic) he also attacked what he called "theological theism" for conceiving of God as a being (even though the most important being) alongside of other beings and for making him an object "bound to the subject-object structure of reality," and, one might add, of language. Tillich thought the problem could be resolved by recognizing that God is not a being but is Being-Itself. Failure to see the concept in this way makes God into an all-powerful and all-knowing tyrant, such as a Hitler or a Stalin. See *The Courage to Be* (New Haven: Yale University Press, 1952), pp. 182–90, esp. p. 185. Calling the true God "Being-Itself" puts him above the God of theological theism according to Tillich. He also called God the "Ground of Being" and the "Power of Being" to resist nothingness. See the index to his *Systematic Theology*, vol. 1 (Chicago: University of Chicago Press, 1951), Bentham would have made sport of Being-Itself for reasons that will become manifest in part 3.

52. The component 'experimental' in the term 'extra-experimental', which Bentham uses frequently in the second part of the *AINR*, encompasses the empirical, but it must be remembered that the empirical here refers only to the kinds of experiences provided by the organs of sense. It does not encompass, for example, what the well-known theologian Rudolf Otto meant by "*deeply felt religious experience*, as little as possible qualified by other forms of consciousness" (emphasis added). See his influential book *The Idea of the Holy*, trans. John W. Harvey, 2nd ed. (London: Oxford University Press, 1950), p. 8. Nobody has summarized better what Otto meant by experiencing the "numinous," that is, the presence of deity, and by experiencing the *mysterium tremendum*, some at least of whose meaning is transparent in the Latin, than anthropologist Paul Radin, author of *Primitive Religion: Its Nature and Origin* (New York: Dover Publications, 1957):

> From fear, according to Otto, came awe, the terrible, the feeling of being overpowered and overwhelmed, crystallizing into what he [Otto] calls the tremendum and the majestas [what I call the monarchic principle in religion]; out of the sense of helplessness, of powerlessness, of insignificance, came that creature-feeling so well described in the OT, and out of compensation fantasies arose, finally, the concept of that completely other [i.e., the Holy] which is rooted in the familiar and which is yet entirely new. From the compulsion implied in coercion there developed eventually that willing sense of subjection which is implied in fascination. All the ingredients are here from which the supernatural arose. Merged and interpenetrated with what is always primary, the implications of living and the economic struggle for existence in an inimical physical environment, they gave us primitive religion. (p. 9)

On the same page, Radin also writes of Otto, "Being a theologian and a mystic he naturally misunderstood the true nature of these concepts and of their genesis." Had Bentham been able to know of this quotation, he would have applauded it. One must admit that the experience of gooseflesh on the arms and the feeling of hair standing erect on the nape of the neck are empirical in their way. One must also admit that such experiences occur to some people some of the time in the presence of the (believed-in) sacred or the supernatural. However, such experiences are not what Bentham meant by the empirical, nor can they play a role in experimentation that is designed to separate fact from fiction. Such experiences, in short, are not instrumental in discovering truths about the world.

53. Specifically, vol. 13, no. 3 (1993).

54. In his "Can God's Existence Be Disproved?" *Mn* (April 1948): 176–83, J. N. Findlay argues that "Divine Existence can only be conceived, in a religiously satisfactory manner, if we also conceive of it as something inescapable." Put slightly differently, a religiously adequate deity for modern humans must have all the characteristics attributed to him by the natural theologians Bentham had in mind plus the characteristic of necessary existence. Unfortunately for such theologians the concept of God predicated in this way can have no verbal significance and can refer to nothing. Hence, to conceive of God as religion requires nowadays is to produce a concept with no referent.

55. See *Creeds of the Churches: A Reader in Christian Doctrines from the Bible to the Present*, ed. John Leith (Garden City, NY: Doubleday, Anchor Books, 1963), pp. 57–58.

56. *ET*, s. v. "Trinity, Divine, the," part B, "The Doctrine of the Magisterium," pp. 1757–58.

57. Bernard J. Otten, *A Manual of the History of Dogmas*, 3rd ed. (St. Louis: B. Herder, 1922), pp. 272–73.

58. *ET*, see especially Karl Rahner's comments, pp. 690–91.

59. Søren Kierkegaard, *Concluding Unscientific Postscript*, trans. David F. Swenson, completed by Walter Lowrie (Princeton, NJ: Princeton University Press, 1941), p. 188.

60. Ibid., p. 191.

61. St. Ephrem the Syrian, *Mary in the Documents of the Church*, ed. Paul F. Palmer (Westminster, MD: Newman Press, 1952), pp. 16–17.

62. In Catholic theology, hyperdulia is the precise degree of adoration that ought to be accorded to the Blessed Virgin Mary.

63. *ET*, s. v. "salvation," part 4A, "Theology," esp. pp. 1519–26, and part 5, "Soteriology," pp. 1526–30.

64. Kai Nielsen, "Eschatological Verification," *CJT* 9, no. 4 (1963): 271–81, attacks his stated topic precisely as he would, for example, have attacked the doctrines of the Trinity, Incarnation, and Atonement. His carefully reasoned, but spirited, conclusion is that one cannot have faith in a proposition that one does not understand. To illustrate, the statement, "The Holy Ghost (coeval with the other two members of the Trinity) proceeds from both," cannot be comprehended. Lacking intelligible meaning, it cannot be believed, no matter the loud protestations of the faithful to the contrary.

65. The expert in question was my colleague, Robert R. Rea, PhD, professor emeritus of history at Auburn University, author of more than fifty-five historical

monographs, including "The North Briton and the Courts of Law," *TAL* 12, no. 4 (October 1951): 415–21, esp. p. 416.

66. Priestley (1733–1804), having departed orthodoxy, came to preach Unitarianism (as opposed to Trinitarianism) even though he did not serve as a pastor to an exclusively Unitarian congregation in England. Moreover, his leadership in various churches was focused on the homiletic and the catechetical functions of the ministry rather than on its pastoral aspects. Nevertheless, he is close enough to have served as a (or the) model for Bentham's minister of natural religion. According to Basil Willey, Priestley came to disbelieve (as unscriptural) each of the following corruptions of Christianity: the Trinity, the miraculous conception of Jesus, original sin, predestination, the Atonement, and the plenary inspiration of Scripture. See Willey, *Eighteenth Century Background*, p. 188. Philosophically, there was much in common between Bentham and Priestley, and though Bentham had no warm feeling for Priestley personally (See *Memoirs of Bentham*, in *WJB*, 10:571) he paid tribute to him for the idea of utility. Bentham wrote, "He [Priestley] had already written several philosophical works; and in the tail of one of his pamphlets I had seen that admirable phrase 'greatest happiness to the greatest number', which had such an influence on the succeeding part (which some erroneously call the afterpart) of my life" (*WJB*, 10:46). Also, "In the phrase, 'the greatest happiness of the greatest number,' I then saw [in Bentham's twenty-second year] delineated, for the first time, a plan as well as a true standard for whatever is right or wrong, useful, useless, or mischievous in human conduct, whether in the field of morals or of politics" (*WJB*, 10:79). Despite the indebtedness Bentham felt toward Priestley (for supplying the "true foundation of morals and politics" [*WJB*, 10:79–80]), he was prepared to devastate every deistical idea Priestley preached together with his specifically Christian beliefs in Jesus as the supreme moral teacher, in Jesus' resurrection, and in the general resurrection of all believers, or perhaps of all people. Priestley had Universalist leanings as well as Unitarian convictions. Bentham, of course, did not give a fig for the idea of universal salvation, and we have already seen what he made, on empirical grounds, of the deists' conception of a god.

67. Note 38 above refers to a quotation revealing Tillotson's deism, and he was not alone among Anglican clergymen.

68. Morton Smith, historian and biblical scholar, approaches the historical Jesus as a wonder-worker in his *Jesus the Magician* (New York: Harper and Row, 1978). Even a cursory reading of the four Gospels will show that Jesus was often portrayed in a matrix of marvels, miracles, and wonders.

69. St. Paul appears to have started Christianity down this slippery slope. In 2 Cor. 12:4, he wrote, "How that he [Paul himself] was caught up into paradise, and heard unspeakable words, which it is not lawful for a man to utter." So, Paul heard ineffable words which, even if he had wanted to make known, he could not reveal, being forbidden by law (what law?). On the basis of this (and of similar visions and revelations vouchsafed to him alone) he recommended himself above people whom he sarcastically referred to as the "very chiefest apostles," (v. 11), people who knew much more of Jesus' teachings than he, and to whom he came as a rival. The point is that Paul offered his doctrines to others to take on faith in his authority, the essence of dogmatism. See part 2 of this work.

70. See the *GEL*.

71. William F. Arndt and F. William Gingrich, *GELNT* (Chicago: University of Chicago Press, 1957) p. 200.

72. Heb. 6:4–6 indicates that it is impossible to bring to repentance a second time those who have once believed and fallen away, i.e., apostates.

73. Joseph McCabe is a classic example of a priest who became an apostate and in many, many books told all. For a brief biographical sketch see *EU*, s. v. "McCabe, Joseph Martin."

74. Respecting voices in one's own head, see chap. 4, "The Bicameral Mind," and chap. 5, "The Double Brain," of book 1, as well as chap. 5, "Schizophrenia," of book 3, of Jaynes's *Origin of Consciousness*. Jaynes believes that the brains of archaic humans were organized differently from those of most modern humans, the principal exception being schizophrenics. According to him the voice heard in one's head was that of a god. I shall return to this topic toward the end of this chapter.

75. Regarding Galileo, see *RNCSE* 12, no. 4 (1992), which says, "After 13 years of study, on October 31st a Vatican panel reported that Galileo had been wrongfully condemned by the Inquisition in 1633" (p. 9). The earth, it seems, does move around the sun, rather than vice versa.

In addition to the notorious case of Muslim treatment of the author Salman Rushdie, the following reports are noteworthy: "Farouk Mohammed Ibrahim, professor of biology at the University of Khartoum, has been jailed and tortured for teaching students about evolution" (Andy Coghlan, "Sudan Jails Biologist for Teaching Darwinism," *NS*, March 17, 1990, p. 21). Adverting to Rushdie, *SHB* 6, no. 2 (1990) carried the following news item: "Youaaf Awssik, a former Tunisian professor now living in Paris, may soon join Salman Rushdie on Islam's hit list. Awssik composed a children's version of the Koran in comic book form, titled *If The Koran Were Told to Me*. The book has been condemned as 'heresy' and 'sacrilegious' by the secretary-general of an organisation representing Muslims in 46 nations" (p. 8). Moreover, according to *CS* 45, no. 10 (1992): 3, the government of Saudi Arabia executed a man for insulting Muhammad; and "A Catholic accused of insulting Mohammed has been convicted of blasphemy and sentenced to die in Pakistan according to church officials in that country" *CS* 46, no. 1 (1993): 17.

76. See Delos B. McKown, *The Mythmaker's Magic: Behind the Illusion of "Creation Science"* (Amherst, NY: Prometheus Books, 1993).

77. By Percival Davis and Dean H. Kenyon (Dallas: Haughton Publishing, 1989).

78. See esp. chap. 8 of McKown, *Mythmaker's Magic*.

79. Ibid., esp. chaps. 2 and 3.

80. Not bothering to distinguish natural theology from Christian dogmatic theology, James E. Crimmins, "Bentham's Unpublished Manuscripts on Subscription to Articles of Faith," *BJECS* 9 (1986) says that in the *AINR* Bentham "sought to disprove the logic of Christian theology" (p. 33). Bentham did disprove it in the sense of showing its illogicality, but those who have an appetite for it, perhaps including Crimmins, fail to notice this, not wanting it to be so.

Chapter 3

Criticisms

The *AINR* is, quite simply, inadequate as a philosophy of religion. This is not due to Bentham's philosophical materialism, empiricism, or nominalism, and certainly it has nothing to do with his inability to grasp "higher spiritual truths," whatever these might be.[81] It has to do rather with excessive reliance on reason, with a concomitant lack of empiricism in his approach to religion, with a lack of feeling for those who have what are called religious needs, and with the inability to comprehend to the fullest that complex of psychological phenomena that is religion. It can be said without fear of contradiction that no thinker of Bentham's time could have understood the whole of religion; perhaps nobody in the twentieth century did either. In any case, some progress can be made toward answering the question, what is wrong with Bentham's philosophy of religion?

In 1970, the *Southern Humanities Review* published a contribution of mine to a symposium prepared for the annual meeting of the American Academy of Religion. The topic was "Religion as a Humanizing Force in Man's History." Two scholars spoke for the affirmative, two for the negative, mine being one of the contributions on the negative side.[82] By the late 1960s I had concluded that the phenomena of religion are too multifarious to be encapsulated in any one definition. I claimed, however, that religion can be characterized in five ways and went on to argue that it appears in its fullest form only when all five are present. Here is what I wrote:

> First, if its intellectual aspects are isolated, religion is, figuratively speaking, anchor, gyroscope, and compass, all rolled into one. It is closely associated with the production and authoritative maintenance of frames

of reference which typically include causal explanations and teleological interpretations of basic physical and social realities or events. Religion is, as it were, a trainer whose task is to domesticate the universe and to tame whatever is significantly problematical to mankind.

Second, religion is intimately bound up with the human being's sense of oughtness, with the world as it ought to be, with visions of splendor and perfection. This type of vision often includes a portrait of a former golden age from which the present has devolved, will include in most cases the portrayal of a future time of joyous unity for the elect, and may even supervene upon the present with sufficient visual allure to enable the beholder, who believes what he sees, to enter the vision and dwell therein, aesthetically at least, while remaining physically in the mundane world.

Third, religion functions as a gray eminence whose principal daily task is to support and celebrate a given mode of social existence. Prophetic criticism, though significant in Western tradition, is the religious exception rather than the rule. Generally, there is no doubt as to which side the deity will be on. To illustrate, I have sought in vain for a segregationist with an integrationist god and for an integrationist with a segregationist god. Religion functions typically to sacralize the traditional, to hedge the forbidden with taboos, and to fix standards of discernment whereby the status and behavior of others can be evaluated ethically.

Fourth, religion combines the functions of funnel, pipeline, and pump. As a funnel it collects such attitudes as reverence and awe and such emotions as love and devotion; as a pipeline, it conveys these attitudes and emotions to, and puts them in the service of, whatever is taken to be supremely valuable; as a pump, it increases the pressure of the attitudes and emotions involved and delivers the entire mixture to the object of worship with the added force of commitment and dedication.

Fifth, religion operates as a spiritual jack-of-all-trades, sleight of hand artist, and savior in regions of human need and helplessness. It can accomplish acts of forgiveness and purification, for example, which transcend all the capacities of human jacks-of-all-trades. Religion also has the mythopoeic power to transmute intolerable situations into shining examples of divine favor. Furthermore, in crucial circumstances, religion is a last resort which functions most vigorously when all other energies are spent. In conclusion, through ritual, prayer, and penitent acts, types of work are accomplished which science, technology, and profane ingenuity leave undone. Moving mountains is the least that faith can do.[83]

As I look back at this somewhat dated and euphuistic effort, I realize now that I seriously underplayed three features upon which I should have expanded. The first is the role of paranormal experiences, so-called, in the causes for and reinforcement of religion. The second is what I have subsequently come to call the monarchical principle.[84] The third is the role of ritual, not simply in religion as practiced now, but as a progenitor of it.

These constitute topics to which I shall advert over and again in the paragraphs that follow. Despite these sins of omission, my conviction that religion is multifarious has persisted during forty years of study. It is clear that it must also be seen as issuing from more than one source.

Imagine my pleasant surprise to discover in a work by Michael S. Gazzaniga, a prominent neuroscientist, the contention that the human brain is not a single organ but a society of related organs.[85] Respecting the (to him) mistaken notion that the brain is a single, unified organ that allows problem solving to proceed in a "linear, unified conscious experience," Gazzaniga writes, "In contrast, I argue that the human brain has a modular-type organization. By modularity I mean that the brain is organized into relatively independent functioning units that work in parallel. The mind is not an indivisible whole, operating in a single way to solve all problems."[86] Among the modules in question (that inhibit, override, or release one another at varying times and in varying circumstances) Gazzaniga selects one module for special attention: "In short our species has a special brain component I will call the 'interpreter'. Even though a behavior produced by one of these modules can be expressed at any time during our waking hours, this special interpreter accommodates and instantly constructs a theory to explain why the behavior occurred."[87] Gazzaniga concludes these observations by stating, "The dynamics that exist between our mind modules and our left brain interpreter module are responsible for the generation of human beliefs."[88] "Believing," he says, "is what we humans do best."[89] It is obvious that there is a close relationship between believing and religion. So, it should not come as a complete surprise that this neuroscientist includes in his book on the brain a chapter entitled "On the Inevitability of Religious Beliefs."[90]

I am not contending that just as Gazzaniga has discerned physical modules in the brain in mechanistic interaction with one another, so religion comes in physical modules that interact mechanistically. What I am suggesting is that just as I have called religion multifarious and he has approached the human brain on the same (or on a similar) assumption, so there may be heuristic value in continuing to approach the former as he has approached the latter. It is this that I shall attempt to explicate in the pages following immediately and in the process shall be able to reveal most clearly Bentham's inadequacies on religion. For one who takes this kind of approach there is no temptation to round up all religious phenomena to make them huddle together under the explanatory umbrella of some one principle or other. Nor should it be surprising to discover that one of the principal functions of religion (i.e., forgiveness) individually runs counter to one of its principal social functions (moral judgment and control), of which, more later. To approach religion as irreducibly multifarious is to give up hope of tying all loose ends together tidily.

Bentham quoted the "pious Addison" in a footnote as follows: "Religion is the highest species of self-love."[91] Since 'highest' may be self-serving, let us agree to call it, rather, the most intense or the most sincere form of self-love. Bentham himself recognized that, in addition to having a social aspect, religion was "self-regarding."[92] Without doubt, self-love is to be expected as natural of most human beings in most of life's circumstances; also species-pride in relation to other animals. Though some animals are divinized and totemized, it is a rare religion, indeed, that views the universe as having been created primarily for animals or that sees their salvation as the foremost goal of its deity. William James put it best when he wrote, "Religion, in short, is a monumental chapter in the history of human egotism."[93] This was written neither in anger nor in criticism; he meant it to be taken as descriptive.

When Gazzaniga first introduces the concept of the "interpreter" module of the brain, he does so in the context of explaining one's own behavior to oneself. He contends (it must be remembered) that other brain modules can, episodically, express themselves in behavior at any time during one's waking hours. These would be unnervingly mysterious if the "interpreter" were not ever ready to supply a satisfactory explanation(s). The "interpreter," however, is not limited to explaining one's own behavior. It also addresses the world at large and the whole range of human experiences. Three points can be made about the "interpreter" that Gazzaniga does not make explicitly. First, the "interpreter" is profoundly anthropomorphic. It sees the world (not empirically, as Bentham understood seeing, but) structurally in the sense of viewing things on a human model, ever and anon. That which "knows" its own mind and heart (what we call our self-consciousness) projects itself, that is, its own humanity, into objectivity, as Ludwig Feuerbach (1804–1872) contended long ago.[94] In this manner, the universe is shot through with characteristics that we recognize as humanoid. To continue, if one inspects one's own mind and feelings one finds a spirit, so to speak, certainly not a body. Our brains reveal neither their substance nor their physiological operations to our inspection. It is as though we were disembodied centers of mind and emotion housed in the alien substances of flesh, blood, and bone. The "interpreter," quite naturally, explains the happenings presented to our consciousness as though they were activated by centers of mind and emotion scattered throughout the everyday empirical world. "There are gods everywhere," Thales (640–546 B.C.E.), the first philosopher, is supposed to have said.[95]

Second, the "interpreter" is not limited to the anthropomorphic. It can call at will upon the biomorphic and the sociomorphic for models.[96] Objects in the world that we moderns take to be inanimate are to the animistically inclined "interpreter" alive in varying ways and degrees. For example, there is a living stone at one place in the Bible that has the power to hear, remember, and bear witness, should certain Hebrews forget, or otherwise break, their agreement.[97] This is biomorphism in the extreme. To continue, the spirits that populate the world need not dwell in isolation. They can be understood as related to one another as humans are related in extended families and, when seen politically, can be organized into hierarchies. Hence 'sociomorphic', not that I coined it, meaning to be modeled on human social patterns in one way or another. Thus, we project not just ourselves upon the universe but life in general and human social relations as well.

Third, it is important to note what the "interpreter" is not. The "interpreter" is not in a position to know that it is a brain module, nor does it know of other brain modules as areas of specialized tissue within the heads of other people. Moreover, the "interpreter" does not know its own function nor why its person believes its explanations so readily. Historically, it could know nothing of itself, even by inference, until the advances in neuroscience achieved by the mid-twentieth century. The "interpreter" is born and may survive its entire existence in a magical ambience without knowing anything resembling scientific method. Nor does it know the importance of suspended judgment. The "interpreter," you see, is very naive. It can call upon and make much of the most quixotic of coincidences, the most tenuous of associations, and the most fabulous of reports. This "interpreter" is not out to tell the unvarnished truth, nor even to know it, but to please its person (and its person's peers) with acceptable, if not altogether agreeable, reasons and explanations. Though it may chance upon truth occasionally, it is not in business to confirm or to disconfirm hypotheses with an eye to literal accuracy.

If each "interpreter" were equal with respect to the legitimacy of its explanations of the external world and were idiotic in the sense of being peculiar unto itself with no requirement to conform to others, it is impossible to see how human beings could have lived in organized groups with common language, rituals, and culture and, lacking these, how the human species could have survived.[98] That our species has prevailed, its members finding organized life natural to them, indicates that on occasion, if not often, each "interpreter" is willing to accept authorized interpretations from elsewhere. Even more, it has an appetite to do so. "Human beings are absurdly easy to indoctrinate—they *seek* it," according to Edward O. Wilson.[99] Given the appropriate circumstances of time, place, peer pressure, willingness to conform, and acceptance of authority, the "interpreter" appears to demand nothing more of that with which it suffers itself to be indoctrinated than it demands of its own madcap explanations.

In the spirit of parallel processing, I turn next to the topic of the sacred. Bentham had no reason to believe that 'sacred' named anything objective in the world nor any property thereof, because he had no empirical evidence that it did. Abstracting 'sacred' from any alleged referent(s), he found it to be of "loose, and therefore the more convenient signification, nothing more than that the subject to which it was attached, was or was not to be accounted an object of distant awe and terror."[100] Awe and terror are surely involved with the sacred, powerful taboos and frightening retributions ordained to protect it from profane violations.[101] The sacred, however, can also be enormously attractive, uplifting individuals, gladdening their hearts, and uniting them as nothing else can. Nor must it be distant. It can be very close indeed and can present itself in varying degrees of intensity. The human creativity needed to establish and maintain the sacred far exceeds, I think, the creativity required for any other of our greatest achievements in the arts, visual, musical, literary, etc.[102]

It is very difficult, if not impossible, to write adequately about the sacred. Moreover, the way it comes to pass still eludes our complete understanding. I should like to approach it here only obliquely. Karl Marx once wrote, "Real dollars have the same existence imagined gods have. Has a real dollar [bill] any mode of existence other than in conception, though in man's general or rather communal conception? Take paper money into a country where this use of paper is not known, and everyone will laugh at your subjective concept. Come with your gods into a country where other gods prevail, and people will prove to you that you are a victim of fictions and abstractions."[103] The sacred is like paper money in that it cannot be created by one person acting alone but requires a community of like-minded people, and though it is subjective in concept, it cannot be merely subjective but must take on a kind of objectivity in the eyes of those whose communally subjective creation it is. Although grist for sacralization is enormously varied—a word, a doctrine, a person, a place, a thing, an event, a ritual, a tradition, etc.—no one item has ever been sacred for all human beings everywhere, even though all ethnic groups may have busied themselves in creating sacred things. Despite such universal human activity in groups, some individuals, such as Bentham, recognize nothing as sacred. His eyes, for example, saw only light, hue, value, and shape; never the sacred.

Another oblique approach to the sacred can be illustrated in a parable written by Philip Wheelwright, a prominent American philosopher who flourished during the middle years of the twentieth century. This parable was designed to undercut the naturalism of all who, like Bentham, deny that there is anything intrinsically sacred to be recognized, apprehended, or intuited. The parable has it that there was once a remote isle inhabited by a unique human group that worshiped music. On holy days these folk would assemble to play instruments and sing holy songs. Over a period of time, alas, they were progressively afflicted by loss of hearing, some individuals in succeeding generations being more afflicted than others, some less. While communication came progressively to consist of sign language and writing, the religious tradition of congregating on holy days and of going through the motions of playing instruments and singing holy songs continued. Eventually, some modernists began to question the faith of the fathers and to criticize these apparently pointless activities. Finally, only the priests of the religion, who, of course, had vested interests in upholding tradition, and a tiny minority who could still hear sounds ever so faintly kept up the sacred practices:

> These last were dubbed mystics, and when noticed at all were made the butt of ridicule. Psychologists built ingenious theories to expose the causes of their delusion, while semanticists [like Bentham] started a campaign to have words like *music, tone,* and *harmony* eliminated from common speech, on the ground that they were semantic blanks, mere vacant sounds without any referents in actual [empirical] experience. . . . The whole thing was accepted as clear proof of social and intellectual progress. And of course no one heeded or understood when once in a while a music lover, goaded into argument, would reply (in sign language presumably): "It is not we who are deluded, but you, my friends, who are deaf!"[104]

Whether there is anything sacred to see (or otherwise to sense) or not, the bulk of religious people believe that there is more to the world than meets the empirical eye. Not more in the sense of unseen galaxies to be seen in the future by better telescopes, nor unexpected cosmic phenomena to be detected by and by, nor more in the sense of finding, at the other end of the spectrum, ever greater numbers of evanescent particles in the nuclei of atoms smashing, but more of the sort envisioned by William James:

> Summing up in the broadest possible way the characteristics of the religious life . . . includes the following beliefs:—
>   1. That the visible world is part of a more spiritual universe from which it draws it chief significance;
>   2. that union or harmonious relation with that higher universe is our true end;
>   3. that prayer or inner communion with the spirit thereof—be that spirit 'God' or 'law'—is a process wherein work is really done, and spiritual energy flows in and produces effects, psychological or material, within the phenomenal world.[105]

Bentham cannot be faulted, in my view, for sticking to his empiricist/rationalist guns, but he might have aimed his guns so as to have achieved greater gains. That the means for explaining religion in psychological terms were not fully available to him does not excuse his lack of intent in investigating such possibilities. Understanding religion was, of course, not as important to him as replacing it with secular utilitarianism. But if religion is to be replaced (a dubious goal indeed), then understanding it would seem to be the preferred way to start.

If the four following quotations could have been presented to Bentham for his ratification, he would surely have assented. The first:

> The spectacle of what religions have been in the past, of what certain religions still are today, is indeed humiliating for human intelligence. What a farrago of error and folly! Experience may indeed say "That is false," and reasoning "That is absurd." Humanity only clings all the more to that absurdity and that error. And if this were all! But religion has been known to enjoin immorality, to prescribe crime. The cruder it is, the more actual space it occupies in the life of a people.[106]

Taking such theological statements as, "Hear, O Israel, the Lord our God, the Lord is One," and "Jesus Christ is the Son of God," as examples of sacred assertions, consider the second quotation:

> Propositions such as these sacred sentences are peculiar. Since their terms have no material referents, they are not amenable to verification but neither are they vulnerable to falsification. They are, in a strict logical positivist sense, nonsense.[107]

Referring to religion as a "strange pattern of animal behaviour" and to the gods as "invented,"[108] another author writes,

> Religion has also given rise to a great deal of unnecessary suffering and misery wherever it has become over-formalized in its application, and wherever the professional "assistants" of the god figures have been unable to resist the temptation to borrow a little of his power and use it themselves.[109]

And from the pen of yet another author comes the final quotation:

> The enduring paradox of religion is that so much of its substance is demonstrably false, yet it remains a driving force in all societies. Men would rather believe than know, have the void as purpose, as Nietzsche said, than be void of purpose.[110]

The first of the four quotations immediately above comes from French philosopher Henri Bergson, the second from American anthropologist Roy A. Rappaport, the third from English ethnologist Desmond Morris, the fourth from American sociobiologist Edward O. Wilson. If we could assume that each of the four knew (or knows) Bentham's *AINR*, we could safely conclude that each has found (or finds) much truth in it. Where they would part company with him would be over his almost total ignorance of the sacred, of how it functions in social groups, and of how it has facilitated (and still facilitates) human survival.

At no point of which I am aware does Bergson say flatly that humanity could not have survived without religion; but he does say, "[H]umanity has never subsisted without religion."[111] Also important to our discussion are each of the following three quotations:

> The closed society is that whose members hold together caring nothing for the rest of humanity, on the alert for attack or defence, bound, in fact, to a perpetual readiness for battle. Such is human society fresh from the hands of nature. Man was made for society, as the ant was made for the ant-heap.[112]

> [O]bedience of everyone to laws, even absurd ones, assures greater cohesion to the community.[113]

> [W]e have . . . seen that the myth-making function, innate in the individual, has as its object the consolidation of society; but we know that it is also intended to support the individual himself, and that, moreover, such is the interest of society.[114]

That which Bergson leaves implicit but obvious, Rappaport makes explicit when he says, "Neither history nor anthropology knows of societies from which religion has been totally absent."[115] He continues by saying, "We must agree with Durkheim . . . that anything which is universal to human culture is likely to contribute to human survival," and concludes, "Indeed . . . our thesis here is that religion has not merely been important but crucial to human adaption."[116]

Desmond Morris writes: "At first sight, it is surprising that religion has been so successful, but its extreme potency is simply a measure of the strength of our fundamental biological tendency, inherited directly from our monkey and ape ancestors, to submit ourselves to an all-powerful, dominant member of the group. Because of this, religion has proved immensely valuable as a device for aiding social cohesion, and it is doubtful whether our species could have progressed far without it."[117]

Edward O. Wilson puts it most bluntly when he says, "We are religious to survive; we surrender to the tribe and its sacred rites in a gamble for both personal and genetic immortality."[118]

So the four authors quoted above are repeatedly at one with Bentham in criticizing religion from the standpoint of modern scientific thought but arrive nevertheless at a description of its benefits that go far beyond his narrow purview. It is easy to see why his outlook was so limited. He died eleven years before Darwin and Wallace introduced the world to the idea of biological evolution. Bentham could, quite simply, not relate religion to genetics, or to human adaptation, selection, and survival.

If Bentham had been asked to comment on the topic of mysticism, he would have done so with disdain or derision. 'Mysticism' seldom issued from his lips or pen. There is, as might be expected, no entry for it in the Index to the *WJB*, volume 11. But, in dismissing mysticism as inconsequential at best and as fraudulent at worst, he limited his understanding of religion and diminished the value of his critique thereof. In establishing the truth of these claims I must turn to a consideration of mysticism while resisting the temptation to write more than is useful (to the reader) about the various experiences that pass as examples of this mode of consciousness.

The best guide to mysticism in my view is Anglo-American philosopher Walter T. Stace (1886–1967), who taught at Princeton for more than twenty years. Stace weeds the garden of mimics and pretenders to the mantel of mysticism with a vengeance. To him genuine mysticism is something neither misty nor vague, nor is it "mystery mongering."[119] Equally, it has nothing to do with intramental visions and voices, and it cannot be equated with the "occult" or to any sort of hocus-pocus. Moreover, mysticism has nothing to do with "spiritualism, or ghosts, or table turning. Nor does it include what are commonly called para-psychological phenomena such as telepathy, telekinesis, clairvoyance, [or] precognition."[120]

A small but not inconsequential minority of people throughout much of history in various, if not all, cultures have been able to reach a state of mind that is declared by them to be utterly nonsensuous (i.e., "formless, shapeless, colorless, odorless, and soundless") and is totally without content in that no idea or recollection of an idea is present.[121] This state of consciousness, though ineffable at the point of being experienced, is not (to Stace) ineffable when recollected after the individual has returned to normal sensuous and content-freighted experience. He identifies two ways of reaching the mystic experience, the "extrovertive" and the "introvertive." Using the former approach, the practitioner, as it were, commences with ordinary sensations of the external world as a way to pass to the nonsensuous and contentless state of mind (called mystical by Stace), whereas the practitioner using the introvertive method looks inward and away from the empirical world at the outset, using techniques that are well established.[122]

Those who can reach a state of nonsensuous, contentless consciousness (one that is also spaceless and timeless) call it a state of pure consciousness.[123] This they commonly equate to pure (absolutely undifferentiated) unity and in turn to pure ego.[124] In such a state the private, pure ego (or individual self) is experienced as losing, yet as retaining, itself as it dissolves into what is known (or taken to be) the universal ego (or cosmic self),[125] an intrinsically paradoxical experience, utterly irreconcilable with any applicability thereto of the laws of logic.[126] This experience brings to the mystic the peace that "passeth all understanding."[127] That numerous mystics from different times, climes, and cultures are unanimous about the foregoing is not at issue. The issue for Stace is whether the experience described above is what he calls intramental (such as hallucinatory experiences and dreams) or whether it is extramental in that a person in the mystic state encounters an objective reality, but a reality that can be encountered only in this way.[128]

Stace's concern, however, is not ours, not at least as far as this book is concerned; our concern is with interpretations or explanations of the mystic experience. Of this Stace writes, "The undifferentiated unity is interpreted by Eckhart and Ruysbroeck in terms of the Trinitarian conception of God, but by Islamic mystics as the unitarian God of Islam, and by the leading school of the Vedantists as a more impersonal Absolute. And when we come to Buddhism we find that the experience is not interpreted as any kind of God at all.[129]

So, as surprising as it may seem, there can be atheistic mystics. Accordingly, mysticism can be dissociated from religion, though in fact the two are usually so tightly associated that the mystic experience is taken as self-certifying evidence of a supreme being and is either a source of religion or a powerful reinforcer thereof. It is unfortunate for Bentham's analysis of religion that he ignored the stratum of human experience existing at this level.

Beneath the pristine procedures of the introvertive mystics and their ineffable experiences, unalloyed by sensuousness, lie a rabble of procedures and (to Stace) some very questionable experiences indeed, even though to most people these too would be classified as mystical. For example, one bright morning in May of 1953, the writer and aesthete Aldous Huxley swallowed, as he said, "[F]our-tenths of a grain of mescalin [sic] dissolved in half a glass of water and sat down to wait for the results."[130] Half an hour later he became aware of "a slow dance of golden lights," then "sumptuous reds" pulsating in continuously changing patterns.[131] "I was," he writes, "seeing what Adam saw on the morning of his creation—the miracle . . . of naked creation," of "Is-ness"[132] at the "mind's antipodes."[133] Spatiality ceased to be of importance to Huxley as new intensities of existence and profundities of significance overwhelmed him.[134] He experienced himself becoming his "not-self," and proceeded deeper into egolessness.[135] Eternity, infinity, and the Absolute presented themselves to him.[136] Except for numerous references to what he saw,[137] Huxley's experiences were much like those reported by the introspective mystics featured by Stace. "Visionary experience," Huxley notes, however, "is within the realm of [logical] opposites, whereas "[true] mystical experience is beyond it."[138]

Apart from any further concern with what to Stace and, to some extent, to Huxley is genuine mystical experience (and its relation to religion), the latter makes an extraordinarily important point when writing, "The urge to transcend self-conscious selfhood is, as I have said, a principal appetite of the soul. When, for whatever reason, men and women fail to transcend themselves by means of worship, good works and spiritual exercises, they are apt to resort to 'goof pills' in the modern West, alcohol and opium in the East, hashish in the Mohammedan world, alcohol and marijuana in Central America, alcohol and coca in the Andes, alcohol and the barbiturates in the more up-to-date regions of South America."[139] He clinches this point by quoting Philippe de Félice's *Poisons Sacrés, Ivresses Divine* (Sacred Poisons, Divine Inebriations) to the effect that anybody who hopes to understand "what religion is" and what the "deep needs" are which it is expected "to satisfy" must come to grips with the ingestion of chemical agents that alter normal experience.[140] The English-speaking authors of our standard texts in comparative religions seem to be nearly as ignorant of this connection as was Bentham.[141] Here I am not simply referring to the drugs themselves that have been used in religious practices at all times and places but to the perceived needs of human beings to which religion, including the drug-related variety, ministers.

If Huxley were alive today he could not stop (as does Stace) with self-induced (introvertive) mystical states nor with drug-induced states but would also have to consider Persinger's helmet, which "induces mystical experiences by stimulating the temporal lobes [of a person's brain] with magnetic forces."[142]

Anybody who has read Bentham's *AINR* or my distillation above will know that he found asceticism odious. Throughout the entire first chapter of part 2, he berated natural religion for the four mischiefs of "inflicting unprofitable suffering," of "imposing useless privations," of "impressing undefined terrors," and of "taxing pleasures, by the infusion of preliminary scruples and subsequent remorse." Elsewhere he wrote as follows of the "fear [suffered by ascetics] of future punishment at the hands of a splenetic and revengeful Deity:

> These [ascetic] exercises consisted in so many contrivances they had for tormenting themselves. By this they sought to ingratiate themselves with the Deity. For the Deity, said they, is a Being of infinite benevolence: now a Being of the most ordinary benevolence is pleased to see others make themselves as happy as they can: therefore to make ourselves as unhappy as we can is the way to please the Deity. If anybody ask them, what motive they could find for doing all this? Oh! said they, you are not to imagine that we are punishing ourselves for nothing: we know what we are about. You are to know, that for every grain of pain it costs us now, we are to have a hundred grains of pleasure by and by. The case is, that God loves to see us torment ourselves at present: indeed he has as good as told us so. But this is done only to try us, in order just to see how we should behave: which it is plain he could not know, without making the experiment. Now then, from the satisfaction it gives him to see us make ourselves as unhappy as we can make ourselves in this present life, we have a sure

proof of the satisfaction it will give him to see us as happy as he can make us in a life to come.[143]

Both Bentham and the unnamed ascetics he quoted were excessively rationalistic and, thus, missed a motive for mortifying the flesh.

In *Heaven and Hell* Huxley writes, "Asceticism . . . has a double motivation. If men and women torment their bodies, it is not only because they hope in this way to atone for past sins and avoid future punishments; it is also because they long to visit the mind's antipodes and do some visionary sight-seeing. Empirically and from the reports of other ascetics, they know that fasting and a restricted environment will transport them where they long to go. Their self-inflicted punishment may be the door to paradise.[144] In a matter-of-fact way Huxley notes the double advantage of fasting in procuring visionary experience: (1) It removes nicotinic acid ("a known inhibitor of visions") from the blood, and (2) it reduces the "amount of available sugar," lowering the brain's biological efficiency and so makes possible the entry into consciousness of material possessing no survival value.[145]

Huxley, by no means an enemy of visionary mysticism (as Bentham would have been), proceeds to demystify it further. Observing that "*all* our experiences are chemically conditioned," he proceeds to itemize "the internal conditions favorable to spiritual insight."[146] Respecting flagellants, who have appeared episodically in Christian history and are present today in Shi'ite Islam in Iran in particular, he notes that large quantities of histamine and adrenaline are released while the whip is being applied.[147] Such internal chemical outpourings are followed by festering wounds that produce toxins resulting from the decomposition of protein. He writes, "But histamine produces shock, and shock affects the mind no less profoundly than the body. Moreover, large quantities of adrenalin [sic] may cause hallucinations, and some of the products of its decomposition are known to induce symptoms resembling those of schizophrenia. As for toxins from wounds—these upset the enzyme systems regulating the brain."[148]

Respecting Yoga, or other meditative practices involving decreased breathing patterns, Huxley observes that long suspension of breath raises the concentration of carbon dioxide in the blood which in turn affects the brain, permitting the "entry into consciousness of experiences, visionary or mystical, from 'out there.'"[149]

To summarize, there is method of a spiritual sort, so-called, in what to Bentham was ascetic madness. Fasting, prolonged loss of sleep, sensory deprivation, reduced availability of oxygen, and shock, whether from flagellation, locomotion on the knees, or other wounding practices, enable some people some of the time to enjoy paranormal experiences. In his classic work, *The Psychology of Religious Mysticism*, James Leuba even adds extreme sexual deprivation and/or erotic frustration to the mix.[150] Bentham, of course, cannot be blamed for his ignorance of the changes in brain chemistry occasioned by the causal factors treated above nor of their manifestations in what can only be called abnormal consciousness. However, insofar as such "mystical" experiences are interpreted in religious terms, as they usually are,[151] insofar as they may be originative of religion in some cases at least,[152] and insofar as those who have mystical experiences are looked to by the many who do not as authority figures having special types of religious knowledge (or revelations), a whole stratum of religious phenomena emerges that is impervious to the sort of rationalistic attack that Bentham launched.

We have now descended on the ladder of paranormal experiences that are typically interpreted in theological terms, from the "pure," self-induced, introvertive mysticism of Stace to the visionary mysticism of Huxley associated with mescaline and other drugs (together with Persinger's magnetic helmet) to what may be, perhaps, types of rather "impure" mystical experiences aided and abetted by shocks, fatigues, and deprivations of various sorts. Without any further descent one might move laterally to experiences induced by trance states, ritual dancing, and liturgical exercises that narrow or otherwise alter consciousness.[153] It is not necessary for present purposes to pursue each of these avenues to understanding the etiology of religion. I would, however, like to descend one more rung, if that is the maneuver indicated, from visions to voices.

Lily Tomlin, the actress/comedienne, was once quoted in the popular press, I think, as having said, "When you talk to God, it is called prayer; when he talks to you, it is called schizophrenia."[154] Exactly so, Professor Julian Jaynes would say, based on his book *The Origin of Consciousness*, where he contends that the gods were voices heard as surely as epileptics and schizophrenics hear voices:[155]

> The voices in schizophrenia take any and every relationship to the individual. They converse, threaten, curse, criticize, consult, often in short sentences. . . . As in bicameral civilizations, they are recognized as gods, angels, devils.[156]

> Occasionally in what are called acute twilight states, whole scenes, often of a religious nature, may be hallucinated even in broad daylight. The heavens standing open with a god speaking to the patient.[157]

> [W]e could say that before the second millennium B.C., everyone was schizophrenic.[158]

> And why do these hallucinations of schizophrenics so often have dramatic authority, particularly religious? I find that the only notion which provides even a working hypothesis about this matter is that of the bicameral mind,

that the neurological structure responsible for these hallucinations is neurologically bound to substrates for religious feelings, and this is because the source of religion and of gods themselves is in the bicameral mind.[159]

"Bicameral" as used above refers to the two hemispheres of the human brain. To make a long and complex theory short—but not, I hope, too simple for present purposes—Jaynes believes that the brains of most modern humans are neurologically different from those of our not-so-distant ancestors four thousand years ago.[160] The development of language and the invention of writing, he thinks, have had much to do with this alteration.[161] In any case, as he sees it, the neurological bases for what we now call hallucinations had much freer rein then than now. Jaynes believes that moments of stress, in particular, induced magisterial voices to speak to our not-so-distant ancestors from within their brains' right hemispheres.[162] The point here is neither to sketch the whole of his theory nor to judge the evidence for it, but rather to recognize the role of auditory hallucinations in the etiology of religion.[163] The kind of empirico-rationalistic assault Bentham launched against theology had (and has) no impact at all upon people who hear commanding voices in their heads, voices they take, more often than not, to express the will of a (or the) god.

Though countless pious people today have never heard "Thus saith the Lord" booming from within their heads, they believe that others, such as the holy prophets of yore and contemporary charismatic religious leaders did (or do) hear these words, issuing, presumably, from outside their heads— and from on high. To continue in like manner, although countless Christians, for example, have never really had a born-again experience or felt themselves washed in the blood of the Lamb, they speak endlessly as though they have, using the vocabulary of the favored few who have had such experiences and interpret them theologically. Thus do the religious, ranging from the fervent to the tepid and from the genuine article to the mimic reinforce one another. Once the ingredient of time is added to mixes of these kinds, traditions begin. Few things, it should be noted, are easier to sacralize than a tradition, its very persistence over a long time sanctifying it.

In the preceding pages I have itemized various experiences extending from pure introspective mysticism through drug-induced visions to spontaneous auditory hallucinations. We who have not had such experiences and who have approached religion academically, focusing narrowly on scripture and theology, usually think of the aforementioned experiences as paranormal and, holding them in suspicion, discount their importance to the etiology and reinforcement of religion. This is a great mistake, for such experiences, over time, have been enormously important. They are not, of course, the whole story. Surrounding these are vast numbers of common, even daily, experiences happening to ordinary people that can best be called spooky, a term I use advisedly. These too aid and abet religion over and again, but they need not deter us from turning at once to two further considerations of extreme importance.

A great, if not the greatest, weakness of Bentham's philosophy of religion stems, no doubt, from his total disinterest in soteriological themes. The great bulk of humanity, however, have the keenest interest therein. "Religion," Alfred North Whitehead wrote, "is a force of belief cleansing the inward parts."[164] But, in his matter-of-fact way, Bentham's inward parts consisted of his heart, lungs, liver, spleen, etc., and these needed no cleansing. Moreover, belief could not have done the job for Bentham anyway. In the same passage, Whitehead also said, "But in some sense or other, justification is the basis of all religion." Bentham, however, felt no need to be absolved from anything and sought no rehabilitation of a religious sort. Not believing himself to be an inheritor of original sin nor a locus of total depravity, he suffered no guilt over being human and sought no forgiveness for his condition in life. Being an honorable man devoted to truth and to human betterment through the ethics of utility, he sought no moral guidance and accepted no ethical dicta from any monarch, earthly or heavenly. Possessed of comfortable means (especially from his middle years onward) and as much in control of life as one can expect to be, he sought no divine benisons and feared no demonic designs.[165] Loving his life but not dreading death (at the ripe old age of eighty-four), he succumbed with equanimity, despite his pain. Such a person is very ill equipped to understand the common human appetite for salvation and the lust for something for nothing.

Not aware of the load of guilt the normal course of socialization can engender in people, he turned to the depredations of priestcraft as the obvious source of guilt. Priests, according to Bentham, pretend to knowledge they do not possess and arrogate to themselves the power of the one they profess to represent. Professionally interested in ensuring an abundant and continuing supply of presumed offenses against their deity, they prohibit the very acts that people are most frequently and powerfully tempted to commit, even when these are innocuous. Portraying their deity as irritable and vindictive, if not capricious, they render people guilt-ridden, insecure, and helpless. They then appear as the messengers of divine forgiveness (the good news of the Gospel and salvation, perhaps, by faith alone). Mendacity being their stock in trade they work to sunder required beliefs (dogma) from daily empirical experiences. When necessary to ensure the submission and docility of the laity, priests conspire with the crown "to neutralize all hatred of slavery and facilitate the business of [economic] spoilation." The ruling class return the favor by supplying the clergy with physical protection and "compulsory tribute," that is, church taxes obligingly extorted from the common people.[166] Despite the truth in this indictment, and it is substantial, priestcraft is not the sole cause of guilt and the resultant craving for forgiveness. Parents, peers, and potentates also contribute to the psychosocial conditions that cause people to yearn for justification, redemption, and salvation.

If Bentham had been as empirical about religion as his epistemology indicates he ought to have been, he would have taken time out from his European journeys to visit "holy" places. If he had gone to holy mountains, holy cities, holy shrines, and had sought out holy things, he could have witnessed how very needy human beings, by the droves, perceive themselves to be—and how possessed of the beggar's proclivities. Perhaps one visit to Lourdes would have sufficed. People, from all over the world, flock to such places to witness prodigies such as the appearance of the Virgin Mary in the clouds of heaven, the weeping icon of some saint or other, the image of Jesus on a tortilla chip, in the bark of a tree, on the mottled surface of a water tower, etc. Even when such prodigies fail to occur as expected, many pilgrims, most perhaps, will still feel that they have received a "spiritual" blessing merely for having been where rumor has it the prodigy at issue occurred or is still occurring. The proverbial bottom line, it would seem, is to get something for nothing.[167]

Christianity yields to no religion in its reinforcement of the beggar's mentality. In its Pauline version (which is the source and center of Christian orthodoxy), the recipient of divine grace (i.e., of unmerited love) receives almost everything for next to nothing.[168] This takes some explaining: I say almost everything, because Christianity does not promise an easy life on earth. Matthew 10:16–22 predicts its rigors, and 2 Corinthians 11:24–29 recounts the sufferings of Paul as though in fulfillment of the predicted rigors. Moreover, Christianity, unlike Platonism and other reincarnationist theologies, does not claim that we have lived prior to this life and that we were with God in the beginning (*Phaedrus* 245c–250c; *Phaedo* 72e–87a).[169] But it does teach that the saved of earth will receive the free gift of God, which is eternal life (Rom. 6:23; Gal. 6:8). This is to be possessed for next to nothing I say, because it is exceedingly easy to have faith in a doctrine which one is pleased to believe anyway. Over and again, Paul tells the recipients of his letters that Christians are justified by faith apart from the works of the Mosaic law (Rom. 3:28; 5:1) or any moral effort on their own part and that the promise of God is to be enjoyed through the righteousness of faith (Rom. 8:1–3). On one occasion he even tells his readers that Christians are saved by hope (Rom. 8:24). Well, why not? Why should hope not gain eternal life for us as efficaciously as faith? In summation, then, Christianity is a kind of pious panhandling for holy handouts—the most desired handout being everlasting life with God in bliss.[170]

Early in the *AINR*, Bentham proposed to see whether or not the good effects, if any, of an allegedly revealed religion might suffice to neutralize the bitter fruits he had shown, logically, to stem from natural religion. Just as a psychotherapist would counsel an otherwise healthy person in early or mid-life to stop brooding over old age, sickness, pain, debility, and death, so Bentham counseled the natural religionist to stop brooding about what it would be like after death to fall into the clutches of the Deity of natural religion. Such brooding to him was clearly contrary to utility in that it added the unnecessary pains of doleful anticipation to a life that might otherwise be happy, due to a favorable balance of pleasures over pains. Since the Deity of natural religion is almighty and equally capricious and has not written into the ways of nature any moral prescriptions for humans, there is no way, prudentially, to prepare oneself to encounter him on any posthumous occasion. Hence, in this life, one should eat, drink, and make merry (largely in accordance with social approbation), totally suppressing postmortem considerations. This was a major part of Bentham's prescription for a happy life, whether natural religion is true or false.

Hard though it is to fault Bentham's logic, it is clear that he underestimated or otherwise misunderstood the prowess of such an allegedly revealed religion as Christianity. For the overwhelming majority of its devotees, it clearly neutralizes the "bitter fruits" of natural religion. For this task it matters not one whit as to whether Christianity is truly a revealed religion or not. A brief consideration of kathenotheism will show why this is so. 'Kathenotheism', coined by Max Müller (1852–1935), an eminent German theologian and historian, means "one-at-a-time" theism. Ancient polytheists, it is obvious, turned from god to god depending on the area governed by each deity and the pressing human needs of the moment. In times of peace and stability, ancient polytheists turned to fertility gods; in times of bellicosity, to war gods; at the time of death, to funerary deities; etc. The one and only god of the Judeo-Christian-Islamic tradition had perforce to assimilate all of these functions unto himself. In times of war, the Lord became a man of war (Exod. 15:3); in times of peace and stability, the stern upholder of traditional values and the avenger of broken taboos; and at the time of death, the loving heavenly father who has established a paradise for his own.

I can do no better in clinching the point above than to quote myself in criticism of Karl Marx's failure to understand religion. There is an irony herein, for Marx was contemptuous of "the archphilistine, Jeremy Bentham," yet each was wrong at the same point for the same reason:

> The god of infinite power is also a god of love and hence need not be feared by the pious. If there are tricksters about, well, there are also guardian angels. The good god cannot really be capricious, for his goodness will not permit. The deity who demands righteous conduct is good enough to reveal objective standards so that men will know precisely what

to do. In cases of human failure he is, happily, quick to forgive. The god of the dead is a threat but only to the wicked. As for Satan, he will get his just deserts in due time, and the good God will at last have no rival. Should the great high God become too remote and alien, a Mediator will come. Should the Mediator become assimilated to the Godhead, there is always the blessed Virgin. Consider too the treasure troves of merit which the saints have accumulated for us men and our salvation. If all else fails, there are always penances to be performed, rituals to be undertaken, good works to be done, and heartfelt prayers to be said. The gods which Marx assumed that people believe in are more nearly their devils than their gods. Few, if any, go to devils for consolation.[171]

The same mythopoeic power of human beings that creates any one god of polytheism creates any and all of the rest of them—so too the complex character of the "One True God" of Judaism and Christianity and the deity of the ninety-nine names of Islam.[172] If the top line of religion is the monarchical principle (more on this in parts 2 and 3), the bottom line is the soteriological principle, a principle which proclaims redemption, or justification, or salvation unto eternal life, or enlightenment, or the merger of individual egos with the One, call it what you please.

Bentham was aware of certain Christian rituals, such as infant baptism and the Lord's Supper (or Holy Communion), but he had not a glimmering of the role of ritual in the misty origins of religion. It is now taken for granted that in biological terms there is a continuity in ritualized performances between subhuman animals and the earliest human animals. Although it is not known whether or not Neanderthals had language, they participated in at least one formalized procedure—the ceremonial burial of their dead, a ritual performed perhaps as early as one hundred thousand years ago.[173] The likelihood is that they had other rituals, principally dances for the hunt, for war, and modes of "mating display."[174]

In any case, rituals cry out for explanation, eliciting etiological myths as surely as do the mysterious and awesome powers of nature with which our earliest (and subsequent) ancestors had to contend. One can be confident that the myth-making process began as early as human beings developed language. Anthropologist Roy A. Rappaport writes in his final major work, "[R]eligion emerged with language. As such, religion is as old as language, which is to say precisely as old as humanity" (emhasis added).[175] Since Bentham was intensely preoccupied with language (as part 3 will reveal), he ought to have found this extremely revealing, could it have been vouchsafed to him. He did not, of course, have the findings of modern scientific anthropology available to him, nor ethnological studies of ritual, subhuman and human. Thus, he could not link such performances, the emergence of language, and subsequent myth-making processes with religion.

He did not fully realize that the participants in religious rituals think they are, thereby, accomplishing holy works, nor did he appreciate the feelings of satisfaction they enjoy when the work is (to all appearances) rightly done. To him the mouthings and performances of ritual activities were sheer magic, productive of nothing.

As my readers will remember, Bentham took the total divorcement of one's beliefs from one's ordinary empirical experiences to be complete insanity, lesser degrees of divorcement being tantamount to lesser degrees of insanity. Instead of using 'insanity', he would have been well advised to use 'religion-specific irrationality', or 'RSI' for short. He could not have done this, however, since I believe myself to have originated this less colorful but more accurate term. To continue, he could not see how the mental depravity or "prepared imbecility" of religious indoctrination could fail to blight the whole of a believer's thought processes.[176] He could have allayed his fears, however, had he understood the common human proclivity for compartmentalizing thought. In addition to the common ontological duality of body and soul and the age-old division of entities into the sacred and the secular that is presupposed by religious people, Bentham ought to have recognized a common epistemological duality, also presupposed by religious people, which allows them to entertain RSI unnoticed while remaining largely rational in the nonreligious aspects of their lives.

The blithe separation of truths into two varieties, spiritual and ordinary (or worldly), makes this possible. "Spiritual" truths, whether based on Scripture, pope, prophet, guru, personal revelation, mystical visions, auditory hallucinations, or drug-induced states, etc., are never put to the same tests as are ordinary claims to truth in everyday life, or in alien religions, or by boards of inquiry, or in courtrooms, or in scientific investigations. Everything is taken as evidence for a "spiritual" truth, by those believing it, and nothing is ever specified as disconfirmatory of it. People who seek "spiritual" truths, unlike those who seek scientific truths, never specify a method (beyond psychological satisfaction) for attaining them, or for knowing when success has crowned the search, or when failure has rendered it futile. Deplorable as this situation may have been to Bentham, RSI does not necessarily (and, perhaps, not usually) afflict the whole of a believer's thought processes. Leibniz and Newton (the latter narrowly religious) illustrate the truth of this clearly, through the brilliance of the calculus that each devised apart from the other. Religious people can be eminently rational in all areas that are not ideologically threatening to their faith.

Bentham's philosophy of religion remains unfinished at the conclusion of the *AINR*. Surprising though it may be, that which completes it is only hinted at therein. One has to look elsewhere to find what is missing—the application of his philosophy of language and theory of fictions to metaphysical propositions in general and to theological assertions in particular. Since the theological propositions he analyzes are overwhelmingly Christian, it seems good to me to turn next, in part 2, to his treatment of St. Paul, leaving the application of his philosophy of language until part 3.

NOTES

81. James E. Crimmins in his "Bentham on Religion: Atheism and the Secular Society," *JHI*, 47, no. 1 (1986) writes, "Bentham's utilitarianism with its materialist and nominalist underpinnings could not encompass the 'internal' and 'mysterious' and this impoverished his analysis [of religion] (p. 100)." Moreover, in *Secular Utilitarianism: Social Science and the Critique of Religion in the Thought of Jeremy Bentham* (Oxford: Clarendon Press, 1990), Crimmins, citing Thomas Carlyle, mentions "the barren wastes of materialism" and proceeds to opine that an empirical analysis of the sort Bentham employed is "an inappropriate method to use in relation to spirituality" (p. 278). Granted that Bentham's analysis of the etiology, nature, and practice of religion is inadequate, is it inadequate because Bentham was a materialist? Does Crimmins want us to fancy that we humans would be a different sort of creature than we are, if materialism were true? Does he want us to believe that human beings would not be religious if materialism were the case? Put differently, does human religiosity presuppose the truth of some idealistic system of metaphysics or other? Surely not! Precisely the same sort of rejoinder can be made to the complaint that Bentham was a nominalist. In *DP*, s. v. "Nominalism," one finds it defined, in part, as follows: "In scholastic philosophy, the theory that abstract or general terms, or universals, represent no objective real existents, but are mere words or names, mere vocal utterances, 'flatus vocis.' Reality is admitted only to actual physical particulars." See also the appropriate entries in *DPR* and *EP*. Crimmins would be more convincing if he could show precisely how human religiosity predicated on the existence of universals would differ from religiosity based on the truth of nominalism. It is regrettable that he does not attempt this. How very enlightening it might be, if he could do it! Along the same lines, he will be taken sorely to task in part 2 for what he says about "spirituality" when criticizing Bentham on St. Paul.

82. Delos B. McKown, "Religion as a Humanizing Force in Man's History: A Negative Response," *SHR* 4, no. 3 (1970): 206–14.

83. Ibid., 207–208. While still on the subject of defining religion, the following needs to be noted. Durkheim's definition of religion (see n. 15 above) is overwhelmingly, if not totally, social in outlook. Alfred North Whitehead, on the contrary, once wrote, "Religion is what the individual does with his own solitariness. . . . If you are never solitary you are never religious" (*Religion in the Making* [New York: Macmillan, 1927], pp. 16–17). If one turns to a dictionary to settle the issue, one will find only limited assistance, for therein one will merely find yesterday's definition based on the way literate people were using the word then. Clearly, Whitehead was not using the dictionary's definition. He was stipulating his own, and anybody else can do likewise. Stipulative definitions can be wildly various, but on the other hand may occasionally come closer to the essence of what is being defined than does the dictionary. One could make this point effectively by

using John Dewey's *A Common Faith* (New Haven, CT: Yale University Press, 1934), esp. the opening pages of chap. 1, "Religion versus the Religious."

84. I am not alone in stressing the monarchical principle in religion; see Walter Burkert, "Hierarchy," chap. 4 in *Creation of the Sacred: Tracks of Biology in Early Religions* (Cambridge: Harvard University Press, 1996).

85. Michael S. Gazzaniga, *The Social Brain: Discovering the Networks of the Mind* (New York: Basic Books, 1985).

86. Ibid., p. 4.

87. Ibid., p. 5. Gazzaniga locates the interpreter in the "left dominant hemisphere of right-handed humans."

88. Ibid.

89. Ibid., p. 3.

90. Ibid., chap. 11.

91. *Introduction to Morals and Legislation*, in *WJB*, 1:56.

92. Ibid.

93. William James, *The Varieties of Religious Experience: A Study in Human Nature* (New York: Modern Library, 1994), p. 534.

94. In *The Essence of Christianity*, trans. George Eliot, with an introduction by Karl Barth and a foreword by Richard Niebuhr (New York: Harper and Brothers, Torchbook, 1957), pp. 29–30, Feuerbach contends that human beings project their own unique essence (i.e., their self-consciousness) onto the world, bring it into such sharp focus that it becomes objective, and then bow down to worship that which they have created, unaware of their deed. Needless to say the deity thus created has the same value system as that of its creators. Should they not eat pork, he will conveniently command them not to eat pork. Should they revere milk cows, he will esteem milk cows too, and so on ad infinitum. Should they advance in morals over time, he would progress to the same degree, but later, quite likely.

95. Cited in G. S. Kirk and J. E. Raven, *The Presocratic Philosophers* (Cambridge: Cambridge University Press, 1962), p. 93.

96. When I was a doctoral student in the philosophy of religion at Columbia University in 1959–60, 'sociomorphic', meaning to be modeled on human social relations, was a common term used for referring to the families (or family relationships) of gods. This term does not appear to have caught on and is now dated, but useful nonetheless.

97. Josh. 24:27. The context is that of a meeting at Shechem between the Israelites who were led out of Egypt (but by this time were under Joshua, not Moses) and some kindred people whom they had encountered. The covenant made between these two groups is heard by a particular rock that will serve as a witness against them, should the occasion arise.

98. A personal anecdote should suffice to make this perfectly clear. Upon departing graduate studies in the philosophy of religion at Columbia, I bade farewell to an acquaintance who was doing a residency in psychiatry. Upon being asked what I would teach when taking up teaching duties at the University of Idaho, I replied that among other things I would teach elementary logic. The soon-to-be psychiatrist said, "Well, that should be fairly easy, because people naturally tend to think in terms of Aristotelian logic." Then he added, "Come with me to the mental

hospital where I work, and you will find that each different patient has his or her own system of logic." It should be clear that it would be impossible to create a society composed of individuals each of whom has a unique system of logic. Communication would be impossible; so too would cooperation.

99. Edward O. Wilson, *Sociobiology: The New Synthesis* (Cambridge: Harvard Univeristy Press, 1977), p. 562.

100. *Principles of Penal Law*, in *WJB*, 1:506. Bentham took 'sacred' and 'holy' to be synonyms (*Bentham to Fellow-Citizens*, in *WJB*, 4:438).

101. In 2 Sam. 6:6–7, one can see how dangerous the sacred is even to the well-intentioned. Therein a man named Uzzah puts out his hand to steady the ark of the Bible-god, lest it fall, and was struck dead for his considerateness. In 2 Sam. 1:6–15, we find the story of an Amalekite who out of mercy acceded to the wishes of the wounded King Saul and slew him. When David learned that this man had laid hands on the Lord's anointed king, that is, on a sacred personage, he had him slain.

102. Anselm Atkins, PhD, a Trappist monk and priest, was also an essayist, novelist, and artist in stained glass. He wrote of the Roman Catholic Church in particular much as I have written of the sacred in general. In his "From City of Man to City of God," *THu* 42, no. 5 (1982): 26, he wrote, "[A]s for the Church as a whole, a historical institution in all its frailty, I shall now damn it with faint praise: it is the most magnificent work of art ever constructed by man."

103. Karl Marx, "Notes to the Doctoral Dissertation: Reason and the Proof of God," in *Writings of the Young Marx on Philosophy and Society*, ed. and trans. Loyd Easton and Kurt Guddat (Garden City, NY: Doubleday, Anchor Books, 1967), p. 65.

104. This parable first appeared as the article, "The Failure of Naturalism," *KR* 3 (autumn 1941): 460–72. Later it appeared in Philip Wheelwright, *A Critical Introduction to Ethics*, rev. ed. (New York: Odyssey Press, 1949), pp. 398–99.

105. James, *Varieties of Religious Experience*, p. 528.

106. Henri Bergson, *The Two Sources of Morality and Religion*, trans. Ashley Audra and Cloudesly Brereton (London: Macmillan, 1935), p. 102; also see n. 25 above.

107. Roy A. Rappaport, "The Sacred in Human Evolution," in *Explorations in Anthropology: Readings in Culture, Man, and Nature*, ed. Morton H. Fried (New York: Thomas Y. Crowell, 1973), p. 409. Also see his "Ritual, Sanctity, and Cybernetics," *AA* 73, no. 1 (1971): 59–76. When referring to positivism, he probably had A. J. Ayer in mind. In chaps. 1 and 6 of *Language, Truth, and Logic*, 2nd ed. (London: Victor Gollancz, 1946), Ayer defined metaphysical sentences as those expressing neither empirical hypotheses (explanatory sentences that could be true or false; sentences for which, in principle at least, confirmatory or disconfirmatory evidence could be provided) nor tautologies (i.e., logical truths; sentences that either repeat themselves wholesale or in which nothing appears in the predicate that is not already in the subject). As such, metaphysical sentences (including theological sentences) can be neither true nor false, because, quite simply, they are neither empirical nor analytical in nature. Since, to Ayer, empirical and analytical sentences (declaring that something or other is the case) are the only ones that can be cognitively significant (or sensible), it follows that sentences that do neither are, technically speaking, nonsense. On the basis of this analysis, Ayer writes, "And our view that all utterances about the nature of God are nonsensical, so far from being identical with, or even

lending any support to, either of these familiar contentions [those of atheism and agnosticism], is actually incompatible with them. For if the assertion that there is a god is nonsensical, then the atheists' assertion that there is no god is equally nonsensical, since it is only a significant proposition that can be significantly contradicted. As for the agnostic, although he refrains from saying either that there is or is not a god, he does not deny that the question whether a transcendent god exists is a genuine question" (pp. 115–16). In this fashion, Ayer sought to make agnosticism, as well as atheism, logically impossible. The entire analysis turns on whether or not a sentence in which 'god' (begun with or without a capital letter) can serve as the logical subject (not to be confused with the grammatical subject) of a cognitively significant sentence. Ayer's analysis can be bypassed and rendered irrelevant by a slightly different approach. Rather than beginning with 'god', used as the subject of a relevant sentence, one can begin with 'universe' and proceed to ask whether or not the universe is an artifact or sufficiently like one to require, i.e., presuppose, an artificer. Proceeding in this manner, the atheist is one who says that the universe is not an artifact; the theist says that it is; and the agnostic says that there is not enough evidence to claim knowledge one way or the other. In this way the possibility of the three positions can be preserved and no metaphysical assertion needs to be involved. Although Bentham did not put the matter in quite this way, his analysis of religious language (to be taken up in detail in part 3) preserves these three possibilities and avoids the absurdity of telling atheists and agnostics that they are logically impossible, as it were. Rappaport, whose claim that metaphysical/theological statements can never be confirmed or disconfirmed, goes further in "The Sacred in Human Evolution," claiming that when such statements are taken in a given society to be unquestionably true, one comes upon the "sine qua non of sanctity," i.e., one treads upon the threshold of the sacred (p. 409). Moreover, in "Ritual, Sanctity, and Cybernetics," he says, "If a proposition is going to be taken to be unquestionably true, it is important that no one understand it." One is reminded here of Karl Rahner's perplexity over the doctrine of the (adorable?) Trinity. This social phenomenon goes quite beyond Bentham's comprehension; it is something the rationalist cannot fathom.

108. Desmond Morris, *The Naked Ape* (New York: McGraw-Hill, 1967), pp. 178–79.

109. Ibid., p. 181. Bentham made the same point, but at much greater length in the *AINR*.

110. Wilson, *Sociobiology*, p. 561.

111. Bergson, *The Two Sources of Morality and Religion*, p. 108.

112. Ibid., p. 266.

113. Ibid., p. 24.

114. Ibid., pp. 198–99.

115. Rappaport, "The Sacred in Human Evolution," p. 404.

116. Ibid., pp. 404, 405.

117. Morris, *The Naked Ape*, p. 180

118. Edward O. Wilson, "Biology's Spiritual Products," *FI* 7, no. 2 (1987): 15.

119. See Walter T. Stace, *The Teachings of the Mystics* (New York: New American Library, Mentor Books, 1960), p. 10.

120. Ibid.

121. Ibid., p. 12.

122. Stace says of the extrovertive route to the mystical consciousness, "The extrovertive mystic with his physical senses continues to perceive the same world of trees and hills and tables and chairs as the rest of us. But he sees these objects transfigured in such a manner that the Unity [of all things] shines through them." He quotes Meister Eckhart (c. 1260–1329): "'Here [i.e., in this experience] are blades of grass, wood, and stone, all things are one."' (pp. 15–16). In Stace's book *Mysticism and Philosophy* (Los Angeles: Jeremy P. Tarcher, 1960), p. 85, Stace notes that when attention is sharply focused (as in a fast-paced, exciting game) people can be hurt and not know it; only later is the discomfort felt. Obviously, then, some mental states exclude ordinary modes of awareness that would otherwise be recognized at once. Introvertive mysticism requires that all sensations be excluded from awareness, all recollections thereof, "all abstract thoughts, reasoning processes, volitions, and other particular mental contents" (pp. 85–86). This can be done with help, training, and discipline by commencing initially by concentrating, for example, "on the stream of one's own breath," by repeating a mantra, that is, a short formula of words," over and over, or by practicing detachment from "self-centered desires." See *The Teachings of the Mystics*, pp. 18–19. The literature by mystics and about mysticism, collectively, is vast. Readers interested in learning more about the subject, as Stace has delineated it, would do well to read works of or about the philosopher Plotinus, the philosophically sophisticated Catholic Meister Eckhart, the Protestant Jacob Boehme, the Quaker George Fox, the eminent poet Tennyson, and the writer and former Marxist Arthur Koestler. Gershom Scholem has written major works on Jewish mysticism. Respecting topics rather than figures, it is most instructive to learn of Patanjoli's Raja Yoga, of the meditative practices and discipline of Theravada (or Hinayana) Buddhist monks, and of Sufism. Respecting Zen, D. T. Suzuki is eminent. Major American scholars who have written perceptively about mysticism are philosopher/psychologist William James and psychologist James Leuba. The works of Richard Maurice Bucke on cosmic consciousness and of R. C. Zaehner are also recommended. These scratch only the surface of the topic.

123. Stace, *Mysticism and Philosophy*, p. 86.

124. Ibid., p. 147.

125. Ibid.

126. Ibid., pp. 65, 268.

127. Ibid., p. 315.

128. Ibid., pp. 14, 194.

129. Stace, *The Teachings of the Mystics*, p. 24.

130. See Huxley's two books in one, whose pages are numbered sequentially, *"The Doors of Perception" and "Heaven and Hell"* (New York: Harper and Row, 1954), p. 12.

131. Ibid., p. 16. For corroboration of drug-induced experiences, also see Malachy McCourt's memoir, *A Monk Swimming* (New York: Hyperion, 1998), pp. 88–90.

132. Huxley, *"The Doors of Perception,"* p. 17.

133. Ibid., p. 95.

134. Ibid., p. 20.

135. Ibid., pp. 22, 26.

136. Ibid., pp. 35–36.

137. Ibid., pp. 19, 22, 25, 27.

138. Ibid., p. 138.

139. Ibid., p. 67. In the *The Origin of Consciousness in the Breakdown of the Bicameral Mind* (Boston: Houghton Mifflin, 1976), p. 332, Julian Jaynes endorses Huxley's view of the importance of transcendence to human beings.

140. Huxley, *"The Doors of Perception,"* p. 67.

141. Perhaps embarrassment is more at issue here than ignorance. In the half-dozen texts of comparative religions that I can reach without leaving the chair in which I sit while writing these words, scant attention is paid to the relation of religion to intoxicants and drugs. The books in question are Edwin A. Burtt, *A Man Seeks the Divine*, 2nd ed. (New York: Harper and Row, 1957); John Clark Archer, *Faiths Men Live By*, rev. by Carl E. Purinton (New York: Ronald Press, 1958); John A. Hutchison and James Alfred Martin Jr., *Ways of Faith* (New York: Ronald Press, 1960); John A. Hutchison, *Paths of Faith* (New York: McGraw-Hill, 1969); John B. Noss, *Man's Religions*, 4th ed. (London: Macmillan, 1969); and Ninian Smart, *The Religious Experience of Mankind* (New York: Charles Scribner's Sons, 1969). Of these six, only two mention either peyote or mescaline. Smart devotes three sentences to peyotism (p. 536) but does so only in the context of rapid social changes suffered by certain American Indian tribes. Burtt devotes two pages to Bacchic cults in which he notes a Mexican variant thereof "centered around a drink made from the button of a small cactus called the peyote" (p. 59). Respecting the much more famous soma (or haoma), now believed to have been a mixture of milk and the juice of a hallucinogenic mushroom, drunk by ancient Hindus in India and by Zoroastrians in Persia, Archer has nothing to say; Burtt mentions it twice (pp. 59, 190); Hutchison, writing with Martin, mentions it several times on a single page (p. 99); Hutchison, writing alone, mentions it on four different pages (pp. 67–69, 302); Smart devotes about one page of text to it (p. 66–67); and Noss refers to the drink (whether called soma or haoma) on nine occasions (pp. 90, 92, 95, 345–46, 350, 353–54, 356). In contrast John M. Allegro, *The Sacred Mushroom and the Cross* (New York: Doubleday, 1970), believes the mushroom *Amanita muscaria* to "have become the center of a mystery cult in the Near East which persisted for thousands of years [involving both Judaism and early Christianity]. There seems good evidence that from there [the Near East] it swept into India in the cult of Soma some 3,500 years ago; it certainly flourished in Siberia until quite recent times, and is found even today in certain parts of South America" (p. 39). Only one of the comparative religions texts above has an index entry for drugs (Smart, p. 67). Only one has an entry on intoxicants in relation to religious practice (Burtt, pp. 37, 58).

142. "Mysticism and the Brain—The New Controversy," *RW* 4, no. 3 (1989): 2–3. See also Dennis Stacy, "Transcending Science," *Om*, December 1988, pp. 54 ff., for an article about Professor Michael A. Persinger, head (at the time of writing) of the neuroscience lab at Laurentian University of Sudbury, Ontario, Canada. A metal cap that gives its wearer mystical experiences when magnetic forces are exerted and focused on certain brain areas might be seen as answering Stace's question as to

whether such experiences are intramental or extramental. Religionists and others who are interested in asserting the extramental nature of at least some mystical experiences (the genuine ones à la Stace) have attacked Persinger's work and the rather obvious conclusion that stems from it. Persinger, however, has responded as follows according to Stacy (p. 116): "Even if there are real, other-dimensional wonders out there, he says, there must be a physical mechanism by which their voices come through. 'And', he adds, 'even if there are no aliens, no gods, no old hags, our human need to escape the mundane dictates that we conjure them—be it from the temporal lobes or the astral plane.'" A revealing interview with Professor Persinger by British journalist Ian Cotton can be found in "Dr. Persinger's God Machine," *FI* 17, no.1 (1996–97): 47-51, wherein Cotton quotes Persinger (p. 50) as follows, "The fact that we can actually insert [into consciousness] a God experience [via the helmet] doesn't change the fact that the process is there for some functional or evolutionarily significant reason. If one accepts that God created the universe, then why not have a brain mechanism whereby these experiences take place?" Persinger also adds, "Social disruption, confusion, disorientation; and then, in tandem . . . great surges of paranormalism. The Great Depression of the thirties, for instance, was a fine source of Charismatic belief" (p. 51).

143. Bentham, *Introduction to Morals and Legislation*, in *WJB*, 1:4, 6; and *Defense of Usury*, 3:16.

144. Huxley, *"The Doors of Perception,"* p. 88.

145. Ibid., p. 87.

146. Ibid., p. 155.

147. See *NCE* for a short but excellent article on flagellants (and flagellation) in Christendom, a topic not much relished by religionists. For an insight into a particularly brutal form of it in Islam, see John Kifner, "Iran Obsessed with Martyrdom," *NYTM*, December 16, 1984, 36 ff.

148. Huxley, *"The Doors of Perception,"* p. 153.

149. Ibid., pp. 143–44. William James, *Varieties of Religious Experience*, pp. 556–57, notes that it is the nature of mystical experiences to emerge from subconsciousness with such force as to appear to the recipient to be objective (or "extramental" in Stace's terminology).

150. James Leuba, *The Psychology of Religious Mysticism* (New York: Harcourt, Brace, 1929), pp. 137–55, esp. 138, 149, 151. See also pp. 185, 193. Leuba agrees with Huxley on the roles of isolation, food and sleep deprivation, and self-inflicted tortures on achieving states of ecstasy (pp. 11, 14). On p. 161 he writes, "The human being is so complex that there is no *a priori* difficulty in accepting a statement affirming that something very painful is also highly enjoyable."

151. It can hardly be surprising that mystics interpret their experiences theologically, for as George A. Coe wrote long ago, "The mystic brings his theological beliefs to the mystical experience; he does not derive them from it" ("The Sources of the Mystical Revelation," *HJ* 6 [1907–1908]: 367). By the same token Arthur Koestler, a nonbeliever, did not come away from his mystic experiences with a theological explanation of them (see Stace, *The Teachings of the Mystics*, pp. 232–34), nor do nontheistic Buddhist monks become theists as a result of their mystical experiences.

152. James, *Varieties of Religious Experience*, pp. 429–34.

153. For trance states, see Leuba, *The Psychology of Religious Mysticism*, esp. pp. 181–83, 275; for ritual dancing, see ibid., pp. 13–15. The whirling Dervishes come to mind first, but one must also remember the Shaking Quakers in Christian England and America together with the Holy Jumpers (or Rollers) of American Pentecostalism. For liturgical exercises, see Morton Smith, *The Secret Gospel* (New York: Harper and Row, 1973). In the short first chapter called "The Preparation" Smith draws certain conclusions from repeated experiences of worship at the Greek Orthodox monastery of Mar Saba in Israel. While there he came to a new understanding of worship as "a means of disorientation." He writes, "The words of this worship too—the enormous hymns of the Greek monastic offices—were unmistakably hypnotic . . . dazzling the mind and destroying its sense of reality" (p. 6). He found the attitudes undergirding the Orthodox liturgies to be "basically magical" (p. 7).

154. This appeared, I believe, in *Parade*, a supplement to many Sunday newspapers, sometime within the last six months of 1993.

155. Jaynes, *The Origin of Consciousness*, pp. 73–74.

156. Ibid., pp. 88–89.

157. Ibid., p. 92. In keeping with this, Noss includes in his *Man's Religions* the following amazing material in a footnote, pp. 164–65: "Once [Tumo Geshe Rimpochhe, a celebrated Tibetan yogin who died in the 1930s], while traveling in Tibet with a large retinue, caused to appear in the sky a wonderful phantasmagoria of the Buddha Maitreya and His attendant Bodhisattvas. The phenomenon, which was visible for miles around, lasted for several hours. Not only was the whole country-side bathed in celestial radiance, but flowers resembling lotuses came raining down. These latter, though they could be picked up and handled, appeared to melt into the air after about half an hour. . . . Many of those who were eye-witnesses are still alive and the substance of their united testimony is not lightly to be rejected." This suggests that the same or very similar hallucinations may be communal in nature, on occasion at least.

158. Jaynes, *The Origin of Consciousness*, p. 405.

159. Ibid., p. 413.

160. Ibid., pp. 101–108. See especially what he writes about Wernicke's area, an area of specialized brain tissue, associated with language, on the left side of the brain and its apparently missing complement on the right side of the brain in modern humans.

161. Ibid., pp. 63–64, 67, 134, 217–19. Note especially what he says about narratization and its relation to consciousness. Also see what he has to say about the impact of writing, pp. 198, 208, 302.

162. Ibid., pp. 86, 93–94, 258–59. Note especially the relation of novelties in social experience (what might best be called cognitive dissonance) to the induction of stress.

163. The range of evidence Jaynes calls upon is as vast as it is varied, ranging from neuroscience to etymology, from schizophrenia, epilepsy, and hypnosis to ancient iconography and the exegesis of the *Iliad*.

164. Whitehead, *Religion in the Making*, p. 15.

165. Bentham was extremely fearful of ghosts during his childhood and well into his maturity. He says that it was a "permanent source of amusement [to his par-

ents' servants] to ply him with horrible phantoms" (*Memoirs of Bentham*, in *WJB*, 10:18). To a large extent he overcame his fears by realizing that all the ghosts he had "seen" were clothed, indicating that there must be ghost clothes—a notion which is patently absurd. (*WJB*, 10:587).

166. Karl Marx was but a lad of four when Bentham wrote of the upper classes and their exploitation of the lower classes, using religion. See Delos B. McKown, *The Classical Marxist Critiques of Religion: Marx, Engels, Lenin, Kautsky* (The Hague: Martinus Nijhoff, 1975), p. 58.

167. As I look into the files I keep on such goings-on, it is hard to know where to begin and how to proceed. Despite the fact that the Shroud of Turin, taken by many to be the burial cloth of Jesus, has now been declared unauthentic by the Catholic Church, no less a person than Anastasio Cardinal Bellestrero, Archbishop of Turin, has declared, "I can assure you that the holy shroud has produced miracles and continues to." To many it has proved inspirational, and more than a few trace cures to it (*NYT*, October 14, 1988). In Medjugorje, in what was once Yugoslavia, alleged appearances of the Virgin Mary brought out as many as one hundred thousand people a day and about three million in all from 1981–1985. According to Archbishop Frane Franic of Split, the visionaries seeing her had "done more for the Catholic faith in the archdiocese than our pastoral work in forty years." Said one person, "We used to curse a lot, but not any more" (*NYT*, November 18, 1985). The *NYT* wrote, "Authentic or not, there is little doubt that the Medjugorje apparitions have changed many lives" (September 28, 1990). Marija Pavlovic (one of the visionaries from Medjugorje) came to the Hospital of the University of Alabama in Birmingham to donate a kidney to her ailing brother. While recuperating near the tiny town of Sterrett, east of Birmingham, apparitions of the Virgin began to appear, whereupon "Hundreds of pilgrims from Florida, Louisiana, Arkansas, and other states braved rain and chilly winds . . . to be near . . . Marija." One Maria Gonzolez, a native of the Canary Islands, drank, for its alleged curative powers, about a dozen glasses of water that had pooled on a sodden cow pasture near where the Virgin was said to have appeared (*BPH*, January 16, 1989); also see the same paper for January 27, 1989). In the *AJC* of December 25, 1992, the reader is told that the Blessed Mother "has been spotted in the sun above a Denver hilltop, in a field near Kettle River, Minn., in a back yard in Marlboro, N. J., and in a kitchen window in Oxnard, Calif." The Virgin's increased and ready availability has, according to the paper, "produced a spiritual renewal." In an article titled, "The Vision that Wasn't. Or Was It?" (September 2, 1992), the *NYT*, commenting on an apparition in Cold Spring, Kentucky, that was not very convincing to the eight thousand people who turned out to see it, thinks that such marvels are not very important in themselves but are ways of drawing people to prayer and faith in Jesus. One priest/theologian who was present (though he saw nothing) described the occasion as "a profound experience of peace and serenity." During the past decade, the longest running visions of the Virgin Mary seem to have occurred in Conyers, Georgia, where Nancy Fowler lived. She had visions of, and received messages from, the Virgin on the thirteenth of each month beginning in 1987 (both Fowler and the Blessed Virgin have now departed Conyers). For example, with five thousand people looking on she received a message on January 13, 1994, which

consisted of the following: "As you make the sign of the cross I will bless you and everything you have with you." Of this one person said, "It was a wonderful experience, real peaceful, real spiritual." On November 13, 1993, the sheriff's department estimated that eighty thousand people showed up to witness the proceedings and to be blessed thereby (*BN*, January 16, 1994). Meanwhile, Jesus has also been active in making appearances, it would seem. According to the *NYT* of May 25, 1991, he appeared first to one Joyce Simpson in a fork full of Pizza Hut spaghetti pictured on a billboard in Atlanta, Georgia. Subsequently, others saw his image too, accepted it as a miracle, and were benefited by it, just as she was, to hear their testimonies. Some less convincing reports of the Savior's appearance can be found in the *SS*, April 18, 1983; in the *BPH*, August 21, 1986; and in the *KS*, July 25, 1987. Even in the atheistic Soviet Union (before its dissolution), pilgrims were going to St. Petersburg to visit the tomb of a certain Ksenya, yet to be canonized by the Russian Orthodox Church. Despite this lack of official status, many claim to have been helped by her. According to the *NYT*, December 18, 1986, "'People come here because if you believe in her, she will help you,' said a well-dressed, middle-aged Russian woman. 'My life has changed since coming here. It has become good.' . . . Handwritten messages, most barely legible, cover every inch of the fence. 'Dear Ksenya,' reads one, 'preserve my brother from Alyona.' 'Help me find a one-room apartment,' reads another. 'Blessed Ksenya,' writes a lovelorn Tanya, 'please help me marry Maikov.' Grigory, a student in vocational school, writes, 'Blessed Ksenya, help me, a sinner, excel in deeds and in love.' A message nearby, in a child's hand, is less demanding: 'Help me finish fifth grade.'" Meanwhile, back in America, a small Orthodox church in Chicago, for a time in the mid-1980s, was drawing upward of five thousand people a day, some from as far away as Sri Lanka and Pakistan, to see an icon (of the Virgin with Child) weep (*NYT*, December 22, 1986). Four years later, an icon of St. Irene, in an Orthodox cathedral in Queens, New York, also became lachrymose for a season. "The roving eye of a seven-year old girl" was said to have been healed by this icon. Another person felt it had transformed her life (*NYT*, November 5, 1990). Even a dry-eyed statue of the Madonna can work wonders. According to the *NYT*, July 17, 1986, "'The Blessed Mother over there, she takes care of everybody,' said Rosa Morrone. . . . 'Maybe you got a son looking for a good job. Or your son's trying to get off drugs. Maybe you've been sick. You come and pray and the Blessed Mother takes care of you.'" A relative of Mrs. Morrone, an engineer and an educated man, "attributes his survival from a case of double pneumonia during childhood to the Madonna's intercession." Such reports could go on endlessly. Even when no prayers are answered, together with no apparition(s), pilgrims of the sorts mentioned above often feel that they have been benefited just by being where they are. Believing in the supernatural as they do, they do not accord to what they would regard as the merely psychological (both personal and social) forces at play to explain their sense of peace, tranquility, etc. Nor do they recognize the temporary reduction in the level of their stress. William W. Dressler, an anthropologist who is a professor of behavioral and community medicine in Alabama and who has written extensively on hypertension, cardiovascular diseases, and the social and cultural contexts of coping with stress, told a reporter for the Associated Press that "superstition, if not overdone, can help some people overcome stress." It is a way, he thinks, of introducing greater predictability (and hence less stressful uncertainty) into life. (I saw the Associated Press report in my local paper, the *OAN*, July 12, 1984.) In his book *Stress and Adaptation in the Context of Culture: Depression in a Southern Black Community* (Albany: State University of New York Press, 1991), he found that "higher levels of religious participation are related to greater self-reliance in terms of coping with problems, when just the opposite [logically] might be anticipated" (p. 143).

168. Although it can be said that without Jesus there would have been no St. Paul, once the latter took his version of the Christian message to the Gentile world, Jesus was changed forever. A large body of scholarly opinion believes that the original message of Jesus passed into the keeping not of Paul but of Jesus' brother James and the so-called Jerusalem church. It is widely believed that this original church with its pristine message was destroyed by the Romans along with the Jewish nation in the war beginning in 67 and ending with the destruction of Masada in 73. For an introduction to this topic see the index entry "James" and the subentries "dynastic factor," "leadership of Church," "relations with Paul," and "zeal for the Torah," in particular, in Samuel G. F. Brandon, *Jesus and the Zealots: A Study of the Political Factor in Primitive Christianity* (Manchester, UK: University of Manchester Press, 1967). For a much more recent exploration of some of the same themes but from a decidedly different vantage point, see Barbara Thiering, *Jesus and the Riddle of the Dead Sea Scrolls: Unlocking the Secrets of His Life Story* (San Francisco: HarperSanFrancisco, 1992).

169. For a detailed discrimination between the concepts at issue see Oscar Cullmann, *Immortality of the Soul and Resurrection of the Dead* (London: Epworth Press / Macmillan, 1958), pp. 28–47.

170. The *MA*, June 9, 1984, carried an unsigned article titled "Poll Suggests Most Americans Have Self-Serving Religion." George Gallup, the pollster, is quoted as saying that interviews with 1,610 adults gave "evidence of a self-centered kind of faith." What, one may wonder, did he expect? The same paper, January 2, 1993, claims that 76 percent of Catholics and 84 percent of Protestants believe in life after death.

171. McKown, *The Classical Marxist Critiques of Religion*, p. 54.

172. Among the ninety-nine names of Allah are (1) the Compassionate, (2) the Merciful, (3) the King, (22) the Abaser, (25) the Humiliator, (28) the Judge, (35) the Rewarder, (61) the Giver of Death, and (81) the Avenger (*DCR*, pp. 306–307).

173. Burkert, *Creation of the Sacred*, p. 12.

174. Ibid., p. 20.

175. Roy A. Rappaport, *Ritual and Religion in the Making of Humanity* (Cambridge: Cambridge University Press, 1999), p. 16. In chap. 2, the author devotes forty-five pages to an investigation of ritual among human beings. Readers interested in pursuing this subject further will find a long and very useful bibliography in this book. A classical work on the subject of language and myth is Ernst Cassirer, *Language and Myth* (New York: Harper and Brothers, an unaltered reprint of the first Dover edition, 1946), esp. chap. 4, "Word Magic."

176. James E. Crimmins, "Bentham's Metaphysics and the Science of Divinity,"

HTR 73 (1980), quotes (p. 394) from one of Bentham's unpublished manuscripts as follows: "That state of prepared imbecility which is necessary to a mind for the tranquil reception of one parcel of Nonsense, fits it for another. . . . A man who after reading the scriptures can bring himself to fancy the doctrines of the Athanasian Creed. . . . [H]is mind if not already blotted over with hieroglyphical chimeras is a sheet of blank paper, on which any one who will press hard enough may write what scrawls he pleases (UC xcvii. 48)."

Part 2

Not Paul, but Jesus:
How Bentham Exposed the
Would-Be President of Christianity

Chapter 4

Introduction and Distillation
with Commentary

In 1823, in England, publisher John Hunt brought forth a book entitled *Not Paul, but Jesus* (hereafter referred to as *NPBJ*). Its ostensible author was given as Gamaliel Smith. Although the surname "Smith" denoted legions (and thereby conferred anonymity), "Gamaliel" named but few and signified not a little. In Acts 5:27–39, following the arrest of Peter (and other apostles), we learn that a certain Gamaliel, a Pharisee and an honored teacher of the Mosaic law, advised his coreligionists as follows: "And now I say unto you, Refrain from these men [i.e., Jewish and perhaps also some Gentile Christians] and let them alone: for if this counsel or this work be of men, it will come to nought: But if it be of God, ye cannot overthrow it; lest haply ye be found even to fight against God."[1] We also learn in Acts 22:3 that Saul of Tarsus sat, in his student days, "at the feet of Gamaliel, taught according to the perfect manner of the law of the fathers." Forsaking the benign tutelage of the tolerant Gamaliel, Saul, the extremist student, sallied forth "breathing out threatenings and slaughter against the disciples of the Lord" (Acts 9:1). This Saul "made havoc of the church" (8:3), "binding and delivering into prison [various disciples of the Lord], both men and women alike" (22:4). In Philippians 3:6, Paul confirms Acts by confessing to having persecuted the church.

Just as the Gamaliel of Acts counseled his fellow Jews to be patient and tolerant of the Christian movement burgeoning within their ranks, so, too, would the Gamaliel of *NPBJ* have counseled Saul of Tarsus to temper his opposition to Christianity and to quash his murderous intentions against messianic believers in Jesus, innocent of any crime. The biblical Gamaliel would also have advised the converted Paul neither to attempt a takeover of the Christian movement nor to justify himself in so doing with fabricated revelations, likely stories, and convenient miracles. Hence the fittingness of the "Gamaliel" in "Gamaliel Smith." But, enough of this digression into what's in a name. The more important inquiry lies in identifying Gamaliel Smith. Gamaliel Smith was none other than Jeremy Bentham using Francis Place, a well-known English atheist, as his amanuensis.

Francis Place (1771–1854) was a self-educated, self-made man who began in trade as a leather-breeches maker. Later he became a kind of labor organizer and political activist. Still later he became a successful businessman and bibliophile but not to the exclusion of his enduring interest in radical social reform. Despite his nonintellectual origins and lack of formal education, he came to travel in elevated circles, being a friend of James Mill; an associate, for a time, of Robert Owen; and a valued disciple of Bentham from 1812 onward.[2] There is not much controversy as to his contribution to *NPBJ* and his relation to Bentham in its production. Place claimed in his own copy of the book that during August and September of 1817 he put the substance of it together "at Mr. Bentham's request" and from the latter's extensive writings on the relation of Paul to Jesus; on the relation of the Gospels to Acts and certain Pauline epistles; and on the history of the primitive church. The entire work cannot, however, have been finished in 1817, and much that Bentham wrote on the aforementioned subjects was left out at his request.[3] The result is a 440-page book detailing the differences between Jesus and his religion on the one hand and Paul and his on the other. The pages of this book are not very big, and the type is not very small, so the book, though considerable, is not nearly as extensive as it would at first seem to be, based on the number of its pages.

The brains behind "Gamaliel Smith" were discerned almost immediately (by one Unitarian clergyman at least), and within the first year after its publication *NPBJ* suffered, in print, a handful of ignorant brickbats.[4] Acute apologists for and defenders of the faith could perceive in it implicitly what Place wrote of it explicitly, to wit: "[T]his book is calculated to do infinite injury to the Establishment."[5] It did, of course, no such thing, but it did incite some to leap to the defense of their hero, St. Paul. Although not himself a member of the Triune Godhead nor the fruit of a virginal mother's womb (the virgin herself immaculately conceived), St. Paul's dicta, nevertheless, became as canonical in due time as the teachings of Jesus. Even when, with uncharacteristic modesty, Paul delivered himself, admittedly, of his own opinion, rather than that of the Bible-god (e.g., 1 Cor. 7:25), his writings became holy Scripture. It was unthinkable to the faithful that an amanuensis so favored by the Most High could have possessed character defects of the sort Bentham detected. Bentham's principal mistakes it seems (if mistakes they were) lay in approaching Paul as an entirely human being rather than as an inspired instrument of deity, in seeing his writings as the expression of one man's personal agenda rather than as the grand design of the presumed maker of heaven and earth, and in seeing Paul's ambitions for his deity as ambitions for himself—on occasion unscrupulous ambitions. Those who strove to strike *NPBJ* down might as well have saved their exertions, for if there were ever a flash in the pan, it would be this book. It slipped into oblivion almost at once.

Nor has history, so to speak, treated it more kindly.[6] Since *NPBJ* is rare and relatively hard to acquire, at present, the average reader is incapable of knowing whether or not the criticisms launched against it have hit their marks. Accordingly, it seems good to me in the pages that immediately follow to provide a distillation of it. Once this is accomplished we may then take an informed look at Bentham's foray into New Testament scholarship, together with criticisms of it, in the light of contemporary scholarship.

That the person known as St. Paul changed from being a "destructive persecutor" of the Christian way (within Judaism) to being a collaborator, largely on his own terms, is a point of ancient history as well established as any.[7] Although this is indisputable, there remains a question as to whether or not the three accounts of his conversion in Acts allow one to infer confidently that his conversion was *inner* as well as outer. Respecting these three accounts (9:1–9, 22:3–11, and 26:9–20), the latter two are presented as speeches (one spontaneous, the other studied) that Paul delivered, whereas the first is presented as biography, penned by the author of Acts (hereafter referred to as the A-h, the Acts historian).[8] Nowhere else in the New Testament does anything resembling even the gist of these conversion accounts appear. Paul's epistles never allude to it, even though they present numerous opportunities for its recitation.

Tedious though it may be, the individual assertions in each of the conversion stories need to be separated one from another, and the stories as such juxtaposed so as to reveal clearly the inconsistencies therein:

Conversion Story I (Acts 9:1–9):

1. Saul (later Paul), with animus against Jesus' disciples, went to the (Jewish) high priest.
2. Saul desired letters to be sent to synagogues in Damascus.
3. These documents would authorize him to arrest Christian men and women for transportation to Jerusalem.
4. Nearing Damascus, there suddenly shone a light from heaven.
5. Saul fell to the ground.
6. He heard a voice saying, Saul, Saul, why do you persecute me?
7. Saul asked the voice to identify itself.

8. The voice said, I am Jesus whom you persecute: it is hard for you to kick against the pricks [or prods].
9. Trembling and astonished, Saul asked what he should do.
10. The voice said, Arise, go into the city, and you shall be told.
11. Speechless themselves, the men accompanying him heard a voice, but saw no one speaking to Saul.
12. Saul arose from the ground, eyes opening but seeing no man.
13. His companions, taking his hand, brought him to Damascus.
14. He remained there three days, sightless, neither eating nor drinking.

CONVERSION STORY II (Acts 22:3–11), presented as spontaneous:

1. I (Paul) am a Jew of Tarsus, was brought up in Jerusalem, studied the law under Gamaliel, and was zealous for God.
2. I persecuted the Christian way unto death, binding and delivering men and women to prison.
3. I received letters from the high priest (who can attest thereto) to brethren in Damascus to bring prisoners to Jerusalem for punishment.
4. Journeying thither, nearing Damascus at about noon, there shone from heaven a great light about me.
5. Falling to the ground, I heard a voice.
6. It said, Saul, Saul, why do you persecute me?
7. I asked the voice to identify itself.
8. The voice said, I am Jesus of Nazareth whom you persecute.
9. My companions saw the light and were fearful.
10. They did not hear the voice speaking to me.
11. I (Saul) asked the lordly voice what to do.
12. It said to arise, to go to Damascus, and there to learn of the things appointed unto me to do.
13. Being led by the hand by my companions, because I was unable to see, due to the glory of the [aforementioned] light, I came to Damascus.

CONVERSION STORY III (Acts 26:9–20), presented as studied:

1. Believing that I should act in ways inimical to Jesus, as I was doing in Jerusalem, I imprisoned many of his followers.
2. I received authority for this from the chief priests.
3. As the imprisoned were put to death, I testified against them.
4. I punished them often in every synagogue and made them blaspheme.
5. I persecuted them even unto strange cities.
6. I went to Damascus with the chief priests' authority and commission.

7. En route at midday I saw a light from heaven brighter than the sun shining around me and my traveling companions.
8. We all fell to the ground.
9. I heard a voice in Hebrew saying, Saul, Saul, why do you persecute me? It is hard to kick against pricks [or prods].
10. I asked the voice for identification.
11. It said, I am Jesus whom you persecute.
12. Rise and stand; I (Jesus) have appeared to you (Saul) to make you a minister of mine and a witness to what you have seen and will see as I appear to you in the future.
13. I (Jesus) will deliver you from the people (i.e., the People of Israel) and from the Gentiles to whom I send you.

Each time the conversion story is told, it is "adapted to the occasion" (p. 2). What does this imply about its veracity on any occasion of its telling, and where did the A-h get the story? The well-known "we-passages" in Acts indicate that the A-h joined Paul's entourage from time to time.[9] In Acts 16:8, the pronoun "they" in a description of certain peregrinations changes (two verses later) to "we." This is followed in verse 14 by "us" rather than by "them." At the beginning of chapter 17, the "we" changes back to "they," and together with "us," drops out for a time (Bentham seems not to have remembered chapter 16 of Acts perfectly, for he locates the first "we-us passages" in chapter 20). Though slipshod, this is not a major mistake, the point being that the A-h was not with Paul at the time of the latter's alleged conversion experience. Whence, then, came the story in the first place? Only from Paul. None of his fellow travelers is said anywhere to have come forward with corroborating evidence, certainly none respecting any *inner* conversion of his. Since Paul must have been the source of the story for the A-h, and since the story is altered to suit the audience, on two occasions at least, why may it not have been a convenient tale composed out of whole cloth by Paul from the outset? How scrupulously honest in such matters, we must ask, was the source?

In addition to questions about the trustworthiness of Paul are similar questions about the A-h. What qualifications had he for receiving critically a (or the) conversion story from Paul? It is one thing to write of Paul's presumed commission from the chief priest(s) or of his journey to Damascus (items that could have been verified, in principle at least); it is something quite different to write of a conversion experience (as history) in one version of which Paul's companions heard the "heavenly voice" he was supposed to have heard (story I, number 11) and in another version of which (story II, 10) they did not. If conversion story II, 10 is true, only Paul could have been the original source of information about the alleged experience. Lacking all possibility of corroboration, the event (if event it was) was subject to Paul's misunderstanding, misinterpretation, misrecollection, or to any other mental or moral frailty he may have been suffering at the time. Accordingly, we must ask of the A-h what historiographic skills he possessed for evaluating Paul's "receipt of a *supernatural* commission [from Jesus] for the [eventual] delivery of a fresh body of doctrine . . . a supplement containing matter never revealed to . . . his [other] Apostles. . . . [A]t no time in all the personal conferences he had with the Apostles was any such story told by Paul, as is related by the author of Acts" (pp. 5–6).

A story about a heavenly light seen by one or more people at midday does not, of course, become true even when it is told thrice, in identical fashion, but when the light goes from being just a light (story I, number 4) to being a great light, (II, 4), to being a light brighter than the sun (III, 7), notice needs to be taken. Since in Paul's day, there was likely no light brighter than the midday sun on a clear day, the light he allegedly saw must have been miraculous. If so, how can one explain the deficiency in reporting this in story I, number 4? If on the other hand, the light grows ever brighter with the retelling of the tale, as an embellishment to heighten its dramatic effect, what becomes of truth?

Questions raised by the three stories of Paul's conversion as to who in his entourage saw the light and who did not, as to who heard a disembodied voice and who did not, and as to who fell to the ground and who did not are minor queries in relation to whether or not Paul actually had a conversion experience of some sort or other at some point in his life, but they are nevertheless, vexatious to historians who would like to know, as nearly as possible, what really happened.[10] But major are the questions having to do with the identity of the voice and the contrariety in what it told Paul to do. Apparently all it took to convince Paul that he was hearing the voice of Jesus was for the voice to say so. Taken at face value this reveals credulity (or gullibility) of a high order.[11] To move from improbability to impossibility, it should be remembered that in the story I, number 10, the disembodied voice told Paul to go into Damascus, and in I, 13, he obeyed, being led because he had been blinded. In II, 12, the voice told him the same thing, and in II, 13, he obeyed, being led by another because blinded. In conversion story III, however, the voice told him to do no such thing but gave him, unblinded, his marching orders forthwith (III, 12) and assured him that he would be delivered from the Jewish people and Gentiles alike (III, 13). Nothing necessitates that any of this is true, but the law of contrariety necessitates that if the first two stories are true about the blinded Paul's entering Damascus to await further instructions, then the third story is false at that point, and vice versa.

It is one thing for a person, bathed in a light brighter than any known to exist at the time, to converse with a disembodied voice; it is quite a different thing for that person's companions to see the light too, or hear the voice, or both. Such occurrences, however, pale in comparison with coordinated voices addressing *two* individuals, unknown to one another, at a distance, and over a period of several days. Yet that is what Acts 9:8–18 would have us take as historical.[12] While Saul lingered in Damascus in darkness, with something like scales on his eyes (a condition unknown to medicine),[13] a certain Ananias was said to have encountered the Lord (Jesus? God?) in a vision (v. 10). The Lord of the vision ordered him to go to Straight Street (v. 11) to ask for the house of a certain Judas, a house that harbored the sightless Saul. This would be like going to Oxford Street or to Westminster Street in a fair sized English city and asking for the house of William or Richard. Saul meanwhile, with prodigious "foresight," had seen (in a vision?) a hitherto unknown man named Ananias coming to him to lay hands on him that he might, in this magical way, regain his sight (v. 12).

At first Ananias remonstrated with the lordly voice bidding him to go to Saul. Ananias, it seems, had heard of how much evil Saul had wrought among the saints (i.e., Christians) in Jerusalem and of how he had acquired authority from the chief priests to bind such folk (vv. 13, 14) in (or associated with) synagogues (v. 2). If Ananias were a real person (and not a convenient fiction whereby the A-h could lend credibility to Saul's alleged conversion experiences), then he knew something suspicious. Under what circumstances, if any, could the chief priests of the Jerusalem Temple (Roman Quislings) send a self-professed Pharisee (Phil. 3:5) into a foreign jurisdiction (Damascus) to synagogues (Pharisaic religious and educational centers) having no organic relation to the Jerusalem Temple and its hierarchy?[14]

Up to this point, the role of Ananias (never mentioned in any of Paul's epistles) has been recounted by the A-h as history. However, in Acts 22, Paul is presented as giving one of his two versions of the same (alleged) history. Herein Ananias is not pictured as having been favored by a conversation with the (disembodied) Lord, telling him where to go and what to do; he simply materializes out of nowhere at Paul's side (v. 13). Also, unlike the version in chapter 9, wherein Ananias is identified simply as a disciple (of Jesus), in chapter 22, he is extolled (v. 12) as a devout man according to the law [a Pharisee perhaps], having a good report of all Jews that dwelled there [Damascus]. Why, one wonders, was such an excellent man as Ananias (with whom the Lord also conversed) not sent to the Gentiles (rather than Paul)? The situation is as obvious as it is simple: It was Paul who, in fact, went to the Gentiles, taking with him an unauthorized, heretical form of Christianity, and it was Paul who, after that fact, needed all the legitimizing he could get.[15] In a most obliging way, the A-h provided it for him through the fiction of Ananias. It should be noted that in Paul's second telling of his conversion (Acts 26:9–20), no intermediary appeared. Paul, to hear him tell it, received his marching orders on the spot directly from the voice of the disembodied Lord. Of course, in the third of the three versions, Paul needed no help in getting rid of the (alleged) scales on his eyes, for he had not been blinded by any light in the first place.

Respecting baptism, a clear regression occurs in the three stories of Paul's conversion. In Acts 9:18, it is said that he arose (after shedding something like scales from his eyes) and was baptized. In Acts 22:16, after receiving his sight (no scale-like things being mentioned), he was commanded to arise and be baptized, but he is never said to have done so. In Acts 26, he is not even told to be baptized and is not said to have done so. Such peculiarities, not to say inconsistencies, in the "history" of Paul's conversion are nothing compared with the larger issue of how it is that a natural act (such as being dipped in or sprinkled with water) can lead to a supernatural effect (such as having one's sins nullified). In Bentham's words, "[A]nd thus it is, that from a mere physical operation of the most trivial nature, we are called upon to infer a spiritual and supernatural effect of the most awful importance; the spiritual effect stated as if it were produced by the physical operation, to which it has no perceptible real relation—nothing but the mere verbal one thus given to it; produced by it, and following it, as of course—just as if sins were a species of dirt, which by washing, could as surely be got off as any other dirt (pp. 41–42).[16] Moreover, "[I]f impunity could indeed be thus conferred by the sprinkling a man with water or dipping him in it, then would it be a matter of serious consideration—not only what is the *verity* of that religion, but what the *usefulness* of it, what the usefulness—with reference to the present life at any rate, not to speak of a life to come: What the usefulness of it; and on what ground stands its claim to support by all the powers of factitious punishment and factitious reward, at the hands of the temporal magistrate" (p. 43). It is a dubious doctrine that holds that misdeeds and their consequent sufferings can be nullified by a dip in some water or by a dab of it upon one's brow, even when accompanied by fervent faith.

After hearing a voice (intra- or extramentally) or only saying that he (Paul) had heard it (no corroborative witness coming forward); after being blinded or maybe not; after being visited by Ananias, or maybe not; after recovering his sight, or maybe not; after being baptized, or maybe not; after having his sins washed away, or maybe not; and after being converted inwardly (as well as outwardly), or maybe not, Paul is pictured as being ready to receive his commission as an apostle of Jesus. In Acts chapter 9, the commission is not given directly to Paul but to Ananias in the form of a promise. Paul, it seems, was chosen by the Lord Jesus "to bear my [i.e., Jesus'] name before the Gentiles, and kings, and the Children of Israel: For I will shew him how great things he must suffer for my name's sake (vv. 15–16). Of this talk about suffering, vague though it is, the obvious intent is to exalt Paul as a hero—in accordance with his own wishes, no doubt.[17] That such exaltation at the hands of the A-h (and of others) was accomplished is a historical fact, but did this achievement put the A-h in a position to know whether or not Paul received a revelation (i.e., a self-disclosure) from the Almighty? Among the purposes of *NPBJ* is that of satisfying the reader not only that Paul received no such revelation but "[T]hat, on pretense of his having received it from the Almighty by a special revelation, he preached . . . a certain doctrine; but that this doctrine was partly one of his own, contrary to that of Jesus's apostles, and therefore contrary to that of Jesus: and that, in the way of revelation, he never did receive anything; neither that doctrine . . . which he preached, nor any thing else" (pp. 48–49).

To recapitulate certain salient points, here is what passes for history in the A-h's accounts of Saul's conversion. In Acts chapter 9, Saul saw a great light (but his companions did not) and heard a disembodied voice identifying itself as Jesus.[18] In due time, while Saul was blinded and in Damascus, Ananias arrived having experienced a coordinated voice, maintaining that Saul was to be a chosen instrument of the Lord (Jesus) and was to bear his name to the Gentiles, kings, and Jews, suffering much in so doing. After being baptized and strengthened with food, Saul, now Paul, straightaway preached in the local synagogues that Christ is the Son of God (v. 20). There is an important problem with this. It is nowhere said in the "history" above that this is (or was) a (or the) message that was revealed to him supernaturally. *No doctrinal content was delivered.* The "revelation," such as it was, was given to Ananias, and it is clearly different from the proclamation that Christ is the Son of God. Moreover, in Acts 22, wherein Paul is pictured as giving the spontaneous account of his conversion, no mention at all is made of any preaching activities in Damascus. In Acts 26:20, in the studied account of his conversion, Damascus is mentioned, but the message allegedly preached is different than the one in Acts 9:20. From all of this it is safe to conclude that Paul received no self-disclosure of any divine will conveyed to him supernaturally. What one sees in Acts, chapters 9, 22, and 26, is whatever the A-h thought useful or edifying to say in heightening Paul's reputation and in furthering his end(s).

In Galatians 1, Paul adverts to his former life in Judaism in which he persecuted the church (v. 13).[19] The deity who had (presumably) set Paul apart before his birth (v. 15) revealed his Son in Paul that he might preach to the heathen (v. 16). After receiving this revelation he did not, by his own boastful admission, confer with flesh and blood, nor go to Jerusalem to solicit guidance from those who were apostles before him (vv. 16–17). Indeed, Paul's gospel was not man's gospel in the sense of not having been conveyed to him by others (v. 11). To hear him tell it, his gospel came directly from Jesus by revelation (v. 12). Anyone, even Paul himself (at a later time in his life) or an angel from heaven (v. 8), who preached a message contrary to his initial message to the Galatians was to be accursed, in Greek to be anathema (v. 9).[20] A similar outburst with exaggerated claims on his own behalf can be found in 2 Corinthians 11:4–23.[21] If Paul had received any such revelation as he claimed to have received, why did he not proclaim it in the synagogues of Damascus shortly after his conversion? What better time could there have been? Yet, if Acts 9:20 can be believed, he merely preached that Jesus Christ (i.e., King Jesus) was the Son of God. This was a humdrum message in that it was, most likely, what Jesus' original disciples had been preaching all along.[22] Paul's failure at this time to lay out, point by point, the body of doctrine revealed to him, and apart from any human transmission, indicates that he had received no revelation. The message that he came to preach, which separated him sharply from Jesus' authentic disciples and the apostles of the Jerusalem church, was exclusively of his own making. Jesus as merely the earthly Messiah (or King) of the Jews held little or no appeal for him.[23]

Paul's failure to proclaim *his* gospel in the Damascus synagogues shortly after his baptism (or did he actually get his idiosyncratic gospel elsewhere and in a more mundane way?) was not his only failure. Equally conspicuous was his failure in Galatians to dazzle Peter and James, the brother of Jesus (Gal. 1:18), and, later, other apostles (Gal. 2:2) in the Jerusalem Church with some version or other of his experiences in and around Damascus. He had, after all, traveling companions who also fell to the ground with him when the bright light appeared; there was a lordly voice speaking that could only have been that of Jesus; he suffered something like scales on his eyes, blinding him; there was the coordinated voice of Jesus speaking to Ananias as well as to him, predicting his (Paul's) future mission, accomplishments, and sufferings; and he absolutely amazed the Jews (Christian as well as otherwise?) in the synagogues of Damascus with his conversion, his preaching, and his "proof" that Jesus was the King, the Son of God. But, to none of this did he advert in Galatians. The best he could do was to say that he had received a revelation (Gal. 1:12). This, alas, is a very uncertain term that may mean no more than a feeling in the bones, a certitude of mind, some awareness of a calling, etc. Why should he have chosen this frail, ambiguous term when he could have recounted his wondrous experiences in and around Damascus? The reason is simple: No such events occurred there or anywhere else. During the rancorous days when he first sought the approval and cooperation of the original apostles he had not yet made up the "miraculous" but inconsistent conversion tales for consumption by the gullible A-h (or the A-h had not yet made them up, on Paul's behalf, to inflict on other gullible people).

It is instructive to look in, imaginatively, upon Paul's life (as a Jew) just before and during the persecutions he launched against Jesus' disciples. It must be supposed that he was well informed about these Christian enemies of his. Acts 2:41 says that (shortly after Pentecost) about three thousand souls were added to the church in one day alone. Moreover, Acts 6:7 says that the number of disciples multiplied greatly. So, a considerable number of people, *plus their wealth*, were in existence by the time Paul set out to destroy some or all of them. Being knowledgeable, no doubt, he must also have heard of one Simon Magus, a magician who amazed the nation of Samaria, a scant forty miles from Jerusalem (Acts 8:9–11). In due course Simon became a Christian, and it was then his turn to be amazed, amazed at the signs and the great miracles wrought by a Christian evangelist named Philip whose preaching had converted him (Acts 8:13). But this was not all. The apostles Peter and John came to Samaria to pray over and to lay their hands on the converts there that they might receive the Holy Ghost. When Simon saw this wondrous transfer of power, he offered money to gain the same power (Acts 8:17–19). Bentham comments, "To Paul's alert and busy mind—the offer, made by the sorcerer, to purchase of the Apostles a share in the government of the church, could not have been a secret"[24] (p. 90).

Thinking on these matters, it occurred to Paul (whether on the road to Damascus or not) that his object should be to gain control over Christians, not to destroy them. Using the police powers granted him by the chief priests and applying threats and the extortion of money, he began to realize his new-found goal: "With the assistance thus obtained, the plan was—to become a declared convert to the religion of Jesus, for the purpose of setting himself at the head of it; and . . . to preach, in the name of Jesus that sort of religion, by the preaching of which, an empire over the minds of his converts, and, by that means, the power and opulence to which he aspired, might, with the fairest prospect of success be aimed at" (p. 93).

Whether Paul experienced an inner conversion to the religion of Jesus or merely decided to exhibit an outer conversion to hide ulterior motives, one thing is clear: He double-crossed the chief priests, if, indeed, he was ever carrying out a punitive mission for them.[25] Moreover, if his persecutions of the Christian community were as ferocious as he would have us believe (Gal. 1:13), then a period of continuing suspicion among Christians must have followed his conversion, inner or outer. The first and third accounts of it, in Acts, indicate that he preached in Damascus (9:19–22 and 26:20), thus allaying, one would suppose, some of the fearful suspicions entertained of him. The second conversion account (in Acts 22), however, gives no hint of any such preaching. After being told to be baptized (v. 16) he shows up next (in v. 17) in Jerusalem, an indeterminate amount of time intervening. A somewhat similar pattern appears in Galatians 1:13–16. Here Paul goes from being a persecutor of the church to being the recipient of a revelation that converts him.[26] No mention is made of any preaching in its immediate aftermath, but one may infer that his conversion, such as it was, occurred in Damascus, for in verse 17, he says that he returned to

Damascus after a sojourn in Arabia.[27] Only then (after three years) did he go up to Jerusalem. Surely his quietude and good behavior in Arabia, if known about, served to allay continuing Christian suspicions. But more was gained by his retreat than that, according to Bentham: "Arabia, a promising field of enterprise—Arabia, a virgin soil, opened to his view. There he would find none to abhor his person—none to contradict his assertions: there his eloquence—and, under the direction of his judgment, his invention—would find free scope: in that country the reproach of inconsistency could not attach upon him: in that foreign land he beheld his place of quarantine—his school of probation—the scene of his novitiate. . . . [H]e would initiate himself in, and familiarize himself with, the connected exercises of preaching and spiritual rule" (pp. 94–95). Having become sanitized in his behavior, having settled upon his course, but having built no bridges to the Christian leadership (for according to Gal. 1:16 he had not conferred with flesh and blood), it was now time for him to enter into a "sort of treaty" with these disciples; hence the trip to Jerusalem (Gal. 1:18).

The sojourn in Arabia also provided him, one may infer, with physical protection. Before considering his first visit to Jerusalem as his own sort of Christian, more needs to be noted about his less than graceful departure from Damascus. Of this the A-h gives one version; Paul himself, another, leaving us to wonder who, if anyone, is telling the truth. As will be seen increasingly in the pages that follow, Paul's ministry was a contentious one, provoking attacks from Jews, Jewish Christians, and Gentiles alike. Respecting these, it always suited his purposes, and those of the A-h, to make it seem that the trouble invariably arose from the simple preaching of the gospel of Jesus—this and nothing more. Acts 9:22 would have us believe that Paul so confounded (and thus enraged) the Jews of Damascus (with his preaching of Jesus) that they plotted to kill him (v. 23). With murderous Jews watching the gates of the city, day and night, to rid the world of Paul (v. 24), Jesus' disciples took him by night and put him over the city wall in a basket (v. 25). The second book of Corinthians 11:33 corroborates this unseemly mode of egress but gives a different reason for it: rather than murderous Jews waiting to fall upon him, it is no less a person than the governor of Damascus, acting to arrest Paul at the behest of King Aretas. Paul, it would seem, had done, or was perceived to have done, something illegal, not simply something heretical.[28]

Whether Paul was in Arabia for three full years (Gal. 1:17–18) or for one full year plus a part of the preceding year and a part of the following year (equivalent in the reckoning of the time), the question of how he earned his keep comes up. Did he ply his trade of tent making? It seems unlikely that he went to Arabia for that reason, but if he did support himself in that way, while there, it is odd that he failed to glorify himself for it.

He was never shy in grasping at the last straw of credit. As to the source of his subsistence, the answer has already been implied. "[F]rom the purses of those, whom, having had it in his power, and even in his commission, to destroy, he had saved." Bentham continues,

> When ever we get a Temperamental and psychological view of Paul, we see verified the deductions of the author of this treatise, that he was a transparent impostor. An unscrupulous adventurer, with talent well adapted to dogmatically command the attention of the ignorant and especially well those of organized hereditary idolatry, the extreme vanity, the vainglorious pretensions of this new priest was well adapted to obtain obsequious complacence from such people. He always presents himself in a controversial spirit of self-exaltation.
>
> His egotistic diction could hardly be made more manifest than in the terms above quoted, to wit:—"I robbed other churches taking wages of them that I might minister unto you, etc. [2 Corinthians 11:8]." It presents a striking contrast to the benevolent and fraternal spirit of Christ and his disciples. (p. 107)

In each of the three conversion accounts in Acts, there is an abrupt transportation, textually, of Paul from activities in and around Damascus to Jerusalem. In Acts 9:25–26, Paul is no sooner let down over the city wall in a basket than he appears in Jerusalem. No mention is made as to how long it took him to get from one place to the other, nor is there any hint of intermediary peregrinations. In Acts 22:16–17, he is no sooner told to rise and be baptized than he materializes in Jerusalem. In Acts 26:19–20, he no sooner announces his obedience to the "heavenly vision," vouchsafed to him, than he claims to have preached repentance in Damascus first, then in Jerusalem. Moreover, Acts 26:21 has him claiming to have been seized by murderous Jews in the Temple—an act that could only have occurred in Jerusalem. None of these arrivals in Jerusalem even hints at Paul's sojourn in Arabia (alleged in Gal. 1:17) followed by a return to Damascus before venturing on to Jerusalem for the first time as a Christian. Attempts at determining how many visits he paid to Jerusalem (and more or less when and with whom) are made no easier by the inconsistencies between Acts 9:27ff. and Galatians 1:18ff.[29] In the former passage, it is a certain Barnabas who brings him to the Apostles upon his first visit to Jerusalem as a Christian. In Galatians 2:1, Barnabas is relegated to the second visit, fourteen years after the first one (Gal. 1:18), at which time Paul would seem to have gone alone. He claims to have remained fifteen days and to have seen only the top leaders, that is, Peter and James. As though his veracity had been impugned concerning this (presumed) visit, Paul felt it useful to assure his Galatian readers that he was not lying (1:20). How good, one wonders, is such assurance?

It is not so important for us to concern ourselves with the exact number of his visits to Jerusalem and his conferences with the leaders of the Christian community (within Judaism) as it is for us to ask whether or not the record shows that the leadership accepted his conversion and his commission to the Gentiles—*inner* conversion that is and a *revealed* commission, bypassing the leadership. The record will show that his claims were disbelieved. In order to show this, Acts will be followed below in detailing Paul's visits to Jerusalem. Herein they are four, to be called for convenience (1) the Reconciliation Visit (9:26–30), (2) the Money-bringing Visit (11:25–30), (3) the Deputation Visit (15:1–29), and (4) the Invasion Visit (21:15–40). Acts chapter 20 needs to be read as a prologue to the Invasion Visit, and chapters 22–26 need to be read as an epilogue, or as a continuing saga. From the first of these visits to the fourth, some seventeen years may be supposed to have passed.

When Paul double-crossed the Temple authorities (if he was ever an official in their employment) and went over to the Christian side, he may have done so from the outset with an eye to gaining a leadership role for himself.[30] However, coming into a movement with a bad name and with no allies legislates against a rapid rise to the top; hence his need for acceptance by the apostles of the Jerusalem church and a reconciliation, if possible, of outstanding differences. Despite overweening confidence in his own views, he must have approached such people as Peter and James with some trepidation. "To them was known, everything that, in relation to Jesus was unknown to anyone else: and moreover, in unlimited abundance, particulars not capable of being known by any one else" (p. 171). "To perfect success it was necessary, that not only these shepherds of the Church pasture, but, through them the whole flock, should thus be brought under [his] management" (p. 175). What import could Paul's "revelation" on the Damascus Road have held for Peter and James, especially if it contradicted their preaching and the theological positions they held? Moreover, what, Paul must have wondered, would their attitude toward him be over events in Damascus? Did he really say something that enraged the Jews in the synagogues there? Would the original apostles have preached Jesus in the same provocative way? Since Peter and James did not cease to be Jews when they became disciples of Jesus, they might have found ample ground for sympathy with the Jews of Damascus. Would they also have been offended by Paul's preaching? Or, was it King Aretas whom Paul had provoked and through whose fingers he had slipped? This might have strengthened his credentials in the Jerusalem church.

In any case, in due time, Paul took it to be in his interest to go to the Christian leadership in Jerusalem, the headquarters of the movement.[31] Perhaps he had a "revelation" that conformed nicely with his self-interest in Christianity. If the first visit mentioned in Galatians 1:18 is historical, it appears to have accomplished little or nothing toward rapprochement. The same is true of the first visit, (the Reconciliation Visit) detailed in Acts 9:26–30. Herein Paul is not even pictured as speaking for himself: it is a certain benefactor named Barnabas who brings him to the apostles and tells them (v. 27) that Paul had seen the Lord. This is a significant change, for in the three conversion stories in Acts, he sees only a *bright light*. Representing him to the disciples and apostles as having seen the Lord initiates (however weakly) the process of elevating Paul to parity with them in this particular. He himself claims the same prerogative in 1 Corinthians 15:8, wherein he notes that the Lord also appeared to him, untimely born though he was. One wonders how Barnabas came to know that the Lord Jesus had appeared to Paul. Just as the Corinthians did—from Paul himself! Leaving Barnabas to speak before the disciples and apostles on this matter, rather than taking the floor himself, provided Paul with an advantage. It enabled him to avoid "cross-examination" by those who had known Jesus best. Just how impressed could these people who had walked and talked with Jesus have been by Paul's alleged visionary encounters with their Lord? Not very impressed, one would surmise.

Nothing is said in Acts' account of the Reconciliation Visit about any harmonization of doctrines and goals between Paul and the apostles. They are not portrayed as having rejoiced in his claim of having seen the Lord. They granted no blessing that would have made him one with themselves. No mention is made about spheres of influence—of the original disciples' staying home to proclaim Jesus to Jews and of Paul's going abroad to proclaim him to Gentiles. In fact, in Acts 9:28–29a, he is said, immediately after meeting with the Christian leadership, to have preached Jesus boldly in *Jerusalem* and to have disputed the Grecians (or Hellenists), who were probably Greek-speaking Jews of the Diaspora who had become Christians, people with whom he ought to have had much in common. Yet, he is said to have angered these Grecians so greatly that they sought to kill him (v. 29b), a common reaction, it would seem, to Paul's preaching.[32] Acts 9:30 concludes the saga of the Reconciliation Visit by saying that the brethren brought him down to Caesarea and sent him forth to Tarsus. The account in Galatians, which has Paul visiting Jerusalem in the company of Barnabas, ends quite differently. After what would appear to have been an exceedingly rancorous exchange initially (Gal. 2:1–5), we are led to believe that the Jerusalem leadership accepted Paul's mission to the uncircumcised (Peter to continue his mission to the circumcised) and extended the right hand of Christian fellowship to Paul (2:7–9). When a geographical place is next identified, it is Antioch, not Caesarea or Tarsus. So much for the history in sacred history.

Anyone approaching Paul as Bentham did will find inadvertent humor in the juxtaposition of verses 30 and 31 in Acts 9. Verse 30, as noted above, says that the brethren brought him down to Caesarea and sent him off to Tarsus.[33] So, says verse 31, the church throughout Judea, Galilee, and Samaria had peace.[34] Yes, indeed, a principal troublemaker was temporarily out of the way. Being sent to the hinterlands of the Christian movement must have been difficult for Paul to bear, for "the prime object of his ambition—the situation of President of the Christian Commonwealth—had never quitted its hold on his concupiscence." It is easy to picture him in Tarsus scheming to return to the center of ecclesiastical politics in the infant church. Paul's return to Jerusalem, according to Acts, came in two stages. First, some Christians of Cyprus and Cyrene preached the gospel of Jesus to Greeks, converting a great number of them, perhaps to everyone's surprise. When word of this reached the Jerusalem church, it sent Barnabas to Antioch to investigate. Discerning at once, it would seem, that this was a case for the self-appointed apostle to the Gentiles, Barnabas went all the way to Tarsus in search of Paul, not a difficult quarry to track down, one must surmise. Upon finding Paul, Barnabas brought him to Antioch, where the two remained for a year and where the disciples of Jesus were first called Christians (Acts 11:20–26). Then came to Antioch a man named Agabus, who foretold in the Spirit that there would be a famine in the days of the emperor Claudius. Since his reign lasted from 41–54, it was a good bet that there might be some lean times during those years. In any case, the disciples of Antioch resolved to take up a collection so that relief might be sent to the brethren in Judea.

So, it came to pass that the second stage of Paul's return to Jerusalem was made possible by an eleemosynary opportunity. It was probably not hard to persuade Paul (together with Barnabas) to convey this largesse to Jerusalem. It was in his interest not only to be successful on the mission field but also to be perceived as charitable, showering gifts of money on those with whom he had contended acrimoniously. In Galatians 2:10, after a rancorous dispute with the Jerusalem leadership, he wrote, conveniently enough for his purposes, that he was eager to remember the poor.[35] The Money-Bringing Visit, if historical, may also have provided him the opportunity of saying that it is more blessed to give than to receive, a saying he attributed to Jesus, but one that the Gospel writers failed to note. Ah, well, Paul received direct revelations from the Lord, so there should be no surprise in a saying of Jesus known only to him. What is really surprising is that Paul never seems to have found occasion in any of his epistles to boast of this charitable deed—something in which he might have been expected to take legitimate pride. No matter how grateful the members of the Jerusalem church may have been, the A-h fails to note any increase in belief in what Paul was preaching. Thus, he left Jerusalem and returned to the mission field in what is now Turkey.

Paul's third visit to Jerusalem as a Christian, the Deputation Visit, was fraught with significance for the expanding church, if this visit ever occurred.[36] Recounted in Acts 15:1–29, this visit, it should almost routinely go without saying, cannot be reconciled with his second visit to Jerusalem as presented by him in Galatians 2:1–10. The reason for linking these two passages (from different New Testament writings) is that the topics they cover are similar, including the question of jurisdiction, that is, about who it is who is to evangelize among Jews and who among non-Jews. As dubious as one may be of Paul's veracity on every occasion, it is to be preferred to "a multitude of anonymous narratives" in Acts.[37] When we encounter Paul in Acts 15:1–29, at the so-called Jerusalem Council, it is important to remember that he had already completed his first missionary journey, on which it must be supposed that he met with considerable success.[38] Gentiles and/or Greek-speaking Jews were being converted, were being baptized in Christ, and were in receipt of the Holy Ghost, whatever that may mean. In short, the Jewish Christian movement was being swelled, if not overwhelmed, by non-Palestinian Jews and, perhaps, even by non-Jews.[39] When chapter 14 of Acts ends we find Paul telling the Christians of Antioch how God had opened the door of faith to Gentiles. Into this happy situation come some men from Judea (Acts 15:1) telling the Gentile brethren that they must be circumcised to be saved.[40]

Nothing illustrates more graphically the Jewishness of Jesus' original disciples than the claim that male Gentile converts would have to be circumcised. That this item of ceremonial law should be put on a par with the moral law (epitomized by the Ten Commandments) is, to the modern mind, astounding.[41] According to Acts 15:2, Paul and Barnabas entered into no small dissension and debate with those who claimed the needfulness of circumcision. Unable to settle so grave an issue in what to Christians was the frontier town of Antioch, the local leadership sent Paul and Barnabas to the apostles in Jerusalem. On the way, through Phoenicia and Samaria, these two, according to Acts 15:3, reported the conversion of the Gentiles, strengthening their hand and setting more sharply on edge the teeth of those in the circumcision party. Upon arriving in Jerusalem, Paul and Barnabas, whether they were really welcomed or not (v. 4), fell silent as Peter took center stage. Whether the A-h made up a convenient speech for the occasion or Peter actually said some such thing, he is portrayed as claiming (v. 7) that in the early days of the Christian movement he was given jurisdiction among the Gentiles that they might hear the Gospel. Then, sounding much like Paul, Peter claims (v. 11) that it is through the grace of the Lord Jesus (not through circumcision) that people are saved. Circumcision, to hear him put it (in v. 10), was a "yoke upon the neck of the disciples, which neither our fathers nor we are able to bear." This is surely false of the Jewish fathers of such people as Peter, James, and the other apostles. It was, however, a great burden upon any in Peter's generation who would proselytize among potential converts who were adult, male, and non-Jewish. After this, the A-h allows Paul to say (v. 12) in effect that nothing succeeds like success, signs and wonders, presumably, having accompanied the conversion of Gentiles. Surely, signs and wonders accompanying the results of a policy can be taken as the Bible-god's ratification of that policy! Then, James, the Lord's brother and real leader of the Jerusalem church, brings the dispute to a resolution, saying that the Gentiles should be told to abstain from "pollutions of idols, from fornication, and from things strangled, and from blood" (v. 20). This is a strange amalgam of the moral and the ceremonial laws of the Jews and one made even more curious by the exclusion of any ruling on the topic that started the controversy—circumcision.[42]

The A-h puts the best face possible on events immediately following the decisions of the Jerusalem Council. The leadership picks two stalwarts, Judas Barsabas and Silas (Acts 15:22), to accompany the "beloved Barnabas and Paul" (v. 25) on their return to Antioch, there to repair the damage done by those who had unsettled Gentile Christians (v. 24) with the claim that they must be circumcised to be saved. Bentham comments, "[C]harged with this letter [containing the decisions of the Jerusalem Council], carrying with it the authority of the whole fellowship of the Apostles. Paul himself—he [the "beloved"] Paul—what sort of regard did he pay to it? *He wrote against it with all his might.* No more Jewish rites! No more Mosaic law! Such is the cry, that animates the whole body of those writings of his which have reached us" (p. 224). After an unspecified time in Antioch, Paul determined to revisit those he had converted on his first missionary journey, and he invited Barnabas to accompany him (v. 36). But then there arose a contention so sharp between the "beloved" Paul and the "beloved" Barnabas that they split asunder (vv. 39–40), each going his own way.

As noted earlier, the alleged events of Acts 15, in which there is a suspicious degree of sweetness and light, cannot be dropped until they are seen in the harsh light of Galatians 2:1–16. Here, by Paul's reckoning, he visited Jerusalem for the second time as a Christian. Here, too, Barnabas was with him (v. 1) and a certain Titus, an uncircumcised Greek. Unlike Acts 15:3, wherein Paul and his companion(s) were sent by the church in Antioch to Jerusalem, here, in Galatians 2:2, he went up on the basis of his own personal communication from the Bible-god. Once there, he met privately with those who were of repute and told them what he preached (v. 2), not asking of them leave to preach differently than they. But, then, someone secretly brought in "false brethren" to spy out (so as to tattle on?) Paul's freedom from the law (i.e., his antinomianism) granted him in Christ Jesus. Merely disagreeing with Paul is all it would have taken (to him) for one to be a false brother. Could these "false brethren" have been members of the circumcision party? Could they have been Jewish Christian believers in the importance of the ceremonial law as it related to persons with whom a Jew could sit at table? The text, as we have it now, does not deign to tell us. In any case, not only did the men of repute add nothing to Paul (v. 6), they perceived, miraculously one must suppose, that he (Paul) had been entrusted with the gospel to the uncircumcised (v. 7). What choice had they (who had merely been with Jesus, who had merely been his disciples, but who were not getting daily revelations from him) except to extend the right hand of fellowship (v. 9) to Paul—and to Barnabas? None it would seem, so overpowered were they by Paul's character and his obvious successes. Overpowered perhaps in that he got his way, but did they really believe in his inner conversion, in revelations vouchsafed to him alone? In any case, what might be called the partition treaty was effected; Paul was to have the Gentile mission field; Peter, James, and John, the Jewish mission field. Acts, it should be noted, contains no mention of any such treaty.

Galatians 2:11 finds Paul in (or back in) Antioch. Peter himself, the alleged rock on which the church is built, arrives (v. 11) and is opposed to his face by Paul, the Johnny-come-lately who preaches a different gospel. Peter, it seems, had on some occasion(s) eaten with Gentiles, thus breaking a commandment in the ceremonial law respecting food and those with whom it could be eaten.[43] Then had come certain men from James (of the circumcision party), and Peter, fearing them, henceforth refrained from further infractions of the ceremonial law. If the facts of the case were as they are represented by Paul, then Peter was guilty of hypocrisy, something upon which Paul could seize to good effect. Having once lived as Gentiles lived, that is, having once eaten with them, Peter was in no position, according to Paul (v. 14) to require Gentile converts to Christianity to live as Jews. Human beings are not justified (whatever this may mean) by works of the Mosaic law, according to Paul (v. 16), but by faith in Jesus Christ (in whatever manner this is supposed to be efficacious).

Before turning to Paul's fourth visit to Jerusalem, the Invasion Visit, a recapitulation from Bentham is in order:

> In no place can this man exist, but to exercise hostility or provoke it: with no man can he hold intercourse, without acting towards him, if not in the character of a despot, in that either of an open and audacious, or in that of a secret adversary, or both. Against Peter, at Jerusalem, in his Deputation Visit, he is intriguing, while he is bargaining with him. With the same Peter, when arrived at Antioch, he quarrels: for, at Antioch, Peter was but a visitor—a stranger; Paul, with Barnabas for his constant supporter, was on his own ground: no betrayed rulers *there* to fear—no persecuted Christians. He quarrels—so he himself informs his Galatians—he quarrels with the chief of the Apostles: he 'withstands him to his face.' Why? because, forsooth, 'he was to be blamed.' In conclusion, to such a pitch,—by the degree of success,

whatever it was, which by this time he had experienced,—to such a pitch of intemperance, had his mind swelled—he quarrels even with Barnabas: with Barnabas—in all his three antecedent visits to Jerusalem, his munificent protector, and steady adherent: with that Barnabas, in whose steady company, and under whose wing, one of his missionary excursions had already been performed. Acts 11:19–27, Ib[id]. 2:37–40.

At Antioch, the number of his competitors could not but be considerable: at Antioch, the number of years, which he appears to have passed in that city, considered,—the number of his enemies could not be small. He accordingly plans, and executes, a new missionary excursion. He stands now upon his own legs: no Barnabas now,—no necessary protector, to share with him in his glory: to share with him, in equal or superior proportion, in the profit of his profession: in that profit, the image of which, in all its shapes, was flitting before his eyes,—and which we shall accordingly see him gathering in, in such unequaled exuberance. He now looks out for a humble companion—an assistant: he finds one in Silas: that Silas, whom, with Judas Barsabas, we have seen come to Antioch, deputed by the Apostles and their disciples, to conclude, in that second metropolis, the negotiation, commenced in the first metropolis, of the new Christian world. Deserter from the service in which he was sent, Silas enlists in that of the daring and indefatigable adventurer. Thus much, and no more, do we learn concerning him: for, in the picture drawn in the Acts, no character is given to him, except the being found in company with Paul, in some of the places which Paul visits: except this exercise of the locomotive faculty, nothing is there to distinguish him from the common stock of still-life. (p. 252)

Between the conclusion of the Deputation Visit (Acts 15) and Paul's arrival in Jerusalem (Acts 21:17 ff.) at the beginning of the Invasion Visit, he had conducted two extensive missionary journeys.[44] Whether or not the apostolic pillars of the infant church ever entered into a partition treaty with Paul (Gal. 2:7–9), giving him the Gentile world to proselytize, whether or not a heavenly voice ever promised him the Gentile world to evangelize (Acts 26:16-18), Paul went to the Gentile world and enjoyed, at first at least, astonishing success therein, preaching his own gospel. Nor did he limit himself to the Gentiles, for he was ever and anon preaching to the circumcised in their synagogues (see Acts 14:1, 17:10, 17:17, 18:4, 18:19, 18:26, and 19:8) in the Gentile world. Taking advantage of his knowledge of Greek and of his familiarity with the Gentile world, Paul had clearly gained the upper hand over the apostolic leaders of Christian Jews in Judea.[45]

Paul's fourth visit to Jerusalem, the Invasion Visit, calls for an inspection of his motives. Following the Deputation Visit in Acts 15 and the partition treaty in Galatians 2 (which treat of similar topics), he undertook his second missionary journey (Acts 15:36-18:22). Presumably Peter, James, and John were to take the gospel to the Jews while Paul was to take it to the

Gentiles. Yet in the chapters of Acts devoted to his second missionary journey, we find him going to synagogues, not, it would seem, to strengthen disciples (i.e., Jews who had become Christians) therein, but to convert Jews to his brand of Christianity. If so, he was clearly not observing the partition treaty. In Acts 17:2–3 we find him spending three weeks with Jews of one synagogue, trying to persuade them to accept his gospel. Acts 17:11 pictures him as having considerable success with certain Jews in Beroea (in Macedonia) who were (in his view) of a more noble stripe than some he had encountered. Acts 17:17 places him in a synagogue in Athens, his spirit sorely vexed, arguing about the idols of Athens (as though the Jews of Athens could do anything about the idols of Athens, erected by Greeks). Acts 18:4 finds him in Corinth arguing in a synagogue every Sabbath (for an unspecified time), persuading both *Jews* and Greeks. When these Corinthian Jews turned on him, he exploded according to Acts 18:6b, saying, "Your blood be upon your own heads; I *am* clean: from henceforth I will go unto the Gentiles. Why from henceforth? Why had he not been honoring the partition treaty all along?

To make matters worse he did not keep his word to the Corinthian Jews. In Acts 19:8, while on his third missionary journey, he entered a synagogue (in or around Ephesus) speaking boldly, arguing and pleading his case about the kingdom of God for a span of three months. Two verses later the A-h announces that all the residents of Asia, both *Jews* and Greeks, heard the word of the Lord, largely because of Paul's efforts, one must presume. Paul even condemns himself inadvertently in 1 Corinthians 9:20–21: "And unto Jews I became as a Jew, that I might gain the Jews; to them that are under the law, as under the law, that I might gain them that are under the law; to them that are without the law . . . that I might gain them that are without the law." This may seem to some to be commendable flexibility. It can equally be interpreted as duplicity and hypocrisy, to say nothing of treachery against James, Peter, John, and the other original apostles in the Jerusalem church.

The simple fact is that Paul had created a religious empire in Syria, Asia Minor, Macedonia, and Greece. His constituency appears to have consisted of (1) a motley throng of Gentiles who found his message of salvation appealing; (2) (Pharisaic?) Jews, living in the Gentile world and speaking Greek, who had been persuaded by his exegeses of Old Testament prophecies to accept Jesus as their King (Messiah) and the Son of God (Acts 17:1–3, 11–12); and (3) disciples of Jesus who, while remaining Jews, had been baptized into the baptism of repentance (Acts 19:2–5) but who had later turned to Paul's idea and practice of Holy Ghost baptism.[46] Taken together, this possibly populous conglomeration of coreligionists may have outnumbered those in the original Jewish Christian empire in Judea. Moreover, it may have been increasing its lead daily not in numbers alone but in affluence and influence as well. As it grew in power so too did its undisputed leader—Paul. Two centers of power remained to be conquered (Acts 19:21), one a center of religious power antithetical to him (Jerusalem), the other a center of supreme political power (Rome). By the time we encounter him on his third missionary journey, he was not yet prepared to storm the ramparts of Rome, but he was prepared, albeit with fear and trembling, to march on Jerusalem.

What business had he, the self-appointed apostle to the Gentiles, in going to Jerusalem, the jurisdiction of James, Peter, and John? He had no business there except to further his own agenda, to extend his power. His pretext for going was to deliver charitable contributions, raised in the Gentile world, to the poor in Judea. Let us now ask, deferring the answer for a bit, whether or not there is any evidence that the money was ever delivered. In Bentham's words,

> The common objects of political concupiscence—money, power, and vengeance—were all before his eyes. . . .
> In a general point of view, ambition,—rival ambition,—the same motive which sent Caesar to Rome, may be stated as having sent Paul, at this time, to Jerusalem: to Jerusalem—the metropolis of the Christian world by design; and thence, eventually and undesignedly, to the metropolis of the whole civilized world. (pp. 266–67)

Paul's agreement in Galatians 2:10 to remember the poor in Judea (as he proselytized among the Gentiles) and his claim that this was something he was eager to do gave him carte blanche to return to Jerusalem whenever he had amassed enough money and thought the time ripe. He knew perfectly well, as he said in 1 Corinthians 16:3, that he could send the Gentiles' monetary contributions by others accredited by them to take it. There was no compelling reason for him to go (where he was clearly not wanted) unless there was something for him to gain thereby. Romans 15:25 shows him resolving to take the contribution himself to the poor among the saints in the Jerusalem church (see also 2 Cor. 8:1–4). It is telling that the A-h has nothing to say in Acts about any charitable motives underlying Paul's Invasion Visit (except for a passing reference in Acts 24:17). Extolling such charity (if it ever occurred) would have served to elevate the reputation of his hero—St. Paul. The simple fact is that this money, which might have bought Paul considerable influence, was never turned over to the Jerusalem leadership.[47]

Acts 20:17 ff. finds Paul (near the end of his third missionary journey) in Ephesus. He announces that he is going to Jerusalem *bound* by the (Holy) Spirit to go, not knowing what shall befall him there except that the Spirit reveals imprisonment and afflictions ahead. Why should one motivated by charity and arriving with largesse expect to be treated so shabbily by the apostles, disciples, and poor men of the Mother Church? Upon disembarking at Tyre in Syria, Paul sought out some disciples who, through the revelations of the same Spirit, one must suppose, told Paul not to go to Jerusalem.[48] "Oh! what a useful word this word *spirit*! Let a man say plainly and simply, I shall go, or be going, to Jerusalem—or, Don't go to Jerusalem,—his words go for no more than they are worth: in either case, with a proper proposition to introduce it, add the word 'spirit', the matter becomes serious. Out of a word or two, you then add to the Godhead a third person, who talks backward and forward for you, and does for you whatever you please" (p. 271). Whatever Paul wanted to do badly enough, the Holy Spirit conveniently told him to do. Well, poor man, what could he do but obey? The Holy Ghost whom all the rest of the church had for their advocate was no match for the Holy Ghost whom Paul had for his adviser:

> That, to the advancement of religion—of the religion of Jesus—no such presence of his was necessary;—that no good could result from it;—was obvious to all eyes. Of the original number of the Apostles,—for aught that appears, not less than eleven were still remaining on the spot: men, to every one of whom, all acts and sayings of Jesus were, by memory, rendered so familiar:—men, on the part; of some of whom, and, at any rate, on the part of the Chief of them, Peter,—there was no want of zeal and activity. While to these men a single city, or, at the utmost, one small region—composed the whole field of exertion—the whole earth besides is left open by them to Paul: still, such is the ravenousness of his ambition, nothing can content him, but he must be intruding himself—thrusting his restless sickle into their ripening harvest. (pp. 271–72)

According to the A-h, Paul claims (Acts 21:13) that he is ready to die at Jerusalem for the name of the Lord Jesus. Such bravado may elevate our hero in the minds of his epigoni, but it can hardly have been his real reason in going there. "What was he to die for?" "Was it then really to die for the name of Jesus? was it not rather to live? to live for his own name, for his own glory, for his own profit, and for the pleasure of depriving of their flock those shepherds of souls, by whom his pretensions had been disallowed, his glory disbelieved, his advances received with that distrust and jealousy, for which the long and bitter experience they had had of him, afforded so amply sufficient a warrant? men, in whose eyes, though in the clothing of a shepherd, he was still a wolf?" (p. 281).

In spite of an opposing Spirit telling Paul not to go to Jerusalem (Acts 21:4); in spite of concerned people who begged him not to go (v. 12); in spite of his own unhappy premonition, were he to go (20:22–23); in spite of confirmation from the mouth of a prophet who predicted his arrest once there (21:11); and in spite of his dread of ferocious wolves that would (upon his departure from the Gentile mission field) scatter his flock with false doctrine (i.e., with anything he had not taught); what did Paul do? He went to Jerusalem! What stakes could have been so high as to compel him to do this? Upon arrival, whether he was greeted gladly, as the A-h would have it (21:17) or not, he waited a day and then met but one apostle (v. 18), James, the one apostle best positioned to contend with Paul successfully.[49] "Salutations performed, he [Paul] addresses the assembly in that strain, which was so familiar to him: boasting upon boasting, and above all things, boasting that he does not boast: 'declaring,' says his historian;—declaring? declaring what? declaring what was his business at Jerusalem? declaring what service, in his eyes the cause stood in need of, at his hands? Not he, indeed: to any such effect, declaration might not have been altogether so easy. What he declared, and that *'particularly,'* was—what 'things God had wrought' among the Gentiles by his ministry" (pp. 289–90). Not being able to castigate James for hypocrisy, as he had done effectively with Peter (Gal. 2:11 ff.), Paul played his highest card: He pointed to his astonishing successes in the Gentile mission field, a feat James, perhaps, could not match among the circumcised. James, however, trumped Paul, saying, "Thou seest how many thousands [*myriads* in Greek, so tens of thousands] of Jews there are which believed [in Jesus]; and they are all zealous of the law [the Torah]. And they are informed of thee, that thou teachest all the Jews which are among the Gentiles to forsake Moses; saying that they ought not to circumcise their children, neither to walk after their customs [such as food laws]" (Acts 21:20–21).

Standing before James and all the elders of the Jerusalem church, Paul was meek and tractable, this in spite of his claim that his gospel came not from human beings but from God (Gal. 1:11–12) and in spite of his claim that his discipleship was superior to that of any other disciple (2 Cor. 11:23).[50] When told (Acts 21:24) to purify himself ritually and to pay the expenses of four others, probably Christian Nazirites (or Nazarites), so that they could shave their heads and purify themselves too, he complied without resistance, betaking himself and the four to the Temple on the following day.[51] The object of these ritual goings-on was to show that he was observant of Mosaic law and not one who would (as accused by some) teach Jews to be dismissive thereof. Bentham commented,

> If the case was that he had taught it; let him have purified himself ever so purely, whatsoever was meant by purification,—let him have purified himself ever so completely, let him have paid ever so much money, let him have shaved his head ever so close,—by any, or all of these supposed meritorious acts, how could that be caused, not to have happened, which in fact had happened? by what means could they afford proof of his performance of any ceremony, other than those very same purifications ceremonies themselves? (p. 301)

> But in so doing, thus much also we know: namely, that he consented to, and betook himself to one of two things: an act of perjury, if the effect of the ceremony was to convey an assertion, that he had never taught, that a Jew, on being converted to the religion of Jesus, *need* not circumcise his children, or walk after the Mosaic customs: an act of apostasy, if the effect of it was an engagement never to teach this same doctrine in the future. (p. 303)

Paul, like Peter, whom he had excoriated earlier (Gal. 2:11-12), was a hypocrite—on occasion at least.

Shortly before the seven days of purification were completed (for Paul and the four whom his [perhaps enforced] charity had supported), Jews from Asia inflamed the local populace against him (Acts 21:27 ff.). He who had taught (in Gal. 2:16) that nobody is justified (or saved) by the works of the (Mosaic) law was seen in the Temple perjuring himself by carrying out a work of the (ceremonial) law. Moreover, it was believed by some, at least, that he had even taken a Gentile into the Temple with him, a capital offense (vv. 28–29).[52] This would not have been surprising, for he had apparently done so earlier with Titus, a Greek and, at least at the time, uncircumcised (Gal. 2:3). In any case, the aforementioned Jews of Asia, who had possibly followed Paul to Jerusalem, incited the locals to such an extent that he was seized, dragged from the Temple, and beaten with murderous intent (vv. 30–31). Roman authorities saved but also arrested him, pending a resolution to this (to them) mystifying attack. The identity of the Asiatic Jews is uncertain. They may have been Jewish Christian converts rather than ordinary (Pharisaic?) Jews who had not accepted Jesus as their King.[53] It can hardly be surprising that Paul's visit to the Temple at James's command ended as it did: "Stay in the same town [Jerusalem], and in the same company with them [the Jerusalem Nazarenes], [Paul] could not,—without being either their known *adversary*, or their known *associate*. Their known *adversary* he could not be, without either continuing himself to be an object of universal horror, or else rendering *them* objects of horror, to the whole body of their disciples. Their *associate* he could not be, without involving *them* in that odium, with which he himself was, by the confession of his own adherent and historiographer, covered" (p. 308).

Upon being conducted to Roman barracks for safe keeping, Paul asked to speak to the people (Acts 21:37). This granted, he attempted to justify himself in what we have come to know as the second telling of his conversion story. Since this has been examined in detail above, it can be bypassed here, except to note that it did not convince those who heard it (if the A-h can be trusted here to be recounting history), for the people said, "Away with such a *fellow* from the earth: for it is not fit that he should live" (Acts 22:22). Clearly, disbelief in Paul's apostleship continued unabated. It should be noted in passing that Paul, to avoid torture at the hands of the Romans to extract information from him, declared himself to be an uncondemned Roman citizen (Acts 22:25). This ended all threats of torture and prompted the Roman tribune in charge to remark on how he had bought his citizenship at a great price. Paul, however, insisted that he was born a Roman citizen.[54]

The events recounted in Acts as occurring between the episode above and Paul's departure for Rome (Acts 27:1), on what is called his fourth missionary journey, need not detain us for long, because they do not address the major issue. In outline, these events are (1) Paul's defense before a council of Jews (including the chief priests) assembled by the aforementioned tribune to inform this person of the reasons for the dispute (Acts 22:30–23:10). During this defense Paul sets the Sadducees on the council against the Pharisees on it over belief in the resurrection of the dead, the former not believing in it (23:8), the latter believing in it and finding Paul innocent on this head (v. 9). (2) Forty Jews swear an oath not to eat until they have killed Paul, a plot overheard by his nephew and foiled by Paul's removal under military escort from Jerusalem to Caesarea (Acts 23:12–35). (3) In Caesarea, Felix, the Roman governor of the province, entertains a delegation from Jerusalem including the chief priest. Paul is accused of agitating for insurrection among Jews all over the (Roman) world, of being a leader of the Nazarenes, and of profaning the Temple.[55] Paul responds by claiming that he believes everything in the law and that he is on trial only for his belief in the resurrection of the dead (Acts 24:1–21). (4) Felix delays judgment, then brings his Jewish wife in to hear Paul, then delays judgment again, hoping to be bribed, believing Paul to have money (Acts 24:22–26). How, one wonders, could a traveling evangelist who supported himself by the tent-maker's craft amass enough money to tempt a Roman governor? (5) Felix having been replaced, the new governor, Festus, encounters the chief priests and leading men of the Jews who inform him against Paul. They want Paul returned to Jerusalem, planning to ambush and kill him along the way. Festus instead permits a delegation to question Paul in Caesarea. He defends himself by saying that he has neither offended against the Mosaic law, nor the Temple, nor Caesar (Acts 25:1–11). (6) King Agrippa and Queen Bernice arrive in Caesarea to greet and to congratulate the new governor on his appointment. Paul's case comes up, and plans are made for him to defend himself before the royal pair (Acts 25:13–27). (7) In his speech, which includes the third telling of his conversion experiences, Paul claims that the Jews have seized and sought to kill him only because he has preached to Jews and Gentiles alike that they should repent their sins and turn to God (Acts 26:1–32).

With respect to the stressful interval between Paul's arrest in the Temple and his departure for Rome, there is no knowing how much of what the A-h included in Acts was contrived for that purpose and how much, if any, Paul actually said. In either case, outright deception results, for what is said in Paul's defense, whatever the source, is beside the point. It is made to seem (in Acts 23:6b, 24:14–15, and 25:19) that he is on trial for preaching the resurrection of the dead. This is categorically false. Pharisees would not have persecuted each other for a belief common to them. Moreover, there is little evidence that the Sadducees, who did not subscribe to this belief, ever prosecuted (or persecuted) anybody just for believing in it.[56] Such a belief was simply not an actionable offense against the law. As for the complaint that Paul was being persecuted for preaching repentance to Jew and Gentile alike, there is no validity at all (Acts 26:19–21). The complaints lodged against him upon his arrest are uniformly ignored by the A-h. These complaints were that he was teaching Jews in Gentile lands to forsake Moses, that is, not to circumcise their sons and not to walk after the (sacred) customs of Israel (Acts 21:21); that he was teaching everywhere against the Jewish people; and that he had profaned the Temple (v. 28). Paul's writings indicate abundantly that these charges were accurate, exempting only the profaning of the Temple. Let us let him convict himself from some of his writings, each of which predates his arrest.

> I know and am persuaded by the Lord Jesus, that there is nothing unclean of itself; but to him that esteemeth anything to be unclean, to him it is unclean, . . . For the kingdom of God is not meat and drink; but righteousness, and peace, and joy in the Holy Ghost. (Rom. 14:14, 17)

> *By the deeds of the law there shall no flesh be* justified in [God's] sight; for by the law is the knowledge of sin. (Rom. 3:20)

> Where is boasting then? It is excluded. By what law? of works? Nay: but by the law of faith.—Therefore, we conclude, that *a man is justified by faith without the deeds of the law.*—Is *he* the God of the Jews only? is *he* not the God of the Gentiles? Yes, of the Gentiles also:—Seeing it is one God, which shall justify the circumcision by faith, and uncircumcision through faith.—*Do we then make void the law through faith? God forbid: yea, we establish the law.* (Rom 3:27–31)

> [I]f thou shalt confess with thy mouth the Lord Jesus, and shalt believe in thine heart that God raised him from the dead, thou shalt be saved. . . . For there is no difference between the Jew and the Greek; for the same Lord over all is rich unto all that call upon him.—For whosoever shall call upon the name of the Lord shall be saved. (Rom. 10:9, 12)

> [O]ne believeth that he may eat all things: another who is weak, eateth herbs.—Let not him that eateth despise him that eateth not; and let not him which eateth not judge him that eateth; for God hath received him.—

One man esteemeth one day above another: another esteemeth every day alike. (Rom. 14:2)

All things are lawful unto me, but all things are not expedient: or *profitable,* all things are lawful for me, but I will not be brought under the power of any.—*Meats for the belly, and the belly for meats,* but God shall destroy both it and them. (1 Cor. 6:12)

For though I be free from all men, yet have I made myself servant unto all, that I might gain the more.—*And unto Jews I became as a Jew, that I might gain the Jews;* to them that are under the law, as under the law, that I might gain them that are under the law:—*To them that are without law, as without law,* being *not without law to God but under the law to Christ, that I might gain them that are without law.*—To the weak I became as weak, that I might gain the weak: I am made all things to all men, that I might by all means save some.—And this I do for the Gospel's sake, that I might be a partaker thereof with you. (1 Cor. 9:19–23)

Seeing then that we have such hope, we use great plainness of speech.— And not as *Moses, which put a veil over his face, that the children of Israel could not steadfastly look* to the end of *that which is abolished.* But their minds were blinded; for until this day remaineth the same veil untaken away in the reading of the Old Testament; which veil is done away in Christ.—But even unto this day, *when Moses is read, the veil is upon their heart.*—Nevertheless *when it shall turn to the Lord, the veil shall be taken away.*—Now the Lord is that spirit; and where the spirit of the Lord is, there is liberty. (2 Cor. 3:12–17).

Now as to circumcision in particular:

For *circumcision verily profiteth, if thou keep the law: but if thou be a breaker of the law, thy circumcision is made uncircumcision.*—Therefore if the uncircumcision keep the righteousness of the law, shall not his uncircumcision be counted as circumcision?—And shall not uncircumcision which is by nature, if it fulfill the law, judge thee, who by the letter and circumcision doest transgress the law?—For he is not a Jew, which is one outwardly, neither is that circumcision which is outward in the flesh:—But he is a Jew, which is one inwardly: and circumcision is that of the heart, in the spirit, and not in the letter; whose praise is not of men, but of God. (Rom. 2:25–29)

What advantages then hath the Jew? or what profit is there of circumcision?—Much every way: chiefly, because that unto them were committed the oracles of God. (Rom. 3:1–2)

Cometh this blessedness then upon the circumcision only, or upon the uncircumcision also? for we say that faith was reckoned to Abraham for righteousness.—How was it then reckoned? when he was in circumcision, or in uncircumcision. Not in circumcision, but in uncircumcision.—And he received the sign of circumcision, a seal of the righteousness of the faith which *he had yet* being uncircumcised: that he might be the father of all them that believe, though they be not circumcised; that righteousness might be imputed unto them also:—And the father of circumcision to them who are not of the circumcision only, but who also walk in the steps of that faith of our father Abraham, which he had being *yet* uncircumcised. (Rom. 4:9–12)

Now I say that Jesus Christ was a minister of the circumcision for the truth of God to confirm the promises made unto the fathers. (Rom. 15:8)

Is any man called being circumcised? let him not become uncircumcised. *Is any called in uncircumcision? let him not be circumcised.—Circumcision is nothing, and uncircumcision is nothing, but the keeping of the commandments of God.* (1 Cor. 7:18)[57]

Inquiry into Paul's career from a temporal perspective (i.e., from his outward conversion on the Damascus road to his fourth missionary journey) leaves some topics unexamined. Prime among these are three falsehoods he foisted on others: (1) the multiplication of witnesses to Jesus' resurrection, (2) predictions concerning the end of the world, and (3) the invention of the Antichrist. Respecting the first of these points Bentham wrote in a footnote,

The account given by Luke of the resurrection and ascension of Jesus is contained in the last chap. 24:[1]–53.[58] According to this account, by no men was Jesus seen in the interval between those two events, besides the eleven Apostles and a few others, all together not more than enough to sit down together at meat, in one of the houses of a village, Luke 24:9, 28, 29, 30. Number of the occasions on which Jesus was seen by the Apostles, two: the company the same without addition, and both occasions having place within twenty-four hours. Between these two occasions it is that Paul sticks in the one of his own invention, in which Jesus was seen by above five hundred brethren at once [1 Cor. 15:6].

　　Point-blank on this head is the contradiction given to the story of Paul's, by his own attendant and historiographer, namely, in the account put into the mouth of Peter, speaking to Centurion Cornelius, Acts 10:39 to 42. Expressly is it there said, ver. 40, 'Him (Jesus) God raised up the third day, and showed him openly;—Not to all the people, but unto witnesses chosen before of God even to us, who did eat and drink with him after he rose from the dead.' When in the year 62, or some posterior year, the author of the Acts was writing his history, nothing, it will be inferred, did he know of the contradictory account given by his hero, in writing in a letter written in the year 57. (p. 334)

In 1 Corinthians 15:3–5, Paul summarizes the essential doctrines of Christianity (the so-called *kerygma*, meaning 'proclamation' in Greek), which he received not from personal revelation but from believers, one may safely suppose.[59] This is followed by assertions about appearances that are found nowhere else in the New Testament, the most outlandish of which is that Jesus was seen by more than five hundred brethren at one time (v. 6).[60] Had Paul been writing to Judeans rather than to Corinthians he would have had to limit himself with appearances to fewer than twenty people (in line with living memory as reflected, most likely, in the Gospels and Acts), but how would the Corinthians have known whether Paul was lying or not? 'Five hundred' was as easily written as 'twenty': "Meantime, while Jesus was thus magnified, Paul was not to be forgotten. Insufficient still would be the cloud of witnesses, unless himself were added to it. 'Last of all', says he, 1 Cor. 15:8, 'he,' Jesus, 'was seen of me also'. Seen by him Paul? at what place? at what time? At the time of his conversion, when hearing a voice and seeing a light, but nothing else?" (p. 337). How magnanimous of the Lord to have gone out of his way to appear to one, alas and alack, untimely born as was Paul (v. 8), and how useful to Paul's credibility as a preacher of new and unauthorized doctrines![61]

The second (of the three falsehoods mentioned above) that the "disordered brain" of St. Paul foisted on the gullible was his prediction concerning the end of the world, a *"delusion"* to which he gave the name of *"knowledge."*[62] In 1 Thessalonians 5:2–10 he wrote apodictically,

> For yourselves know perfectly [merely because Paul had said so] that the day of the Lord so cometh as a thief in the night.
>
> For when they shall say, Peace and safety; then sudden destruction cometh upon them, as travail upon a woman with child; and they shall not escape.
>
> But ye, brethren, are not in darkness, that that day should overtake you as a thief.
>
> Ye are all the children of light, and the children of the day: we are not of the night, nor of darkness.
>
> Therefore let us not sleep, as *do* others; but let us watch and be sober.
>
> For they that sleep sleep in the night; and they that be drunken are drunken in the night
>
> But let us, who are of the day, be sober, putting on the breastplate of faith and love; and for an helmet, the hope of salvation.
>
> For God hath not appointed us to wrath, but to obtain salvation by our Lord Jesus Christ,
>
> Who died for us, that, whether we wake or sleep, we should live together with him.

Not only did Paul not know that the world was about to end (after all, it did not), his perfidious proclamation thereof resulted in two undesirable conditions depending on the cast of mind of those gullible enough to believe him: (1) "terror and self-mortification" on the one hand and (2) "confidence and mischievous self-indulgence" on the other (p. 344). Self-indulgence, of course, fitted well with antinomianism.[63] Although Paul preached salvation, in season and out, he can hardly have been as concerned about the terror and self-mortification his prophecy caused, in some at least, as about the confidence and mischievous self-indulgence it caused in others. A scant four verses later (v. 14) he felt compelled to admonish the *idle* (so identified in the RSV and several other modern translations) not to be idle but to work, making it seem that some, believing his prophecy, had decided not to work any more while awaiting the Lord's speedy return on the clouds of heaven with salvation for the faithful. Nor did the problem go away with the receipt of 1 Thessalonians, for by the time he wrote 2 Thessalonians, he was still addressing the same problem (see 3:11).[64] In the interim he had heard again, it would seem, that some are living in idleness, doing no work. His rather draconian recipe for this is that if there be any who do not work, then let them not eat (v. 10).

The third of the three falsehoods (mentioned above) that Paul foisted on his credulous converts in Thessalonica was necessitated by the second. Having written of the nearness of the Lord's return (1 Thessalonians 4:15–17) and preached of it too, no doubt, he had unintentionally created sloth on the part of some Christians. These idle ones, however great or small their numbers, had clearly created a problem for the church. Accordingly, Paul had written in 1 Thessalonians 5:14 to exhort the brethren there (i.e., the leadership) to admonish the lawless (i.e., those who were shirking their duties). Nobody was to await the Lord's return indolently, it would seem. Then had come word (referred to in 2 Thessalonians 2:1–3a) that some Thessalonians had been shaken in mind or unduly excited with the idea that the day of the Lord had already come! This news was said to have arrived variously by a spirit, or word, or letter purporting to be from Paul. This he denied, telling them that they should not be deceived. The day of the Lord will not come, according to our apostle, until there is a falling away (an apostasy) and the man of sin, the son of perdition is revealed (2 Thessalonians 2:3b). This unidentified (and to date unidentifiable) personage, antithetical to true deity, is at some future time to arrogate to himself divinity and sit in the temple of God (v. 4).[65] Paul then reminds the Thessalonians that he had spoken of these singular matters (singular in that they appear nowhere else in his writings) when he was among them (v. 5). One presumes that the Thessalonians who had heard Paul address this general subject (if ever he did and was not deceiving them about it) would know that the "son of perdition" was currently being restrained (vv. 6–7) by an unidentified agency. Once its restraining power is relinquished, the "lawless one" will be revealed. Jesus will then slay him (v. 8), paving the way for his own return. The "ape of Satan" which Paul thus created (in v. 9) served him well; it kept him from being exposed as the false prophet he was (p. 348). With this newly contrived and most convenient "ape" at hand, he could continue predicting the coming day of the Lord, filled with glorious promise for those who believed in his gospel, and still be able to explain why, alas, its coming was being delayed and why, in the meantime, the idle Thessalonians should return to gainful labor.[66]

In an age with a voracious appetite for the miraculous, it is to Paul's credit that he did not recommend his gospel with claims based thereon. Bentham noted,

> Observations applying to the whole [topic] together [respecting miracles in general and in particular] are the following:
>
> 1. Not by Paul himself, in any one of his own Epistles, is any such general assertion made, as that he had received from God or from Jesus,— or, in a word, that he was in possession of, any such power, as the power of working miracles.
> 2. Nowhere in the account given of his transactions by the author of the Acts, is he in any of his speeches represented as making reference to any one act of his in the character of a miracle.
> 3. Nowhere in the same account, is he represented as stating himself to be in possession of any such powers. (p. 355)

"He who makes so much of his *sufferings* [2 Cor. 11:24–27], had he wrought any miracles, would he have made nothing of his *miracles*?" (p. 358). Surely, he would have boasted of these, time and again, had there been any.

In Acts, the A-h, however, provides his hero with miracles in the amount of an even dozen.[67] Bentham grouped them according to periods of time in Paul's career as a self-appointed apostle:

> In the first [period] are included—those which are represented as having had place during the time when at the outset of his missionary expedition, Paul had Barnabas for his associate. Of these there are two, viz. 1. At Paphos, A.D. 45. Sorcerer Elymas blinded [13:6–12]. 2, At Lystra, A.D. 46, cripple cured [14:8–11].
>
> In the second period are included—those, which are represented as having had place, during the time when Paul, after his separation from Barnabas, had Silas for his associate, and the unnamed author of the Acts for an attendant. This ends with his arrival at Jerusalem, on the occasion of his fourth visit—the Invasion Visit.
>
> In the current accounts, this event is placed in the year 60. Within this period, we have the seven following supposed marvels: 1. At Philippi, A.D.

53, divineress silenced [16:16–18]. 2. At Philippi, A.D. 53, earthquake: Paul and Silas freed from prison [16:19–40]. 3. At Corinth, A.D. 54, Paul comforted by the Lord in an unseen vision [18:7–11]. 4. At Ephesus, A.D. 56, diseases and devils expelled by Paul's foul handkerchiefs [19:1–12]. 5. At Ephesus, A.D. 56, Exorcist Scevas bedeviled [19:13–20]. 6. At Ephesus, A.D. 56, magic books burned by the owners [19:19–20]. 7. At Troas, A.D. 59, Eutychus found not to be dead [20:7–12].

In the third period are included—those which are represented as having had place, in the interval between his forced departure from Jerusalem and his arrival at Rome.

In the current accounts, this event is placed in the year 62. Within this concluding period, we have the following supposed marvels: 1. On ship-board, A.D. 62, Paul comforted by an angel [27:20–25]. 2. At Malta, A.D. 62, a reptile shaken off by Paul without his being hurt [28:1–6]. 3. At Malta, A.D. 62, Deputy Publius's father cured by Paul of some disorder [28:7–10].

Is it or is it not a matter worth remarking—that, of all these twelve supposed occurrences, such as they are,—in not more than four is the hero represented,—even by his own attendant, historian, and panegyrist,—as decidedly taking any active part in the production of the effect? (pp. 393–95)

As useful as Paul might have found signs, wonders, and miracles with which to bolster his newly contrived doctrines on no occasion do we find him calling into his aid, so much as a single one of all these supposed irrefragable evidences.

Of the two prodigies in the first set above, it is sufficient to note that a moderate sum of money would have sufficed to engage a sorcerer (already a fraud) to declare himself struck blind for a short while (Acts 13:11) and an even more moderate sum to cure a cripple so long as a vagrant was to be found, who, without any risk, could act a part of this sort for a few pence (14:10) in an age so fertile in imposture.

Of the seven prodigies in the second period four deserve further comment. Respecting the earthquake that delivered Paul from prison on a particular occasion (16:25–26), we can only marvel at its ability to pick locks: "Earthquakes in these latter days, we have but too many, in breaking open doors they find no great difficulty; but they have no such nicety of touch as the earthquake, which produced to the self-constituted Apostle a family of proselytes: they are no more able to let feet out of stocks, or hands out of hand-cuffs, than to make watches" (p. 368).

While in Ephesus, Paul is supposed to have wrought certain *special*, that is, uncommon, miracles (19:11–12). One of these had to do with healings occasioned by taking articles of his personal linen to the sick, causing evil spirits to depart the afflicted. Diseases cured, evil spirits driven out, by handkerchiefs and aprons!—by handkerchiefs and aprons brought from a man's body! Diseases cured and devils driven away by foul linen![68]

The tale of the seven sons of Sceva (reputedly a Jewish high priest) is difficult for modern minds to countenance (19:11–16). Learning of the magical powers to be had by pronouncing the name of Jesus, these reckless boys ventured to pronounce his holy name over certain persons with evil spirits indwelling. One such spirit talked back to these (to that spirit) unknown boys. Immediately following this unlikely conversation, the possessed man leaped on all seven stripping them to the skin of their raiment, while in each case the remaining six looked on, impotent to do anything.

The story of Eutychus, in Troas (20:7–12), shows how easily the A-h could abide a contradiction. Eutychus, put to sleep by Paul's extra long sermon, tumbled out a third story window and was taken up dead. But Paul falling on him (figuratively) and embracing him, announced that he was not dead.[69]

Of the three episodes in the third period, two deserve notice. While Paul was on board a ship bound for Rome, a dreadful storm arose (27:14 ff.). Despite howling winds, he was able to make a little speech (miraculous in itself) which heartened one and all. An angel, it seems, had stood before him, favoring him with a communication to the effect that since he had to stand before Caesar, none of his fellow passengers needed to fear shipwreck.

> But is it really to be believed, that this angel, whom, in a deckless vessel, for the vessels of *those* times were not like the vessels of present time, no person but Paul either saw or heard, was really sent express from the sky by God Almighty, on such an errand? If not, then have we the additional proof—if any additional proof can be needed,—to help to satisfy us,— that, where a purpose was to [be] answered, falsehood, or as *he* would have called it *lying* was not among the obstacles, by which Paul would be stopped, in his endeavors to accomplish it.
>
> Once upon Malta (28:1–6), safe from the sea, a fire of sticks being kindled, a reptile, here called a viper, is represented "as coming out of the heat, and fastening on Paul's hand." Having shaken it off without harm being done, the barbarous Maltese concluded that Paul was a god.
>
> Of this story, what is to be made? At this time of day, among Christians in general, what we should expect to find is; that it passed for a miracle. But if by miracle is meant, not merely an accident, somewhat singular and extraordinary,—but, by a special act of Almighty power, an effect produced, by means disconformable to the uniform course of nature,—it might be too much to say, that even by the reporter himself, it is for the declared purpose of its being taken for a miracle, that it is brought to view. (pp. 386–87)

Of this viper, it may be said that it was misidentified; if really a poisonous snake, perhaps it had recently expended its venom on another or, perhaps, it had lost the 'appropriate tooth.' (p. 388)

In concluding this distillation of *NPBJ*, it is appropriate to reiterate one of Bentham's major contentions, to wit: in relation to Jesus, Paul was at the beginning of his ministry what Judas was at the end of his—a traitor. He was himself the Antichrist![70]

NOTES

1. The Gamaliel of the New Testament (or, more formally, Rabban Gamaliel Ha-Zahen), grandson of the great Hillel, lived during the first half of the first century of the Common Era and was a leading Pharisee as well as president of the Sanhedrin. See *EJ*, s. v. "Gamaliel, Rabban." Hyam Maccoby, *Revolution in Judaea: Jesus and the Jewish Resistance* (New York: Taplinger, 1980), underscores his importance by saying, "Gamaliel was not just a Pharisee leader; he was the head of the whole Pharisee party" (p. 68).

2. *DNB*, s. v. "Place, Francis." Bentham was sufficiently fond of Place to write to him with bantering irony as follows: "Son Francis, you are a good child: but I will not be accessory to Sabbath-breaking. Continue your devotions undisturbed today. I shall look for you with more than usual confidence tomorrow" *CJB*, vol. 9, ed. Stephen Conway, p. 9.

3. James E. Crimmins, *Secular Utilitarianism: Social Science and the Critique of Religion in the Thought of Jeremy Bentham* (Oxford: Clarendon Press, 1990), esp. pp. 227–29. Also see the index of this work for entries on Francis Place and look into Crimmins's "Bentham on Religion: Atheism and the Secular Society," *JHI* 47, no. 1 (1986): 101, n. 28.

4. Crimmins, *Secular Utilitarianism*, p. 227, esp. n. 1, 229, esp. n. 13, 230; also see James Steintrager, "Morality and Belief: The Origin and Purpose of Bentham's Writings on Religion," *MNL* 6 (spring 1971): 11, also n. 47.

5. Quoted in Steintrager, "Morality and Belief," p. 10.

6. See Alfred William Benn, *The History of English Rationalism in the Nineteenth Century*, vol. 1 (New York: Russell and Russell, 1962), pp. 302–303. Benn criticizes Bentham for being out of date with the then current biblical scholarship, for disgracefully bad scholarship himself, and for being ignorant of the higher criticism, largely German, at the time. Higher criticism is defined as the "critical study of the literary methods and sources used by the authors (esp.) of the Old Testament and New Testament." (*ODCC*, p. 648). In our time, Crimmins has criticized Bentham for being so unspiritual as to be unable "to come to grips with the spiritual content of religion" ("Bentham on Religion," p. 95). This is presumably compounded by the fact that where Paul is concerned, "[I]t mattered little to Bentham whether history was on his side or not." (*Secular Utilitarianism*, p. 280). These criticisms, together with Benn's, will be subjected to detailed criticism toward the end of this part.

7. Although I know of no biblical scholars, Christian or otherwise, who think that this is all that was involved in his so-called conversion (or call), some eminent scholars have, without intending to do so, added support to Bentham's position. In "The Apostle Paul and the Introspective Conscience of the West," *HTR* 56, no. 3 (1963), Krister Stendahl (former dean of Harvard Divinity School) writes,

> A fresh look at the Pauline writings themselves shows that Paul was equipped with what in our eyes must be called a rather "robust" conscience. In Phil. 3, Paul speaks most fully about his life before his Christian calling, and there is no indication that he had any difficulty in fulfilling the Law. On the contrary, he can say that he had been "flawless" as to the righteousness required by the Law (v. 6). His encounter with Jesus Christ—at Damascus, according to Acts 9:1–9—has not changed this fact. It was not to him a restoration of a plagued conscience; when he says that he now forgets what is behind him (Phil. 3:13), he does not think about the shortcomings in his obedience to the Law, but about his glorious achievements as a righteous Jew, achievements which he nevertheless now has learned to consider as "refuse" in the light of his faith in Jesus as the Messiah. (p. 200)

In a similar vein, Martin Hengel, *The Pre-Christian Paul* (London: SCM Press, 1991), writes, "[A] psychological interpretation of Paul's conversion must be ruled out. Paul gives no indications in this direction. We do not learn that at the bottom of his heart he had been influenced by the crucified Messiah or the Christians whom he persecuted, nor do we know anything of discontent with the law and its strict demands or of inner struggles which prepared the way—on the contrary, he knew that he was 'as to the righteousness of the law blameless,' as is shown by the last decisive statement in the climactic chain in Phil. 3:6, which shows the firm basis of his former self-confidence. No one who is afflicted by depression talks like that" (p. 79). The more one rules out Paul's having a dysfunctional religion, or his having a guilty conscience, or his suffering cognitive dissonance, etc., as a prelude to his so-called conversion, the greater the scope remaining for the real reason (to Bentham) why Paul stopped persecuting the Church and began promoting it—that reason being his ambition to control it. It is somewhat speculative, but enticing, to consider that that segment of the church over which Paul might most easily have achieved control was the very segment of it which he was persecuting most strenuously. Hengel writes, "As the result of the agitation of the new messianic Jesus movement, or more precisely the Jewish Christian 'Hellenists' [i.e., Hellenized Jewish Christians living in Judea at the time], in the Greek-speaking synagogues of Jerusalem, considerable unrest developed there and there was an energetic reaction. The proclamation of the Greek-speaking followers of the messiah Jesus of Nazareth . . . which was critical of the ritual parts of the Torah and the cult, was a provocation to the majority who were loyal to the law" (p. 85). Apart from a new direction for Paul's ambition, which is all that Bentham noticed, Paul's "conversion" seems to have consisted in an acceptance of Jesus as the Messiah, despite a lack of distinctive messianic accomplishments on Jesus' part (to that date) and an altered way of regarding the law, especially in its ritual aspects.

8. The prologues to Luke and to the book of Acts are prima facie so similar as to make it seem obvious that the author of the one was the author of the other, a common opinion among New Testament scholars then and now. Bentham did not concur. To him, not even an author capable of changing Paul's conversion experience twice in a single document, as the occasion demanded, could end one document (Luke) and begin another (Acts) with an inconsistency as great as the one that appears between the two. To illustrate, in Luke 24 the events alleged of Jesus' post-Resurrection life on earth are pictured as happening in a day, whereas in Acts 1 they are stretched over forty days. So great a contrariety (in Bentham's view) overcame the standard reasons for identifying the author of Luke with the author of Acts. He wrote, "With all this before him, does the editor of the edition of the [KJV] Bible called Scholey's Bible, in a note to the commencement of the Acts, very confidently assure us, that 'from its style, and other internal marks, it is evidently the production of Luke': quoting for his authority, Bishop of Lincoln's *Elements of Christian Theology*, IV." It is unimportant to Bentham's dissertation on the relation of Jesus and his original disciples to the "spiritual" renegade Paul whether or not the author of Luke also wrote Acts. Bentham sidestepped any further concern with authorship by simply denominating the author of Acts as the "Acts historian" and by never referring to the author of Luke by the same name. The controversy over authorship, however, continues. I have before me an article by Lucan expert James M. Dawsey (a friend and former colleague at Auburn University) titled "The Literary Unity of Luke-Acts: Questions of Style," *NTS* 35, no. 1 (1989): 48–66. In addition to some stylistic differences that Dawsey notes, he writes, "It is quite remarkable how this message of Jesus [in Luke] is so thoroughly replaced by the message about Jesus [in Acts]. The concept of the Kingdom of God becomes surprisingly vague, and the teaching parables and miracles of Jesus which dominate the gospel almost completely disappear in Acts. The anger at the rich and powerful that seems so much a correlative to the proclamation of good news in Luke is lost. . . . The good news, in fact, becomes the good news to Gentiles. The ones who do not perceive are not necessarily the rich and the powerful . . . but rather the jealous Jews who do not accept the teachings about the Lord Jesus" (p. 58). In the course of his exposition Dawsey notes that the ancients did not link Luke and Acts, that it was eminent New Testament scholar Henry J. Cadbury, writing in the 1920s, who "deserves much of the credit for popularizing the idea that Luke and Acts were intended as two parts of the same work," and that it was Bible scholar Albert C. Clark who last attempted (in 1933) to establish significant stylistic differences between Luke and Acts. In any case, Bentham's denial of Lucan authorship of Acts has not put him out on a limb alone. Massey Hamilton Shepherd Jr. notes the contradiction between the one day of Luke and the extended time (if not exactly forty days) of Acts in his article "Paul and the Double Resurrection Tradition," *JBL* 64 (1945): 236, and he also writes, "Chapters 1 and 2 [of Acts] show clear signs of redaction: the original preface has been altered; 1:15–26 is a combination of two, originally separate, stories which have been tied together by the double Scriptural citation of v. 20; and 2:5–11 fits well with 2:1–4, 12, 14."

9. Morton Scott Enslin, *Christian Beginnings* (New York: Harper and Brothers, 1938), part 3, p. 419, argues pointedly that the person who put Acts in the form in

which we now have it (Bentham's A-h) is not the same person as the one who, upon joining Paul's entourage from time to time, changed the pronouns from "they" to "we" and "them" to "us" and back again in a written source, such as a diary or journal, that the A-h later incorporated when writing Acts. The "we-passages" are to be found in Acts 16:10–17, 20:5–15, 21:1–18, and 27:1–28:16. Edgar J. Goodspeed, as eminent in New Testament scholarship as Enslin, wrote in his article "The Editio Princeps of Paul," *JBL* 64 (1945) (at a time when Enslin was on the editorial committee of that journal), "It seems to me overwhelmingly more probable that the writer of Acts uses the first person in Acts just as he does in his preface to refer to himself" (p. 196). This debate has continued; see James L. Price, *Interpreting the New Testament* (New York: Holt, Rinehart, and Winston, 1961), pp. 97–98. No matter how this dispute may be resolved, it will have no impact on Bentham's thesis, namely, that the A-h was in no position to judge accurately as to whether or not Paul's conversion/call was associated with inner as well as with outer changes.

10. Charles W. Hedrick, "Paul's Conversion/Call: A Comparative Analysis of the Three Reports in Acts," *JBL* 100, no. 3 (1981): 415–32, gives an excellent survey of more recent thought on the subject. Hedrick wonders how Luke (assumed here to be the author of Acts) can have been so insensitive to the contradictions that appear in three presentations of Paul's conversion/call in Acts, chapters 9, 22, and 26: "It is unclear why the contradictions would not trouble Luke, since he evidently intended each subsequent account to build on the preceding account(s). . . . Further, if the contradiction is a problem to modern readers, why should one assume that it would not trouble discerning earlier readers?" (p. 430). His answer is not persuasive: "Therefore, it seems better to regard the tensions and non-agreements among the three accounts as Lucan corrections and improvements, both theologically and stylistically motivated, rather than 'contradiction', if by contradiction one means error, mistake, or oversight. Certain features are clearly contradictory in a *formal* sense but when viewed in light of Luke's literary method they should be understood in an *essential* sense as improvements and corrections" (p. 432). How, one wonders, is this appraisal an improvement over Bentham's recognition that the A-h altered the conversion narratives to suit the occasion, casting doubt on the historicity of each and all? Hedrick would have us believe that the A-h's theology justified contradictory assertions of fact and that his literary style justified inconsistencies in presentation. J. G. Gager, "Some Notes on Paul's Conversion," *NTS* 27, no. 5 (1981): 697–704, approaches Paul's reported conversion psychologically, with respect to type, emphasizing the importance of stress and anger in the "transvaluation of values," such as occurred in Paul's case. Bentham's point is that the Damascus Road event, if it was an event at all, is so uncertain historically that one can know only that Paul's behavior toward Christianity changed at some point in his life from persecution to the promotion of his own brand of Christianity at least.

11. Hearing a disembodied voice and taking what it says at face value raises a serious epistemological issue. This can best be illustrated by the following event that, with much digging, could be confirmed in part by an article in *The Auburn Plainsman*, the student paper of Auburn University. A former student of mine appeared one day (probably in the very early 1970s) with a middle-aged waif in tow. The student (now deceased) and the waif (almost certainly deceased) came to

me to "test a spirit," as Christians are bidden to do in 1 John 4:1. On the basis of his understanding of John (Gospel) 7:37–38, the waif had been drinking his own urine for some time. When I showed him conclusively from John that what he had taken to be literal was intended by the author to be metaphoric, he announced, after a pregnant pause, that Jesus himself had told him to drink his own urine. To this I said, But how can you be sure it was Jesus and not the Devil disguised as Jesus who told you to do as you are doing (see 2 Cor. 11:14 for Paul's description of the Devil's prowess as a deceiver)? The waif, clearly shaken by the application of what I call the Devil-in-Disguise (DID) Principle fell silent for a time. Then confidently, serenely he assured me saying, "Oh, it was Jesus all right." Having done my best to "test the spirit" in question, I bade my visitors farewell. Even if we grant that Paul heard an extramental voice addressing him on the Damascus Road, why did he not apply the DID Principle? Why did the A-h not make inquiries about this and tell us how Paul verified the genuineness of the voice?

12. This poses no problem for the eminent Ernst Haenchen in *The Acts of the Apostles: A Commentary*, trans. Bernard Noble and Gerald Shinn (Philadelphia: Westminster Press, 1971), who refers to the description of the alleged episode "as belonging to the Hellenistic narrative technique [called] the 'double dream'" (p. 108), a literary device known well enough to have a name.

13. Medical science still knows nothing of anything like scales that might, upon falling from blinded eyes, permit restored vision. Paul T. Manchester, PhD and P. Thomas Manchester Jr., MD, address the medical aspects of Paul's blindness in their article "The Blindness of Saint Paul," *AO* 88, no. 3 (1972): "There are not many conditions that will cause sudden blindness in both eyes for three days, followed by permanent scotomata [the condition they attribute to Paul due to hints in his epistles that he had subsequent difficulty seeing well]. Those that can produce sudden blindness in both eyes, however, are as follows: Acute expansive lesions in anterior cranial fossa, Occlusion of the remaining carotid, Chiasmal arachnoiditis, Optic neuritis, Ocular conversion reaction, Actinic choroiditis (solar retinitis), Takayasu's pulseless disease, and Bilateral homonymous hemianopsia" (p. 318). The authors seem to favor solar retinitis: "One condition does seem to fit the entire picture: This is irradiation injury to the eyes resulting in ultraviolet burn initially, and symptoms of solar chorioretinal burn later" (ibid.). This explanation is reminiscent of annual explanations in the popular press of the bright star that supposedly led the Magi to the baby Jesus (Matt. 2:2b, 9, 10). This wondrous star was, it is often hypothesized, not really a single star but the result of the seeming merger of Jupiter, a comet, and a supernova into one extraordinarily bright star. That might explain its brightness, but what about this star's ability to lead the Magi to the very spot where the baby Jesus lay (Matt. 2:9)? Solar retinitis might well explain Paul's blindness, but what about the something-like-scales that fell from his eyes three days later? One can put about as much confidence in the Manchesters' diagnosis as one can in a star that not only shone brightly but that also led seekers to the precise spot they were hoping to find. The reader is invited to try to follow the sun or the moon to a particular place. The same problem would have confronted the Magi, no matter how bright the star. (I am indebted to Dr. Emil Wright, MD, my often-visited ophthalmologist, for information leading to the Manchesters' article.)

14. Hyam Maccoby, *The Mythmaker: Paul and the Invention of Christianity* (London: Weidenfeld and Nicholson, 1986), makes much of this—far more than is relevant to the point raised by Bentham. Although the temple priesthood had some police powers, Maccoby writes, "Outside Judaea . . . the High Priest had no such police authority, and it is . . . difficult to understand how any 'letters' he might give to Saul 'authorizing him to arrest' followers of Jesus would have any validity. The difficulty is all the greater in that Damascus . . . was not even under Roman rule, having been ceded by Caligula (A.D. 37). It belonged to the independent Arab kingdom of Nabataea, under the rule of King Aretas IV (9 B.C.–A.D. 40). This king, who was jealous of his independence, would hardly have taken kindly to the entry into his territory of an emissary of the Roman-ruled area of Judaea for the purpose of arresting and dragging away citizens or even aliens who were under his protection" (p. 86). Maccoby, not a fan of St. Paul, is not alone in this. Hengel, *Pre-Christian Paul*, says, "Here Paul [in his persecution of the church] is given a decisive function in the supreme organs of Jewish justice, and at the same time—probably contrary to historical reality—it is presupposed that Jerusalem courts could impose and carry out death penalties without further ado" (p. 67). He continues on the same page, "Luke is evidently exaggerating somewhat here to heighten the drama of his account, a practice of which he is also fond elsewhere."

15. Though dubious of Paul ever and anon, Bentham did not doubt the historicity of Jesus, nor shall I, at least in the confines of this book. If Jesus suffered execution under Pontius Pilate, it must have been between 26 and 36, the dates of his procuratorship. Most New Testament scholars seem content to put the date at about 30. There is considerable evidence that in believing himself to be the Jewish Messiah (the long-awaited king sent by the Bible-god to deliver Israel from her enemies and to restore her national sovereignty), he simultaneously became seditious in Roman eyes, hence the inscription on the cross, "The King of the Jews" (see Mark 15:26, Matt. 27:37, Luke 23:38, John 19:19). The Jesus movement within Judaism survived the shock of its Messiah's death, continuing to exist in Jerusalem and elsewhere in Judea among Pharisaic or Pharisaically inclined Jews. Although Peter (Cephas) remained a leader of the Jesus movement, James, the brother of Jesus, gained ascendancy. Morton Smith, *Jesus the Magician* (New York: Harper and Row, 1978), writes, "[Jesus] was executed as a would-be 'Messiah,' that is, an anointed [or crowned, in our terms] king. The title was hereditary, and he was childless, so his brothers found themselves saddled with his claims. More than a half century later, some of their descendants were rounded up and interrogated by the Romans, and only then dismissed as harmless" (p. 25). Samuel G. F. Brandon is at odds with Smith on some points respecting the importance of messianism; nevertheless, in *Jesus and the Zealots: A Study of the Political Factor in Primitive Christianity* (Manchester, UK: University of Manchester Press, 1967), pp.165–66, 168, agrees with Smith on the authority of James and the familial reasons for it. After the execution of James in 62 at the hands of Ananus, the High Priest, the leadership of the Jerusalem church is said to have passed to Symeon, a cousin of Jesus (p. 166). According to Brandon (pp.167–68), James was famous for being rigorously observant of the Torah (the law of Moses); that is, he remained a practicing Jew while being a messianist, while believing that Jesus, though executed, would return

somehow to deliver Israel. Brandon also made this point in great detail in his article "The Death of James the Just: A New Interpretation," in *Studies in Mysticism and Religion*, presented to Gershom Scholem (Jerusalem: Magnes Press, 1967), p. 67. In the manuscripts that were to become *NPBJ*, Bentham relied primarily on Paul's epistles to the Galatians, Corinthians, Romans, and on Acts. What he discovered on a prima facie reading, devoid of all reverential inclinations, was an intense ideological and ecclesiastical (i.e., political) struggle between Paul on the one hand and, on the other hand, James, Peter, the Jerusalem church, and its satellites inside and outside of Judea. Taking the latter as being in the best position to know what Jesus taught, the former, to Bentham, could only be seen as an apostate. Said Brandon, in *Jesus and the Zealots*, "From the Jewish [and Jewish-Christian] point of view, such a presentation [as Paul's] of the death of Jesus [of which, more later] was not only theologically outrageous, it amounted to apostasy of a most shocking kind, involving both race and religion" (p.185). Michael Grant, *Saint Paul* (New York: Charles Scribner's Sons, 1976), writes, "[Paul] was denounced by Jews as the greatest apostate of all time; and rightly, from their point of view, because had it not been for him Christianity might have been absorbed into Judaism" (p. 96). Donald Riddle, "The Jewishness of Paul," *JR* 23, no. 4 (1943), writes, "[H]e was, from any point of view other than his own, at best a poor Jew and at worst a renegade" (p. 244). Clearly Bentham has not been left without scholarly support. What must be recognized is that James, the brother and successor of Jesus, may have been more conservative than Jesus and that the Jerusalem church under him may not have been the perfect yardstick for measuring Paul's doctrinal deviations from the original teachings of Jesus (to be discussed later).

16. At the broadest philosophico-scientific level, Bentham was quite right to have asked how a natural act (such as some kind of washing in or with water) could dispose of a person's moral mistakes (and the consequences thereof) in a super-, extra-, or nonnatural way. The problem is that the washing away of sins with baptism is not what Paul taught about it, at least not in his best authenticated letters, although he may have believed this too (see Titus 3:5). What he taught requires a mechanism, as it were, far more magical. The passages most relevant to Paul's concept of baptism are Rom. 6:3ff., 1 Cor. 12:12f., Gal. 3:26ff., and Col. 2:9–3:4. Granting the disputed Pauline authorship of Colossians, the doctrine of baptism therein conforms nicely with Paul's teaching elsewhere. Romans 6:3ff. provides the most complete exposition of the doctrine in question. We learn in verses 3 and 4 that believers who are baptized *into* Christ die to the sins of the natural, fleshly life, are buried (through total immersion in water) as Jesus was buried in a sepulcher, and are raised up to live in a new mode of life even as he was resurrected from the dead. Those who might like to see death and burial above as merely symbolic can hardly wish the new life promised, that is, the spirit-filled life with Christ, to be merely symbolic. Surely Paul did not see any of it this way. The magic here is not that of washing away moral or ritual pollution with an application of ordinary, yet holy, water, but of an individual's dying, being buried, and being raised into a new form of existence (that is, identified with or participating in Jesus Christ) while remaining metabolically and homeostatically the same as before. Next (v. 5), Paul assaults modern sensibilities by presenting as indubitable fact a hypothetical asser-

tion, based on faith alone, whose antecedent fails to entail its consequent. He writes, "For if we have been planted [united or joined] together *in the likeness* of *his* death, we shall be also in the likeness of his resurrection" (emphasis added). We *know*, he claims (v. 6), that the Christian's old self was crucified with Christ so that the old sinful body might be destroyed, such that the Christian is no longer enslaved to sin. Here 'sin' is not merely the name of the class of each and every intention and/or act proscribed by the Bible-god but is hypostatized into one of two sovereign entities, the other being Paul's deity. Hypostatization, a common fallacy in Paul's writings, is treated superbly by William Werkmeister, *Introduction to Critical Thinking* (Lincoln, NE: Johnsen, 1948), as an elementary fallacy in thought and defined as one "committed whenever abstract concepts—such as 'truth', 'beauty', 'humanity', 'justice', 'science', 'progress', 'whiteness', 'hunger', etc.—are treated as if they designated specific and concrete entities capable of independent existence and of producing empirical effects" (pp. 27–28). This is precisely the way Paul treated sin, along with his treatment of the Bible-god. He would have us believe that sin was busy working death in him (Rom. 7:13), that he was sold (out?) under sin (7:14), and that sin lived in him (7:17). "Let not sin . . . reign in your mortal body," he says (in Rom. 6:12). Sin, as an active agent in human affairs, will have no dominion over Christians, because being dead to their former lives, they are no longer under (Mosaic) law (and thus no longer answerable for their sins) but are under grace, having been justified (Rom. 6:14). From that point until the end of the chapter (with v. 23), he develops the notion that human beings are not autonomous but are slaves either of sin (hypostatized) or of the Bible-god. Baptism as described above conduces to a union with Christ (and with other Christians constituting the body of Christ) through the "Spirit." For more on baptism and its relation to the giving and receiving of the "Spirit," see Morton Smith, *The Secret Gospel* (New York: Harper and Row, 1973), esp. p. 101, and also the whole of chapter 11. Elsewhere, Smith writes in summation, "Such rites, beginning with an imitation death and ending with resurrection by receipt of a divine spirit, to a new life, are familiar in magical material [i.e., in documentary evidence relative to magical practices in the ancient world]" ("Pauline Worship as Seen By Pagans," *HTR* 73, nos. 1–2 [1980]: 242). Acts 18:24–19:7 bears two testimonies to the association of proper Christian baptism with the descent of the Holy Ghost (whatever this may have meant to the A-h) upon believers. In 18:24–25, we learn of a certain Apollos, a Jew, taught in the way of the Lord but knowing only the baptism of John the Baptist, a baptism of repentance followed by ritual washing. Moreover, in 19:1–7, Paul comes upon some disciples of the Lord in Ephesus who were baptized into John's baptism, not knowing proper Christian baptism. Upon hearing Paul expatiate on the topic (authoritatively one must suppose), they underwent baptism in the name of Jesus and received the Holy Ghost. The reader is invited to hypothesize as to what this means, if anything, beyond heightened emotionalism of some sort or other. Most revealing of all, perhaps, of the magic of the times is baptism on behalf of the dead (1 Cor. 15:29). Paul mentions it only in passing and does not tell us whether or not he believed in the efficacy of this practice, but he does not criticize it. His failure to criticize the practice and the concept behind it should be taken as significant, for he was not slow to criticize. It is noteworthy that many Mormons today are zealous in being baptized on behalf of the dead, basing their practice on this verse. If such baptism is efficacious, why can one not be baptized on behalf of those living now but in circumstances that prevent their hearing the Gospel and believing therein? As a general rule one should not think that the ancients, Paul included, were less credulous than those modern Americans who believe what they read in the sensationalistic tabloids on sale at any supermarket. I had no sooner written these words than I came upon the following in *AR* 39 (July–August 1994): 23. A poll conducted by the National Opinion Research Center at the University of Chicago found that 70 percent of Americans believe in miracles and 40 percent "claim to have contacted the dead." Surely, the ancients were not less inclined toward fantasy, unbridled speculation, and credulity than are modern Americans as indicated by the information above.

17. "Paul, in fact, is the hero of Acts, which was written by an admirer and follower of his," writes Jewish scholar Maccoby, *The Mythmaker*, p. 4. "Paul was Luke's hero," agrees Christian scholar E. F. Bruce, "The Enigma of Paul," *BR* 4, no. 4 (1988): 32. John Clayton Lentz Jr., *Luke's Portrait of Paul* (Cambridge: Cambridge University Press, 1993), contends that Luke (or Bentham's A-h) was trying to exalt Paul (in Acts chapters 21–23) by painting a picture of him as a person "of high social status and implied wealth and prestige" (p. 59). Presenting Paul as a Roman citizen from birth (22:25, 27–28), as a citizen of the essentially Greek city of Tarsus (21:39), and as a member of a strict Pharisaic family (23:6) raises serious difficulties according to Lentz. Noting that the ordinary "pagan" duties of citizenship in any Greek city would have been all but impossible for a strict Pharisee, Lentz writes, "[T]he evidence indicates that Jews who would have aspired to or held these citizenships were not, as a rule, included among those who would have been perceived as among the strictest, more zealous, law-abiding Jews. Yet, this is precisely the difficulty of the portrayal in Acts—he claims that he [Paul] has been all three from birth! In other words, while each of the specific claims, in and of itself, is not problematic, the combination of the three in one person is doubtful" (p. 60). Lentz writes further, "[W]hat seems to be of greater concern to Luke is not just Paul the [loyal] Jew, but Paul the Tarsian and Roman [citizen] who showed himself to be comfortable in the company of the high and the mighty of the first century Greco-Roman world. In Acts, Paul is always in control. His authority is not only recognized among Christians. He is also acknowledged as a man not to be taken lightly by the secular leaders as well. Luke is also intent on emphasizing that Paul, before his conversion, was a wild and zealous persecutor, yet after his conversion Paul is a model of sobriety, piety, and bravery" (p. 2). Surely, this is too good to be true! In elevating Paul's status unduly in the minds of the readers of Acts, the A-h again exhibits his undependability as a biographer and historian.

18. Putting the best face on it, we would today, no doubt, say that Paul experienced an auditory hallucination that he took to be the voice of Jesus. Quite apart from any divinely intended interpretation, a miracle would have had to occur to put a particular person at a particular time and place and in a particular set of circumstances into such a brain state as to allow the reception of a specific message issuing from beyond that brain. Bentham acceded to none of this. Such to him were Paul's ambitions and deceits that he fabricated the voice and duped the A-h, a hero

worshiper more than willing to be duped. So, in the recapitulation above, it would not have been correct to say, using modern terminology, that Paul and Ananias (also a fabrication) had auditory hallucinations. In the main, the real people allowed into the pages of Acts were so gullible as to believe in Paul's reputed visions. He was only too well aware of this and happy to take advantage of it. His visions, it should be remembered, always served his purposes ever so conveniently.

19. Even allowing for some exaggeration on Paul's part, why, one wonders, was his persecution of the Jesus movement (or way) so ferocious? In Gal. 1:13b he confesses to having persecuted the church "beyond measure," wasting it (also see Phil. 3:6). The A-h presents much the same picture even though he was either ignorant of, or chose to ignore completely, the letters of Paul. Acts 8:3 says that Paul made "havoc of the church," Acts 22:4 has it that Paul persecuted the way unto death, and 26:11 has him, in fury, compelling Christians to blaspheme (see also 9:1). This is most puzzling, because nothing the Jerusalem church believed or was doing was actionable in law. Smith, *The Secret Gospel*, writes,

> Why should the early Christians have been persecuted not only by the Jewish authorities, but by private pietists like Paul? There seems no likelihood that Christianity ever posed a serious threat of political revolution—certainly it did not do so after Jesus' death. The persecution by Jews, not only in Jerusalem, but also throughout the Roman empire, has to be explained on religious grounds. But holding odd beliefs about the Messiah is no offense against Jewish law. And the reasons given by Acts are mostly inadequate. This raises the suspicion that something is being concealed. We may suspect that what was concealed was the teaching that the kingdom had already come and the [Mosaic] law had been abolished for those in Jesus. (p. 121)

The notion that the kingdom had already come in some mysterious manner, even though King Jesus had been executed and was not physically present, is known as realized eschatology, that is, in some "spiritual" manner the end of the age had already been inaugurated, though not yet fully realized. It was a common belief that when Messiah came, the Mosaic law would be abolished. Since 'law' was usually translated into Greek by *nomos*, those who thought they had been freed from the law were called antinomians. Smith argues strongly that both Jesus and Paul, in varying degrees, were antinomian. 'Antinomian' refers both to the moral and to the ceremonial aspects of the law of Moses. When used of Jewish Christians it referred to people, like Paul, who thought that such legal prescriptions as circumcision and avoiding nonkosher foods (also eating kosher foods with Gentiles) had no applicability for Christians.

20. In summoning up the gall to announce himself as one who had been set apart before birth to carry out a divine mandate, Paul put himself in company with the great prophets Isaiah (see Isa. 49:1, 5) and Jeremiah (see Jer. 1:5), no mean feat, and by claiming that the God of Israel had revealed his son *in* him (Paul), Paul was able to say, in effect, that those who would know the mind of God and the mind of the Son of God had but to look to or at him (Paul)! After all, if Christ was really

revealed *in* Paul, then what God had revealed in Jesus was there for all to see in Paul. How, then, could Paul's converts go wrong as long as they beheld him and listened to what he had to say? They could not. Little wonder that he could anathematize all the Christians who pursued him, trying to undo his message, teaching another gospel than the one he taught.

21. Paul, lauded by legions of Christians for centuries for writing 1 Cor. 13 (the famous chapter that extols love), exhibited no scintilla thereof toward those in Corinth, for example, who questioned his apostolic status and the authority derived from it. In 2 Cor. 11:3-4 he expresses the fear that even as Eve was seduced by the serpent, so his Corinthian brethren might, all too compliantly on their part, be corrupted by someone (or anyone for that matter) who might preach a different Jesus (or interpretation thereof), or proclaim a different gospel than the one he had been preaching, or offer a different "spirit" than his. He then announces that he is not one whit inferior to the highest or chiefest apostles, whoever they may be, if not James, or Peter, or their emissaries (v. 5). There is considerable dispute among scholars as to the precise identity of these chiefest apostles. See Jerry W. McCant, "Paul's Thorn of Rejected Apostleship," *NTS* 34, no. 4 (1988): 553-54. Having achieved parity, in his own view at least, with any and all apostles, Paul resolves (v. 12) to continue his course as before in order to undercut those who presume to work on the same (apostolic) terms as the ones he claims for himself. He brands his Christian competitors as false apostles and deceitful workmen (v. 13). Even worse, they are agents of Satan. Even as the Prince of Lies masquerades as an angel of light, so his servants disguise themselves as the exemplars of righteousness (v. 15). Rather than loving these contenders for leadership in the church, as 1 Cor. 13 indicates that he should have, Paul takes considerable pleasure, one can perceive, in announcing that their (unhappy) end will correspond to their nefarious deeds (2 Cor. 11:15). Six verses later he asks rhetorically if his religious competitors are Hebrews, Israelites, descendants of Abraham, and servants of Christ and answers himself saying that even if so, so is he, but that he is a *better* servant of Christ than they (vv. 22-23). The vitriol above is set in the context of boasting, more about which can be learned in Christopher Forbes, "Comparison, Self-Praise, and Irony: Paul's Boasting and the Conventions of Hellenistic Rhetoric," *NTS* 32, no. 1 (1986): 1-30. Even if Paul could not love the (to him) miscreants who were denying him apostolic authority, why could he not have taken his own advice in Phil. 2:12 and left his opponents and the Corinthians alike to work out their own salvation with fear and trembling? The rather obvious likelihood is that he was less concerned about the salvation of the average Christian than he was about the maintenance of his own control not only over the church in Corinth (and in Galatia too) but over the churches in the whole Gentile world, the world to which he was, in his own view, the apostle par excellence. Of course, he could not say this in so many words in his letters, so he represented himself as the one in whom the truth of Christ was pleased to dwell (2 Cor. 11:10, 13:3). Accordingly, those who disagreed with him had no truth in them, but were servants of Satan. Noting Paul's "vehement" defense of his apostleship in the Corinthian letters, David M. Hay writes, "He typically assumes and insists that others admit his right to define doctrines and wield discipline" ("Paul's Indifference to Authority," part 1, *JBL* 88 [May 1969]: 36). In an

ecclesiastical organization, the ability "to define doctrine and to wield discipline" is the ability to control the members thereof—in short, to exercise power over them. Whatever else Paul may have intended, this desire loomed large in his life. In the same article, Hay contends that even if the Jerusalem leadership had condemned Paul, he would have gone on doing whatever he was doing "despite their opinions" (p. 42). That Paul was busily engaged in exercising control over communicants in the churches he regarded as his own can best be seen in 1 Cor. 5:1–5, a passage that seems to have escaped Bentham's attention. Herein a report reaches Paul claiming that a man in the church is cohabiting with a (former?) wife of that same man's father, no other details concerning this incest being available. Paul takes this as an instance of immorality that exceeds anything of which pagans are capable! At least as important as this kind of incest itself is the apparent perception of it in the Corinthian church. In verse 2 Paul asks if the recipients of his letter ought not to mourn rather than being puffed up. Puffed up about what? It looks as though the church had said of this incest, So what? In verse 3, Paul notifies them that he has *already* pronounced judgment and that the miscreant is to be delivered to Satan for the destruction of his flesh (v. 5). The end of this action is, of course, a good one. It is to be done that the wretch's soul may be saved in the day of the Lord Jesus. This is precisely the object of the infamous autos-da-fé, featured in the Inquisition. It detracts from the author of 1 Cor. 13 to learn that the inspiration for the Inquisition lies in 1 Cor. 1:1–5 (also in 1 Tim. 1:20, though Paul is not now thought to be the author of this letter). Those with literal minds can hardly keep from visualizing a pickup service in which an imp or demon goes about in a little (red?) wagon picking up the excommunicated for additional punishment or execution. As might be expected scholars have interpreted 1 Cor. 5:5 differently. Adela Yarbro Collins, "The Function of 'Excommunication' in Paul," *HTR* 73, nos. 1–2 (1980), notes that the most "common interpretation is that Satan was expected to cause the man's sudden death or a slower one by illness [just how dependable Satan was in such matters one may wonder!] that his death would expiate for his sin and thus his immortal soul or his inner, true self would be saved" (p. 257). Collins does not espouse the standard interpretation wholeheartedly but does not provide as clear an alternative interpretation as one would like. What she does do clearly is to make the point that if the incestuous deed were theological in nature and "defiant of Paul's authority," then "discipline within the community may also have been an issue" (p. 263). As she makes crystal clear, incest of the sort involved was violative both of Roman and Mosaic law, but Paul, it must be remembered, taught that Christians were no longer under the law (of Moses at least). Christians have, presumably, died to the law, its relevance and efficacy alike abolished for them (Gal. 2:19–21). So the Corinthian man, living incestuously, may have flouted the law on purpose, believing himself on firm (antinomian) ground in doing so. After all, if faith in Christ abrogates the ceremonial law, respecting circumcision for example, why does it not also abrogate the moral law? Paul makes no explicit distinctions when referring to the law. Peter S. Zass, "Catalogues [of Vice] and Context: 1 Corinthians 5 and 6:2," *NTS* 34, no. 4 (1988): 625, seems to favor excommunication as all that Paul had in mind in the way of punishment. Whatever the precise nature of the punishment, Paul's authority over both the offending individual and the Corinthian congregation seem to have been at issue, and he determined to dominate both. Morton Smith, *Jesus the Magician* (New York: Harper and Row, 1973), p. 110, thinks that Paul was practicing the blackest sort of magic, this giving of people over to the spirits of the underworld for punitive purposes. Also see Smith, "Pauline Worship as Seen by Pagans," *HTR* 73 (1980), wherein he writes that the idea that a man can be given over to Satan "for the destruction of his flesh" is an "idea expressed, with some of the same words, by magical curse tablets" (p. 249), common to the magical literature and practices of the time. Even more interesting is Smith's suggestion in his article "Paul's Arguments as Evidence of the Christianity from Which He Diverged," *HTR* 79, nos. 1–3 (1986): 255, that the incestuous man may have been a ringleader in the church, rather than a mere eccentric, arguing that those who have died with Christ are free from law. Two other examples of Pauline animosity, also falling far short of 1 Cor. 13, come to mind. First, in Gal. 5:12, while fixing his attention on certain people who were unsettling his Galatian converts, he expresses the wish that they would castrate themselves or have themselves castrated. Although the Greek *apokopsontai* can by extension also refer to circumcision, the context makes this unlikely. In either case, Paul's bitter wish does not imply a benefit to those he hopes will mutilate themselves. See William R. Reed's entry in *IDB* s. v. "Mutilation." Paul's animosities did not exhaust themselves on enemies within the church but also extended to Jews outside the Jesus movement. His bitterest outburst against Jews is found in 1 Thess. 2:14–16, where he speaks of those who killed both the Lord Jesus and their own prophets and (prior to the time of writing) drove Paul and his associates out (out of what, out of where?) and have hindered him and his party from preaching salvation to the Gentiles. Having filled up their quota of sins as usual, Paul takes satisfaction, one can discern between the lines, in believing that the wrath of their God is upon them to stay. In "Rehabilitating Renan," *AS* (spring 1989) (i.e., Ernst Renan, 1823–92, eminent French philologist and biblical scholar), Wallace Fowlie cites him on the differences between Jesus and Paul, a differentiation that would have delighted Bentham. Fowlie writes of Renan, "In this controversial book [*The Life of Jesus*] he writes [in 1862] a pastoral story treating Jesus as a handsome man unable to keep people from loving him, unable not to perform miracles in the midst of children and people acclaiming him. Then later, in the third volume of *The History of Christian Origins* (1869), Renan wrote the story of Saint Paul, whom he looked upon as a fanatic able to set fire to a village and massacre the inhabitants" (pp. 253–54). He who extolled love so magnificently in 1 Cor. 13 wrote three chapters later (16:22), "If any man love not the Lord Jesus Christ, let him be anathema [i.e., cursed]."

22. Not only was it humdrum, it may have been the only major point that separated Jesus' disciples (in the Jerusalem church under James's leadership of the time) from the Pharisees. See also note 32 below for more on the Pharisees. Moreover, 'Son of God' did not refer only to supernatural beings as in Gen. 6:2, 4; it also was used in reference to King David (2 Sam. 7:14) and to the line of Davidic kings (Ps. 89:26–27). See the *IDB* s. v. "David" and "Davidic Kings." Also, for various meanings of 'Son of God,' see *IDB* s. v. "Son of God." Jews in the synagogues of Damascus may have been amazed at Paul, if he ever preached there (Acts 9:21), but not because he confounded them and not because he *proved* that Jesus was the

prophesied King of Israel (v. 22). This was an open question, the Christian Jews saying that he was, the non-Christian Jews saying that he was not.

23. It is astonishing how little one can learn about Jesus of Nazareth from Paul's epistles. Granted that (with the exception of Romans) these documents were all written in response to specific problems that had arisen in the churches Paul had founded or influenced mightily, that all were topical and occasional in nature, and that none was thus a thorough and systematic exposition of Christian theology, still and all, the so-called Jesus of history is given very short shrift therein. On this point one can hardly do better than to quote G. A. Wells, *Who Was Jesus? A Critique of the New Testament Record* (La Salle, IL: Open Court, 1989):

> None of the letters ascribed to Paul that are now accepted as genuinely written by him make any allusion to Jesus's parents, let alone to the virgin birth. They do not refer to a place of birth or residence (e.g., by calling him "of Nazareth"). They mention neither John the Baptist (even though Paul stresses the importance of baptism), nor Judas, nor Peter's denial of his master (They do, of course, mention Peter, but do not imply that he, any more than Paul himself, had known Jesus, while he had been alive.) They give us no indication of the time or place of Jesus's earthly existence. They never refer to his trial before a Roman official, nor to Jerusalem as the place of his execution. And one could never gather from these letters that he had been an ethical teacher, even though they are full of ethical admonitions. Paul is also totally silent about Jesus's miracles, even though he believed in the importance of miracles as a means of winning converts. (p. 188)

This is reinforced by Grant's *Saint Paul*: "He shows . . . *an almost complete lack of interest* in the words and acts of Jesus" (p. 58). Furthermore, Bradley H. McLean, "The Absence of an Atoning Sacrifice in Paul's Soteriology," *NTS* 38, no. 4 (1992), states of Paul, "[H]is writings are not motivated by biographical interest, much less a concern for historical authenticity. It is safe to assume that when Paul passes on what would seem to be a historical fact concerning Jesus' crucifixion, such as the suffering and death of Christ, he is actually making a theological statement" (p. 548).

24. Bentham's reference to government here is a bit perplexing. Peter and John were surely governing officials among the disciples of the Lord, and they, together with other apostles, had a monopoly on transferring the Holy Ghost (whatever this means and however it was, or is, done), but granting this power to Simon Magus would not seem to have constituted a transfer of ecclesiastical control as such. In any case, Paul eventually acquired this power (according to Acts 19:6) and may be supposed to have been pleased to have it.

25. If the change in Paul's behavior toward the church, which Bentham accepted as historical, can be coordinated with a visit to Damascus, then the following sequence of events occurred upon conversion, according to Acts and Galatians. Upon seeing the light (but which light, Bentham wondered?), Paul descended into Arabia (to the south and east of the Dead Sea) for a time following the change

that overcame him; returned to Damascus; and finally went up to Jerusalem where he met privately with Peter and James, the Messiah's brother (Gal. 1:17b–18). A span of time lasting up to three calendar years is associated (by Paul) with some or all of these events, but ambiguously. After leaving Jerusalem, a fourteen-year period is supposed to have ensued before Paul, acting under divine direction, returned to lay before the leadership of the Jesus movement the gospel that he (alone?) was preaching (Gal. 2:1–2). What all, we may wonder, transpired in Paul's thoughts during the three-year period mentioned before his appearance in Jerusalem in private with Peter and James? We shall, of course, never know, but there was plenty of time for motives ulterior to religious to have developed, to have been pondered, and to have been espoused. If ulterior motives did develop in Paul, at this time or later, they were surely not the sort of thing he would have adverted to openly in his letters. Hence, the silence of the letters on any such topic(s) is not evidence that there were none. Similar questions can be asked about what went through his mind theologically during the fourteen years leading up to the visit to Jerusalem at which time he laid *his* gospel (*his* good news) before the leadership of the Jerusalem church. Did he, for example, develop self-consciously a gospel that he believed would be acceptable to the Roman occupation of Judea—smacking less of sedition than did the gospel of Peter and James? Did he deliberately forge good news that would be more palatable to Hellenized (i.e., Greek-speaking) Jews living outside Judea than contained in the original gospel of Jesus? Did he contrive to create a theology whose message would be good enough to entice Gentiles more effectively than anything the Jerusalem church could offer? Did he attempt knowingly to universalize certain otherworldly themes that when preached in Judea had a this-worldly, parochial ring? It taxes the imagination excessively to believe that an extremely domineering person such as Paul entertained only religious motives—and these in the purest fashion. In any case, Bentham would have none of it. He discerned behind the plaster saint of subsequent Christian history a man lusting for prestige, power, and possessions. This man, with a mania to persuade others to believe what he believed, would have had plenty of time, during the fourteen-year period mentioned above, to have observed which themes associated with the Jesus movement were most persuasive and which were less, and to have incorporated the most persuasive into his theology well before the first of his missionary journeys.

26. Although Stendahl does not suspect Paul of ulterior motives, he does contend, as we have seen, in his article "The Apostle Paul and Introspective Conscience," that Paul had a "robust" conscience and that it was not hurting him due to "any difficulty in fulfilling the Law" (p. 200). The extent to which a guilty conscience, cognitive dissonance, or other psychological source did not prompt Paul to convert to Christianity is the extent to which the field is opened for other motives, including the unhappy motives attributed to him by Bentham. It is, of course, possible that Paul came to believe in Jesus as the Christ simply because, intellectually, he changed his mind and thought himself mistaken in his views while still a persecutor of Christianity. No less an expert in theology than Joseph Fletcher wrote of himself while still a believer, "[A]lthough I accepted the faith, although I said 'I believe,' it was always without religiosity. I thought it theologically, but I did not feel it religiously" ("An Odyssey: From Theology to Humanism," *RH* 13, no. 4 [1979]:

148). It is logically possible that the same was true of Paul, yet his apparent craving for justification (whatever this is) makes it seem unlikely that he became a Christian for intellectual reasons alone. In any case, the extent to which emotional factors of the sort usually associated with religion are denied is the extent to which seven devils, as it were, are invited in. In short, by the time Paul commenced his missionary labors, he may have been much more calculating than pious New Testament scholars have ever imagined.

27. Arabia here does not refer to the whole Arabian peninsula but to the land of the biblical Nabataeans, usually believed to lie to the east and south of Damascus. See *IDB*, s. v. "Arabia," also s. v. "Nabataeans."

28. Maccoby, *The Mythmaker*, writes, "No doubt some activists [against Roman occupation] still remained in [the] Judaea underground and were receiving help and advice from their comrades in Damascus, who were proving a thorn in the flesh of the High Priest. Saul, the trusted police officer of the High Priest, was therefore sent with a band of mercenaries to put an end to this menace by illegally entering Damascus and carrying off the ringleaders of subversion" (p. 86). This might have been enough to prompt the government in Damascus to attempt to arrest Paul. Howard C. Kee and Franklin W. Young, *Understanding the New Testament* (Englewood Cliffs, NJ: Prentice-Hall, 1957), pp. 214–15, theorize that Aretas may have been trying to ingratiate himself with potential allies, hence his willingness to attempt to arrest Paul.

29. The number of visits Paul made to Jerusalem after becoming a believer in Jesus as Messiah is a matter of dispute. John Knox, *Chapters in a Life of Paul* (Nashville, TN: Abingdon Press, 1950), esp. pp. 33–40, claims that on the basis of Gal. 1:15–2:10, 1 Cor. 16:1–4, and Rom. 15:25–32, Paul was in Jerusalem on only three occasions. Acts has him there on at least four occasions (detailed by Bentham in the text cited) and maybe on a fifth, depending on what 18:22 is taken to imply. In "The Pauline Chronology," *JBL* 58, no. 1 (1939): 23, Knox dates the visits as follows: Assuming conversion in 37, the first visit occurred in 40, the second in 51, and the third in 53. Some scholars are dubious of the Jerusalem conference that in Acts 15 occasions the third of four or possibly of five visits that the A-h mentions.

30. In the course of persecuting the primitive church or elements thereof, Paul may have had occasion to evaluate the Christian leadership and to have judged it weak (a point missed by Bentham). If so he may well have envisioned a rapid rise for one as able and domineering as himself. Given the double-cross of the High Priest(s), given Christian anger and fear over his former depredations, and given that he had enraged the Jews of Damascus enough for them to have wanted to kill him, it seems likely that once his basket hit the ground he fled immediately, seeking safety and solitude.

31. Why could Paul not have been content simply with having been justified, in the eyes of his deity, and with being a simple Christian, earning his daily bread by making tents, doing good works, and awaiting the return of the Lord? Moreover, why could he not simply have conformed to what was being taught by the Christian Jews in Jerusalem? It can hardly be denied that Paul strove for leadership in the Jesus movement. Why? For "spiritual" reasons?

32. The mention of Grecians makes it important at this point to develop two

catalogs, one concerning where's where and the other who's who. The area at the southeastern edge of the Mediterranean Sea known as Palestine (at the time of the first Roman war, 66–73) extended from Lake Semechonitis ten to fifteen miles north of the Sea of Galilee to a line beginning about ten miles north of the southern tip of Lake Asphaltitis (the Dead Sea) and stretching irregularly westward to the Mediterranean. For most practical purposes Palestine can be said to have been bounded on the east by the River Jordan. In geopolitical terms the area was divided into three sections stacked, as it were, on a north-south axis. In the north, Galilee, the smallest of the three regions, did not extend as far west as the Mediterranean. In the center was Samaria extending fully from the Mediterranean on the west to the Jordan on the east. The Samaritans and their quasi-Mosaic religion can safely be ignored as far as this work is concerned. In the south was Judaea (or Judea) stretching fully from the Mediterranean to the Jordan and the Dead Sea except for the tiny enclave of Ascalon. The (second) Temple in Jerusalem (the capital of Judea) was the national cultic center of the Jewish people. On average the Jews living in Judea were less Hellenized (influenced by Greek culture) than those elsewhere. Jews in Galilee were far more Hellenized, and their region was a hotbed of insurrection against Roman rule. Outside of Palestine lived the Jews of the so-called Diaspora, of the dispersion, that is, Jews dispersed outside their traditional Palestinian home-land. On average they were the most Hellenized Jews of all (in the West) and in some cases and for a variety of reasons were pro-Roman. If Paul came from Tarsus, as he claimed, then he was himself a Jew of the Diaspora. With respect to sedition and insurrection in Palestine he was clearly pro Roman (see Rom. 13:1–7). More-over, if his first base of missionary operations was in Syrian Antioch (close to where modern Turkey and Syria meet at the extreme northeast shore of the Mediter-ranean), then he dwelt among Jews of the Diaspora (as well as among Gentiles) who were Hellenized to a considerable degree. Respecting who's who we must attempt to get straight on Sadducees, scribes, Pharisees, Essenes, Zealots, Herodians, God-fearers, Grecians (or Hellenists), and Gentiles. The complete story differenti-ating Jewish groups in Palestine would require a recognition that some Jews were even caught up in tensions involving urban versus rural interests. There is no dis-pute as to who the Sadducees were and what their agenda was. Donald J. Selby, *Introduction to the New Testament* (New York: Macmillan, 1971), writes of them suc-cinctly: "The Sadducees . . . were the wealthy minority of the landed gentry who controlled the Temple priesthood. Basically conservative, they had little interest in adding interpretations to Torah. Hence they rejected the growing body of tradition known as 'oral Torah'. They rejected also all belief in angelic beings and the resur-rection" (p. 11). They collaborated with the Roman occupation and were seen by many as Quislings. Maccoby, *The Mythmaker*, says that the High Priest (always drawn from Sadducean ranks during this period) "was not just a ceremonial official with jurisdiction over the Temple; he was also, in effect, a chief of police with his own armed forces, his own police tribunal which was concerned with political offenses [against the Roman regime in particular], and his own penal system including prisons and arrangements for flogging prisoners" (p. 58). Maccoby takes the "*chief* point of conflict between Jesus and the Sadducees [to be] political rather than religious" (pp. 34–35). Joseph Klausner, *From Jesus to Paul* (London: George

Allen and Unwin, 1944), adds the following: "The Sadducees . . . hated the Nazarenes [primarily, if not exclusively, Jewish believers in Jesus] mostly because the latter made belief in the resurrection of the dead the cornerstone of their faith; sometimes they persecuted the Nazarenes, but for the most part they despised and scorned them" (p. 443). In *Jesus the Magician*, Smith writes of the scribes, "They were almost certainly a professional class, not a party (in contrast to the Pharisees and Sadducees), nor a small distinct social group (in contrast to the high priests). What the members of this profession did is not completely clear. They were authorities on the Pentateuch [the first five books of the Old Testament including the Torah], and probably on most of the rest of . . . the Old Testament (p. 30). They are portrayed in the New Testament, according to Smith, as hostile to Jesus because he transgressed the law (eating with sinners, etc.), pretended to supernatural powers, and practiced magic. Scribes are not to be compared to or contrasted with Pharisees. A Pharisee by religious party could be a scribe by profession as one who was literate, learned, and trained in the law. A scribe might be, but did not need to be, a rabbi. It has now become clear that our traditional view of the Pharisees has been skewed. Toward the end of the first century and the beginning of the second, the period during which the four Gospels and Acts are believed to have been written, the Pharisees, newly dominant over the Sadducees, were in vigorous conflict with the church. However, earlier in the first century, during the time of Jesus, there does not seem to have been significant animosity between the Pharisees and the Jews of the Jesus movement. Indeed, one could have been both. Maccoby asserts in both *Revolution in Judaea* (p. 98) and *The Mythmaker* (pp. 29–43) that Jesus was taught in the Pharisaic way, that Jesus himself taught as a Pharisee, and was a Pharisee. Without going this far Rudolf Bultmann, *Jesus and the Word*, trans. L. P. Smith and E. H. Lantero (New York: Charles Scribner's Sons, 1958), pp. 57–60, has detailed ways in which Jesus taught as a rabbi. In the process of helping to create the institution of the synagogue, a place for the study and teaching of the Torah, the Pharisees were the founders of congregationalism, their leaders not being hereditary priests but proven wise men, master teachers (i.e., rabbis) coming from any social stratum. Though not totally dismissive of the Temple and its national cult, the Pharisees were often opposed to the Sadducees and unwilling to pollute themselves through collaboration with the Roman occupation. In varying degrees, ranging from passive resistance to outright revolutionary activity, they were anti-Roman. Although sticklers for the Torah (both written and oral) and for purity in its observance, they were theologically liberal, even adventuresome in religious speculation. Like Jesus they believed in the resurrection of the dead unto reward or punishment and in angels and angelic activity on earth. In our day and time the identity of no Jewish religious group has occasioned more intense inquiry and rancorous dispute than the Essenes. We are fortunate in that as far as this work is concerned we do not need to know who they were and what they were up to. By way of tantalizing the reader, I recommend John M. Allegro, *The Dead Sea Scrolls and the Christian Myth* (Amherst, NY: Prometheus Books, 1984). See especially chap. 13, "Will the Real Jesus Christ Please Stand Up?" and Barbara Thiering, *Jesus and the Riddle of the Dead Sea Scrolls: Unlocking the Secrets of His Life Story* (San Francisco: HarperSanFrancisco, 1992), esp. chap. 2. The Zealots did not constitute a religious party but were rather Jews drawn from many quarters (but not from Sadducean ranks) who were not content to wait passively for the "God of Israel" to deliver his people from the heathen, and who were not content to engage merely in passive resistance, but who were intent on driving the Romans out of Palestine violently, if need be. Brandon, *Jesus and the Zealots* writes, "[T]he inclusion of Simon the Zealot in the Apostolic band actually points to the probability that Jesus was not a Zealot, and that his movement was not an integral part of the Zealot resistance against Rome. However, the presence of a Zealot among his disciples has also another significance: it means that Jesus deliberately chose a professed Zealot for an apostle which, in turn, indicates that the profession of Zealot principles and aims was not incompatible with intimate participation in the mission of Jesus" (p. 355). Respecting Herodians, one can do no better than to quote the first sentence of the appropriate entry in *HBD*, by M. S. and J. L. Miller (New York: Harper and Brothers, 1952), to wit: "Herod . . . [was] the name of a dynasty of princes who in various capacities ruled all or parts of Palestine and neighboring regions from c. 55 B.C. to A.D. 93." That the leading Herodians were at best only princes bears testimony to Roman permission and manipulation. The various ruling members of Herod's dynasty, their families, their courts, supporters, and hangers-on were collectively known as Herodians and were, on average, the most Hellenized of Jews or, better yet, of half-breed Jews. Herod Agrippa II (great-grandson of Herod the Great, who ruled from 37–4 B.C.E.) was the prince before whom Paul was brought (in Acts 25:12–26:32), if the A-h may be trusted. How many an itinerant tent-maker–evangelist would have been brought before royalty, we may well wonder? Could Paul have been well-to-do at this time and known to be so? As likely as not, in promoting the Christian cause, the A-h thought Paul ought to have been brought before royalty and thought he ought to have said what he is reported to have said. Although Judaism, the religion of a subset of Semitic peoples, was not and is not an evangelistic faith, it was and is possible for non-Jews to become Jews religiously, if not ethnically. In addition to instruction in the faith, this required the extirpation of one's previous life, ritual washings, and, in the case of men, circumcision, the last a deterrent to many. It is commonly believed that in New Testament times some Gentiles, attracted to Judaism but unwilling to be circumcised, entered into the category of God-fearers (see Acts 10:22). Richard Rubenstein, *My Brother Paul* (New York: Harper and Row, 1972), expresses no doubt as to their existence: "All authorities agree that there was a class of men known as *sebamenoi*, or 'God-fearers', attached to the synagogues of the Diaspora, who accepted Jewish monotheism and attempted to live in accordance with Jewish moral precepts, but who did not commit themselves to circumcision or full observance of Jewish law" (p. 70). Maccoby, *The Mythmaker*, agrees: "The 'God-fearers' were regarded, too, as having their own covenant with God, just as valid in its way as the Torah: namely, the covenant made with Noah (Genesis 9), which, in Pharisee exegesis, comprised a kind of Torah for the Gentiles, and was called the Seven Laws of the Sons of Noah [or the Noahide laws], Noah being regarded as the patriarchal ancestor of the Gentiles, just as Abraham was the patriarchal ancestor of the Jews" (p. 134). However, Alan F. Segal, *Paul the Convert: The Apostolate and Apostasy of Saul the Pharisee* (New Haven, CT: Yale University Press, 1990), believes the term to be ambiguous, referring to anything from "minimal financial support to preproselyte status" (p. 204). The spectrum of views on the God-fearers is completed by A. T. Kraabel "The Disappearance of the 'God-fearers,'" *Nu* 28 (1981): 113–26, who views this classification as Luke's invention, a device for showing how Christianity had progressively become a Gentile religion. John G. Gager, "Jesus, Gentiles, and Synagogues in the Book of Acts," *HTR* 79, nos. 1–3 (1986), agrees: "Luke uses the 'God-fearers' for his own theological purposes, specifically to justify his view that Gentiles have replaced Jews as the chosen people of God" (pp. 98–99). None of this would have surprised Bentham, who clearly regarded the A-h as a most dubious historian. The extent to which the theologian in the A-h overcame the historian in him is the extent to which we are justified in doubting or disbelieving what he wrote in Acts, whether of Paul or other Christians. When I was in seminary, preparing for the Protestant ministry, the so-called Judaizers were portrayed as blind guides at best and as villains at worst. They were presumably benighted Jewish-Christian conservatives hampering the enlightened, progressive Paul. A collective sigh of relief wafted its way from the classroom up to the heavens when it was pointed out that the misguided Judaizers had failed spectacularly in trying to prevent the onward, upward march of "true" Christianity, the kind we had inherited. There was no hint that the Judaizers were merely being true to Jesus, whereas Paul was as egregious a heretic in relation to original Christianity as he was an apostate to Jews. The precise identity of the Judaizers is never made clear in the New Testament. The term itself is not biblical but is a scholar's name for certain people who pursued Paul on the mission field, preaching a gospel different than his (Gal. 1:6–9) and trying to undo the damage they perceived him to be doing. Klausner, *From Jesus to Paul*, writes,

> The "Judaizers" did not recognize [Paul's] mystical teachings, which involved a negation of Judaism; they did not recognize baptism of Gentiles into Christianity without having first become Jews; they did not recognize the apostleship of Paul; and they did not recognize annulment of the ceremonial laws, particularly annulment of circumcision—that symbol of a holy covenant which God impressed in the flesh of the race of Israel and the flesh of those proselytes who joined themselves with Israel [by cutting off the end of their penises]. And when the "Judaizers," by way of compromise, though with great reluctance, agreed to exempt baptized Gentiles from circumcision and the rest of the ceremonial requirements (the "apostolic decree"), they did not intend by any means to exempt from these requirements baptized Jews and their children. (pp. 385–56)

Johannes Munck, *Paul and the Salvation of Mankind*, trans. Frank Clerk (Richmond, VA: John Knox Press, 1955), pp. 87–134, has argued at length that the Judaizers were not Nazarenes, as Klausner believes, but Gentile converts who, as is often the case with converts, became more zealous for Judaism than the average run of Jews. Anyone who has undergone circumcision as an adult in order to espouse Judaism only to be told by the like of Paul that it profits nothing (Gal. 6:15) can be expected to take umbrage at the notion that his pain was for nought. W. Smithals has even argued that the Judaizers were Jewish-Christian Gnostics (believers in salvation through esoteric knowledge), thus further complicating the picture (see Jack T. Sanders, "Paul's 'Autobiographical' Statements in Galatians 1–2," *JBL* 85, no. 3 [1966]: 340). Morton Smith, "Pauline Problems: Apropos of J. Munck, *Paulus und die Heilsgeschichte* (Paul and salvation history)," *HTR* 50, no. 1 (1957), concludes as follows, "In sum, the Pauline epistles and Acts agree in reporting a Judaizing movement of which there are traces in a number of the Pauline communities. This movement had connections with Jerusalem and was represented there by a group which was influential, though James, Peter, and John did not belong to it" (p. 120). Whoever they were, the Judaizers believed that before people could become Christians they had first to become Jews. See the following note to learn more of the Gentiles. Finally, the Grecians (or Hellenists) of Acts 6:1, 9:29, and 11:20 were most likely Greek-speaking Jews, originally from the Diaspora but living in Judea, who had been converted to the Nazarene movement. For more, see the following note.

33. Granted that there may be some hyperbole in the "murderous intentions of the Hellenists," Paul stood to gain by disputing them then and there. In fact it may have seemed to him to have been part of the price of admission he had to pay to enter the movement whose leadership he hoped to seize. The theory that lay behind his attack on the Hellenists, which may have been trumped up, is that the enemy of my enemy is my friend. The likelihood, as noted above, is that the Hellenists were Greek-speaking Jews (like Paul himself) who had come to Judea for various reasons from the Gentile world and had become Christians (*IDB*, s. v. "Hellenists"). Maccoby, *The Mythmaker*, p. 79, agrees but sees no reason why they were less loyal to the Torah than were the Hebrews, that is, the contemporary Jews, like Peter and James, who spoke Aramaic and who had become Christianized Jews. There is, however, the possibility that the A-h used the term 'Hellenist' to refer to "Greeks by race and upbringing" (i.e., to Gentiles) who had become Christians (see Price, *Interpreting the New Testament*, p. 137). Even if the former meaning is the correct one, there may still have been grounds for strife. Price goes on to say, "It is quite understandable that the 'Hebrews' in the Church should have viewed with alarm the growing minority of 'Hellenists'. . . . The Hellenists did not share the forms of piety so dear to the Pharisees of Judea and the priests of Jerusalem" (p. 138). The Hellenists may also have had legitimate grounds for dispute (see Acts 6:1). Thiering, in *Jesus and the Riddle*, p. 139, makes the dispute much more specific. She believes that the Hellenists were of two varieties; those in the peace (with Rome) movement (which included Paul) and those in the war movement, there being ample grounds for contention. Bentham, who was aware of the possible meanings of 'Hellenists' (or 'Grecians') but who did not appear to know of partisan differences over war with Rome, failed to focus on Paul's attack on the Hellenists in Acts 9:29. He would, however, have found nothing out of character here. Whether Paul picked a specious fight with the Hellenists on purpose or had legitimate, even long-standing, grounds for controversy, the side he took may have been carefully calculated to endear him, however slightly, to the Christian leadership. He was, after all, willing to become all things to all men to gain his ends (1 Cor. 9:22).

34. According to the RSV.

35. There is an element of irony here. Along with 'Nazarene', 'Ebionite' was one of the earliest terms used to name the original Jewish Christians. It comes from the

Hebrew *evyonim*, which means "poor men." When Paul expressed a desire to help the poor in Gal. 2:10 he did not use the term *evyonim*, but rather *ptochon*, 'beggars' in Greek. Since Gal. is written in Greek, Paul would have had no occasion to insert the Hebrew/Aramaic *evyonim* into his text, but it is of more than passing interest that the Ebionites believed Paul to be a false apostle. A show of financial assistance for them might well have been useful for him (see Maccoby, *The Mythmaker*, pp. 175–83, esp. 180). Thiering, *Jesus and the Riddle*, specifically identifies the poor in Gal. 2:10 and Rom. 15:26 with the Ebionites (pp. 45, 412–13, n. 14).

36. Grant, *Saint Paul*, pp. 16, 164, is dubious of the historicity of the Jerusalem Council, as are many other scholars.

37. In *Saint Paul*, Grant agrees with Bentham that Paul is to be preferred over the A-h whenever there is a disagreement over historical fact. This is a commonplace in New Testament scholarship. Richard I. Pervo, *Profit with Delight: The Literary Genre of the Acts of the Apostles* (Philadelphia: Fortress Press, 1987), writes, "For many the chief obstacle to viewing Acts as a work of history arises from its content rather than its style and form. After all excuses have been made for the presumed lack of ancient concern for strict truth, Acts is still lacking. More than a few of the incidents appear to have been invented, good sources were not used even if available, and the characterization of both people and events can often be shown to be either highly improbable or contrary to known facts" (p. 8). Donald T. Rowlingson, "The Jerusalem Conference and Jesus' Nazareth Visit," part 2, *JBL* 71 (June 1952), includes a list of differences between what Acts says of Paul and what Paul says of himself, in Galatians in particular. Rowlingson writes, "At several points it can be proved that Luke's version of Paul's career is inaccurate," and, "We should without hesitation prefer the total perspective of Paul in Galatians to that of Acts in seeking to understand Paul's movements and activities between the conversion and the [Jerusalem] conference visit" (p. 72). David B. Bronson, "Paul and Apocalyptic Judaism," *JBL* 83, no. 3 (1964), not only adverts to some of the distortions of truth in Acts but also gives reasons for these:

> And the greatest difference between Acts and the epistles is that Acts was written after the first Roman war [against Jews in Judea, 67–73]. Acts is pro-Roman, for people living in the shadow of the Jewish armed rebellion. . . . Acts, therefore, represents Paul as a Jerusalem man, not because he was one, but for the theological reason that salvation starts from Jerusalem. Paul is further represented as loyal to the traditions of his people to the point of being a collaborationist with the occupation authorities, a man . . . of unimpeachable political purity. The opposition to him is [depicted as] Jewish, and the Romans are represented as either neutral or favorable. This picture is, of course, motivated by an apologetic concern. . . . For Luke the vital choice was between a distinct and thorough pro-Romanism and a policy of sedition and insurrection." (pp. 290–91)

Edvin Larssen, "Paul: Law and Salvation," *NTS* 31, no. 3 (1985), provides the following list of differences between what Paul says of himself and Acts says:

The real Paul, the Paul of the letters, claims to be an apostle. In Acts he is depicted as subordinate to the Twelve, for whom the title apostle is reserved. In Galatians and Romans, Paul takes up a strongly polemical attitude to the Jewish Torah and to circumcision. The Paul of Acts circumcises Timothy (16:3). And he declares his solidarity with the law, the prophets and the people of Israel (23:6; 24:14 f.; 26:6, 23; 28:21). In his epistles Paul strongly emphasizes the significance of the death of Christ. He proclaims its atoning effect for all mankind (Rom. 3:24 ff.; I Cor. 1:18 ff.; 15:3; II Cor. 5:18 ff.; Gal. 3:13). The author of Acts seems to regard the suffering and death of Jesus, the servant of God, almost as a test, which he had to undergo before "entering upon his glory." (p. 425)

To the A-h's theological assumptions, apologetic interests, and intentions both to elevate Paul to equality with Peter and to harmonize the views of each must be added his penchant for routinely strewing signs, wonders, and miracles throughout his "history."

38. This journey, to be constructed from narratives scattered throughout Acts 13:1–14:26, took Paul from Antioch in Syria to Salamis and Paphos in Cyprus, thence to Pamphylia on the seacoast of what is now southern Turkey, to Pisidian Antioch in central Turkey, to Iconium and Derbe somewhat to the east, then a retracing of steps back to Pamphylia, and finally to Syrian Antioch.

39. This kind of problem exists to a large extent today in the spread of Mormonism, a homegrown American religion founded by white people of northern European extraction. It is now becoming a world religion with about eleven million members, approximately half of whom live outside the United States and many of whom are people of color (Gustav Niebuhr, "A Ceremony in Mexico City Shows Growth in Mormonism," NYT, December 11, 1994). From rural roots, it has become urban. Its exclusively male leadership is being challenged by women (Dirk Johnson, "Growing Mormon Church Faces Dissent by Women and Scholars," NYT, October 2, 1993). Earlier its exclusively white leadership was successfully challenged by blacks, but only at a low level. Robert Lindsey, writing in NYTM, January 12, 1986, pp. 19 ff., says, "On June 9, 1978, president of the Mormon Church Spencer Kimball said God had revealed to him that black males, formerly excluded because they carried 'the curse of Cain' should be given full status in the Church." To be more specific, they could henceforth hold the priesthood as this is understood in the Mormon Church.

40. Among my prized possessions is a cartoon showing a bearded man standing on a mountain top. He wears a long robe and holds a crude staff, or perhaps a shepherd's crook, that has seen better days. His eyes look to the heavens, under perplexed brows, and he says, "Now let's get this straight—you want us to cut the ends of our dicks off?" (Although the cartoonist's first name is illegible, to me at least, his last name seems to be Dole). The source of the cartoon is unknown to me. This cartoon is the perfect foil to the theological mystification behind this form of sexual mutilation and should be called to mind hereafter, whenever Paul belabors the topic, making it seem to be of extreme significance, even though he claims that for the non-Jewish Christian it has no significance at all.

41. Unless otherwise indicated, 'law' in this part will be taken to mean the Mosaic law (i.e., the Torah), that set of 613 directives, some positive and some negative, that constitute the traditional, distinctive Jewish way of life. These are commonly divided into two types, the moral and the ceremonial. The moral law is typified by the Decalogue (the Ten Commandments). Here two points must be remembered: First, some of these commandments are not exclusively moral, if at all, but rather are theological. For example, "Thou shalt not make for yourself a graven image" (Exod. 20:15) is not moral in the sense in which "Thou shalt not steal" (Exod. 20:15) is moral. Second, there are numerous directives in the Torah that are moral but that are not in the Decalogue. For example, "If there be among you a poor man of one of thy brethren . . . thou shalt not harden thine heart, nor shut thine hand from thy poor brother" (Deut. 15:7) is moral but not one of the Ten Commandments. Perhaps the most famous of the ceremonial laws is expressed as follows: "Every man child among you shall be circumcised" (Gen. 17:10), and "[T]he uncircumcised man child whose flesh of his foreskin is not circumcised, that soul shall be cut off from his people" (Gen. 17:14). Circumcision proved to be one of the most contentious issues between Paul on the one hand and orthodox Jewish Christians of the Mother Church in Jerusalem plus the so-called Judaizers on the other. Another important law of the ceremonial sort is found in Lev. 17:10: "And whatsoever man *there be* of the house of Israel or of the strangers that sojourn among you, that eateth any manner of blood; I will even set my face against that soul that eateth blood, and will cut him off from among his people." Other examples of ceremonial law follow: "Thou shalt not plow with an ox and with an ass together" (Deut. 22:10); "Thou shalt not wear a garment of diverse sorts" (Deut. 22:11), of, for example, wool and linen, as idolatrous priests were believed to do; "Six days shall work be done: but the seventh day is the sabbath of rest, an holy convocation ye shall do no work therein: it is the sabbath of the Lord in all your dwellings" (Lev. 23:3); "Ye shall not offer unto the Lord [in sacrifice] that which is bruised, or crushed, or broken, or cut" (Lev. 22:24); "Thou shalt not seethe a kid in his mother's milk" (Exod. 23:19b); "Ye shall kindle no fire throughout your habitations upon the sabbath day" (Exod. 35:3); "Ye shall eat nothing leavened; in all your habitations shall ye eat unleavened bread" (Exod. 12:20); "And the flesh that toucheth any [ritually unclean or tabooed] *thing* shall not be eaten; it shall be burnt with fire" (Lev. 7:19); "All the firstling males that come of thy flock thou shalt sanctify unto the Lord thy God: thou shalt do no work with the firstling of thy bullock, nor shear the firstling of thy sheep" (Deut. 15:19); "Thou shalt not offer the blood of my sacrifice with leaven; neither shall the sacrifice of the feast of the Passover be left unto the morning" (Exod. 34:25); and "If a man find a damsel *that is* a virgin, which is not betrothed, and lay hold on her, and lie with her, and they be found; Then the man that lay with her shall give unto the damsel's father fifty *shekels* of silver, and she shall be his wife; because he hath humbled her, he may not put her away all her days" (Deut. 22:28–29). The few injunctions above are but the tip of the tip of an enormous iceberg, theological, moral, cultic, agricultural, commercial, marital, military, etc., and various combinations thereof. Readers interested in the law and its interpretation should seek out and spend some time with the Talmud or the Code of Maimonides, the latter being more readily accessible, to the first-time reader at least.

42. The pollution of idols refers to meat offered to idols. Such meat was viewed as ritually unclean and was not to be eaten by an observant Jew. Also the flesh of an animal was taken to be ritually impure if the animal in question had been put to death by strangling. Such meat would retain the animal's blood in it, and such blood was to be avoided. (As though kosher meat were free of all blood!) To this odd mixture of food laws, sexual impurity was added as something to be avoided by Christians, Jewish or Gentile. If such food taboos were observed, Christians of all kinds could, presumably, sit at table together and partake of common meals. For more on this topic see J. Brunt, "Rejected, Ignored, or Misunderstood? The Fate of Paul's Approach to the Problem of Food Offered to Idols in Early Christianity," *NTS* 31, no. 1 (1985): 113–24.

43. Maccoby, himself a Talmudic scholar, writes in *The Mythmaker*, "1. Certain foods (more precisely, certain forms of meat and fish) were forbidden to Jews by the Bible (which, however, does not forbid these foods to non-Jews). 2. It was forbidden to Jews to eat any food from which an offering or libation had been made to an idol; at pagan meals, such offerings were usually made. 3. *At certain times*, it was necessary for an observant Jew to be in a state of ritual purity, and this was possible only if he shared his meal with others observing ritual purity" (p. 134).

44. Paul's second missionary journey, which can be traced in Acts 15:40–18:22, took him from Antioch north to Tarsus, then west through what is now central Turkey to Troas, then across the Aegean Sea to Macedonia, thence to Athens and Corinth, back to Asia to Ephesus and Cnidus, then by ship to Caesarea, and back to Antioch. His third missionary journey (Acts 18:23–21:17 ff.) largely retraced the steps of his second journey.

45. Orthodox Jewish Christians did not give up in their struggle with Paul. They or their emissaries almost certainly pursued him to some places in the Gentile mission field and sought to undo his perversions of Jewish Christianity. In 2 Cor. 11:4 (as in Gal. 1:6) Paul shows angry awareness of people who are preaching a different Jesus than he. In 2 Cor. 11:5, he announces that he is not in the least inferior to these highest or chiefest apostles. Since he was *the* apostle to the Gentiles, who could these chiefest apostles be but James, Peter, John, or their emissaries? He announces (v. 12) that he will undercut their efforts, for they are false apostles and perfidious workmen (v. 15). All it took to be so vile was to disagree with him. Then he prophesies threateningly that their end will correspond to their deeds (v. 15). Continuing in this manner he boasts that he is as much a Hebrew as they, as much an Israelite, as much a descendent of Abraham (v. 22). The difference is that, by his own admission, he is a *better* servant of Jesus than they (v. 23). In his megalomania he has all but said: I am better than James, the Lord's brother; I am better than Peter; I am better than John; I am better than the whole lot of them. He then points to his more assiduous labors and more grievous sufferings (vv. 23–27) as though working indefatigably makes one doctrinally pure and as though being beaten up repeatedly certifies the truth of idiosyncratic doctrines. Also see 2 Cor. 12:11–12, wherein he reiterates what a splendid apostle he is. In Gal. 1:8 he reaches the epitome of fanaticism in condemning himself in advance should he ever change his mind and thereafter preach a gospel contrary to the one he had been preaching. Naturally he lays the same curse on others (even on angels from heaven) who might preach a different Jesus than the one he had preached.

46. It was a commonplace for Jews to engage in a variety of washings to remove ritual impurities, and it was required of Gentile converts to Judaism to do likewise (see Maccoby, *The Mythmaker*, pp. 125–26). Then came John the Baptist upon the scene with a baptism of repentance (Matt. 3:2), a baptism to which Jesus submitted (vv. 15–16). In view of such a tradition of washings, it is not surprising that, after Jesus' death an apostle such as Peter should preach repentance and command baptism in the name of Jesus Christ (Acts 2:38). After repentance and baptism, the Jews who had believed Peter were, according to the A-h, supposed to receive the Holy Spirit, whatever this means. The Holy Spirit at issue is hard to comprehend. Sometimes it fell on people; other times it was poured upon them, resulting in glossolalia, or speaking in tongues (Acts 10:44–45). The order of its appearance varied. For example, on one occasion some Samaritans had been baptized in the name of the Lord Jesus but had not been favored with the Holy Spirit (Acts 8:16) and did not receive it until Peter and John laid their hands on the baptized Samaritans, still lacking the Spirit (v. 17). How this magic (to all appearances) worked is never made clear. On another occasion (Acts 10:47), the Holy Spirit arrived before baptism, no hands being needed. On yet another occasion Paul came upon some disciples of Jesus who had not even been baptized with Christian baptism (which was supposed to convey the Holy Spirit, Acts 11:16) but only with the baptism of John the Baptist, a baptism of water and repentance. Paul saw to their proper baptism and then laid his hands on them, acting as a conduit for the Holy Spirit, it would seem, after which the new Christians spoke in tongues and prophesied (Acts 19:2–6). It seems unlikely that Pharisaic Jews in Judea, upon accepting Jesus as their Messiah, would have spoken (or would have needed to speak) in tongues, interpreted speaking in tongues, or needed to work miracles (including healings), yet Paul takes these phenomena for granted (1 Cor. 12:29–31). In short, he was prepared to march on Jerusalem backed not only by what may have been larger numbers of converts and (much?) more money than the Jerusalem church could put up but also by fervor and phenomena it could not match Paul probably believed, and certainly wanted others to believe, that he could convey the Holy Spirit with greater dependability and force than could the like of James, Peter, and John.

47. Gerd Lüdemann, *Opposition to Paul in Jewish Christianity*, trans. M. Eugene Boring (Minneapolis: Fortress Press, 1989), pp. 59–62, also notices the failure of Acts to assert that the collection was delivered and received. However, he thinks that the reason for this is that the leadership of the Jerusalem church rejected it, thus showing hostility to Paul and a breakdown in relations between Paul's Gentile churches and the Jerusalem church. For a variety of views on the collection see the extensive footnotes, pp. 106–17 and 249–51. In effect, Bentham has picked up considerable support for his belief that the money was never delivered but not for the reason he gave. His reason, however, remains a viable possibility.

48. In Acts 21:10–14, a certain prophet named Agabus came from Judea to Caesarea, where Paul had gone from Tyre by the way of Ptolemais. This prophet announced a revelation of the Holy Spirit, to wit: the Jews of Jerusalem would bind Paul and deliver him into the hands of the Gentiles. This, in fact, is just the opposite of what happened, if the A-h can be believed. So, in addition to speaking "backward and forward," as Bentham put it, as the occasion arose, the Holy Spirit could reveal a falsehood without apparent strain.

49. Brandon, *Jesus and the Zealots*, says,

> Concerning the outlook of James, the testimony of Paul and Acts seem in accord. He was rigorous in maintaining strict observance of the Torah among Jewish Christians. If the later traditions, preserved by Hegesippus [a second-century Church Father who wrote a history of Christianity], are to be trusted, he enjoyed a high reputation among the Jews generally for his exceeding devotion to the practice of Judaism, a reputation that may possibly be confirmed by Josephus. . . . In his dealings with Paul, during his visit to Jerusalem, he appears to have been very astute. Paul's presence in the city was obviously an embarrassment to James. (p.167)

Brandon, *The Fall of Jerusalem and the Christian Church* (London: S. P. C. K., 1951), comments at length on this astuteness:

> [James] proposed the test which was designed to put Paul in a fatal dilemma. If he refused to give this proof of his orthodoxy [carrying out a prescribed Temple ritual], then he was in effect declaring himself an apostate from Judaism and thus would merit excommunication. On the other hand, he had come to Jerusalem, with a delegation of converts, as the champion of Gentile's right to full participation in the new faith; if, therefore, he submitted to the order of James and provided evidence of his orthodoxy, his position in the eyes of his Gentile followers would be gravely compromised, for they would know that he, their champion, recognized his subordination to the Jerusalem authorities and proclaimed his adherence . . . by the performance of an obscure Jewish ritual act. (pp. 150–51)

See also Samuel G. F. Brandon, "The Death of James: A New Interpretation," in *Studies in Mysticism and Religion* (Jerusalem: Magnes Press, 1967), p. 60.

50. After his exaggerated claim that his gospel was not man's gospel and that those of repute (i.e., the apostles of Jerusalem) added nothing to him (Gal. 2:6), it might seem odd to some, not to say contradictory, that in 1 Cor. 15:3–8, he detailed what he had received of Christian doctrine (the so-called kerygma) from others, to all appearances, and not from Jesus by direct, personal revelation.

51. A Nazirite (or Nazarite) is one who is consecrated or set apart, to some extent at least, from ordinary life and occupations. As a sign thereof, such a person lets his hair grow (except for subsequent ritual cuttings) and avoids strong drink. In early times the Nazirite was taken to be a sacred person (see esp. Num. 6:2, 6–8, 12; Judg. 13:5, 7; 16:17), but by New Testament times one could take Nazirite vows for limited periods without assuming a lifelong status (see *IDB*, s. v. "Nazirite"). Despite the syntactical ambiguity of Acts 18:18 (not letting the reader know for sure to whom "his" refers), it would appear that near the end of his second missionary journey, Paul cut his hair due to a (Nazirite?) vow. Such a vow, according to Bentham, would by nature have been a promissory oath. How curious it is that Paul did not seem aware of Jesus' express command not to swear any oaths (Matt. 5:34).

James 5:12 repeats the same command. Could there have been a slip-up in personal revelation from Jesus to Paul on this point? However unsettling this thought may be, Paul still had to undertake a concluding ritual he had vowed to perform, provided that Acts 18:18 is historical. If Paul's vow was Nazirite, he had to complete the purification process by going to the Temple in Jerusalem with his *Asham-Nazir*, his Nazirite guilt offering (Klausner, *From Jesus to Paul*, p. 398; see also Segal, *Paul the Convert*, pp. 238, 346, nn. 20, 23). Maccoby, *The Mythmaker*, thinks that Paul did not take a Nazirite vow but merely had to go to the Temple for the usual purification of "one arriving in the Holy Land from abroad" (p. 219, n. 3 to chapter 13). To have paid to assist others in fulfilling their vows would have shown extra piety as well as charity. Such acts of piety, purity, and charity might have negated, or at least blunted, the charges leveled against Paul, but they did not. Perhaps James knew that this ploy would fail, and he had in reality been trying all along to make Paul play the hypocrite. If so, James succeeded admirably.

52. Klausner, *From Jesus to Paul*, says, "The best face one can put on Paul's perjury is to call it accommodationistic, the worst to call it egregious hypocrisy" (p. 399). Peter Richardson, "Pauline Inconsistency: I Corinthians 9:19–23 and Galatians 2:11–14," *NTS* 26, no. 3 (1980), writes, "The issue, then, is this: if Paul views accommodation as a legitimate principle for himself, and if Peter in Antioch has already shown some measure of adaptability as well [see esp. Gal. 2:11–12], why does Paul reject so vehemently Peter's understanding of the need to adapt yet once more when some come from James [who opposed Peter's eating with Gentiles]? A similar hypothetical question could be posed: what would Paul have done had a group of Gentile Christians from Galatia visited the Jerusalem church at the very time he was undertaking the Nazirite vow? . . . Peter's action should not be viewed as hypocrisy but as an attempt (obviously unacceptable to Paul) to engage in a similar kind of accommodation to that which Paul espouses" (p. 348). Apropos the same point, Sanders, "Paul's 'Autobiographical' Statements," writes, "One should recall at this point how insistent the 'Apostle to the Gentiles' can be that he is an Israelite, when it is necessary to be an Israelite in order to be an Apostle" (p. 343). By the same token, he was free of the Mosaic law whenever it suited him. In this light the accommodationism so famously expressed in 1 Cor. 9:20–21 is outright hypocrisy.

53. Maccoby, *The Mythmaker*, p. 157.

54. Ibid., p. 161. Here he questions Paul's claim that he had Roman citizenship by birth. First, in 2 Cor. 11:25, Paul says he was beaten thrice with rods, "i.e., by Roman lictors" or officials. Why, one wonders, did he not claim Roman citizenship before these beatings as he did in Acts 22:25? Second, Paul never mentions Roman citizenship in his letters, something he might have been expected to do. Third, he was probably in possession of considerable money, into which he could easily dip, due to the contribution he had for the Jerusalem church. So he may have bought Roman citizenship shortly before arriving in Jerusalem. Maccoby writes, "It is likely that he held back a considerable sum, in addition to the money he spent on purchasing Roman citizenship, in case it was needed to fund his own church" (p. 162). If any of this is true, it would confirm Bentham's belief that the contribution never reached the right hands. In passing, it might also be remembered that Acts 20:16b says that Paul was hastening to Jerusalem so that he might arrive in time for Pente-

cost, the traditional birthdate of the Nazarene movement. What better time, what more fitting day of the year than Pentecost for him to convert the Jerusalem church to his doctrine or for him to found his own church in spite of James et al.! With either option, money would have been a great asset. Not even as important a scholar as Haenchen in *Acts of the Apostles*, p. 588, recognizes that Paul may have had an ulterior purpose in arriving in Jerusalem on Pentecost, but rather attributes his desire to be there by that date to Paul's having been a "pious Jew." Was Paul still a pious Jew at the time in question? Although Haenchen notes that the A-h drops the Pentecost theme at once, he fails to observe that the A-h also drops the theme of the collection of money, leaving us in doubt as to whether or not it ever reached the hands for whom it was ostensibly intended.

55. It may come as a shock to the average Christian and even to the average unbeliever that there is substantial evidence that Jesus was seditious in relation to Rome. Brandon, *Jesus and the Zealots*, writes, "Ironic though it be, the most certain thing known of Jesus of Nazareth is that he was crucified by the Romans as a rebel against their government in Judea. . . . That the founder of their faith had been put to death on a charge of sedition could hardly have been invented by Christians. . . . The early Christians had . . . a strong motive for suppressing so embarrassing a fact" (p. 1). Later he continues, "The Romans could have executed Jesus on one or more of a number of other charges; but the fact that all four Evangelists agree that he was condemned for *sedition*, and that the *titulus* on his cross reading 'The King of the Jews' must be accepted as authentic" (p. 328; emphasis added). At this point in his text Brandon cites Robert Eisler, *The Messiah Jesus and John the Baptist*, trans. A. H. Krappe (London: Methuen, 1931). Eisler was a pioneer in approaching original Christianity as a political movement against Rome as well as a religious movement. See also Brandon, *The Fall of Jerusalem*, esp. pp. 114–19. In *The Mythmaker*, Maccoby writes, "As far as Jews in general were concerned, the Jesus movement was a resistance movement against the Romans, pious and extremist" (p. 157). Furthermore, "When Paul declared himself a Roman citizen, this was the end of his uneasy association with the 'Jerusalem Church.' The announcement would have come to James and the other Jerusalem leaders as a great shock. The Jesus movement was an anti-Roman movement" (p. 163). Archibald Robertson, *The Origin of Christianity*, rev. ed. (New York: International Publishers, 1962), writes, "If we consider that in all the Gospels Jesus rides into Jerusalem as messianic king a few days before his death, that in three of the four he is welcomed with the seditious cry of *Hosanna* —'Deliver us!'—we can infer for ourselves the events which the original narrative related and which the Gospels suppressed" (p. 87). Later, he continues, "The earliest strata of the Gospels . . . point both to a revolutionary movement led first by John the Baptist and then by Jesus the Nazoraean, and aimed at the overthrow of Roman and Herodian rule in Palestine and the establishment of an earthly 'kingdom of God'" (p. 93). Hugh J. Schonfield, *Those Incredible Christians* (New York: Bantam Books, 1969), writes, "It would be underestimating the security consciousness of the Romans to imagine that they thought of the Christian movement as either negligible or harmless. . . . There is ample evidence in Christian, Roman, and Jewish sources that the emphatic messianism that gave Christianity its name was very quickly recognized as politically pernicious and that measures were taken to cope

with it" (pp. 104–105). Maccoby, *Revolution in Judaea,* writes, "If we fix our attention on the *facts* of Jesus's life and death (as opposed to the interpretation of the facts added by the Gospels) we shall see that Jesus was a Jewish Resistance leader of a type not unique in this period" (p. 94). Maccoby, pp. 126–30, interprets the confusing event in Jesus' life called the Transfiguration (Matt. 17:1–8, Mark 9:2–8, Luke 9:28–36) as a "spiritualized" (i.e., fictionalized) account of Jesus' actual coronation as King of the Jews. The list of citations above, taken from Jewish and non-Jewish scholars, is not meant to be exhaustive; it is merely meant to show the reader who is unfamiliar with New Testament scholarship that a sizable body of reputable scholarship believes that Jesus' original disciples were messianic, Pharisaic Jews looking for deliverance in this world, not in a heaven somewhere in the skies, from Roman domination. Two verses from the New Testament can be quoted along these lines with telling effect: "Think not that I am come to send peace on earth: I came not to send peace, but a sword" (Matt. 10:34); "I am come to send fire on the earth; and what will I, if it be already kindled?" (Luke 12:49) The RSV puts the last half as, "Would that it were already kindled."

56. The Romans, who are pictured as blameless in Paul's case, would, however, have been most interested in getting to the bottom of any claims that the King of the Jews, whom they had executed, was still alive. It is conceivable that the Nazarenes, who believed in Jesus' resurrection and in his speedy return to assume royal prerogatives, might have preferred to remain silent about this when in company with Romans. In light of this, Paul may have been perceived by them to be altogether too outspoken on the matter for comfort. The Sadducees not only rejected the idea of the resurrection of the dead in general but would also have been disturbed by the idea of a resurrected king of Israel in particular for the same political reasons that would have disturbed the Romans.

57. Knowing Greek well, Bentham made his own translations from the New Testament when it pleased him. These are much like the KJV translation but are not identical. In the many verses designed to show that the charges against Paul were true, he used the KJV, in some versions of which, various words in the text appear in italics. Bentham italicized at will for emphasis, not following the King James in all respects. He appended footnotes to three of the biblical passages cited. Of Rom. 10:9 he wrote, "A cheap enough rate this, at which salvation is thus put up. Of what use then morality? Of what use abstinence from mischievous acts, in what degree so ever mischievous? 'Oh! but,' says somebody, 'though Paul said this, he meant no such thing': and then comes something—which it may suit the defenders' purpose to make Paul say." The emperor Constantine is famous, or perhaps infamous would be better, for delaying conversion to Christianity and baptism until he was on his deathbed. In this manner, believing Paul, he could sin safely throughout his entire life until he had no strength to sin further and could then submit to baptism at the last minute, being sure to have all his sins washed away for such a trifle as faith. See *NCE,* s. v. "Constantine." Respecting Rom. 9:12, Bentham wrote, "Another receipt for making salvation still cheaper than as above. Not so Jesus, Matt. 7:21, '*Not every one that saith unto me, Lord, Lord, shall enter into the kingdom of heaven*; but he that doeth the will of my Father which is in heaven.'" Here we have what would appear to be another breakdown in revelation between the Lord Jesus and the (self-appointed)

apostle to the Gentiles. The third note was appended to Rom. 14:5: "Behold the degree of importance attached by Paul to Sabbaths." This amounted to making no distinction between the holy day to be kept sacred in the Mosaic law (Exod. 20:8) and ordinary work days. It is all very well to elevate every day to the level of the sacred, but to pretend that this is not a departure from Jewish law is deceitful.

58. I corrected a mistake in the quotation. The original refers to Luke 25:9, 28, 29, 30, but there is no twenty-fifth chapter in Luke. The reference ought to have been to 24:9, 28, 29, 30. Bentham turns to the Gospel of Luke because it contains the most textual material alleging Jesus' post-Resurrection appearances. In some ancient manuscripts of Mark (ending with 16:8) no appearances are asserted. In other versions in which verses 9–20 are added, Jesus appears to Mary Magdalene (v. 9), then to two unidentified people (v. 12), and finally to the remaining eleven original disciples (v. 14), at most fourteen people. In Matthew, Mary Magdalene and another Mary (28:1) are encountered by Jesus (v. 9). Later his eleven disciples are said to have seen him (v. 17), in all, thirteen people. In John Mary Magdalene sees Jesus after his death not knowing that it is he (20:14), then Jesus appears on three occasions to his original disciples (vv. 19, 24, and 26). Also see 21:1, 14. In Acts, assumed by most contemporary scholars to have been written by the author of Luke, Jesus is portrayed as being with his chosen ones for forty days off and on but is not said to have been seen by others individually or by any group.

59. 'Kerygma' has come to be understood in New Testament scholarship as the kernel, or essence, of the original Christian proclamation of beliefs about (or faith in) Jesus. Using it as the baseline, subsequent developments in theology can be identified and the degree of development measured. See Henry Cadbury, "Acts and Eschatology," in *The Background of the New Testament and Its Eschatology*, ed. W. D. Davies and D. Daube (Cambridge: Cambridge University Press, 1956), pp. 313–14.

60. Paul makes it seem (in 1 Cor. 15:5) that the risen Jesus appeared to Peter first, then to the twelve. In the Gospels, however, he appears to Mary Magdalene first, then to some unidentified persons, then to the eleven, Peter not being singled out for first or primary contact with Jesus at all. Also, Paul has Jesus appearing to the twelve (v. 5), not knowing, it would seem, the fate of Judas Iscariot, who dies in two different ways in the New Testament (see Matt. 27:5 versus Acts 1:18). Then come the five hundred–plus brethren who see Jesus, then James, and then the apostles. James, by the way, is never mentioned in the Gospels and in Acts as having seen the resurrected Jesus. Last, but by no means least, Paul gets to see the Lord. It does not take much insight to recognize that Paul has put himself on a par with Peter and James in this way. He then proceeds to boast about how he has worked harder for the Lord than the others (v. 10).

61. Immediately following 1 Cor. 15:3–11 (wherein appears the kerygma, the alleged appearances of the resurrected Jesus, and a bit of modest Pauline boasting), Paul says (v. 12), "Now if Christ be preached that he rose from the dead, how say some among you that there is no resurrection of the dead?" Of this Bentham wrote in a footnote, "Follows a sample of Paul's logic wrapped up as usual in a cloud of tautologies and paralogisms, the substance of which amounts to this:—Jesus resurrects; therefore all men will do the same. Admitting the legitimacy of this induction, what will be the thing proved? That every man, a few days after his death, will come to life again, and eat, and walk in company with his friends."

62. Bentham seldom missed an opportunity to compare Paul unfavorably with Jesus. Respecting expectations of the end of the (then) present world order, if not the whole world itself, he overstepped himself in criticism, for if we may believe the so-called synoptic Gospels (i.e., Matthew, Mark, and Luke) Jesus also expected a sudden, dramatic alteration in human affairs. *Eschaton* in Greek means (in respect to time) 'the last' or 'that which ends something'; accordingly eschatology means the doctrine of last things or of the end time. There is now no doubt that the synoptics were written in an eschatological framework. If Bentham had read the Gospels as closely as he had read Acts and certain of Paul's letters, he would have seen this for himself (see Matt. 24:2–51, Mark 13:2–37, and Luke 21:5–33). Whatever Jesus may have thought about his Messiahship (as distinct from what the Gospel writers thought forty to sixty years later), the earliest Jewish community of his disciples apparently expected the "almost immediate return of Christ [the Messiah] to end the present evil age and usher in the Kingdom of God" (Donald J. Selby, *Introduction to the New Testament: The Word Became Flesh* [New York: Macmillan, 1971], p. 31; also see p. 33). For the extreme Jewishness of this expectation see Ernest Lohmeyer, *The Lord of the Temple*, trans. Stewart Todd (Richmond, VA: John Knox Press, 1962), esp. pp. 111 ff. This is not to say that Paul's eschatology was identical to that of Jesus, to that of the earliest disciples, or to that of the synoptics (see Enslin, *Christian Beginnings*, pp. 241–44). What it does say is that Bentham should not have singled Paul out for special opprobrium for entertaining eschatological delusions. It goes without saying, of course, that whatever Paul believed was as good as demonstrated in his "disordered brain," as Bentham put it, and was to be taken as fact by his credulous converts. He was a classic hypocrite, telling others to test all things (1 Thess. 5:21) but never doing so himself in any methodologically respectable way.

63. Ronald Russell, "The Idle in 2 Thess. 3.6–12: An Eschatological or a Social Problem?" *NTS* 34, no. 1 (1988), thinks the Greek term in 1 Thess. 5:14 and in 2 Thess. 3:6, 7, 11 that is normally translated as 'to be idle' or 'to be a loafer' is better translated as 'to be disorderly', "because it refers to what contravenes nature, the gods or reason" (pp. 107–108). If so, what we may see here is the old bugaboo, antinomianism, all over again. If Christians are set free from the law in Christ, and if the Lord Jesus is about to return at any moment bringing a new kingdom, delivered from the law, with him, why not live it up now, so to speak? The disorderly in Russell's preferred translation may, then, have been in part at least the excessively indulgent as well as the shiftless.

64. Whenever the corpus of Paul's letters comes up, questions arise as to how many he actually wrote, how many other people wrote feigning his authorship, and which is which. The four-letter hypothesis maintains that Galatians, 1 and 2 Corinthians, and Romans are the only authentic letters Paul wrote. The seven-letter hypothesis accepts these four and adds 1 and 2 Thessalonians as well as Philippians. Although Bentham gave no sign of knowing anything about this, the overwhelming majority of scriptural citations in *NPBJ* come from what are now taken to be the best authenticated of Paul's epistles. Citations from 1 and 2 Thessalonians constitute the principle exception to this. Of these two letters, 2 Thessalonians is most in doubt at present. This is due to an obvious change in content in two letters that seem other-

wise to have much in common and to have been written over a short span of time. Eminent scholars are arrayed on both sides of this dispute. For example, Klausner, *From Jesus to Paul*, writes, "Paul was a man of unusual temperament—intense and emotional and acrid. It is inevitable that a man like this, in a time of excitement, in anger, or in a flight of imagination, should experience changes of opinion that would flash into his mind in a moment of intense thought" (p. 238). However, Segal, *Paul the Convert*, p. 164, says flatly that 2 Thessalonians was probably not written by Paul. In this vein, Karl P. Donfried and I. Howard Marshall, *The Theology of the Shorter Pauline Letters* (Cambridge: Cambridge University Press, 1993), write, "Our understanding is that 2 Thessalonians is non-Pauline in the technical sense but that it *is* related to a concrete situation in Thessalonia" (p. 86). James M. Reese, preface to *1 and 2 Thessalonians* (Dublin: Veritas, 1979) counters, "Those who argue for its non-Pauline origin have not provided a satisfactory motive for its existence." David L. Mealand, reporting on conclusions derived from a sophisticated stylo-metric analysis, in his "Positional Stylometry Reassessed: Testing a Seven-Epistle Theory of Pauline Authorship," *NTS* 35, no. 2 (1989), concludes that the seven-epistle hypothesis "comes out almost as successfully as a four-epistle theory from the first set of tests, and rather better than a four-epistle theory on the second set of tests" (p. 285). Stylistically, then, 2 Thessalonians cannot be ruled out as non- (or deutero-) Pauline. Bentham's acceptance of 2 Thessalonians as Paul's and his treat-ment of the two Thessalonian letters cannot be dismissed out of hand simply as uninformed; scholarly opinion is still too divided to settle the issue.

65. Paul never used 'Antichrist' in any of his extant writings to name the man of sin, the son of perdition, or the lawless one. To find this term in the New Testa-ment, one must turn to 1 John 2:18–22, 4:3; and 2 John 1:7. At a later time in church history, 'Antichrist' came to be used of whatever John was presumed to have had in mind and of whatever Paul was alluding to with the terms above. Ernest Best, perhaps the leading authority in English on 2 Thessalonians, devotes more than twenty pages to a word-by-word, case-by-case, tense-by-tense examination of the contents of 2 Thess. 2:1–9. The apostasy (v. 3) cannot be identified, the man of sin (or of lawlessness) and the son of perdition (v. 3) cannot be identified, the temple in which he is to take his seat may have been the Temple in Jerusalem or an even more glorious one in the heavens (v. 4). The restraining power (v. 7) that prevents him from revealing himself cannot be identified. Even the term *katechon*, usually translated as 'restraining', may be a mistranslation. See Ernest Best, *A Commentary on the First and Second Epistles to the Thessalonians* (New York: Harper and Row, 1972), pp. 280–306. There is also a considerable puzzle among New Testament scholars as to why the return of Jesus was pictured as imminent in 1 Thessalonians but is pictured as delayed indefinitely in 2 Thessalonians. If the two letters were written by Paul and at about the same time, this shift in eschatological viewpoint concerning the coming (the *parousia*) of Jesus is dramatic. Bentham of course sup-plied an answer, if not *the* answer, but one that was not (and would not now be) very palatable to most New Testament scholars and one that, as far as I can ascer-tain, they have not considered. It is hard for them to think that our saint could have contrived a convenient deceit to save his prophecy to the Thessalonians concerning the speedy return of Jesus. I shall return to this topic later when defending *NPBJ*

against its critics. In any case, if Paul's readers knew what he was writing about, eschatologically speaking, in 1 Thessalonians, then he wrote about it falsely. If, on the other hand, he wrote in 2 Thessalonians to obfuscate, and thus to spare himself the embarrassment of being proved wrong by events and of being made to answer for it, he succeeded admirably.

66. There is a similar failure of Pauline prophecy in 1 Cor. 7:25–31:

> Now concerning virgins I have no commandment of the Lord: yet I give my judgment as one that hath obtained mercy of the Lord to be faithful [in other words, God might as well have told him what to say]. I suppose therefore that this is good for the present distress [the time just before the *eschaton*, the end of the present world order] I say, *that it is* good for a man so to be. Art thou bound unto a wife? seek not to be loosed. Art thou loosed from a wife? seek not a wife. But and if thou marry, thou hast not sinned; and if a virgin marry, she hath not sinned. Nevertheless such shall have trouble in the flesh [i.e., worldly trouble]: but I spare you. But this I say, brethren, the time *is* short: it remaineth, that both they that have wives be as though they had none; And they that weep, as though they wept not; and they that rejoice, as though they rejoiced not; and they that buy, as though they possessed not; And they that use this world, as though not abusing it: for the fashion [form or mode] of this world passeth away [with the return of Jesus from heaven].

To make short work of the point, Paul was advising his married converts no longer to copulate with their duly married spouses. To be overtaken in erotic activity by the return of the Lord was clearly something to be avoided. It is unfortunate that Paul never tells us exactly why this would have been so disadvantageous. Any considerable delay in the Lord's return (necessitating celibacy in marriage) to end the age of evil in which people were then living would, no doubt, have led to sexual restiveness on the part of married Christians. By the same token any such delay might have increased idleness (and who knows what else) among Paul's converts. Worse still, any delay in the Lord's return put his prediction in peril and jeopardized his trustworthiness as a prophet capable of predicting the future. Judging from the fecundity of Christians, only relatively few of them ever heeded the apostle's injunction on the importance of celibacy in marriage—and they for only a short time. He had, of course, given this advice to the married of Corinth (presumably living at the end of the age) as his own, and not as the Lord's and would thus have been able to extricate himself from a failed prophecy a bit easier than he could have done with the Thessalonians, to whom no qualification was made. To them he had spoken as the Bible-god might have spoken, and some of them, seeing the logic in his teaching, had simply stopped working, becoming thereby burdensome to their brethren. It should go without saying that the apostle to the Gentiles, whether speaking for himself or for the Bible-god, could not abide being wrong about anything. Hence, he suffered the keenest need to be able to have his cake and eat it too. The day of the Lord was indeed at hand, but the Antichrist was, most perversely, delaying its coming. With this ruse, Paul could die, even of old age, before any definitive disconfirmation of his rash prophecy occurred. Needless to say, his obscure reference to "the man of perdition" has proved to be a treasure trove for Christian conspiracy-theorists and their ilk throughout all subsequent ages. Any pope, religious leader, or world figure sufficiently odious in the eyes of the faithful can simply be dubbed the Antichrist, and when any given one passes from the scene another one can easily be found.

67. After criticizing Bentham's *NPBJ* trenchantly, Benn, *History of English Rationalism*, writes, "Yet even in this unaccustomed field [of New Testament scholarship] his wonderful sagacity shows itself. For not only has the antithesis between Paul and the Jerusalem church, of which so much is made, turned out a valuable clue to the solution of problems involved in the early history of Christianity, but in one instance he has even detected the artificial parallelism between the legends of Peter and Paul which is one of the most unquestionable merits of the Tübingen School to have worked out in detail" (1:303). The "Tübingen School" refers to a group of theologians under the leadership of F. C. Baur at the University of Tübingen (esp. from 1826 to 1860, beginning their work near the close of Bentham's life and more than a decade after he had written the manuscripts that Place put together as *NPBJ*) who approached New Testament literature under the influence of Hegel's philosophy of history. To illustrate, Peter and the other original apostles constituted the thesis, that is, the initial proclamation of the original church, Paul the antithesis, that is, a viewpoint set over against the original proclamation, and Acts (together with other works attempting a reconciliation) the synthesis of the earliest Christian movement. For an excellent thumbnail sketch of this approach, see Virgilius Ferm (ed.), *ER*, s. v. "Tübingen School." One need not adopt the Hegelian pattern of history to see the artificial parallelism that Acts presents between Peter and Paul. One has only to approach the text naturalistically (as Bentham did), or in rhetorical terms (as some modern scholars do), or both. For an example of the rhetorical approach see Pervo, *Profit with Delight*, esp. p. 134. Pervo writes, "Historical monographs with convincing affinities to Acts are difficult to identify. Novels that bear likenesses to Acts are, on the other hand, relatively abundant. For the type of audience Luke apparently addressed, the edifying historical novel was the genre most appropriate to his purposes and most available" (p. 137). Pervo notes, with neither criticism nor rancor, that the author of Acts had little in common with "historians of scrupulous accuracy and penetrating acumen" (p. 138). Bentham knew this perfectly well. Examples of the parallelism at issue in Acts follow: (1) Peter with a companion (John) heals a cripple unable from birth to use his feet well, if at all. After the cripple stands up, being made well, Peter addresses the crowd, 3:1–10. Paul with a companion (Barnabas) heals a cripple from birth who had never walked. After the healing Paul speaks to the people and is taken for a god, 14:8–10. Peter, on another occasion (10:25) is worshiped as well. (2) Peter, having been arrested and incarcerated, is approached by an angel; Peter's chains fall off, and the iron gate to the prison opens of its own accord, 12:3–17. Paul, having been arrested, escapes after an earthquake shakes the prison's foundations, opens all doors, and unfastens the prisoners' fetters, 16:23–35. On a different occasion (27:23), an angel appears to Paul. (3) A certain Simon, seeing that the Holy Spirit is given by the laying on of apostolic hands (such as Peter's) offers money to possess this power. Peter curses

him, 8:18–24. Elymas, a magician, withstands Paul who in turn curses him, leaving Elymas blinded for a time, 13:6–12. Paul also practices the laying on of hands after which certain folk receive the Holy Ghost, 19:6. (4) Peter falls into a trance on one occasion, 10:10; not to be outdone, so does Paul, 22:17. (5) Peter has a vision coordinated with a vision experienced by another, the Roman centurion Cornelius. These coordinated visions deal with ritual purity in matters of food and of Jews eating with Gentiles, 10:1–35. Paul has a vision coordinated with a vision vouchsafed to Ananias at the time of Paul's conversion, 9:1–18. (6) Peter raises Tabitha, a dead woman, 9:36–42; Paul seems to play a significant part in the recovery of Eutychus, near death, if not dead, 20:7–12. (7) The sick are brought so that Peter's shadow may fall on them; those so fortunate are healed, 5:14–16. Paul's dirty linens are taken to the sick whereupon diseases leave those so fortunate, and evil spirits depart them, 19:11–12. In the "historical novel" called Acts (more novelistic than historical and always propagandistic) it is clear that the signs, wonders, and miracles done by Paul match those even of the chiefest apostle, and in all, as Robertson has pointed out in *Origins of Christianity*, "miracle runs riot" (p. 101). Had Paul written Acts he would simply have said to Peter, "Anything you can do, I can do better."

68. The transportation of Paul's "cast-off habiliments," their "precious effluvia thus conveyed" to the infirm and the demonically possessed, reminds the author of American evangelist and spiritual jack-of-all-trades Oral Roberts, who, during the first half of 1948 alone provided thirty thousand "anointed handkerchiefs," better known as prayer cloths, for healing purposes. This Pentecostal practice is based directly on Acts 19:11–12. David Edwin Harrell Jr., Roberts' biographer, writes, "Oral repeatedly mailed 'prayer cloths,' as he had in years past. A cloth sent in 1979, along with a letter asking for a thirty-eight-dollar donation for the City of Faith, included the imprint of Oral's hand and the instruction: 'As you place your hand on the imprint of mine, immediately look to the Healing and Restoring Hand of the Living Christ'" (*Oral Roberts: An American Life* [San Francisco: Harper and Row, 1985], pp. 111–12, 119).

69. This reminds me, once a clergyman serving in the mountains of eastern Kentucky, of the two degrees of violent death recognized there: being killed, and being killed dead. There was a fair chance of recovering from the first, but none from the second. Eutychus, clearly, had suffered being killed by his fall, but not being killed dead. Wherein, then, lay the miracle?

70. Bentham made this point over and again in *NPBJ*, but never so economically nor so elegantly as in *CECE*. It is worth noting that Friedrich Nietzsche, though disdaining utilitarianism, agreed with Bentham very largely in appraising Paul. Nietzsche believed our saint to be a forger having no interest in historical truth, a dishonest person who foisted hallucinations, such as his alleged Damascus Road experience, on others, a man greedy for power, and an apostle of revenge. See *The Antichrist* (New York: Arno Press / New York Times, 1972), esp. pp. 36, 40.

Chapter 5

A Defense

As I have written elsewhere, "Except for hard drugs and for falling in love with absolutely the worst sort of person, nothing so scrambles the human brain as does religion."[71] This addling of the intellect is especially liable to occur whenever the favored faith is under attack. In witness thereto, consider the treatment of Bentham meted out by historian of philosophy Alfred William Benn (1843–1915) in *The History of English Rationalism*.[72] In the space of just two pages therein, one encounters several ill-conceived and jaundiced judgments, one of which follows: "Under the title *Not Paul but Jesus* [Bentham] attempts to discredit the personal character, and with the character the doctrine of the great Apostle of the Gentiles, who was also the favorite Apostle of the Evangelicals.[73] In the judgment above our historian of philosophy, who should have known better, engaged in not a little hero worship of the "great Apostle." Moreover, could Benn have meant to refer to "the Evangelicals" or to the Evangelists (i.e., to the authors of the Gospels)? If he meant the former, the reference is irrelevant, because ignorant; if the latter, he was opening a can of worms, for the extent to which Paul influenced the authors of the synoptic Gospels (i.e., Matthew, Mark, and Luke) on the one hand and influenced the author of John's Gospel on the other are moot points. More important by far is Benn's contention that Bentham was trying to discredit Paul's doctrine by discrediting his person. Anyone who knows how Bentham applied his philosophy of language to theological assertions will know that he viewed Paul's doctrines as nonsensical, not to say lunatic, whether Paul was saintly or sinister. The same would have applied to Jesus' theology, had it become an issue.

Benn continues, "[*NPBJ*] is not, what the title might have led us to expect, a comparative view of the two entirely different religions respectively embodied in the Epistle to the Romans and in the Sermon on the Mount, but rather a historical investigation of the true relation subsisting between Paul and the original disciples of Jesus."[74]

Bentham's choice of a title for his work on Paul may not have been the most prescriptive one possible, but a moment's reflection ought to have dissuaded Benn from thinking that he was to find in *NPBJ* a "comparative view of two entirely different religions." After all, Jesus and Paul were both Jews, the former remaining one until death, the latter retaining much of his Jewishness until death, despite his conversion. Moreover the Sermon on the Mount is not the sum and substance of Christianity. The Jerusalem church was not unique in accepting the Beatitudes, but in the beliefs its members held *about* Jesus Christ, about his person, work, death, resurrection, and expected return, bearing salvation. In Romans, Paul is also preoccupied with beliefs *about* Jesus Christ, about his person, work, death, resurrection, and expected return, bearing salvation.

In reading Acts on the one hand, and Galatians and 1 and 2 Corinthians (but *not* Romans) on the other, Bentham noticed a sharp and enduring conflict between Peter, James, and John, leaders of the Jesus (or Nazarene) movement within Judaism, and Paul, the Johnny-come-lately who would, though uninvited, become an apostle. It should not have surprised Benn that Bentham believed that Jesus' original disciples were in a better position to know the mind of their master than was Paul and to know the purposes of the Nazarene (or Ebionite) movement better than he. In contrasting Paul's views unfavorably with the beliefs and goals of the Nazarene movement, Bentham was not trying to advance Ebionite Christianity, even though it denied deity to Jesus. There were, however, certain nontheological beliefs in the Gospels that he endorsed strongly, making Jesus superior in his view both to Moses and to Paul.

Bentham never spoke ill of Jesus in *NPBJ*, though he had ample opportunity for doing so, referring to Jesus by name no fewer than 146 times. This name appears most often in such phrases as "the religion of Jesus," "the gospel of Jesus," or "the disciples (or apostles) of Jesus" and sometimes in combination with the title "Christ," meaning literally 'messiah' or 'king'. In a perfectly straightforward way Bentham referred to Jesus occasionally as "the Lord." Similarly, he mentioned the resurrection of Jesus with no hint of skepticism and the ascension of Jesus into heaven as a simple historical fact. In one instance in the context of weaning Jews away from strict adherence to the Mosaic law (i.e., to the ceremonial aspects thereof) Bentham referred to Jesus as "the great original." Jesus' antinomianism was a theme to which he adverted approvingly more than once. This alone made Jesus preferable to Moses. Bentham also endorsed most heartily Jesus' teaching in Matthew 5:43: "But I say unto you, Swear not at all."[75] Bentham's animus against forcing people to swear oaths is well known and will be taken up in the final part of this book. Also, the Gospels report that Jesus came eating, and drinking, and countenancing marriage (i.e., came teaching in nonascetic ways). This provided Bentham with a good reason for preferring Jesus to Paul who, as we already know, made a point of his celibacy (1 Cor. 7), urging it on others. Given Paul's domineering personality, it is not difficult to think that he might have attempted to enforce celibacy on some, at least, of his converts, had he had the power to do so. This is not to say that Bentham would have endorsed all of Jesus' ethical teachings nor *any* of his theological doctrines. As James Crimmins has written expressing Bentham's view," [I]f all of us seek to do good to others whenever and wherever we can then we would destroy ourselves; by neglecting our labours to serve others we would give up all security and the requirements for our own preservation."[76] It merely says that for the most part Jesus' teachings (as delivered by his *original* apostles) were not at issue in the *NPBJ*, except as a yardstick for measuring, episodically, the *doctrinal* waywardness of Paul, the heretic, the Antichrist.

Bentham not only ignored most of Jesus' ethical teachings and all of his theological teachings, he also refrained from trying critically and thoroughly to examine what passes for thought in St. Paul's writings.[77] Of this Stevan L. Davies has written pointedly, "With [Paul's] particular frame of reference much of this thinking makes logical sense. Outside his frame of reference he cannot make sense." Davies goes on to say that to understand Paul one must "willfully suspend disbelief for a period of time."[78] Needless to say, Bentham was unwilling to suspend disbelief even for a second and was not about to enter Paul's frame of reference constituted (as Bentham believed it to be) of an absurd concatenation of preposterous ideas. What Bentham wanted to do was to show the extraordinary extent of Paul's heresies and to explain the motivation thereof. That the result was unflattering to our saint can only have been pleasing to Bentham—it was high time for Paul to be cut down to size. If Christianity were to be cut down in the process, well, that would be no great loss. Secular utilitarianism was more than ready to take its place, among rational people at least.

Benn continued his criticism stating, "The result [of Bentham's approach to Paul] is to exhibit the converted persecutor of the Church as an ambitious and worldly-minded intriguer, who joined the infant community in order to use its resources for the attainment of his own selfish ends. Even in Bentham's youth such an interpretation would have been entirely out of date."[79] The first part of this charge is exactly correct, but what did Benn think had happened in biblical scholarship about 1765 (when Bentham was a youth) to make his view of Paul so dated? We are never told. Progress in technology, for example, is fairly easy to chart. Once the self-starter was wed to the internal combustion engine in automobiles, the hand crank was instantly out of date. Scarcely anybody cranks a car by hand nowadays. Progress in biblical studies, however, does not occur in the same lineal way. Disputed topics can linger long, and only occasionally and incrementally do bits of new evidence tilt the balances one way or another.

A comparison of Bentham's already "dated" views on Paul with some of the views of certain of our contemporaries can be quite instructive concerning progress in biblical studies. As I survey the 440 pages of *NPBJ*, I find the following characterizations of Paul: He was rebellious against established Christian authorities, had an alert and busy mind, became a declared convert so as to set himself at the head of Christianity, desired power and opulence, was a transparent impostor, an unscrupulous adventurer, was egotistic in the extreme, a self-constituted apostle for the sake of power, was continually in contradiction with himself and others, had an audacious temper, was despotic, sought money, power, and vengeance, exhibited both spleen and ambition, was boastful and perfidious, and pretended to communicate with God.

In 1986 Jewish scholar Hyam Maccoby, apparently not having heard of how "dated" such views were, wrote of Paul as follows: he was "not above deception" (*The Mythmaker*, pp. 6, 15, 151, 161, 167), was an "adventurer" (ibid., pp. 15, 183), "the founder of Christianity" (p. 16), "a compound of sincerity and charlatanry" (p. 17), made up Christianity out of a "brilliant concoction of Hellenism and Judaism" (p. 18), "transformed the historical event of Jesus into the cosmic myth of Christ" (p. 40), was "naturally ambitious" (p. 98), "lacked logical ability" (pp. 99, 101), had strong motives "to aggrandize his role" (p. 148), had "dubious visions" (p. 150), would have held back money (from the famous collection for the Jerusalem church) to buy Roman citizenship (p. 162), would have done the same to found his own church (ibid.), had "great presence of mind but lacked scruples" (p. 165), was a "false prophet to the Nazarenes or Ebionites" (p. 180), was "a falsifier of Jesus" (p. 181), and "a fantasist" (p. 204). What a shame Benn did not tell us what had happened in Bentham's youth to make dated the above views of Paul, views presented as recently as 1986!

More understanding, perhaps, and certainly more accepting of Paul than Maccoby, Joseph Klausner, in his classic work of scholarship *From Jesus to Paul*, has this to say: Paul was "not philosophical but was intense, emotional, and acrid" (p. 238); possessed of a "stormy temperament" (p. 335); had "clever schemes" (p. 356); was "two-faced to the Judaizers" (pp. 385–86) and "a usurper" (p. 394); was "guilty of hypocrisy" (p. 398); was "an extremist" (p. 424); was "boastfully condescending" (ibid.); "loved having his own way," that is, was an "authoritarian spiritual tyrant" (p. 426); was "extremely abusive of his opponents" (ibid.); was "cunning and deceitful in money matters" (p. 427); was "inconsistent" (p. 505) and "opportunistic" (p. 565); and was "one who cursed, reviled, and abused his enemies" (p. 586).

Alan Segal, *Paul the Convert* (among the most appreciative treatments of Paul by a Jewish scholar), characterizes him as follows: he was "inconsistent" (p. xii), used "ferocious, angry rhetoric" (pp. 140, 282), was an "apostate to Judaism" (pp. 218, 223), created in Christianity a "Jewish heresy" (p. 205), was "vituperative" (p. 206) and a "hypocrite" (p. 239), was "imprecise in language" (p. 262), and used "deliberate ambiguity" (p. 281). Another contemporary Jewish scholar, Richard L. Rubenstein, finds common cause of a psychological sort with Paul and, like Segal, treats him with great understanding. Nevertheless, Rubenstein observes that Paul was "impatient, harsh," and at times "furiously angry," only "not malicious."[80] Morton Smith, not Jewish, reinforces this opinion somewhat when he notes that despite Paul's "intense hostility" in Galatians, there is no clear indication of personal rivalry.[81]

Jewish New Testament scholars are not alone, however, in appraising Paul much as Bentham did, on certain points at least. English scholar Michael Grant says of our apostle in *Saint Paul* that the man's mind was "undisciplined" and "ambiguous" in expression and that he "commit[ted] flagrant self-contradictions" and paid "scant attention to the niceties of rational coherence."[82] Moreover, Grant writes that Paul's letters "display a startling mixture of conciliatory friendliness and harsh, bitter, inexorable bullying," that he was given to "violent, stubborn outbursts," and that he was "devoid of any consideration [of those who disagreed with him] or sense of humour" (ibid., p. 22). Because of his "virulent abuse" of Jewish law, calling it *skubalon* (i.e., 'shit', to do full justice to the Greek) in Philippians 3:8 (pp. 95–96), he was denounced by Jews as the "greatest apostate of all time." He was characterized ever and anon by "fanatical insistence" on "his own special position" (p. 116).

Turning to the topic of veracity, Morton Smith says flatly, "[T]here is no doubt that Paul was not scrupulous about minor misrepresentations of fact: Paul himself admits it, II Cor. 9.2 ff."[83] The Reverend C. L. Mearns writes in the same vein: "We may infer from some of Paul's strongest affirmations and most emphatic denials when in controversy with opponents, that the opposite of what Paul is saying had been argued by these opponents. Paul says in I Thess. 2.3: 'Our appeal does not spring from error or uncleanness, nor is it made with guile.'"[84] Mearns continues, "This implies that Paul therefore had been charged with evasiveness and dishonesty."[85] Edvin Larsson adds, "When Paul claimed that he believed everything in the Law and the prophets and that he had never done anything against the Jewish law and people he could hardly be taken seriously by Jews and by some Jewish Christians."[86] He was in effect perfidious when this was needed for what to him were worthy causes, a practitioner of "holy guile . . . trying to avoid confrontation."[87]

Respecting matters of status, Paul was "[F]rom any point of view other than his own at best a poor Jew and worst a renegade."[88] Moreover, within the Christian church as a whole he was not really an apostle in the eyes of his opponents.[89] Nowhere can one see more clearly the Janus-face Paul presented to the world than in 1 Corinthians 7:19, wherein he wrote, "Circumcision is nothing, and uncircumcision is nothing, but the keeping of the commandments of God." Of this Frank Thielman has written, "How can Paul say to his readers in one breath that circumcision is nothing and in the very next tell them to keep the commandments of God? Is not circumcision one of the most prominent of the Pentateuch's commandments?"[90]

Respecting Paul's opportunism, Jack T. Sanders writes of the would-be apostle's posturing in Galatians 1:13–2:10 as follows:

> The oath in [Galatians] 1:20 on the one hand and the hazy relationship with Acts on the other have tended to lead interpreters of the passages to assume that Paul is narrating historical fact in the modern sense. This he is not doing. He is proving his apostolic rank and independence. Had the situation been such that Paul could better have proved his apostleship by showing how *many* times he had been in Jerusalem [rather than how few], he would no doubt have been able to argue equally well in that vein. One should recall at this point how insistent the "apostle to the gentiles" can be that he is an Israelite, when it is necessary to be an Israelite in order to be an apostle.[91]

Paul's moral flexibility whenever an opportunity for self-aggrandizement arose plus the fact that he was not really as antinomian as he sounded[92] and the fact that he often found himself having to develop a theological answer to some problem or other among the congregations of his converts combined to put him in temptation's way—the temptation, that is, to rationalize theological positions rather than to think in an inquiring manner. No wonder he failed to develop a coherent system of theology.[93]

Given Paul's character and ambitions on the one hand and on the other the stumbling blocks that various leaders in the primitive church laid on his path, it is no wonder that he wrote Galatians, for example, in what J. Louis Martyn has called "a state of white-hot anger." Martyn says additionally, "And while all are pleased with the letter's celebration of freedom, some interpreters feel somewhat embarrassed that Paul should have written the letter in a state of unrepentance for the inflexible and even hostile words he spoke to Peter in the presence of the entire church of Antioch (Gal. 2:11–14). All of these factors, and others as well, have led a number of interpreters to a degree of regret that Paul should have written such an angry, unbalanced, and unrepentant letter."[94] Nor was Galatians alone in this respect. Of 2 Thessalonians, 1 Corinthians, and 2 Corinthians (especially chapters 10–13), as well as Galatians, Edgar Goodspeed writes, "And above all, what biting, disagreeable letters some of them were! How could anyone at Corinth or in Galatia think of putting into circulation documents so damaging, before the generation that called them forth was gone?"[95]

And what of Paul and money? Does contemporary scholarship lend any credence to Bentham's charge that Paul never turned over to the Jerusalem church the money that he had, presumably, collected for that purpose? We have already seen a similar suspicion in Maccoby.[96] More of the same can be found in the opinion of Lindsey P. Pherigo: "The chief trouble was caused by the financial campaign. Some in Corinth who mistrusted Paul had convinced many others that he was only a clever thief. Not accepting money for his preaching was merely a subterfuge for a much bigger program. They suspected his disposal of the fund raised ostensibly for the poor of Jerusalem. That he had seemingly avoided them [the Corinthians] after Titus had gotten their contribution, and did not visit them as promised, confirmed their suspicions. The charge is plain at several points (II Cor. 10:2; 11:7–11; 12:11–18; 13:1), and the key is in 12:14–18."[97]

And, suffusing this whole litany of peccadillos, shortcomings, character defects, and worse is pervasive, insufferable boasting.[98]

Among non-Jewish scholars of the first rank, none was more appreciative of Paul than Albert Schweitzer: "Paul is so great that his authority has no need to be imposed upon anyone. All honest, accurate, and living thought about Jesus inevitably finds in his its center."[99] However, Schweitzer also knew Paul to be vehement and on occasion uncompromising:

> The personal authority which the Apostle to the Gentiles could oppose to the Jerusalem church was not great. At moments violent, and then again extremely submissive, he can have organized no considered resistance. He is only a thinker, not a tactician. His violence no less than his submissiveness puts him in disadvantageous positions. The reflections, open or indirect, which he makes upon the original Apostles go so far that they put him in the wrong and give them a weapon which can be turned against him. He indulges in irony about the respect which is paid to them; charges one of them, Peter, with hypocrisy before all the believers of Antioch; claims a higher place than they, because he has done and suffered more; hints that they are in favor of circumcision in order to avoid the persecutions which the true teaching of the Cross of Christ brought upon those who preached it; and finally asserts, in the terrible excitement in which he threw off the second Epistle to the Corinthians [especially chapters 10–13], nothing more or less than that they in their blindness, and deceived by Satan, are actually serving Satan's cause against the church.[100]

In view of the pages immediately preceding, neither A. W. Benn nor anyone like him can dispose of Bentham's unflattering views of Paul on the ground that they are out of date or based on a "low view of human nature." Ignorant of this and undaunted, Benn next criticizes Bentham for his "absolute isolation from the intellectual currents of the age" and for "his entire ignorance of history."[101] It is unfortunate that Benn does not identify the various "intellectual currents" ignorance of which (presumably) detracted from Bentham's treatment of Paul. Counter to this, Stephen Conway says that Bentham was "reading widely in preparation for . . . writing" *NPBJ*.[102] It is equally unfortunate that Conway did not (probably because he could not) itemize the sources Bentham had read relative to Paul's multifaceted conflict with the original apostles, especially the secondary sources that influenced him directly. An examination of the relatively few footnotes that grace *NPBJ* reveals that Bentham had not read much, if anything, of prime importance in biblical scholarship in general and in New Testament scholarship in particular, or, if he had, he was chary with his acknowledgments.

He knew the *Historical Geography of the Old and New Testaments* by Edward Wells (1687–1727); a work on Mosaic law called *Origines Hebraicae*, by Lewis Thomas (1687–1749?); an edition of Scripture called Scholey's Bible; *The Elements of Christian Theology*, by the Bishop of Lincoln (no additional information supplied); and the famous concordance of Alexander Cruden (1701–1770).[103] Attention to Bentham's letters shows that he possessed Archdeacon William Paley's *Horae Paulinae* (subtitled *The Truth of the Scripture History of St. Paul Evinced by a Comparison of the Epistles Which Bear His Name with the Acts of the Apostles and with One Another*); that he knew to some extent the *Canon of the New Testament*, by Nathaniel Lardner (1684–1768); knew (or knew of) *A Critical History of the Text of the New Testament* (2 vols.), by French Hebraist Richard Simon (1638–1712); and at least knew something of eminent German Bible scholar Johann David Michaelis (1717–91).[104] Of these only two, Simon and Michaelis, merit inclusion in German New Testament scholar Werner Georg Kümmel's very valuable "biographical appendix," and American New Testament scholar William Baird thinks Nathaniel Lardner worthy of a half-dozen pages.[105]

Benn's claim that Bentham did not know what was going on intellectually and that therefore *NPBJ*, by implication, is ill- or uninformed is but a criticism of the most carping kind. Any intelligent contemporary could have done what Bentham did, given three necessary conditions: first, one would have had to know how to read the Greek New Testament or some reasonably good translation thereof (Bentham could do both); second, one would have had to be able to approach Peter, James, Paul, and the A-h as human beings having various perspectives and agendas and being subject to ordinary human frailties (Bentham had no trouble doing so); and third, one would have had to divest oneself (temporarily at least) of any theological attachments (Bentham had none).[106] In short, to write historically of the early church, one needed (then as now) to sever 'Saint' from 'Paul', 'Holy' from 'Scripture', and 'Sacred' from 'History'. Bentham's "entire ignorance of history," alleged by Benn, was largely beside the point. Bentham had met the necessary conditions for doing history, and there was not much to be learned from his contemporaries on the subject to which he addressed himself. The most important German scholar from whom Bentham could have learned (but apparently did not) was Johann S. Semler (1725–1791).[107]

Noting that NPBJ identifies Luke as one of the twelve apostles (he was not) and takes Aquila and Priscilla to be two female disciples of Paul (one was male, according to Acts 18:2), Benn writes triumphantly of Bentham's scandalously poor scholarship (though neither of these minor mistakes detracts from NPBJ's thesis), "Naturally the higher criticism is unsuspected. 'Of Paul's epistles the genuineness is out of dispute.'"[108] At the end of the paragraph containing these criticisms, Benn refers to the "merits" of the Tübingen school (of New Testament scholarship) and in so doing convicts himself of profound ignorance. Taken together these criticisms are so absurd it is hard to know where to start to set the record straight. In short, the "unsuspected" (by Bentham) higher criticism has done much to reinforce, rather than to undercut, his views of Paul. The genuineness of the traditional set of Paul's epistles is in great doubt due in large measure to the founder of the Tübingen school, F. C. Baur, who limited the genuine Pauline epistles to four, Galatians, 1 and 2 Corinthians, and Romans. Almost by "divine inspiration" it would seem, these are the four epistles that Bentham quoted or referred to most often in NPBJ; Galatians at least forty-eight times, 1 Corinthians at least 15 times, Romans at least 12 times, and 2 Corinthians at least 9 times. To the suspect epistles he referred scarcely at all. And all without the benefit of the "higher criticism" as practiced by the scholars of the Tübingen school! They, alas, did not begin their work on the relation of the "supremely self-devoted evangelist" to the original apostles until a generation after NPBJ was written and a decade after Bentham had died.[109] Benn seems to have known little more of Tübingen than the name. He had little excuse for his ignorance, for he, unlike Bentham, lived well *after* the Tübingen school had commenced its work.

A contemporary scholar too important to ignore in the criticism of Bentham on religion is James E. Crimmins. Crimmins quotes Benn (much as I did above) to the effect that Bentham (1) was already out of date in biblical scholarship, (2) was isolated from the intellectual currents of his time, (3) was ignorant of history, and (4) had a low opinion of human nature, believing, as he did, that even "spiritual" people could be motivated by pecuniary interests. Crimmins, to his credit, writes, "We might demur from one or two of the charges contained in this attack, but the theory of imposture . . . had been completely discredited by the time Bentham wrote."[110] It is regrettable that Crimmins does not tell us (1) whose theory of imposture is at issue; (2) what, precisely, the theory claims; (3) what the data are that discredit it; and (4) whether or not this alleged discrediting still stands in contemporary scholarship. If the theory contends that Paul was a pretender at every point, that he knew that he had received no personal, divine revelation but said nevertheless that he had, and if he knew that he had never been commissioned as an apostle of Jesus but posed as one anyway (all for the sake of ulterior motives alone), then the theory of imposture has been and remains discredited. But the situation is hardly as clear-cut as this.

Paul marched into the Christian camp not merely claiming that he was a convert, not merely professing faith in Messiah Jesus, but announcing, in no uncertain terms, that he had been appointed an apostle (i.e., an emissary) on a par with any and all other apostles, and that, moreover, he was called to be the director of foreign missions for the Jesus movement. He may not have said all of this with his first breath as a convert, but it all came out over a period of time, if his letters may be believed. From the outset of his claim to be an apostle, he knew that not all Nazarenes accepted him as being what he claimed to be.[111] He admitted as much in 1 Corinthians 9:2: "If I be not an apostle unto others, yet doubtless I am to you; for the seal of mine apostleship are ye in the Lord." Let us ask how those to whom he was not an apostle viewed him. As an impostor, of course! It did not matter to the faithful who rejected him how sincere he was in his beliefs, how cocksure he was in his teachings, or how successful he was on the mission field.[112] Those who had known Jesus personally, or who had known others who had walked and talked with their Messiah, viewed Paul as a fraud and an impostor. Paul responded in kind, branding those officials of the Jesus movement who sought to counteract his influence as false apostles (2 Cor. 11:13). All it took to be a false apostle in Paul's view was to disbelieve *his* gospel, to attempt to undercut *his* theologicoecclesiastical position, and to refuse to submit to *his* authority.

So, respecting a theory of imposture, what are the criteria? In other words, what does it take to make one an impostor? Must one know that one is a pretender, or is it enough to preach a message seriously at odds with the message of the group allegiance to which one professes? In Paul's case, the issue was complicated by power politics of the ecclesiastical kind. Whether his motives were completely ulterior to his newly professed religion, partially ulterior (as seems most likely), or purely and selflessly responsive to what he took to be a divine commission, his theologicoecclesiastical party eventually triumphed, becoming orthodox for Christianity in the process. At the uncertain time of his death, however, his side was in eclipse, the

Jerusalem church having largely succeeded in regaining control.[113] It took 350 years for Paulinism to establish itself as Christianity.[114]

Although Crimmins criticizes *NPBJ* much as Benn did, there are two points at which the former tempers the criticisms at issue.[115] First, Crimmins became aware (as Benn apparently did not) of eminent French scholar Ernst Renan, who discerned sharp differences between the teachings of Jesus in the Gospels and those of Paul in his epistles. These differences, of course, so clear to Bentham, laid the basis for the conflict between Paul and Jesus' original disciples. Writes Crimmins, "[E]vents can be construed religiously or naturalistically—which leaves room for the kind of interpretation that Bentham provides."[116] In this connection, one can hardly do better than to quote English scholar F. C. Burkett of Cambridge: "We must be prepared to find the whole drama of the rise of Christianity more confused, more *secular*, in a word more appropriate to the limitations of its own age, than we should gather from the epic selectiveness of the creeds and the theological manuals" (emphasis added).[117]

Benn (1843–1915), twenty years the junior of Renan (1823–92) could easily have learned that Bentham's position on the Jesus-Paul question enjoyed powerful, independent support from the French scholar, both in taking a naturalistic (i.e., a historical) approach to the New Testament and in discerning remarkable differences between the teachings of Jesus and Paul. Renan, of course, was not alone. A host of German scholars, beginning with F. C. Baur (1792–1860) in particular, adopted the same naturalistic approach and discerned the same doctrinal animosities between Paul and the Jerusalem church.[118]

Second, Crimmins became aware (as Benn did not) that those who take a naturalistic (or historical) approach to New Testament studies, rather than a religious (or, to be more specific, a Christian) approach, find not only that Paul was seriously out of step with the Jerusalem church doctrinally, but also that Jesus, very likely, had other, more specifically Jewish goals for his life's work than those asserted of him by the pro-Roman, mystical, idiosyncratic theologian Saul of Tarsus. Crimmins's reference to Maccoby's *Revolution in Judea: Jesus and the Jewish Resistance* shows his awareness of the "Zealot hypothesis" for interpreting the life and teachings of Jesus, a hypothesis (involving sedition) not very palatable to Christians of the Paulinist persuasion.[119] Crimmins tiptoes around this hypothesis when writing, "But it is also possible to see Jesus simply as a self-appointed prophet who got mixed up in politics, clashed with the Jerusalem rabbis, and therefore had to be eliminated."[120] "Mixed up in politics" is putting it mildly, if the Zealot hypothesis has any merit. Moreover, if it is true, it would not have been the rabbis who quarreled with Jesus but the Sadducees and their Roman overlords. Anyone who seriously thought himself to be the Jewish Messiah (or let himself be persuaded of this potentially seditious role) was liable to be on a collision course with more than rabbis of the Pharisaic stripe.[121]

The Zealots, from whom the theory takes its name, espoused violence in ridding Israel of its pagan rulers. The most distinguished English-speaking representative of this hypothesis in recent times, Samuel G. F. Brandon, writes,

> Ironic though it be, the most certain thing known about Jesus of Nazareth is that he was crucified by the Romans as a rebel against their government in Judaea. The fact is recorded in the four Christian Gospels, and the execution, on the order of Pontius Pilate, is mentioned by the Roman historian Tacitus. . . . The Christian attestation is particularly significant. That the founder of their faith had been put to death on a charge of sedition could hardly have been invented by Christians; for such a fact obviously caused the Roman authorities to view the faith with suspicion. . . . The early Christians had, indeed, a strong motive for suppressing so embarrassing a fact. That they did not do so surely attests both to its authenticity and notoriety.[122]

In granting some merit to the "naturalistic" approach to New Testament studies (after all, even Renan had used it, as well as Bentham) and in recognizing the possibility of a mundane, political, nationalistic element in Jesus' life and work (Maccoby noticed this as well as Bentham), Crimmins tempers Benn's criticisms of *NPBJ*. However, Crimmins holds fast to the charge that Bentham was unspiritual and in so doing makes his most important criticism—one that will require a rather lengthy and detailed analysis. Consider Crimmins's litany of complaints: Bentham lacked "any sense of man's incorporeal nature, religious or otherwise"[123] and could not understand the mysterious,[124] bringing to the "mysteries of religion" nothing more than the tawdry logic of "courtroom tactics."[125] "Bentham could not countenance any common ground between the spiritual world of religion and the perceptible world of physical experience; they are, he believed, mutually exclusive worlds."[126] Nor could he comprehend adequately "the inner spirit which motivates the truly religious person."[127] His "complete inability to come to grips with the spiritual content of religion and its meaning for the pious believer" led him to strip "religious beliefs of their spiritual content."[128] "He simply ignored the fact that religious knowledge ultimately depends on faith."[129] However, before acceding too readily to Crimmins's evaluation of Bentham as a blind guide on religion in general and on Paul in particular, it is admonitory to contemplate Morton Smith's incisive quip, "When a theologian talks of a 'higher truth,' he is usually trying to conceal a lower falsehood."[130] To this I would add that when a pious defender of the faith mentions "spiritual truths," as does Crimmins, he is usually, at the same time, dismissing claims about *ordinary* personal/emotional experiences and/or psychosocial phenomena of perfectly *natural* types. As a general rule, one should not leap to the "spiritual" until one has first exhausted the physical, and one should not resort to the "supernatural" until one has depleted the natural.

In defending Bentham against the charge of being unspiritual, it is necessary to analyze what it means to be spiritual. This, in turn, forces one to come to grips with the so-called spirit world and its etiology. In doing so, there is no one more instructive with whom to begin than Plato, the inventor of natural (i.e., philosophical) theology.[131] In the tenth book of *The Laws*, we find him trying out certain arguments designed to persuade unbelievers that there really are gods.[132] In 886, a man named Clinias says to the Athenian, "Why, to begin with, think of the earth, and sun, and planets, and everything! And the wonderful and beautiful order of the seasons with its distinctions of years and months! Besides, there is the fact that all mankind, Greeks and non-Greeks alike, believe in the existence of gods."[133]

The Athenian, however, fears that there is a lack of persuasive power in these arguments. There are, after all, certain "modern men of enlightenment" who do not accept the divinity of the sun and moon, planets, and earth, regarding these as but earth and stones "incapable of minding human conduct."[134] Not even the "universal prostrations and devotions of mankind," with their joint implication that the gods are realities and not fictions, can be depended on to persuade certain evil, unbelieving persons and their recruits.[135] What is needed, especially when focusing on nature—that is, on earth, air, fire, and water (the elements of ancient Greek physics)—is a demonstration of the priority of soul (i.e., of psyche)[136] in relation to body (or matter). Moreover, soul must be shown to be as eminently natural as it is primordial.[137] Soul, then, is the prime source of the various changes and transformations in bodies. Opinion, judgment, foresight, deliberation, wisdom, law, and art are all prior to and independent of such qualities of bodies as hard and soft, heavy and light, and other properties of matter. Thus does Plato, through a mixture of bad reasoning and (understandable) ignorance, help to armor-plate that age-old dualism called the "mind-body problem," which routinely puts the cart before the horse.

The refutation of the proofs for the existence of God, gods, and goddesses is child's play. First, Clinias's argument from the motion of the planets and the orderly flow of the seasons is an early example of the so-called argument from design for the existence of a supreme being. Refusing at the outset to consider that repetitive (i.e., orderly) sequences in the cosmos may be natural to it, Clinias jumps to the conclusion that order in nature must be the result of intelligent design superimposed upon it. Second, although the universal prostrations and devotions of Greeks and non-Greeks alike may tell us much about the anthropology and psychology of the human animal, they need tell us nothing at all about the putative object(s) toward which or whom such pious actions are directed. In short, one may bow and scrape before the creations of human imagination as easily as before nonmental entities. (In essence, this is what all false gods are.) Third, to put it epigrammatically, although one can lose one's mind without literally losing one's head, one cannot be beheaded without being "beminded." Knowing no biology, it had not occurred to Plato that he had never encountered a mind (or any of its artifacts) without encountering a functioning brain, supported and nourished by a living body.[138] Ignorant of this and relying on introspection alone to know within himself the presence of thought, judgment, intention, will, and passion, he concluded that something nonphysical dwells in human bodies, controls these bodies (on occasion at least, if not always), and exhibits feelings and emotions through them. From this point on, a single hasty generalization served to invest each thing in nature with a soul, each motion with an intention, and each process with a goal. Thus there are gods everywhere (according to the Greek philosopher Thales), and some, if not all, of us have entertained angels (outdwelling spirit entities) unawares (Heb. 13:2). When such souls (or spirits or ghosts), with their various likes and dislikes, focus their ever-seeing attention on human beings, there is much to fear—but equally much to hope for, if the nonphysical entities in question can be appeased, or, better yet, be enlisted in human pursuits.

Meanwhile, over in Palestine, in ways roughly parallel to Plato's natural theology, the Psalmist was singing (Ps. 19:1), "The heavens declare the glory of God; and the firmament sheweth his handiwork"; and the prophet was prophesying (Jer. 31:33b–34)," I will put my law in their inward [i.e., spiritual] parts, and write it on their hearts; and will be their God, and they shall be my people. And they shall teach no more every man his neighbor, and every man his brother, saying, Know the Lord, for they shall all know me, from the least of them unto the greatest of them, saith the Lord"; and the Bible-god was being portrayed (Gen. 1:2) as the disembodied, primordial spirit (or soul or mind) acting as the agent of creation and change, bringing order out of chaos. Hebrews 11:3 embroiders this, adding, "[T]he worlds were created, beautifully coordinated, and now exist, at God's command; so the things that we see did not develop out of mere matter."[139] Also roughly parallel to the Greek use of *psuche* (more commonly *psyche* in English transliteration) as breath is the Hebrew word *ruach*, meaning "breath." Genesis 2:7 says, "And the Lord God formed man out of the dust of the ground, and breathed into his nostrils the breath [*ruach*] of life; and man became a living soul [*nephesh*]."[140] Although the dualism of body and soul (or spirit) was not so sharp in ancient biblical thought as it was in the Platonic tradition, it was no mere tendency but was rather an established fact in the way in which people of that time and place saw themselves.

At this point I can do no better than to appropriate a few words from an unpublished manuscript of mine.[141] A primitive man's keen image of himself as a dualistic creature, as a body motivated by invisible, intangible, indwelling forces, and his apprehension of inexplicable powers at work in the world are two important factors in the development of religion. Eminent English anthropologist E. B. Tylor was among the first to argue that the earliest religion, or "animism" as he called it, arose from the vague apprehension of our remote ancestors that they were all dualistic creatures. In his work *Religion in Primitive Culture*, Tylor claims that our aboriginal ancestors became religious, that is, believed in spirits and/or souls, because of their own experiences of psychic phenomena.[142] Looming large among these, to him, was the dream life. The primordial human took to bed each night and awoke on the same pallet next morning, but remarkable events had often intervened. In dreamland the dreamer had paddled his canoe to distant places and had ventured into fantastic lands, had fought and triumphed or fled in fear, and had encountered friends and enemies from among the dead as well as from among the living. Such dream experiences, feigning reality, must have contributed, Tylor thought, to the concept of the soul (or ghost) as separable not just from one's sleeping body but from one's dead body as well.

Another psychic factor that made belief in the soul credible to the ancients was the experience of strong emotion, the experience of being possessed, of being mastered by violent outbreaks, for example, of rage, terror, or passion. As E. Washburn Hopkins wrote, "The first conception of soul is that it is *power*, not a spirit in the body, but a power inherent in the body and manifested in life and action" (emphasis added).[143]

In addition, anything that conduces to human ecstasy, that is, to the experiences of standing outside oneself or of transcending one's ordinary being, produces and/or reinforces belief in dualism, and in naive minds, belief in *outdwelling* spirits. Among the causes of ecstasy are frenzy, however induced (such as in religious dances or other collective rituals); epilepsy (or other forms of "divine madness"); and the use of psychotropic drugs (or various techniques that induce psychedelic experiences). Put epigrammatically, soul travel cannot occur (while leaving the body behind or below) unless there is a soul to travel. Even among sophisticates today, knowing one's mind is not knowing one's brain, and finding one's inner self is not the same as catching one's neurotransmitters in the act—in the act, that is, of making it all possible. In spite of enormous advances in the neurosciences, and in spite of the fact that most philosophers specializing in the philosophy of mind are now in full cry against Cartesian dualism, Professor Crimmins, it would seem, remains a naive dualist, not to say an animist.[144] Whereas Bentham's philosophies of mind and human nature would have made him quite at home in today's scientific world, Crimmins's philosophies of mind and human nature place him squarely in pre-Benthamic, prescientific, wholeheartedly animistic times.[145] His criticisms of Bentham on religion must be appraised in this light.

Although *NPBJ* downplays Paul's "spiritual teachings," focusing rather on the self-appointed apostle's ecclesiastical activities, it should be very instructive, in defending Bentham, to confront Crimmins with some of Paul's "spiritual teachings," a number of which may prove difficult for him to accept. It must be remembered that Paul lived at a time and place when and where the dualism of spirit (or soul or ghost) and body was par for the course; that he was acquainted with both the Hellenistic and Judaic versions thereof; and that he was an archdualist himself, if not an adherent of trialism, of the threefoldness of the human being.[146] In witness thereto, 1 Corinthians 14:14 (IB version) says, if "For [*sic*] I pray in a tongue [i.e., in the unknown tongue, technically glossolalia, not merely in a foreign language], the spirit of me prays, but the mind of me is unfruitful."[147] So, granted that human beings either are or have a body, they also are or have a spirit (*pneuma* in Greek, from which 'pneumatic' comes) and a mind (*nous* in Greek, from which 'noetic' comes). Paul even suggests a dualism in the Bible-god himself (see 1 Cor. 2:10 and Rom. 8:27). These and many other citations in the catalog of Pauline beliefs (to follow shortly) illustrate how difficult it often is to know precisely what Paul meant. The reasons for this are fairly obvious.

Mark Twain once provided an essential clue when he wrote, "Adam and Eve had many advantages, but the principal one was, that they escaped teething."[148] In like manner, we can see that St. Paul had many advantages, the principal one being that he escaped any close questioning by acute, tenacious, fair-minded, nonpartisan interrogators, bent on trying to learn exactly what he meant by the astonishing things he said, claiming to know their truth by revelation. Nor did he have the grace or take the time to articulate clearly and fairly the various theological and ecclesiastical positions of his religious opponents and rivals for power. To these points must be added the fact that Paul nowhere organized his teachings, drawn from his various epistles, into a single coherent, well-founded system of thought. The contents of his letters, taken as a whole, are more nearly a mishmash of unchallenged speculations, fabulous notions (familiar to his time and place), and rationalizations transmuted into articles of faith for his converts to believe, all of which he delivered dogmatically to them and to all who heard his voice or read his writings. No wonder the Epicurean and Stoic philosophers who chanced upon him in Athens one day (Acts 17:18) called him a *spermologos*, literally a seed picker, metaphorically a babbler, and descriptively "one who makes his living picking up scraps" of this and that, in his case scraps of metaphysical notions and religious ideas (see the *GEL* for more on this term). The catalog of Paul's "spiritual" beliefs that follows will show, with painful clarity, that this is no idle accusation.

In the context of Pauline dualism, it is now possible to formulate a working definition of spirits and of the spiritual. Paul conceived of spirits as humanoid entities of nonflesh and nonblood, angelic or demonic, that, acting as messengers or agents of this or that, move about the world pneumatically, seeking, when in the role of agents, humans whom they may enter, thereby diminishing or abolishing the moral autonomy of the host and making the human so invaded act as the spirit in question dictates.[149] Paul's deity (having a "Holy Spirit") is conceived to be the Lord of all good spirits, a spiritual monarch who will triumph at the end of the present evil age, despite being opposed in the current dispensation by demonic spirits (or devils) whose Lord's name is Satan, a name used by Paul on a half-dozen occasions.[150]

'Spiritual' poses greater complications. On the one hand, this adjective can be used to modify beliefs, usually metaphysical or moral in nature, and on the other can modify experiences, usually aesthetic or highly emotional in type. It is, after all, commonplace to hear people speak of spiritual truths and of spiritual experiences. The human desire that a belief or an experience be spiritual may also play a part in making it (seem to be) so, and, withal, a keen imagination is essential. However, metaphysical and moral beliefs, aesthetic and other emotional experiences do not qualify as spiritual, in a Christian context at least, unless they are organically related to belief in a supreme Lord of (good) spirits. Subtract this belief from metaphysical and moral beliefs, and they become just that and nothing more. Exactly the same is true of aesthetic and other emotional experiences. Bentham, as we shall see in part 3, subscribed to a certain metaphysical viewpoint, but it was not spiritual. Moreover, with his Principle of Utility, he was ever and anon promoting and trying to practice a moral principle, but nobody would call his brand of utilitarianism spiritual. Finally, when he played or listened to Handel's music, of which he was very fond, Bentham was having aesthetic experiences, but he never thought of these as spiritual, because they were in no way related, in his mind, to any Lord of (good) spirits. Obviously, there is no language-dictator who can force us to limit our use of 'spiritual' to what has just been described, but the further one ventures from the usage suggested above, the further one goes from the mind of St. Paul. Absent a belief in the "spirit world," neither the poetic nor the metaphoric reaches the level of the spiritual.

First, in any catalog of Pauline beliefs, comes the view that a supreme, monarchical, outdwelling spirit-entity—that is, the Bible-god—disclosed, from time to time, his nature, thoughts, and intentions to various people (Rom. 1:17–18, 16:25–26; 1 Cor. 2:10, 14:30; Gal. 3:23), but most especially to him (Paul) and sometimes to him alone (1 Cor. 2:6–7; 2 Cor. 12:1, 7; Gal. 1:16, 2:2). God did not, however, disclose (or reveal) anything of his own psychic nature to Paul different from the then prevailing views of human anthropology and psychology. These views were that the human being was some sort of composite (1 Thess. 5:23) of spirit (*pneuma*), soul (*psuche*), and body (*sōma*, from which comes the English 'somatic'). In 1 Corinthians 14:14–15, Paul adds to this list the mind (*nous*) of a person. But, the Bible-god never disclosed to Paul anything as to whether these four components are separable entities or are merely as many functions of the normal human being, available to introspection. It would, for example, be very desirable if one could know precisely the relation of the soul in a living human body to the spirit of that same body. It is anybody's guess as to why the Bible-god failed to oblige in this way. Why did he not reveal to Paul definitive information as to whether or not *pneuma, psuche, sōma,* and *nous* are *parts* of a human whole or are identifiable *functions* of that whole— a whole that could, conceivably, have been (or be) physical throughout?

To complicate matters further, Paul tells us in 1 Corinthians 15:44 that there are spiritual bodies as surely as there are physical bodies. Relative to those humans who have been (or will be) saved unto eternal life, these bodies make their appearance in a fixed order (v. 46). First, there is the physical body, then the spiritual body, the latter "body" being the one that is resurrectable (vv. 42–44). Paul never tells us precisely what a *sōma pneumatikon* (a pneumatic, or spiritual, body) is—that is, what its defining characteristics are, or how exactly it differs from a flesh-and-blood body, that is, a natural or physical body. Does, for example, the resurrected "spiritual body" preserve and incorporate the same mind (*nous*) and the same soul (*psuche*) that formerly dwelt in the now-dead natural body? Or, perchance, a new *nous* and a new *psuche* are divinely supplied to each resurrected "pneumatic body." Here one must ask an unhappy question: did Paul know what he was talking about? This is no idle question, because the entire passage in 1 Corinthians 15, dealing with what it is of a saved person that is resurrected, is introduced by an old wives' tale, and introduced arrogantly at that. Says Paul (1 Cor. 15:35–38),

> But some *man* will say, How are the dead raised up? and with what body do they come?
> *Thou* fool, that which thou sowest is not quickened, except it die:
> And that which thou sowest, thou sowest not that body that shall be, but bare grain, it may chance of wheat, or some other *grain*:
> But God giveth it a body as it hath pleased him, and to every soul his own body.

That a kernel of wheat or other grain must die before it can germinate is a mistake at least as old as Jesus (see John 12:24), and, no doubt, much older. In retrospect, we can tolerate (or even humor) Paul in his ignorance of plant germination, but we can hardly take such a benign view of those today who wish to transform this biological falsehood into a "spiritual truth." The planting of a seed and its subsequent germination cannot serve as a proper analog to what Paul thought happened to the physical body of the saved Christian and the presumed resurrection of that Christian in a new "spiritual body." Such was Paul's character and such was his certitude that not even the most obvious question as to how anybody could know the truth in any of this ever troubled him. What he was delivering to the Corinthians was, to him, a revealed truth for no better reason than that he believed it strongly. Even given the reality of divine revelation, why would the Bible-god choose to use a biological falsehood to disclose a "spiritual truth"?

Paul's conception of deity was clearly created out of the same anthropological and psychological ingredients that he took to constitute the human being. Paul never says that the Bible-god has a body, a "spiritual body" to be sure, but given that the dead of earth who are saved shall have spiritual bodies and shall inhabit the Bible-god's kingdom, it is reasonable to infer that the Bible-god also has (or is) a "spiritual body" (1 Cor. 15:51–53). And, of course, Paul assures us over and again that his deity has a Spirit (a *pneuma*), just as does a human being, except that it is Holy in the case of the deity. First Corinthians 2:10b–11 says literally, "[F]or [the] Spirit all things searches, even the deep things of God, who For [sic] knows of men the things of a man, except the spirit of a man in him" (IB version). There is widespread agreement among translators that the "deep things of God" refers to thoughts, and thoughts are commonly believed to be the possession of minds.[151] So, it is probably accurate to say of Paul that just as he took humans to be composites of body, mind, and spirit, so too his deity was a composite being, understood in the appropriate "spiritual" sense, but a composite of what? Paul cannot be blamed for not having known what he could not have known in his day and time nor for failing to understand how a human being stores thoughts in memory, calls them up again at will, or considers them introspectively. Nor can he be criticized for hypothesizing (as did many, if not most, of his contemporaries) a homunculus inside the individual or even a more fugitive homunculus inside the homunculus inside the individual (which is about what a spirit that plumbs the thoughts in the mind of a person must be).[152] The points to note are these: Paul did not know what was going on inside his head; he received no revelation about the nature and powers of his brain nor about the nature and powers of his hypothesized deity's "spiritual brain"; and he delivered no "spiritual truths" relative to any of these issues. The most exculpatory claim that can be made on Paul's behalf is that he heard voices in his head. What he taught about body, mind, soul, and spirit were the confused commonplaces of his time and location.

Even assuming that Paul knew what he was writing about, the ontological status of what he called the Spirit remains problematical. In his usage, 'Spirit' (whether capitalized or not, whether modified by 'Holy' or not) remains a catch-all term. Sometimes it is nothing more than a redundancy. For example, to have a spirit of meekness (Gal. 6:1) is nothing other than to be meek; to have a spirit of slumber (Rom. 11:8) is nothing more than being slumberous; and to have a spirit of faith (2 Cor. 4:13) is nothing beyond being faithful. On other occasions, Paul seems more nearly to have had influence in mind. We can all understand how the influence of an individual (especially of a domineering individual like Paul) can be felt at a distance and over time. It was in this sense that he told the Corinthians (1 Cor. 5:3) that although he was absent from them in body, he was present amongst them in spirit. This was to prompt them to do what he wanted done. What was true of Paul's spirit (i.e., of his commanding presence) was undoubtedly true, as he saw it, of the Holy Spirit of his deity. First Corinthians 12:3 provides the clearest example of the presence of Spirit understood as influence. Here Paul writes (according to TBAT), "I must tell you that no one who is speaking under the influence of the Spirit of God ever says, Curse Jesus! and no one can say, Jesus is Lord! without being under the influence of the Holy Spirit." The NEB's translators agree exactly in the choice of 'influence'. Also, Christians who are led by the Spirit (as in Gal. 5:18) are for all practical purposes guided or influenced by it, and in Romans 8:14 we learn that all who are led, guided, or moved by the Spirit are "sons of God." Most often, however, Paul uses 'Spirit' to name an agent and not merely a source of influence, or, even more trivially, a mood, emotion, or attitude.

As an agent the Spirit is a source of power (Rom. 15:13, 19; 1 Thess. 1:5) enabling Paul (1 Cor. 2:4) and others (1 Cor. 12:8) to edify the church in a variety of ways. Various people are gifted by the Spirit to be especially wise and to have special knowledge (1 Cor. 12:8), to possess healing ability (1 Cor. 12:9), and to work miracles, to prophesy, to discern spirits (i.e., to distinguish true from false spirits), to speak in tongues, and to interpret those gifted in tongues.[153] The fruits of the Spirit's activities in Christians are love, joy, peace, long-suffering, gentleness, goodness, and faith (Gal. 5:22). Christians are justified in the name of the Lord Jesus and by the Spirit of God (1 Cor. 6:11), are sanctified (or consecrated or made holy) by the Spirit (Rom. 15:6; 2 Thess. 2:13), and are the recipients of the Spirit's tutelage (1 Cor. 2:13), intercession, and assistance (Rom. 8:26).

Unless Paul was lying to all and sundry in his epistles, he was clearly an ecstatic, one who, depending on the brain state he was in at any given time, believed himself to be possessed now by this "spiritual agency," now by that, a man whose life was a battlefield of conflicting spirits. Moreover, could we have attended a meeting of one of his congregations, we would have witnessed goings-on more akin to those of a Pentecostal tent revival in Appalachia than to those of an Anglican worship service in an English cathedral. A close analysis of 1 Corinthians 12:8–11 and related passages will confirm these contentions.

One wishes to know what wisdom was given to some by the Spirit, what knowledge to others (v. 8). We are never told, hence, have no way of testing the alleged wisdom and knowledge at issue. One thing, however, is clear. Whatever the wisdom and the knowledge may have been, if anything at all, both were compatible with Paul's theology and ecclesiology. If anybody in the Corinthian church had received "wisdom" from the Spirit to the effect that Jesus was the deliverer of Israel only and not the savior of Gentile as well as of Jewish souls, it would not have been wisdom to Paul and would not have been included in any of his letters except in a shower of abuse. Similarly, if the Spirit had revealed to somebody the knowledge that Peter, not Paul, was the true apostle of Jesus, that person would have been squelched, becoming a nobody.[154] In short, we need look no further than Paul's teachings to find "revelations" of the wisdom and knowledge at issue.

In addition to revealing wisdom and knowledge to some in the church, the Spirit gave gifts of healing to others (v. 9). It has often been said that Christianity could not have reached first base in competition with the welter of Hellenistic religions, had it not been associated with, and episodically successful at, healing some people, miracles or no miracles. To some converts, undoubtedly, it came as "strong medicine," but what did it heal? The New Testament contains neither a catalog of maladies that were allegedly healed nor follow-up studies of the individuals said to have been healed of this, that, or the other. What are needed are longitudinal studies showing that those healed "miraculously" through the agency of the Spirit remained well ever after, or at least until death. To illustrate, in the winter of 1951–52, in Lexington, Kentucky, I was made aware of a woman who had been healed many times, according to her husband. She had been diagnosed with chronic appendicitis and when attacked would speed to the altar of her church so as to be there at the next scheduled healing service. It does not seem to have dawned on her that chronic appendicitis comes and goes, that she would, most likely, have gotten better after each attack, and that miracle cures that have to be repeated are neither miracles nor cures. To countless instances of episodic improvement in chronic cases, one must add unnumbered cases of improvement due to the body's own recuperative powers, numerous instances of spontaneous remission (even of cancer), and astronomically large numbers of cases of improvement involving psychosomatic ills. Lacking verification, we do not know that any "miraculous" cases of healing ever occurred in Corinth; even less do we know anything about the healing activities of a disembodied, outdwelling agent variously called the Spirit, the Holy Spirit, or the Holy Ghost.

Next (v. 10), it is written that the Spirit gifted various people in Paul's Corinthian congregation with the power to work miracles (not necessarily limited to healing), the power to prophesy, to discern spirits, to speak in tongues, and to interpret the speaking in tongues. Each of these gifts requires scrutiny.

Nothing is easier than to speak of miracles and of the miraculous. Even today, the secular media, for example, are quick to use these terms in otherwise responsible reporting. A truck plunges off a Mississippi River bridge, falls one hundred feet to the water below, and its driver is "miraculously" rescued. An earthquake buries dozens of people under tons of rubble, and, after a week, a couple of victims are "miraculously" dug out alive. A father and son are trapped by a blizzard raging on the shoulder of a high mountain, and, after nine days, "miraculously" stumble out of an ice cave to the delight of their would-be rescuers. I was told once, in no uncertain terms, that the recovery of good vision in my right eye after a retinal detachment was a miracle. That I sought out the best retinal surgeon at a distinguished medical school to reattach the fallen tissue seems to have been only incidental to this "miracle."

It should be observed that events tend to be viewed as miracles only when they are taken to be beneficial to the one acted upon or to others who vicariously put themselves in the same circumstances. A person, otherwise in good health, who suddenly crashes to the ground because a hip joint has given way is not said to have broken the joint miraculously. An innocent passerby pierced by a bullet that has ricocheted off a metal chimney and thence been deflected by the bill of a swooping bird is not said to have been wounded miraculously. A heavy object accidentally dropped from a highway overpass that crashes through the windshield of a passing vehicle below, killing a passenger within, is not viewed as miraculous. This is very curious, because the definition of the miraculous as that which happens while contravening the laws of nature does not imply that the results must invariably be beneficial.

Even if miracles were always to redound beneficially to some human(s), the problem of criteria remains, that is, the problem of being able to distinguish an event that has contravened natural law from one that is natural but so rare that nobody has ever encountered it before. The first albino piglet born with three heads, six pink eyes, and four tails would, perhaps, qualify. Absent a dependable method for distinguishing events contravening nature from those in accord with it (even though very rare), and absent safeguards against any and all kinds of trickery, Paul could not have recognized a miracle even if he had encountered one. Only if he could have specified an occurrence impossible of achievement by natural means and then besought his deity successfully to bring it to pass could he have recognized a bona fide miracle.

Various people in Paul's congregations were said to have been gifted with prophetic powers. What, precisely, were these powers? What did people having them do that was impossible to ordinary people? Did they attempt to predict the future—in particular the future with reference to the expected return of King Jesus?[155] Did they comment on world events from the presumed standpoint of their deity? Did they admonish the immoral with singular effectiveness, or what? Whatever they did, one thing is clear: prophets in Paul's congregation(s) would have edified the church as *he* understood edification (1 Cor. 14:4–5) and would have proclaimed nothing inimical to *his* teachings, else they would have been attacked, if mentioned at all.

The ability allegedly given by the Spirit to discern spirits (1 Cor. 12:10) means nothing more than the ability to distinguish between true and false teachers, that is, between the orthodox and the heterodox (or heretics). The Spirit need not have bothered giving any gifts for this. All that a reliable discerner would have needed would have been a thorough grasp of Paul's teachings. Anyone disagreeing with him on any point that he regarded as essential to the faith would have had a false spirit.

The "gift" of the Spirit that enabled (and still enables) some to speak in tongues (v. 10) is more complicated than the gift of discerning spirits. Paul was fearful that outsiders and unbelievers who happened to be in church when Christians were exercising this "gift" might think them mad (1 Cor. 14:23). This is one obvious indication that tongues here are not to be confused with foreign languages. Another clear indication is to be found in 1 Corinthians 14:14: "For if I pray in an *unknown* tongue, my spirit prayeth, but my understanding is unfruitful." One could hardly speak in a foreign language without involving one's intellect. What is at issue here is the phenomenon known as glossolalia, something that Paul engaged in more than all the Corinthians (1 Cor. 14:18), according to him. It tells us that he was an ecstatic, episodically at least, and perhaps often. Edifying oneself while speaking in a tongue (1 Cor. 14:4) and communicating with one's deity thereby (1 Cor. 14:2) is all well and good, but what does it disclose of divine truth? Meaning nothing intelligible to ordinary humans, what is said in a tongue reveals nothing to them.

So, the Spirit must also give certain favored individuals interpretive powers (1 Cor. 12:10), either those who speak in tongues themselves (1 Cor. 14:13) or others. Here, as always, when religious claims are made, an ugly epistemological problem intrudes itself. How does the individual whose understanding is disengaged while praying (or declaiming) in a tongue through the Spirit come to know the meaning of the glossolalia uttered?[156] Since to be human is to err, one must be able to apply the appropriate tests to what the mind now says the individual meant when previously vocalizing in ecstasy. The same kind of problem arises when the interpreter is different from the speaker in tongues. How does the interpreter know when the interpretation is right, and even on those occasions when it has been gotten right, how do third parties know which is which? Paul's test would clearly have been that what is said by way of interpretation must be edifying to the church as he understood edification (1 Cor.

14:19). And what would that have been? Whatever supported his theological and ecclesiological positions!

An important instance of the Spirit's being understood as influence, if not taken to be an agent acting directly, occurs in 1 Corinthians 12:3b: "[N]o man can say that Jesus is the Lord, but by the Holy Ghost." Whatever this may imply about human autonomy (or the lack thereof), it becomes extremely curious when juxtaposed with 2 Corinthians 3:17a: "Now the Lord is that [or the] Spirit." As was too often the case, Paul did not write clearly enough to avoid subsequent confusion. In short, are we dealing here with the 'is' of identity or the 'is' of attribution? If the former, then it is correct to say, "The Lord (Jesus) *is* the Spirit, *and* the Spirit *is* the Lord (Jesus)." If the latter, then what one is saying is approximately the following: "The character, intentions, traits, or functions of the Lord (Jesus) are the same as those of the Spirit, but the two remain separable entities." If the first interpretation above is correct, then one might as well say that nobody can call Jesus the Lord except through the influence or agency of Jesus the Lord. Although Paul may have meant this and nothing more, the confusion may equally well be due to the kind of stylistic redundancy one finds in describing the faithful as having a spirit of faith (2 Cor. 4:13).

In some cases, the Lord (Christ) and the Spirit seem to be the same in nature and function. Presumably the Christian is one who has died and risen with Christ. Likewise, writes Paul in Romans 6:11, "[R]eckon ye also yourselves to be dead indeed unto sin, but alive unto God through Jesus Christ our Lord." But, through the Resurrection, Christ became a life-giving Spirit. Says Paul (Rom. 8:9), "But ye are not in the flesh, but in the Spirit, if so be that the Spirit of God dwell in you. Now if any man have not the Spirit of Christ, he is none of his." According to Paul, Christ, then, is in the Christian (Gal. 2:20a): "I am crucified with Christ: nevertheless I live; yet not I, but Christ liveth in me." The Spirit, it should be noted, is also in the Christian. First Corinthians 6:19 says, "What, know ye not that your body is the temple of the Holy Ghost *which is* in you, which ye have of God, and ye are not your own." Similarly, one learns that to walk in the Spirit is to bear good fruit, that is, to exhibit righteousness (Gal. 5:22–23). It should go without saying that the postmortem world where Christians will supposedly be with Christ is the realm of the Spirit.

Despite the identities of nature and function respecting Christ and the Spirit, posited above, the dissimilarities are sharp. For example, nowhere is the Spirit referred to as the Son of God, as Jesus often is (Rom. 1:3–4, 1:9, 5:10, 8:3, 23; 1 Cor. 1:9; 2 Cor. 1:19; Gal. 2:20, 4:4), nor is the Spirit ever represented as incarnated in a particular human body. Moreover, he is never represented as dying for the sins of humanity, nor is he expected to come again in the sense that King Jesus is expected to return. Finally, the Spirit, as Paul uses the term, is never referred to as an agent in creation, nor does Paul make a point of the Spirit's preexistence with the Bible-god, as he does in the case of King Jesus (Phil. 2:5–8) who first was with Paul's deity (equal in form), then came to earth as a man, and finally returned to be with the deity in question.[157]

In his commentary on 2 Corinthians, R. V. G. Trasker tries to resolve the relation between the "Son of God" and the "Spirit of God" functionally, as have many before him.[158] He writes, "The influence of Christ and the influence of the Holy Spirit cannot, therefore, be distinguished."[159] Well and good, but Paul calls the one source of this common influence the "Son of God"; the other source is never called by this name. So, something distinguished, or should have distinguished, the two in his theology. What might it have been, how could he have discovered what it was, and why should the recipients of his letters have believed the "Son of God" and the "Holy Spirit" to have been more than figments of Paul's imagination?

It is tempting for modern Christian liberals, at least, to think that Paul was writing metaphorically (and not literally) whenever he called Jesus the Son of God, that he was merely thinking of an attitudinal, dispositional, or intentional unity between his deity and Jesus the Messiah. However, Philippians 2:6–11 shows that Paul had much more in mind than the kinds of unity suggested above. This passage speaks of Messiah Jesus as follows:

> Who, being in the form of God, thought it not robbery to be equal with God:
> But made himself of no reputation [i.e., emptied himself], and took upon him the form of a servant [or slave], and was made in the likeness of man.[160]
> And being found in fashion as a man he humbled himself, and became obedient unto death, even the death of the cross.
> Wherefore God also hath highly exalted him, and given him a name which is above every name:
> That at the name of Jesus every knee should bow, of *things* in heaven, and *things* in earth, and *things* under the earth;
> And *that* every tongue should confess that Jesus Christ *is* Lord, to the glory of God the Father.

When the verses above are added to Colossians 1:15–19 (which claims that the "Son of God" was the firstborn of creation, was the one by whom and for whom all things were created, and is the one in whom all things cohere) an exalted Christology (or doctrine of Jesus' person) results. It should be noted, however, that these passages cannot make a Trinitarian of Paul in what is now the orthodox sense of that doctrine.[161]

Those Christians who believe in a triune Godhead (and not all do) of three hypostases (Father, Son, and Holy Spirit) justify their belief by reading back into Paul's loose use of language (and the confusion resulting therefrom) their own preconceived notions. In Paul's letters, it is obvious that three distinct, personal nouns (in Greek) are used to name God, Christ, and the Holy Spirit. It is also obvious that the three are identified at times in various ways, but it is equally obvious that each personalized concept in Paul's mind is distinguished from the other two on different occasions. So, as H. Wheeler Robinson says, "Paul does not conceive the Father, Son, and Holy Spirit as three hypostases [or persons in Latin] and one ousia [or essence], three centers on one plane equidistant from the believer. Paul conceived of a line of intensive approach, always in the Spirit, always through Christ, always to the Father."[162] Elias Andrews adds that although there may have been a trinity of expression in Paul's thinking, there certainly was no immanential metaphysical trinity in his mind.[163] In short, Paul was confused about his subject matter, could not have known what he was talking about (in the sense of having warranted beliefs thereof), and was in no position to reveal anything to anybody, whether that person was "spiritually minded" or not.

For Paul the cosmos was a small and tidy affair. Neither he nor any other biblical writer had an adequate cosmology as we now understand this term. Theirs was, more nearly, a cosmogony, a very constricted view of the earth together with its close neighbors, the sun, the moon, and the stars which, conveniently, circled around it—or so it seemed to all unsophisticated eyes, except for those in the polar latitudes. This cosmos was viewed as belonging to its maker just as a clay pot belonged to the potter who molded it. In this little world, however, the paradigm for power was not supplied by the potter alone but also by the proverbial oriental despot. In short, monarchical thinking played a huge part in Paul's day and time. The potter and the potentate were, of course, persons, and persons were constituted by parts, some of which were taken to be physical and some of which were taken to be nonphysical, not to say spiritual. Among the latter constituents were such hypothesized entities as the mind, the soul, and the spirit, all inhabiting animistically (or being closely associated with) some human body or other. In order to rule effectively, despots (then as now) had to be able to communicate with their subjects and did so ordinarily through a hierarchy of underlings and messengers. Among the most effective ways, presumably, whereby the sovereign could communicate with his subjects was through the dispatch of his firstborn son. Surely the king's rebellious subjects would respond to his heir, yet, as might have been predicted, they did not but, instead, killed him (see the parable of the house-despot or landlord who planted a vineyard in Matt. 21:33–46, Mark 12:1–12, and Luke 20:9–19). The despot carried out two actions in response to his subjects' murderous act: (1) He came to slay these rebellious tenants, letting others replace them (see Isa. 5:1–7 as well as the Gospel passages cited above), and (2) he made that which had been rejected (i.e., the firstborn son) into the cornerstone of a new edifice. As it is written in Matthew 21:42 (also see Mark 12:10 and Luke 20:17), "The stone which the builders rejected, the same is become the head of the corner: this is the Lord's doing, and it is marvelous in our eyes."

With an appropriately magical mentality, there is no difficulty in seeing the dead heir of the parable as the living cornerstone of a new edifice, or, better yet, of a new dispensation. The rebellious tenants are, of course, the Jews of the Mosaic covenant. Those who are allowed to replace them in the vineyards of the Lord are Christians, whose church constitutes the new Israel. The cornerstone of the new dispensation, the dispensation of grace, is, as we might expect, the resurrected heir who will come again in the fullness of his power at the end of the present age. The A-h reports (in Acts 2:22–24, 33, 36) that Peter preached as follows on the day of Pentecost:

> Ye men of Israel, hear these words; Jesus of Nazareth, a man approved of God among you by miracles and wonders and signs, which God did by him in the midst of you, as ye know:
> Him being delivered by the determinate counsel and foreknowledge of God, ye have taken and by wicked hands have crucified and slain:
> Whom God hath raised up, having loosed the pains of death: because it was not possible that he should be holden of it. . . .
> Therefore being by the right hand of God exalted, and having received of the Father the promise of the Holy Ghost, he both shed forth this, which ye now see and hear. . . .
> Therefore let all the house of Israel know assuredly, that God hath made that same Jesus, whom ye have crucified, both Lord and Christ.[164]

When contemplating what possible significance the term 'Son of God' might have, it is instructive to contrast our contemporary, scientifically informed worldview with Paul's storybook view, and to do so at four points: (1) His antique Semitic cosmogony versus modern cosmology; (2) his traditional, introspectionistic, dualistic anthropology and psychology (replete with spirit possession) versus modern monistic, materialistic approaches to human consciousness and behavior based on studies in the neurosciences; (3) his theology (not to say mythology) of history, especially of Jewish history, versus modern approaches to historiography; and (4) his eschatological anticipation based on a soteriological fulfillment versus contemporary futurist outlooks based on extrapolations from natural history and current socioeconomic trends.

First, it is clear that our world, unlike Paul's, is no small and tidy affair. We must struggle to comprehend astronomically long periods of time, astronomically great distances, and astronomically large numbers of stellar and quasi-stellar objects. Our worldview must now begin with quarks or even more fugitive building blocks of atomic nuclei, extend to black holes lurking ravenously in the centers of great galaxies, and not stop until the whole of matter (dark as well as light) and also antimatter are encompassed. Ours is not a clockwork universe nicely packaged within a discrete container, constituting space, but is rather an expanding universe of galaxies hurtling away from one another (except when colliding), a world with no stable center such as the earth was naively taken to be in Paul's day.

Second, an equally great contrast appears when one juxtaposes the three homunculi (mind, soul, and spirit) of Paul's theology of human nature with the findings of the neurosciences respecting brain anatomy and physiology. As I write these words, I have before me an article titled "The Brain Manages Happiness and Sadness in Different Centers."[165] Focusing for the moment on happiness and taking it to include joy, I call the reader's attention to Romans 15:13, wherein Paul writes, "Now the God of hope fill you with all joy and peace in believing, that ye may abound in hope through the power of the Holy Ghost." Here is a typical bit of Pauline thought. As a result of believing in correct doctrine (i.e., what he taught), the individual, conceived of as a receptacle, is to be filled with the emotion of joy through the agency of spirit possession, the spirit in this case being one called the Holy Ghost. This is not the way the article in front of me explains the experiencing of happiness. In summary, the article says, "The brain handles happiness and sadness in different areas, not in a single emotional center [the limbic system including the amygdala and the thalamus] as was thought." Positron emission tomography (PET) scans indicate that happiness is experienced when certain decreases in brain activity (associated with forethought and planning) occur. The sharpest decrease in activity is to be found in the right prefrontal and temporal parietal cortex. The point here is not to claim that happiness and joy are identical nor to suggest that scientists can study only instances of secular joy, leaving free rein to the Holy Ghost in cases of religious joy. The point is to show how our worldview is (or can be) informed by science, whereas Paul's worldview was both prescientific and prephilosophical.

Third, the Jews approached their past temporally (not cyclically) and, hence, had a genuine sense of history. They did not, however, study their past to determine precisely what had happened and why, because they already knew on faith, a priori (i.e., theologically), what had happened and why. First, their deity, YHWH, called Father Abraham from Mesopotamia (Gen. 12:1–7; Deut. 26:5–6; Josh. 24:2–15) and made his posterity a chosen people, a holy nation (Deut. 7:6–11). Then, to justify their eventual bloody occupation of Palestine, they arranged, theologically, to have YHWH give them, presumably, the promised land in perpetuity (Gen. 12:7). When their national fortunes went well, it was because their king had done that which was right in the sight of the Lord (2 Kings 18:3, 22:2), and when their national fortunes went badly (which was most of the time), it was because their king (or the whole people) had done that which was evil in the sight of the Lord (2 Kings 17:2, 21:2). When YHWH's three promises that (1) his people were to possess the promised land in perpetuity (Gen. 17:8), (2) were to be as numerous as the sands of the sea (Hosea 1:10), and (3) were to be a blessing to all nations (Gen. 12:3) went unfulfilled, it was because the chosen people had sinned most grievously (Ps. 106:32–46; Ezek. 5:5–11). When decimated by stronger, rival, neighboring states, it was because YHWH was using the triumphant nations as a rod of his anger, a staff of his fury (Isa. 10:5) with which to chasten his wayward people. To the eye of faith, the promises would, of course, be fulfilled one day with the arrival of the Davidic Messiah to restore the fortunes of Israel (Jer. 23:5–8). It was in such a theological hothouse as this that Paul's view of history was forged. His novelty was to have invited Gentiles in to share the promises and to have invited non-Christian Jews out. Modern historical studies, when at their best, do not proceed in such a manner. They do not interpret the past with reference to some myth or other of ethnic selection or of national destiny, are not based on theological assumptions, and do not explain current conditions either as a divine reward for previous virtues or as a divine penalty for earlier vices. Nowadays, history is being rewritten continuously as new data and new varieties of evidence come to light, as earlier assumptions prove themselves inadequate, and as the demands of patriotism and the constraints of culture are relaxed. World history can no longer be subsumed under "sacred history," though elements of myth still cling to historiography.[166]

Fourth, for Paul, at his juncture in history, the reign of Satan and sin was about to end (Rom. 16:20; Phil. 3:20–21; 1 Thess. 1:10), death was about to be conquered (it is tempting to say that death was about to die; see 1 Cor. 15:26, 54–56), and the power of flesh and the law was about to end (1 Cor. 15:56b–57).[167] When all was in readiness, in the immediate future, the following would occur, according to 1 Thessalonians 4:14–17:

> For if we believe that Jesus died and rose again, even so them also which sleep in Jesus will God bring with him.
>
> For this we say unto you by the word of the Lord, that we which are alive *and* remain unto the coming of the Lord shall not prevent them which are asleep.
>
> For the Lord himself shall descend from heaven with a shout, with the voice of the archangel, and with the trump of God: and the dead in Christ shall rise first:
>
> Then we which are alive *and* remain shall be caught up together with them in the clouds, to meet the Lord in the air: and so shall we ever be with the Lord.

Such were Paul's futurist expectations about 1,950 years ago. The theme was soteriological; the hope was to live in the heavens with the Lord after one had died on earth, together with all other true Christians. Modern futurists have rather different expectations. In one issue of *The Futurist*, vol. 29 (1995), I found such articles as "Seven Doomsday Myths about the Environment"; "Nanoplastics: How 'Intelligent' Materials May Change Our Homes"; "Building Tomorrow's Empires of Technology"; and "Planning for Career and Life: Job Surfing on the Tidal Waves of Change." Life in space, life in the oceans, life in various kinds of planned communities, new opportunities for work at home, being wired to the world of cyberspace; these and other similar themes dominate modern futurist thought. Hardly a word is said about the end of the world or of the human species (though devastating microorganisms may lurk in our future); nothing is envisioned as to redemption either of a chosen people or of all peoples; not a hint of levitating into the heavens to be with Jesus. Alas, such is the nature of clouds that they cannot bear aloft even so insignificant a figure (in world history) as a Jewish king, nor can they support the indeterminate weight of those who are dead in Jesus and are (presumably) levitating in their post-mortem state.

As was pointed out in part 1, it is logically possible that the universe is an artifact or sufficiently like one to allow the inference that it is the work of an artificer (or a creator). It is also logically possible that the inferred artificer persists until this very day and that he, she, or it has some regard for the universe, including the human contingent therein. However, the mind-boggling magnitudes and the confounding complexities of the universe (touched upon four paragraphs above) prevent the Bible-god from being a serious candidate for the position at issue. Much though the Bible lauds its deity's wisdom and extols his power, a close examination of the scriptures reveals that the Bible-god knew nothing about the world not known by the Bible's archaic authors. Needless to say, they knew very little about it. Obviously, knowledge of the universe has expanded astronomically since the biblical canon was closed. The inescapable conclusion is that the Bible-god, the deity of Paul, was far too ignorant, not to say too stupid, to have made this world. His knowledge of mathematics, physics, and chemistry appears to have been nonexistent; his knowledge of astronomy, geology, and biology, minuscule at best and muddle-headed. If it were humanly possible to catch a glimmer of what the essential conditions would have had to have been for anything to qualify as the artificer of the universe, what sense could then be made of the assertion that he, she, or it had a human, male offspring and that Jesus of Nazareth, the alleged king of the Jews, was that offspring? For nearly two millennia, we in the West have heard 'Son of God' intoned so often and so gravely that it has seemed to name a particular being in a straightforward way. But, upon reflection, nothing could be more problematic. Of all the points that could be made relevant to this, the clearest one is that Paul *knew* nothing of any such offspring, no matter how fervent his faith. Moreover, it does not matter how 'Son of God' is interpreted, metaphorically, morally, metaphysically, or physically. Insuperable problems of meaning, verification, and knowledge (understood as warranted belief) persist.

Since 'Spirit of God', 'Holy Spirit', and 'the Spirit' flowed from Paul's pen more often than did 'Son of God', and since the saint's hypothesized deity and the deity's male offspring were presumed to share the same Spirit, it is important to approach 'Spirit of God' as 'Son of God' was approached in the preceding paragraph. We must also come to grips with 'Mind of God', a term which I wish to examine before turning to 'Spirit of God'.

Any purposive entity that could have designed the universe to be as it is and to function as it does must possess (or have possessed) surpassingly great intelligence. As feeble and inadequate as the greatest human minds may be (in relation to such intelligence), they constitute, nevertheless, the *only* avenue of comprehension open to us. So, in analyzing 'Mind of God', we must first analyze the mind of a human being. This, of course, lands us in the midst of the mind-body problem or, better yet, the mind-brain problem. To say 'my mind' and 'my body' is to say much the same thing in that the same owner is posited and some sort of possession is claimed in each case, but one's experience of consciousness (or one's awareness of awareness) is very different from one's experience of one's body or some part thereof. English ratifies the difference by forcing us to distinguish between mind and brain by providing (and also by limiting) us with two different vocabularies that can scarcely be intermingled, if at all. When speaking of the conscious mind, we speak of attending to this or that; of intending to do this or that; of contemplating x or y; of seeing, hearing, tasting, touching, or scenting something or other; of feeling this way (emotionally) or that way; of having one mind or of having two minds about some stimulus or other; of remembering, fantasizing, or dreaming; etc. When we speak of a living human brain, we speak of an organ weighing about three pounds; of functioning tissue of specialized sorts; of a wet-cell battery; of electrochemical energy; of neurotransmitters shuttling to and fro over synapses between neurons; of certain brain centers inhibiting or releasing other brain centers, as the case may be; and of, in correlation with feelings of happiness, for example, the decrease of activity in the centers of forethought and planning in the right prefrontal and temporal parietal cortex. When, in evolutionary terms, we contemplate the success of our species in surviving (or even in flourishing), one point is obvious: we have not needed nor have we been able to know by direct intuition anything at all as to how our brains work or what they are doing at any time.

Given the great gulf between experiencing our minds and experiencing our bodies, and given the chasm between the vocabularies of mind and body, the inevitable question arises as to how, in one person, we are to relate the two. Among contemporary scientists and philosophers there is a tidal wave in favor of materialism, of biologizing the mind, and of seeing it as an achievement of the brain.[168] If to explain the mind of a human being, nowadays, we must advert to the brain of that person, what are we to understand by 'Mind of God'? Does it entail that there is a Big Brain somewhere (i.e., occupying space) which by functioning biologically could explain the thoughts Paul attributed to the Bible-god or the thoughts attributed to the artificer of natural theology? If so, this is but the first of many uncomfortable questions.[169]

A more popular attempt at resolving the brain-mind problem than materialism lies in theorizing some sort or degree of interaction between radically dissimilar realities. This approach is at least as old as its most famous proponent, French philosopher, René Descartes (1596–1650), who defined any sort of body as an unthinking (i.e., nonconscious) somewhat extended in (or occupying) space and any mind (human or divine) as a thinking (i.e., conscious) somewhat not extended in (or occupying) space. How the two "somewhats," one a material substance, the other a mental substance, for want of a better term, could interact in a person occupied much of Descartes' time. The result of this radical bifurcation was ridiculed by English philosopher Gilbert Ryle as the "ghost in the machine theory."[170] Much thought has been spent in trying to avoid the Cartesian extremes of definition while still maintaining that the brain and the mind, being separate entities, interact. According to this the mind does not simply result from brain function but is something in its own right. Given Paul's persistent dualism (or even trialism), this attempt at resolution would no doubt have satisfied him more than the idea that the mind is a brain function. But, upon reflection, his likely preference resolves nothing theological, because it posits two entities (God and the Mind of God) and tells us nothing as to how the two might differ yet interact in creating a supreme, divine, conscious person. It seems likely that, if pushed on this point, Paul would have said that his deity had a spiritual body. This, however, is an incoherent idea. Even if we had the slightest inkling as to what the term might mean, we would still not know how the mind of the hypothesized being could interact with the spiritual body of the same being. For all we can tell, these are merely words—words signifying nothing. Were Bentham alive today, he would make just this point.

At first blush, the best maneuver might be to deny dualism altogether respecting Paul's or any other deity. One could posit unity by saying that 'Mind of God' is just a way of referring to whatever is meant by 'God', that 'Spirit of God' is just a way of referring to whatever is meant by 'God', and that 'Mind of God' is just a way of referring to whatever is meant by 'Spirit of God', and vice versa in each case. Then, one could deny that any of these terms refers to anything physical, bodily, or material. This, however, would be no more than a verbal solution. Positing such a unity within a disembodied mind is not the same as demonstrating its reality. The extent to which faith would have to be called upon to maintain this idea of divine mental unity is the extent to which all knowledge of it would be absent. The greater the advances in the neurosciences, in computers, and in artificial intelligence, the more difficult it will become for informed people to entertain the idea of a disembodied mind, even if divine. The inevitable question will be, how does it work? The almost inevitable answer will be, by some kind of mechanism, as it were. Needless to say, this is not what Paul had in mind.

Any thorough analysis of 'Holy Spirit' takes us deeper than Paul's stated beliefs into the realm of his experiences. This does not require us to rely on the A-h's conversion accounts (on the Damascus Road) or on Paul's reference to the man taken up into the third heaven in 2 Corinthians 12:3 (to be discussed more later). Although Bentham thought the only demonstrable change in Paul's life was the one from being a persecutor of Christianity to being a promoter of it, this is mistaken. Paul's epistles indicate an additional change, an inner change. Paul says of himself that he was (1) a Hebrew born of Hebrews (Phil. 3:5; Gal. 2:15; 2 Cor. 11:22), (2) circumcised on the eighth day (Phil. 3:5), (3) a member of the tribe of Benjamin (Phil. 3:5; Rom. 11:1), (4) a Pharisee (Phil. 3:5), (5) a zealous advocate of the traditions of his fathers (Gal. 1:14), (6) a zealous persecutor of the church (Phil. 3:6), and (7) a blameless person, righteous under the Mosaic law (Phil. 3:6). He was also, by his own admission, advanced in Judaism beyond many of his own age (Gal. 1:14). The A-h reiterates some of this by calling him (or letting him call himself in speeches) a Jew (22:3), a Pharisee (23:6, 26:5), and a persecutor of the church (26:9, 11).

The characteristics above fall naturally into two distinct classes, those that are accidents of birth (for which one can take neither credit nor blame) and those that are not (for which one can take either credit or blame). It is very significant, I think, that when describing his moral and religious life in Judaism, Paul never attributed anything he did to the indwelling of the "Holy Spirit," yet, presumably, his deity possessed a Holy Spirit before and during the time Paul remained a devotee of Judaism. (In view of Paul's style of expression as a Christian thinker, one might have expected him to say that he had a *spirit of zeal* for the Mosaic law, not just that he was zealous for it, or that he had a *spirit of attainment* rather than just being ahead of his peers in the practice of Judaism, or that he was moved by a *spirit of persecution* toward the church rather than that he persecuted the church.) At some point in his life, whether on the Damascus Road, in the third heaven, or elsewhere, Paul began to have some intense emotional experiences that shook him out of Judaism (part way at least) and that led to the spirit-dominated argot that we have come to associate with his ponderings as a Christian. Whatever the cause of these intense emotional experiences, they could only have been interpreted by him (given his uncritical time, place, and person) as instances of possession, of spirit-possession, of possession by the one spirit (in particular) that he chose to call the Holy Spirit (or Ghost). Paul measured the holiness of this ghost by the perceived benefits that accrued to him from his Christian belief and behavior. Among these perceived benefits were justification by faith (Rom. 5:1, 6, 8), deliverance from the bondage to sin which leads to death (Rom. 6:14, 16), and the promise of endless life in bliss after physical death (1 Cor. 15:51–57).

The importance to Paul of being justified in the presence of his deity (whatever, precisely, he meant by justification) cannot be overemphasized. But, why had he not been justified (or felt that way) while still a zealously observant Jew? Unless Philippians 3:6 (wherein he claims to have been righteous in the law and blameless) is just another example of Pauline braggadocio, he ought (while still a zealously observant Jew) to have been justified (or to have felt that way) and thus been at peace with himself, satisfied with his religion, and in harmony with the presumed will of his deity. In Romans 2:13 he tells us that it is not hearers of the law that are justified but doers of it. Since he was a zealous doer of it, by his own admission, he ought to have been justified. However, his writings indicate that he had not been at peace with himself for some time prior to becoming a Christian. What could have caused his (extreme?) unease and (intolerable?) cognitive dissonance? Perhaps it was his murderous persecution of those of his fellow Jews who were Nazarenes.[171]

No theological reason has ever been found that would have explained his confessed savagery toward the church. Since Paul seems to have been pro-Roman all along and zealous for the traditions of Judaism (while still an observant Jew), it is tempting to theorize that at first sight he perceived in the church's proclamation that Jesus was the Messiah something inimical to Rome and potentially dangerous for the Jews—sedition. The danger to the Jews would have been Roman military force used in suppressing the sedition at issue. This theory, though perhaps mistaken, may explain his persecution of those who believed in the crucified Nazarene.[172] A rapid change in primitive Christian expectations may have led Paul to modify his perception of any politicomilitary threat associated with belief in Jesus. The extent to which Jesus was believed to be the religiopolitical messiah from David's line was the extent to which his disciples' hopes were dashed by his ignominious, unmessianic execution.[173] But, believing Jesus still to be alive though no longer present in the flesh, the church rallied quickly, in theological terms, by coming to view his death as a necessary prelude to a temporary withdrawal to heaven in preparation for his triumphal return (or second coming) to usher in the reign (or kingdom) on earth of the Bible-god. For their part, the Romans would have found such a heavenly reign far less disturbing than they would have found the terrestrial agitations of a messianic pretender afoot in Palestine.

A somewhat parallel change may (indeed, must) have occurred in Paul's perceptions. Jesus, for him, ceased to be merely a claimant to the Jewish throne and equally a (proposed) deliverer of Israel from her enemies, preeminently Rome, and became a deliverer (or *soter* or savior) of all human beings from death and personal destruction in the grave (Rom. 5:18–21). In believing this, Paul not only worked strenuously to bring Gentiles into the Christian fold but also felt himself freed from the Mosaic law by the coming of the messianic age that Jesus had presumably inaugurated. Gentile Christians, of course, had never been under this law, and Jewish Christians henceforth could (and should) be delivered from its bondage by substituting faith in Christ for legalistic observation. With this new faith in Jesus Christ as the savior of the world, Paul felt justified. His cognitive dissonance was gone, and emotional peace was restored to his life.

Just how this evolution in religious thought was accompanied by (or punctuated with) experiences of "Holy Ghost" possession we will never know. Did the experience of possession come first, followed by changes in belief and thought, or did changes in belief and thought begin to change first, followed by episodic experiences of possession? Or was there such an intermingling of the two, each reinforcing the other, that it does not matter which came first and which came second? In any case, Paul's change from a zealous, observant, but non–spirit-possessed Jew to a zealous, nonobservant (of the ceremonial law), spirit-possessed Christian was profoundly significant psychologically. But does one have to go beyond the psychological domain to explain the possession he experienced over and again? The answer is no. Does one have to go beyond the sociobiological creature that is the human being to some "spiritual" realm or other to explain the glossolalia Paul engaged in, more than all others (1 Cor. 14:18)? Again the answer is no. Does one have to hypothesize the existence of a supernatural agent to explain the radical religious reorientation of St. Paul? The answer is a decisive no. That he would have answered yes to these three questions merely indicates how he grasped at an explanatory fiction to explain his experiences. That he did so is understandable. That others subsequently dogmatized his explanation, taking it on faith, is also understandable, but unfortunate. That we should continue to explain such experiences by resorting to a "spirit" of this or that is absurd. Personal and social psychology plus the neurosciences will suffice. Not only is there no need to hypothesize an outdwelling, extranatural agent to explain "spirit possession" and related phenomena, to do so is to violate the Law of Parsimony (which holds that the simpler of any two equally adequate explanations is to be preferred), to thwart any possibility of rational inquiry into the nature of the alleged agent, and to turn the inquiry over to magical thinking, which, in this context, would almost certainly be called spiritual.[174]

What was true of Paul in terms of personal psychology was also true of the social psychology that developed in the Christian congregations that welcomed him on his missionary journeys in the Hellenistic world or in congregations that he founded while traveling about. Such was Paul's personality, such the kinds of people he converted to his persuasion, and such were the times in which he and they lived that his experiences of being possessed became infectious. Just as he had felt the power that can radically reorient one's life, so, too, did his converts, or some of them at least. Just as he could feel cleansed, forgiven, justified, or saved, so, too, could they, or some of them at least. Just as he could become ecstatic, speaking in the unknown tongue, so, too, could they, or some of them at least. Just as he could participate in psychosomatic healings episodically, so, too, could they, or some of them at least. Just as he could prophesy (whatever this may mean), so, too, could they, or some of them at least. It is little wonder then that he came to associate what he called the Spirit of God with the power to accomplish a variety of (to him) religiously desirable works. In Romans 15:19 he wrote, "Through mighty signs and wonders, by the power of the Spirit of God; so that from Jerusalem, and round about Illyricum, I have fully preached the gospel of Christ." In 1 Corinthians 4:20 he wrote, "For the kingdom of God *is* not in word, but in power." In 1 Thessalonians 1:5, in a similar vein, he wrote, "For our gospel came not unto you in word only, but in power and in the Holy Ghost." In 1 Corinthians 1:18, he capped it off writing, "For the preaching of the cross is to them that perish foolishness; but unto us which are saved it is the power of God."

Second (in the catalog of Paul's "spiritual" beliefs) to the quadripartite nature of his deity (i.e., God, the Mind of God, the Son of God, and the Spirit of God) is the quadripartite set of evil agents (i.e., Satan, Sin, Flesh, and Death). It is surprising how seldom 'Satan' issued from Paul's pen— fewer than a dozen times, including one use of 'Belial' as another name for the same malign agent (2 Cor. 6:15). Reserving references to the Devil and to demons for later consideration, we learn that Satan seeks to gain advantage over us (2 Cor. 2:11); that he may tempt married people through lack of self-control (1 Cor. 7:5); that Paul was pleased on one occasion to deliver an evildoer (probably an antinomian libertine) to Satan for the destruction of the miscreant's flesh (1 Cor. 5:5); that on one occasion Satan hindered Paul and his party from visiting the Thessalonians (1 Thess. 2:18); that Satan sent a vexatious messenger (a thorn in the flesh) to buffet Paul (2 Cor. 12:7); that Satan was, in some surpassingly mysterious way, delaying the arrival of the lawless one, the man of perdition, whose coming had to precede the arrival of the eschaton (2 Thess. 2:9); and that Satan was *soon* to be crushed by the peace of God beneath the trampling feet of Christians (Rom. 16:20).[175] In Paul's treatment of Satan we find the same mistakes in reasoning that blight his treatment of God, the Mind of God, the

Son of God, and the Spirit of God. Paul, giving no justification for hypothesizing a malign "spiritual" entity, lapsed into unwarranted dualism, created an explanatory fiction, unwittingly violated the Law of Parsimony, and failed to analyze the lessened degree of moral accountability that, logically, ought to attach itself to those who are subjected to satanic infestation through no necessary fault of their own.

Sin, in Paul's thought, is best approached with a mixture of exposition, analysis, and criticism. On two occasions he created a catalog of individual sins. First, in Romans 1:29–31 we find unrighteousness, fornication, wickedness, covetousness, maliciousness, envy, murder, debate (i.e., quarrelsomeness), malignity, whisperings, backbiting, animosity toward God, spitefulness, pride, boasting, the inventing of evil things, disobedience to parents, lack of understanding, covenant-breaking, lack of natural affection, implacability, and unmercifulness. Second, in Galatians 5:19–21 we find adultery, fornication, uncleanness, lasciviousness, idolatry, witchcraft, hatred, variance, emulations, wrath, strife, seditiousness, heresies, envyings, murders, drunkenness, revelings, and the like.

Ease in communication requires that we create and use abstract nouns to name classes (or sets) of things and of activities. For example, we use 'justice' to name the class (or set) of all just actions, 'truth' to name the class (or set) of all true assertions, and 'beauty' to name the class (or set) of all beautiful things or activities. It is not clear that Paul was aware of the logical differences between classes (or sets) and the members that constitute them, nor do his letters show the acumen to recognize that what is true of a class (or set) is not necessarily true of its members and vice versa. In any case, he did not commit the common fallacies of composition and division, but respecting sin what he did was far worse.[176] Instead of treating 'sin' as the name of the class (or set) of all individual sinful behaviors, he hypostatized it, took it to be *alive*, and transmogrified it into a malign agent. Here again, a form of spirit possession characterizes his thought.

Romans 6:6–23 accords to sin an active role largely parallel to that accorded to the Bible-god. Verse 12 says, "Let not sin therefore reign in your mortal body, that ye should obey it in the lusts thereof." Verse 16 adds, "Know ye not, that to whom ye yield yourselves servants to obey, his servants ye are to whom ye obey; whether of sin unto death, or of obedience unto righteousness?" Here the whole of life is portrayed as one or the other of two servitudes, as slavery to sin or as slavery to the Bible-god. No moral autonomy is accorded to a human being except for the sole choice of a master. Sin, we learn in Romans 7:8, took occasion by the commandment, "Thou shalt not covet," to work all manner of concupiscence in Paul. He wrote in Romans 7:11, "For sin, taking occasion by the commandment, deceived me, and by it slew me." It is in the context of what might be called "sin-possession" that he wrote the famous, but puzzling, lines in Romans 7:19–24:

For the good that I would I do not: but the evil which I would not, that I do.

Now if I do that I would not, it is no more I that do it, but sin that dwelleth in me.

I find then a law, that, when I would do good, evil is present with me.

For I delight in the law of God after the inward man:

But I see another law in my members, warring against the law of my mind, and bringing me into captivity to the law of sin which is in my members.

O wretched man that I am! Who shall deliver me from the body of this death?

Yes, Paul was a wretched man, because he came through misunderstood experiences to believe in spirit possession and lost his moral autonomy thereby yet retained forebodings of culpability, even though it was the spirit possessing him that was evil and not he himself. Paul could (and may) have found an unhappy precedent for his anxiety in the disastrous end of the Pharaoh of the Exodus. Respecting this end, it is never clear as to whether it was Pharaoh who brought destruction upon himself by hardening his heart against the Children of Israel (Exod. 8:15, 32) or whether it was the Bible-god who hardened Pharaoh's heart against them (Exod. 10:1, 20). Whatever the explanation of Pharaoh's motivation, he paid the ultimate price (Exod. 14:17–28), if this story is, in the main, historical.

According to Morton Smith, it was commonly believed in Paul's day that possession by an evil agent, for example, could make people "act foolishly or criminally, sometimes hurt themselves, sometimes even commit suicide."[177] In emotional terms, then, Paul had good reason to be anxious about the consequences to himself of doing (or of having done in and through him by an evil agent) that which he would not have done left to himself and of not doing (or of not being permitted to do by an evil agent) that which he would have done of his own volition. Theologically, however, he had no reason to indulge in such histrionics as calling himself a wretched man, for by the time he wrote Romans, he had long since come through faith to think himself in possession of the good, saving Spirit of Jesus—or so his theology would have it.[178] When referring to the body of this death (in Rom. 7:24), Paul was giving vent to his idea that death was (and is) the result of the original sin of Adam and not the natural end of all organic creatures. Of this bit of Pauline theology Rudolf Bultmann writes: "Human beings are subject to death even before they have committed any sin. And to attribute human mortality to the fall of Adam is sheer nonsense, for guilt implies personal responsibility, and the idea of original sin as an inherited infection is subethical, irrational, and absurd."[179] What is true of Paul's thought in this particular is true of his theology in general.

'Flesh' is a term in Paul's theological vocabulary that exceeds most, if not all, other terms in the number of its meanings. Some of these are non-problematic; some are problematic but contextually comprehensible (in light of his Judaism); and some are problematic and hard, if not impossible, to comprehend. A sampling of nonproblematic uses of 'flesh' follows: When he told the Philippians that he wanted to depart this life to be with Jesus but that he would abide in the flesh that he might minister to their ("spiritual") needs (Phil. 1:23–24), he merely meant that he would remain alive on their behalf. When he told the Colossians that though he was absent in the flesh but was with them in spirit (Col. 2:5), he meant no more than that he was not physically with them despite his abiding influence (see also 1 Cor. 5:3). When in Romans 1:3 he wrote of Jesus as being of the seed of David according to the flesh, he meant that the former was a physical descendant of the latter. When he wrote in 1 Corinthians 8:13 that he would not eat flesh if that action were to offend his brother (in Christ) he meant that he would not eat meat (also see Rom. 14:21). When (in 1 Cor. 15:39) he distinguished between the flesh of humans, of beasts, of fishes, and of birds, he was announcing approximately what we would mean by saying that animal tissue from different species, genera, etc., is not identical.

Other nonproblematic uses of 'flesh' are (or were) metaphorical. To have a thorn in the flesh (2 Cor. 13:7) is so commonplace as to need no comment. When in 1 Corinthians 15:50 he declared that flesh and blood cannot inherit the Kingdom of God, he meant that the physical and the mortal cannot inherit the nonphysical (or spiritual) and the everlasting (or immortal). When in 1 Corinthians 1:26 he observed that not many of his Corinthian congregants were wise as to the flesh (or in the flesh) he probably meant that not many Christians there were intellectuals—literate, learned, and logical (in the sense of having mastered rhetoric). When in Colossians 3:22 he told slaves to obey their lords according to the flesh, he probably meant that Christian slaves were to obey their masters in worldly (i.e., secular) affairs as befitted their status (but were not necessarily to obey them in "spiritual" matters). When in Galatians 4:13 he wrote of the infirmities of the flesh, he was referring to some malady or disability that plagued him physically, and when in Romans 13:14 he mentioned the lusts of the flesh, he was referring to such moral weaknesses as drunkenness and (sexual) wantonness (see also Gal. 5:19–21). While on the subject of sex, it must be acknowledged that Paul probably thought that he was writing literally, not metaphorically, when he wrote, in 1 Corinthians 6:16, that he who joins himself to the body of a harlot becomes one flesh with her (see also Rom. 6:19). Nowadays, however, this can only be taken metaphorically, for we know that the exchange of bodily fluids during sexual intercourse cannot suffice to cause two people to merge magically into one.

The surprising use of 'flesh' (in Paul's theology) to mean circumcision is a problematic but contextually comprehensible utilization. It is problematic in that no rational reason is ever given as to why the Bible-god chose this form of penile mutilation as an emblem of belonging to his "chosen people" (see Gen. 17:11). Why not a lopped-off right ear lobe or a lopped-off third toe on the left foot in lieu of a lopped-off foreskin? Clearly, such mutilation is not a precondition for "spirituality." Otherwise how could one explain the spirituality of Paul's Gentile (i.e., uncircumcised) male converts? Contextual comprehensibility, however, emerges from the recognition that Paul had, on a regular basis, to cope theologically with three classes of people: (1) Jews who practiced the ceremonial law (among whose rituals circumcision was paramount) but who spurned the Jesus movement; (2) Jews who practiced the ceremonial law and espoused the message of the Jesus movement; and (3) non-Jews who espoused the teachings of the Jesus movement and spurned the ceremonial law. Episodically he also had to deal with antinomian Christians, of whatever extraction, but that topic is treated elsewhere. It is not necessary to understand all the nuances of Paul's theological coping to recognize that in addition to all the meanings of 'flesh' above, he sometimes used it simply to mean circumcision. This can hardly be clearer than in Romans 2:25–29, wherein he compared those Jews and Jewish Christians who were outwardly circumcised in the flesh (i.e., in the penis) but were not circumcised inwardly (in the heart) with Gentiles who were not circumcised outwardly but were inwardly. To continue, when in 2 Corinthians 11:18 he wrote of those who glory after (or in) the flesh, he was referring to circumcision and to religious pride taken therein (see also Gal. 6:12–13). This is not a use of 'flesh' that would readily occur to the average, modern, English-speaking person. Everything that has been written about 'flesh' above, however, is but a prologue to incomprehensibilities to come, incomprehensibilities that must be grappled with, because in some mysterious way Flesh, in Paul's theology, stands on a par with Satan and Sin as a malign agent standing between the individual and salvation.

The meaning of 'flesh' in Romans 8:1–13, the most sustained exposition Paul ever gave of the subject, is different from the previous meanings and puzzling to say the least.[180] The verses in question follow, together with my asides and questions:

1. There is therefore now no condemnation [an article of Paul's faith, but unconfirmed] to them which are in [i.e., in unity with, but what kind of unity with?] Christ Jesus, who walk not after the flesh, but after the Spirit [flesh and Spirit seen as opposing principles, powers, or agents].
2. For the law of the Spirit of life in Christ Jesus [what law, what kind of law (natural, statute, moral), and how articulated?][181] hath made me free from the law of sin and death [as though death does not afflict the righteous (or those in unity with Jesus) just as it does the unrighteous].

3. For what the law [of Moses] could not do in that it was weak through the flesh [how so?],[182] God sending his own Son in the likeness [only in the *likeness*, but not really?] of sinful flesh [as though one were sinful just for being embodied], and for sin, condemned sin [understood how, as an agent, as a principle, as the name of the class of all sins, or what?] in the flesh [meaning what, merely being embodied?].

4. That the righteousness of the law [of Moses] might be fulfilled [meaning what, accomplished how?] in us [Christians of Paul's persuasion], who walk not after the flesh, but after the Spirit.

5. For they that are after the flesh do mind the things of the flesh, but they that are after the Spirit the things of the Spirit.

6. For to be carnally minded *is* death [understood how, literally, figuratively, or both?] and to be spiritually minded is peace [which means what in this theological context?].

7. Because the carnal mind *is* enmity against God: for it is not subject to the law of God [how can it not be, how can anything escape the decrees and sanctions of the deity of Paul's conceptualization?], neither indeed can be [why not, what prevents it?].

8. So then they that are in [unity with] the flesh [not the same as being embodied it would seem] cannot please God.

9. But ye [those to whom Paul writes] are not in [unity with] the flesh [even though embodied] but [in unity with] the Spirit, if so be that the Spirit of God dwell in you. Now if any man have not the Spirit of Christ, he is none of his [so, what follows from this?].

10. And if Christ *be* in you, the body [but not the flesh?] is dead [in what sense?], because of sin [understood how, as the set of all sins or as something more?]; but the Spirit *is* life [meaning what?] because of righteousness [whose, the (presumed) righteousness of Jesus or of the individual believer, and how does this righteousness operate to achieve life?].

11. But if the Spirit of him [a presumed entity] that raised up Jesus from the dead [an article of unconfirmed faith] dwell in you, he that raised up Christ from the dead shall also quicken [meaning what?] your mortal bodies [the same as mortal flesh or not?] by his Spirit that dwelleth in you [literally, figuratively, or what?].

12. Therefore, brethren, we are debtors, not to the flesh [how could one be indebted to flesh in any of its meanings, even if one wanted to be?], to live after the flesh.

13. For if ye live after the flesh, ye shall die [shall we not all die anyway?]: but if ye through the Spirit do mortify the deeds of the body [which deeds, mortified how?], ye shall live [meaning what and for how long?].[183]

In concluding this exposition of flesh as a metaphysical power, I can do no better than to quote Oscar Cullmann:

> Body and soul are both originally good [to Paul] in so far as they are cre-
> ated by God; they are both bad in so far as the deadly power of the flesh
> has hold of them. Both can and must be set free by the quickening power
> of the Holy Spirit.
>
> Here, therefore, deliverance consists not in a release of soul from
> body but in a release of both from flesh. We are not released from the
> body; rather the body itself is set free [from flesh].[184]

Death is the fourth in the quadripartite set of malign metaphysical
agents in Paul's theology. In his letters the word 'death', like 'flesh', sometimes has the ordinary meaning of no longer living; on other occasions it
has meaning(s) unique to Paul. Three examples of the ordinary use of
'death' follow: (1) When in Romans 1:32 Paul mentioned that those who
committed certain sins (detailed in vv. 29–31) were worthy of death, he
meant that they were deserving of capital punishment; (2) when in Philippians 2:8 he referred to the death of the cross, he was referring to a method
of execution practiced by the Romans; and (3) when in Philippians
2:25–30 he referred to a colleague who had been sick unto death, he was
referring to a person whose illness on one occasion had nearly been fatal.

When, however, he mentioned how death entered the world by (or
through) man (Rom. 5:12; 1 Cor. 15:21), how it proceeded to reign for a
certain historical period (Rom. 5:14), working its pernicious way in human
beings (2 Cor. 3:7, 4:12), and how one day soon it was to be defeated and
destroyed (1 Cor. 15:26), losing its dominion (Rom. 6:9), he was clearly
using 'death' in extraordinary ways. Before expanding on these departures
from the verbal norm, some context must be supplied. Paul was totally
ignorant of human evolution, of physical anthropology, and of world history. He knew nothing, for example, of Chinese and Indian civilizations,
civilizations at least as old as Semitic civilization and in each case more
extensive and influential, at least until after Paul's time. Lacking such crucial information, he turned uncritically to the mythological and legendary
past of the Jews, as presented in their scriptures, and took this idiosyncratic
saga, in a self-serving way, as the history of humankind, especially insofar
as the topics of sin, condemnation, death, and salvation were concerned.

Ignoring the biological kinship between humans and animals, creatures that have been dying from time immemorial, and prepared to use
'death' metaphorically as well as descriptively (and thus ambiguously)
when applied to humans, Paul claimed, so it seems, that Adam and Eve had
been created to live forever. But, then, they rebelled against the Bible-god,
bringing death into the world as a punishment for their sin (Rom. 5:12).
Once in the world, it reigned even over those who had not sinned (Rom.
5:14), even though all have sinned (Rom. 5:12). If the text is accurate, we
have here an example of Paul's respect for logical consistency. So, from

Adam until Moses (not normally recognized as a distinct historical period by non-Jews), sin was in the world but was not recognized as such. Nevertheless, death as the punishment for sin reigned over sinners who did not know that they were sinners (Rom. 5:13–14).

People could not know that they were sinners until receiving the Mosaic law telling unsuspecting sinners what was against the law and was therefore sinful (Rom. 5:13). The upshot is that for a long but indeterminate time (from Adam to Moses), all humans were being punished by death for committing acts that they did not and could not recognize as sinful, because the Bible-god had not seen fit to reveal the law to Adam at the commencement of human life but had waited a millennium or more until Moses appeared. What this says about the moral nature of Paul's deity is left to the reader's judgment.

But, once the law was given, however tardily, did matters improve? No. Did those who strove to fulfill all the demands of the law find justification for their pains? No, Paul knew that he had not and assumed the same of others. Did they receive the Holy Spirit? No, not according to him. In Galatians 3:19 he wrote of the law, "It was added because of transgressions, till the seed [i.e., Jesus, the descendant and heir of Father Abraham] should come to whom the promise [of salvation through faith] was made." The law according to this was never meant to remain the sacred core of Jewish life in perpetuity; it was, according to Galatians 3:24–25, to be merely a pedagogue, a term variously translated as attendant, trainer, schoolmaster, custodian, tutor, and disciplinarian. This pedagogue was primarily designed to bring Jews to the point at which they would be receptive to Paul's message of grace and justification through faith. By faith, of course, is meant faith in the life, death, and resurrection of Jesus. In rising from the dead, Jesus triumphed over death (Rom. 6:9). But that, of course, is not all. Believers in Jesus can also participate in his triumph over the enemy. Paul summarized his position in 1 Corinthians 15:55–56: "The sting of death is sin; and the strength of sin is the law. But thanks be to God, which giveth us the victory [over death] through our Lord Jesus Christ."

Compared to the orthodox Jews in the Jesus-movement who thought that salvation was for them alone (or was in some sense limited to Israel), Paul appears to exemplify a generous universalism, for he also welcomed Gentiles as candidates for salvation, provided they accepted his gospel. However, since the end was near (Rom. 13:11–12, 16:20; 1 Cor. 7:26) and the time for evangelism was short, only a few of the world's teeming masses could hope to hear the gospel, believe it, and thus triumph over death with the Lord. When one adds these hopeless multitudes to all those who from Moses to Jesus groaned in vain under the Mosaic yoke (which lacked the power to save), one can see that Paul's universalism was very narrow, not to say mean-spirited. Commenting on a closely related topic, namely, Jesus' alleged resurrection and triumph over death, Bultmann wrote, "The *resurrection of Jesus* is . . . difficult, if it means an event whereby a supernatural power is released which can henceforth be appropriated through the sacraments. To the biologist such language is meaningless, for he does not regard death as a problem at all. The idealist would not object to the idea of a life immune from death, but he could not believe that such a life is made available by the resuscitation of a corpse. If that is the way God makes life available for man, his action is inextricably involved in a nature miracle."[185] It is very curious to think of death as an opponent of Paul's deity. Since he is presumed to be eternal, how can death be his enemy? In attempting to clarify this point on Paul's behalf, Cullmann writes, "Nevertheless, death *as such* is the enemy of God. For God is Life and the Creator of life. It is not by the will of God that there are withering and decay, dying and sickness, the by-products of death working in our life. All these things according to Christian and Jewish thinking came from human sin."[186] This indeed may be what Paul thought, but how can it be made to stand? It is, after all, Paul who wrote in Romans 5:12, "Wherefore, as by one man sin entered into the world, and death by sin; and so death passed upon all men, for that all have sinned." Why should such punishment be an (or the) enemy of the righteous, punishing deity? Or is it that in some fugitive, inchoate way death in Paul's theology is a malign *agent* in its own right in opposition to the Bible-god and lurking about awaiting a point of entry into the world—a point which was provided by Adam's original sin of disobedience? Surely, the Bible-god does not require a malign agent to wreak just vengeance upon those who disobey him! Nevertheless, when Genesis prescribes death for Adam, were he to eat the fruit of the tree of the knowledge of good and evil, the text does not say that the Bible-god will slay him, only that death shall befall him (Gen. 3:3). We have good reason to believe that Paul knew this passage, and, given his animism, may have interpreted it to mean that death was a kind of agent, adjunct to the Bible-god, on occasion at least, and prepared to carry out his sentence of death for rebellion. Whatever his precise point, as in almost every case, Paul has some explaining to do that never gets done.

The third set of Paul's "spiritual" beliefs, as I have organized them, is more of a grab bag than the previous two sets. Even so, coherence of a sort characterizes his beliefs in demons or devils, elemental spirits, principalities and powers, rulers of this world, and angels. He also believed in the efficacy of certain magical practices and in the reality of ascension into the heavens. Although Paul seldom used the Greek *daimonion* (translated variously as 'demon' or 'devil'),[187] Mary E. Andrews shows no hesitation in asserting of Paul's beliefs, "Man lives in a demon-ruled universe (Col. 2:8–15). It is of fundamental importance that he be able to control these hostile powers. The Christian had a means of control by virtue of the indwelling *pneuma* [spirit]."[188]

More perplexing, not to say astounding, was Paul's apparent belief in *stoicheia tou kosmou*, literally 'the elements of the cosmos'. The word *stoicheia* appears twice in Galatians, once in 4:3 and once in 4:9, and is used as though the Galatians would know exactly what he meant by it. The term (in one grammatical form or other) also appears twice in Colossians, once in 2:8 and once in 2:20, again as though there were no possibility of misunderstanding. Prior to writing each of these letters Paul may well have made his understanding of *stoicheia* crystal clear to the recipients thereof, but we today cannot know what meaning he intended. The appropriate entry in a Greek dictionary, such as the *GEL*, will make this abundantly clear, as will the wide range of construals in various translations of the letters in question. The translators of the RSV, together with James Moffatt in his translation of the Bible, think the term at issue should be translated as "the elemental spirits of the universe." In TBAT, Goodspeed favors "material ways of looking at things." In his translation of the New Testament, Williams gives it as "the world's crude notions," and the translators of the MLB take it to mean "the world's elementary teachings." To make matters worse, the Greek word itself, apart from any unique theological twist, can refer to the elements of the natural world—that is, to earth, air, fire, and water—and even to heavenly bodies. Once again, one of Paul's "spiritual" notions plunges us into deep confusion.

The context of Galatians 3 and 4 provides some clues. Here, as everywhere it seems, we find Paul wrestling with the problem of what to do with the Jewish law, particularly with its ceremonial components. As a devotee of the law, Paul found it holy and spiritual (Rom. 7:12, 14), but it had not brought him justification. He found that happy state through faith in Christ, apart from the law, and preached this message to the Gentiles (Rom. 3:28). Yet he could not view the law as being inconsequential. So, theologically, he attempted an end run past Moses back to Abraham, who lived long before the law was handed down but who was nevertheless justified by faith (Rom. 4:3; Gal. 3:6). Christians living long after the law was handed down were (or are) no more justified by it than Paul but, as the true heirs of Abraham, are also justified by faith. In this convenient way Paul bypassed the law theologically but found it essential to preserve it in some way or other (Rom. 3:31). As Galatians 3:24 makes clear, he preserved it in the role of the pedagogue, or stern taskmaster, leading both Jews and Gentiles to Christ. So much for the contextual background leading up to the crucial passages in Galatians 4 relative to the elemental spirits of the universe.

In Galatians 4:1, Paul compares the heir to an estate with a slave, as long as the heir remains a minor. In that condition the heir is under guardians or trustees who control his legacy until he is of age and can control it himself. In like manner, according to Paul, human beings while still children (i.e., while still under the law) were slaves to the elemental spirits of the universe.

Likening the *stoicheia* to guardians or trustees personalizes (or anthropomor-phizes) whatever Paul had in mind when he used this term. In view of his persistent animism and dualism, this anthropomorphizing should surprise nobody. In any case, he tells the Galatians (in 4:4) that in the fullness of time God sent forth his Son, born of a woman, born under the law, to redeem those under the law (something that it could not do) that they might receive adoption as sons (i.e., that they might become heirs of the promises made to Abraham, promises that he took on faith and faith alone).

At the time of his angry letter to the Galatians, some (or, perhaps, most) of these converts were in danger of backsliding into Jewish ortho-doxy, to some extent at least. This was an ecclesiastical crisis with which Paul had to deal decisively. The following three verses (8–10) taken from the RSV (together with my clarifications) will make the essential points about the elemental spirits: "Formerly, when you did not know God [i.e., before the Galatians had accepted as true what Paul told them on the sub-ject], you were in bondage to beings [not to principles or teachings it should be noted] that by nature are no gods [i.e., are not on a par with the Bible-god]; but now that you know God [i.e., believe what Paul told them] . . . how can you turn back again to the weak and beggarly elemental spirits ['beggarly' modifies beings much better than principles or teachings], whose slaves you want to be once more? You observe days, and months, and seasons, and years [i.e., you adopt once again practices prescribed by the ceremonial law]." Christianity, of course, as Paul preached it was sup-posed to set the faithful free from such bondage.

Upon subjecting Galatians 4:1–11 to penetrating scrutiny, Bo Reicke, a Swedish biblical scholar, was forced by the evidence to conclude that in Paul's theology there is a "relative identification of law and the 'elements' of the universe."[189] By "relative identification" he means that to Paul the words in the text "'under the law' are synonymous with the expression 'to the ele-ments of the universe.'"[190] In practical terms this means that those who are slaves of the one (i.e., the unredeemed) are slaves of the other. "We see here also," he continues, "that Paul actually considers all the non-Christian world, both Jewish and heathen, to be subject to the Law or 'elements' of the universe."[191] 'Universe' as used here, of course, is not to be understood nat-uralistically but as meaning that which is of the world or is worldly; as such it stands in opposition to the deity of Paul's conceptualization. The upshot is that the Jews, who have the Mosaic law objectively, and the Gentiles, who presumably have it written upon their hearts (Rom. 2:14–15), are arrayed on one side as worldly, sinful, enslaved to the law, and unredeemed, whereas on the other side are Christians who are spiritual, forgiven of their sins, free from the law, and redeemed. Reicke writes, "If these concepts [of law and of elements] are regarded as independent of one another, Paul's train of thought does not seem at all logical; but if the elemental spirits are

placed above the Law as *agents* of its origin and supervisors over its contin-
uation, and if they also be conceived as representatives of the Law, we can
more easily grasp the logic of this conception (emphasis added)."[192]

To Reicke, then, the elements of the cosmos are angels, hence the cor-
rectness of 'elemental spirits' as the translation of *stoicheia*. Moreover, and
this is breathtaking, they are identical to the mysterious angels in Galatians
3:19 who, according to Paul ordained the law.[193] But, had not all Israel,
from time immemorial, proclaimed something quite different? Maccoby
writes, "Despite the convoluted arguments of scholars, there is no parallel
to this [i.e., Paul's radical assertion] in Jewish sources, which all insist that
God was the sole author of the Torah and that it was God Himself, not
angels, whose voice was heard on Mount Sinai 'giving' the Torah.[194] Who
was Paul to have changed this hoary doctrine, and what was he trying to
accomplish with his singular assertion that it was angels (whatever they
are) that gave the law?

Neither Paul, while still a faithful Jew, nor his fellow Jews escaped illu-
sions about the Mosaic law. Neither could see it as merely the codification of
the folkways and mores of a particular group of Semites. Neither could recognize the kinship between the moral aspects of their law and the moral
aspects of other codes, such as the Code of Hammurabi, and neither could
recognize that such ceremonies as circumcision might have been borrowed
from neighboring people, such as the Egyptians. Oh, no, the Jewish law was
uniquely sacred and as such could only have come from the one true or only
real deity. Such sacralizing of a given way of life is commonplace among
tightly knit ethnic groups, such parochialism endemic, such arrogant idio-
syncrasy a form of patriotism, the ways of all others becoming, in consequence, outlandish and inferior. But, somewhere and at some point in Paul's
life, something dramatic happened to him. He became an ecstatic or, in his
own words, Holy Spirit–possessed and began to reap emotional benefits that
had been denied him under the law. Having been forgiven (in his own mind
at least) for persecuting the church and no longer subject (in his own mind
at least) to the ceremonial law, he became joyous and (in his own mind at
least) free and redeemed. This must have surprised him! Certainly it required
an explanation, one that came in the form of theological musings.

Being a Jew of the Diaspora and more sympathetic toward Gentiles
than were the Jews in Judea, he began to share his ecstatic "new-life experiences" with others (Jews and Gentiles alike) through successful persuasion and conversion. Thus, he opened the Christian door to all and told
motley multitudes that they could be redeemed through faith in Christ
without having to subject themselves to the law, especially to certain ceremonial aspects of it that required circumcision and scrupulosity in matters
of foods and the partaking thereof. Some Jewish Christians as well as Gentiles probably found this message appealing; but some (such as the Gala-

tians) who at first fell under Paul's spell yearned occasionally (for whatever reasons) to return to the rigorous practice of the law. Such backsliding, from Paul's point of view, undercut his theology and threatened to depopulate his congregations. Since he could not tolerate losing intellectual dominance over his converts and could not stand idly by while his congregants stole (or were stolen) away, he had to devise a plausible theological ploy for retaining his hard-won converts. This involved finding a way of having his cake and eating it too. The result was the clever rationalization found in Galatians 4:1–11.

Since, to Paul, the law could not have been a human artifact, evolving over centuries of practice, and since it retained enormous significance for him even after he became a Christian, it had to have a supernatural origin, but it did not have to have the ultimate supernatural origin. Angels, lesser but still divine beings, could fill this bill nicely! Had Paul's eternal deity really revealed the law to his "chosen people" in perpetuity, then Paul could not validly have experienced release from it through faith in Christ and Holy Spirit–possession. So, though the law could no longer be viewed as eternal and immutable, it could take on the most important role in history—that of preparing humanity for the coming of Christ and of bringing sinners to him for redemption, release, and everlasting life.[195]

Unless far more powerful evidence exists (or is forthcoming) for the reality of angels (or of elemental spirits of the world) than any I have seen to date, then it is safe to say that Paul, despite his saintliness, knew *nothing* of what he wrote in Galatians 4:3 and 4:9, or in Colossians 2:8 and 2:20.[196] Certainly he had no information as to any role played by such dubious beings in the creation of the Mosaic law, either in its moral demands or its ritual prescriptions. Once again the "spirituality" of an idea fails to confirm its truth.

Other denizens of the "spiritual" bestiary of Paul's beliefs include principalities and powers in heavenly places (Eph. 3:10), power(s) in the air over whom Satan rules as a prince (Eph. 2:2), and rulers of darkness (Eph. 6:12).[197] In 1 Corinthians 2:8 Paul tells us that the princes of the world would not have crucified Jesus if they had known the mysteries and hidden wisdom that he (Paul) knew. For in trying to kill Jesus, they overstepped their bounds, and he, in turn, triumphed over them and over death, the dominion they had hitherto exercised over humanity.[198] Some might say that "princes of the world" refers to various Caesars and other earthly potentates, but not so. Ephesians 6:12 tells us, "[W]e wrestle not against flesh and blood, when we wrestle against principalities, against powers, against the rulers of the darkness of this world, against spiritual wickedness in high *places.*" Moreover, regarding earthly potentates and political authority, Paul endorsed obedience and quietism, as Romans 13:1–7 amply demonstrates. No, principalities and powers in Paul's theology are not human; they are evil "astral forces," the "Lords of the planetary spheres."[199]

As a taxonomist of angels, Paul leaves much to be desired. However, often, if not usually, angels would appear to have been (or to be) good, else why would Satan disguise himself as an angel of light, the more deceptive to become (2 Cor. 11:14), and if angels were not good, what could Paul have meant when writing in Galatians 4:14b that despite his condition, the Galatians received him as an angel of God, *even as* Jesus Christ? Yet angels cannot all have been (or be) all good all the time, for in Romans 8:38–39 he mentions angels, among other agencies, that cannot separate the Christian from the love of God. Why should angels, if they are good, even try to do such a dastardly deed? Moreover, confusion reigns in 1 Corinthians 11:10, where Paul seems to tell women to keep their heads covered because of the angels (see note 193). It is not clear who is being spared. Would angels find women offensive in some way if their heads were uncovered, or would women whose heads were uncovered be in some danger from angels? Whatever the case, Paul makes an astonishing point in 1 Corinthians 6:3a, when he writes rhetorically, "Know ye not that we shall judge angels?" It would seem that the tables will be turned one day on these agencies that have varying degrees of control over human beings. How, one wonders, did Paul gain this information, and what is the point of certain humans' lording it over angels? Pure vengeance, perhaps.

In concluding this analysis of certain of Paul's beliefs relative to the topics of God, the Mind of God, the Son of God, and the Spirit of God; to Satan, Sin, Flesh, and Death as malign agents; to principalities and powers; rulers of darkness; and to angels, some good, some perhaps not so good, and some, most certainly, evil, we would do well to ponder Morton Smith's contention that early Christianity was a "combination of theoretical monotheism with practical polytheism."[200] This was surely true of its Pauline version, and in passing it should be noted that "practical polytheism" is no less spiritual than "theoretical monotheism."

Paul adopted, adapted, and practiced certain rituals as dubious as any of his doctrines. The most important of these are baptism and the Eucharist (or sacred meal). If his letters adequately reflect his mind, then he never saw baptism as a symbolic washing away of sins, let alone their actual washing away. His contrary views on the subject are most fully expressed in Romans 6:2–11 and echoed in Colossians 2:12–14. In summary, these passages claim that the believer in the process of being baptized is dying to the world, is being buried in water as though in a sepulcher, and is being resurrected to a new life delivered from sin because free from the law. This is pure magic, not magic as it is practiced today for entertainment but magic as practiced in the time and place of the birth of Christianity. Says Morton Smith, a leading expert on ancient magic, "Such rites, beginning with an imitation death and ending with resurrection by receipt of a divine spirit, are familiar in magical material."[201] He also comments, "Paul's baptism . . .

is a way of uniting with Jesus the Messiah, whom Paul conceives as 'the spirit' (2 Cor. 3:17; 1 Cor. 15:45). So Paul conceives union with the Messiah as possession by a spirit. The spirit lives inside the baptized and acts through them (most conspicuously, it speaks through them, making incomprehensible noises—a common symptom of schizophrenia). Thus the body of each possessed Christian is in effect a part (a 'member', that is a hand or foot or whatever) of the body of the Messiah, who lives and acts in them all."[202]

Smith also discerns a clear case of "substitutionary magic" in 1 Corinthians 15:29, wherein baptism on behalf of the dead is adverted to.[203] In view of such notions of baptism, of the practice of recalling the spirits of the dead,[204] of the Eucharist (to be taken up next), etc., it is not surprising that "the emperor Julian, himself experienced in magic and far from prejudiced in Paul's favor, would describe him as 'the man who surpassed all magicians and deceivers that ever were, anywhere.'"[205]

Christianity's sacred meal, as practiced by Paul, cannot merely have been symbolic to him. This extraordinary departure from the practice of Judaism in which human flesh is never eaten and blood is never drunk is most fully described in 1 Corinthians 11:23–33 (see also 1 Cor. 10:16–17).[206] The verses from this passage most germane to my contention that the Lord's Supper cannot merely have been symbolic to Paul are 27–30, wherein he wrote,

> Wherefore whosoever shall eat this bread, and drink *this* cup of the Lord unworthily, shall be guilty of the body and blood of the Lord.
>
> But let a man examine himself and so let him eat of *that* bread and drink of *that* cup.
>
> For he that eateth and drinketh unworthily, eateth and drinketh damnation to himself, not discerning the Lord's body.
>
> For this cause many *are* weak and sickly among you, and many sleep [i.e., have died].

Of this potentially pernicious food and drink, Morton Smith writes, "Such consumption of food identified as the body and blood of a god was a familiar form of love magic. As in the case of baptism, no other ancient parallels to Paul's words are as close as those in the magical texts."[207]

Lesser "spiritual" oddities that bear notice in passing are the marks or brands of Jesus that Paul claimed to bear upon his body (Gal. 6:17), the buffeting to which he says he subjected his body (1 Cor. 9:27), and his fear of being found naked (i.e., without a body) in death (2 Cor. 5:1–9). The Galatians, no doubt, knew what Paul meant by the stigmata (the marks or brands) of Jesus on Paul's flesh, but we do not. Morton Smith opines that these were magical tattoos, indeed, "the same that Jesus had carried."

According to Smith the magical papyri contain instructions for magicians to write "spells and the like on their flesh."[208] We must not, however, underestimate Paul. Rather than tattoos, he may have been able to simulate the wounds of Roman crucifixion on his body. Lesser people than he in more recent times have, quite certainly, been able to effect such stigmata. What Paul meant by buffeting his body is also ambiguous. In Attic Greek it meant literally to strike under the eye or to give a black eye. Metaphorically it meant to "treat roughly, torment, [or] maltreat."[209] Perhaps the five sets of thirty-nine lashings Paul claims to have received (2 Cor. 11:24) were not enough. Perhaps on occasion he flagellated himself. Many people of lesser "spirituality" have done so. Insofar as Paul entertained the concept of the soul of a person, he thought it important that it be clothed at all times, clothed in this life, so to speak, in a tabernacle (or tent) of flesh and clothed in the next (presumed) life in a solid house (i.e., a permanent spiritual dwelling) made by the Bible-god.[210] At physical death, it seems, Paul believed the soul to be unclothed, i.e., naked or bodiless. Of this Albert Schweitzer wrote,

> The soul [at death] has put off its fleshly body, and has still to await the heavenly body. As he thinks of this nakedness, even for the soul of the righteous, as a rather miserable existence, he holds that those who remain alive up to the Return of Jesus, and then immediately undergo the transformation from the natural state of existence to the supernatural, are better off than those who having "fallen asleep" in the meantime, have to pass through a period of this nakedness, and the kind of shadowy existence associated with it. He himself eagerly desires to be found alive at the Return of Jesus Christ, in order to be reclothed without being first unclothed.[211]

Surely, no one can deny the "spirituality" of these views of St. Paul.

Apart from the fantastic and dubious doctrine that the (alleged) maker of heaven and earth sired a male child and the equally fantastic and dubious doctrine that the (presumably) saved of earth shall live a conscious existence after death, there is nothing more fantastic and dubious in Paul than his account of a man, whom he knew, who was caught up into the third heaven, to paradise itself, and lived to tell about it, more or less (2 Cor. 12:2–5). As is not uncommon with Paul, this passage is a riddle wrapped in an enigma:

> I knew a man in Christ above fourteen years ago, (whether in the body, I cannot tell; or whether out of the body, I cannot tell: God knoweth;) such an one was caught up to the third heaven.
>
> And I knew such a man (whether in the body, I cannot tell: God knoweth;)

How that he was caught up into paradise, and heard unspeakable words, which it is not lawful for a man to utter.

Of such an one will I glory; yet of myself I will not glory, but in mine infirmities.

Who is this mysterious man? For a time, Morton Smith believed him to be Jesus, but later became less convinced.[212] The current predominant view is that Paul is referring to himself.[213] William Baird writes, "This use of the third person, of course, does not imply that Paul is talking about someone other than himself. That he is describing his own experience is clear from v. 7, where he recognizes that he, Paul, might 'be too elated by the abundance' of his revelations—including this one."[214]

Whatever the case, whoever the man, we have here the idea that a living human being can ascend at least to the third heaven and return to earth to describe the trip. Baird identifies two kinds of heavenly sojourning: "(1) the journey of the soul, wherein the body is left behind, and (2) bodily ascension, whereby the whole person is transported to heaven."[215] As if this were not enough, the next surprise consists in learning that belief in such goings-on was commonplace in Paul's time and location. There was, in fact a considerable amount of literature telling the would-be traveler to heavenly places how to make the trip.[216]

In trying to explain what was actually happening, Baird resorts to hallucination, Smith to "some sort of hypnotic technique" leading the traveler and others to the illusion of heavenly ascension, and Segal, quite simply, to ecstasy (literally, to standing outside oneself).[217] Clearly, the modern interpreter cannot escape resorting to human psychology in general and to paranormal experiences (and their corollary brain states) in particular (however caused). To the one who travels to the heavens, the trip (i.e., the experience) is its own warrant; for the rest of us, the traveler never gets off the ground but remains locked inside her head. For those who make such "trips," 'spiritual' is the term of choice.

The foregoing analysis of Paul's "spiritual" beliefs and related practices is by no means exhaustive, though the reader may have found it exhausting. It was undertaken to put us in a position to assess accurately some of Crimmins's criticisms of Bentham on Paul. These criticisms were, it should be remembered, that Bentham (1) "could not countenance any common ground between the spiritual world of religion and the perceptible world of physical experience," (2) lacked "any sense of man's incorporeal nature, religious or otherwise," (3) ignored "the fact that religious knowledge depends on faith," (4) applied the logic of the "courtroom" to the "mysteries of religion," (5) stripped "religious beliefs of their spiritual content," (6) misunderstood "the inner spirit which motivates the truly religious person," (7) and held a low opinion of human nature, believing that even "spiritual" people could be motivated by pecuniary interests.[218] Each of these charges deserves critical comment.

Crimmins's first criticism, charging that Bentham allowed no common ground between the religious world and the empirical world, can best be approached by a circuitous route. On November 4–7, 1993, a "Re-Imagining" conference was held in Minneapolis, Minnesota. Peter Steinfels of the NYT writes that the conference "was billed as an opportunity for Christians, especially women, to rethink their concepts of God, Jesus, church, family, sexuality, community and ministry."[219] During one service the attendees called upon Sophia, identified by Steinfels as a "female personification of the divine" to "bless each major speaker."[220] He writes,

> At the conclusion on Sunday morning, participants shared milk and honey in a ritual with overtones of a communion service and prayed in language meant to affirm women's sexuality and sensuality:
>
> "Our mother Sophia, we are women in your image; with the hot blood of our wombs we give form to new life," the group prayed. "With nectar between our thighs we invite a lover," they continued, and "with warm body fluids we remind the world of its pleasures and sensations."[221]

When members of the United Methodist Church in general learned that the Women's Division of their own United Methodist Board of Global Ministries had paid the way of forty-six top staff members to attend this conference, a flood of complaints ensued. This furor was duplicated in the Presbyterian Church (USA). Officials in each denomination, alarmed by the "Re-Imagining" conference, hastened to reaffirm their commitment to the "traditional Christian faith in a Trinitarian God of Father, Son, and Holy Spirit."[222]

Given today's cultural climate, it is understandable that American churchwomen should wish to reimagine masculine, patriarchal religious conceptions so as to make these more compatible with their feminine sensitivities. It is equally understandable that traditionalists, women and men alike, should hasten to reaffirm the traditional conceptions. What the women at the "Re-Imagining" conference do not seem to have realized and what the traditionalists are not about to reveal is what reimagining says about theology in general. After all, one cannot *reimagine* something that has not first been imagined differently. Bentham allowed no common ground between the religious world and the empirical world, because, to him, the former was (and remains) a fabulous and fictitious world of imagination, whereas the latter is what we know through our senses of the physical environment in which we live.

For Crimmins to criticize Bentham in this way is known in common parlance as a cheap shot. If Crimmins wishes to add credibility to his charge, let him show beyond reasonable doubt that the universe is artifactual, that its artificer revealed his disposition through the codification of Hebrew folkways and mores, that he procreated (in whatever sense) a male child whom he resurrected from the dead, and that such terms as 'angels', 'demons', 'powers', and 'principalities' do more than name religious imaginings. Let him show that there are extramental, outdwelling referents for these names.

Crimmins's second criticism is that Bentham lacked "any sense of man's incorporeal nature, religious or otherwise." Quite apart from whether or not man's "incorporeal nature" comes in religious and nonreligious varieties are the twin issues of what Crimmins means by this negative characterization and how he learned about it in the first place. He proceeds as though all it takes to vanquish Bentham is to use the term "incorporeal nature" as a sort of magic wand. There is no mystery in where Crimmins got the idea of man's "incorporeal nature"; it stems from thousands of years of Western culture, based on naive introspection, in which such powers (not to say entities) as mind, soul, or spirit are taken to have causal efficacy over matter. During this entire period, moreover, matter has most often been denigrated as *mere* matter, its nature grossly misunderstood until very recently, its potentialities not even dreamt of. Contrary to three millennia of culture and even more millennia of naive introspection, it is premature to say that human beings have an incorporeal nature. The breathtaking advances in the neurosciences are not based on this idea (with its implicit dualism) but are squarely based on monistic materialism. Respecting method and epistemology, it is risky to turn to man's "incorporeal nature" for an explanation of any phenomena, before his corporeal nature is fully fathomed. Whereas Bentham's philosophy of human nature is being validated daily by the neurosciences, Crimmins's philosophy of human nature is being vitiated daily by the explanatory fiction of incorporeality.

Crimmins's third criticism is that Bentham ignored "the fact that religious knowledge depends on faith." In the English New Testament, 'faith' is most often used to translate the Greek *pistis*, which means essentially 'to have trust or confidence in' somebody (such as Jesus or Paul) or in something (such as a teaching of Jesus or a pronouncement of Paul). Crimmins seems to be saying that a person's subjective experience of trust is a warrant for the trustworthiness of the one in whom confidence is being placed or in the truth of the doctrine(s) being presented for acceptance. In Mark 9:1 (see also Mark 13:30; Matt. 10:23; Luke 21:32), Jesus is reported to have said, "I say unto you, That there be some of them that stand here, which shall not taste of death, till they have seen the kingdom of God come with power." Paul expressed a similar eschatological conviction in 1 Corinthians 7:25–26, 29, 31 (see also 1 Cor. 10:11 and Rom. 13:11), when he advised single Christians to remain single and married Christians to forego sexual relations, because of the impending distress. "The fashion [or form] of this world," he said, "is passing away." If Crimmins is right (despite the intervening nineteen hundred years), all it takes to make Jesus and Paul trustworthy in this particular and all it takes to make their teachings about it true (i.e., to constitute knowledge) is for somebody to have trust or confidence in these religious promulgators and their promulgations about the speedy end of the present world order. Surely, there was a slip of Crimmins's pen when he wrote that "religious knowledge depends on faith." What he meant to write is that what is believed without adequate evidence depends on faith.

While on the subject of knowledge, Crimmins might have examined the three warrants Paul used to confirm his pronouncements—as needed: (1) direct, personal revelation (Gal. 1:12, 16, 2:2); (2) proof texts from the Old Testament prefaced by "as it is written" or a parallel phrase (Rom. 11:8, 26, 15:9; 1 Cor. 1:19, 2:9, 10:7; Gal. 3:10, 3:13); and (3) alleged signs and wonders (Rom. 15:19; 2 Cor. 12:12). A critical word about each is in order. Except for 2 Corinthians 12:4, in which he wrote of hearing unspeakable words, Paul did not clinch his pronouncements, in his letters at least, by saying that he had actually heard the voice of his Lord. It was enough that he assert his authority (2 Cor. 10:8) and announce convincingly that Christ was speaking in him (2 Cor. 13:3). Such representations and the willingness to command his converts to do this or that (1 Cor. 5:5; 1 Thess. 5:27) were, however, and still are inadequate warrants for the truth of what he was claiming. Grossly delusional people often comport themselves in such a manner. How shall we tell which is the case? One cannot know that Paul received divine disclosures just because he said so. Even he may have recognized this on occasion; else why would he have bothered to quote the Old Testament to clinch some point or other? Citing the Old Testament may have a telling effect on those who believe it to be divinely authoritative, but this alone cannot serve to confirm the truth of any of its contentions. Moreover, Paul used it hypocritically. It is written in Genesis 1:28 that Adam and Eve (and by extension other Hebrews) were to be fruitful, and multiply, and replenish the earth, but that did not stop Paul from advising the Corinthians to live as he, celibately (1 Cor. 7:1, 6–7). Obviously, he cited the Old Testament when it served his purposes and ignored it when it did not. When all else failed, he could claim to be an apostle (and thus trustworthy) by virtue of signs, and wonders, and mighty deeds that occurred among his converts when he was present. Some of these phenomena almost certainly referred to "spirit possession," i.e., to ecstatic experiences that he was able to unleash on occasion, perhaps often. Nevertheless, these do not validate the existence of the "spirit world" but point rather to the vagaries of human emotionality.

Crimmins's fourth criticism is that Bentham applied the "logic of the courtroom" to the "mysteries of religion." Just as apologists for religion denigrate matter to *mere* matter, so, too, do they denigrate logic to its basest level, in this case to the level of courtroom tactics, a level so low that it cannot possibly be used to assail religion—or so it is hoped. It is more telling, however, that Crimmins failed to notice that 'mysteries of religion' has a double meaning. On the one hand, it can mean that there is still much that is puzzling about the nature and origin of religion in general; on the other hand, it can mean that individual religions present their devotees with mind-boggling doctrines and with rituals whose efficacy can only be psychological at best and magical at worst.

An example of the first meaning can be found in the "Re-Imagining" conference described above. How is it, one wonders, that a group of modern, well-educated, economically comfortable women can go to a conference to reimagine earlier religious imaginings, remain ignorant of what they are doing, and come away moved and spiritually uplifted? Now that is a mystery, a mystery for the solution of which it is appropriate to turn to anthropologists, psychologists, comparative religionists, and kindred researchers. And, of course, logic alone is not up to this task, sophisticated empirical research being requisite.

An example of how a given religion (Christianity) can present its devotees with a mind-boggling mystery is the doctrine of the Trinity, which was analyzed in part 1. A simpler and (for our purposes) equally useful doctrine is the Roman Catholic teaching which claims that the Blessed Virgin Mary was (or is) the Mother of God. If so (as noted in part 1) then her mother, St. Anne, must have been God's grandmother and so on back to Eve, the primordial great-grandmother, who, according to Genesis 2:21–22, was created by God from one of Adam's ribs. How one can create one's own great-grandmother is indeed a mystery, but is it a genuine mystery, or is it a man-made mystery manufactured through the agency of language? Courtroom logic is quite adequate for probing verbal mysteries.

An example of a magical ritual is the Lord's supper. In the early church, the physical elements of this meal were sometimes called the food—and other times the medicine—of immortality. Although Paul did not do so, John 6:51, 53–58 did, for all practical purposes, when he wrote what he claims Jesus said, to wit:

> I am the living bread which came down from heaven: if any man eat of this bread, he shall live forever: and the bread that I will give is my flesh, which I will give for the life of the world.
>
> Then Jesus said unto them, Verily, verily, I say unto you, Except ye eat the flesh of the Son of man, and drink his blood, ye have no life in you.
>
> Whoso eateth my flesh, and drinketh my blood, hath eternal life; and I will raise him up at the last day.

> For my flesh is meat indeed, and my blood is drink indeed.
> He that eateth my flesh, and drinketh my blood, dwelleth in me and I in him.
> As the living Father hath sent me, and I live by the Father: so he that eateth me, even he shall live by me.
> This is that bread which came down from heaven: not as your fathers did eat manna, and are dead: he that eateth this bread shall live forever.

Whether the bread and the wine consumed ritually become the actual body and blood of Jesus, as in Catholic dogma, or are only symbolic of Jesus' sacrifice, the question remains the same: how does this holy nutrition work? By what mechanism does it confer immortality?

To approach the same questions from the opposite position, we remember that in 1 Corinthians 11:29–30 Paul warned against any unworthy consumption of the sacred food, lest illness or death ensue. Seekers after truth will wish to know how the body and the blood of the Lord become pernicious under such a circumstance. What kind of toxin do they become? When we read on a death certificate that the deceased died of prostate cancer, we can have confidence that oncologists have a fair idea of how the dreaded tumor did its fatal work, and when someone dies of AIDS or bubonic plague, again, one can have fair confidence that medical specialists will know about the progress of the disease(s). Supposing one were to come upon a death certificate of one who expired because of the unworthy consumption of the body and blood of the Lord Jesus. Can one have fair confidence that Christian theologians will know *how* this cause worked? No, for such a demise would be a great mystery even to them— and magical as well.

Crimmins's fifth criticism is that Bentham "stripped religious beliefs of their spiritual content." Even assuming that we can usually distinguish religious from nonreligious beliefs, there is still a further distinction to be made, if Crimmins is right—namely, the distinction between religious beliefs that retain their "spiritual content" and those that have had it stripped away. An example from Galatians should help clarify the issue. Herein we find Paul being pursued by certain Judaizers who insisted on circumcision as part of the price of admission to Christianity and to the redemption it promised. Paul, fervently denying this, opened wide the gates of Christian redemption to the uncircumcised as well as to the circumcised. Given two contradictory assertions, one would think that each would strip the other of its spiritual content, but not so. The Judaizers remained fervently devoted to their convictions about circumcision, and Paul remained equally fervently devoted to his. Put differently, the Judaizers related themselves religiously to the (to them) crucial importance of circumcision while Paul related himself religiously to its denial. Bentham did not give a fig for circumcision or the lack thereof in relation to redemption, because he did not believe in redemption, taking it to be nothing but an unwarranted idea. His negative position, however, did not strip the "spiritual content" from the religious beliefs of either party, because content is not at issue. What is at issue is *how* individual believers relate themselves to the beliefs in question, not the content of what is believed.

Bentham did not imagine the world to be as the Judaizers imagined it to be, nor did he imagine it to be as did Paul. He did not imagine the universe to be artifactual, nor did he relate himself to its alleged artificer as do subjects to their sovereign. The king of England was royalty enough (or more than enough) for him. He did not beat his breast in contrition for being a fallible human, did not hold out his hands in supplication, seeking eternal bliss, and did not fear any pains of retribution after he had ceased to be. The difference between Bentham and orthodox Jewish Christians on the one hand and Pauline Christians on the other was not a difference of "spiritual content"; it was a difference between imaginings and such emotions as hope and fear. Crimmins may be able to show that Bentham was mistaken in the way he envisioned the world and that he was deficient in appropriate emotions, but he cannot show that Bentham stripped "spiritual content" from "religious beliefs," for this is not a property they possess.

Crimmins's sixth criticism is that Bentham misunderstood "the inner spirit which motivates the truly religious person." There is an element of truth in this, but it is obscured by Crimmins's phraseology. The term 'truly religious person' is not as dependably descriptive as he seems to think but is rather highly evaluative. An evaluation of this sort can be made only on the basis of some paradigm or other of what the evaluator accepts as truly religious. For example, religious members of Planned Parenthood hardly viewed Mother Theresa in the same light as did members of the College of Cardinals. Moreover, 'spirit', 'spiritual', and 'spirituality' are vague terms that religious people often use when they do not know quite what else to say or when they do not want to risk definition by synonym. Even though there may be no perfect synonyms for these terms, there are approximations in the vocabulary of the emotions. 'Awe', 'fear', 'deep respect', 'self-abasement', 'hope', 'exaltation', 'ecstasy', 'yearning', 'unity', and 'love' come to mind. The emotions being referred to thereby (and numerous combinations thereof) are intimately associated with responses to the imagined objects of religion. One could have found little, if any, fault with Crimmins's characterization had he said that Bentham misunderstood both the range and the intensity of such emotions in motivating the sincerely religious person.

Crimmins's seventh and last criticism (one shared with W. A. Benn) is that Bentham held a low opinion of human nature, believing that even "spiritual" people could be motivated by pecuniary interests. This is the most innocent, not to say naive, of all criticisms of Bentham on religion in general and on Paul in particular. The issue is not whether Bentham held a low or a high opinion of human nature but whether he held an accurate view. Respecting "spirituality" and its compatibility with keen pecuniary interest, his view was accurate. Although "spirituality" is often associated with material privation, voluntary or involuntary, it need not be. When in 1987 televangelist Jim Bakker was laid low by scandals, an article in the *NYT* quoted Professor Samuel S. Hill, an expert on evangelical Christianity, as saying, "Mr. Bakker is not the first Christian leader to claim divine support for capitalism. Such disparate denominations as Baptists, Calvinists, and Presbyterians all embraced the idea that 'God created the free enterprise system.'"[223] In point of fact, the denominations identified here are not very disparate. One can easily expand this set by adding the Mormon, Christian Science, and Episcopal churches.[224] In short, piety can flourish among the privileged as well as among the impoverished. In the same *NYT* article, its author, Samuel G. Freedman, wrote of Bakker that his genius was "to deny any conflict between the checkbook and the good book." Also, "By his own example, Mr. Bakker preached that the world's material allures were not trappings of Satan but rather the wages for piety. When critics questioned Mr. Bakker's lavish surroundings, he often replied, 'God wants his people to go first class.'"

Although Bakker may have lived more opulently than his fellow televangelists, they shared his pecuniary interests then and, in his absence now, still do.[225] The reason is obvious. A religious establishment that is neither state supported (i.e., surviving on church taxes) nor an entity within a larger religious setting, receiving subsidies therefrom, must concern itself with money to survive and grow. On this basis alone, as repugnant as it may be to some, a unity can be established between the Reverend Jim Bakker and the apostle to the Gentiles, between televangelists and the Paulinist movement within early Christianity.

Numerous religious leaders throughout history have worshiped mammon, not necessarily to slake their cupidity but to extend their power. Paul, it must be remembered, received no government support and, probably, very few, if any, subsidies from the Jerusalem church. Not only did he have to finance his extensive travels, he also had to struggle against enemies without (such as the Judaizers) and within (such as the antinomians). Against this background his statement in 2 Corinthians 11:8 that he robbed other churches to serve the Corinthians can be seen in a penetrating light as can the collection he was at pains to garner, ostensibly for the Jerusalem church. Even if his motives were largely charitable, charity can be used to buy people off, to silence critics, to forge new alliances, and to extend power. This can hardly have been lost on St. Paul. Nor should it be lost on the reader that he was a one-man, charismatic creator of a religious empire that he sought to dominate. Those who doubt that he assumed an authoritarian position and took a commanding role have but to read 1 Corinthians 4:21, 5:5, 7:17; 2 Corinthians 8:8, 10:6, 8, 13:10; Philippians 2:12; 1 Thessalonians 5:27; 2 Thessalonians 3:6, 10, 12; and Philemon 1:8.

In summary, Professor Crimmins seems to have thought that he could spare St. Paul (and save true religion too, no doubt) by showing such egregious "spiritual" deficiencies and insensitivities in Bentham that the latter could in no way be trusted to appraise the former accurately. Although Bentham can be justly criticized, as I have already shown and shall show below, Crimmins's criticisms of him are largely jejune. Moreover, Bentham would have taken it as an honor to be accused of being unspiritual.

NOTES

71. Delos B. McKown, *The Mythmaker's Magic: Behind the Illusion of "Creation Science"* (Amherst, NY: Prometheus Books, 1993), p. 25.

72. Alfred William Benn, *The History of English Rationalism in the Nineteenth Century* (New York: Russell and Russell, 1962), 1:302.

73. Ibid.

74. Ibid.

75. It is especially noteworthy that the same teaching appears in the Epistle of James, believed to be by (or under the heavy influence of) James the brother of Jesus. Hence, its credentials are good as being a bona fide teaching of the early church. For whatever reason, Bentham ignored James 5:12, in which the injunction against swearing oaths reappears. In any case, his opposition thereto can also be found in *WJB*, 5:219, 221; and 10:582.

76. James E. Crimmins, *Secular Utilitarianism: Social Science and the Critique of Religion in the Thought of Jeremy Bentham* (Oxford: Clarendon Press, 1990), pp. 233–34. Going the second mile, turning the other cheek, giving away one's cloak as well as one's coat, taking no thought of the morrow, refraining from judgment, etc., are all so inimical to ordinary life and a stable social order that Albert Schweitzer concluded that with these teachings Jesus was putting in place an interim ethic between the time of his proclamation of the coming Kingdom of God and its actual supernatural appearance. In *The Mystery of the Kingdom of God*, trans. William Montgomery (New York: Macmillan, 1954), he writes, "[T]hey [items of the interim ethic] make one meet for the Kingdom of God. Only, they constitute a climax [between now and then in the near future] in the attainment of the new righteousness, inasmuch as they render one meet not merely for entrance into the Kingdom but for bearing rule in it" (p. 55). A few pages later, he says, "The ethics of Jesus . . . is 'conditional,' in the sense that it stands in indissoluble connection with the expectation of a state of perfection which is to be supernaturally brought about" (p. 57). In other words, humans do not help in building a divine kingdom on earth. It is a gift of divine power, in Jesus' thought.

77. What passes for thought for Paul is rationalization, always clever, some-

times brilliant, but rationalization, nonetheless, in the most pejorative, Freudian sense of the term. Later in the text, I shall make this abundantly clear when responding to Crimmins's criticisms of Bentham's treatment of our saint.

78. Stevan L. Davies, *The New Testament: A Contemporary Introduction* (San Francisco: Harper and Row, 1988), p. 65.

79. Benn, *History of English Rationalism*, 1:302.

80. Richard Rubenstein, *My Brother Paul* (New York: Harper and Row, 1972), p. 116.

81. Morton Smith, "Paul's Arguments as Evidence of the Christianity from Which He Diverged," *HTR* 79 (1986): 260.

82. Grant, *Saint Paul* (New York: Charles Scribner's Sons, 1976), p. 6.

83. Morton Smith, "Pauline Problems: Apropos of J. Munck, *Paulus und die Heilsgeschichte*," *HTR* 50 (1957): 111, n. 10.

84. C. L. Mearns, "Early Eschatological Development in Paul: the Evidence of I and II Thess.," *NTS* 27, no. 2 (1981): 145.

85. Ibid.

86. Edvin Larssen, "Paul: Law and Salvation," *NTS* 31 (1985): 433.

87. Michael D. Goulder, "ΣΟΦΙΑ in 1 Corinthians," *NTS* 37, no. 4 (1991): 520.

88. Donald Riddle, "The Jewishness of Paul," *JR* 23 (1943): 244.

89. Smith, "Paul's Arguments," p. 258.

90. Frank Thielman, "The Coherence of Paul's View of the Law: The Evidence of First Corinthians," *NTS* 38, no. 2 (1992): 237, esp. n. 7. For more on Paul's ambivalence about the law and the real reason for his being persecuted, see also Morton Smith, "The Reason for the Persecution of Paul and the Obscurity of Acts," in *Studies in Mysticism and Religion* (Jerusalem: Magnes Press, 1967), pp. 261–68.

91. Jack T. Sanders, "Paul's 'Autobiographical' Statements in Galatians 1–2," *JBL* 85 (1966): 343.

92. Smith, "The Reason for the Persecution of Paul and the Obscurity of Acts," p. 262.

93. For inconsistencies in Paul's thought see Heikki Räisänen, *Paul and the Law* (Tübingen: Mohr, 1983), esp. pp. 10–11, 65, 94–96, 103, 109, 154; and E. P. Sanders, *Paul, the Law, and the Jewish People* (Philadelphia: Fortress Press, 1983), esp. pp. 3, 123, 147. For more on Paul's opportunism and accommodationism, see Peter Richardson, "Pauline Inconsistency: 1 Corinthians and Galatians 2:11–14," *NTS* 26 (1980): 347–62. Also see James D. G. Dunn, "Works of the Law and the Curse of the Law (Galatians 3:10–14)," *NTS* 31, no. 4 (1985): 523–42; and J. C. Beker, "Paul's Theology: Consistent or Inconsistent?" *NTS* 34, no. 3 (1988): 364–77.

94. J. Louis Martyn, "Apocalyptic Antinomies in Paul's Letter to the Galatians," *NTS* 31, no. 3 (1985): 410.

95. Edgar J. Goodspeed, "The Editio Princeps of Paul," *JBL* 64 (1945): 201.

96. Hyam Maccoby, *The Mythmaker: Paul and the Invention of Christianity* (London: Weidenfeld and Nicholson, 1986), p. 162.

97. Lindsey P. Pherigo, "Paul and the Corinthian Church," *JBL* 68, no. 4 (1949): 348.

98. Christopher Forbes puts what may be the best face on Paul's boasting in

"Comparison, Self-Praise, and Irony: Paul's Boasting and the Conventions of Hellenistic Rhetoric," *NTS* 32 (1986): 1–30. Also see Jerry W. McCant's treatment of boasting, irony, and parody in "Paul's Thorn of Rejected Apostleship," *NTS* 34 (1988): esp. 556–60; and Dunn's treatment of the "boasting Jew" in "Works of the Law and the Curse of the Law," esp. pp. 529–30.

99. Albert Schweitzer, *The Mysticism of Paul the Apostle*, trans. William Montgomery (New York: Macmillan, 1955), p. 395.

100. Ibid., pp. 156–57; see also p. 325 for more on Schweitzer's opinion of Paul.

101. Benn, *History of English Rationalism*, 1:302.

102. Stephen Conway, Introduction to *CJB*, vol. 9, p. xvii.

103. Upon first encountering the title "Scholey's Bible," one might take it to be a translation of the Bible by an obscure biblical scholar/translator named Scholey, but not so. A glance at the one copy in academic custody in the United States (at the College of William and Mary) shows that Robert Scholey was merely a bookseller who commissioned the project and published it in 1809. Scholey's Bible was simply the result of combining the KJV with bits of information taken from the "works of the most approved commentators (British and Foreign)," resulting in various tables of biblical weights, measures, and other kinds of useful information. Among the "approved commentators" drawn upon was the eminent Johann David Michaelis, of whom Bentham had at least a passing awareness.

104. Conway, Introduction to *CJB*, vol. 9, p. xvii; *CJB*, 9:90, 93.

105. See Werner Georg Kimmel, "Biographical Appendix," in *The New Testament: The History of the Investigation of Its Problems*, trans. S. McLean Gilman and Howard C. Kee (Nashville, TN: Abingdon Press, 1970), pp. 466–97; and William Baird, *History of New Testament Research: From Deism to Tübingen*, vol. 1 (Minneapolis: Fortress Press, 1992), pp. 160–65.

106. These conditions had already been met by several English deistic authors in the late seventeenth and early eighteenth centuries, such as John Mill (b. 1645), John Toland (b. 1670), and Thomas Morgan (b. 1680?). Closer to Bentham's time was Peter Annet (1693–1765), who, in addition to finding numerous discrepancies in the Bible, attacked Paul in his book *The History and Character of St. Paul*. Because of his doubt of Paul's veracity, Annet took Acts to be more reliable on matters of fact than Paul's epistles. Subsequent scholarship has shown this to have been a serious mistake. Thomas Morgan (d. 1743), contrary to Bentham, thought that it was Paul (and not Peter and the Jerusalem church) who had preserved the "true religion" of Jesus. Another serious mistake (see Baird, *History of New Testament Research*, p. 52). Thomas Chubb (1697–1747), more in harmony with Bentham, thought Paul responsible for theological deviations from original Christianity. Although (according to Baird, p. 56) the English deists were not "bona fide biblical scholars," they nevertheless "raised a variety of historical-critical issues: the relation of the New Testament and the Old Testament; the authorship and order of the Gospels; Jesus versus Paul; the history of early Christianity." Bentham was squarely in this tradition. Deistic rationalism next confronted the Christian world in Germany, but this time bolstered with immense scholarly knowledge.

107. Believing Semler to be the "most important biblical scholar of the eighteenth century," Baird, *History of New Testament Research*, writes of him, "Antici-

pating the work of F. C. Baur, he believed the early church to have been made up of two parties: a Jewish faction represented by Peter, and a Hellenistic group under the leadership of Paul—two parties which, at the end of the second century, were merged into the catholic church" (p. 126).

108. Benn, *History of English Rationalism*, 1:302–303.

109. Ibid. This reference to Paul by Benn could hardly be more true, ironically speaking: Paul was excessively devoted to himself and to the theological artifacts of his imagination.

110. Crimmins, *Secular Utilitarianism*, p. 238.

111. Maccoby, *The Mythmaker*, reporting on the contents of an Arab manuscript (discovered by Schlomo Pines) which gives the Ebionite position on Paul, writes, "The standpoint . . . is that of the Ebionites: belief in the continuing validity of the torah, insistence on the human status of Jesus as a prophet, and strong opposition to Paul as the falsifier of Jesus' teachings" (p. 181).

112. Remembering the adage that nothing succeeds like success, we need to ask whether Paul had confidence in his (forthcoming) success on the mission field because of his "divine" commission or whether he became increasingly sure of his "divine" commission because of success on the mission field. Perhaps it was his missionary success that led him to believe in the "truth" of his gospel, rather than vice versa.

113. Grant, *Saint Paul*, writes of Paul,

At first, [i.e., at the very end of his life] his career seemed to have been an almost total failure. His churches among the Dispersion do not seem to have prospered or even in most cases to have survived, at least in the form that he had ordained for them. Instead, the Christian communities of all those cities gave their allegiance to the apostles [just as though Paul were not one of them]—the leaders and figureheads of that Jewish Christian Church which he had so stongly opposed. Likewise, Paul's extremely daring views . . . failed almost completely to gain acceptance; because the Jewish Christian doctrine was manifestly so different. (p. 189)

114. Krister Stendahl, "The Apostle Paul and the Introspective Conscience of the West," *HTR* 56 (1963), writes, "It has always been a puzzling fact that Paul meant so relatively little for the thinking of the church during the first 350 years of its history. To be sure, he is honored and quoted but—in the theological perspective of the West—it seems that Paul's great insight into justification by faith was forgotten" (pp. 203–204).

115. At one point in *Secular Utilitarianism*, Crimmins gives as his own opinions certain views that Benn had expressed long before. Crimmins fails to acknowledge his debt to Benn and does not seem to be aware of paraphrasing him closely. Compare the following two paragraphs, the first from Benn, *History of English Rationalism*, the second from Crimmins, *Secular Utilitarianism*:

[*NPBJ*] is not, what the title might have led us to expect, a comparative view of the two entirely different religions respectively embodied in the

Epistle to the Romans and in the Sermon on the Mount, but rather a historical investigation of the true relation subsisting between Paul and the original disciple of Jesus. The result is to exhibit the converted persecutor of the Church as an ambitious and worldly-minded intriguer, who joined the infant community in order to use its resources for the attainment of his own selfish ends. (1:302)

In *Not Paul, but Jesus*, then, we have what purports to be a comparative view of the two entirely different religions embodied respectively in Paul's Epistles (particularly Romans) and in Jesus's Sermon on the Mount. In actual fact what we are given is a historical investigation of the relations between Paul and the original Apostles intended to discredit the motives and actions of the former. Paul is portrayed as the converted persecutor of the Church, ambitious, worldly, an intriguer, ready to manipulate the community of Christians in order to attain his own selfish ends. (p. 237)

116. Crimmins, *Secular Utilitarianism*, p. 232.

117. F. L. Burkett, quoted in Hugh J. Schonfield, *The Passover Plot* (New York: Bantam Books, 1967), pp. 11–12.

118. For an excellent overview, see Victor Paul Furnish, "The Paul-Jesus Debate: From Baur to Bultmann," in *Paul and Jesus: Collected Essays*, ed. A. J. M. Wedderburn (Sheffield, UK: JSOT Press, 1989). The editor also contributes four informative essays on the subject at issue in this volume.

119. Crimmins refers to Hyam Maccoby's *Revolution in Judaea: Jesus and the Jewish Resistance* (New York: Taplinger, 1980) in *Secular Utilitarianism*, p. 232, n. 25. Crimmins does not seem to know that Maccoby is not the only, and by no means the most important (historically) scholar adopting the Zealot hypothesis. In addition to Samuel G. F. Brandon, named in the text above, there are also Robert Eisler, author of *The Messiah Jesus and John the Baptist*, trans. A. H. Krappe (London: Methuen, 1931), and J. Spencer Kennard Jr., author of *Politique et religion chez les Juifs au temps de Jesus et dans l'église primitive* (Politics and religion among the Jews in the time of Jesus and the primitive church), rev. ed. (Paris, 1927). For a book giving thumbnail sketches and penetrating criticisms of this and other hypotheses put forward in New Testament studies, see Eldon Jay Epp and George W. MacRae (eds.), *The New Testament and Its Modern Interpreters* (Philadelphia: Fortress Press, and Atlanta: Scholars Press, 1989). It does not seem to have occurred to Crimmins that Jewish scholars, no matter how religious, tend to approach Jesus and any messianic claims he may have made in what to Crimmins would be a "naturalistic" (i.e., nonreligious) way. Their approach takes account of the political and other mundane aspects of messiahship as well as the religious, but not the religious à la Paul. Klausner, *From Jesus to Paul*, writes, "[Y]et there was in his messiahship . . . a *genuinely political element*, as testifies his having as a disciple the 'Zealot,' and as testifies also one of the first verses of Acts [1:6–7; see also Luke 6:15]. In the last analysis any Messiah is King-Messiah, that is to say, he is to free his people from subjection to foreign powers, being therefore also a 'son of David' from the liberated and liberating royal house of Israel" (emphasis added; pp. 437–38). To be the Messiah in the

exclusively Jewish context of first-century Palestine was not the same as being the Incarnated Lord or the Redeemer of the world in the Christological context of St. Paul. Crimmins seems to think that only the latter is religious. Following the researches of James Steintrager (whose work will be discussed more in part 3), Crimmins writes "According to Bentham, Christ's real mission was not to establish a religion or to advance a specific morality, but to acquire sovereign power over the Jewish nation. It was only when his movement began to fail that he developed the notion of a spiritual kingdom as a cover or refuge to prevent the detection of his revolutionary plot before it was sufficiently advanced" (*Secular Utilitarianism*, p. 231). Bentham was not and is not alone in these views. If it turns out that they are wrong, it will not be because of their irreligion, and if they turn out to be right, it will not be because of their naturalism—they will become right or wrong depending on the support or lack of support of historical evidence.

120. Crimmins, *Secular Utilitarianism*, p. 232.

121. Rabbis in local synagogues would not necessarily have taken exception to messianic claims. Indeed, many might have welcomed such claims, whether from Jesus or some other plausible claimant. It would, rather, have been the members of the priestly class, that is, the Sadducees, in league with the Romans, who would have taken sharp, even violent exception to Jesus.

122. Samuel G. F. Brandon, *Jesus and the Zealots: A Study of the Political Factor in Primitive Christianity* (Manchester, UK: University of Manchester Press, 1967), p. 110.

123. Crimmins, "Bentham on Religion," p. 110.

124. Ibid., p. 100.

125. Crimmins, *Secular Utilitarianism*, p. 252.

126. Crimmins, "Bentham on Religion: Atheism and the Secular Society," *JHI* 47 (1986): 97.

127. Ibid., p. 99.

128. Ibid., p. 95; Crimmins, "Bentham's Metaphysics and the Science of Divinity," *HTR* 79, no. 4 (1986): 407.

129. Crimmins, "Bentham's Metaphysics and the Science of Divinity," *HTR* 70 (1986): 410.

130. Morton Smith, *Jesus the Magician* (New York: Harper and Row, 1978), p. 165.

131. John Rexine, *Religion in Plato and Cicero* (New York: Philosophical Library, 1959), calls the contents of the tenth book of *The Laws* "the foundation of all subsequent 'natural' theology, the first attempt in the literature of the world to *demonstrate* God's existence and moral government from the known facts of the visible order" (p. 24).

132. As I point out in "Deception and Development in Plato's Theology," *SJP* 5, no. 3 (1967), "*The Laws* of Plato is truly a god-intoxicated work. 'God' or 'gods' and 'goddess' or 'goddesses' appear at least 250 times. . . . Furthermore, a number of specific gods including Zeus, Apollo, Athena, Dionysus and several others (including some foreign deities such as Isis) are mentioned in aggregate at least 88 times, and such terms as 'deities', 'daemons', 'nether-gods', 'god-like', and 'godly-fear' are commonplace" (p. 179, n.45). Plato's failure to see polytheism versus monotheism as a problem can be disconcerting to the modern thinker.

133. Plato, *The Laws*, trans. A. E. Taylor, *The Collected Dialogues of Plato*, Bollingen Series 71, ed. Edith Hamilton and Huntington Cairns (New York: Pantheon Books, 1961), 886a.

134. Ibid., 886d–887a.

135. Ibid., 887c–888a.

136. Psyche (or, more accurately, *psuche*) means variously "breath of life, ghost, vital principle, soul, anima," according to F. E. Peters, *Greek Philosophical Terms* (New York: New York University Press, 1967), pp. 166–67. Julian Jaynes, *The Origin of Consciousness in the Breakdown of the Bicameral Mind* (Boston: Houghton Mifflin, 1976), pp. 270–71, 288–92, traces its evolution from the verb *psychein*, meaning 'to breathe', to the full-blown appearance in thought of the separable soul, and writes, "So dualism, that central difficulty in the problem of consciousness, begins its huge haunted career through history, to be firmly set in the firmament of thought by Plato, moving through Gnosticism into the great religions up through the arrogant assurances of Descartes to become one of the great spurious quandaries of modern psychology" (p. 291).

137. Plato, *Laws*, 892a–e.

138. St. Paul was in a similar position. It is not surprising that he failed to associate the mind of a given human with the brain of that same human. Even as great a thinker as Aristotle dissociated the two altogether, believing the brain and top of the head to be involved in cooling the body and balancing the warmth-producing area around the heart. Aristotle more nearly believed the heart to carry out the functions that we now associate with the brain (see *Aristotle: Parts of Animals*, trans. A. L. Peck, Loeb Classical Library [Cambridge: Harvard University Press], 647a–b9, 652b16–653 all, 656a22–30). Even more important for Paul, the biblical books at his disposal did not associate the mind with the brain (see *IDB*, s. v. "Mind").

139. Here I have followed the translation of the New Testament by Charles B. Williams (Chicago: Moody Press, 1955).

140. As I have written in "What Does the Bible Say about Abortion?" *FI* 11, no. 4 (1991): 29, "The theme that associates spirit, breath, and life occurs elsewhere in the Old Testament. Elihu, one of Job's friends, says of his own origins, 'The spirit of the Lord hath made me, and the breath of the Almighty hath given men life' (Job 33:4). Moreover, Isaiah 42:5 refers to the Bible-god as him 'that giveth breath unto the people upon it [the earth], and spirit to them that walk therein.' Most graphic, in support of this view, is the story of the valley of dry bones in Ezekiel 37." Regarding *nephesh*, the *IDB*, 4:428–29, thinks it likely that this word came from the Akkadian, meaning 'neck' or 'throat' and, by association, 'breath'.

141. The manuscript referred to is the thesis I wrote to complete the requirements for the Bachelor of Divinity degree at what is now Lexington Theological Seminary in Kentucky. It is titled "A Critical and Historical Examination of the Concept Holy Spirit" and was submitted in the spring of 1955.

142. E. B. Tylor, *Religion in Primitive Culture*, vol. 2 (Gloucester, MA: Peter Smith, 1970), esp. chap. 11.

143. E. Washburn Hopkins, *Origin and Evolution of Religion* (New Haven, CT: Yale University Press, 1923), p. 110.

144. The mind-body problem, which was once almost exclusively the intellectual domain of philosophers, has now increasingly been invaded by scientific trespassers. For an overview, see John Horgan, "Can Science Explain Consciousness?" *SA* (July 1994): 88–94. Upon taking down my file on the mind-body problem, I find the following titles (among many others) that will illustrate the point: "Brain Defects Seen in Those Who Repeat Violent Acts," *NYT*, September 17, 1985; "Clues to Suicide: A Brain Chemical Is Implicated," *NYT*, October 8, 1985; Daniel Goleman, "Investigations of the Brain Finding Clues to the Mind," *NYT*, April 22, 1986; "Brain Wound Eliminates Man's Mental Illness," *NYT*, February, 25, 1988; "Biology of Brain May Hold Key for Gamblers," *NYT*, October 3, 1989; "Key to Post-Traumatic Stress Lies in Brain Chemistry, Scientists Find," *NYT*, June 12, 1990; "Studies Find a Link between Aggressiveness and Cholesterol Levels," *NYT*, September 11, 1990; "Feeling Cheerful? Thank the Brain's Left Lobe," *NYT*, February 2, 1991; "Brain Yields New Clues on Its Organization for Language," *NYT*, September 10, 1991; "Nerve Cell Rhythm May Be Key to Consciousness," *NYT*, October 27, 1992; "Scanner Pinpoints Site of Thought as Brain Sees or Speaks," *NYT*, June 1, 1993; "Old Accident Points to Brain's Moral Center," *NYT*, May 24, 1994; "Tracing the Brain's Pathways for Linking Emotion and Reason," *NYT*, December 6, 1994; "In Work of Intuition, Gut Feelings Are Tracked to Source: The Brain," *NYT*, March 4, 1997; "Brain of Chimpanzee Sheds Light on Mystery of Language," *NYT*, January 13, 1998; "Scientists Track Process of Reading through the Brain," *NYT*, March 3, 1998; "Mapping Thoughts and Even Feelings," *NYT*, May 22, 1999; "Study Finds Region of Brain May Be Problem Solver," *NYT*, July 21, 2000; and "Brain-Updating Machinery May Explain False Memories," *NYT*, September 19, 2000. In the article of April 22, 1986, written by Daniel Goleman, there is a report on the research of neurophysiologist Benjamin Libet that ought to make Crimmins's blood run cold. In part Goleman writes of Libet, "His research . . . shows that appreciable brain activity precedes all voluntary acts. The activity not only seems to trigger the acts, but—most surprising—it also precedes the instant at which a person decides to act. This means that the brain actually decides for the mind, rather than the brain['s] executing some conscious decision the person makes. What most people think of as free will in his view, is actually an illusion, occurring after the brain has made a decision to act." Bentham's philosophy can incorporate these findings without difficulty. Crimmins's philosophy, which is at least as old as Plato's, and no more modern, cannot.

Jacques Monod, French Nobel laureate in physiology and medicine in 1965, situates all theists in what he calls the "animist tradition." In his book *Chance and Necessity* (New York: Alfred A. Knopf, 1971), he writes, "Modern societies accepted the treasures and the power that science laid in their laps. But they have not accepted—they have scarcely even heard—its profounder message: the defining of a new and unique source of truth, and the demand for a thorough revision of ethical premises, for a total break with the animist tradition, the definitive abandonment of the 'old covenant,' the necessity of forging a new one. Armed with all the powers, enjoying all the riches they owe to science, our societies are still trying to live by and to teach systems of values already blasted at the root by science itself" (pp. 170–71). Crimmins's criticisms of Bentham indicate that, unlike his target, he is an animist mired in the "old covenant."

145. See Thomas Nagel, review of *The Rediscovery of Mind*, by John Searles, *NYRB* March 4, 1993, p. 37. Nagel, a distinguished philosopher, notes that dualism is now rare among philosophers, "most of whom accept some kind of materialism." This is bad news, indeed, for Crimmins and for some of the criticisms he lodges against Bentham on religion.

146. In "What Are Spiritual Phenomena?" the presidential address given to the American Philosophical Association, Pacific Division, David Stern writes, "But . . . with the Jewish Alexandrines [such as Philo of Alexandria] and Saint Paul the concept of the πνεῦμα or spirit appears already dematerialized, and there one finds also the root of the trichotomy of the *spiritual*, the *psychical*, and the *physical*" (See *PAAPA* 39 [1965–1966]: 43). There is yet another dualism in Paul, in 2 Cor. 4:16, where he writes of the outward man and the inner man (also see Rom. 7:22 and Eph. 3:16). Hans-Dieter Benz has investigated this dualism exhaustively in "The Concept of the Inner Human Being (ὁ ἔσω ἄνθρωπος) in the Anthropology of Paul," *NTS* 46, no. 3 (2000): 315–41. Benz argues (p. 340) that Paul's distinction between the inner and the outer human being does not place him in any recognizable philosophical position of his time. Or of any time, I might add.

147. Glossolalia (or speaking in the unknown tongue) is the utterance of syllables, singly or in combination, that are unrecognizable as words in any known language, that are linked according to unknown rules (if any) of grammar, and that assert nothing intelligible in any natural or artificial language. This definition does not imply that instances of glossolalia have no effect on the emotions of the speaker or on the listener(s). The speaker commonly appears to be in a trance-like state. It is also common, but not necessary, for instances of glossolalia to inspire some one among the auditors to attempt a translation into a common tongue. For a great deal more on this topic see Watson E. Mills, *Theological/Exegetical Approach to Glossolalia* (New York: University Press of America, 1985). Also see Virginia H. Hine, "Pentecostal Glossolalia: Toward a Functional Interpretation," *JSSR* 8, no. 2 (1969): 211–26; and in the same source, Felicitas D. Goodman, "Phonetic Analysis of Glossolalia in Four Cultural Settings," pp. 227–39.

148. See *Mark Twain Laughing*, ed. Paul M. Zall (Knoxville, TN: University of Tennessee Press, 1958), p. 62, entry 135.

149. Respecting anthropomorphism, Paul yielded to no one in the New Testament. In his writings, human beings relate themselves to angels and to devils (or demons) much as they do to other humans. In Gal. 4:14 Paul notes that the Galatians received him as an angel of God (even as Jesus Christ), indicating a kinship between superhumans and humans, at least in the person of Paul. In 1 Cor. 13:1 Paul implies that both angels and humans have language, and in 4:9 he speaks of himself as having become a spectacle to angels and men, so, in some sense, angels can see or perceive as humans do. In 1 Cor. 10:20 Paul urges the Corinthians not to have fellowship with devils, implying the personhood, even if evil, of the latter, and in 10:21, in the context of the Eucharist, announces that a Christian cannot drink the cup of the Lord and also of devils, nor partake of the Lord's table and of the table of devils.

Angels have traditionally been seen as messengers or heralds of the Bible-god (as in Luke 1:11 and 2:13–15). Although Paul found no occasion to say just this, there is no reason to believe that he would have rejected this view. It is a common-place in modern New Testament scholarship to see good spirits and evil spirits as being able, in the ancient view of things, to enter people and work their will. Emi-nent New Testament scholar Rudolf Bultmann, *Kerygma and Myth: A Theological Debate*, ed. Hans-Werner Bartsch, trans. Reginald H. Fuller (London: S. P. C. K., 1972), writes, "Man is not in control of his own life. Evil spirits may take posses-sion of him. Satan may inspire him with evil thoughts. Alternately, God may inspire his thoughts and guide his purposes. He may grant him heavenly visions. He may allow him to hear the word of succour or demand. He may give him the supernat-ural power of the Spirit" (p. 1).

The Greek *pneuma*, originally meaning 'wind', 'blowing', 'breath', or 'breathing', is the term Paul most often used to mean 'spirit'. *Pneumatikos* ('pneu-matic' in English) in the New Testament means "spiritually, in a spiritual manner, in a manner caused or filled with the Spirit" (*GEL*, pp. 680 ff).

Regarding the entry of spirits into humans, Bultmann, *Kerygma and Myth*, con-trasts the present view of the matter with that of the New Testament writers: "Sick-ness and the cause of diseases are . . . attributable [nowadays] to natural causation; they are not [as in New Testament times] the result of daemonic activity, or of evil spells" (p. 4). Sin, sickness, and death were intimately related to the indwelling presence of demons. Redemption, good works, and freedom were, on the other hand, the result of the indwelling presence of the "Holy Spirit."

Ancient belief in the frequent indwelling presence of outdwelling spirits is what we would now call possession. Smith, *Jesus the Magician*, writes, "Once in pos-session of a man [evil spirits] may not only cause disease or loss of faculties, but also act and speak through their victims; they often make them act foolishly or criminally, sometimes hurt themselves, sometimes even commit suicide. Men are 'led' or 'driven' by indwelling demons" (pp. 126–27). Evil spirits are not alone in being able to possess a person; good spirits may do so as well. Smith writes, "Paul's theology is mainly an extension of the notion of possession" (p. 127). This is a point that cannot be overemphasized. Howard C. Kee and Franklin W. Young, *Understanding the New Testament* (Englewood Cliffs, NJ: Prentice-Hall, 1957), ratify this point: "The helpless plight of man, Paul continues, is not merely the result of human weakness; man is under the dominion of superhuman forces of evil at work in the world. Paul's belief about these demonic forces lies behind his words to Gen-tile hearers about the enslaved condition from which they were delivered by Christ" (p. 234).

150. In 1 Cor. 15:24, Paul writes, "Then *cometh* the end, when he [Jesus] shall have delivered up the kingdom to God, even the Father; when he [Jesus] shall have put down all rule [opposed to the Father] and authority [of satanic evil against the Father] and power [including the power of Satan and his legions]."

Jeffrey Burton Russell, *The Devil: Perceptions of Evil from Antiquity to Primitive Christianity* (Ithaca, NY: Cornell University Press, 1977), writes, "The Devil [or Satan] is a creature of God, the chief of the fallen angels, but he most of the time acts as if he had far greater power. He is lord of this world, chief of a vast multitude of powers spiritual and physical, angelic and human, that are arrayed against the Kingdom of God. Satan is not only the Lord's chief opponent; he has under his generalship *all* opposition to the Lord. Anyone who does not follow the Lord is under the control of Satan" (p. 247).

For Paul's use of the name Satan, see Rom. 16:20; 1 Cor. 5:5, 7:5; 2 Cor. 2:11, 11:14, 12:7; 1 Thess. 2:18; and 2 Thess. 2:9.

151. Edgar J. Goodspeed translates "deep things" as "thoughts" in TBAT. So, too, does James Moffatt in his translation of the Bible, and Charles B. Williams in his translation of the New Testament. The translators of the RSV agree as do the translators of the MLB, the LB, and the NTIV.

152. In a less than pellucid passage (Rom. 8:26–27), Paul says (according to the NEB), "[T]he Spirit comes to the aid of our weakness. We do not even know how we ought to pray, but through our inarticulate groans the Spirit himself is pleading for us, and God who searches our inmost being knows what the Spirit means, because he pleads for God's own people in God's own way." Here the tables are turned: it is not the Spirit that is plumbing the "deep things" of God, but God who is plumbing the deep things of the Spirit. To the ordinary believer, this may seem profound; to the ordinary logician, without prior religious commitments, it simply seems confused. The TBAT and the WNT agree with the translation above, as does the MTB.

153. Speaking in tongues (i.e., glossolalia), it must be remembered, is the ecstatic utterance of syllables (singly or in combination) that belong to no known language (natural or artificial), that conform to no known grammar, and that are prima facie meaningless. Some people within a believing community may claim the power to translate glossolalia into the vernacular, but whether translated or not, the believing community will likely claim that instances of it reveal hidden "spiritual" truths that are edifying to that community or congregation (see note 147).

154. 1 Cor. 1:12 indicates not only that there was factionalism in the Corinthian church but also the very real possibility that a man named Cephas (who was the apostle Peter, according to John 1:42) was there for a time in person (see Smith, "Paul's Arguments," pp. 254, 259–60).

155. If "gifted" prophets in Corinth were prophesying (i.e., predicting) the quick return of the Lord Jesus to judge the world, as Paul had been doing (see Rom. 13:11–12, 16:20; 1 Cor. 1:7, 3:13, 7:26, 7:29–31, 10:11, 11:26, 15:24; 2 Cor. 1:14; Gal. 1:3; Phil. 1:6, 2:16, 3:20, 4:5; 1 Thess. 5:2; and 2 Thess 1:7, 2:2), then they were as egregiously mistaken as he. All biblical messianists to date, including Paul, have been wrong in their expectations, and there seems little likelihood that any of them will ever prove to have been right. Being mistaken in this, Paul and his fellow messianic prophets can hardly have received a true revelation concerning the eschaton, the end of the age. When Christian messianists are confronted with this, their classic theological dodge is to repeat 2 Pet. 3:8b: "[O]ne day *is* with the Lord as a thousand years, and a thousand years as one day." The unintended result of this is to dash any hope of receiving a revelation concerning the timing of the eschaton. For example, if when Paul wrote (in 1 Cor. 7:29), "But this I say brethren, the time *is* short: it remaineth, that both they that have wives be as though they had none," a short time as reckoned by humans might be several thousand years long as reckoned by the Bible-god, then no revelation was received by the humans in question. If all married, potentially child-bearing Christians had taken seriously Paul's estimate of the remaining time before the end of the age and had forthwith lived celi-

bately, Christians today would be about as numerous as the Shakers. It must be recognized as a general principal that if the Bible-god understands his revelation to mean one thing whereas the recipients of it understand another, then no self-disclosure of divine truth occurs. Respecting the failure of the eschaton to occur as anticipated, nobody has put it more succinctly than Bultmann, *Kerygma and Myth*: "The *mythical eschatology* is untenable for the simple reason that the parousia (return) of Christ never took place as the New Testament expected. History did not come to an end, and, as every schoolboy knows, it will continue to run its course" (p. 5). Bultmann must have had European schoolboys in mind: many of the American variety still, today, believe in the factuality of Noah's Ark and take similar biblical fictions as literal fact.

156. A noteworthy moment in my professional quest to understand religion occurred in the early 1950s when, in the mountains of eastern Kentucky, I heard both an instance of glossolalia and the (or an) interpretation thereof. The setting was a Pentecostal revival meeting held in a tent on a hot summer's night. What is called the Spirit (but seemed to me to be a kind of emotionalism) was moving mightily that night. Without preamble, a woman in the congregation arose from the chair she had been sitting on and began to speak in the unknown tongue, while appearing to be in a trance. The syllables came smoothly and rapidly but were joined to one another in such a way that, though they were English in sound, they were unintelligible. No recognizable word in English, not even an article or a preposition, was uttered. After several minutes, the speaker sank down on her chair, seemingly spent. After a moment's pause, another lady, several rows in front of the first, arose and began to utter what sounded like verses from the Old Testament, perhaps from one or another of the major prophets, something about how sinners ought to beware and how saints ought to be hopeful and joyous. If the interpretation was correct, the revelation in the unknown tongue was banal in the extreme. It did, however, indicate the Spirit's endorsement of English as it was used in 1611, when the KJV was hot off the presses. Although I was a Christian and a clergyman at the time, I found it impossible to have much confidence either in the mysterious tongue or in the alleged interpretation of it that I had heard. More tellingly, I was not edified.

157. Col. 1:15–19 speaks of "God's Son," "Who is the image of the invisible God, the firstborn of every creature: For by him were all things created, that are in heaven, and that are in earth, visible and invisible, whether *they* be thrones, or dominions, or principalities, or powers: all things were created by him and for him: And he is before all things, and by him all things consist. And he is the head of the body, the church: who is the beginning, the firstborn from the dead; that in all *things* he might have preeminence. For it pleased the *Father* that in him should all fullness dwell." Nothing similar is said of the Spirit in Paul's other writings. There is, however, a question as to whether Colossians is from Paul's hand. The very passage just cited is sometimes taken as one of the reasons for doubting the authenticity of this epistle, the point being that the Christology herein (i.e., the doctrine of the person of Christ) is more advanced than any of Paul's creation in his other writings. The authenticity of Colossians, however, has many defenders. See Morton Scott Enslin, *Christian Beginnings* (New York: Harper and Brothers, 1938), pp. 291–92. Also see

Stephen Neill and Tom Wright, *The Interpretation of the New Testament: 1861–1986* (Oxford: Oxford University Press, 1988), who say of British scholarship that it is "almost unanimous in accepting the authenticity of Colossians" (p. 63).

158. A classic source for functional identity can be found in Auguste Sabatier, *The Apostle Paul* (London: Hooder and Stroughton, 1903), p. 285. Two decades later, eminent German scholar Adolph Deismann said essentially the same thing in *The Religion of Jesus and the Faith of Paul*, trans. William E. Wilson (New York: George H. Doran, 1923), p. 175. Twenty-five years later, well-known British scholar C. H. Dodd, *The Meaning of Paul for Today* (London: George Allen and Unwin, 1949), pp. 127–37, endorsed this view.

159. R. V. G. Frasker, *The Second Epistle of Paul to the Corinthians*, Tyndale New Testament Commentaries (Leicester, UK, and Grand Rapids, MI: William B. Eerdmans, 1963), p. 66.

160. This is the so-called kenosis doctrine, the doctrine that holds that the "Son of God," preexisting with the Father in heaven, emptied himself of equality and became a human being in order to complete a unique soteriological role.

161. In 1 Cor. 15:24–28, Paul refrains from positing an identity between his deity, his deity's male offspring, and his deity's (Holy) Spirit:

> "Then *cometh* the end, when he [Christ] shall have delivered up the kingdom to God, even the Father; when he [Christ] shall have put down all rule and all authority and power. For he [Christ] must reign, till he hath put all enemies under his feet. The last enemy *that* shall be destroyed *is* death. For he hath put all things under his feet. But when he saith all things are put under *him*, *it is* manifest that he [the Father-deity] is excepted, which did put all things under him [Christ]. And when all things shall be subdued unto him, then shall the Son also himself be subjected unto him [the Father-deity] that put all things under him [Christ], that God may be all in all."

This is a clear case of subordinationism, that is, of subordinating the Son to the Father, a position inimical to the doctrine of the Trinity, which posits equality of essence between the Father-deity, the Offspring-deity, and the (Holy) Spirit of the deity.

162. K. R. Hagenbach writes in *A Text-Book of the History of Doctrines*, trans. Henry B. Smith, vol. 1 (New York: Sheldon, 1861), "[T]he word οὐσία (*essentia, substantia*) denotes what is common to the Father, the Son, and the Holy Spirit; the word ὑπόστασις (*persona*) what is individual, distinguishing the one from the other. Each person possesses some peculiarity (ἰδιότης), by which it is distinguished from the other persons, notwithstanding the sameness of [their] essence. Thus, underived existence (ἀγεννησία) belongs to the Father, generation (γέννησις) to the Son, and procession (ἐκπορεύσις, ἔκπεμψις) to the Holy Spirit" (pp. 264–65). Stated as such, no subordination of one person to another occurs.

The quote is from H. Wheeler Robinson, *The Christian Experience of the Holy Spirit* (New York: Harper and Brothers, 1930), pp. 230–31.

163. Elias Andrews, *The Meaning of Christ for Paul* (New York: Abingdon-Cokesbury Press, 1949), p. 263.

164. See also Acts 7:51–53.

165. This article, which appeared in the *NYT*, March 26, 1995, is by Daniel Goleman concerning a recent publication in *The American Journal of Psychiatry* by Dr. Mark George, a researcher at the National Institute of Mental Health. The study focuses on PET scans of the brains of women. Men were excluded in this study so as not to complicate the research with any sex-based brain differences in human beings.

166. I would argue, for example, that excessive amounts of Freudianism persist in much psychohistorical writing, and, of course, patriotic demands still skew the history of one's own country (any country) and people (any people).

167. Oscar Cullmann, in his famous little book, *Immortality of the Soul and Resurrection of the Dead* (London: Epworth Press / Macmillan, 1958), pp. 33–34, wrote, "[F]or Pauline theology, flesh and spirit in the New Testament are two *transcendent* powers which can enter into man from without; but *neither is given with human existence as such*. On the whole it is true that the Pauline anthropology, contrary to the Greek, is grounded in *Heilsgeschichte* [i.e., salvation-history]. 'Flesh' is the power of sin or the power of death. It seizes the outer and the inner man *together*." And as 1 Cor. 15:56b makes absolutely clear, the power of sin is the Mosaic law. Also see Rom. 4:15, 5:13, and 7:5, 13.

168. To get a feel for the tidal wave of materialistic resolutions of the mind-brain problem, see Daniel C. Dennett, *Consciousness Explained* (Boston: Little, Brown, 1991); Gerald M. Edelman, *Bright Air, Brilliant Fire: On the Matter of the Mind* (New York: Basic Books, 1993); Paul Churchland, *Matter and Consciousness: A Contemporary Philosophy of Mind* (Cambridge, MA: MIT Press, Bradford Books, 1988) and *The Engine of Reason, the Seat of the Soul* (Cambridge: MIT Press, Bradford Books, 1995); Patricia Churchland, *Neurophilosophy: Toward a Unified Science of Mind-Brain*, rev. ed. (Cambridge: MIT Press, Bradford Books, 1986), Antonio R. Damascio, *Descartes' Error: Emotion, Reason, and the Human Brain* (New York: G. P. Putnam, 1994); Stephen Priest, *Theories of the Mind* (Boston: Houghton Mifflin, 1992); and Francis Crick, "The Recent Excitement about Neural Networks," *Na* 337 (January 1989): 129–32.

169. If there is a Big Brain able to account for the big bang and the subsequent evolution of the universe, where is it? Does it require a body to house, support, and nourish it, as is the case with human brains? Is it functioning biologically in splendid isolation or is it also social, and if the latter, whence the necessary society? Could the Big Brain become addled for a time, such as the brain of King George III of England, and then recover temporarily before death? Could a Big Brain of the sort hypothesized be eternal and immortal? Countless other disturbing questions could follow, but these should be sufficient to illustrate the problem involved in taking the so-called Mind of God to be a function of a divine Big Brain.

170. Descartes is famous for having picked what is now known as the pineal body (or gland) as the point of contact between body and nonbody (i.e., between brain and mind), in part because it is a unitary body (not divided into hemispheres as is the brain) and in part because it is so delicate that (to him) the slightest contact of mind (soul or will) upon it could send "animal spirits" coursing from it to cause physical effects throughout the human body. See Descartes, *The Passions of the*

Soul, trans. Stephen Voss (Indianapolis: Hackett, 1988), Articles 31–46, pp. 36–44. Taking the well-known "ghost in the machine" depiction (see Gilbert Ryle, *The Concept of Mind* [London: Hutchison; New York: Barnes and Noble, 1949] as accurate, we have but to ask the following question: would a ghost (unextended and massless) be able to manipulate the gear selection lever in a car with an automatic transmission easier than it would be able to shift gears in a car with a manual transmission? Since the answer is no, Descartes clearly failed to resolve the mind-brain problem. The pineal gland has, however, come in for considerable attention recently as a powerful factor involving hormonal changes in adolescence. Harold M. Schmeck Jr., "As Scoffing Fades, Pineal Gland Gets Its Due," *NYT*, January 31, 1984, writes, "Some elements of Descartes' observations seem remarkably close to today's views. He said the pineal gland receives messages from the outside world through 'strings' between the eyes and the center of the brain, and reacted by sending 'animal humors' down tubes to the muscles, where they produced appropriate responses. In fact the pineal body in mammals does receive nerve signals relayed by the brain from the eye, and does send its principal hormonal product, melatonin, elsewhere in the body, where it elicits important responses."

171. Paul confessed to persecuting the church in 1 Cor. 15:9 and in Phil. 3:6, to doing so violently in Gal. 1:13, 23, and murderously, if Acts 22:4 can be taken as historical.

172. There is considerable scholarly disagreement as to why precisely Paul persecuted the church. Martin Hengel, *The Pre-Christian Paul* (London: SCM Press, 1991), says flatly, "[Paul] persecuted the Jewish Christian Hellenists in Jerusalem because he saw what was most holy in Israel [the ceremonial law] threatened by their proclamation and their conduct" (p. 80). Hengel continues, "The proclamation of the Greek-speaking followers of the messiah Jesus, . . . which was critical of the ritual parts of the Torah and the cult, was a provocation to the majority who were loyal to the law" (p. 85). However, Arland J. Hultgren, "Paul's Pre-Christian Persecutions of the Church: Their Purpose, Locale, and Nature," *JBL* 95 (1976): 97–111, argues against Hengel's position. Noting that a "partial consensus" has appeared among New Testament scholars to the effect that Paul "persecuted the Hellenistic wing of the Church" (p. 97), Hultgren argues nonetheless that Acts gives no hint that "the Christian Hellenists set themselves against the law" (p. 98). Moreover, the A-h gives no hint as to why Paul persecuted the church (p. 99). Hultgren also writes, "A second affirmation is that Paul persecuted the Christian movement as a threat to Jewish existence in the Roman Empire; the stir that it caused among the Jewish people could have had dangerous political consequences, especially since it was a Messianic movement" (p. 104, n. 14).

173. It is important in this connection to stress the Davidic descent of Jesus as *the* Messiah. Morton Smith, "What Is Implied by the Variety of Messianic Figures?" part 1, *JBL* 78 (March 1955): 66–72, has shown that in some ancient Jewish texts 'messiah' is made plural, that the High Priest is sometimes called a messiah, and that some messiahs appear in no relationship to eschatological hopes. This, of course, complicates the picture enormously.

174. I use 'extranatural' here rather than 'supernatural' because the latter is loaded with traditional theistic connotations that might better not be brought up

at this point. What one wants is more nearly a neutral term that can be set in opposition to the natural. 'Nonnatural' will not do, because unless explained properly, it gives the wrong impression. If the universe is at all like a human artifact, it is its artificer that (or who) is natural. The universe, being the product of the artificer, is nonnatural in the sense of being artificial, rather than natural. It is, however, dauntingly difficult to think of the universe (or of nature) as being nonnatural.

175. Paul nowhere writes that Satan is the Devil and vice versa, even though 'Satan' and 'Devil' are generally assumed to refer to the same entity/agent. Paul never used the word 'Devil' (*diabolos* in Greek) in any of his best authenticated letters. This word (in one grammatical form or another) appears only in Eph. 4:27, 6:11; in 1 Tim. 3:6–7; and in 2 Tim. 2:26, letters whose Pauline authorship is suspect to say the least.

176. Paul's mysterious thorn in the flesh is usually believed to have been some physical affliction, with epilepsy ranking high among the favored diagnoses. See Terrence Y. Mullins, "Paul's Thorn in the Flesh," *JBL* 76 (December 1957): 299. However, McCant, "Paul's Thorn of Rejected Apostleship," writes, "The hypothesis defended in this essay is that the thorn in the flesh was the Corinthian Church's rejection of the legitimacy of Paul's apostolate" (p. 572). Earlier, McCant writes, "Paul is engaged in a life-and-death struggle with persons who deny the legitimacy of his apostolate [2 Cor.] 12:12. For Paul this is a conflict between God and Satan; Paul is an 'ambassador' for Christ (2 Cor. 5:20) and anyone who questions his authority as an apostle becomes an 'angel [or messenger] of Satan' (2 Cor. 12:7). The battle is not less intense when Satan masquerades as an 'angel of light' (11:14)" (p. 572). In either case, whether physical affliction or Corinthian rejection of Paul's apostleship, the thorn is taken as the doing of Satan understood as a malign agent.

The informal fallacy called composition occurs whenever what is true of the individual members of a class (or set) is inferred to be true of the class (or set) taken as a whole. It would be a composition fallacy, for example, to argue that because the rate of (sinful) revelings is increasing, the class (or set) composed of all different kinds of sins has grown larger. This, of course, does not follow. The fallacy of division occurs whenever what is true of a class (or set) is inferred to be true of the members making it up. It would be a division fallacy, for example, to argue that because the class (or set) of sins has diminished by one type (because witchcraft, shall we say, is no longer practiced), individual sinners are committing fewer sins than before. However, this does not follow.

177. Smith, *Jesus the Magician*, pp. 126–27.

178. Ibid., p. 127. Here Smith writes, as quoted earlier, "Paul's theology is mainly an extension of this notion of [spirit] possession."

179. Bultmann, *Kerygma and Myth*, p. 7.

180. Two quotations should suffice to clinch the points at issue. First, Heikki Räisänen, "Galatians 2:16 and Paul's Break with Judaism," *NTS* 31, no. 4 (1985) writes, "In theory, Paul did not require Christian Jews to give up Torah observance. Actually, however, he expected them to do just that whenever the observance interfered with the intercourse with Gentile Christians, as Gal. 2 shows. God's eternal decrees, then, were no longer fully valid" (p. 549). Second, Samuel Belkin, "The Problem of Paul's Background," *JBL* 54, no. 1 (1935) writes, "According to Paul, however, once a Gentile had been circumcised he became obliged to fulfill all the

commandments of the written and oral law, 'I warn every man [Gal. 5:3] that gets himself circumcised that he is under obligation to fulfill the whole law'" (p. 44). The same view was also held by the Pharisees. Such a Gentile could, of course, become a Christian after being a converted Jew. Hence the theological complications that ensued over questions of the flesh understood as circumcision!

181. John Murray, *The Epistle to the Romans* (Grand Rapids, MI: William B. Eerdmans, 1959), declares, "'The law of the Spirit of Life' is . . . the power of the Holy Spirit operative in us to make us free from the power of sin which is unto death" (p. 276). If this is what Paul really meant, then law has been given a meaning never before entertained—one that defies classification.

182. Ibid., p. 277. Here Murray claims that the Mosaic law could not condemn sin in the flesh but that the Bible-god could and did. Granted that any promulgator of law can act in ways that the promulgated law cannot, why, in this case, should the Mosaic law have been impotent to condemn sin in the flesh? One would think that this is precisely what it could have done best. Murray states that the impotence of the law means that it has no redemptive power (ibid.). This is almost certainly true in the larger Pauline perspective, but it is not a satisfactory explanation of what Paul wrote in Rom. 8:3.

183. J. E. Frame stated long ago in his article "Paul's Idea of Deliverance," *JBL* 49 (1930), "Sin and flesh are *interchangeable*, if not quite identical terms, for the same results are ascribed to each" (p. 4; emphasis added). Much more recently, Stevan L. Davies, *The New Testament*, writes, "Fallen Humanity is in a body of flesh, and flesh, like a possessing demon, tempts it to sin" (p. 66). It should be noted here that Davies is not just saying of Paul that he believed each unredeemed individual was in a body of flesh (whatever this may mean) but that the collective "Fallen Humanity" was in a body of flesh, a much more complicated and dubious idea.

184. Cullmann, *Immortality of the Soul*, pp. 35–36.

185. Bultmann, *Kerygma and Myth*, p. 8.

186. Cullmann, *Immortality of the Soul*, p. 29.

187. Only in 1 Cor. 10:20–21.

188. Mary E. Andrews, "Paul, Philo, and the Intellectuals," *JBL* 53 (1934): 163. Paul does not use the Greek 'diabolos' in any of the epistles now believed to be authentically his. The term does appear in Eph. 4:27 and 6:11, but this letter, though Pauline in outlook, is no longer believed to be his by leading New Testament authorities.

189. B. Reicke, "The Law and This World According to Paul," part 4, trans. William B. Schaeffer, *JBL* 70 (December 1951): 260. This article was regarded as so important that the *JBL* broke its rule of not publishing articles that had previously been published elsewhere.

190. Ibid., p. 259.

191. Ibid.

192. Ibid., pp. 262–63.

193. See also Acts 7:38 and esp. 7:53, which refers to the Jews "[w]ho have received the law by the disposition of angels but have not kept it." The A-h may well have received this novel information from his hero, either directly or indirectly. The extent to which he knew of Paul's Galatian letter, if at all, is uncertain.

For the claim expressed in the text, see Reicke, "Law and This World," p. 262. Jason David BeDuhn, when "Because of the Angels: Unveiling Paul's Anthropology in 1 Corinthians 11," *JBL* 118, no. 2 (1999), complicates Paul's bizarre view of angels: "*Paul is attributing the separate formation of woman from man to a creative act of angels, not of God*" (p. 308), adding later, to "insulate God from . . . the imperfection of gendered existence" (p. 317).

194. Maccoby, *The Mythmaker*, p. 189.

195. Joseph Klausner, *From Jesus to Paul* (London: George Allen and Unwin, 1944), writes,

> Lest someone should say, "The Law is from God; how is it possible to abolish something divine and hence very important?"—Paul is ready with this answer: the Law was not given by God at all; it was given by the angels. . . . And lest someone should say, "The Law is the guide of life for individual and nation," Paul has this reply: the Law was a "nurse" or "tutor" to Israel only up to the time of the Messiah; but now that he has come, died, and risen, there is no longer any need of it. Now there is no longer any need of circumcision, of avoiding forbidden foods, of keeping Sabbaths, feasts, or new moons. "For if righteousness is through the Law, then Christ died for nought." Men can be "justified" only "by faith in Christ, and not by the works of the Law; because by the works of the Law shall no flesh be justified." (pp. 501–502)

196. Although the legitimacy of Colossians is doubted by some scholars (because its theology may be more advanced than was Paul's), its two references to elemental spirits (in 2:8 and 2:20) cohere with Gal. 4:3 and 4:9. This is especially true of Col. 2:20, whose rendition in the RSV, together with my clarifications, will make this evident: "If with Christ you died to the elemental spirits of the universe [i.e., to the angelic agents responsible for the law], why do you live as though you still belonged to the world [i.e., to the worldly, to the sinful]? Why do you submit to its regulations [i.e., to the requirements of the law]?"

197. Although Ephesians is no longer believed by leading scholars to have come directly from Paul's hand, it does contain much Pauline content. Edgar J. Goodspeed, "Ephesians and the First Edition of Paul," part 4, *JBL* 70 (December 1951), writes, "[T]he nine letters [of Paul] supply virtually all that [Ephesians] contains except for a line or two from the Septuagint or the Acts of the Apostles" (p. 285). So, though Ephesians contains more and more detailed references to principalities and powers than does any authentic letter of Paul, it does not introduce an alien idea at this point. See also Rom. 8:38, 1 Cor. 2:8, and Col. 1:16.

Regarding Satan, Klausner, *From Jesus to Paul*, writes, "Satan is for Paul 'the prince of the powers of the air'" (p. 471).

198. See Rubenstein, *My Brother Paul*, p. 156.

199. For "astral forces," see Frame, "Paul's Idea of Deliverance," p. 2; and Brandon, *Jesus and the Zealots*, p. 11, esp. n. 4. For "Lords of the planetary spheres," see E. F. Bruce, *Paul: Apostle of the Heart Set Free* (Grand Rapids, MI: William B. Eerdmans, 1977), p. 422.

200. Smith, *Jesus the Magician*, p. 126.

201. Smith, "Pauline Worship," p. 242.

202. Smith, *The Secret Gospel*, p. 99.

203. Smith, "Pauline Worship," p. 242.

204. Ibid., pp. 243–44. Readers interested in this esoteric subject should also see Collins, "The Function of 'Excommunication' in Paul," pp. 255–56; for even more, see esp. n. 8 on p. 255.

205. Smith, "Pauline Worship," p. 249.

206. Smith, *Jesus the Magician*, p. 123.

207. Smith, "Pauline Worship," pp. 247–48.

208. Smith, *Jesus the Magician*, pp. 47–48.

209. GEL, s. v. ὑπωπιάζω.

210. Alan Segal, *Paul the Convert: The Apostolate and Apostasy of Saul the Pharisee* (New Haven: Yale University Press, 1996), p. 39, writes, however, that Paul had no clearly developed idea of the soul. Why does this not surprise us?

211. Schweitzer, *The Mysticism of Paul*, p. 131; see also pp. 130 and 132.

212. Smith, *Jesus the Magician*, p. 179; Segal, *Paul the Convert*, p. 314, n. 7.

213. Ibid., p. 58. Here Segal writes of Paul as follows: "He does not admit to the ascent personally. Apart from the needs of his rhetoric, rabbinic rules also forbid public discussion of mystic phenomena." A first-century date for this rule would explain why Paul could not divulge his experience in his *own* name at that place.

214. William Baird, "Visions, Revelation, and Ministry: Reflections on 2 Corinthians 12:1–5 and Galatians 1:1–17," *JBL* 104, no. 4 (1985): 654.

215. Ibid., p. 654.

216. Those interested in pursuing the topics of ascension to the heavens (in Paul's time) and to "throne-chariot" (or *Merkabah*) mysticism among the Jews should see Segal, *Paul the Convert*, esp. pp. 39–71, as well as the index entry on the *Hekhaloth* literature (guides for making the heavenly journeys), p. 363. Smith, *The Secret Gospel*, pp. 84–88, takes up similar topics, mentions the *Hekaloth* books and adverts to the concentric heavens believed to surround the earth. In *Jesus the Magician*, pp. 124–25, Smith shows that ascension to the heavens was also important to Hellenistic (i.e., to pagan) peoples as well as to the Jews.

217. Baird, "Visions, Revelation, and Ministry," p. 652, n. 2; Smith, *The Secret Gospel*, p. 108; Segal, *Paul the Convert*, pp. 58–61.

218. Crimmins, "Bentham on Religion," p. 97; ibid., p. 110; "Bentham's Metaphysics," p. 410; *Secular Utilitarianism*, p. 252; "Bentham on Metaphysics, p. 407; "Bentham on Religion," p. 99; *Secular Utilitarianism*, p. 238. This last claim is a view that Crimmins attributes to Alfred William Benn but one with which he appears to agree. In any case, it is useful to take it up at this point.

219. Peter Steinfels, "Female Concept of God Is Shaking Protestants," *NYT*, May 14, 1994.

220. Ibid. Information about Sophia (actually a Greek word meaning 'wisdom') can be found principally in Prov. 8:22–31. Wisdom is not, however, pictured therein as a female personification of the divine but as a female companion, the firstborn of creation.

221. Ibid. There is no doubt that the "Re-Imagining" conference was "spiritu-

ally" significant. The Reverend Heidi Hudnut-Beumler, an ordained Presbyterian minister, was quoted in the *AJC*, May 21, 1994, as follows: "For me it was a very positive experience, spiritually enlightening, deepening. It increased my Christian faith and I would say it refreshed and renewed my call to the ministry."

222. Steinfels, "Female Concept of God." For the traditionalist side, the *AJC*, May 21, 1994, quoted Kathy Kersten, "a board member of the Institute on Religion and Democracy, in [the] magazine *First Things*," as writing, "From November 4 to 7, 1993, the Minneapolis Convention Center was home to a spiritual Disneyland. In this fantasy world, well-heeled women with strings of graduate degrees pretended together that they inhabit a dark and oppressive world, a world where 'hope burns through the terror'. How odd to pin one's hope for salvation in such dire circumstances on a goddess whose chosen milieu seems to be women's bodily fluids." Kersten does not seem to recognize that the corporate, participatory faith of Christians worshiping anywhere is also "pretending together." Furthermore, the bodily fluids wherein a goddess operates are no more insubstantial than the body and blood of the Bible-god's only begotten boy. The major difference is that the one "pretending together" has a long, powerful tradition behind it; the other does not. It is instructive to learn that a decade before the "Re-Imagining" conference, a woman named Kathleen R. Fischer, a Catholic, was writing a book titled *The Inner Rainbow: The Imagination in Christian Life* (New York: Paulist Press, 1983). A Paulist Press catalog (whose date I failed to note) quotes a reviewer, Bernard Cooke, as saying of *The Inner Rainbow*, "This book is an important addition to our literature about the religious function of imagination." Moreover, the Sheed and Ward Academic Catalog of 1996, p. 3, advertises a book by Gerald J. Behar, *Faith as Imagination: The Contribution of William F. Lynch, S.J.* Verily, verily, I say unto Professor Crimmins that a not-so-holy cat has been let out of the bag by some people who know not what they are saying and doing.

223. Samuel G. Freedman, "How Bakker Widened the Eye of the Needle," *NYT*, June 14, 1987.

224. Fawn Brodie, preface to *No Man Knows My History* (New York: AAK Fellowship, 1968), wrote of founder of Mormonism Joseph Smith, "No one more ingeniously than he combined Jewish and Christian mysticism with the goal of perpetual prosperity" (p. ix). Martin Gardner, *The Healing Revelations of Mary Baker Eddy* (Amherst, NY: Prometheus Books, 1993), pp. 101–102, 107, adverts to eight important early defectors from Christian Science who left in part because of Eddy's "love of money" and writes of what a "shrewd businesswoman" she was, also stating that she was "extremely knowledgeable about stocks and bonds." The connection between Episcopalians, wealth, and privilege is too well known to merit further comment.

225. There is nothing to be gained in denying "true Christianity" to Bakker. In the first place there is no universal agreement as to what it is, and in the second place there is no reason to doubt that Bakker's worldview was (and is) based squarely on Christian myths and metaphysics. He too was, and is, a "spiritual" man, a dualist, and for all practical purposes an animist.

Chapter 6

Criticisms

As unexpected as it may seem, Bentham read the Bible much as though he were an American fundamentalist; that is, he read it literally. Belief in its religious content was, of course, never an issue with him, nor did he try to reconcile apparently (or truly) inconsistent passages. Nor did he alter the obvious meanings of unsettling verses by "spiritualizing" them, that is, by allegorizing or otherwise tinkering with them until they became palatable. He took the text straight, as we would say, having no motivation to rationalize, reconcile, or allegorize any parts of it nor any reason to flinch at what he saw. The major problem with taking a text straight is that not all texts (nor all parts of a given text) are meant to be taken straight. Some, for example, may be ironic and others may be expressed in religious symbolism amounting to a code, purposely unintelligible to outsiders.[226] To illustrate, in Matthew 7:6, Jesus is reported to have said that one should not give that which is holy to dogs nor to cast pearls before swine. But, do 'dogs' and 'swine' here really refer to the animals so named, or, perhaps, to Gentiles in general or to the Romans in particular, and what does 'pearls' refer to? Even more esoteric are Paul's unique references to the man of sin, the son of perdition (2 Thess. 2:3) and to the *katechon*, the restraining force (2 Thess. 2:7).[227] Bentham was too unsympathetic toward biblical religion to care to get to the bottom of its "sacred" texts, especially when they did not mean what they seemed to say.

Although he had an excellent reason (based on his philosophy of language) for dismissing theology in general and for rejecting Paul's "thought" in particular, this philosophical reason plus his untempered literalism prevented him from becoming a credible New Testament scholar. If he had wanted to contribute to New Testament studies he would have had to change his outlook dramatically: first, he could not have persisted in his literalism; second, he would have had to become sensitive to literary styles and conventions that were foreign to him; and third, he would have had to develop the sympathy and patience requisite to becoming a successful historian of ideas, especially of ideas that he thought absurd.

Such was Bentham's outlook that if confronted with the claim that every document in the canon with Paul's name on it issued directly from Paul's pen, Bentham, like the fundamentalist, would most likely have assented. To claim this, however, is to saddle Paul with ideas that may not have been his, and this is clearly unscholarly and unfair. Before deciding which ideas are genuinely Paul's and which are not, one has to decide which of the biblical documents attributed to him are really his. As noted earlier, when Bentham cited Paul, it was almost always from one of the following four epistles, Galatians, 1 and 2 Corinthians, and Romans—the four about whose authenticity there is, today, the least scholarly dispute. Bentham, however, did not hew to these four out of commendable concern for authenticity but because it was herein that he found Paul attacking his theological and ecclesiastical enemies most vehemently, thus supporting one of Bentham's contentions about the self-appointed apostle to the Gentiles.

To have gained credibility as a New Testament scholar, he would have had to use the four epistles above (and in more ways than one) as the baseline for appraising other candidate documents presumed to be Paul's. On the basis of these authentic letters, he would, at the very least, have had to develop a list of Paul's favorite words (i.e., his typical vocabulary), to identify his characteristic syntax, and to become aware of what is nowadays called positional stylometry.[228] He would also have had to know enough relevant history to have detected evidence internal to some of the epistles indicating that they were written after Paul's time.[229] Furthermore, he would have had to master Paul's thought well enough to have distinguished it from developments stemming from it but not directly Paul's.[230] A glance at *NPBJ* shows that he did no such thing.

Even more elusive than determining an ancient writer's typical vocabulary, syntax, and positional stylometry (especially when the surviving documents are few) are his uses of once conventional rhetorical devices (such as parody) that are now dated, having long since fallen into disuse. An example may be Paul's boastfulness, a presumed characteristic of the saint that Bentham found particularly odious. The most concentrated instances of Paul's boasting and references to boasting (that of others as well as his own) are to be found in 2 Corinthians 10:8, 13, 15, 16, 17; 11:10, 12, 16, 17, 18, 30; and 12:1, 5, 6, 9. Read at face value, as Bentham typically read them, these passages, portray the saint as insufferably vain, thus blackening his character. For at least a generation, however, several scholars have argued forcefully that some of the boasting herein is meant to parody the boasting of others—more precisely the boasting of rival apostles claiming authority over the Corinthian church.[231] If, by boasting, Paul was parodying the boastfulness of his rivals (especially if according to certain accepted rules of rhetoric), then there is irony in at least some of his boasting. Ironic expressions, of course, can never be taken at face value.

Bentham's distaste for theology and his lack of sensitivity toward mystagogy (i.e., the teaching of mysteries, commonplace in Paul) led him to blame our apostle for an instance of perfidy that may have been the fault of another. His literalistic but superficial reading of Acts led him (as it does every unsuspicious person) to believe from the "we-passages," such as 16:10 and 20:6, that the Λ-h had episodically attached himself to Paul's entourage. Since none of the conversion stories (in Acts 9, 22, and 26) contains a "we-passage," how, Bentham wondered, could the A-h have known what had happened to Paul on the Damascus Road? Bentham concluded that the only possible source of this conversion story was Paul himself, but since he trusted neither Paul's veracity nor the A-h's ability to confirm the truth of what Paul had told him, Bentham held the story suspect, especially the parts of it having to do with an inner change in Paul. Bentham, of course, already knew that the A-h altered the story with every retelling, thus weakening any claim to historicity it may have had. Although Bentham could not have known that scholarly doubt would one day be cast even upon the identification of the A-h with the author of the "we-passages," he could have noticed, even in his day and time, additional reasons for being suspicious of the role played by the A-h relative to Paul's conversion story.

A more penetrating inquiry than any Bentham initiated into the relationship of Acts to Paul's epistles would have revealed some startling facts. Acts shows little, if any, awareness of Paul's distinctive theology, shows no awareness of any of his epistles, and presents a chronology of events between the time of his conversion and his first missionary journey that cannot be reconciled with Paul's own chronology of the same events. Moreover, Edvin Larsson has noted: "The real Paul, the Paul of the letters, claims to be an apostle. In Acts he is depicted as subordinate to the Twelve, for whom the title apostle is reserved. In Galatians and Romans Paul takes up a strongly polemical attitude to the Jewish torah and to circumcision. The Paul of Acts circumcises Timothy (16:3). And he declares his solidarity with the law [a claim that the letters strongly belie], and the people of Israel."[232] To continue in this vein, Donald T. Rowlingson, claiming that the A-h's "omissions amount to inaccuracies." gives the following example: "A case in point is the first Jerusalem visit (Acts 9:26–30 and Gal. 1:18–24), as well as the general circumstances of Paul's career immediately following the conversion. The differences are too great to be reconciled, and everything favors giving the palm to Paul's report. Luke's [i.e., the A-h's] mention of a decree at the Jerusalem Conference is another example. Paul knows nothing about it, and Acts itself is inconsistent; when Paul returns to Jerusalem for the last time he is informed of the decree as though he had not previously heard of it (Acts 21:25).[233]

Other salient differences between the contents of Acts and Paul's epis-tles come readily to mind: (1) Paul's letters never mention a conversion experience as such, whereas Acts makes much of one; (2) Paul mentions Damascus twice (2 Cor. 11:32 and Gal. 1:17) but never associates it, as does the A-h, with a blinding light, a fall to earth, or a voice from heaven; (3) Paul asks rhetorically (but most ambiguously) in 1 Corinthians 9:1, "[H]ave I not seen Jesus Christ our Lord?" but he does not mention, as does Acts in 9:4, 22:7, and 26:14, that he heard his Lord's unseen voice; and (4) Paul's most mystical experience (i.e., his ascent into the third heaven in 2 Cor. 12:1–4, where he hears things that cannot be told) is unlike the rational conversation he presumably had with the unseen voice, taken to be the Lord's, in Acts 9, 22, or 26. In view of all these differences, it is not surprising to read Pervo's conclusion, respecting these matters, in which he says in part, "Historical monographs with convincing likenesses to Acts are difficult to identify. *Novels* that bear likenesses to Acts are, on the other hand, relatively abundant" (emphasis added).[234]

In view of how little Paul's letters tell us, even between the lines, about his cognitive, emotional, and moral states of mind leading up to his aban-donment of Judaism and espousal of Christianity and in view of how little the A-h seems to have known about Paul (judged by the text of Acts), how confident can we be about the experiences Paul is supposed to have had when nearing Damascus on a certain trip?[235] It may, however, have been Bentham who was gullible. The A-h may have *invented the entire episode*, which he embroidered at will, to make vividly pictorial (and even enter-taining) for his readers the way Paul, metaphorically, saw the light![236]

Finally, before turning to the four serious mistakes Bentham made in his treatment of Paul, one further topic needs consideration. When using 'Judaism' and 'Christianity', language may deceive the unwary into thinking that these terms referred (in the first century of our Common Era) to monolithic, unified religions, all and only Jews on one side, so to speak, and all and only Christians on the other. Within both groups, however, there were many shades of opinion, there being as Morton Smith has written, no "one, definitive, Jewish teaching" even on, for example, such an important issue as the Mosaic law.[237] Respecting this law, Hugh Schonfield has shown that the Pharisees, usually typed as highly legalistic, were also often metaphysically speculative and theologically adventuresome, making some of them, at least, resemble Paul, and vice versa.[238] There was also great variety in early Christianity, there being so-called circles of Peter and

John and the schools of Matthew, James, and Paul.[239] Both the Jews and the early Christians had to come to grips with the Hellenism pervasive in Palestine, as well as with the larger Greco-Roman world, both had members more or less welcoming to outsiders, and both had communicants either pro-Roman or anti-Roman, the latter sometimes advocating violence.[240] Such were the Zealots who constituted a party within Judaism. According to Luke 6:15, Jesus included a Zealot among the Twelve. Moreover, the problem of establishing harmonious relations in early Christian congregations between Palestinian-Jewish-Christians, non-Palestinian-Jewish-Christians, and Gentile (i.e., non-Jewish) Christians sorely vexed the church.[241] Even more significant, perhaps, was the first Roman war (67–73) against the Jews (and who knows how many Christians?). Although it is not mentioned in the New Testament, it was nonetheless profoundly significant. It prompted the Christian church to dissociate itself from Judaism, not wanting to suffer Roman reprisals for what the nationalistic, rebellious Jews had done. Paul's letters, all from before the war, show him to have been pro-Roman and politically quiescent (see Rom. 13:1–7).[242] While attributing political quiescence to Paul, Acts, which is universally believed to have been written after the war, makes him pro-Jerusalem and theologically loyal to Jewish traditions.[243] It is not just that the A-h was a poor historian; he was a propagandist. He not only elevated Paul to parity with Peter, as we have seen, he also altered Paul's persona in light of postwar events. Bentham could not have known all the points above, but he could have been more aware than he was of the religious complexity of the times, more perceptive of theological currents, and more penetrating in reading the New Testament texts.

Although the criticisms above detract from *NPBJ*, they do not seriously damage its major contentions about Paul in relation to the Jesus movement. Let us now turn to the criticisms that inflict considerable damage on Bentham's position, criticisms of which Benn and Crimmins might, validly, have made much.

Bentham's biggest blunder was to think that Paul's shift in behavior from persecuting to promoting the church was outer (i.e., self-serving) alone, being accompanied by no inner (i.e., emotional) change. To give Bentham his due, he was not the only one to think Paul duplicitous. On three occasions (Rom. 9:1; 2 Cor. 11:31; Gal. 1:20), our saint felt the need to assure his readers that he was not lying. Moreover, despite his claim to being an apostle, he knew that he was not accepted as such by all Christians (1 Cor. 9:2), these detractors believing him to be perfidious, and, finally, he felt the need to blunt the charge that he was crafty and guileful (2 Cor. 4:2, 12:16; 1 Thess. 2:3). At no point, however, did Paul feel the need to repudiate any criticism to the effect that he remained a Jewish wolf in the sheep's clothing of Christianity. Being denied the rank of apostle to the Gentiles by his detractors is, after all, not the same as being denied the status of a disciple of Christ, and even though Paul was pursued by Judaizing Christians bent on undoing certain aspects, at least, of his teaching, he was not accused of disbelieving in Jesus Christ. Given Paul's intensely polemical nature, we can confidently assert that he would have alluded to such charges while denying them vociferously, had any been lodged.

So much for the negative evidence against Bentham's claim that nothing can be inferred as to any inner change in Paul upon his joining the church. The positive evidence against it, though oblique, is far more impressive. As pointed out earlier (in a slightly different context), this evidence consists of two different vocabularies that Paul used systematically, un-self-consciously, and without fail whenever, on the one hand, he described his life as a Jew and, on the other hand, described his life as a Christian. Respecting Judaism here again is what he said of himself: a Jew by birth (Gal. 2:15); a Hebrew, an Israelite, a descendant of Abraham (2 Cor. 11:22), circumcised on the eighth day; of the people of Israel, of the tribe Benjamin, a Hebrew of Hebrews; a Pharisee, blameless under the law (Phil. 3:4–6); one who was advanced beyond many in Judaism, zealous for the traditions of his fathers (Gal. 1:14); a violent and zealous persecutor of the church (Gal. 1:13, 1 Cor. 15:9, Phil. 3:6); and one who lived constricted by the law that acted as a pedagogue or custodian until Christ came (Gal. 3:24). In the descriptions above, one word of extreme religious significance is missing: 'spirit', whether understood as an outdwelling entity and agent, or as an indwelling presence (possessing the believer), or both is nowhere to be found.

When writing of himself as a Christian, 'spirit' peppers Paul's letters as it did, no doubt his sermons and pious, theological conversations. The reason why his Jewish vocabulary was devoid of 'spirit', whereas his Christian vocabulary was full of it was precisely the inner change that Bentham denied. Put differently, even though Paul was blameless (and thus self-satisfied) in the practice of the law and even though he felt righteous in promoting Judaism by persecuting the church, elements of religious life that he later came to prize above all were absent from his Jewish experience of life. Judaism did not provide him with the experience of sublime contentment that he called justification, nor did it lead to the emotional manifestations that he called receiving the Holy Spirit and bearing its fruits. In Galatians 2:16 he announced that a man is not justified by works of the law but by faith in Jesus Christ, and in 3:2 he asked rhetorically, "Received ye the Spirit by the works of law, or by the hearing of faith?" In 2 Corinthians 3:6b, he announced that the letter (of the law) kills whereas the spirit gives life, and in Romans 7:6 he wrote, "But now we are delivered from the law, that being dead wherein we were held; that we should serve in newness of spirit, and not in the oldness of the letter." The whole point is summarized in Romans 9:4, where Paul says that the glory of Israel lay in being the chosen people, in receiving the covenants or law (of Moses), and in various divine promises, but Israel, whatever her virtues, is never said to have received the Spirit. That was reserved for Christians alone.

If Paul had claimed that he alone had received the "Holy Spirit," then he would have had ample room to lie, to claim to have undergone an inner change from Jew to Christian when in fact he had not. But, this was not the case. The gift of the Holy Spirit was to be shared with and possessed by his converts (Rom. 5:5; 1 Cor. 2:4, 3:16, 19; 2 Cor. 1:22; Gal. 4:6; 1 Thess. 4:8, 5:19) who were, henceforth, to exhibit its fruits (1 Cor. 12). It was even transferable from Paul to others, if Acts 19:2–7 can be believed. Paul made much of not preaching his gospel by words alone but by demonstrations of "spirit" and power, that is, by inducing emotional states in others that he took to resemble his own (1 Cor. 2:4, 4:20; 1 Thess. 1:5). Almost certainly, he took the Pentecostal contagion that others contracted from him to be a certification, perhaps the principal certification, of his apostleship (1 Cor. 9:2, 2 Cor. 3:2–3, 12:12).

Bentham was ill prepared to assess Paul's Pentecostalism accurately, let alone sympathetically. His intellectualism and rationalism, the emotional constraints of his socioeconomic class, and the formalistic creedalism of the Anglican Church, wherein he was raised, all legislated against any understanding on his part of "spirit-filled" religion. To have grasped it at all well, he would have had to immerse himself for a time in the corporate life of a group such as the Shakers, led in Bentham's youth by Mother Ann Lee and her disciples. In their communal worship they routinely became ecstatic, shaking, and quaking, believing themselves to be possessed by a (or the) "divine spirit" and to have power over diseases. Failure to understand the psychological conditions that might, for example, have led an Anglican theologian, previously hostile to Shakerism, to espouse this kind of Pentecostalism prevented Bentham from understanding Paul's conversion and the integrity that most likely, if not almost certainly, accompanied it.

Bentham's second major mistake was to think that Paul's personal characteristics, as revealed in his epistles, were incompatible with an inner, genuine conversion to the religion of Jesus. To Bentham, the self-appointed apostle to the Gentiles was insatiably ambitious, audacious, avaricious, domineering, fractious, perfidious, and splenetic—a man who contrived trances to receive "revelations" whenever and wherever needed and who readily confused nonsense with profound mysteries. To make matters worse, he promulgated these "revelations" and "profound mysteries" with galling dogmatism. Such characteristics of personality and behavior, however, are in no way incompatible with genuine conversion from one religious worldview to another, either in general or in particular in Paul's case.

In short, Paul was as religious after his conversion as he had been before, but obsessed with new and different religious objectives.

At some point he who had not been a disciple of Jesus while Jesus trod the earth became a disciple by joining the infant church. Once a member, he could remain a follower or attempt to become a leader. He chose the latter. Believing himself to be the recipient of divine revelations significantly different from the teachings of the Jerusalem church, always prone to confusing his psychological certainties with truth, and eager to set his leadership abilities against the genuine apostles' abilities, confrontation and conflict were inevitable.[244]

Of course he was insatiably ambitious and audacious. How could a Johnny-come-lately who wanted to be a Christian leader have succeeded otherwise in the time of the original apostles? Even though he may not have been avaricious personally, he became avaricious for his cause. He had to be. It cost money then, as now, to develop and maintain a far-flung religious empire. He had to travel extensively to influence old congregations and to create new ones in his own image. He had to travel repeatedly to put out the fires of false doctrine. He had to travel to recapture straying congregations and to reassert his authority. He had to pay for the travel of his lieutenants whom he sent hither, thither, and yon. He had to spend money on the costs of communication. He learned early, no doubt, that money was an aid, in more ways than one, in promoting his cause and in maintaining personal control. If he had been spending his own money, he would surely have boasted of it. Since he did not, we can be sure that it was money he raised or appropriated in some way or other. Yes, he was domineering: in his letters, he orders people about, extolling this and proscribing that. Yes, he was fractious: his teachings were not the standard fare of the original church. It is not surprising that he was pursued and harassed by various people who were trying to undo the damage they perceived him to have done and trying to wean congregations from him. It must always be remembered that whatever else religion is, it is a species of partisanship. As such, its devotees are always on the brink of self-defense and counterattack. People who are scrupulously honest in personal dealings may lapse into propaganda in defense of their faith, dissembling here and telling outright lies there—all, of course, for the best cause in the world—their own religion. What is a little fib, after all, when eternal life is at stake or where the health of the one true church (always one's own) is at risk? As for being splenetic, one has only to read 2 Corinthians 10–13 to be assured of that.

Although it is logically possible that for reasons of self-aggrandizement alone Paul remained a crypto-Jew and became a pseudo-Christian, there is not only no evidence that requires this conclusion, there is none that makes it even probable. It is always a great threat to a legalistic religion, such as Judaism, that any one of its members might break any one of its strictures and not feel guilty; it is an even greater threat that any one of its members might break any one of its strictures and not only not feel guilty but also feel liberated. This appears to have been the case with St. Paul who compounded his antinomianism (which gave him a sense of freedom) with not one but numerous Pentecostal experiences that gave him a sense of power. That he wished to share his freedom from the law and his Pentecostalism with others is in no way incompatible with the fact that he wanted to be a major, if not the supreme, leader of Christendom.

Third, Bentham went too far when accusing Paul of being the Antichrist, a "spiritual Judas" in relation both to Jesus' teachings and the faith of the Jerusalem church. Bentham was right, of course, in recognizing the vast difference between the cosmic Christ of Paul's contrivance and the more modest Jesus of the synoptic Gospels (but not John's). Moreover, he did not claim that there was no unity at all between Jesus and Paul. He noted approvingly that both were antinomian, trying to wean Jews "from their attachment to the Mosaic laws: for thus he [Paul] copied Jesus: and in copying did not go against, but only beyond, the great original."

The problem is that Bentham did not look as hard for unity between Jesus and Paul as he looked for disunity. Antinomianism is not the only point to notice; the fact that they both neglected the law in varying degrees must also be seen in association with a welcoming attitude toward outsiders. In Jesus' case the outsiders were largely outcasts from proper, law-abiding society such as tax (or toll) collectors and sinners (Matt. 9:10–12; Mark 2:15–17; Luke 15:7), demoniacs and lepers (Matt. 10:8, 11:5; Mark 5:1–3), adulteresses and prostitutes (John 8:3–11, 4:7–30; Luke 7:36–50), and Samaritans (Luke 10:29–37). In Paul's case it was the uncircumcised of the world, unclean persons whose presence made table-fellowship impossible for the Jewish Christians who still adhered zealously to the law.[245]

A doctrinal theme that united Jesus and Paul was the theological conviction that the Bible-god was about to terminate the present, wicked, devil-infested age and inaugurate a new, righteous, messianic era. It is now widely believed by New Testament scholars that the synoptic Gospels were written in a common eschatological framework. Matthew 16:28 and Mark 9:1 agree, almost word for word, that there were some standing in Jesus' presence (or living at his time) who would not die before the Kingdom of God came with power. Other ways of making the same point were to say with Matthew 10:23 that the disciples would not have evangelized throughout the tiny land of Israel before the end came or to say with Mark 13:30 and Luke 21:32, in common phraseology, that the current generation would not pass before the end came. Eschatological themes (or allusions and references thereto) appear in most of Paul's major epistles ranging from those believed to be early (see Gal. 1:4; 1 Thess. 1:10, 2:19, 5:2, 5:23; 2 Thess. 1:7–9, 2:1) to those of his mid-career (see 1 Cor. 1:7–8, 3:13, 4:5,

7:25–31, 10:11, 11:26, 15:24; 2 Cor. 1:14) to those generally believed to be late (see Rom. 8:18–19, 13:11–12, 16:20; Phil. 1:6, 2:16, 3:21, 4:5).

Two rituals of the greatest importance to Christianity linked Paul to Jesus: baptism and the sacred meal known as the Lord's Supper. In all four Gospels, John the Baptist appears (before the commencement of Jesus' ministry), baptizing sinners with water (Matt. 3:11; Mark 1:8; Luke 3:16; John 1:26). Three Gospels say specifically that his was a baptism of repentance (Matt. 3:11; Mark 1:4; Luke 3:3) and, one supposes, cleansing of a moral or religious sort. The same three say that Jesus came to John to be baptized (Matt. 3:13–16; Mark 1:9; Luke 3:2). The Gospel of John refrains from saying that Jesus submitted to John's baptism, but it does put him in John's company (1:19–36) and says twice (3:22, 3:26) that Jesus also baptized, then abruptly denies it (4:2), saying that it was only Jesus' disciples who baptized. A curious partial parallel appears in 1 Corinthians 1:13–17, wherein Paul admits to having baptized a few people, then claims that he was not sent to baptize (but to preach the gospel), and finally expresses gratitude lest in baptizing converts some of his critics might accuse him of baptizing in his own name. Whether Paul baptized or not, he regarded baptism as important and developed a unique theology explaining what happened in this magical ritual. In Romans 6:4–11 we learn, as noted earlier, that those who are baptized into Christ are baptized into his death, that they are buried with Christ in the waters of baptism, and that they who descend into this watery sepulcher will automatically be resurrected into newness of life even as Christ arose triumphant over death from the tomb.

Baptism as just described is very different from John's baptism of repentance and cleansing.[246] At first blush it might seem that here again is an instance of Paul's betrayal of Jesus (insofar as Jesus espoused John's baptism), but Morton Smith has argued that Jesus did not merely espouse John's baptism but created a new baptism, a baptism into "the mystery of the Kingdom of God," a baptism associated with spirit possession, one that led straight to Paul.[247] Bentham could not have known about what Smith presents as Jesus' esoteric teachings and secret baptismal practices, but he could have seen plainly enough that Paul retained baptism and in the practice thereof preserved elements, at least, of a ritual important to Jesus.

The Lord's Supper is the second ritual linking Jesus to Paul. The extent to which (if any) Paul's epistles influenced the Gospel writers is a moot question. Goodspeed denies any such influence.[248] If none, it is all the more striking that both Paul and the synoptic Gospels present similar information on what Jesus did and taught his disciples to do on the occasion of their final meal together.[249] It is doubly striking that Paul claims to have received his information about this meal directly from the Lord and not from any source in the primitive church (1 Cor. 11:23). If Jesus identified some bread with his body (about to be broken), identified a cup of wine with his blood (about to be shed), and commanded his disciples to eat and drink thereof (establishing a new covenant), and if Paul continued the practice with a similar rationale, then another strong link between Jesus and Paul is forged. Morton Smith writes, "But one of the strongest traits of Israelite tradition is the tabu against blood; blood in food was strictly forbidden (Gen. 9:4, and often). That the blood of the sacrifice of the covenant should be drunk (!) is by traditional Jewish standards an atrocity that can have been conceived only by a circle bent on demonstrating its freedom from the Law."[250]

Fourth and finally, Bentham failed to analyze the factors that have made Paul the most influential writer of the first century and quite likely the most influential theologian in history. Bentham's failure is understandable. On the one hand, Paul never came closer to literal truth than when he observed that those who marry will have worldly problems (in 1 Cor. 7:28; divine revelation hardly being necessary for such a banality); on the other hand, no fact (or set of facts) that can be known or shown to be true undergirds Paul's theological imaginings, and no line of sound reasoning necessitates any of it. Divorced from empirical experience and bereft of logic, Paul's theology was, to Bentham, a tangled web of fabulous and fictitious notions—that and nothing more. Accordingly, having brushed Paulinism aside as humbug, Bentham failed to inquire as to how it was that the religion of Jesus, irrevocably altered by Paul, could become the most successful faith of all time—up to now at least. In short, what did Paul do to transform a sect of Judaism into a world religion?

Fortunately, Morton Smith undertakes the analysis that Bentham left undone. One cannot do better than to let Smith speak for himself. He identifies, among others, nine points worthy of our attention: (1) "Prayer and praise are usually directed to one god at a time, and peoples and persons are often represented as, or appear to have been, particularly devoted to a single god."[251] (2) "The god being worshipped is regularly flattered—that is to say, exalted."[252] (3) "He maintains by rewards and punishments the moral order, but he is independent of it and can pardon sin at will."[253] (4) Regularly compared to "the most powerful objects known to a culture," he is "the father and king of his people, his child [or children] whom he especially favors."[254] (5) "[T]he god described by prayer is everywhere the god who will do the things which are most prayed for by the people who have most cause to pray."[255] (6) "[T]he god of worship is just as well as merciful, an object . . . of fear as well as love. His justice has accordingly expressed itself in the law, both . . . of his cult and . . . of the land."[256] (7) Since the gods were conceived as humanoid, "[I]t was expected everywhere that a god would punish men who offended him and would reward those who did what he wanted; this, moreover was what he was for."[257] (8) "Because of their [presumed] contractual relationship with the gods, people gave attention to the prophets who everywhere claimed to know by revelation the country's state of obedience or disobedience and the rewards or punishments soon to be allotted."[258] (9) The "prophets often foretell . . . the coming of a good king who will save his people."[259]

Five of Smith's nine points above call for modification or expansion. First, relative to point 1, Paul was not quite as henotheistic as, for example, Joshua when (in Josh. 24:1–15) the latter acknowledged the existence of other gods but, nevertheless, chose only one saying: "[B]ut as for me and my household, we will serve the Lord." Paul, however, came close when he wrote, "For though there be that are called gods, whether in heaven or in earth (as there be gods many and lords many,) But to us there *is but one* God, the Father" (1 Cor. 8:5–6a). And, of course, he peopled his world with spirits galore.

Second, with reference to points 3 and 6, Smith did not emphasize enough the importance to religion (modern as well as ancient) of divine mercy. An almighty deity who is perfectly just and punishes humans accordingly would be almost as great a horror as the almighty but quixotic deity claimed by Bentham, in the *AINR*, to be the logical result of natural theology. From a religious standpoint the most important assertions made by Paul are soteriological. Take for example Romans 8:38–39:

> For I am persuaded, that neither death, nor life, nor angels, nor principalities, nor powers, nor things present, nor things to come,
> Nor height, nor depth, nor any other creature, shall be able to separate us from the love of God, which is in Christ Jesus our Lord.

Even more telling is Romans 10:9–10:

> [I]f thou shalt confess with thy mouth the Lord Jesus, and shalt believe in thine heart that God hath raised him from the dead, *thou shalt be saved.*
> For with the heart man believeth unto righteousness; and with the mouth confession is made unto salvation. (emphasis added)

These verses provide the loophole through which sinners with their dying breath can still escape the just but negative sanctions deserved by bad behavior. For all its vaunted support of morality, Paulinism, as noted before, offers almost everything (eternal salvation) for next to nothing (confession and belief). It is impossible to overemphasize the magnitude of this appeal and the hope engendered thereby. *Kyrie eleison*—Lord have mercy. And, lo, it is so—in imagination at least!

Third, with reference to point 4, Smith did not emphasize sufficiently the importance to religion, modern as well as ancient, of likening the deity to a sovereign, to a King of kings. This is what I have called elsewhere the monarchical principle. The springboard of Pauline theology is the court and country of the oriental despot and all the relationships personal, emotional, and social existing therein.

Fourth, with respect to point 8, Paul's theology transcended such constrictions on religious expansion as the nation, the state, or the country, and, above all, the ethnicity of potential believers. Paul, in effect, threw open the whole world, as he knew it, to Christian penetration. If he had not done this or if it had not been done effectively by any other like-minded missionaries, Christianity would have remained a sect of messianic Jews, with a long life perhaps but with a very narrow appeal. The importance of Paul's universalism cannot be overestimated.

Fifth, with respect to point 9, Smith did not make enough of the importance to religion of eschatology, of the yearning for the coming of the Messiah in whose kingdom the crooked will be made straight, all will be well, and the saved of the earth will live happily ever after. In one way or another, Paulinism gives us all of this and more, including mind-body dualism and spirits set free from matter. Little wonder then that the Juggernaut (as Bentham called it) of Christianity plows on unimpeded by modern knowledge, crushing all secular opposition to it.[260] Bentham knew its power but did not bestir himself sufficiently to understand it.

Since Bentham wrote many pages critical of Paul that were not included in NPBJ and since the Bentham Project (mentioned in the Prologue) is attempting to bring all or nearly all of Bentham's writings to light, it is, as one might say, a waiting game until his entire treatment of Paul is made known.[261]

NOTES

226. See Christopher Forbes, "Comparison, Self-Praise, and Irony: Paul's Boasting and the Conventions of Hellenistic Rhetoric," NTS 32 (1986): esp. 1–2.

227. Traditionally, the mysterious "restraining force" was thought to have been the Roman government, or perhaps, more particularly, the Emperor Claudius (see Ernest Best, A Commentary on the First and Second Thessalonians [New York: Harper and Row, 1972], p. 296). However, William Neil, The Epistle of Paul to the Thessalonians (New York: Harper and Brothers, 1950), writes, "[T]here is much to be said in favour of looking for the clue to the restraining force, not in history, but in some kind of theological or even mythological speculation" (p. 169). Why does this not surprise us? See also James M. Reese, 1 and 2 Thessalonians (Dublin: Veritas, 1979), p. 95, for another interpretation.

228. The importance of word study can be illustrated by Paul L. Hammer, "A Comparison of Kleronomia in Paul and Ephesians," part 3, JBL 79 (September 1960): 267–72, in which he shows that Paul consistently used this word (meaning inheritance) in a way different from its use in Ephesians, indicating that the latter is not directly Paul's. A similar point could be made of 2 Thessalonians, in which the text

refers to "the man of perdition" and to the "restraining force," terms that Paul did not use elsewhere, thus casting some doubt on the authenticity of 2 Thessalonians.

David Mealand, "Positional Stylometry Reassessed: Testing a Seven-Epistle Theory of Pauline Authorship," *NTS* 35 (1989), tests the various theories as to how many authentic epistles of Paul we have by looking at "the relative frequency of particular words in the sentence." He writes, "In this paper I am considering only the use of four words in the first or second position in the [Greek] 'sentence.' The four words are καί, δέ, γάρ, and εἰ and the positions are first, second, second, and first respectively" (p. 268). Bentham's treatment of Paul's epistles was light-years away from the attention to detail and the subtlety revealed in Mealand's paper.

229. Edgar J. Goodspeed, "Ephesians and the First Edition of Paul," *JBL* 70 (1951), writes, "A minute comparison of Ephesians, line by line and phrase by phrase, with the other nine letters shows unmistakably that it has made use of every one of them, a most important finding as to its own evidence to its origin. But more remarkable still,—the nine letters supply virtually all that it contains except for a line or two here and there from the Septuagint or the Acts of the Apostles. This shows unmistakably that it is not the work of Paul" (p. 285). A similar point could be made about attempts at dating the so-called Pastoral Epistles. Howard C. Kee and Franklin W. Young, *Understanding the New Testament* (Englewood Cliffs, NJ: Prentice-Hall, 1957) write, "A number of later New Testament writings show marked evidence of this struggle with false teaching—I and II Timothy and Titus, for example. These writings, which are commonly called the Pastoral Epistles, were traditionally attributed to Paul. . . . It is generally acknowledged today, however, that they were written later than the time of Paul, although they may contain fragmentary phrases from lost Pauline writings. The language and theology of these epistles show some similarity to Paul, but the differences are far more striking" (pp. 341–42).

230. As noted earlier, the Christology of Col. 1:15–20 is taken by some scholars to be more advanced than Paul's Christology and, hence, most likely, a later articulation. The same point is made by James L. Price, *Interpreting the New Testament* (New York: Holt, Rinehart, and Winston, 1961): "[Certain scholars] consider that the type of [theological] error at Colossae hardly existed in Paul's lifetime; that the letter presents—in a distinctive style and manner—a view of Christ and the Church not developed in other letters of the Pauline collection" (p. 431).

231. See E. A. Judge, "Paul's Boasting in Relation to Contemporary Professional Practice," *ABR* (October 1968): 37–50, and Forbes, "Comparison, Self-Praise, and Irony," pp. 1–30. Also see Jerry W. McCant, "Paul's Thorn of Rejected Apostleship," *NTS* 34 (1988): esp. 556–60.

232. Edvin Larssen, "Paul: Law and Salvation," *NTS* 31 (1985): 425.

233. Donald T. Rowlingson, "The Jerusalem Conference and Jesus' Nazareth Visit," part 2, *JBL* 71 (1952): 72.

234. Richard I. Pervo, *Profit with Delight: The Literary Genre of the Acts of the Apostles* (Philadelphia: Fortress Press, 1987), p. 137.

235. J. E. Frame, "Paul's Idea of Deliverance," *JBS* 49 (1930), writes, "Unfortunately, there are no letters of Paul from the earlier and major part of his Christian life. And again unfortunately, the extant letters do not disclose unambiguously his pre-Christian attitude; they do not explain that revelation or vision which con-

vinced him that Jesus lives; nor do they permit us to trace the steps taken after the revelation by which he arrived at the mature outlook that the surviving letters substantially presuppose" (p. 2).

236. Pervo, *Profit with Delight*, p. 11. Also see Alan F. Segal, "Paul's Thinking about Resurrection in Its Jewish Context," *NTS* 44, no. 3 (1998): "Paul's ecstatic conversion [account] in Acts is a product of Luke's literary genius" (p. 404). In the same issue of *NTS*, Alexander Loveday, "Fact, Fiction, and the Genre of Acts," pp. 380–99, says that in respect to fact and fiction, Acts falls "uncomfortably" on the boundary. Dennis R. MacDonald continues the indictment of Acts as history in "The Shipwrecks of Odysseus and Paul," *NTS* 45, no. 1 (1999): 88–107.

237. Morton Smith, "Pauline Problems: Apropos of J. Munck, *Paulus und die Heilsgeschichte*," *HTR* 50 (1957): 125.

238. Hugh Schonfield, *Those Incredible Christians* (New York: Bantam Books, 1967), pp. 242–58.

239. E. Earle Ellis, "Dating the New Testament," *NTS* 26, no. 4 (1980): 501.

240. For Hellenism in Palestine, see ibid., p. 497; for Jews and Christians welcoming to outsiders, see A. J. M. Wedderburn, "Paul and Jesus: Similarities and Continuity," *NTS* 34, no. 2 (1988): 164, 167.

241. Jack T. Sanders, "Who Is a Jew and Who Is a Gentile in the Book of Acts?" *NTS* 37, no. 3 (1991): 441–42. Also see J. Brunt, "Rejected, Ignored, or Misunderstood? The Fate of Paul's Approach to the Problem of Food Offered to Idols in Early Christianity," *NTS* 31 (1985): 113–24.

242. David B. Bronson, "Paul and Apocalyptic Judaism," *JBL* 83 (1964): 288.

243. Ibid., p. 291.

244. In "Paul's Indifference to Authority," *JBL* 88 (1969), David M. Hay writes, "We may ask, however, what response he would have made if the 'men of repute' [i.e., the Jerusalem authorities] had condemned his gospel or called it inadequate. Surely the whole tone of Gal. 1–2 implies that he would have gone on preaching it despite their opposition (Peter's stand at Antioch did not move him!)" (p. 12). In short, Paul was not about to be dissuaded from doing what he was doing as a Christian evangelist, whether the Jerusalem church viewed him as a legitimate apostle or not.

245. See A. J. M. Wedderburn, "Paul and Jesus: Similarities and Continuity," *NTS* 34 (1988): esp. pp. 164–67. Also see J. D. G. Dunn, "Mark 2:1–3:6: A Bridge between Jesus and Paul on the Question of the Law," *NTS* 30, no. 3 (1984): 412–13.

246. All four Gospels contrast John's baptism with Jesus' baptism, saying that the latter baptized (or would baptize) with the Holy Spirit (see Matt. 3:11; Mark 1:8; Luke 3:16; John 1:33). The reader should hardly need much reminding of the importance to Paul of the Holy Spirit and possession thereby. Smith's short but erudite book, *The Secret Gospel* (New York: Harper and Row, 1973), introduces the reader to the world of first-century religion as practiced in the general area of the eastern Mediterranean. This world is bizarre beyond anything that a rationalistic, prima facie reading of the New Testament indicates and equally beyond what is usually presented in most treatises of New Testament scholarship written, as they are, by people in, or close to, the Christian faith. Smith was not burdened in this way. His book needs to be savored to the fullest and not subjected to summarizing by anyone else. In a chapter called "The Secret Baptism," pp. 97–114, he makes the following points:

"1. Paul's baptism was . . . a ritual for [mysterious, metaphysical] union with Jesus. . . . 2. The union in Paul's baptism was affected by the Spirit [of Jesus], and the spirit was the cause and characteristic of Jesus' ministry. 3. The closest parallels to Paul's baptism are found in magical material, and there is considerable evidence that Jesus practiced magic. 4. Paul's baptism was connected with ascent into the heavens: Jesus was believed to have ascended, perhaps already in his lifetime. 5. Finally, Paul's baptism freed the recipient from the law, from which Jesus' disciples had been freed."

247. Ibid., pp. 97–99. Concomitant with receiving the Holy Spirit is freedom from the law. Smith, "The Reason for the Persecution of Paul and the Obscurity of Acts," in *Studies in Mysticism and Religion* (Jerusalem: Magnes Press, 1967), writes "Liberation from the Law is effected by a magical ceremony, baptism, in which the recipient is identified with Jesus (Rom. 6:1–11; Gal. 2:19f., 3:27)" (p. 262).

248. Edgar J. Goodspeed, "The Editio Princeps of Paul," *JBL* 64 (1945): 193.

249. Information about the Last Supper can be found in 1 Cor. 10:16–17, 11:23–31; Matt. 26:26–28; Mark 14:22–24; Luke 22:17–19. John mentions a meal associated with Passover and links it to Judas's betrayal but does not mention the establishment of a new covenant in the body and blood of Jesus whose tokens are bread and wine.

250. Smith, *Jesus the Magician* (New York: Harper and Row, 1978), p. 123.

251. Morton Smith, "The Common Theology of the New East," part 3, *JBL* 71 (September 1953): 137–38.

252. Ibid., p. 138.

253. Ibid., p. 141.

254. Ibid.

255. Ibid., p. 142.

256. Ibid.

257. Ibid., p. 144.

258. Ibid., p. 145.

259. Ibid.

260. It continues to do this even among those who should be epistemologically sophisticated and should understand scientific methods for acquiring and validating knowledge. On April 3, 1997, there appeared in the *NYT* an article by Natalie Angier titled "Survey of Scientists Finds a Stability of Faith in God." This article reported on information taken from a commentary in the journal *Nature* of the same date. A survey of scientists undertaken in 1916 by distinguished psychologist James Leuba found that 41.8 percent of those responding believed in a personal deity to whom one might pray in "expectation of receiving an answer." This survey was recently repeated with the result that 39.3 percent of the scientists responding believe similarly. In 1916, 50.6 percent of the scientists polled believed in immortality; now only 38.0 percent. If scientists can discard their methods so easily, thus compartmentalizing their minds, what hope is there that the general population can or will do better? Leuba, called a "devout atheist" by the *NYT*, entertained the naive belief that as progress in science and in science education occurred, one ought to expect diminished religious faith on the part of the educated classes at least. Verily, verily, the fields are still white for the harvest, and the pale Galilean continues to triumph—with singular assistance from St. Paul.

261. See the Internet address given in the preface to this book on how to keep abreast of the work being done by the Project.

Part 3

Church-of-England Catechism Examined:
How Bentham's Philosophy of Language
Undercuts Theology

Chapter 7

Introduction and Distillation with Commentary

In 1818 there appeared in England an eight-hundred-page book whose full title was *Church-of-Englandism and Its Catechism Examined preceded by Strictures on the Exclusionary System as pursued in the National Society's Schools: interspersed with Parallel Views of the English and Scottish Established and Non-Established Churches: and concluding with Remedies Proposed for Abuses Indicated: and an Examination of the Parliamentary System of Church Reform lately pursued and still pursuing: Including the Proposed New Churches.* To this massive, rambling, turgid, but incendiary work, Bentham boldly affixed his name, even though he had been advised not to publish it, and even though he knew that its appearance could jeopardize him legally.[1] Some protection from prosecution was gained, perhaps, by the fact that he never criticized Jesus therein or the "religion of Jesus." Moreover, he identified himself neither as an agnostic (a name not yet invented) nor as an atheist. An outraged theist could have written this book, though not an orthodox Christian theist. *Church-of-Englandism* as a whole will not concern us in part 3 but, rather, an eighty-page segment of it. This segment, in addition to its original appearance in 1818, was published independently of the rest in 1824 and again in 1868, bearing the title *The Church-of-England Catechism Examined* (hereafter referred to as *CECE*). Seldom if ever has the catechism of an Established Church been examined more logically and found more wanting. However, given the work's stilted, forbidding language, its small circulation, and the distaste of the average Anglican for applying logic to his religious beliefs, it achieved no more, in practical terms, than a popgun's volley against one of His Majesty's gunboats.

Before examining Bentham's attack in *CECE* in detail, two introductory topics need to be addressed: The first has to do with the Thirty-nine Articles of Religion of the Church of England and with the Catechism (or instruction) for would-be communicants based thereupon; the second relates to Bentham's unhappy encounters with the Thirty-nine Articles while yet a mere boy (even though he was already an Oxford undergraduate) and his subsequent hatred of anybody's having to swear oaths binding on the presumed "Maker of Heaven and Earth."

The Catechism consists of twenty-three questions the catechumen is to answer correctly and two commands to carry out successfully, namely, to state the Ten Commandments and to recite the Lord's Prayer. The famous Thirty-nine Articles of Religion are curious in that they constitute neither a creed to be professed (such as the Apostles' or the Nicene Creed) nor a catechism to be learned and accepted prior to confirmation. Issued by a Church Convocation in 1563, and showing the results of compromise, they are "short summaries of dogmatic tenets, each article dealing with some point raised in current controversies and promulgating the Anglican view."[2]

The Anglican Catechism is a type of instruction in the form of questions crucial to the faith and their approved answers. Presumably consistent with the Thirty-nine Articles, the Catechism is primarily intended for young catechumens, baptized as infants, but not to the exclusion of those of "riper years" converted to the Church of England. Bentham had no objection to the voluntary catechizing of adults who thought they understood what they were being asked and had some theological inkling of what they were supposed to say in response. It was on the catechizing of children who had not the vaguest notion of religious metaphysics that he vented his spleen.

However thoroughly or haphazardly the young Bentham might have been catechized, ecclesiastical requirements would not have forced him, as a private citizen, to subscribe to the Thirty-nine Articles. In his day, only members of the Anglican clergy plus students at Oxford and Cambridge had to subscribe thereto.[3] But, alas, it was to Oxford that Jeremiah Bentham sent his little philosopher.[4] So, it was all but inevitable that Bentham, the undergraduate, and the Thirty-nine Articles would collide. Even if he had not been in full cry against the Established Church before matriculation at Queen's College, Oxford, he certainly became so while there, for to remain a student and be graduated, he had to subscribe to religious doctrines in which he did not believe.[5] This brings us to the second point of introduction that should be considered before proceeding to his meticulous and unsparing dissection of the Catechism.

Upon being required to subscribe to the Thirty-nine Articles, young Bentham, perforce, swore that he believed the Thirty-ninth Article, a clear and comprehensible article whose latter part ends with, "[S]o we judge that

Christian religion doth not prohibit, but that a man may swear when the magistrate requireth, in a cause of faith and charity, so it be done according to the prophet's [which prophet's?] teaching, in justice, judgment, and truth." In so swearing, Bentham, who knew the scriptures disconcertingly well, realized that he (and others in his situation, including clergymen) were rendering null and void Jesus' teaching in Matthew 5:34–37:

> But I say unto you, Swear not at all; neither by heaven; for it is God's throne:
>> Nor by the earth; for it is his footstool: neither by Jerusalem; for it is the city of the great King.
>> Neither shalt thou swear by thy head, because thou canst not make one hair white or black.
>> But let your communication be, Yea, yea; Nay, nay: for whatsoever is more than these cometh of evil.

When Bentham, together with his fellow university students and all Anglican clergymen, subscribed to the Sixth Article, they affirmed the canonicity of the Gospel of Matthew, that is, affirmed its authenticity and authority over Christian faith and life. However, for hundreds of years, citizens hailed before the bar of English justice had been (and still were) required, for a variety of reasons, to swear oaths to tell the truth. In so doing, they presumably activated a (or the) divine sanction—potentially against themselves. It appears that it was not enough for English courts to threaten witnesses with prescribed penalties of perjury and public shame; they also had to be filled with "the fear of God." But what was the ingenious theologian to do when a forceful admonition of Scripture conflicted directly with a time-honored practice?[6] In this case, it was simply a matter of tinkering with Scripture.[7] The opening sentence of the Thirty-ninth Article, contains the words, "[W]e confess that *vain and rash* swearing is forbidden Christian men by our Lord Jesus Christ" (emphasis added). A glance at Matthew 5:34–37, however, reveals that Jesus' admonition is sweeping in scope and absolute in prohibition. Moreover, Matthew 23:16–22 reports that Jesus said, "Woe to you, to those, that is, who made such nice distinctions, calling them blind guides and fools."[8] As though to clinch the point, the Epistle of James (5:12) says, "But above all things, my brethren, swear not, neither by heaven, neither by earth, neither by any other oath: but let your yea be yea; and *your* nay be nay; lest ye fall into condemnation."[9] Linking Matthew 5:34–37 and James 5:12 to the Commandment not to take the Lord's name in vain (Exod. 20:7), Bentham wrote, "Says God to man,—thou shalt not perform any such ceremony. Says man to God,—I do perform this ceremony, and thou shalt punish every instance of disregard to it. Suppose the Almighty prepared to punish every or any

instance of disregard to this ceremony, you suppose him employed in sanctioning disobedience to his own express commandments."[10]

In addition to swearing an oath to swear oaths when good Anglicans
were legally required to swear oaths and as a good Christian never to swear
any oaths, Bentham also swore that he believed in articles of faith in which
he disbelieved, thinking them false. Moreover, he had to swear that he
believed in articles that were incomprehensible, being allegedly divine mysteries. Among the Thirty-nine Articles in which Bentham disbelieved were
three that bear special scrutiny. First, the Second Article asserts that the
eternal God took man's nature in the womb of the blessed Virgin such that
two whole and perfect natures, the Godhood and Manhood, were joined
together in one person. The Third Article claims that after his death and
burial, but before his Resurrection, Christ went down into hell, paying a visit
to the infernal regions.[11] Finally, the Fourth Article (contradicting St. Paul in
1 Cor. 15:37–38, 50) asserts that Christ in emerging alive from the tomb
took again his body, with flesh, bones, and all things appertaining to the
perfection of man's nature, wherewith he ascended into heaven." Prime
among the Articles Bentham thought to be incomprehensible were the First
and Third, which in tandem assert the unity of the Godhead in which there
be Three Persons of one substance, power, and eternity and yet such that one
of these Persons, the Holy Ghost, is found always to be proceeding from the
other two, the Father and the Son, while these two never proceed singly or
together from the Holy Ghost or from each other. This hints at something
less than perfect unity. That nobody knows what this blessed mystery means
did not prevent young Jeremy from having to swear an oath that he believed
it.[12] Thus, to him, did mendacity triumph and perjury prevail![13]

The swearing of oaths to do this or not to do that is so deeply rooted
in the West and so grave an undertaking that people seldom perceive, as
Bentham did, that the ceremony of swearing oaths is but a "magical incan-
tation."[14] By virtue of mere words intoned and gestures made (such as an
uplifted arm or a hand placed on a holy book) the oath-taker not only
enters a new relationship (it is presumed) with those who impose the ceremony but also with the "Maker of Heaven and Earth," who, without con-
sultation, is dragged in as a third party and is thereafter bound to punish
any infraction on the part of the swearer. Bentham wrote, "On the suppo-
sition that, by man, over the Almighty, *power* should, to this or any other
purpose, be exercised or exercisable, an absurdity, than which nothing can
be greater, cannot be denied to be involved:—man the legislator and judge,
God the sheriff and executioner;—man the despot, God his slave."[15]

It should be obvious that promissory oaths (or vows) to do this or that
need not always be administered by an agent of some court or other. An
individual who believes in the efficacy of "magical incantations" can also
initiate a promissory oath to her deity, making the latter a private "sheriff

and executioner." A notorious example is Jephthah's vow in Judges 11:30–31. Said he to the Bible-god, "[I]f thou shalt without fail deliver the children of Ammon into mine hands, Then it shall be that whatsoever cometh forth of the door of my house to meet me, when I return . . . shall surely be the Lord's, and I will offer it up for a burnt offering." Upon returning home victoriously, the first creature Jephthah saw was his only child, a daughter, come with timbrels and dances to welcome him home. After two months, says verse 39b, he did with her *according* to his vow. Well, a vow *is* a vow, binding on both the swearer and his deity. Was the Bible-god pleased to be a party to Jephthah's vow? Was he happy with the burnt offering that resulted? We do not know, because gods bound by oaths are not asked in advance to evaluate the morality (or lack thereof) of the object(s) in view. They are merely to look favorably on the swearer of the oath, if kept, and to punish him, if not kept, though greater good might have come from a broken vow(s).

In addition to the evil with which a vow like Jephthah's ensnares the Almighty, consider the "divine" dilemma experienced when two people swear oaths calling upon the Almighty to uphold the sanctity of contradictory vows. Bentham provided the following illustration: Let England be the geographical place and let religion be the political field. Then introduce two claimants to the throne, a certain James who has sworn, when crowned, to exalt and magnify the old religion (i.e., Roman Catholicism) and a certain George who has sworn, when crowned, to exalt and magnify the new religion (i.e., Church-of-Englandism). Bentham wrote, "[T]wo swearers, swearing, and thus respectively engaging themselves, to direct their utmost endeavours to the production of two opposite and altogether incompatible effects. By the draughts thus drawn for eventual punishment, what, according to the current theory, is the effect produced upon the Almighty? What but that he is *compelled*, or, if that word be too plain and clear, *engaged*, to lend his power, at the same place and time, to the productions of these same opposite and incompatible effects?"[16]

Bentham was, of course, much less concerned about how any "Almighty" being might cope with the problems above than with the mischiefs done to citizens not only by requirements to swear oaths invoking the Almighty but also by kindred legal disabilities placed on the members of religious minorities and by the more or less continuous pressure on all dissenters to the Established Church to conform to its dogmatic standards. Focusing broadly on these topics, he wrote, "Under English law, there are various instances in which, though not under the name of punishment, restrictions are imposed on certain classes of persons. Catholics were formerly not allowed to exercise either the profession of the law or that of medicine. Persons refusing to take the sacrament according to the rites of the Church of England, were excluded from all public offices."[17] Unitarians, who would not subscribe to the doctrine of the Trinity, could not attend Oxford or Cambridge; Quakers, who would not swear any oaths, suffered legal disadvantages at times in English history; and atheists could not serve as witnesses to crimes nor give testimony in English courts.[18]

Bentham was particularly galled by the courts' treatment of atheism and the evils resulting therefrom. Although it would be easy to summarize the essence of his rancor, he might better be allowed to speak for himself:

> Answering to his call, this man places himself in the witness's box. The learned counsel has his instructions. "Sir," says he, "do you believe in God?" What follows: Answering falsely, the proposed witness is admitted; he cannot be rejected: answering truly, he is silenced, and turned out with ignominy. The martyr to virtue, the martyr to veracity, receives the treatment given to a convicted felon. . . .
>
> A murderer (suppose) is on his trial: necessary to conviction is the testimony of an individual, who has just mounted the box. Before the oath is tendered,—"First, (may it please your Lordship,) let me ask this man a question," says the counsel for the murderer. Thereupon comes the dialogue. Counsel—"Sir, do you believe in a God?" Proposed witness— "No, sir." Judge—"Away with him; his evidence is inadmissible." Out walk they, arm-in-arm, murderer and atheist together, laughing: murderer, to commit other murders, pregnant with other fees [for attorneys and court costs].[19]

Finally, as to the enormity of this *"mischievousness"*:

> Of the immense mass of evil constantly flowing from this source, a part, and but a part—has as yet been presented to the view of the Honourable House:—namely, under the last head, the head of *mendacity:*
>
> 1. By so simple a process as the declining to act a part in this ceremony [of swearing oaths in court to tell the truth], any man, who has been the sole percipient witness to a crime may, whatever be that crime— murder, or still worse—after appearing as summoned, give impunity to it: without the trouble or formality, producing thus the effect of pardon: sharing thus with his majesty this branch of the prerogative, and even in cases, in which his said majesty stands debarred from exercising it.
>
> 2. By the same easy process, in a case called *civil*, may any man give to any man any estate of any other man.
>
> Not quite so easy (says somebody.) For would not this be a contempt? and would he not of course be committed?
>
> May be so: but when the murderer has been let off, or the man in the right has lost his cause, would the commitment last for life?—in a word, what would become of it?
>
> But to no such peril need he expose himself. A process there is in which is still easier: *"I am an atheist."* He need but pronounce these four words. The pardon is sealed; or Doe's estate is given to Roe.[20]

Although more could be written about Bentham's attacks on the evils of coerced oaths, especially when these reinforce the status quo, preventing innovation and reform, enough has been offered to introduce the main subject of part 3 of this book—the logical demolition of the Anglican Catechism. Nothing disgusted Bentham more than the pious practice of adults who, in the role of godparents (or sponsors), make vows (i.e., utter promissory oaths) on behalf of infants and who then turn them over in due time to catechists to finish the odious work.

Question 1 of the Catechism asks the catechumen for his name; question 2 for the source of the name. The authorized answer is, "My godparents in baptism: wherein I was made a member of Christ, the child of God, and an inheritor of the kingdom of heaven." Not being able to resist or refuse baptism as an infant, the Anglican catechumen (as young as seven years old in some cases) is surely correct in alluding to his baptism but then is induced by the catechist to assert as true the (alleged) effects of that baptism, to wit, becoming a member of Christ, a child of God, and an inheritor of the kingdom of heaven. These assertions are clearly incomprehensible to the child and dubious of truth, to say the least. Thus begins the lesson in insincerity.

Question 3 asks what the godparents did for the catechumen.[21] Instead of doing something they could have done, namely, vow to help the child live the desired kind of life, they vow something that cannot be done. Here is what the hapless catechumen says *falsely* that they did: "They did promise and vow three things in my name: first, that I should renounce the devil and all his works, the pomps and vanities of this wicked world, and all the sinful lusts of the flesh; secondly, that I should believe all the Articles of the Christian faith [i.e., the Thirty-Nine Articles of Religion of Anglicanism]; and thirdly, that I should keep God's holy will and commandments, and walk in the same all the days of my life."

It is an unwarranted assumption that godparents can in this way fasten upon infants, with no regard to their consent, a set of obligations the breaking of which would lead presumably to the most horrific consequences—the everlasting flames of hell. "The notion of a power derived from the Almighty to cast infants into such bondage" merely by a formulary uttered by third parties is "absurd and indefensible" (*CECE*, p. 4). When and on what occasion was such power ever given? Where is the slightest evidence of it?

Even assuming that godparents can swear promissory oaths in general in the names of infants, how can they swear in particular that the infants in question will renounce the Devil? At the outset, it would have to be shown that 'Devil' and 'Satan' are not like 'Jupiter' and 'Juno', names now recognized never to have named beings. To whom does 'Devil' refer? What precisely is he? Where does he reside? Will the child, in whose name so much is promised, ever see the Devil? Furthermore, what are his works more than the works of Jupiter and Juno? How can infants and children renounce all the Devil's works any more than they can renounce all the works of Jupiter and Juno? Let the "Archbishop of Canterbury tell us precisely and in detail what the Devil is, what are his works, and how they are renounced!" (p. 7).

While he is about it, this very reverend personage might recount in detail what, precisely, the vanity of this wicked world is, vanity being the vainest of all vain words, so vacuous is it. As for pomps, he and his fellows among the Lords Spiritual know exactly what is at issue, for in their "theatrical piety" they revel in pomps repeatedly, as do the Lords Temporal. "Under the word *pomp* are comprised all those factitious appendages by which factitious dignity,—when combined with the visible and tangible fruits and marks of opulence,—is, in the hands of the ruling few, employed to distinguish them from the *subject many*" (p. 11). Behold the Lords Temporal with their *titles*, their *coronets*, and their *armorial ensigns*. Behold the Lords Spiritual, those living pageants, with the *fine linen* on their shoulders, the *purple* on their *liveries*, the *purple* and the *mitre* on their *equipages*. If these are not pomps, in what do pomps consist? Thus is hypocrisy added to mendacity in the Catechism.

Hard upon the heels of the renunciation of *the Devil and all his works* and the renunciation of *the pomps and vanity of this wicked world* comes the renunciation of *all the sinful lusts of the flesh*. What sense are children (lately in their cradles) to make of this renunciation taken on their behalf? What, exactly, are these lusts of the flesh they have, perforce, vowed through others to eschew? Are all lusts of the flesh sinful or only some? These are among the secrets in the Catechism made known to none. Thus catechumens find themselves having renounced they know not what.

Question 4 asks, "Dost thou not think that thou are bound to believe and to do as they have promised for thee?" The authorized answer for catechumens to parrot is, "Yes, verily: and, by God's help, so will I. And I heartily thank our heavenly Father that he hath called me to this state of salvation, through Jesus Christ our Saviour. And I pray unto God to give me his grace, that I may continue in the same to my life's end." The catechist then bids the catechumens to rehearse the articles of their belief, and they do so under command, regurgitating the so-called Apostles' Creed. With or without a glimmer of comprehension, each catechumen says, "I believe in God the Father Almighty, Maker of heaven and earth; and in Jesus Christ his only Son our Lord, who was conceived by the Holy Ghost, born of the Virgin Mary, suffered under Pontius Pilate, was crucified, dead, and buried; he descended into hell; the third day he rose again from the dead. He ascended into heaven, and sitteth at the right hand of God the Father Almighty; from thence he shall come to judge the quick and the dead. I believe in the Holy Ghost; the Holy Catholic Church; the communion of the Saints; the forgiveness of sins; the resurrection of the body, and the life everlasting. Amen." The Eighth Article says that the Nicene Creed ought also to be believed.[22] The first five Articles blend elements of the two creeds, though the Catechism leaves out some of the Nicene Creed.

The first thing to notice about the Apostles' Creed is that it is "a forgery" and, as presented, a fraud (p. 15). No emissary (i.e., apostle) of Jesus ever recited, wrote down, or taught this creed. Its content does not appear as material unifying the four Gospels. Moreover, at least since the time of Bishop John Pearson (1613–1686), the Anglican Church has known this, but has promulgated the creed, nevertheless, as apostolic.[23]

Respecting the so-called Apostles' Creed, what are very young catechumens, only recently conversant with English, to understand by the assertion that Jesus Christ *was conceived by the Holy Ghost*? What conception of conception are young children expected to have? And what of the idea that Jesus was born of the *Virgin Mary*?[24] Mary, of course, began life as a virgin, but could hardly have been so at the point of Jesus' conception. *Suffered under Pontius Pilate* would, of course, cause no particular problem, neither would *crucified, dead, and buried*, until the question arises as to who or what it was that died. Since question 5 of the Catechism (asked in full below) requires catechumens to assert that they believe in God the Father, God the Son, and God the Holy Ghost, what precisely happened to God when Jesus Christ died? Did the God of the Christians die? If, perchance, catechumens were to hear of heathen gods, immortal and not subject to death, would the God of the Christians not seem inferior among deities? If God the Son were mortal, what should preserve his Father from being mortal too? If the Father were to die, perhaps taking turns with the Son, what would become of the world and all that live therein?

The solution to the problem, if solution it be, lies in the doctrine of the two natures.[25] The catechumen must be told (and of course must believe) that Jesus had two natures. "He was a man and he was a god," or better yet, "the one true God" (p. 19). It was the man only that was crucified, dead, and buried. The God did not die, death not being possible for him. Was Jesus, then, two persons, one mortal and one immortal? No such thing. One human person plus one divine person (in this unique case) do not make a being of two persons but rather of two natures in one person. The catechumen, to be confirmed as a Christian, must assert that God and man together were one and the same.[26]

To force a child to declare most solemnly and seriously that she believes in the existence of a being having two natures in one person just as surely as she believes in the (one) person of the catechist who forces these words to be swallowed and then regurgitated is a mischief as real as "the pretended belief is false" (p. 20).

The child is next required to say of Jesus that after his death he *descended into hell*. Even admitting the truth of this assertion, no part of the

New Testament directly relevant to the life and death of Jesus ever makes this claim. One might as well say that the Devil ascended into heaven. The Gospels know nothing of any such divine descent, nor does Paul. The feeble foundation on which this absurd claim is based is to be found in 1 Peter 3:18–20, in which it is announced that Jesus, after dying, went in the Spirit to certain spirits in prison to announce good tidings.[27] The Greek *phulake* means a place of guarding and is described in Revelation 20:7 as a haunt for all kinds of unclean spirits and birds—yes, *birds*.[28] It is not to be translated into English by 'hell', because the place of guarding is never understood as a place (or condition) wherein the damned are tormented.[29] To claim that God the Son visited the place of fiery torment appointed for the Devil and his angels is to babble, to mouth inarticulate sounds.

The charade continues when catechumens are required to say that they believe in the *Holy Ghost*. Granting that 'Holy Ghost', 'Holy Spirit', and 'Spirit of God' mean the same, what then is this Spirit of God in which one must believe in addition to believing in God? What sort of reagent is it that has the effect of decomposing a human person, for example, into two persons, one of which is himself, the other his spirit? If believing in God is not enough without also believing in his Spirit, what is to be done with the biblical terms 'hand of God', 'arm of God', and 'finger of God'? (p. 23). The writers of the Catechism have strung words upon words upon words and then believed, or pretended to believe, that a real, existent object is named by each of the noun-substantives they have fancifully contrived. The result is that the Holy Ghost is the same as God yet distinct from God, and when pictured in didactic art is portrayed as a pigeon hovering in the air in a spot of light.[30] Pictures of God the Father, looking like an old man, and God the Son, looking like a young man, and God the Holy Ghost, looking like a pigeon, are not less bizarre, pictorially, than is the creedal assertion, intellectually, that these images are meant to illustrate. It is flagitious to force children to utter a senseless vow.

When catechumens are called upon to declare, "I believe in the Holy Catholic Church," no guidance is given as to where they should look to find this Church in which their belief is lodged. Although the Church of England might have been omnipresent in England, it was hardly catholic (i.e., universal). Moreover, young catechumens could easily confuse this "Universal Church" with the Roman Catholic Church, a church of Papists, 'Papist' being a term of disapprobation.[31] Furthermore, the Papists' church, when in power, burned alive as many of the catechumens' Protestant ancestors as it could lay its hands on. Could this be the Holy Catholic Church so blithely referred to in the Catechism? To continue, could 'Holy' in 'Holy Catholic Church' have the same meaning as 'Holy ' in 'Holy Ghost'? No, no meaning at all, just "a string of sounds and [alphabetic] characters, void of all sense" (p. 25), baffling and wearing to the young mind.

The catechumens will also say that they believe in *the communion of saints.* Here we have a riddle which, unhappily, is not explicable but which, happily, is not worth explication. Some vague notion of the communion service will probably come to mind, and saints, one supposes, will be communing, whatever this may mean, but who or what are saints? Nearly everyone in the New Testament of value to the later church will be called a saint, and the catechized child will have seen many pictures of holy saints. But what about the saint called Paul? At the beginning of his career, he was much like Judas at the end of his, a traitor to Jesus.[32] Yet Paul will be included as will hundreds of postbiblical individuals such as St. Dunstan, among whose saintly accomplishments was that of seizing the Devil's nose with tongs and of pulling the "unclean spirit" this way and that.[33]

No Christian catechism could end properly without having the uncomprehending catechumen vow to believe in *the forgiveness of sins, the resurrection of the body,* and *the life everlasting.* Each of these three affirmations presents an obvious and undeniable demand for an explanation, but none gets one. Doubtless those who penned these words had some more or less determinate subject matter or object in view, and thus some meaning in mind, but in the mind of a young child forced to say these words, it is quite different. The hapless child "believes in whatever is thus forced into his mouth without knowing so much as *who* it is that put it where it is, much less *what* it is" (p. 25).

Question 5 of the Catechism asks the catechumen, "What dost thou chiefly learn in these articles of thy belief?" The parrot responds, "First, I learn to believe in God the Father, who hath made me and all the world. Secondly, in God the Son, who hath redeemed me and all the world [i.e., all mankind]. Thirdly, in the Holy Ghost, who sanctifieth me and all the elect people of God." The parrot also learns concomitantly "the art of *gratuitous assertion*—the art of speaking and writing without thinking—and the art of making *groundless inferences*" (p. 29). Moreover, the unfledged parrot learns to overlook contradictions in what has been forced down its gullet.

Yes, the catechumen has learned, no doubt, to believe in God the Father and in God the Son, but how can the catechumen learn to believe in God the Son who *redeemed* her *and all mankind*? First, there is no mention of redemption in the so-called Apostles' Creed that the catechumen has been forced to rehearse. Whence, then, comes anything about redemption?[34] Second, there is a contradiction between this assertion and the Eighteenth Article. This Article says, "They are to be had [i.e., held] accursed, that presume to say, that every man shall be saved by the law [what law?] or sect which he professeth, so that he be diligent to frame his life according to that law, and the light of nature [what light of nature?]. For holy Scripture doth set out unto us only the name of Jesus Christ, whereby men must be saved." So, whereas the Catechism implies universal salvation when it speaks of God the Son's redeeming *all mankind* (or the *whole world*), the Eighteenth Article denies it. The catechumen of tender years may be induced, easily enough, to believe in contradictions, but those (in Bentham's day) who eventually entered Holy Orders or who were enrolled either in Oxford or Cambridge had to declare in writing their belief in the Thirty-nine Articles. These pawns of religious compulsion had already been forced, in more tender years, to profess belief in the Catechism. Could they have failed to notice the contradiction that orthodoxy and mendacity were compelling them to profess? Not in Bentham's case!

Thirdly, the catechumen is led to say that she *believes in God the Holy Ghost who sanctifieth* her *and all the elect people of God.* Here another rabbit is pulled from a theological hat. Not only is redemption (whatever it is) not to be found in the Apostles' Creed, neither is sanctification (whatever it is), yet God the Son redeems and God the Holy Ghost sanctifies.[35] God the Father, it must be remembered, creates and sustains. So the three equal and coeval Persons in one undivided Supreme Triune Being divide the labor among themselves, the one creating and sustaining, the other redeeming, and the third sanctifying.

The word 'sanctifieth' in the Catechism is in the present tense. Accordingly, it points to some sort of process going on in the one who has learned to profess belief in it. One wonders how the process of being sanctified (i.e., of being made holy) feels to catechumens. What difference in life's experiences would there be if catechumens were not being made holy? And, then, alas, those who profess belief in being sanctified by God the Holy Ghost keep on sinning just as before, and when they go to church they learn that they are "miserable sinners" (p. 32). How can those being made holy be miserable sinners? To make matters worse, if the person forced to confess faith in sanctification truly feels sanctified, that is, truly feels holy, what then keeps this person from being a schismatic, errant Methodist? If the person does not feel sanctified, that is, does not feel holy, does not feel any different than otherwise, why should that person be forced to say so and in so saying have to lie?

Other grotesqueries follow. Question 6 begins with an assertion and ends with a command: "You [the catechumen] said that your godparents did promise for you, that you should keep God's commandments: tell me how many there are." The answer, of course, is "Ten."

Question 7 asks which they are, and the catechumens mouth the words, "The same which God spake in the twentieth chapter of Exodus, saying I am the Lord thy God, which brought thee out of the land of Egypt, out of the house of bondage. Thou shalt have none other gods but me." Is one really to think that the catechumens or their Anglican ancestors were *brought out of the land of Egypt* and *out of the house of bondage*? This is manifestly absurd. It is to the biblical Hebrews alone (and by extension to their Jewish progeny) that the Ten Commandments were delivered. These Commandments were not delivered to Anglicans, who were never in bondage in Egypt, nor by extension to any Anglicans-in-the-making. What must those who penned the Catechism have had in mind? The Anglican catechumen who understands the content of the First Commandment must realize that it was delivered to others, not to his ilk, making it inapplicable to all those who were not delivered from Egypt.[36] If it is just the utterance of the formulary that is important, just its form and not its content, then the catechumen is being made to mouth an "insignificant assemblage of words" (p. 35).

Absurdity and hypocrisy run rampant whenever the Church of England requires would-be Anglicans to obey the Second Commandment. This Commandment, delivered to Hebrews and to them alone, says in part: "Thou shalt not make to thyself any graven image, nor the likeness of anything that is in heaven above, or in the earth beneath, or in the water under the earth." Meanwhile, as everyone knows, living in a country in which the religion of Jesus is not only professed but established, and even forced upon people by law, the making of graven images and the myriad results of the graphic arts are not only practiced and allowed, but are also encouraged by public authority. The Church of England has never observed the Second Commandment, except in the breach thereof.

Theologians who have noticed that what is sauce for the corporate body (i.e., the Anglican Church) is not supposed to be sauce for the individual members thereof have rationalized the situation as follows: individual Anglicans are not to make any graven images or likenesses of anything, lest they should bow down and worship them. This dodge, however, is easily refuted. If the Bible-god had been concerned with this alone, he could have commanded the Jews not to bow down nor worship any graven image or likeness of anything, whether made by them or by Gentiles. But the Second Commandment, as it stands, is a simple conjunction, composed of two parts: (1) not to make any graven images nor likenesses of anything and (2) not to bow down and worship any such things. Whether or not any Christians anywhere at any time have bowed down and worshiped such things, they have certainly made them and still make them wholesale, having routinely ignored the first part of the Second Commandment, at least since the beginning of the third century of the Christian era and throughout the entire history of the Church of England.[37]

Question 8 asks, "What dost thou chiefly learn by these commandments?" The authorized answer is, "I learn two things: my duty towards God, and my duty towards my neighbour." Question 9 asks, "What is thy duty towards God?" The answer is, "My duty towards God is to believe in him, to fear him, and to love him with all my heart, with all my mind, with all my soul, and with all my strength; to worship him, to give thanks, to put my whole trust in him, to call upon him, to honour his holy name and his word, and to serve him truly all the days of my life."

Granted that belief in God means belief that the selfsame God exists, a question, nevertheless, arises as to whether or not belief is under the control of will. If one entertains the belief that God exists, then that is simply an autobiographical fact. Any alleged obligation to believe is irrelevant and ineffective. If, on the contrary, one does not entertain the belief that God exists, how is mouthing a vow to believe in God going to transform unbelief into belief? It is never made clear how the training given to catechumens can bring about the desired effect.

Doubtless, catechumens can be made to say that they are duty-bound to fear and love God. But can they be made to do so? If the God in question is infinitely powerful, as Christianity teaches (together with being wrathful), then boundless fear is the appropriate emotion. It is hard to understand how feelings of terror can blend with love for the source of the terror. It is even harder to understand how one can be *obliged* to love such a fearsome being.

According to the Catechism, appropriate love for God enlists all of one's heart, mind, soul, and strength. This is indeed an impressive assemblage of words, heaped upon one another, but what do they name? What, in reality, distinguishes heart from mind, heart from soul, and heart from strength, to say nothing of the distinction between mind and soul? One is never told.[38] Moreover, it is made to seem that the proper love of God involves difficulty, even striving and straining. In what other circumstance, when the emotion of love is present, does it have to strive and strain?

To continue, to put one's *whole* trust in God, taken as the primary cause of all things, implies that one has no trust remaining to put in any of the secondary, lesser causes in the world, such as parents, siblings, other relatives, friends, and even strangers. Experience indicates that Christians do place some trust, at least, in others, and rightly so. Again, as is so often the case, the Catechism indulges in nothing but verbal bombast.[39]

Question 10 asks of the catechumen, "What is thy duty towards thy neighbour?" The following wordy formulary gives the answer: "My duty towards my neighbour, is to love him as myself, and to do to all men as I would that they should do unto me. To love, honour, and succour my father and mother. To honour and obey the king, and all that are put in authority under him. To submit myself to all my governors, teachers, spiritual pastors, and masters. To order myself lowly and reverently to all my betters. To hurt nobody by word or deed. To be true and just in all my dealings. To bear no malice nor hatred in my heart. To keep my hands from picking and stealing, and my tongue from evil speaking, lying, and slandering. To keep my body in temperance, soberness, and chastity. Not to covet nor desire other men's goods; but to learn and labour truly to get mine own living, and to do my duty in that state of life, unto which it shall please God to call me."

So beautiful is this formulary that the eye shrinks from traveling over it in search of imperfections, but why should the Catechism retain the particularizing, localizing term 'neighbor' when Christians are taught to love all men (i.e., all human beings) everywhere? What is the point of distinguishing neigh- (or nigh-) dwellers (i.e., neighbors) from the most distant of foreigners?

Following immediately upon the answer to Question 10, the catechist bids the catechumen to recite the Lord's Prayer and then asks, "What desirest thou of God in this prayer?" The canned answer is as follows: "I desire my Lord God, our heavenly Father, who is the Giver of all goodness, to send his grace unto me and to all people, that we may worship him, serve him, and obey him, as we ought to do; and I pray unto God, that he will send us all things that are needful both for our souls and bodies; and that he will be merciful unto us, and forgive us our sins; and that it will please him to save and defend us in all dangers both of soul and body; and that he will keep us from all sin and wickedness, and from our spiritual enemy, and from everlasting death: and this I trust he will do of his mercy and goodness through our Lord Jesus Christ; and therefore I say, Amen: so be it."[40]

The catechumens are made to say, among other things, that they desire *grace* and deliverance from *everlasting death*. Here, more rabbits leap from a theological hat. Neither of these concepts is to be found in the Lord's Prayer, nor is either implied by it. It is more than curious, is it not, that the recitation of a prayer prompts catechumens to try to advert to something absent from that same prayer? It is, in fact, a misrepresentation foisted on innocent minds! The catechist knows that the subject matter in question is missing, as may the catechumens, yet the latter are forced to declare most solemnly that it is there. To recite as true what the catechumens see (or can see) to be untrue is what they from infancy are compelled to practice and to reckon among their duties. From such pious instruction as this comes no new knowledge but rather a (deeply) rooted and "habitual deprivation of the mental faculties" (p. 45).

As far as *grace* is concerned, whether in the Lord's Prayer or not, it is a mere expletive (i.e., a mere verbal filler), adding nothing to the sense of the prescribed answer.[41] "Yet upon the ground of this expletive, systems have been built, controversies raised, swords drawn, and blood made to flow in torrents" (p. 46).

Question 11 asks the unfledged parrot, "How many sacraments hath Christ ordained in his Church?" The hapless parrot answers, "Two only, as generally necessary to salvation: that is to say Baptism, and the Supper of the Lord." Thus does the Church of England (claiming only two sacraments) seek to distinguish itself from the Roman Catholic Church, against which it revolted, the latter claiming seven.[42] The answer, in fact, is none. Jesus instituted no sacraments. In evidence thereto, on what occasion, in the Greek (of the New Testament) in which he is represented as having spoken, did he ever use a term meaning what the English word 'sacrament' now means? Never! 'Sacrament', derived from the Latin *sacramentum*, is a theological term of modern invention, a kind of metaphysical term whose object is to enshroud a religious ceremony with a sense of mystery.[43]

Take baptism, for example. As practiced by Jesus, it was a ceremony for aggregating believers into the religious society whose head he was and for reminding them of their inclusion. In the unlettered community of his time, it was a substitute for entry in "a *register* or *memorandum book*" (p. 47). But, by an all too natural misconception, the mere sign or evidence of this aggregation was taken to be the efficient cause of the benefits (presumably) produced by it. Subsequently, all manner of questions were raised as to the circumstances that should accompany this ceremony of aggregation, to wit: was one to be immersed in water totally or only partially; if only partially, which fingers were to be used in applying the liquid; and what form should the resulting wet mark make? The asininity of these questions can be illustrated very easily. For example, suppose aggregation into Jesus' movement to have been by entry in a register-book. If the writing of a man's name, signifying his inclusion, was to be done by quill, then should it be by "*goose*-quill or *crow*-quill"; if upon paper, "demy or foolscap"; if bound, calf's hide or sheep's hide (p. 48)?

Contradictory to the Catechism, Jesus not only did not ordain baptism as a sacrament (of which, more below), he did not institute it in the sense of creating a new ceremony for membership in his movement, nor was he the first to practice it. At the beginning of his ministry, he submitted himself to the baptism of John the Baptist and only later practiced it or caused it to be practiced on others.[44] Those who force this falsehood on catechumens must hope that these little Anglicans-in-the-making never read the Gospels. Should this happen, the perfidy of the Catechism and its catechists will be manifest to all.

Question 12 asks, "What meanest thou by the word Sacrament?" The catechumen regurgitates, "I mean an outward and visible sign of an inward and spiritual grace, given unto us, ordained by Christ himself as a means whereby we receive the same, and a pledge to assure us thereof." The Rome-sprung vocable 'sacrament' was no more invented by Jesus than by Satan. 'Sacrament' (meaning "holy thing" in English) became the manufactured box (or category) into which two transactions of Jesus (his baptism and the final meal with his disciples) were dumped willy-nilly. What kind of a property is it that can attach itself alike to two unlike transactions?

In one transaction, Jesus accepts the baptism of John the Baptist, then is represented (in the Gospels) as directing converts to his own movement to be baptized, and, presto, out pops something under the generic appellation of 'sacrament' or, in other words, something possessing the attribute of holiness.[45] In the second transaction, Jesus participates in a farewell meal with his disciples, consumes bread and wine, and, abracadabra, when Anglicans nowadays perform a highly ritualized version of the same transaction, they participate in a sacrament, in an act having the property of holiness. What is this mysterious property that makes Jesus' immersion in water holy, but not holy, some unbelieving heathen's immersion in water? What is it that makes the ritual act of memorializing Jesus' sacrifice sacred but a similar act of a pagan theophagy not sacred? In fact, nothing at all. As a property, holiness is vacuous; 'sacrament' an empty sound, a pure invention.

Under the pretended name 'grace' (or 'a grace'), something good is represented as being given to participating believers (no matter the quality of their conduct) that is no mere *sign* as the Catechism indicates, but is rather an *efficient cause*. Imagine the Almighty laid hold of and made to enter into a contract (under what penalty is not mentioned), pledging himself, binding himself, to give to this pretended *efficient cause* a pretended *real effect*. Thus it is that the "sham science" (of theology) grows; thus it is that "the wilderness is formed, in which the wits of those who are destined to travel therein are destined to be lost" (p. 50).

Question 13 asks, "How many parts are there in a sacrament?" "Two," pipes the innocent neophyte, "the outward visible sign, and the inward spiritual grace." A compound made out of a *real* and *visible ceremony*, to which, by the force of imagination, is attached an *invisible* and *unintelligible* effect—such is the *whole*: and now comes the unfledged parrot, and with his tongue is required to split it into two parts.

Question 14 asks, "What is the outward visible sign, or form in Baptism?" The bird answers, "Water; wherein the person is baptized, in the name of the Father, and of the Son, and of the Holy Ghost." To say that the water itself wherein one is baptized is the sign of aggregation into Jesus' movement is as absurd as saying that a blank sheet of paper in a baptism book is a sign of aggregation. It is the physical operation of immersion in water that is the sign of aggregation. Similarly, it is the name written in the baptism book that is the sign of membership. In itself, nothing can be more trifling than such an inaccuracy in the catechetical question at issue. The real matter of regret is that in this body of pretended instruction (composed by a man who did not understand what he wrote) a child should be forced to declare himself to understand that which neither understands, because the whole is unintelligible.

Having been induced to misidentify water as the visible sign of the inward grace at issue, the unthinking catechumen next mouths words that indict the whole Anglican Church. Respecting the baptismal water, the parrot says *"wherein,"* not *"wherewith,"* the person is baptized. Horrors! What a scene of horror is presented by the recognition that legitimate baptism is by total immersion in the baptismal water, not by pouring, sprinkling, or dashing some of it on the catechumen's head, which act is rendered null and void by the Catechism itself. The Church of England, it seems, does not *really* baptize anybody.[46]

While performing an act that Anglicans call baptism (their substitute for Christian baptism), the reverend clergyman doing the baptizing claims his action to be done *in the name of the Father, and of the Son, and of the Holy Ghost.* Here one hears a mouthful of air making sounds that function as names in a sentence. The deluded and deluding clergyman, however, cannot show that the names he has used, in his pious formulary, are more than fictions. Were the priests of Baal to undertake some ritual in his name, or the priests of Zeus to carry out a directive on his behalf, or the priests of Osiris to do some sacred thing at his behest, the Anglican clergy and their catechumens alike would hoot in derision at what, to them, would be mere magical incantations.

Question 15 asks, "What is the inward and spiritual grace?" The unfledged bird warbles, "A death unto sin, and a new birth unto righteousness; for being by nature born in sin, and the children of wrath, we are hereby made children of grace." The long and the short of it seems to be this: the Almighty God, maker of all things visible and invisible, also makes, perforce, the infant human who comes into this world a child of wrath. The Maker of heaven and earth promptly determines to consign the newborn wretch to endless torture, but then, a reverend clergyman appears agitating the air with certain vacuous words and slopping a dollop or two of water on the child. Moved by these vacuous words (and also by the dollop[s] of water, one presumes), the all-wise Being alters his design and, though not appeased, vouchsafes to the infant, nevertheless, a chance of escape. Thereupon the infant dies to its old sinful nature and is born anew as "a child of grace" (p. 53), a child of righteousness. Should a child fail to believe this oft-told tale, as though belief were under the control of volition, this child will face an endless future of unremitting torture.

Question 16 asks, "What is required of persons to be baptized?" The regurgitated answer is, "Repentance, whereby they forsake sin; and faith, whereby they steadfastly believe the promises of God made to them in that sacrament." Sensitive, it would seem, to embarrassing questions that might be raised as to how a young child can repent of the sinful nature into which it was presumably born, a nature which was none of its own making, the Catechism hastens to the next question.

Question 17 asks, "Why then are infants baptized, when, by reason of their tender age, they cannot perform them?" The uncomprehending catechumen makes the following sounds: "Because they promise them both by their sureties: which promise, when they come to age, themselves are bound to perform." Perform *them*? Perform *what*?[47] These words constitute a cloud of obscurity and ambiguity derived from a purely grammatical source, a source unrelated to reality. Infants no more than a week or two old (typically the time for Anglican baptism) cannot repent of anything and cannot have faith. Not being able repent of anything, they cannot *perform* repentance; not being able to acquire faith, that is, belief in this or that, they cannot *perform* it. Into the breach, the infants' sureties, the godparents, throw themselves making promises that adult converts might easily make, but that infants can never make. So muddy is the answer to question 17 that the infants to be baptized appear to be sureties for their own sureties.

In Jesus' day, those who understood his message and had faith therein acquired the motive for repentance. With repentance attendant upon this faith, they expected to enjoy God's promises and avoid the threats made against the faithless and unrepentant. One step only remained; baptism as the sign of aggregation into Jesus' movement. However, in the topsy-turvy world of the Catechism, the act of baptism precedes the motive for it, and the requirements that ought to precede it follow it. Since godparents are so adept at promising repentance and faith on behalf of their spiritual wards and so puissant in saddling obligations upon these wards to believe what the selfsame wards might not otherwise believe, why should the godparents not really repent and really believe *on behalf* of their spiritual wards, no matter what the wards eventually come to do or to believe? In this way their spiritual wards could enjoy the promises of God, no matter what.

Question 18 asks, "Why was the sacrament of the Lord's Supper ordained?" In answering, the fledgling twitters, "For the continual remembrance of the sacrifice of the death of Christ, and of the benefits which we receive thereby." Here the Catechism-maker presents the Anglican with another impossibility. No Anglican, whether an unfledged catechumen or a fully fledged communicant, can *remember* Jesus or do anything in *remembrance* of him or his sacrifice. Only those who actually knew Jesus personally or knew of him from close contemporaries could *remember* him. It requires an active imagination, indeed, for any Anglican (at any time) to pretend to be remembering Jesus, when participating in the so-called sacrament of the Lord's Supper.

Of all those who knew Jesus personally and who knew of him (from contemporary sidelines, as it were), he selected only twelve disciples, his most intimate and confidential friends, to share a farewell repast. Moreover, it was with these same disciples (minus Judas) that he expected to eat bread and drink wine anew when the Kingdom of God came. Matthew 26:29 and Luke 22:14–18 make this explicit and fail to suggest the inclusion of any outside the eleven remaining disciples. Yet the manufactory of Anglican theology, being as deceptive as it is, has turned this farewell meal into a "sacramental" banquet for all communicants at all times and into a means for receiving grace.

The act of receiving grace (i.e., of receiving various spiritual, supernatural, and mystical benefits) presupposes an act of delivering grace. Without any warrant in the Gospels, a type of functionary has arisen in Anglicanism (and elsewhere) competent, and competent alone, to deliver grace.[48] This functionary is the priest. Those competent only to receive grace are the laity.

The theological manufactory of grace produces a commodity which catechumens and communicants alike have been sedulously nurtured by the Catechism and catechists alike to desire. Nor need their desires go unfulfilled, for, lo! there is the priest, holding the patent on the desired product, and prepared to sell it for his own benefit and the benefit of the other patentees, that is, his fellow clergymen and their ilk in the hierarchy.[49]

Question 19 asks, "What is the outward part or sign of the Lord's Supper?" The misled catechumen answers, "Bread and Wine, which the Lord hath commanded to be received." The deception herein lies in "hath," a word in the indefinite present tense, a tense not to be confused with the simple past tense. The New Testament reports that Jesus commanded his twelve disciples to take the bread and eat and to take the cup and drink.[50] But it does not say that he commanded anybody else to do so, nor does it imply as 'hath' would imply that he commanded all of his followers and potential followers everywhere and at all future times so to do.

Ever after Jesus' execution, his eleven remaining disciples must have felt an especial poigniancy in breaking a common loaf and in raising a common cup in his memory. His announcement that the broken bread was his body and that the poured cup was his blood was understood by them, of course, as metaphorical. At a later, indeterminate date, however, Christian theologians transmogrified the metaphorical into the literal and the physical into the metaphysical. In so doing, they created "the grossest nonsense" (p. 64). Taken literally, Jesus broke his body into a dozen or so morsels, gave these to his disciples, and then stood about in the flesh while he and they consumed his flesh. Taken literally, Jesus shared his blood with his disciples, and then stood about with the whole of it still coursing through his blood vessels while he and they drank of it. Taken metaphysically, as the Catholic edition of Christianity is wont to take it, the morsel of communion bread becomes the actual flesh of Jesus, magically, and the wine his actual blood. Every child about to enter the Anglican fold is made to declare herself persuaded of this cannibalism.[51]

Question 20 asks, "What is the inward part, or thing signified?" Out of the catechumens' mouths comes the grimgribber (i.e., gibberish), "The body and blood of Christ, which are verily and indeed taken, and received by the faithful in the Lord's Supper." So, when the catechumens have mastered the Catechism and are ready to participate then and henceforth in the Lord's Supper, the testimony of their senses must be denied. What looks like a morsel of bread (or is a wafer) is not what it looks to be, but is, rather, the flesh of Jesus Christ. What looks, smells, and tastes like wine is not wine, but is, rather, the blood of Jesus Christ. This pernicious nonsense is what the Roman Church calls Transubstantiation. Between the 'trans' and the 'sub' there is not a shade of difference worth thinking about. The whole concept is absurd, and the Lutheran doctrine of Consubstantiation is worse.[52]

Question 21 asks, "What are the benefits whereof we are partakers thereby?" The parrot, almost fully fledged in divine science by now, answers, "The strengthening and refreshing of our souls by the body and blood of Christ, as our bodies are by the bread and wine." Ah, yes; if only the bread were metaphorically Christ's flesh, the wine were metaphorically his blood, and the refreshment metaphorical as well! With the metaphorical, all things are possible. But, alas, with either Transubstantiation or Consubstantiation, the metaphorical gives way to the physical and the metaphysical. The answer to question 20, one must remember, assures all and sundry that *the body and blood of Christ are verily and indeed taken, and received by the faithful in the Lord's Supper.* To gain refreshment therefrom, the communicant must, it would seem, digest these holy foods as though they were ordinary flesh and blood. But, no; this is not quite what is meant. To rescue us from this puzzle, 'spiritual' (and its sibling, 'spiritually') are at hand. To the carnal (or physical) sense of things and to their temporal sense may be added at will a new dimension of reality, that is, the spiritual sense of things. In this convenient way, whatever things are false physically or temporally are (or can be) true spiritually.[53]

Should pedagogues or institutions have minds, young or old, to subdue, weaken, or render less rational than would otherwise be the case, they have but to conjoin 'spiritual' with 'sense'. Then out pops a "moulding board" with which the softened wax can be shaped into the desired form. Therewith, no matter how absurd the beliefs, no matter how false the doctrines, eternal truths result, or so it will seem to minds suitably stultified. However, those who cling to their empirical experiences, no matter the moulding, and who still manage to retain their wits, no matter the catechizing, will find the spiritual sense of things identical to the nonsensical sense of things.

Question 22 asks, "What is required of them who come to the Lord's Supper?" The catechumen rattles off the following lengthy answer: "To examine themselves, whether they repent them truly of their former sins, steadfastly purposing to lead a new life, have a lively faith in God's mercy through Christ, with a thankful remembrance of his death, and be in charity with all men." Thus do Anglican catechists force and fasten five allegedly divine duties on their catechumens, duties which the latter may, but most likely will not, comprehend. Nevertheless the catechumens must claim to understand what they are coerced to say. The above ceremony of asking children a theological question and then of extorting from them an authorized answer is (whether Catholic or Anglican) a latter-day invention, a mere fiction having no historical foundation. Should catechumens ever read and comprehend the Gospel history relative to the Lord's Supper, they will find no such accessory duties as those contained in the authorized answer. If such palpable and gross impositions can not only be attempted, but also effected by coercive power, what limit can there be to ecclesiastical imposture? Whatever the precise limits to fraud may be, the resulting debility in a catechized child will be the "prostration of the understanding and will" (p. 75).

NOTES

1. Stephen Conway writes in the introduction to *CBJ*, vol. 9, "In January [of 1818] Bentham was still hoping that [Samuel] Romilly [a friend and advisor] would mark passages in *Church-of-Englandism* that were likely to lead to prosecution and suggest suitable amendments. He soon discovered that Romilly was unwilling to undertake this task" (p. xix). Bentham in his old age was bolder and less circumspect than he had been earlier; see James Steintrager, "Morality and Belief: The Origin and Purpose of Bentham's Writings on Religion,"*MNL* (spring 1971): 7. Historian Basil Willey claims that the (or a) booklet on the Catechism originally appeared anonymously. In any case, Bentham was attacked in print twice (as early as 1819) for his analysis of the Catechism, indicating that the identity of its author was not a mystery for long, if ever. See footnote 157 in chapter 8 for more details; see also Basil Willey, *Nineteenth Century Studies* (New York: Columbia University Press, 1949), p. 134. Bentham might have been, but never was, prosecuted for blasphemy, sedition, or libel. So might have been his publisher, Effingham Wilson; see James Crimmins, *Secular Utilitarianism: Social Science and the Critique of Religion in the Thought of Jeremy Bentham* (Oxford: Clarendon Press, 1990), pp. 148, 163.

2. *ODCC*, s. v. "Thirty-nine Articles, the."

3. Ibid.

4. Jeremy's father began calling his son a philosopher when the lad was but six years old; see *CJB*, 2:424.

5. Bentham's bitterest observation on the coerced swearing of oaths is to be found in *The Rationale of Reward*:

> In all matters of conscience, then, let me lay down to myself the following as inviolable rules: not to be governed by my own reason; not to endeavour at the presumptuous and unattainable merit of consistency; not to consider whether a thing is right or wrong in itself, but what *they* think of it [i.e., the officials at Oxford]. On all points, then, let me receive my religion at their hands: what to them is sacred, let it to me be sacred; what to them is wickedness, let it to me be wickedness; what to them is truth, let it to me be truth; let me see as they see, believe as they believe, think as they think, feel as they feel, love as they love, fear as they fear, hate as they hate, esteem as they esteem, perform as they perform, subscribe as they subscribe, and swear as they swear. (*WJB*, 2:262)

In *Memoirs of Bentham and Correspondence*, he wrote of his subscription to *the Thirty-nine Articles*: "I signed: but by the view I found myself forced to take of the whole business, such an impression was made, as will never depart from me but with life" (*WJB*, 10:37).

6. Roman Catholics face, or ought to have to face, a similar dilemma when calling their priests "Father," for Matt. 23:9 says, "And call no *man* your father upon the earth: for one is your Father, which is in heaven."

7. In *Memoirs of Bentham*, he wrote, "But how little do Christians care about the commands of Christianity. Was ever a text more clear than that, 'Swear not at all,'—but it has been caviled away by glosses and meanings which in no other case would be listened to for a minute" (*WJB*, 10:582).

8. The Gospel of Matthew, the most Jewish of the canonical Gospels, is the only one that reports Jesus' prohibition on the swearing of oaths. An insight into this may be gained from Josephus, the Jewish historian, who wrote of the Essenes, "[W]hatsoever they say also is firmer than an oath; but swearing is avoided by them, and they esteem it worse than perjury; for they say, that he who cannot be believed without [swearing by] God, is already condemned" (*The Wars of the Jews*, in *The Works of Flavius Josephus*, trans. William Whiston, [Grand Rapids, MI: Baker Book House, 1974], 1:146). H. M. Pope, in *IDB*, s. v. "Oaths," says of Jesus, "His strictures against oaths by the temple, the temple gold, the altar, or heavens . . . are aimed at the casuistry which attempted to classify oaths, according to degrees of validity." Then, too, if one makes no oath, one breaks no oath, but it seems more likely that Jesus opposed oaths because they would bind the Bible-god to the will of the oath taker, thus limiting divine sovereignty.

9. It is rare in the New Testament for a passage in a Gospel to be so nearly repeated in an epistle, or vice versa. It is also noteworthy that the Epistle of James, the most Jewish letter in the New Testament, may come from the hands of that James who was the brother of Jesus and the leader of the Jerusalem church, or from a disciple, or a school of followers, honoring their leader. In any case, it seems clear that the swearing of oaths was a bone of contention among Jews, including at least some Jews who were Christians.

10. *Justice and Codification Petitions*, in *WJB*, 5:458.

11. Bentham wrote of Christ's descent into hell that one might as well say that Satan ascended into heaven. See Bentham's analysis of the Apostles' Creed later in this chapter.

12. At twelve years of age, Bentham was the youngest student, up to that time, to matriculate in one of Oxford's colleges. He was graduated at fifteen and was already, by virtue of the oaths he was coerced to swear, a seasoned, if angry, participant in theological humbug and religious cant; see Mary Mack, *Jeremy Bentham: An Odyssey of Ideas* (London: Heinemann, 1962), pp. 43, 45.

13. Bentham believed that forcing people to perjure themselves was intrinsically wrong. In *Principles of Penal Law*, he wrote, "But every article of faith is necessarily hurtful, so soon as the legislator, in order to favour its adoption, employs coercive or penal motives" (*WJB*, 1:564).

14. *Swear Not at All*, in *WJB*, 5:192.

15. Ibid. This is a theme to which Bentham adverted on several occasions and in various writings. In *Principles of Penal Law*, he wrote, "[M]an, by imposing an

oath, would exercise authority over God himself. Man ordains a punishment, and it is for the Supreme Judge to execute it: deny this position, and the religious force of an oath vanishes" (*WJB*, 1:567).

16. *Swear Not at All*, in *WJB*, 5:193.

17. *Principles of Penal Law*, in *WJB*, 1:437.

18. Regarding Quakers, in *Rationale of Judicial Evidence*, Bentham wrote, "What is known to everybody, is, that as far as anything can be true that is predicated of men in whole classes, the quakers are the most veracious of mankind." Nevertheless, "Forbidden by his religion, a quaker will not pay tithes: sued in the spiritual court, he is excommunicated. As a witness, he is now incompetent twice over: once by being a quaker, and again by being excommunicate. Why by being excommunicate: Answer, per Mr. Justice Buller: 'Because he is not under the influence of any religion'" (*WJB*, 7:425).

Regarding atheists, Bentham cites the case of *Omychund* v. *Barker*, which holds that that those who disbelieve "in the existence of a God, or in a future state of rewards and punishments, cannot be admitted as witnesses in England" (ibid., p. 421).

19. *Justice and Codification*, in *WJB*, 5:459.

20. Ibid., pp. 456–57. Quakers were disabled much as were atheists with similar miscarriages of justice. In *Swear Not At All*, Bentham wrote of Quakers and their refusal to swear oaths, "For this refusal it is, that, between church and state, matters are so ordered, that, in a case which has afforded no other witness than such as are of this persuasion, justice—criminal justice at least—is deprived of all evidence: license being thereby granted, to all such crimes as from time to time it shall happen to any man to feel himself disposed to commit (other persons out of the question) upon the bodies, or in the presence, of any number of quakers" (*WJB*, 5:201)

21. In Bentham's day at least three godparents were required, of which two were to be of the same sex as the infant being baptized.

22. The Nicene Creed of 325 (with Greek terms transliterated) states,

> We believe in one God All Governing [*pantokratora*], creator [*poieten*] of all things visible and invisible. And in one Lord Jesus Christ, the Son of God, begotten of the Father as only begotten, that is, from the essence [reality] of the Father [*ek tes ousias tou patros*], God from God, Light from Light, true God from true God, begotten not created [*poiethenta*], of the same essence [reality] as the Father [*homoousion to patri*], through whom all things came into being, both in heaven and in earth; Who for us men and for our salvation came down and was incarnate, becoming human [*enanthropesanta*]. He suffered and the third day he rose, and ascended into the heavens. And he will come to judge both the living and the dead. And [we believe] in the Holy Spirit. But those who say, Once he was not, or he was not before his generation, or he came to be out of nothing, or who assert that he, the Son of God, is of a different *hypostasis* or *ousia*, or that he is a creature, or changeable, or mutable, the Catholic and Apostolic Church anathematizes them. (*Creeds of the Churches*, ed. John H. Leith [Garden City, NY: Doubleday Anchor Books, 1963], pp. 30–31).

23. Bentham noted with relish that the learned Pearson knew the creed too well and knew the New Testament too well to call it the Apostles' Creed, calling his famous book of 1659 *Exposition of the Creed* instead; see *ODCC*, s. v. "Pearson, John."

24. Bentham could have been very much more trenchant in his criticism of the so-called Virgin Birth of Jesus, if he had cared to do so. Nobody who can be depended on for accuracy knew (or knows) the details of Jesus' conception. Nothing was easier at the time than to call a great leader or hero divine (or the child of a god), and nothing was more commonplace than to base the supposed knowledge thereof on revelation. The unknown authors of Matthew and Luke were in no position to know anything about Jesus' conception. Jewish tradition from a very early time identified his father as one Pantera (or Pandera or Panthera); see Morton Smith, *Jesus the Magician* (New York: Harper and Row, 1978), pp. 26, 46–48. Mark makes no reference to Jesus' birth, and John specifically identifies his father as Joseph (John 1:45; see also 6:42). This is very significant in that no Gospel has a higher doctrine of (nor emphasizes the actions of) the Holy Spirit more than John. Paul says only that Jesus was made of a woman (Gal. 4:4) in the likeness of men (Phil. 2:7). Nowhere in the New Testament does anybody ever profess faith in the Virgin Birth as part of a creedal statement essential to Christianity. The Anglican Church has much to answer for on this particular.

25. The Nicene Creed attempts to make this clearer when it speaks of "God from God, Light from Light, true God from true God . . . Who for us men and for our salvation came down and was incarnate, becoming human."

26. The Definition of Chalcedon (451) makes the conundrum in question even more pointed when it says in part of Jesus Christ, "This selfsame one is perfect [*teleion*] both in deity [*theoteti*] and also in humanness [*anthropoteti*]; this self same one is also actually [*alethos*] God and actually man, with a rational soul [*psyches logikes*] and a body. He is the same reality as God [*homoousion to patri*] as far as his deity is concerned and of the same reality as we are ourselves [*homoousion hemin*] as far as his humanness is concerned; thus like us in all respects, sin only excepted" (*Creeds of the Churches*, pp. 35–36). Bentham could have made a great deal more than he did of the conundrums surrounding the two natures of the God-man. This position (the dyophysite as opposed to the heretical monophysite position holding that Jesus Christ was of only one nature and that Divine) raises further perplexities. First, the Divine Nature of the Bible-god and the human nature of Jesus (and other men) are not strictly parallel. The Bible-god is never said to have a body, even a "spiritual" body. He does have a Spirit, according to many, many biblical references, and a mind (Rom. 11:34; 1 Cor. 2:16). Antique psychology sometimes divided the human being into body, soul, and spirit, sometimes into body, mind, soul, and spirit. The New Testament never makes clear the distinctions between these non-bodily aspects of the human being, nor the precise relation of any of these to a human body. The fourth-century theologian Apollinarius the Younger argued that though Jesus had a body and a soul, he did not have a human spirit but rather the Logos, the Word of God, dwelt in him. This, of course, denied his perfect humanness. Second, if Jesus Christ (i.e., God incarnate) had a Divine Mind and a human mind (or rational soul), and if will is a characteristic of minds, then he had two

wills. To put it neatly, he was always potentially of two minds. If so, which mind bade him choose to sacrifice himself for us men and our salvation, the Divine or the human? To solve this and related problems, monothelitism (or monotheletism) contended that the God-man had two natures but only one will or one mode of activity. In 680 the Council of Constantinople condemned monothelitism and reaffirmed the existence of two wills in Jesus Christ. The *ODCC* contains an entry for each of the theological terms or positions mentioned above together with many related entries. A vastly greater repository of information about these subjects can be found in the *ERE*. For Bentham, the foregoing was a case of words, words, words, signifying nothing, of useless information having neither good epistemological bases nor practical usefulness. If adults wished to try to believe incomprehensible doctrines, it was their business. To drum such vacuous ideas into the heads of children and then make them assert belief therein was atrocious.

27. In 1 Peter 3:18–20, a little-read and anything but pellucid passage, it is claimed that Jesus went in the Spirit (whatever this means) to an unidentified prison to preach to certain unnamed but rebellious spirits from the antique period of Noah and the flood. Next the eight people allegedly saved through water (during the Noachian flood) are associated with Christians now saved through the waters of baptism (vv. 21, 22). Quite apart from the total lack of logic in the association, the disobedient spirits are not pictured as being in endless, fiery torment, which is what hell is supposed to be.

28. See *GEL*, p. 770.

29. In Matthew hell, hellfire, and fire are mentioned eight times. On five of these occasions (5:22, 5:29, 10:28, 23:15, 23:33), the word translated 'hell' is 'Gehenna', a place where offal and garbage were burned, making it a place of fire and serving as a model for fiery torment; see the entries "Gehenna" and "Hades" in the *HBD* or similar resource. On two occasions Matthew uses 'Hades' (11:23, 16:18). Once he uses the Greek for fire (18:9). Mark uses 'Gehenna' three times (9:43, 45, 47). Luke uses 'Gehenna' once (12:5) and 'Hades' twice (10:15, 16:23). John uses no term that might be rendered by 'hell' in English. Acts uses 'Hades' twice (2:27, 31). As astonishing as it may seem, Paul never uses a term that can be translated as 'hell'. James uses 'Gehenna' once; Revelation uses 'Hades' four times together with 'lake of fire' once (1:18, 6:8, 20:13–14). Theologians in the Anglican Church and the translators of the KJV knew perfectly well that 'prison' in 1 Peter 3:19 could not be translated into the English 'hell', but with a fine disregard for truth proceeded to forcefeed catechumens with the idea that Jesus after death descended *into hell*.

30. In *Jesus the Magician*, Smith observes, "No Old Testament prophets had birds roost on them. Rabbinic literature contains nothing closely similar" (p. 97). However, in various magical texts, he notes that there are extant directions for getting power over spirits that are associated with birds; see *Papyri graecae magicae*, ed. K. Preisenanz and A. Henrichs, 2 vols. (Stuttgart: B. G. Tenberi, 1973–74).

31. The precocious child with an appetite for more theology than the Catechism provides can look into the Thirty-nine Articles and find that the Nineteenth and Twenty-second Articles refer directly and critically to the Roman Catholic Church and that the Fifteenth, Twenty-eighth, and Thirtieth Articles refer indirectly but critically to it.

32. Part 2 of this work makes plain the nature of Paul's betrayal of Jesus, as Bentham saw it.

33. Here Bentham gave vent to a well-known legend that had lingered in England since the late eleventh century. St. Dunstan (924–88), while living as a cenobite in a cubicle 2½ feet wide by 5 feet long, "saw visions and as he believed wrestled with the Tempter himself [i.e., the Devil] in bodily form" (*DNB*, s. v. "Dunstan, Saint"). The *TCE*, s. v. "Dunstan, Saint," is a bit more specific when suggesting that it was believed that he used tongs to seize the Devil's nose.

34. There is something morally amiss when new concepts or words are sprung upon children (or older catechumens) who have been made to learn and regurgitate a creed that does not contain these concepts or words.

35. Though it is true that children (or older catechumens) could learn about the redemption of Christ (i.e., God the Son) from the Ninth and Twenty-eighth Articles, they could learn nothing about sanctification as the unique work of God the Holy Ghost. Neither 'sanctification' nor the concept behind it appears in the Thirty-nine Articles nor in the Apostles' or Nicene Creed. Moreover, in the Gospels none of Jesus' disciples is ever said to be sanctified, either by him or by the Holy Spirit.

36. The First Commandment reflects a time in religious history when henotheism was common, i.e., a time when tribal groups (if not individuals) were able to choose from a variety of gods. Joshua 24:1–28 makes such choosing explicit. Henotheism was not an issue in Judea in Jesus' time, though it could have held some attraction for individual Jews of the Diaspora. In short, choosing between gods was not a viable option for Christians, either in the primitive church or in the Church of England. Those who say that one's god might be one's belly, or riches, or voluptuous living, etc., are mistaking the metaphoric use of 'god' with its literal use in henothistic times and circumstances. Having Anglican catechumens vow to have no other gods above or before the Bible-god was, as Bentham suggested, a vacuous vow. What other gods were available to Anglicans-in-the-making? Christianity had long since seen to it that there were no other gods from which to choose, except metaphoric ones.

37. In *Jesus the Magician*, on a sheet of illustrations following p. 61, Morton Smith includes a picture of a magical gem showing Jesus, in relief, hung by the wrists from a cross. It is in the Pereire Collection and is dated at about 200.

Bentham quit his analysis of the Ten Commandments with the Second. He could have heaped more coals of fire on Anglican heads had he cared to take up the Fourth Commandment: "Remember the sabbath day, to keep it holy." The Jewish sabbath day was and remains that period of time from sunset on Friday until sunset on Saturday. Though Christians eventually came to regard Sunday as the holy day of each week and though Anglicans always observed it as their holy day, there is no biblical authorization to do so. Neither Jesus nor Paul nor any other Christian leader or teacher in the New Testament calls upon Christians to distinguish themselves from Jews by choosing an alternative holy day. Thus when would-be Anglicans vow to heed the Fourth Commandment, they make an empty vow.

38. This list contains what philosophers nowadays call a categorial confusion. Strength is a relative term, widely applicable, that admits of more or less energy, but

no one in Christian theology would refer to a person as having more or less of a mind or more or less of a soul. Depending on the metaphor intended, however, heart might be classifiable with strength. As an organ, some hearts may well beat more strongly than others.

39. The Catechism also calls upon Christians to serve God truly but never tells why the omnipotent, omniscient, perfect, and infinite being of Christian theology needs or could use any help.

40. For reasons that are unclear, Bentham does not number this question separately, but seems to see it as subordinate to question 10.

41. In today's usage, 'expletive' often means an exclamation that is obscene or profane. Bentham, however, used the term here to mean a verbal filler that added no meaning. For example, the sentence *rain is falling now* is equivalent to *it is raining now*. Here 'it' serves as a mere filler, adding no new meaning. Similar are *A good mechanic is hard to find* and *It is hard to find a good mechanic*. Bentham's point is that *I ask God to be kindly disposed toward me* is identical to *I ask God to be kindly disposed toward me and give me his grace*, the bit about grace being redundant and unnecessary. For a history of the use of 'expletive', see the *OED* .

42. The seven sacraments of Catholicism are Baptism, Confirmation, the Eucharist, Penance, Extreme Unction, Orders, and Matrimony.

43. The Greek word *mustērion* (mystery), in one of its forms or other occurs twenty-two times in the KJV of the New Testament, but only once is its use attributed to Jesus (see Mark 4:11). The plural, *mustēria*, is used five times, twice attributed to Jesus (Matt. 13:11, Luke 8:10). These are routinely translated by the Latin cognates mysterium and mysteria in the Nouum Testamentum Latine (the Latin New Testament). However, in Eph. 1:9 (for reasons that are themselves mysterious), the Greek *mustērion* is translated by the Latin *sacramentum*. The same anomaly occurs in Eph. 3:9 and 5:32, also in Col. 1:27, in 1 Timothy 3:16, and in Rev. 1:20 and 17:7. Thus does the camel insert its nose under the tent. It is imperative to learn that the Greek *mustērion* means 'secret, secret rite, or secret teaching', something that could be revealed to those prepared to receive it. It does not mean what we generally mean when we talk, for example, about the mystery of existence, the mystery of a confounding murder, or the riddle of cosmic origins, etc. The Latin sacramentum has distinctly different meanings. In the legal context of the time, it referred to money deposited with the appropriate authorities which in failed suits the defeated party lost. In the military context, it referred to the oath of allegiance newly enlisted soldiers took. Although it may be recognized that there is something sacred about such a binding oath, it is hardly identical to the Greek sense of 'mystery'. In Jesus' time, the Gentile world, so to speak, was rife with religions involving secrets, including secret oaths, as well as secret beliefs and practices. This, however, is a far cry from the theological meaning of 'sacrament', to wit, an outward or visible sign of an inward or spiritual grace. Bentham regarded this use of the concept in the Catechism as a pure invention, a contrivance foisted upon Jesus, who entertained no such thought or intention when he practiced baptism or caused others to practice it. Exactly the same, Bentham believed, was true of the Lord's Supper. Mystagogues had changed both practices long before belief therein was required of unfledged Anglicans.

44. John's baptism was a baptism of immersion in water for the repentance of sins (see Matt. 3:11, Mark 1:4, Luke 3:7, 16). However, from the theological perspective of the two natures in Jesus Christ, that is, true man and true God, there could have been no reason for him to repent. So why should he have wanted to be baptized? Matthew solves this sort of problem by having Jesus say that he was submitting to John's baptism to fulfill all righteousness. But we are never told what this means. Only the Gospel of John fails to assert categorically that Jesus was baptized by John the Baptist (see John 1:29–34), yet his is the only Gospel that asserts that Jesus himself baptized (3:22), yet did not baptize (4:2). Whether or not Jesus actually baptized initiates into his movement or merely presided over their baptism, there is no prima facie indication that his baptizing was different from John's. This in spite of the fact that John the Baptist is made to prophesy that the one coming after him who was greater than he (i.e., Jesus) would baptize with the Holy Spirit and with fire (Matt. 3:11). A great deal of hyperbole can be seen in this prophesy. The movements of John the Baptist and Jesus existed side-by-side, each with its ceremony of inclusion.

45. See Mark 1:9 for Jesus' baptism by John; see Matt. 28:19–20 for Jesus' baptism of converts.

46. Bentham was largely but not totally correct in this criticism. Although catechumens are routinely baptized in the Church of England by the pouring of some pure water on the heads thereof, immersion in the baptismal font can be elected and is permitted as an alternative method. See the instructions for baptism in *The Book of Common Prayer*. The New Testament, however, suggests no such alternatives, nor is any election of a method different from total immersion hinted at. *Baptizō* means 'to dip repeatedly or to dip under'; *baptisma* means 'that which is dipped'; *baptismos* means 'a dipping in water or baptism'; and *baptistēs* means 'one who dips things', for example a dyer. It is to be expected that a dyer of cloth is going to dip entire pieces, not fractions thereof (see the *GEL*). The *GELNT* claims that baptism by pouring was sometimes allowed in cases of necessity, but the fact remains that neither the New Testament in general nor the Gospels in particular hints at the pouring or sprinkling of water as acceptable alternatives to total immersion. From Bentham's point of view, nothing could be more trifling than baptism, but it was not trifling to him that a religious body claiming to be Christian should ignore the New Testament on baptism and substitute an imaginary alternative for it.

47. Bentham's analyses of what to him were Questions 16 and 17 of the Catechism are very complicated and made doubly difficult by the style of his writing. The following historical sketch should make matters clearer. John the Baptist came preaching a baptism that was to be preceded by the repentance of sins. There is no indication that infants and those of diminished responsibility were enticed or accepted by John. Repentance and baptism were for the forgiveness of sins, a presumed benefit in view of the wrath to come that John predicted (see Matt. 3:1–12, Mark 1:4–8, and Luke 3:2–20). As already noted, only in the Gospel of John is Jesus pictured as baptizing (3:22) or associating himself with baptizing (4:2). Moreover, no conditions precedent to baptism are prescribed in John. These may have been similar to those of John the Baptist, at the outset at least. Morton Smith has argued persuasively that Jesus came to practice a secret baptism, open only to members of

his inner circle; see *The Secret Gospel* (New York: Harper and Row, 1973), esp. chap. 12. In any case, Acts 2:38 portrays Peter as saying to interested parties, "Repent and be baptized every one of you in the name of Jesus Christ for the remission of sins, and ye shall receive the gift of the Holy Ghost." Neither in John 3:22 or 4:2 nor in Acts 2:38 is faith emphasized, but it must be supposed to have accompanied repentance. Sins (rather than sin, which is discussed more below) implies multiple wrongdoings of which individual adults were able to repent. Once again, neither infants nor those of diminished responsibility are represented as candidates for baptism. Although 'sin(s)', 'repentance', and 'faith' had not changed by Bentham's time, the conditions for baptism had changed enormously and had done so centuries earlier. Those who had faith in Jesus, repented their sins, and were baptized believed themselves to have been inoculated against any divine wrath to come. It was (and is) natural that such believers would also wish to inoculate their children. Infant baptism, no doubt, began early in Christian history and in multiple places. Meanwhile, St. Paul was changing the equation. It was not that many sins might lead to a more or less permanent state of sinfulness, but, rather, that the state of Sin into which one was born led to individual sins (see Rom. 5:12–21 and 1 Cor. 15:21–22). From such passages in Paul came the doctrines of original sin and total depravity. The doctrine of original sin maintains that all human beings are born into a state of Sin, a state inaugurated by Adam and Eve when they ate the forbidden fruit, thus committing the original sin. The doctrine of total depravity maintains that the whole progeny of Adam and Eve (i.e., everybody) is born into a condition of depravity from which individual sins emanate; see the appropriate entries in the *ODCC* or another relevant work. The author(s) of the Anglican Catechism, like many earlier theologians, retained the words of the aggregation of adults into Jesus' movement, that is, 'faith', 'repentance', and 'baptism', but focused these on infants and conceived of a state of Sin preceding individual sins. Since infants, a week or so old, can know nothing of an alleged state of Sin into which they have been born, they are incompetent to repent of it, and since they have committed no individual sins knowingly, cannot repent of these either, nor can they have faith in this, that, or the other. They can, however, be baptized, either by being immersed in water properly or by having some thrown in their faces improperly. Since baptism in the New Testament never precedes faith and repentance, others (who are adult) must have faith, profess repentance, and accept the promise of salvation on behalf of the infants in question; hence the emergence of godparents as sureties, more or less, for uncomprehending infants who are about to encounter baptismal or pseudobaptismal water. Muddy, indeed, are the waters that lead to such muddles.

48. In the New Testament, it is noteworthy that none of Jesus' disciples nor any of his emissaries (i.e., apostles) is ever portrayed as being a priest or as one carrying out priestly functions.

49. Here Bentham had surplice fees in mind. The *OED* defines these as the dues received by the incumbent (of a parish) for the performance of marriages, burials, and other ministerial offices. He might also have discerned another evil but did not. In addition to being able to charge the incompetent many (the laity) for holy ministrations, the competent few (the clergy) can exercise power by debarring persons from participating in the sacraments, especially the Lord's Supper or

Eucharist. This is the power of excommunication, a power Bentham would surely have scorned; see the appropriate entry in the *ODCC*.

50. See Matt. 26:26–27, Mark 14:22–23, and Luke 22:17–20.

51. Here Bentham failed to distinguish finely enough between the doctrine and practice of the Roman Catholic Church and the doctrine and practice of the Anglican. The Twenty-eighth Article indicts the Church of Rome for departing from the scriptures in believing that the Eucharistic bread is transubstantiated into Christ's flesh, the wine into his blood. Such a repugnant notion, it claims, can lead to superstition. The Anglican Church (on the contrary, but ever so slightly) subscribes to the doctrine of the Real Presence. As the term 'Real Presence' implies at the prima facie level, this doctrine claims that the body and blood of Christ are actually present (mystically?) in the consecrated Sacrament but not by transubstantiation magically. The Anglican doctrine of the Real Presence has never been articulated definitively and remains ambiguous; see the *ODCC*, s. v. "Eucharist" and "Real Presence."

52. Whereas the doctrine of Transubstantiation holds that the consecrated bread becomes in substance the flesh of Christ without losing the appearance (or secondary qualities) of bread, and that the wine becomes in substance the blood of Christ without losing the secondary qualities of wine, the Lutheran doctrine of Consubstantiation holds that the bread and wine, though remaining what they are, are conjoined with the body and blood of Christ into a new unity; see the *ODDC*, s. v. "Transubstantiation" and "Consubstantiation," or a similar reference work. Bentham still failed to recognize the ambiguous Anglican doctrine of the Real Presence of Christ in the Eucharist (John R. H. Moorman, *The Anglican Spiritual Tradition* [Springfield, IL: Templegate, 1983], pp. 27, 122). Had he been aware of it, he would have reviled it and execrated any requirement of children in having to say that they believed in it.

53. For example, in 1 Cor. 15:35–38, Paul addresses the question of how the dead are to be raised. Arrogantly, he cites an old wives' tale to the effect that sown grain cannot come to life unless it first dies (mentioned earlier). Jesus is reported in John 12:24 to have uttered the same chestnut. But, lo and behold! it is false that seeds die before they live again, yet we are assured of its spiritual truth.

Chapter 8

A Defense

On more than a dozen points, Bentham's attack on the Anglican Catechism needs no defense, because it is true. In direct opposition to Matthew 5:34 and James 5:12, which forbid the swearing of oaths, Anglicans swear oaths as godparents in an attempt at saddling infants with religious obligations. With no biblical warrant, they vow that the infants in question shall come to believe in doctrines that neither infants nor children (nor adults for matter) can understand. The doctrine of the Trinity is a notorious example of an unintelligible dogma, as is the doctrine of the two natures (one divine, the other human) in the one person, Jesus Christ. Moreover, godparents swear that infants and small children shall love the appropriate religious object(s) without showing that such an emotion as love is ever under the control of will or that it can be subjected to any kind of obligation or sanction. Compared to these vain attempts at swearing promissory oaths for others to keep, it is a small issue, no doubt, that young Anglicans-in-the-making must swear to believe in doctrines that are not in the Catechism and, moreover, that they must believe in the Catechism even when it contradicts the Thirty-nine Articles.

Furthermore, though Anglicans teach the Ten Commandments to their children, they misappropriate the First and flout the Second. More egregious is their disregard of the New Testament, a prima facie reading of which indicates through silence that Jesus instituted no sacraments as understood and promulgated by Anglicans. They baptize children prior to faith in Jesus and before the repentance of sins can occur (both of which are directly opposite to New Testament texts), routinely use a method of so-called baptism that disregards the Greek meaning of the word, and claim falsely that water is the outward sign of this so-called sacrament. As for the Lord's Supper, Anglicans attach accessory duties to the partaking thereof, something not warranted by the New Testament, claim to *remember* Jesus when participating in it (something no Anglican can do), and claim falsely that bread and wine are the outward signs of the alleged inner benefits of the so-called sacrament, a misrepresentation of the Gospel record. Since mendacity is the hallmark of the Anglican Catechism, it should surprise no one that it falsifies history by incorporating the so-called Apostles' Creed, a verbal contrivance in which no emissary (i.e., apostle) of Jesus participated.

There is, however, a different class of criticisms in *CECE* that might appear, at first blush, to need defense. At points, Bentham seems merely to have been muttering contemptuously at Christianity in general and at Anglicanism in particular, but not so. After an exposition of the philosophy of language that lies behind this class of criticisms, it will be evident that he kept his biggest guns in reserve, preferring, for whatever reason, to devastate the Anglican Catechism with lesser arms. The few who know what these biggest guns consist of will also know that he hinted at them frequently as he dismantled the Catechism. A list of the hints in question should prove instructive.

In his analysis of the Catechism's third question, together with its dictated answer, Bentham questioned how the Anglican-in-the-making could *renounce the Devil and all his works*. How, he wondered, did 'Devil' differ from 'Jupiter' or 'Juno', or the alleged works of the one from the alleged works of the others? In the commandment to rehearse the Apostles' Creed (following the Catechism's fourth question and answer), Bentham found words, such as 'holy', which he said have no meaning at all, vacuous words strung upon other vacuous words, the recitation of which commits one to babbling. The apex of such imbecility occurs when thinking or uttering "Holy Spirit." In the Catechism's eighth question and answer, he found a suspect assemblage of words, composed of 'heart', 'mind', 'soul', and 'strength', with no attempt (on the part of the catechist) at distinguishing any one of these from the others nor any attempt at determining precisely to what each term refers.

Likewise, in his analysis of the Catechism's tenth question and answer, he demoted 'grace' to being a mere expletive. In his criticism of the Catechism's twelfth question and answer, he indicted 'sacrament' for being nothing more than a manufactured box (or pigeonhole) into which the misunderstood rites of baptism and the Lord's Supper could be dumped. This pigeonhole was designed to contain so-called holy things, that is, certain objects, places, beliefs, and practices important to Christianity, but, sad to say, no attempt was made (by the Catechism's creator[s]) at describing or defining the property of holiness. What, for example, makes water holy on some occasions and not on others? Always invoking the holy, as it does, Christian theology could be no more than a sham science, a suspect body of information, better denominated as misinformation.

Finally, he also noted that the concept of Transubstantiation (in the nineteenth and twentieth questions and answers) required a denial of one's sensory experiences. To several of the senses, the communion bread remains bread with all its ordinary properties and the wine remains wine. What, then, can 'Transubstantiation', 'Consubstantiation', or 'Real Presence' (to add the name of the Anglican doctrine of the Lord's Supper) be but mere words, words, words referring to vagrant concepts, muddled to boot? In the Catechism's twenty-first question and answer (as in the fourth above), Bentham came upon 'spiritual', supreme among weasel words. For this word and its kin, that is, 'spirit', 'spiritually', and 'spirituality', he saved his greatest scorn, as will be amply documented below.

There is no better way to discern the biggest guns, kept in reserve, than to quote two passages, well known to Bentham scholars:

> What we are continually talking of, merely from our having been continually talking of it, we imagine we understand; so close a union has habit connected between words and things, that we take the one for the other; when we have words in our ears we imagine we have ideas in our minds. When an unusual word presents itself, we challenge it; we examine it ourselves to see whether we have a clear idea to annex to it; but when a word that we are familiar with comes across us, we let it pass under favour of old acquaintance.[54]

> By habit, whenever a man sees a *name*, he is led to figure himself a corresponding object, of the reality of which the *name* is accepted by him, as it were of course, in the character of a *certificate*. From this delusion, endless is the confusion, the error, the dissension, the hostility, that has been derived.[55]

In the two quotations above lie not only profound insights into human psychology and use of language but also, in embryonic stage, a profound critique of all religions and theologies.

Put most broadly and perhaps crudely, it is one situation when people come upon something experienced in common and agree on giving it a name; it is a situation quite different when people come upon a familiar name and then go in search of that whose name it is—or is presumed to be. In the first situation, the thing is at hand and awaits a name, as it were. In the second situation, the name is at hand, but that which is being named is not at hand or, at least to all appearances, is not.

Whenever names (i.e., certain sounds in the air or marks on or in writing materials) are automatically taken to imply existence, word magic results. To keep from being deceived by word magic, Bentham undertook an extensive analysis of the part of speech he called the "noun-substantive." In grammatical terms, a noun-substantive is a name (acting as the subject of a declarative sentence) that (merely by being communicated) routinely presupposes, assumes, implies, or asserts existence. Once posited as existing, the named item awaits predication by the verbal, adjectival, and adverbial parts of the rest of the sentence in which it occurs. The problem is that noun-substantives are promiscuous. No flag or other indicator accompanies them to reveal what sort of entity is being named on any given occasion. A noun-substantive may, for example, name psychic phenomena, physical objects, mathematical operations, chemical processes, or figments of imagination (theoretical or mythological), with no indication as to which is which.

To illustrate, many in the Western world assume they know that Henry Morton Stanley hailed David Livingston, in darkest Africa, with the words, "Dr. Livingston, I presume." Many in the Western world also assume they know that the angel Gabriel hailed a virgin named Mary with the words, "Hail, thou that art highly favoured, the Lord is with thee" (Luke 1:28). The names above (in this case proper names) are helpless by themselves to determine the existence of the personage(s) named or the historicity implied by the words spoken. Stanley's greeting to Livingston is, however, grammatically similar to Gabriel's Annunciation to the Virgin Mary.

In his attempt at minimizing, if not eliminating, the hocus-pocus inherent in language, Bentham chose 'entity' (and its plural form) as the least revealing noun-substantive available. Here, "least revealing" means about what modern logicians mean by making as slight an ontological commitment as possible, *if any at all*, when asserting something or other about the subject of a declarative sentence.[56] Minimal ontological commitment (and the logical importance thereof) will become clear as the exposition to follow unfolds. Next, Bentham had to flesh out what he meant by 'entity' (or 'entities'). He did this by determining how many kinds there were to which names could be annexed. It is not necessary here to give an exposition of his entire taxonomy of names and their corresponding entities; it suffices to present just enough so that the reader can understand what he was attempting to do and to grasp how he brought his philosophy of language to bear on religion and theology.[57]

The fundamental bifurcation he made resulted in perceptible entities and inferential entities. A perceptible entity is any individual, discrete item of potential sensation detectable through seeing, hearing, tasting, touching, scenting, or some combination thereof.[58] Bentham used 'body' to name any external item presenting itself to sensuous human experience.[59]

If or when a line of reasoning persuades a person of the existence of something or other not generally, if ever, detectable by sense experience, that nonempirical item is an inferential entity.[60] Bentham never demanded formal validity of any line of reasoning leading to belief in a particular inferential entity; only that the reflective process at issue be persuasive to the individual whose reflective process it was (or is). Since normal human beings have much in common, it should be expected that what is persuasive reflection to one person may also be persuasive to others.

Inferential entities are either human or superhuman. "A human inferential entity," wrote Bentham, "is the soul considered as existing in a state of separation from the body."[61] Though not flatly denying that such an inferential entity could be seen, Bentham thought that no reputable person in his day would, upon rigorous interrogation, claim to have seen a soul. In any case, 'ghost' would be the appropriate denomination of a separable human soul, separated in fact from its body and capable of moving about.[62]

A superhuman inferential entity is either supreme or subordinate.[63] The supreme superhuman inferential entity is of course named 'God' in English. That this inferential entity remains unseen not only conforms to human experience but is also sanctioned, according to Bentham, by revelation in the New Testament, that is, by the religion of Jesus and by St. Paul.[64] It was a useful ploy to let Christian teaching help him make the point that God is an *inferential* entity—one not *known* to exist. Undoubtedly, there have been millions of people who have been persuaded of the existence of God by reflection and various attempts at proof. In Bentham's terms, this was (and is) sufficient to establish God as an inferential entity. It should also be remembered that he was content to treat God in the *AINR* as possibly a real entity, even though an entity very different in character from what is normally assumed of deity by the general run of theists. Those who are unpersuaded (by any and all means) that there is a supreme superhuman inferential entity are left, perforce, with the category of nonbeing.[65]

A subordinate superhuman inferential entity is either good or bad, a good one being called an angel, a bad one, a devil. Thus did Bentham provide for the whole heavenly host plus separable human souls. He thought it unproductive to dwell further on the nature of such inferential, pneumatic entities as these.[66]

Having rid himself of the realm of dubious entities or potential entities, Bentham next turned to the sphere of real, that is, of perceptible, entities: "A real entity is an entity to which, on the occasion and for the purpose of discourse, existence is really meant to be ascribed."[67] Perceptible entities come in two types, the physical and the psychical. The realm of physically substantial entities consists of all those bodies around and about us that can be items of sensory experience. Psychical experiences are no less real. These consist of "individual perceptions of all sorts: the impressions produced in groups [i.e., in bundles] by the application of sensible objects to the organs of sense; the ideas brought to view by the recollection of those same objects; [and] the new ideas produced under the influence of imagination, by the decomposition and recomposition of those groups." Bentham also included "the exercise of the art of logic" among psychic realities.[68]

Before turning to his bifurcative method that leads to the all-important category of fictitious entities, the bastard category of fabulous entities demands attention. This category is abnormal in that it does not stem from any line of bifurcative thinking. It simply appears and in doing so poses the threat of confusion with the category of fictitious entities. Wrote Bentham, "Fabulous entities, whether fabulous persons or things, are supposed material objects, of which the separate existence is capable of becoming a subject of belief, and of which, accordingly, the same sort of picture is capable of being drawn in and preserved in the mind, as of any really existent object. Examples would be such imaginary persons as 'Heathen gods, Genii, Fairies, kings such as Brute and Fergus, animals such as dragons and chimeras, countries such as El Dorado, seas such as the Straights of Arrian, and fountains, such as the fountain of Jouvence."[69]

Lest there be confusion between fabulous and fictitious entities, it is imperative to note that the former are always iconic (i.e., picturable and memorable as such), whereas the latter never are, always being abstract.[70] In addition to bastardy in the origin of fabulous entities, there is also miscegenation, for they intermingle with the names of real entities in the sober writing of history and in the imaginative writing of historical fiction.

Whenever the empirical presentation of real entities to a human mind or the ratiocinative presentation of inferential entities to it are not at being contrasted, the fundamental bifurcation is between real entities and fictitious ones.[71] The twelve following brief quotations let Bentham speak for himself about fictitious entities and their supreme importance:

1. Language is the sign of thought, an instrument for the communication of thought from one mind to another.[72]
2. It is only by the means of *names*, viz. *simple* or *compound* that things are susceptible of arrangement.[73]
3. Every fictitious entity bears some relation to a real entity.[74]
4. To language then—to language alone—it is, that fictitious entities owe their existence—their impossible, yet indispensable existence.[75]
5. Abstract entities can no otherwise be expressed than by fiction.[76]
6. Lamentable have been the confusions and darkness produced by taking the names of *fictitious* for the names of *real* entities.[77]
7. Coeval with the very first steps that can be taken in the endeavour to give clear explanation of the nature of language, must be the intimation given to the distinction between real and fictitious entities, and the correspondent distinction between the names of real and the names of fictitious entities.[78]

8. By a fictitious entity, understand an object, the existence of which is feigned by the imagination—feigned for the purpose of discourse, and which when so formed, is spoken of as a real one.[79]
9. A fictitious entity is an entity to which, though by the grammatical form of discourse employed in speaking of it, existence be ascribed, yet in truth and reality existence is not meant to be ascribed.[80]
10. *Fictitious* . . . entities . . . could not be spoken of at all, if they were not spoken of as *real* ones.[81]
11. In the mind of all [people], fiction, in the logical sense, has been the coin of necessity.[82]
12. To say that, in discourse, fictitious language ought never, on any occasion, to be employed, would be as much as to say that no discourse in the subject of which the operations, or affections, or other phenomena of the mind are included, ought ever to be held. . . ."[83]

Except for those noun-substantives that mistakenly name nonentities and for those that name fabulous entities, all noun-substantives that do not name real entities name fictitious ones.[84] The noun-substantives that name fictitious entities are legion. Before listing some of these that Bentham specifically mentioned, a caveat is in order: "Of fictitious entities, whatsoever is predicated is not, consistently with strict truth, predicated (it then appears) of anything but their respective names."[85] In short, the name of any fictitious entity is identical with that entity, when, but only when, properly conceived.

All of the following are fictitious entities or the names thereof: Nature;[86] logical wholes, aggregations, sorts, kinds;[87] kingdom, class, order, genus, species, variety;[88] the Crown, the Church, the Law, the Court, Property;[89] quantity, quality, relation, place, time, motion, rest, action, passion, possession;[90] inertia, friction, gravitation;[91] necessity, impossibility, certainty, uncertainty, probability, improbability, potentiality, actuality;[92] mind,[93] attention,[94] intentions, affections, motives;[95] a faculty (i.e., an intellectual power);[96] obligation, duties,[97] rights (natural, moral, religious);[98] political causes such as command, prohibition, inhibition, pardon, license, warrant, political effects such as exemption, privilege, prerogative, possession, physical and legal;[99] and Law of Nature (i.e., natural law) and the Original Contract.[100] When one adds to this impressive list all the names of qualities, properties, and attributes (including virtually all names in English ending in '-ness' and '-ity'), one has an enormous number of fictitious entities with which to deal and of which to be wary.[101]

Two examples should suffice to help the reader grasp what Bentham was getting at relative to fictitious entities. First, Bentham did not deny that all bodies move, but he did deny that there is any such *thing* as motion, that is, any such object or any such real entity.[102] Although motion cannot exist apart from bodies that are moving, people are obliged to speak of it as though it were a substance.[103] Even worse, whenever a body is said to be put in (or into) motion, a receptacle of some sort is implied. Bentham wrote, "A body is said to be in motion. This taken in the literal sense, is as much as to say, here is a body, called a motion; *in* this larger body, the other body, namely, the really existing body [that is said to be moving], is contained.[104] Since motions come in varieties such as rectilineal and circular and in degrees of speed, named, for example, "slowness and quickness, etc.," there must be a fictitious entity called mobility (a fictitious entity at the *second* remove from the motions of individual moving objects) to compass motion, a fictitious entity at the *first* remove.[105]

Second, there is no such *thing* as a natural right. Put differently, there is no natural guarantee that human beings may do and be what they wish to do and be (assuming no infringement on the "natural rights" of others) simply because they are born and remain human. To believe in natural rights is to believe in "nonsense on stilts."[106] This does not deny that there can be legal (i.e., posited) rights, but these exist only as long as there is a government willing to maintain them for its citizens. "The rights of the governed," wrote Bentham, "and the rights of the government grow up together; the same cause which creates the one creates the other."[107] The following three quotations from *Pannomial Fragments* let him speak his mind eloquently on the subject:

> It is not the rights of man which causes government to be established:— on the contrary, it is the non-existence of those rights. What is true is, that from the beginning of things it has always been desirable that rights should exist—and *that* because they do not exist; since, so long as there are no rights, there can only be misery upon the earth—no sources of political happiness, no security for person, for abundance, for subsistence, for equality. (p. 219)

> The word right, is the name of a fictitious entity: one of those objects, the existence of which is feigned for the purpose of discourse, by a fiction so necessary, that without it human discourse could not be carried on.
>   A man is said to have it, to hold it, to possess it, to acquire it, to lose it. It is thus spoken of as though it were a portion of matter such as a man may take into his hand, keep it for a time and let it go again. According to a phrase more common in law language than in ordinary language, a man is even spoken of as being invested with it. Vestment is clothing: invested with it makes it an article of clothing, and is as much as to say is clothed with it. (p. 218)

> A man is never the better for having such natural right: admit that he has it, his condition is not in any respect different from what it would be if had it not. (ibid.)

Whenever the name of a fictitious entity appears as the noun-substantive of an assertion (i.e., as the subject of a declarative sentence) or as the direct object of a sentence, literal truth cannot be communicated. There are, however, many occasions on which it is important, even imperative, to know the literal truth about some state of affairs or other. This raises the question as to whether or not there is any technique useful in translating assertions containing the names of one or more fictitious (i.e., abstract) entities into assertions containing, as nearly as possible, the names of real entities. Bentham thought, "[I]t ought to be possible to decipher such language into the language of pure and simple truth—into that of fact." Put differently, "To understand abstract terms is to know how to translate figurative language into language without figure."[108]

He called his technique for such translation "exposition by paraphrasis." Paraphrasis, however, does not consist simply in substituting a word (or phrase) in one sentence with its synonym in a second sentence, nor is it paraphrasing willy-nilly. This will never do, because synonymy will result merely in substituting one name of a fictitious entity for another name of the same entity. The point is to rid oneself of abstract terms as nearly as possible and to do so using a precise, logical procedure. He defined paraphrasis as follows:

> A word may be said to be expounded by *paraphrasis*, when not that *word* alone is translated into other words, but some *whole sentence*, of which it forms a part, is translated into another *sentence*; the words of which latter are expressive of such ideas as are *simple* [i.e., not compound or complicated] or are more immediately resolvable into simple ones than those of the former. . . . This, in short, is the only method in which any abstract terms can, at the long run, be expounded to any instructive purpose; that is in terms calculated to raise *images* either of *substance* perceived, or of *emotions*;—sources, one or the other of which every idea must be drawn from, to be a clear one.[109]

Hand in glove with paraphrasis comes what Bentham called archetypation.[110] This consists in finding at least one real entity that acts as a paradigm for deriving some particular name of a fictitious entity. On more than one occasion, he used 'obligation' as an example of how an abstract idea in religion, morality, and law is derived from real psychic entities. The root of 'obligation' in experience and its etymological root in Latin are far from being the same, but they work in concert, as is often the case. The real psychic entities that underlie 'obligation' are the sensations of pleasure and pain: "[T]he emblematic, or archetypal image, is that of a man lying down, with a heavy load pressing upon him, to wit, in such a sort as either to prevent him from acting at all, or so ordering matters that if so it be that he does act, it cannot be in any other direction or manner than the direction or manner in question,—the manner or direction requisite."[111] In short, in a given instance of behavior, wherein moral or legal sanctions are applied, the individual is constrained from doing thus and so or is required to do this or that upon the pains of punishment. Compliance with the relevant sanction(s) rewards one by enabling one to avoid the pains of social or legal disapprobation, or by realizing the pleasures of approbation, or both.

The etymological root of 'obligation' is different, yet related. It comes from the Latin *ligo*, which means 'to bind, bind together, tie, harness, unite, or connect.'[112] Bentham observed that here the experiential archetype was a cord, tie (rope), or band.[113] 'Etymologization' was his name for the various processes whereby the roots of words proliferate into inflected forms and conjugates.[114] For example, consider how Latin *ligo* finds its way into the following incomplete list of related words: The verbs 'oblige', 'obligated', 'am obliged', and 'was obliged'; the adjectives 'obligative', 'obligatory', and 'obliging'; the adverbs 'obligatorily' and 'obligedly'; the nouns 'obligedness', 'obligee', 'obligor', and, most surprising of all, 'religion'!

Over and again, Bentham generalized the pattern above from the names of real entities to the names of fictitious ones:

> There is no name of a psychical entity, which is not also the name of a physical entity, in which capacity alone it must have continued to be employed, long before it was transferred to the field of psychical entities and made to serve in the character of a name of a psychical and most commonly a fictitious entity.[115]

> Almost all names, employed in speaking of the phenomena of the mind, are names of fictitious entities. In speaking of any *pneumatic* (or say *immaterial* or *spiritual*) object, no name has ever been employed, that had not first been employed as the name of some *material* (or say *corporeal*) one.[116]

Examples of what Bentham had in mind are easy to find. To illustrate, consider the Greek root *hag*, which means to 'stand in awe of, to dread, or reverence'. From it comes the Greek, *hagios*, 'holy or saintly', and from thence come the English words 'Hagiographa', 'hagiographer', 'hagiographic', 'hagiology', 'hagioscope', and 'hagioscopic'. Or, take the Greek root *anch*, which means 'to squeeze, press tightly, or cause pain by strangling'. From it come our words 'anguish' and 'anxious'. The third example is of especial interest to me, because it shows how my given name was derived. From the Greek root *di*, which means 'to be bright, shine, or gleam' come the Greek words *delos* (also 'Delos'), which means 'light, clear, evident', and *dios*, meaning 'divine or deity'.[117]

Only one name remains to be examined before returning to Bentham's attack on the Catechism and the Thirty-nine Articles of Religion, an attack less trenchant than he could have made it. It is the name 'nonbeing'. This word names no entity; it stands, rather, for absence, for the inability to denote anything or to refer to any referent.[118] When a person conceives of various attributes, qualities, or characteristics, and when that person has the appropriate names for these attributes, qualities, or characteristics at verbal disposal, yet cannot bring them to focus on anything or find any core around which they may coalesce, as it were, or in which they may inhere, the appropriate name is 'nonbeing'. The name 'nonentity' can also serve, as can 'nothingness'. "Nothing," wrote Bentham, "has no properties."[119]

With this, we return to certain less than explicit criticisms in *CECE* that could have been made fully explicit. In his analysis of the Catechism's third question and its dictated answer, Bentham questioned how the Anglican-in-the-making could "renounce the Devil and all his works." How, he wondered, did 'Devil' differ from 'Jupiter' or 'Juno', or the alleged works of the one from the alleged works of the others? This was a veiled invitation to Anglicans (extending from the Archbishop of Canterbury, to the magisterial theologians of the Church and on to its lowliest catechists) to confront his philosophy of language. Could any ecclesiastic with the wit to understand the relevant aspects of this philosophy have found a mistake of fact undergirding it? Could any such worthy have found logical errors in it? Could Bentham's philosophy of language have been found unsound for any reason? Perhaps, but not likely at the time. Would any Anglican have been so foolish as to contend that 'Devil' or 'Satan' names a real entity of the bodily sort? If so, a severe, if not insuperable, challenge would have awaited.

In the context of one his expositions of nonentities, he wrote, "In the house designated by such a number, [naming it] in such a street, in such a town, lives a being called the Devil, having a head, body, and limbs, like a man's—horns like a goat's—wings like a bat's, and a tail like a monkey's."[120] Where shall arrogant catechists and hapless catechumens alike go to meet this creature? In the case of Zeus (Jupiter) and Hera (Juno), one would at least know where to go. One would ascend Mount Olympus and, not finding them there nor their ambrosia eaten, would await their return. The wait, of course, would have been very long, so long that their total absence there and elsewhere would have conduced to rendering these names the names of nonentities. As Bentham pointed out in *CECE*, no Christian nowadays believes these names ever to have named real entities. How is it different with 'Satan'?

If learned clergymen say that 'Devil' names a being that lives in Hell, the problem for them begins anew. Where shall one look to find Hell? If they say that Bentham himself allowed for inferred entities of both good and bad subordinate pneumatic varieties, it must be pointed out that he was speaking in the context of arguments that were persuasive to some people, not of arguments that were compelling to all.[121] The simple fact is that in some cases, at least, the names of inferred entities eventuate in naming only nonentities. This is clearly true of the names of such fabulous entities as Jupiter and Juno. Moreover, if theologians say that 'Devil' never named a physical entity anyway, but rather a spiritual (or pneumatic) one, more grief awaits them, as we shall see.

In reciting the Apostles' Creed, as the Catechism bids them do, catechumens cannot avoid the suspect word 'holy'. This adjective reaches the apex of imbecility when compounded with 'spirit', as in 'Holy Spirit'. For all practical purposes, 'holy' means 'sacred' and vice versa. 'Holy' and 'sacred', as adjectives, appear to refer to some sort of quality, property, or attribute, and 'the holy' and 'the sacred', as noun-substantives, appear to name some kind of entity, but what kind? Leaving probing questions about holiness and its attributes until later, we must now rely on archetypation to grasp the second half of the compound term 'Holy Spirit'.

Spiro, in Latin, means a gentle blowing, or stirring of the air. *Spirare* means to breathe. From this simple root come such compound forms as 'aspire', which initially meant 'to breathe upon', 'inspire', which originally meant 'to breathe in', and 'expire', which originally meant 'to breathe out', and later, of course, 'to die'. That which is inhaled, and exhaled, and breathed upon others is called *spiritus*.[122] It is, in fact, the earth's atmosphere, composed largely of nitrogen, oxygen, argon, and carbon dioxide, and upon whose oxygen we depend for life.

By archetypation and paraphrasis, we arrive, breathlessly, at the recognition that the Holy Spirit is sacred gas![123] It is but a half-step from this to the related revelation that the doctrine of the Trinity can be reformulated as God the Father, God the Son, and God the Sacred Gas. Apparently, Bentham did not take this final half-step, but he was fully capable of having done so. Doing it for him, as I have just done, is fully in keeping with his "spirit," but not with any separable soul that might at one time have been uniquely associated with the physical body that was his.

Long before Christians began proclaiming their message in Greek and Latin, *pneuma* and *spiritus* had become inflated with metaphysical meanings. The largely parallel development of each term can be followed in the pre-Christian religious and philosophical literature of the Greeks and Romans. Beginning with the stirring of ordinary air and the breathing of it, this development moves to the breath of life, to the animating (or vital) principle of life, to the spiritedness (in emotional terms) of human beings (and animals), to the concept of spirit as a nonmaterial mode of substance, and finally to the immortal essence of the human being, something inferior to but still akin to the nonphysical Deity of Christianity and his quintessential Spirit. Such is word magic!

Much later, but harmoniously, Germanic roots provide German with *Geist* and English with 'ghost', each meaning 'breath, a blast (of air), an incorporeal being, a spirit (whether good or bad), and a (or the) soul in presumed separation from its body'.[124] Eventually, in the West, it becomes practically impossible to tell spirit from soul, soul from ghost, Holy Ghost from Holy Spirit, Holy Spirit from Sacred Gas, and Sacred Gas from Holy Atmosphere. Although the shock of equating 'Holy Spirit' and 'Holy Ghost' to 'Sacred Gas' and 'Holy Atmosphere' raises Christians' hackles, it need never have done so, had the church uniformly catechized its hapless catechumens with the Litany of Father, Son, and Sacred Gas, or Father, Son, and Holy Atmosphere. Each formulation makes as much sense as the other, and each can be equally useful religiously.

Christianity in general, and Anglicanism in particular, could have replaced the litany of Father, Son, and Holy Spirit (or Ghost) with the litany of Father, Son, and Sacred Gas (or Atmosphere) without detriment to the faith. All that would have been required would have been for dogmatists to dogmatize the latter formulary, for catechists to catechize it, for preachers to preach it, for chanters to chant it, for singers to sing it, for painters to paint it, for the pious to propagate it, for parents to promote it, for teachers to teach it, and for society to sanction it.[125] From continually hearing, 'Sacred Gas' and being forced to mouth it, little Anglicans-in-the-making will assume that they know what is being bandied about. By habit, they will associate words with things, and believe that for every name presented them, there is a corresponding object, certified simply by being named, especially in holy tones—even accompanied by music.

When Bentham turned to the Catechism's eighth question and answer, he found a suspect assemblage of words, composed of 'heart', 'mind', 'soul', and 'strength', with no attempt (on the part of the catechist) at distinguishing any one of these from the others, nor any attempt at determining precisely what is being named thereby. If, for example, 'heart' names an organ of a particular human body, then a real, physical entity exists. Even when the word is intended metaphorically, referring to somebody's individual emotions, real entities may be at issue, because the names of individual emotions name real psychical entities. If the word is intended to be figurative, then nobody knows what kind of entity it names. Learned theologians and catechists alike need to elucidate.

Bentham never denied that individual humans perceive sensations, think logically or illogically, recollect images and ideas, use imagination, foresee alternative futures, and do the sorts of things that "minds" do, but he denied that 'mind' names a real entity. 'Mind' names certain attributes of the human body whose "mind" it is and, as such, it names a fictitious entity.[126] To say that one has something *on* one's mind does not imply a platform of some sort or other; to get something *off* one's mind does not imply a launching pad; to have an idea *in* one's mind does not imply a receptacle; to convey information *to* another mind does not not imply travel to a destination; nor does the reception of information *from* another source imply that the receiving mind is a place.

Enough has been written above about spirits and ghosts to obviate any long examination here of what 'soul' names. To those who are convinced that they possess something very like the stirring of wind within their skins, 'soul' is the word, and it names an inferential entity. To those people (likely the same ones) who believe that this gaseous, pneumatic something or other is not only separable from their bodies, but also of the very essence of their conscious selves, and immortal to boot, 'ghost' is the name, and it names an inferential entity. There is, however, something jarring about being told to love the Bible-god with all one's heart, mind, and ghost. To those who are not persuaded that they have a soul, while alive, or that they will be a ghost after death, 'soul' and 'ghost' name nonentities.

'Strength' is a relative term that names some degree or other of energy or power. As such, being a variable attribute of some sort of agent, it can only name a fictitious entity. Being a relative term, applicable to an enormous range of possibilities, it cannot be added to a list of putative, real entities in such a way as to form a coherent list. The simple litany of 'heart', 'mind', 'soul', and 'strength' is anything but simple. There is more at issue here than the simple mistake of adding 'strength' to the list; there is profound uncertainty as to what is being named; and when there is profound uncertainty as to what is being named, nobody knows what is being talked about. One might as well try to add purple to four plus four and expect to derive a particular sum.

While examining the tenth question and answer of the Catechism, Bentham fell upon 'grace'. He promptly demoted this important theological term to the realm of redundant epithets. To illustrate, asking the Bible-god to be merciful toward oneself is equivalent to asking the Bible-god to be merciful toward oneself and to grant his grace. Should the mercy be forthcoming, getting the grace would add nothing. Had Bentham felt the need to justify this demotion, he could have brought the full force of his theory of language to bear upon it.

At the outset, it is instructive to discover what kinds of entities 'grace' does not name. 'Grace' does not name any real physical entity, nor does it name any real psychical entity. Moreover, it cannot name any fabulous entity, since there is nothing in its conception that can be pictured and remembered as such. This narrows the field to two: fictitious entities and nonentities. Here the *Book of Common Prayer* (of the Anglican Church) renders aid.[127] It says of its deity that it is his *property* always to have mercy, and it closely associates mercy with grace.[128] Moreover, it also calls him gracious.[129] Since 'gracious' is an adjective indicating an attribute of that to which the attribute is ascribed, it would appear that 'grace' names a fictitious entity. If so, this kind of entity can no more be separated from that of which it is an attribute than motion can be separated from bodies that move.

The *Book of Common Prayer* often makes it seem that there is an agency named 'grace', interposed between that which is named 'God' and the recipient of the (alleged) love that is named 'divine'.[130] However, it is never shown why the inferred Almighty Author of all creation should need intermediary agencies of any sort.[131] In summary, if the inference in the paragraph above is valid, then 'grace' names a fictitious entity; if invalid, a nonentity. In neither case can pious Anglicans receive something named by 'grace' additional to the individual benisons they are praying to acquire, such as being forgiven, uplifted, or redeemed.

The Catechism's twelfth question and answer raised the specter, to Bentham, of theological inventions, the so-called sacraments. To him, 'sacrament' merely named a holy box, as it were, or a sacred pigeonhole, in which to place baptism (originally a ceremony of aggregation into Jesus' movement) and the Lord's Supper (originally a ceremony of remembrance after his death). Inasmuch as water in the first "sacrament" and bread and wine in the second are involved, real physical entities are present. Inasmuch as believers have various experiences when being baptized and when participating in the Lord's Supper, real psychical entities are also present. The question is, what kind of a property is named by 'holy', what attribute or quality by its synonym 'sacred'? The Catechism never tells anyone but presumes that everyone knows. Bentham did not know and wanted elucidation.

His conviction that 'holy' and 'sacred' named a nonentity is easy to illustrate. Imagine, dear reader, that you possess a pyramidal prism and a crystal globe. Take these around the world and you will find that ordinary people, through sight or tactile experience, will be able to distinguish one from the other according to shape or figure, regardless of differences in language and culture. Next, take a fully grown, ripe eggplant and a ripe Concord grape to the members of any ethnic group on earth, and you will find that ordinary people will be able to discern the difference in size or in the space occupied by each. Then, take a solid silver letter opener and a bird's feather, about equal in length and breadth, and you will find that people everywhere will have no difficulty in discerning which item requires the greater energy to lift. Lastly, take a quart jar full of detritus and a quart jar full of water from the River Jordan. Upon being told the source of the water, many devotees of Catholicism and Eastern Orthodoxy (and maybe a few Protestants) will discern the property of holiness in the water, but the detritus will be seen as secular or profane, for want of better names. The devotees in question may wish to touch the hand that holds the jar of water, may wish to have some of it sprinkled on them, will hope to drink a bit of it, and will likely beseech it for blessings. Those who are not Christians, not Jews, and not Muslims will likely view the water as the muddy liquid it is, water that could have been taken from any of innumerable ordinary sources, will discern nothing holy in it, and will pay it no heed. Although the conception of and belief in the sacred (holy or taboo) is all but universal, no single thing will be agreed upon by all as possessing the (alleged) attribute named by 'sacred'.

The point is painfully clear. The fictitious entities of shape or figure, of volume, and of weight, for example, are all directly related to real entities. They are, in fact, abstractions from those entities. 'Holy', however, names no fictitious entity abstracted from any real entity. Moreover, it cannot be elucidated when defined by synonymy. It helps not at all to learn that being a holy object is the same as being a sacred one. Finally, 'holy' names nothing that implies a genus.[132] So, definition by genus and species (often very useful for elucidation) is impossible. Should the sagacious theologians of the Anglican Church wish to make clear any sentence including 'holy', 'sacred', or their derivatives, they will have to resort to paraphrasis. This they will find a risky business.

Judging by the number of times he turned to deal with it, Bentham found one use of 'holy' especially irksome, namely, its use in 'Holy Mother Church'. What a verbal horror this is, containing an adjective that refers to a nonentity being used to modify a fictitious entity! The Greek word *ekklesia*, from which come 'ecclesiastic', 'ecclesiastical', etc., originally meant 'to summon certain people to assemble, or to constitute an assembly'. The Christian assembly (i.e., those called out from the world) is now named in English by 'church', a term stemming from Greek *kuriakos* and common to the West Germanic family of languages. If understood as the collective name for all Christians, 'church' names a fictitious entity. If subdivisions within this class (taken as a genus) are allowed, then 'church', suitably modified, becomes the name of more than one species within this genus, as in Catholic church, Anglican church, Lutheran church, etc. But, whether genus or species, 'church' names a fictitious entity.

This, however, is but the beginning of the confusions attendant thereto. Under the heading, "Allegorical Idols—(*ad imaginationem*)," taken from his *Book of Fallacies*, Bentham wrote: "The significations indifferently attachable to the word *Church* are—1. Place of worship; 2. Inferior officers engaged by government to take a leading part in the ceremonies of worship; 3. All the people considered as worshipers; 4. The superior officers of government by whom the inferior, as above, are engaged and managed; 5. The rules and customs respecting those ceremonies."[133] Other complications arise when it is realized that 'church' may name "1. [T]he whole body of the persons thus governed [i.e., the laity]; 2. The whole body of the persons thus employed in the government of the rest [i.e., the hierarchy]; and,

3. The all-comprehensive body, or grand total, composed of the governed and governors, taken together."[134]

Of the "Allegorical Idols—(*ad imaginationem*)," mentioned above, Bentham wrote, "The use of this fallacy is the securing to persons in office, respect independent of good behaviour. . . . It consists in substituting for men's proper official denomination, the name of some fictitious entity, to whom by customary language, and thence opinion, the attribute of excellence has been attached."[135] In this artful manner, the often ignorant, fallible priests, bishops, archbishops, cardinals, or popes of the Catholic Church, for example, can hide behind the *infallible* Church.[136] Similarly, when corrupt, they can lurk behind the *incorruptible* Church. Most amazing is the magic that occurs when the members of the Catholic hierarchy, all males when taken individually, constitute a single sacred female when taken collectively, becoming "Holy *Mother* Church." Bentham observed, "Upon contemplating themselves altogether in the mirror of rhetoric, it was found that of all these males put together was composed the beautiful female, the worthy object of the associated affections of admiration, love, and respect—the Holy Mother Church."[137]

In the Catechism's nineteenth and twentieth questions and answers Bentham ran headlong into the names 'Transubstantiation' and 'Consubstantiation'. In light of his philosophy of language, what kinds of entities must such names name? Nonentities, of course! Had he cared to extend his reading beyond the Catechism to any of many weighty tomes of sacred theology, he would have come upon such names as the 'Immaculate Conception', 'substitutionary atonement', 'plenary inspiration of the Scriptures', 'Papal infallibility', 'predestination', 'purgatory', 'Hell', 'the Divine Economy', the 'double Procession of the Holy Ghost', the 'final conflagration', and 'Heaven', to mention but a few.

Had he also cared to look for the scriptural roots of these terms and their kin, he would have found such names as the 'serpent', the 'tempter', the 'forbidden fruit', 'original sin', 'expulsion from paradise', 'total depravity', 'the Noachian flood', the 'flight from Egypt', the 'burning bush', the 'Chosen People', the 'covenant', the 'redemption of Israel', the 'Annunciation', the 'Incarnation', the 'Firstborn of Creation', the 'Transfiguration', 'sanctification', 'eternal life', the 'Antichrist', '666', and the 'second coming', once again to mention the names of but a few.

Integratable with these, he would also have come upon a vast assemblage of names, such as 'Adam', 'Eve', 'Noah', 'Abraham', 'Joseph', 'Moses', 'David', 'Goliath', 'Solomon', 'Isaiah', 'Nehemiah', 'Ezra', 'John the Baptist', the 'angel Gabriel', 'Peter', 'Matthew', 'Judas', 'St. Paul', 'Beelzebub', and the 'man of lawlessness.' Again we must ask, what kind(s) of entities do these names name, real physical entities, real psychical entities, fictitious entities, fabulous entities, or nonentities?

Some of the many names above may name historical figures, however shadowy; some may name events claiming varying degrees of historicity, but in numerous cases, the names above name nothing, especially the names of alleged supernatural events and the theological doctrines based thereon.

For the vast majority of Christians, however, all the proper names above are taken to name real persons, natural or supernatural. All the names of the putative events above are presumed to name actual historical events, even when "miracles" have to be invoked to guarantee their historicity. All the names above having to do with the alleged fallen condition of human beings, the salvation of the saved, the damnation of the damned, and the life everlasting in heaven or hell are taken as factual. Faithful Christians never ask the kinds of questions about naming that Bentham asked. They live unselfconsciously in a vast *word world* created by the religion into which they are born and in which they are catechized or otherwise immersed. Those who convert to a particular faith in their maturity adopt its word world (hereafter referred to as WW) simultaneously with conversion.

Each religion, in fact, provides and requires a WW for and of its devotees, the differences between religions being to a considerable extent the differences in the vocabularies involved. A cursory knowledge of comparative religions will reveal that religious people, whatever their faith, take their religious WW as much for granted as the WW of everyday experience. As Bentham pointed out, when people keep hearing a word they have heard many times before, they believe they have an idea corresponding to it. They do not question familiar words as they might unfamiliar ones, and they assume that every noun-substantive, when looking and behaving like a name, grammatically speaking, must name something.

In his observations concerning the Catechism's twenty-first question and answer, Bentham became particularly vehement. With the use of the compound term 'spiritual sense', he had come upon the worst of word magic, namely, the ability to make the false (seem to be) true through language. He wrote in *CECE* as follows: "So convenient is the use—so admirable the virtue—of the word *spiritual*. By it whatsoever things are *false* may at pleasure be made *true*: false in a *carnal*—false in a *temporal* sense— yes, so let them be:—still, in a spiritual sense, they are not the less capable of being true: whereupon, in that purer and superior sense, if there be any *convenience* in their being true, true they are" (p. 68).

This is linguistic sleight-of-hand of the most pernicious sort, yet it is omnipresent in theology, in sermons, in religious education, and in the pious propaganda religions put forth in self-defense. It is, of course, pure rationalization. Religious people, it must be remembered, live in at least two WWs simultaneously; one, the WW of ordinary experience, and the other, the WW of their religion.[138] Many modern people live, perforce, in a third WW, that of elementary science and technology. In Benthamic terms, a religious WW is a mishmash of words naming variously real entities, fictitious entities, fabulous entities, and nonentities.[139]

Christianity illustrates the point nicely. Insofar as there are historical persons and events reported in the New Testament, the language of real entities is appropriate and available. The same is true of any psychological truths the New Testament may contain, however fancifully expressed in parables or allegories. Insofar as Christians wish to attribute qualities or properties (such as the sacred) to objects or ceremonies important to them, the vocabulary of fictitious entities is available, even though mistakenly so. Insofar as the Devil and his demons are at issue, there is the language of fabulous entities. Fabulous entities will not be recognized as such by the faithful but will be confused with real entities. Lastly, insofar as theological concepts are involved, such as those named by 'Transubstantion', 'Consubstantiation', or 'Real Presence', the language of nonentities is available, though neither recognized nor admitted as such.

The WW of Christianity, together with its messianism and the saga of salvation it proclaims (including the resurrection of the dead), constitutes the *accepted sacred story* of the West. Since this accepted sacred story (hereafter referred to as ASS) is taken to be divinely revealed, it cannot be mistaken. Conflicts, however, may arise between the sacred WW of any ASS and the other WWs in which people are required to live. This is particularly true of the WW of elementary modern science.[140] Apologists for the ASS of the West have at least three ploys to use in rationalizing their faith: (1) they can invoke miracles; (2) they can argue that appearances are not what they seem to be; and (3) they can rely on the "spiritual sense" of things.

The WW of ordinary experience has names for the never-married woman who gives birth to a child. She may be named 'single parent', 'slut', 'bitch', etc., and her offspring may be named 'illegitimate child', 'bastard', or 'mongrel'. The WW of Christian faith cannot permit such terms to be used of Jesus and his mother. Jesus, the son of Mary (Mark 6:3) and the presumed savior of all Christians, cannot have been born the bastard child of a loose woman.[141] The Blessed Virgin Mary (who never had carnal knowledge of any man) must therefore have conceived *miraculously*. By pious fraud, it can be contrived to have God the Father send God the Holy Ghost to overshadow her (however, precisely, this agency operates) and thus create God the Son incarnate (Matt. 1:20, Luke 1:35).

Since in the Roman Catholic version of the ASS of the West, Mary not only began life a virgin, but remained one perpetually, she cannot have known St. Joseph carnally, nor can the brothers and sisters of Jesus have been his blood relatives (Matt. 13:55–56, Mark 6:3). *Here things are not what they seem to be.* Joseph must have been married previously, and these so-called brothers and sisters must have been the children of another woman or of other women. Only metaphorically can they have been Jesus' brothers and sisters. Thus, the New Testament text does not mean what it seems to mean.

Last but not least, there is the ever-ready "spiritual sense" of things to invoke as needed. What, for example, is to be done nowadays with the New Testament idea that a seed must die before it can live again (1 Cor. 15:36, John 12:24)? This mistaken notion provides the paradigm for the death, burial, and resurrection of Jesus and is therefore an important paradigm. It was taken from the WW of ancient agriculture. But, regrettable as it may be, the DNA molecule (named in the modern scientific WW) has been shown to endure over vast periods of time. Since even very old seeds do not, in fact, have to die before they can germinate, the claim of St. Paul (and the same claim ascribed to Jesus by John) that they do die before they germinate must be true in a *"spiritual sense."* In similar fashion, it is unnerving to learn that the human embryo begins life as female and that the production of testosterone is needed to masculanize a fetus at later points in its development. If this is true, what is to be done with the biblical story of Adam's creation, implying the preeminence of the male human, and the subsequent creation of Eve from one of Adam's ribs, thus implying the subordination of the female (Gen. 2:21–24)? It will remain true, of course, but only in a *"spiritual sense."*

The etymological career of 'spirit' from being a noun which initially named an agitation of the air to becoming the adjective 'spiritual' which may mean anything desired, is breathtaking. In its latter form, when combined with 'sense', it can make the false true and the self-contradictory merely paradoxical—in the Christian WW at least. To some extent, Bentham himself was complicit in this breathtaking career, for he was willing to countenance the separation of substance into material and immaterial varieties. The former is known by empirical experience, as the reader will recall, whereas the latter is known (presumably) by ratiocination alone.[142] Bentham's ancestors and ours too did not arrive at the notion of immaterial substance by logical inference. They took it for granted from the moment they first intuited themselves to be dualistic creatures, that is, from the instant they distinguished (and later objectified through language) their "inner selves" of emotion, thought, intention, etc. from their external, material, physical bodies.[143]

It is not surprising that our remote ancestors took their nonflesh, nonblood minds to be as objectively real as their bodies, that they also anthropomorphized gods, angels, imps, animals, plants, and even inanimate objects dualistically, or that they looked for linguistic ways to objectify the elusive some *thing* or other (presumably) inside their skins.[144] Words for the airy, the atmospheric, the gaseous were prime candidates and readily available. Thus does the soul, spirit, or essence of the individual human being become associated with moving air and breath. Moreover, given the common desire to live on after this life, it is not surprising that the verbally objectified "immaterial substance" that (presumably) inhabits the material substance of individual human bodies should be separable from those bodies, movable, and immortal. That all of this is closely associated with religion is obvious.

When people define themselves by "the one true religion" (e.g., Jew vs. Gentile, Christian vs. pagan, Muslim vs. infidel) and when they come into disruptive social contact with people of different (and therefore false) religions, three responses are possible. First, one group may simply try to exterminate the other. Bentham noted wryly that there was nothing in Catholic doctrine that required Catholics to burn to death or otherwise to ill-treat those who differed from them, but this is precisely what they did, over, and over, and over again.[145]

Second, if members of a religious group find themselves in a culture that tolerates religious diversity, there can be a fair amount of picking and choosing (over time) among doctrines, leading to a syncretistic hash of beliefs.[146] Catholic Christians, in particular, have often entwined their faith with elements of indigenous religions found on mission fields; this is particularly true in South America and Africa.

Third, believers in any "true religion" may engage in the twin activities of apologetics and proselytizing. With these techniques, death is not dealt to heretics, infidels, etc., nor does syncretism necessarily occur. Apologetics is that branch of theology whose principle business it is to defend a faith against intellectual attacks upon it. When apological activities are successful, proselytes may also be won to the faith defending itself. Hence, the two activities can be dealt with as one.

Anybody who has read extensively in Christian apologetics, whether ancient or modern, will know that every fallacy ever identified by logicians has been used (and continues to be used) in defense of the faith.[147] Otherwise intelligent, learned, and even keenly logical people will routinely succumb to what I call religion-specific irrationality (hereafter referred to as RSI).[148] Afflicted by RSI, they will simply not apply the same criteria used in assessing the claims of rival religions to the claims of their own. Nothing is easier to document—Bentham could have done the job as easily as I.

Pious Christians who have no trouble believing in the Immaculate Conception of Mary and in the obeisance paid the fruit of her womb by John the Baptist in utero (Luke 1:41–44), will regard as ridiculous the tradition claiming that Lao Tzu (born c. 604 B.C.E.) gestated for sixty-two years, that he was fluent at birth, and that he had the white hair of old age (signifying wisdom) as befitted a Chinese sage.[149] Christians whose credulity is not taxed by the Incarnation of God the Son in the virginal womb of a certain Mary will find their credulity taxed beyond repair by the idea of the many incarnations of the Buddha and his miraculous conception.[150] Christians who will take as factual the claim that Jesus went up into heaven 40 days after his bodily resurrection from the dead (Acts 1:3, 10–11) will repudiate out of hand the claim that the prophet Muhammad ascended into heaven on a white beast "somewhat smaller than a mule yet bigger than an ass, whose every bound carried him as far as his eye could reach."[151] Christians almost without exception will look to Jesus as Messiah, yet to historical inquiry he did nothing more messianic than did Messiah Simeon Bar Kochba, nearly a hundred years later, who also paid with his life.[152] The same applies to Messiah Shabbati Zevi (1626–1676), whose movement was "the largest and most momentous movement in Jewish history subsequent to the destruction of the Temple [in 70] and the Bar Kochba revolt [132–135]." After being imprisoned by the Turks, he was confronted with death or conversion to Islam, Before his conversion to Islam, which was apostasy to Jews, his disciples rationalized his many sufferings as being necessary to the Messiah before he could reveal "himself with miracles and in all his power and glory."[153] American Jews, in particular, have been blessed with a Messianic figure during the recent past: Rebbe (i.e., Rabbi) Menachem Mendel Schneerson of the Habad/Lubavitcher/Hasidic sect. His (nonviolent) death on June 12, 1994, came as a profound shock to his followers; Christians, however, could hardly have cared less about his demise nor about his expected return from the dead in the near future.[154]

The more the people who can be persuaded to believe in such religious absurdities as the above (and similar humbug), the more heartening it is to those who already believe in the selfsame humbug. Nothing is more reinforcing than to harvest many converts. Bentham wrote, "The more flagrant the absurdity, the stronger is each man's interest in engaging as many as possible in joining with him in the profession of assent to it; for the greater the number of such co-declarants, the greater the number of those whose professions the elements of authority are composed, and of those who stand precluded from casting on the rest the imputation of insincerity."[155] Or, we might add, if not the imputation of insincerity, then of foolishness. Those whose religions require belief in absurdities (at least when these are expressed in the WW of ordinary experience or the WW of science) will require a religious WW in which their beliefs can be true in a "spiritual sense." Most people who are afflicted by RSI cannot admit their irrationality without losing self-esteem and jeopardizing their faith.

Having analyzed 'spirit' and 'spiritual sense', there remains only the name 'spirituality' to examine. (The adverbial form, 'spiritually', can safely be subsumed under 'spiritual sense.') Guided by Bentham, let us undertake the paraphrasis of such statements as *the archbishop's spirituality is very deep*, or *the dean of the cathedral manifests a profound spirituality*. If one can backtrack successfully from the complexity of 'spirituality' to the name of some simple archetype, and if from the denominator 'spirituality' (understood as denominating a fictitious entity) one can glean the name or names of one or more real entities, then there is a fair chance that 'spirituality' can be made to cease being the mystery it so often is.

There are three ingredients of spirituality. First, belief in spirits is necessary. Spirits are to be understood in terms of the primitive yet persistent dualism with which religious people view their nature. If the need for belief in spirits is denied, then the "spiritual person" is left with *mere* (my adjective) emotionality. This will not do, since the emotions are now being taken as the manifestations of various brain states, the brain being a perfectly physical object. No, for the "spiritual person," spirituality, now as before, has to transcend (in faith) mere emotions and any physiological bases these might have. If one takes away belief in spirits, one takes away spirituality—in common understanding at least.

Second, the free use of imagination, untethered by any facts and unbridled by any canons of logic (inductive or deductive) is required. When one considers the enormous range of imaginings exhibited in the world's organized religions (past and present) and one considers the manifold mysticisms of people in such relatively unorganized religions as witchcraft, the New Age movement (exemplified by belief in pyramid power and channeling), and the Heaven's Gate group (whose members committed suicides that they might hop a ride on the Hale-Bopp comet), one realizes that imagination, curtailable by nothing, is requisite for spirituality.

Third, although no manifestation of emotion can be ruled out arbitrarily, there must be emotions (or emotionalism) appropriate to a certain context for spirituality to be present. The context in question is constituted by all those emotions appropriate to the condition of the lowliest subject (slave or servant) in the court of the mightiest monarch. Subjects will feel primary fear in the King's presence and secondary fear in anticipation of His future dispositions and behaviors toward them. Subjects will be so awestruck by His Majesty and His magnificent trappings that they will likely be overcome with emotion, on occasion at least.[156] Subjects will feel the need to praise the King as the King of Kings and will fawn upon Him. They will likely raise anthems of praise to His glorious name and will enact ceremonies delightsome to Him. Subjects will fall to their knees (clasping their hands and closing their eyes) or will prostrate themselves before Him and will abase themselves further, noting how unworthy they are and confessing the same, even enumerating individual shortcomings. Subjects will thank the King for his grace and innumerable benisons, reminding Him that he is renowned in all the world for His mercy. Subjects will offer their humble services, vowing to carry out His slightest wishes, even as they laud him for his unsurpassed power. Subjects will beseech the Sovereign, ever reminding him of their wants and wishes, will play the beggar (hands out-stretched, palms up) in anticipation of handouts, will wheedle, bargain, and make unrealistic vows about what they will do in the future to please Him, if only His grace may be enjoyed in the present. Subjects will inter-cede for others, especially family members, loved ones, lovers, and those to whom they are obliged. Subjects will call down the King's wrath upon their enemies, and *His* too, and will remind Him of how storied is His justice. Subjects will acknowledge that though they know only in part, He knows in whole and will assure Him that their faith resides unreservedly in His wisdom and understanding. Finally, subjects will trump His justice with mercy, toward themselves and their loved ones at least.

Anyone who does not believe the characterizations above is invited to read the prayers in the *Book of Common Prayer* of the Anglican Church. If the price were not too high, doubters might even attend church services (over time) to listen to the prayers offered, observe the behaviors of those who pray, and draw reasoned inferences as to the range of emotions experi-enced.

In conclusion, the person who exhibits profound spirituality will be a dualist (a fervent believer in spirits); will entertain gripping and enduring imaginings as to what the spirit world is like and what it requires of one who would enter and abide therein; will be assiduous in doing the deeds of subjects in the presence of their all-seeing, all-powerful, all-wise Sover-eign; and will accordingly experience the range of emotions appropriate thereto.

The nonsensuous experiences engendered by such Eastern meditative techniques as Yoga and Zen are often taken to be spiritual. They can, how-ever, be taken equally well as voluntarily altered brain states and can be studied scientifically. Furthermore, they are not necessarily associated with theism. Hence, I have not included the manifestations thereof as a part of my characterization of spirituality.

The big guns lying behind Bentham's attack on the Anglican Catechism have now been exposed and stand ready to repulse any cleric who would counterattack him. In the year following the appearance of *Church-of-Eng-landism* (1818), the Reverend Hugh James Rose published a slim volume titled *A Critical Examination of Those Parts of Mr. Bentham's "Church-of-Englan-dism" Which Relate to the Sacraments and the Church Catechism.*[157] Barely polite to the source of his anger, Rose dealt with *Mr.* Bentham as though the latter were a theist "because he has professed to hold such belief" (p. xiii). So, the issue of atheism did not roil the waters. Rose was distressed at the profaneness of *CECE* and at Mr. Bentham's "affectation of setting aside all mystery, and making religion a plain and simple matter" (p. ii). Moreover, according to Rose, "all sincere religious feelings, however misguided, deserve respect" (p. xiv). Mr. Bentham could hardly have disagreed more.

Next, Mr. Bentham was drubbed for his "contemptible misrepresentation of the Trinitarian doctrine" (ibid.), due, no doubt, to his "extreme
ignorance on all theological subjects" (p. 29) and his "very confused
knowledge" (p. 30), where he could claim to possess any at all. Since "the
authors of the Catechism were actuated by the sincerest spirit of piety in
composing it" (p. 10), Mr. Bentham ought to have been content with it and
not disposed to accuse its pious authors of trying to deprave the minds of
little Anglicans-in-the-making. Surely, thought Rev. Rose, Christians can
determine "whether or not the Catechism depraves" the minds of catechumens. (p. 13). Stung by Mr. Bentham's attack on the role of sponsors (at
the time of infant baptism) in promising all manner of future godly beliefs
and future good deeds on behalf of the newly baptized, Rose quotes "that
great ornament of the Church, archbishop Bleeker" (pp. 33-34), as
agreeing with Mr. Bentham that no person can make promises for another
person absolutely, but, still and all, there is value in the ritual, that is, in
going through the motions.

The Reverend Hugh James Rose either knew nothing of Bentham's philosophy of language or, knowing of it, was too wary to risk challenging it.
The tenor of his critique is one of simple outrage, not of intellectual
engagement with the fundamental issues at stake, that is, with the naming
role of noun-substantives, with the variety of entities that can be denominated, and with the need to practice paraphrasis on assertions featuring the
names of fictitious entities. The likelihood is that he knew nothing of Bentham's philosophy of language in relation to theological names and the
assertions built thereon and therewith.

Early in 1819, there appeared in the *Quarterly Review* an article titled
"Jeremy Bentham's Church-of-Englandism."[158] Its author, whose name
does not appear in the journal, wrote of Bentham (quoting him at times)
as follows: "He has not that knowledge of human nature, or that sympathy
with it on which moral philosophy must be founded. He is as he tells us,
'a recluse, who forms no part of society,' one who lives 'as if he were
immured in a cell,' and thus separated from his fellow-creatures, he is not
conscious of, and cannot comprehend many of the feelings that reside in
the human heart."[159] Of *CECE*, in particular, the article states, "We shall not
disgust our readers with any specimens of the wretched and impious
sophistry with which its expressions and doctrines are criticized," and the
article proceeds to state, "But in the language of vulgar scurrility, his vocabulary is copious and original, and all the terms of abuse that he can find or
invent are profusely distributed on whatever is within his reach."[160]

It cannot be denied that Bentham's contempt for Christianity in general and for Anglicanism in particular led him to use vulgar and scurrilous
terms (not just occasionally but often) when dealing with the ASS of the
West. However, even if someone were to go through his entire literary

output, excising each ad hominem visited on clerics and each contemptuous comment on theology, his philosophy of language would still devastate the sham science of divinity. The *Quarterly Review* article shows no awareness of this and at no time refutes Bentham on any substantial topic.

John Flowerdew Colls (1801–1878), who for a decade (following 1816) was an amanuensis of Bentham, became disillusioned with utilitarianism, dissociated himself from it, and eventually lapsed into the Anglican clergy. In a letter on the life, death, and philosophy of Bentham, Colls launched a "bitter attack on Utilitarianism."[161] One would think him to have been in the best possible position to have gained some inklings of Bentham's philosophy of language, but "Utilitarianism Unmasked," as his letter was called, fails to address this crucial aspect of Bentham's thought and its relevance to theology. The failure of Christian thinkers to come to grips with Bentham's analysis of theological language is the key to their failure even to begin to refute him.

Those who have read part 2 of this book may remember the name of Alfred William Benn (1843–1905), the historian of philosophy who wrote (in two volumes) *The History of English Rationalism in the Nineteenth Century*. In the first volume, he appraised Bentham's thoughts on religion as these were expressed in the *AINR*, *NPBJ*, and *CECE*. I took him sorely to task for his ill-conceived criticisms of Bentham's handling of St. Paul in *NPBJ*; it is now time to consider his appraisal of *CECE*. As a trained philosopher who had already written extensively on the history of Greek thought, he might have been expected to have appreciated the importance of logic and linguistic analysis to philosophy in general and to Bentham's thought in particular. Of *CECE* he wrote, "As a piece of abstract criticism it is an acute and powerful exposure of the Church's dogmatic teaching; and had the Catechism been then proposed for the first time as a manual of instruction of young children, it would probably not have survived the assault."[162] Here Benn fails to distinguish between dogmatic methods used in teaching when the substance of what is being taught might be true versus dogmatic methods used in teaching when what is being taught is false— even unintelligible. The logical acuteness of Bentham's analysis of the Catechism is based squarely on his philosophy of language; of this Benn appears to have been totally ignorant. In saying that Bentham might have prevailed had the Catechism been some recently hatched technique of religious indoctrination rather than a pedagogic device hoary with age is the same as saying that whatever was good enough for children in 1549 was good enough for more modern children in 1818, when *Church-of-Englandism* was published.[163]

Moreover, suggesting, as Benn did, that it was better to have something with which to catechize children than mere ignorance shows how little he intuited the big guns that lay behind the bombardment Bentham launched against the Catechism.[164] Once Bentham had demolished it, there was no choice between catechizing children with either something or with mere ignorance: it became a choice of catechizing children with pompous religious ignorance or with mere ignorance. Bentham shows very clearly that religious people from the lowliest communicants to the most lordly archbishops and even including the most magisterial theologians do not know *what* they are talking about—and never have! Finally, Benn does not seem to recognize that secular parents can teach their family values, civic virtues, and patriotism very effectively through parental words, feelings, and deeds. Deceitful or unintelligible words (whether religious or nonreligious) are not needed.

To his credit, James Crimmins (whose name will also be familiar to readers of the first two parts of this book) knows about Bentham's philosophy of language and devotes time in his writings to giving it exposition, but in a scattered, truncated manner.[165] He does not, for example, devote adequate time to examining the logic of fabulous entities and the often intense, even fanatical, "spirituality" associated with these entities. He is always at pains to note Bentham's nonspiritual nature, but the spirituality Crimmins has in mind is that of a species, not of a genus. His concern with Bentham's profaneness seems focused on Western idealism, monotheism, and Christianity. This, of course, is only a fraction of the "spirituality" that Bentham's philosophy of language casts in doubt. Crimmins might have spent some thought on spiritualities and mythologies not his own.

Crimmins accuses Bentham of having a descriptive view of language, then leaves the reader to guess as to what the alternative views of language are and which of these he favors as criticizing Bentham's "descriptive view" best.[166] In any case, Bentham would never have agreed that language is limited to communicating descriptions. Far from dwelling on these, he was primarily at pains to understand and to curb the promiscuity of noun-substantives in naming this, that, and the other, as though every instance of naming stood ontologically on all fours with every other instance. Bentham's philosophy of language was much more concerned with analysis, classification, and definition than with description as such. He provided (through paraphrasis) not a technique of description, primarily, but of translation, one whereby assertions bereft of reference (due to excessive abstraction) could be expressed in assertions full of referential terms, free from abstractions. When such translation fails, the recalcitrant assertions that prompt the need for paraphrasis are dubious indeed. Crimmins does not appear to know that the "spirituality" of assertions does not guarantee their truth. It is a hallmark of those afflicted with RSI to think this way.

Crimmins manages to write descriptively of Bentham in such a way as to make the resulting meanings pejorative. He tells us that Bentham was a nominalist, as though we all agree on what a mistake this is.[167] That the reader may know fully the failures of nominalism, Crimmins ought to have expounded his antithetical position so as to refute nominalism. Upon what falsehoods, for example, did Bentham erect his nominalism? What were his mistakes in logic in arriving at it? Can nominalism be driven into a reductio ad absurdum? Until Crimmins answers these questions successfully, nothing is gained by trying to smear Bentham with the name 'nominalist'. Perhaps all right-thinking people are nominalists.

Crimmins writes, "It is evident that Bentham held a narrow, wholly materialistic, conception of what constitutes knowledge."[168] One must presume that Crimmins's readers already know how bad this is. Poor Bentham—by the accident of birth, he came into the world at a time when if he were to be a materialist at all, he had to be a naive one. Were he living today, with even an elementary knowledge of quantum theory and particle physics, he would have to give up naive materialism. But, if he were resurrected today (in more than a "spiritual sense"), he could readily give up naive materialism without destroying his philosophy of language. There are still quantifiable events taking place in nature, still quantifiable levels of energy in the external world, and multitudes of extramental chemical and biological processes occurring in the unnumbered galaxies that constitute the universe. Today's "real entities" (such as neutrinos, gluons, and, perhaps, quantum foam) need names as much as did the old-fashioned "bodies" of Bentham's day. Once our newly conceived real entities (continuously being sought and discovered by scientists) have been named, there will still be the verbal necessity for the names of all the fictitious entities he named, such as quantity, quality, relation, modality, and dozens of others that categorize phenomena. Once again, we must call upon Crimmins to show how his philosophical worldview refutes Bentham's materialism as well as his nominalism.

When Crimmins wrote, "It is evident that Bentham held a narrow, wholly materialistic, conception of what constitutes knowledge," he either misspoke himself or committed an egregious error. Bentham possessed much metamaterialistic knowledge—he knew metaphysics![169] Crimmins himself tells us so and in so saying hoists himself on his own petard: "For Bentham, then, 'metaphysics' meant linguistic analysis. In another early manuscript [in addition to UC lxix. 155] he credited Locke with the invention of 'modern metaphysics' and described it as 'that science which teacheth the signification of words, and the ideas which they signify: which it does . . . [by] shewing how all the ideas we have that are complex, arise from, and are made up of simple ones. Thus it is that . . . every science has its metaphysics: there is no science that has not a set of terms that are more particularly its own'. (UC lxix. 177, ca. 1773)."[170] Crimmins compounds his mistake by adding the following footnote to the quotation above: "In a later MS (ca. 1775) Bentham described 'metaphysics' as the science of the meaning of words and credited Helvetius with its invention (UC xxvii. 1).[171] Since the *meanings* of ordinary linguistic signs (together with the symbols of logic and mathematics) are not physical objects or bodies of any kind, and since Bentham knew the meanings of many, many words and symbols, he entertained much that was not physical knowledge, but rather metaphysical knowledge. An equally good way of putting it is that he had vast *metamaterialistic* knowledge, knowledge of a realm set alongside the materialistic, external realm. Doubtless, the realm of Crimmins's metaphysics is much more densely populated with "spiritual" denizens than is Bentham's, but should it be?[172]

NOTES

54. *Memoirs of Bentham*, in *WJB*,10:74–75. This was written in 1775 when Bentham was only twenty-seven, well ahead of his major writings specifically on religion. In *An Introduction to the Principles of Morals and Legislation*, he wrote, "There is no speaking of objects but by their names: but the business of giving them names has always been prior to the true and perfect knowledge of their natures" (*WJB*, 1:97).

55. *A Table of the Springs of Action*, in *WJB*, 1:205. These words were written in 1815. They show that Bentham had not deviated from the principal thrust of his philosophy of language, particularly with respect to what he called the noun-substantive of a declarative sentence.

56. If, dear reader, I were to exclaim "Zyxpongifeda" or were to write the word on a piece of paper followed by an exclamation point, you would be strongly inclined to think that I was naming somebody or something, in this case excitedly. It would not be clear at first whether or not I was using a proper name to identify a human being, a subhuman animal (such as a pet), or a class of entities such as a genus or species of plant or animal. Hoping to tease more specificity out of me, you would induce me to communicate further on the subject. But, were I to say, for example, "Zyxpongifeda is elusive," you would still not know whether or not the person or pet named is hard to find, because reclusive or, if a species of plant, is hard to find, because rare, growing only in New Caledonia, let us say. Or, to illustrate further, "Zyxpongifeda is not a name often encountered" would leave you equally mystified. However, if you persist, I will sooner or later have to use a singular or plural verb when communicating about Zyxpongifeda and that will reveal something instantly, or I will refer to Zyxpongifeda as he, she, or it, and again you will learn something. Let us say you have concluded that 'Zyxpongifeda', as I am using (or seem to be using) it, refers to an individual of some sort and not to a set (like a species) having members. Is it, then, a rare word, used as a proper name, that can be found only in the *OED*; is it an English transliteration of a name from a little-known foreign tongue; or is it a word I have made up to illustrate a point? If it is my neologism, independent of outside influence, may I not have unwittingly

chosen a transliterated word from a language I do not know or even know about, or may it not be a scientific term hitherto unknown to me, or may it not be the name of a pharmaceutical product of which I am ignorant? Despite the uncertainties created by the foregoing, they pale in comparison with "Zyxpongifeda does not exist." Perplexity accompanies the use of a word to name that which does not exist. Even 'that which' in the previous sentence indicates that something or other is being referred to, only to have it denied by 'does not exist'. Generally speaking, whenever people use a noun-substantive as the verbal vehicle for naming, they assume that the named item has some kind of being or other, is this or is that sort of thing, subsists in some fashion or other, has some sort of essence or other, or at the extreme, possesses some manner of quintessence or other. Since *ontos* in Greek means 'being or having being', 'ontological commitment' means that one routinely presumes that whatever one is naming has some kind of being or other (i.e., has some ontological status) and that when one intends or presumes to engage in naming, one does not mean to name sheer nothingness. The absurdity of committing oneself to believing that every word functioning as a name implies a named item was well illustrated by eminent American logician Willard Van Ormon Quine when he wrote of the assumption behind the so-called Platonic riddle of nonbeing as follows: "Nonbeing must in some sense be, otherwise what is it that there is not?" (*From a Logical Point of View*, 2nd ed. [New York: Harper Torchbooks, 1963], pp. 1–2). An example of mine that may help elucidate the point is, "Witches, being nonexistent, ought not to frighten people." Here, the word magic of English grammar makes it seem that *being* nonexistent implies some kind of being. Modern logicians strive to avoid making ontological commitments (1) by distinguishing sharply between the grammatical subject of a declarative sentence and the logical subject of the assertion being made by that sentence and (2) by dispensing with each noun-substantive found in the primary (i.e., subject) position of declarative sentences. They do this by replacing all names with such variables as x, y, or z and then by binding these to the following quantifiers: something, nothing, and everything (or to their various synonyms). Those who may be mystified by the two statements above but wish to learn more will find clarification in "On What There Is," chap. 1 in Quine, *From a Logical Point of View*. See also Bertrand Russell, "The Philosophy of Logical Analysis," chap. 31 in *A History of Western Philosophy* (New York: Simon and Schuster, 1945). A good overview for the nonprofessional can be found in chapter 9 of Albert William Levy, *Philosophy and the Modern World* (Bloomington: Indiana University Press, 1959). To continue, lecture 2 in Abraham Kaplan, *The New World of Philosophy* (New York: Random House, 1961), is lucid and enjoyable. The entries on modern logic in *EP* and in *REP* are also very informative. For a systematic, elementary exposition of modern symbolic logic, see any of the many editions of Irving M. Copi, *Introduction to Logic*, 7th ed. (New York: Macmillan, 1986). See footnote 185 below for more bibliographical information germane to the subject at issue.

57. A complete and sympathetic exposition of Bentham's philosophy of language in general and of his theory of fictions in particular was given by C. K. Ogden, *Bentham's Theory of Fictions* (London: Kegan Paul, Trench, Trubner, 1932).

58. See *A Fragment on Ontology*, in *WJB*, 8:195. This short work is the most systematic exposition of Bentham's philosophy of language and theory of fictions.

Even so, it was assembled not by him but by his editor from even lesser fragments written in 1813, 1814, and 1821. It is important to note that Bentham's most important writings on religion and theology did not precede his careful ruminations on language but occurred more or less simultaneously with them or subsequently. In short, the big guns he kept in reserve when demolishing the Catechism were already cocked and primed. Mary Mack, *Jeremy Bentham: An Odyssey of Ideas* (London: Heinemann, 1962), writes, "During the decade 1812–22 Bentham wrote thousands of pages on religious subjects, eventually edited and published *Church-of-Englandism* (1818)" (p. 305). Ogden, introduction to *Bentham's Theory of Fictions*, notes that "much of Bentham's best work on language [and logic] was done in the year of Waterloo" (p. clxviii), that is, 1815. See also *An Essay on Language*, in *WJB*, 8:325. Herein he made the point that a real entity of the physical sort (as opposed to the psychic sort) is either a person or a thing, a substance rational or not.

59. One point and one question need to be kept ever in mind while appraising Bentham's analysis of real entities: the point is that he lived and thought in a world of everyday, macroscopic experience—in short, in a Euclidean-Newtonian world, not in today's world of curved space, of quantum mechanics, of subatomic particles such as quarks, etc. Granted that he was very naive as far as modern physics is concerned, the question arises as to whether this naïveté detracts from his attacks on religion and theology. The text above will show that it does not.

60. *A Fragment on Ontology*, in *WJB*, 8:195.

61. Ibid., pp. 195–96. Bentham did not object to the use of 'soul' to refer to the peculiar spiritedness of a given human being, of that person's character, personality, predominating moods, etc. However, when referring to the soul of a person, Christian theology is unconcerned with such meanings, being intent, rather, to claim that each soul lives eternally in heaven or hell after the death of its human tabernacle. Insofar as a soul was understood to be separable from and mobile without its body, Bentham insisted that it was at best only an inferential entity. See also *Chrestomathia*, including an appendix, in *WJB*, 8:189.

62. *A Fragment on Ontology*, in *WJB*, 8:196.

63. Ibid.

64. Bentham, of course, disbelieved in revelation, but it was useful to him to turn the putative revelation in the New Testament, that God, never being seen, is but an inferential entity, back upon the Christians. Let them contend with their own Scripture. He could not have made this case using the Old Testament. Therein, the Bible-god is said to have been seen on several occasions.

65. *A Fragment on Ontology*, in *WJB*, 8:196.

66. Ibid. Although Bentham would have considered the term 'immaterial real object' to be as self-contradictory as 'immaterial matter', he did accept the possibility of incorporeal substance. But incorporeal substance, if such there be, is ratiocinative, not empirical, and hence must be inferential. This, of course, is where the heavenly host belongs. See his *Chrestomathia*, in *WJB*, 8:189. This work was printed between 1815 and 1817.

67. *A Fragment on Ontology*, in *WJB*, 8:196.

68. Ibid., p. 196, and *Essay on Logic*, 8:253. This essay was written between 1811 and 1816.

69. *Chrestomathia*, in *WJB*, 8:126, and *Essay on Logic*, in *WJB*, 8:262–63. The reader, like the author no doubt, will wonder whether or not Bentham might have included any names, places, events, etc. from the biblical tradition to parallel those hinted at from Gentile mythologies. In his introduction to the *LEM*, Robert Graves writes, "Mythology is the study of whatever religious or heroic legends are so foreign to a student's experience that he cannot believe them to be true. Hence the English adjective 'mythical', meaning 'incredible'; and hence the the omission from standard European mythologies, such as this, of all Biblical narratives even when closely paralleled by myths from Persia, Babylonia, Egypt, and Greece; and of all hagiological legends" (p. v.).

70. Bentham wrote, "But . . . names of fictitious entities do not, as do the . . . names of fabulous entities, raise up in the mind any correspondent images" (*Essay on Logic*, in *WJB*, 8:263).

71. Bentham admits to having gotten the term from *être fictif*, used by French philosopher Jean le Rond d'Alembert; see *Logical Arrangements*, in *WJB*, 3:286.

72. *Essay on Language*, in *WJB*, 8:329.

73. *Essay on Logic*, in *WJB*, 8:262.

74. *A Fragment on Ontology*, in *WJB*, 8:197.

75. Ibid., p. 198.

76. *Essay on Language*, in *WJB*, 8:334.

77. *Chrestomathia*, in *WJB*, 8:120.

78. *Essay on Language*, in *WJB*, 8:331.

79. Ibid., p. 325.

80. *A Fragment on Ontology*, in *WJB*, 8:197.

81. *Chrestomathia*, in *WJB*, 8:126.

82. *A Fragment on Ontology*, in *WJB*, 8:199.

83. *Chrestomathia*, in *WJB*, 8:174.

84. *A Fragment on Ontology*, in *WJB*, 8:197.

85. Ibid., p. 199. Bentham devoted a great deal of time and energy to the proper analysis and usage of fictitious entities.

86. *Chrestomathia*, in *WJB*, 8:125.

87. Ibid., p. 121.

88. *A Fragment on Ontology*, in *WJB*, 8:206.

89. *The Constitutional Code*, in *WJB*, 9:76.

90. *A Fragment on Ontology*, in *WJB*, 8:199.

91. *Chrestomathia*, in *WJB*, 8:129.

92. *A Fragment on Ontology*, in *WJB*, 8:210; also see *Rationale of Judicial Evidence*, in *WJB*, 7:77–79.

93. *Essay on Language*, in *WJB*, 8:328.

94. *Chrestomathia*, in *WJB*, 8:122.

95. *A Fragment on Ontology*, in *WJB*, 8:210.

96. Ibid., p. 198; see also *Language*, in *WJB*, 8:327 and *Chrestomathia*, in *WJB*, 8:120.

97. *Pannomial Fragments*, in *WJB*, 3:217; see also *A General View of a Complete Code of Laws*, in *WJB*, 3:181; *Essay on Logic*, in *WJB*, 8:247; and *Chrestomathia*, in *WJB*, 8:126.

98. *Pannomial Fragments*, in *WJB*, 3:209, 218.

99. *A Fragment on Ontology*, in *WJB*, 8:206.

100. *A Fragment on Government*, in *WJB*, 1:268–69. The notion of natural law holds that the order and structure of natural processes contain implicitly certain prescriptions as to how people ought to behave to be moral. The notion of an Original Contract holds that humans emerged from a brutish state, determined to end anarchy, drew up a contract prescribing lawful and unlawful behavior, and thus established civil society. Bentham thought both ideas false or absurd.

101. *Essay on Language*, in *WJB*, 8:332, 337. The list of types of fictitious entities given in the text is incomplete. For the names of certain fictitious entities of the second remove (such as types of motions), see *A Fragment on Ontology*, in *WJB*, 8:197, 207, and Delos McKown, "A Theological Anomaly in Bentham's Ontology," in *MNL* 22, no. 2 (1987): 2–8.

102. In *A Fragment on Ontology*, he wrote, "[N]o body whatsoever is, or ever has been, or ever will be, absolutely in a state of rest" (*WJB*, 8:200).

103. See *Chrestomathia*, in *WJB*, 8:130; *Essay on Language*, in *WJB*, 8:325.

104. *A Fragment on Ontology*, in *WJB*, 8:197.

105. Ibid., and *Essay on Language*, in *WJB*, 8:326.

106. *Anarchical Fallacies*, in *WJB*, 2:501.

107. *Pannomial Fragments*, in *WJB*, 3:219.

108. *Complete Code of Laws*, in *WJB*, 3:181.

109. *Fragment on Government*, in *WJB*, 1:293. Also see *Chrestomathia*, in *WJB*, 8:126–27. Relative to progress in logic in Bentham's day, Willard Van Orman Quine wrote, "Bentham's step [forward] was the recognition of contextual definition, or what he called paraphrasis. He recognized that to explain a term we do not need to specify an object for it to refer to, nor even specify a synonymous word or phrase; we need only show, by whatever means, how to translate all the whole sentence in which the term is to be used" (*Ontological Relativity, and Other Essays* [New York: Columbia University Press, 1969], p. 72). Later in the same work, he wrote, "Bentham's idea of paraphrasis flowered late, in Russell's theory of descriptions. Russell's theory affords a rigorous and important example of how expressions can be made to parade as names and then be explained away as a mere manner of speaking, by explicit paraphrase of the context into an innocent notation" (p. 101).

110. Archetypation, when illustrated or used in context, is so transparent that Bentham felt little need to define it. However, he comes very close to doing so in his *Essay on Language*, in *WJB*, 8:332.

111. *Essay on Logic*, in *WJB*, 8:246–47.

112. *CLD*, p. 319.

113. *Chrestomathia*, in *WJB*, 8:126; and *Essay on Logic*, in *WJB*, 8:247.

114. *Essay on Logic*, in *WJB*, 8:244; and *Essay on Language*, in *WJB*, 8:324.

115. *Complete Code of Laws*, in *WJB*, 3:286.

116. *Chrestomathia*, in *WJB*, 8:120; see also *Essay on Language*, in *WJB*, 8:327; and *Essay on Logic*, in *WJB*, 8:246.

117. See the relevant entries in Thomas Rogers, *A Practical List of Greek Word Roots* (Nashville, TN, and New York: Abingdon Press, 1968). Without mentioning Bentham and, perhaps, without knowing his analysis of entities, American psychol-

ogist Julian Jaynes, *The Origin of Consciousness in the Breakdown of the Bicameral Mind* (Boston: Houghton Mifflin, 1976), esp. chap. 3, has shown how numerous abstract terms arose from the highly physicalistic Greek language of the *Iliad* and that historical period.

118. In *A Fragment on Ontology*, Bentham wrote, "It is through the medium of absence, the familiar and continually recurring idea of absence, that the idea of non-existence . . . is attained" (*WJB*, 8:210).

119. *Essay on Logic*, in *WJB*, 8:246.

120. *A Fragment on Ontology*, *WJB*, 8:198. Bentham made a similar point about location in *CECE*, but he did not confront the reader nor the ecclesiastics of his time with the relevant elements of his philosophy of language, that is, with the various types of names he identified as naming entities of one sort or the other. By now the reader will know that Bentham was at pains to show that Anglicans were not conspicuously biblical in their beliefs, but here, alas, he fell into the same sin. 'Devil' and 'Satan' never (in the New Testament) name an alleged being looking like a composite of human, goat, bat, and monkey. The only time a shape is ever suggested for Satan, it is dragonesque or serpentine. In Rev. 12:9a we read, "And the great dragon was cast out [of heaven], that old serpent, called the Devil, and Satan, which deceiveth the whole world." Here Bentham simply accepted what he had been told and seen presented in Christian books, in stained glass windows, etc. For a recent, spirited summary of the speckled career of the Devil, see Robert Wernick, "Who the Devil Is the Devil?" *Smithsonian*, October 1999, 113–23. For scholarly expositions, see Jeffrey Burton Russell, *The Devil: Perceptions of Evil from Antiquity to Primitive Christianity* (Ithaca, NY: Cornell University Press, 1977), and Elaine Pagels, *The Origin of Satan* (New York: Random House, 1995).

121. *A Fragment of Ontology*, in *WJB*, 8:195–96.

122. See the appropriate entries in the *CLD*, the *OED*, and the entry "Trophy," by Joseph T. Shipley, in the *DWO*. In his *Essay on Language*, Bentham said explicitly that the original meaning of *spiritus* was "air discharged from the lungs" (*WJB*, 8:328–29).

123. Though the words in Greek are different than their Latin counterparts, the nature of the derivation is identical. Proliferating from the root *pnu* or *pne*, meaning 'to breathe or blow air', we get *pneuma* (πνεῦμα), meaning 'wind, air, breath'; then *pneumatikos*, meaning 'of or having to do with air', ending with *Pneuma to Hagion* (Πνεῦμα το Ἅγιον), literally, 'Spirit the Holy'. In a footnote to *Chrestomathia* titled "Pneumatology," Bentham wrote, "From two Greek words: the first of which (πνεῦμα) signifies spirit, i.e., *incorporeal substance*, in the sense in which it is used as synonymous to *mind*: in their original sense, the Latin, as well as the Greek word corresponding to the English word *breath*. In the New Testament, Ἅγιον Πνεῦμα is the name, employed in the original, in designating the object, for the designation of which, in the English version, the compound appelative *Holy Spirit* is employed" (*WJB*, 8:84). In a late work (1830), Bentham wrote of the high ranking clergy, "1. *Bishops, Right Reverend*; II *Archbishops, Most Reverend*. These to distinguish them from the sort of Lords who are Peers, are styled Lords *Spiritual*; to wit, in consideration of the *spirit* they are full of. *Spirit* meant originally *gas*: a kind of thing, one species of which is that which streets are lighted with: in their instance, it means a *sacred* sort.

Sacred means the same as *holy*: so now you understand what they are" (*Bentham to Fellow-Citizens of France*, in *WJB*, 4:438).

124. See the *OED*.

125. Instead of painting a pigeon to represent the descent of the Holy Ghost, all that would have been necessary would have been a cloud or smudge of atmosphere daubed on canvases, preferably against a patch of distant sky.

126. *Essay on Language*, in *WJB*, 8:323, 328. Animals may also have minds. The issue here is not to compare human minds with human minds or human minds with animal minds, but to examine what kind of entity Bentham thought a human mind was.

127. This famous prayer book contains the Catechism and the Thirty-nine Articles of Religion, together with many prayers for special occasions plus quotations from the Old Testament and the New Testament.

128. See the Collects for the First day and the fourth Sunday in Lent.

129. Under "Thanksgivings," see the prayer for "Safe Return from the Sea."

130. In the Order of Confirmation of those who have reached the years of discretion, one learns that the agency named 'grace' gives certain gifts, among which are the spirit of wisdom, the spirit of counsel, and ghostly strength!

131. Those interested in learning how Bentham dealt with the names 'cause' and 'causality' and why he preferred to call the inferred Supreme Entity 'Author' rather than 'First Cause' can find his reasoning in *A Fragment on Ontology*, in *WJB*, 8:208.

132. 'Holy', like 'obligation', has no genus. Information, for example, can be gained as to what human beings are when told that they are rational animals. Here, 'rational' names a species that distinguishes it (and its members) from other species not so distinguished, but all of which belong to the genus named by 'animal'. See *Essay on Logic*, in *WJB*, 8:247; also *Chrestomathia*, in *WJB*, 8:122.

133. *Book of Fallacies*, in *WJB*, 2:448–49.

134. *Essay on Logic*, in *WJB*, 8:249. See also p. 251, wherein Bentham remarked on the slippery use of 'church', sometimes used to refer to the *subject many*, other times to the *ruling few*.

135. *Book of Fallacies*, in *WJB*, 2:448. See also *Rationale of Judicial Evidence*, wherein Bentham wrote, "It has been among the artifices of men in power, to fasten upon some abstract term, to beget upon it some ideal shadowy being, from the influence of which on the imaginations of mankind they could derive respect, and into the darkness of which they could occasionally escape from envy and censure. Ecclesiastics, sons of the church, were liable like other men to be fools—like other men to be knaves—like other men to be liars: but the church, their holy mother, ever one, ever the same, ceased not for a moment to be all-wise, all trustworthy, infallible" (*WJB*, 7:294). In *The Constitutional Code*, he added, "Amongst the instruments of delusion employed for reconciling the people to the dominion of the one and the few, is the device of employing for the designation of persons, and classes of persons, instead of the ordinary and appropriate denominations, the names of so many abstract fictitious entities contrived for the purpose" (*WJB*, 9:76). He illustrated this in part with "Instead of Churchmen,—the *Church*, and sometimes the *Altar*."

136. In *Essay on Logic*, Bentham wrote, "The holy men might, notwithstanding their holiness, have remained fallible; the Holy Mother was found to be infallible. Her title to implicit confidence and its naturally inseparable consequence implicit obedience, became at once placed upon the firmest ground and raised to the highest pitch" (*WJB*, 8:250).

137. Ibid. Also see *Book of Fallacies*, wherein Bentham wrote, "In Catholic countries, the churchmen who compose Holy Mother Church possess one beautiful female by whom the people are governed in the field of spiritual law, with which has been enclosed as much as possible of profane law" (*WJB*, 2:449).

138. If there were a religion totally mythological with no scrap of historicity involved in its beliefs, then it would have little use for the WW of ordinary experience.

139. Highly trained specialists, of course, live in yet another WW, the professional WW of their training and expertise.

140. The so-called scientific creationists illustrate this point well. Their WW (which includes the biblical tale of the creation of the earth, its satellites [such as the sun and the stars], and life itself, all as recently as ten thousand years ago), runs headlong into the WW of paleontology with its dinosaurs, extinct these past 65 million years, to say nothing of astronomy.

141. Morton Smith writes in *Jesus the Magician* (New York: Harper and Row, 1978), p. 26, that to call a man the son of his mother is tantamount to calling into doubt his father's identity.

142. See *Chrestomathia*, in *WJB*, 8:189.

143. The reader is reminded that the dualism at issue is taken up at great length in part 2 at the point at which St. Paul's notions of mind, soul, and spirit are criticized.

144. To Bentham, on the contrary, the mind of an individual is a property of that person's body, the former being no more immortal than the latter, see *Essay on Language*, in *WJB*, 8:323.

145. Nor did the faith of James I require him to burn the "poor Anabaptists" to death; see the *Book of Fallacies*, in *WJB*, 2:451. When writing of witchcraft, for which people were severely punished in England and in Scotland, as late as the early eighteenth century, Bentham wrote, "In those times of terror, women were punished, and always with death, for acts of witchcraft; men for acts of sorcery" (*Rationale of Judicial Evidence*, in *WJB*, 7:101). Christians have not limited their attempts at extermination to members of other religions than their own, but have been especially cruel to so-called heretics within their own faith, broadly conceived (*Introduction to Morals and Legislation*, in *WJB*, 1:5). For a bitter comment on the Inquisition, see *Principles of Penal Law*, in *WJB*, 1:412.

146. Syncretistic processes are not usually the results of self-conscious, decisive choice. An outstanding example of a person who did make a self-conscious, decisive choice of trying to know what he took to be the Divine (or the Absolute) through various religious routes was the Hindu mystic Ramakrishna (1836–1886). Born a Hindu, he also sought unity with "the Divine" through Muslim, Buddhist, and Christian paths. Such a person is relatively rare, but, then, he lived in a society that was tolerant of such attempts. He was even viewed by his fellow Hindus as a

saint or even a divine being. The Vedanta Society traces its origin to him through the Swami Vivekananda. See John B. Noss, *Man's Religions*, 4th ed. (London: Macmillan, 1969), pp. 226–27.

147. An excellent place to begin one's acquaintance with Christian apologetics is in the writings of the ante-Nicean Fathers of the Church. If one prefers modern to ancient apologetics, one has only to read the writings of the "scientific creationists" in their responses to the claims of modern evolutionary biologists, geologists, and cosmologists. Familiarity with the periodical *Reports of the National Center for Science Education* will keep the reader up-to-date on the sources for modern apologetics of the sort mentioned.

148. Religion-specific irrationality in its advanced form is religion-specific insanity. In the *AINR*, Bentham noted that the divorcement of one's beliefs from one's empirical experience is insanity. This, of course, allows for degrees: the greater the divorcement, the greater the insanity; the lesser, the lesser. During the whole of 1999 and into 2000, Israel entertained an increased number of clinically insane people who believed that they were Jesus, Elijah, some other prophet, or the Messiah about to initiate a new, golden age. For more on this affliction, commonly called the Jerusalem syndrome, see the *NYT*, November 26, 1999.

149. See Holmes Welch, *Taoism*, rev. ed. (Boston: Beacon Press, 1965), p. 1.

150. *LEM*, s. v. "Buddhism."

151. See Arthur Jeffrey (ed.), *Islam: Muhammad and His Religion* (New York: Liberal Arts Press, 1958), pp. 35–36. The whole idea of ascending into heaven from a globular planet in orbit around a star that is itself moving in a galaxy that is in spiral motion is hard to accept by those who adopt the current scientific WW of astronomy. If, however, one is sufficiently afflicted by RSI, one can find Jesus' ascension true in a "spiritual sense," as can Muslims respecting Muhammad's ascension.

152. Bar Kochba was the Jewish leader of the second war between the Jews and the Romans that began in 132 and ended in 135. See the entry for Bar Kokhba (spellings vary) in the *ODJR*, p. 100. Also see Hyam Maccoby, *Revolution in Judaea: Jesus and the Jewish Resistance* (New York: Taplinger, 1980), pp. 68–69.

153. See *EJ*, s. v. "Shabbatai Zevi"; or *EOR*, s. v. "Sabbatai Zevi."

154. The depth of messianic aspirations for Schneerson was amply illustrated by a full-page advertisement in the *NYT*, July 8, 1997. Among other assertions, readers are told that he was "liberated from the limitations of corporeal existence" three years earlier, that "his presence among us is more profoundly felt than ever before," and that "mankind's Redemption" is at hand. Readers are assured of the resurrection of the dead and are urged to improve themselves "in order to be ready to greet Moshiach [Messiah] and hasten the hour for which we have all been waiting." Since Christians have already picked their Messiah long since, none of this will fall on receptive ears. For more on Schneerson, see the *NYT*, June 14, 1994. For the same reason, American Christians, by and large, reject another (or any other) Messiah, such as the Reverend Sun Myung Moon of the Unification Church.

155. *Book of Fallacies*, in *WJB*, 2:397–98. This is not universally true of religions. Some are evangelistic; others not. The ethnic nature of Judaism makes proselytizing almost nonexistent. Much the same can be said of some state churches. The Eastern Orthodox churches of Bulgaria, Serbia, Russia, etc. scarcely proselytize

at all. But then, since most people in these societies belong to the same state church from birth, the numbers of communicants do not need augmentation through conversion to reinforce the faith of the faithful.

156. Bentham was well aware of the monarchical political model as the archetype for Christians' understanding of their deity; see *Bentham to His Fellow-Citizens*, in *WJB*, 4:438; *Letters to Count Toreno on the Proposed Penal Code*, in *WJB*, 8:538; and *The Constitutional Code*, in *WJB*, 9:24. Fear, not just of the kingly deity, but also of a host of unseen, invisible agents, plays a large part in religion; see the *Essay on the Influence of Time and Place in Matters of Legislation*, in *WJB*, 1:174.

157. Printed for J. Porter, Pall Mall, London, 1819.

158. "Jeremy Bentham's Church-of-Englandism," *Quarterly Review* 21 (January and April): 167–77. In *Secular Utilitarianism*, p. 2, Crimmins identifies the author as one W. Gifford, the same person, I judge, as the William Gifford who for many years edited the *Quarterly Review*.

159. "Bentham's Church-of-Englandism," p. 168.

160. Ibid., pp. 170, 176.

161. *CJB*, 9:17, n. 2. See also Stephen Conway, "J. F. Colls, M. A. Gathercole, and Utilitarianism Unmasked: A Neglected Episode in the Anglican Response to Bentham," *JEH* 45, no. 3 (1994): 435–47. J. R. Dinwiddy, "Early–Nineteenth-Century Reactions to Benthamism," *TRHS*, 5th ser., no. 34 (1984): 47–69, fails to treat any aspect of Bentham's religious writings to which others took critical exception. William Empson, "Jeremy Bentham," *Edinburgh Review* 78, no. 158 (1843), is also innocent of linguistic reasons why Bentham should have attacked Christian theology as vigorously as he did.

162. Alfred William Benn, *The History of English Rationalism in the Nineteenth Century* (New York: Russell and Russell, 1962), 1:301.

163. 1549 was the date of the Catechism's inclusion in the authorized service book that became the *Book of Common Prayer*; see the *ODCC*, p. 249.

164. Benn, *History of English Rationalism*, 1:301.

165. See James L. Crimmins, "Bentham's Metaphysics and the Science of Divinity," *HTR* 79, no. 4 (1986): esp. 388–96, and *Secular Utilitarianism: Social Science and the Critique of Religion in the Thought of Jeremy Bentham* (Oxford: Clarendon Press, 1990), esp. pp. 43–62.

166. Crimmins, "Bentham's Metaphysics," p. 388.

167. Ibid.

168. Ibid., p. 406.

169. The Greek *meta* means 'alongside' as well as the more familiar 'above and beyond'. My newly coined term, 'metamaterialistic', merely means that in addition to knowledge of the material world, there is also knowledge of another realm alongside it. This realm contains the meanings of language, logic, and the whole of mathematics. One can know, for example, the meanings and properties of a point in geometry without knowing any material object or physical body. So, metamaterialistic knowledge is metaphysical knowledge.

170. Crimmins, "Bentham's Metaphysics," p. 391.

171. Ibid. In his presidential address to the American Philosophical Association, Pacific Division, titled "What Are Spiritual Phenomena?" David Stern clearly

distinguishes the spiritual from the psychical and from the physical in a way that I believe Bentham would have endorsed. He writes,

> What are spiritual acts? Let me give an example: At a banquet table, I pick up my glass of wine and take a sip. This is a physical act. It is accompanied by a psychical phenomenon: the feeling of pleasure associated with the taste of the wine. But when, during the Mass, the priest takes a sip of wine, this is a spiritual act, because it means something other than it is in its immediate physical and psychical reality. Within the context of the Mass, the beaker of wine means the 'calix salutaris' which the priest offers to God, with the attention directed to the prospective transubstantiation of the wine into the blood of Christ. The spirituality of the priest's act subsists even for those who do not believe in the miracle of the Eucharist. It consists in the fact that in the Mass his acts mean something beyond their immediate physical and psychical reality. This meaning is their spirituality." ("What are Spiritual Phenomena?" in *PAAPA* [Yellow Springs, OH: Antioch Press, 1965–66]: 52)

Precisely the same could be written of acts of language. In addition to the act of producing sounds or making marks on paper and in addition to how the receivers of the message feel, some, perhaps, feeling warmed by it, others chilled, the meaning levitates above, beside, or beyond the physical aspect(s) involved and the psychical aspect(s) elicited and dwells in the realm of metaphysics.

172. Whereas Crimmins criticizes Bentham on religion as boldly as he does mistakenly, James Steintrager treats him more as a bit of a bad boy. But he, too, criticizes Bentham's linguistic scheme as being too narrow: "For not only does he misconstrue the functions of language, but he expects far too much from linguistic clarity" ("Language and Politics: Bentham on Religion," *BNL* 4 [1980]: 13). Granted that linguistic clarity is neither the elixir of life nor the panacea for all ills, and granted that Bentham did not direct his attention to all uses of language, still and all, how is it that his "narrow" linguistic scheme failed him in assailing the verbal wilderness of theology in general and the chaos of the Catechism in particular? Bentham dealt with the Catechism and the related Thirty-nine Articles just as they should have been (and should be) dealt with.

Chapter 9

Criticisms

Since Bentham was human (and, thus, fallible), it is to be expected that he made some mistakes and exhibited some inadequacies in his philosophy of language. These shortcomings can be lumped under three headings: the logical, the material (or physical), and the emotional. First, respecting logic, his category of fabulous entities cannot be what he makes it seem to be. The problem can be illustrated by converting the old saw "The emperor has no clothes" into "The clothes have no emperor." If 'Jupiter' and 'Juno', for example, name no entities, that is, name nothing having properties, then these names name nonentities, not fabulous entities. What is left to be named (and is literally fabulous) is the set of all the myths and would-be theologies in which 'Jupiter' and 'Juno' appear. Put differently, it is the verbal attire that is being named as fabulous, not that which the attire is supposed to clothe.

Here a caveat is in order. It is not certain that every figure of mythic or legendary proportions must be consigned to a (or the) one-way street to oblivion. The street may run both ways. If the slightest evidence is found for a person, place, object, or event, hitherto believed to be totally mythic or legendary, then the item named may have to be transferred from the category of fabulous entities to the category of real entities. The legendary figure of Wilhelm (William) Tell can be used to make this point. Many of us grew up believing that there was such a person who, with crossbow and arrow and marvelous aplomb, split an apple atop his son's head without harming the lad. George Albert Wells, a Germanist and biblical scholar, believes that there is now ample evidence to conclude that there never was

357

any such person nor any such episode.[173] If so, then the Wilhelm Tell of legend is a nonentity, leaving only the fabulous stories about him and his exploits to exist. However, should new evidence appear, such as a hitherto unknown document (attesting to his historicity) or a likely crossbow, if not the very apple-splitting arrow itself, then Wilhelm Tell might have to be reclassified. The same is true of the Abominable Snowman of Himalayan legends, the Sasquatch of the American northwest, and the ETs of Roswell, New Mexico. Bentham could have avoided this problem by recognizing a category of legendary entities, embedded in fabulous tales, whose historicity might be possible, in part at least. Leaving the door ajar to legendary entities would not be tantamount to inviting all the gods of mythology to materialize out of oblivion.

Returning to the unstable category of fabulous entities, as Bentham conceived it, a pressing question arises. Why did he not include Yahweh (the Bible-god) in the pantheon of pagan deities together with Jupiter and Juno, the two he named? Reasons both positive and negative indicate that he ought to have done so. Except for reputed disinterest in erotic affairs, Yahweh is as transparently humanoid as any of the pagan deities—and as little historical. Although the Hebrews were forbidden to depict him (using the graphic and plastic arts), Christian iconographers have suffered no restraints, from an early time onward, in picturing him now as a mature, sapient man with long whiskers and again as a medieval pope with equally long whiskers, and always looking splendidly monarchical. On the negative side, Yahweh is not portrayed in the Bible as an inferential entity, but as a revelatory one, a deity who, for example, accosted Moses with murderous intent (Exod. 4:24) and allowed the latter to behold his hinder parts (Exod. 33:23). Nor is Yahweh identical to the Author and Creator of nature whom Bentham contemplated in his *Fragment on Ontology*, nor to the deity inferred in the *AINR*.[174] Since Bentham, by innuendo at least, classified Satan (with Jupiter and Juno) as a fabulous entity, why not Yahweh? There is no clear answer. One point, however, is clear: There is no logical reason why the inferential entity of natural theology must be identical in (alleged) properties to the clearly fabulous Bible-god.

The category of fabulous entities is not the only one to vex Bentham's philosophy of language. The category of inferential entities also poses problems. The reader will remember that Bentham acceded to the medieval idea of spiritual substance. Under this category he arrayed the souls of human individuals as entities conceived to be separable from their respective bodies, the superhuman inferential entity (i.e., God), and the subordinate spiritual entities, good and bad, called angel and demons. Even granting the legitimacy of whatever class is named by 'spiritual substance' (dubious at best) and agreeing that its members ought to be limited to the three types named above, what is to be done when naming other sorts of inferential entities, the ones subsumable under the class of material sub- stance? Bentham made few, if any, linguistic provisions for inferential enti- ties related to the behavior of bodies, that is, to the inferential (or theoret- ical) entities of the hard sciences. Although he was an amateur chemist and was philosophically in full cry when John Dalton was laying the founda- tions for modern atomic theory (in 1805), he never imagined the extent to which theoretical entities relative to material bodies would be needed (and discarded) in future attempts at the scientific understanding of nature and natural processes. Here, too, as with fabulous entities, allowance has to be made for a great deal of traffic, traffic on the one hand to oblivion and on the other hand to the realm of real entities. For example, the inferential entity phlogiston disappeared with Priestly's, Lavoisier's, and Dalton's experiments with "dephlogisticated air"—that is, with oxygen—which thereupon came into its own, while the former disappeared from thought.

Corrective of all traditional metaphysics though it is, the category of fictitious entities in Bentham's thought is not without problems. One of these can be illustrated by arraying the names 'perspicacity' and 'probity' on the one hand and 'temporality' and 'gravity' on the other. Each of these words is a noun-substantive, each is abstract, each names at least one class or set of closely related items, none names a body (in Bentham's termi- nology), and none names a fabulous entity. So much for the similarities. The differences, however, are considerable, indicating that not all abstract nouns are born equal, logically speaking. Probity can do double duty by naming two sets. One set is constituted by each and every instance of hon- esty, another by each and every person said to have probity or to be honest. Here the moral character of the constituents is at issue, something, so to speak, that persists over time as a trait. Though persisting in this manner, the possession of or exhibition of probity in a given person's life has an episodic quality and is subject to the judgment of others. It is dubious that a sleeping person has probity. A person in an irreversible coma neither has nor exhibits it. Moreover, drugs and alcohol can change a person's char- acter, and finally, spongiform encephalopathy, for example, can destroy it. Exactly the same analysis can be applied to perspicacity, indicating that these two abstract nouns are born equal, though possessed of different meanings. It is quite different with gravity and temporality.

To keep the analysis manageable, let us look in, imaginatively, upon Isaac Newton sitting under the legendary apple tree. As any number of apples fall about him, Newton can invent conceptually and name a class for all unsupported bodies traveling toward the surface of the earth. Con- sidering that an oriental Newton, even then, might be sitting under a plum tree in China, seeing plums fall, it is not so much that unsupported objects fall toward the surface of the earth (as perceived by an individual) as it is that they move toward its center, regardless of the varying directions of each falling fruit relative to one another. Moreover, Newton can extend his newly named class to include what would happen if there were unsupported bodies on the moon and on planets everywhere. But this is not enough to populate his newly contrived class of moving bodies. He also has to consider the movement of each moon in relation to its planet and each planet in relation to its sun. The population of the set of all instances of moving and orbiting bodies has by this time become astronomical in size. Yet Newton cannot stop here. He has to consider the attraction of the earth for himself as he sits beneath the apple tree. Had his body no mass, the slightest breeze would waft him away. But, no, there he sits stably on his fundament, and as he sits there, blood pools a bit in his posterior parts. Moreover, his internal organs are being dragged down, energy is required when he lifts a limb, his neck grows weary when he tilts his head (in thought) too long, the bags below his eyes are pulled upon, and every flake of dandruff that falls from his head, unimpeded, attests to a mysterious phenomenon that appears to be universal in fact (not merely in thought) and constant, quite unlike episodes of probity or perspicacity. How starkly different it would be for the body of a modern-day Newton launched aboard the space shuttle, where, while in space, he could float weightlessly, free from earth's gravitational pull, and where apples could not fall! 'Gravity' seems to name far more about the universe than individual instances of moving bodies, whether in orbit or falling unsupported toward centers of attraction. It will be necessary to advert to this when criticizing Bentham below from a material or physical perspective.

To make matters even more complicated, temporality is not to gravity as perspicacity is to probity. Moreover, temporality appears to be more than the name of a grab bag (or set) of related instants. Hand clapping can illustrate much that is relevant to time, namely simultaneity and succession. If I propose to move my arms in such a way as to strike the flat of my right hand with the flat of my left hand, and vice versa, and do so, the two hands strike one another simultaneously. If I enjoy this clap (no pun intended) so much that I wish to do it again, the following clap is never simultaneous with the first, but succeeds it, and never precedes it. The arrow of time, it is said, moves in one direction only. This topic will recur when criticizing Bentham from a material or physical point of view. There is more to succession, of course, than discrete episodes arrayed as a chain of events, such as somebody's clapping or dribbling a basketball; there are also unnumbered physical processes, more or less continuous. The conception, birth, infantile development, juvenile maturation, adulthood, senescence, and death of individual organisms and the evolutionary appearance and disappearance of species illustrate continuous succession. More important to this analysis than any of the foregoing examples is the fact that gravitational activities occur temporally (i.e., in time). Temporality, however, does not necessarily occur (pass or proceed) gravitationally. This is not to say time is totally independent of gravity (more on that later).

To summarize, not only are there significant logical differences between probity and perspicacity on the one hand and temporality and gravity on the other, there is also a profound difference between temporality and gravity.[175] The point is that Bentham created a logically unmanageable set when he conceived of the class of fictitious entities. To make it manageable, he ought to have created subsets within it and been prepared to see some so-called fictitious entities fly the coop, coming to roost elsewhere. Two likely escapees are gravity and temporality.

Readers will remember the following points Bentham made about fictitious entities: (1) "Every fictitious entity bears some relation to a real entity," (2) fictitious entities owe their existence to language, and (3) since we cannot think without fictitious entities, these must be seen, linguistically, as a "coin of necessity."[176] But suppose that some fictitious entities are not necessary to thought at all! What then? It is easy to illustrate this point. It would be a nightmare if every time one wished to convey the concept of motion (for which there was as yet no name) to an interlocutor, one had to point to an indeterminate number of moving bodies until the interlocutor finally got the point. Once the point is made that every moving body has something in common with every other moving body and that this commonality can be named (in this case by 'motion'), then thought can proceed felicitously.

The same is true of the concept of a line. If one did not have 'line' at one's linguistic disposal but had to point to an indefinitely large number of the edges of bodies to get the idea across to an interlocutor, thought would be paralyzed. To make matters worse, it would be maddening to try to distinguish between 'edge', 'line', 'surface', and 'texture'. To understand this point, the reader has only to try to make these fictitious entities intelligible to a child just learning to speak English or to any person whose mother tongue is not English. Ditto for any other natural language.

In contrast to the fictitious entities 'motion' and 'line', consider the fictitious entities 'natural rights' and, possibly, 'holiness'. The latter two are not necessary to thought at all. As we know, Bentham thought natural rights "nonsense on stilts" and holiness (or sacredness) a fraudulent property. To illustrate, a human being in isolation (and thus unconstrained and unrestrained by other human beings) may do or be whatever she wishes to do or be (given requisite power) without any reliance on natural rights. Even supposing these to exist, natural rights would make no difference to the desired doing or being. Moreover, a human being in community (i.e., constrained or restrained by societal sanctions) who can do or be what he wishes to do or be, but without detection and fear of punishment, needs no natural rights to do or be whatever is desired, nor would such a person know what to do with natural rights in this situation, again assuming their existence. Finally, human beings who enjoy posited rights, established and maintained by laws in a civil society, may do or be whatever is permitted without jeopardy and may expect protection against the infringements of others on the guaranteed freedoms at issue. Once again, even assuming natural rights to exist, they would add nothing to the posited rights enjoyed.

Since the idea of a natural right is not abstracted from any real bodies (as is motion from moving bodies or as are lines from the edges of bodies), from what is it derived? Alas, neither looking into the etymologies of 'natural' nor of 'right' will reveal the origin. Most likely, it lies in the imaginations of those who wish to justify their behavior or to preserve some status quo which benefits them at the expense of others. For example, how splendid for men in patriarchal systems, if it can only be shown that "Nature and Nature's God" intend for men to dominate women naturally or by divinely imputed rights. The ASS of the West is filled with heartening justifications of male dominance and of the treatment of women and children as chattel.[177]

There is no bifurcation more important to religious people than that between the holy and the unholy or, put differently, between the sacred and the secular. Since 'holiness' names a class whose members (allegedly) possess a certain attribute, it must be taken, at first blush at least, to be a fictitious entity. It is instructive to see how holiness relates to 'quickness' and 'slowness', names of fictitious entities that appear in Bentham's writings.[178] 'Quickness' and 'slowness', of course, do not name absolutes and are largely dependent on man as the *measurer* of all things. Still and all, there is a vast difference in speed between the blink of an eye and the movement of a glacier, the first real entity above exhibiting quickness, the second exhibiting slowness, with all manner of degrees in between. It is not the same with holiness, there being nothing about it that is abstracted from any real entity. For example, there is nothing about the city of Jerusalem that permits one to abstract holiness from it (resulting in the "Holy City") the way one can abstract a measure of speed from a reflex action and call it quick as a wink.

As with 'natural rights', the source of that which is named by 'holiness' lies elsewhere. An examination of its etymology will doubtless be of some use but, in the end, insufficient. Far from being an attribute abstracted from real entities, holiness is a status conferred by imagination on singular persons and places, writings and rituals, not to exclude other candidates. It is a way of sheltering these items of potential weal and woe from profane hands. Holy items, in short, are taboo items. Being taboo, however, is not like being quantified as either massive or minuscule, according to some scale or other. The various and varying "holy" entities in the history of the world's religions are important grist for anthropologists and social psychologists, but they are not necessary to thought.

In short, no set that includes probity, perspicacity, gravity, temporality, and sanctity can be left as it is without further logical distinctions. Bentham had the wit to refine the necessary distinctions but could somehow never find the time to do so.

In an invited address titled "Jeremy Bentham and the Nature of Psychological Concepts," P. McReynolds points out an inconsistency in Bentham's concept of real entities.[179] In one instance, Bentham wrote, "In the case where to the object thus spoken of, existence is actually an object of one of the five senses and in particular the sense of touch or feeling,—the only one without which man cannot exist, say, in a word, where the object is a tangible one; here there is no fiction,—as this man, this beast, this bird, this fish, this star;—or this sort of man, this sort of beast, this sort of bird, this sort of fish, this sort of star,—the object spoken of may be termed a real entity."[180] In another instance, he wrote, "A real entity is an entity to which, on the occasion and for the purpose of discourse, existence is really meant to be ascribed."[181] This second construal is not only different from the first, it cannot be maintained, because when religious people make theological assertions, they mean to ascribe reality to the object(s) of their faith. Christians, for example, may speak of this instance of God's grace, this sacred object, this divine revelation, this angelic visit, this act of blasphemy, this unforgivable sin, etc. Here names are being imported from the WW of Christian faith and are made to function as do "this man, this beast, this bird, this fish, and this star," expressed above. Bentham was seriously mistaken if he thought that the *intention* to assert existence suffices to guarantee it.[182]

Thinking it unlikely that any writer was less misled by word magic than Bentham, C. K. Ogden strove to include him in the great tradition of British philosophy, epitomized by Bacon, Hobbes, Locke, Berkeley, Hume, Mill, Bradley, and Russell. Properly positioned between Hume and Mill, he was in some respects, according to Ogden, "the most original representative of this tradition," a tradition concerned ever and anon with the linguistic bases of philosophy.[183]

Contemplating Bentham's role in advancing the logic of his day, eminent American logician Willard Van Orman Quine writes,

> Bentham's step [forward] was the recognition of contextual definition, or what he called paraphrasis. He recognized that to explain a term we do not need to specify an object for it to refer to, nor even specify a synonymous word or phrase; we need only show, by whatever means, how to translate all the whole sentence in which the term is to be used.[184]

> Bentham's idea of paraphrasis flowered late, in [Bertrand] Russell's theory
> of descriptions. Russell's theory affords a rigorous and important example
> of how expressions can be made to parade as names and then be
> explained away as a mere manner of speaking, by explicit paraphrase of
> the context into an innocent notation.[185]

Although Bentham's concept of paraphrasis flowered in Bertrand Russell's theory of descriptions, Russell (1872–1970) did not take the rootstock from Bentham nor did any other of the founders of modern mathematized (or symbolic) logic. Beyond applying insights from his philosophy of language and theory of fictitious entities to the classical Aristotelian logic of his day,[186] Bentham did little more than tinker with it, and complain of its shortcomings and undue influence.[187] Similarly, Russell thought it historically significant but long since a dead-end and an impediment to clarity of thought.[188] When one remembers Bentham's dates (1748–1832) and compares these with the dates of the founders of modern logic, it is clear that he lived too soon to take advantage of the revolution in thought about to occur. It is also noteworthy that this revolution came more from the hands of mathematicians than from philosophers, either in the rationalistic or the empirical tradition. Consider the following: Augustus De Morgan (1806–1871), English mathematician and logician; George Boole (1815–1864), English mathematician and logician; Georg Cantor (1845–1918), German mathematician; Gottlob Frege (1848–1925), German mathematician and logician; Giuseppe Peano (1858–1932), Italian mathematician and logician; and David Hilbert (1862–1943), German mathematician and logician.

Although the early half of De Morgan's life overlapped the latter half of Bentham's, his most important logical works did not begin to appear until after Bentham's death. Much the same can be said of George Boole, the inventor of Boolean algebra, whose first important work appeared twelve years after Bentham's death. Gottlob Frege, commonly believed to be the most influential of the founders of modern logic, was born one hundred years after Bentham's birth and did not publish his first important book on logic until almost fifty years after Bentham's death. Frege's "introduction of quantifiers binding variables has been termed [by some] the greatest intellectual achievement of the nineteenth century."[189] Bentham, in short, was bypassed in the development of modern logic and was, thus, rendered largely irrelevant. Had he lived a hundred years later, he would not have developed the philosophy of language that is the hallmark of his thought.

Having been untimely born (to have taken advantage of the rise of modern symbolic logic) does not, of course, excuse Bentham from criticisms—criticisms made easier by some of the discoveries and techniques of that new logic. A hundred years after Bentham's death, English philosopher John Wisdom (b. 1904) took Bentham to task for a number of mistakes, and no list of Bentham's shortcomings relative to the naming of different kinds of entities would be complete without noting at least some of these.[190] Broadly speaking, Wisdom believes that Bentham contradicted himself occasionally, on other occasions fell into muddles, and on still other occasions was misled.

In *Interpretation and Analysis*, Wisdom discerns various contradictions: first (pp. 89–92), he quotes Bentham to the effect that the names of fictitious entities (i.e., of abstractions feigned by the mind to facilitate communication) constitute a "sort of verbal reality." Verbal reality bothers Wisdom for its vagueness, but worse, he believes it to be contradicted by Bentham's assertion that (excluding proper names and names of fabulous entities) there are but two kinds of names: "names of real entities—names of fictitious entities." Wisdom writes, "This passage [mentioning the two kinds of nameable entities above] contradicts the 'verbal reality' view . . . and lays the fictitious entities which are 'objects' which are not 'real existing ones' open to the charge which the verbal reality theory was designed to meet."[191] Whether or not the mistake at issue is a contradiction, an unanswered question arises, namely, does "a sort of verbal reality" interpose itself as a third sort of reality between real physical and psychical entities on the one hand and fictitious entities, feigned by the mind, on the other.

Wisdom writes (p. 106) of another contradiction he discerns as follows: "[Bentham] again contradicts himself and makes fictitious [entities] = fabulous [entities] when he says that plants which do not exist are not real entities." What Bentham wrote, in part, was this: "But the *aggregate* conceived of as composed of all plants, present, past, and future put together, is manifestly the work of the *imagination*—a pure fiction."[192] Since such an aggregate cannot be visualized, it can hardly be a fabulous entity to Bentham, no matter what Wisdom thinks it to be.

Wisdom finds (p. 130) a serious inconsistency, if not a contradiction, in Bentham's views on the various contents entertainable by a human mind. At one point, Bentham places in the class of perceptible real entities "the impressions produced in groups by the application of sensible objects to the organs of sense," recollections, and the fruits of imagination.[193] Three pages later, we find, "Of nothing, therefore, that has place, or passes in our mind, can we speak, or so much as think, otherwise than in the way of *fictions*." Individual sensations reported upon as such are, of course, not abstractions and hence not fictions. Wisdom does not notice (or care to call attention to) the fact that in the same paragraph Bentham exempted the "sentiments of pleasure, or . . . sentiments of displeasure." Nevertheless, damage is done. Except for this lapse, Bentham meant by mental fictions abstractions such as "faculties, powers of the mind, disposition,"[194] "mind itself,"[195] and "understanding itself."[196] When he wrote "or so much as think," he undoubtedly meant to think with or about the abstractions at issue. Moreover, if one were to *think* or *speak* about (one's) perceptible real entities, beyond merely reporting them, one would have to use fictions as well.

When Bentham illustrated a point, saying, "That apple is ripe," while denying that the ripeness named any quality existing independently of the apple identified, he erred.[197] With only the slightest reliance on paraphrasis, if any, the statement *that apple is ripe* (or *that apple possesses ripeness*) becomes *that apple is in a (transient) condition such that its seeds are mature enough to sprout, given conducive conditions.* Here Bentham's mistakes are three: (1) He would have us believe that the quality of ripeness is being predicated on the name 'ripeness' rather than on the apple in question (if such were the case, nobody would bother to plant apple seeds, yet there are apple orchards aplenty); (2) in focusing on a particular apple as the only real entity involved (while in its ripened condition), he failed to focus on its seeds, the most reliable indicator of its ripeness; and (3) he failed to make clear that a series of events in a recognizable, dependable, predictable process (such as the ripening process of apples) can legitimately be singled out and treated verbally as being as objective as any individual object.[198]

Failing to devise a new kind of entity (such as might name the sort of identifiable, repetitive process identified above) to stand midway between real entities (individual bodies) and fictitious ones (the qualities of bodies), Bentham, according to Wisdom, fell into ambiguity. Focusing on 'ripeness' (but not analyzing it as I did in terms of the process of maturing seeds in an apple), Wisdom discerns a different kind of seeds, the seeds of confusion in Bentham's thought: "We shall find two importantly different classes of case in which Bentham would talk of fictitious entities. There is the case where a noun names some entity though the entity is not an individual thing, e.g., Ripeness. And there is the case where the noun names nothing . . . , e.g., the average man, obligations, existence, necessity, probability, and potentiality" (p. 119).

Clearly, there is a stark difference between the concepts of ripeness (in fruit) and that of the average man (in intelligence, let us say, following Wisdom's example, pp. 74–75). This can be illustrated by the following propositions: (1) the average ripe apple is sweet, and (2) the average American male has an IQ of 100. The latter is derived mathematically by adding all the scores arrived at when the members of an unbiased sample take an IQ test and the sum of the individual scores is then divided by the number taking the test. Although there may be one or more individuals in the unbiased sample who score exactly 100, there is no need for anybody to do so to establish the average of 100. The former, however, is determined empirically (by human tongues) in response to the level of fructose in apples at the time in their development when their seeds become mature. Wisdom thinks (pp. 119–120) that Bentham became aware of problems like this when he distinguished between "fictitious qualities" and "real qualities" but that he failed to rectify the situation.[199]

Although Wisdom's criticisms of Bentham are far more exhaustive than the examples above might indicate, the reader by now may be quite exhausted and care for no more. Yet, one final example may help and also serve as a turning point to some criticisms made necessary by modern science. Bentham wrote that it was indubitable that 'motion' names a fictitious entity.[200] Furthermore, the phrase 'in motion' seemed to him to lead to the conclusion that motion, somehow or other, is a receptacle *in* which an object may move.[201] To this Wisdom responds triumphantly, "And I *should* like to say this to Bentham: If there is one thing we not only see but also feel more than another it is a motion. 'I felt the motion of the car'" (p. 92). This is a singularly inept attempt at refutation. Bentham never denied that human bodies move, whether on foot or in some sort of conveyance: "[N]o body whatsoever is, or ever has been, or ever will be, absolutely in a state of rest, i.e., without being in motion with reference to some other body or bodies.[202]

There is a far better way to show the mistake in Bentham's notion that the phrase 'in motion' presupposes a receptacle in which bodies move. It comes from his own life and concerns his travels (in Europe) to Russia.[203] Once there, he could theoretically have kept going east, over hill and down dale, fording rivers and sailing oceans, until he returned to his home in England. Moreover, his route to Russia took him first to the south of Europe, then east to the Balkans and Turkey, then north to Poland, and finally east to Russia. At any point in his peregrinations, he could theoretically have proceeded north or south and returned to any given starting point along his route. Apart from the particular conveyances in which he found himself, his peregrinations were not undertaken in a box named by 'in motion'. Given this biographical information (upon which Wisdom could have drawn), it defies belief that he thought he had landed a solid blow on Bentham by describing his (Wisdom's) experiences of motion in a motor car.[204]

The foregoing instances of logical criticism, given first by me and then by reference to John Wisdom's *Interpretation and Analysis*, show that there are problems in Bentham's theory of fictions. He knew this and knew that there was more to be done, yet he failed to complete the task. The type of logical criticisms given above, however, cannot provide comfort to those who would rehabilitate theological assertions using the WW of any religion. Moreover, Bentham's attack on the theological use of language does not depend greatly on the success of his theory of fictitious entities but more, rather, on the relations between the names of nonentities and fabulous entities on the one hand and the names of real entities, physical and more especially psychical, on the other. When called on to elucidate what they mean (by using other words), theologians find that they cannot employ paraphrasis legitimately but have to resort to synonymy, using other words from their own religous WW. Trying to explain a holy object by saying that it is a sacred object, or vice versa, elucidates nothing.

To a considerable extent, then, the logical criticisms of Bentham above are tangential to his criticisms of the Thirty-nine Articles of Religion and the Catechism of the Anglican Church—and to the theological mouthings of any other church, temple, or mosque.

Due to an accident of birth and, therefore, through no fault of his own, Bentham's scientific views were no better than those of the highly educated, worldly amateur of his day. Although not a scientist, either by inclination or training, he looked to science for much of his worldview. The relevant elements of it follow:

- Space is both absolute (i.e., infinite) and relative to one's location.[205]
- 'Substance' names a class of real entities (i.e., bodies), whereas 'matter' names a class of fictitious entities (i.e., qualities of material bodies).[206]
- Existence is a predicate of naked (material) substance. Put differently, 'substance' names a homogeneous, undifferentiated substratum that can assume the various material qualities, characteristics, or attributes that we experience in objects and deal with daily.[207]
- Bodies are composed of "solid matter" and "empty space."[208]
- Within bodies and between their atoms (or particles) are to be found not only "empty spaces" but also the "attraction of cohesion" and "intertestine repulsion." These are among the "powers of nature."[209]
- The "attraction of cohesion," commonly called gravity or gravitation, is a force drawing all matter together. Repulsion prevents the collapse of matter.[210]
- All bodies in the universe are in motion, there being no absolute rest, although many bodies are at rest relative to one another.[211]
- The earth, globular in shape, moves through space with its sibling planets; the sun moves; and so too do the so-called fixed stars.[212] Stellar and planetary motions are endless, whereas certain other motions are terminating.[213]
- Respecting endless motion, there is no first mover or cause, 'cause' being but the name of a fictitious entity.[214]
- When a body previously at rest in relation to another body (or bodies) is set in motion, inertia and often resistance must be overcome.[215]
- Although the moon is the only constant power to raise water on earth, it is not related to the flux and reflux of that water, because whereas the former is a real entity, the latter two are but fictitious ones.[216]

- To account for the differences between bodies in point of distance and with respect to intervals of time, we humans arrive at the abstract idea of motion. Never distinct from bodies moving, and not a body itself, motion is a fictitious entity.[217]
- Since people are misled by the term 'in time', time, like motion, is spoken of as though it were a receptacle. On the contrary, it can only be spoken of legitimately as a modification of space and, withal, a fictitious entity.[218]
- Balancing the repulsion of particles of matter in any mass, say, of Newton's apple, is the attraction of gravity, keeping the particles of the apple positioned as they are. This species of force, which also draws planets and stars together, is a fictitious entity.[219]

Trying to integrate what he knew of the "forces of nature" with his beloved theory of fictions, Bentham fell into an irredeemable error. To illustrate this error in starkest fashion, consider the following quote: "For the purpose of rendering, in the best manner in which we are able, an account of the motion of such bodies as are in motion, and of the rest of such as are at rest, certain fictitious entities are, by a sort of innocent false-hood, the utterance of which is necessary to the purpose of discourse, feigned to exist and operate in the character of causes, equally real with, and distinct from, the perceptible and perceived effects, in relation to which they are considered in the character of causes."[220] If there were the slightest truth in this, then the celebrated laws of gravity, articulated by Newton, would apply not to planetary bodies in orbit around a central star nor to unsupported bodies moving, for example, toward the center of the earth; the laws of gravity would, rather, apply to certain innocent false-hoods feigned by the mind to facilitate communication. They would apply to fictitious ideas!

The absurdity of such a notion can best be illustrated by considering the situation among our prehistoric ancestors prior to the time when they had the wit to invent abstract nouns and, thus, before they could name fic-titious entities in communication. In such benighted times, we may sup-pose that unsupported bodies in the earth's gravitational field would not have fallen to earth as now but might have swooped up and down, zig-zagged this way or that, or followed any of a number of oblique angles in their peregrinations. Likewise, the planets in our solar system would not have been constrained to transcribe ellipses in their routes around the sun but might have careened this way or that way, speeding up or slowing down at random. This will not do. The laws of gravity do not apply to (nor are they of) a certain class of noun-substantives.

Were Bentham resurrected long enough to grasp the drift of modern science, he would find it enormously more hostile to elements of his worldview (including his theory of fictions) than any threat posed by the science of his time. He would find substances expunged and essences discarded from scientific thought. He would learn that 'existence' does not name a predicate that can be added to the properties of bodies. He would learn that what he had thought of as atoms (i.e., the smallest units of solid matter) had been smashed long since, yielding ever more minute and evanescent particles. He would come to understand that photons of light sometimes appear to be particles and at other times to be waves but that, whatever they may be, they are bent while streaming past powerful sources of gravity. He would learn that to such "powers of nature" as gravity and electromagnetism would have to be added two more fundamental forces of nature, the strong and weak nuclear forces. He would be made aware of the convertibility of matter and energy, of the conjunction of space and time, and of the curvature of the former and the relativity of the latter.[221] He would hear of gravitons and of a link between gravity and time. He would be faced with Einstein's General Theory of Relativity, with bafflements of quantum mechanics, and of the current impossibility in uniting the two in a satisfactory TOE (i.e., a theory of everything). He would be made aware of our expanding universe; of the singularity from which it exploded in a "big bang"; of dark matter and black holes; of string theory; and of the uncertain (but very distant) destiny of the cosmos, whether it continues expanding forever or eventually contracts into a "big crunch." It would be easy to go on and on in this vein, but there is no need to beat the dead horse that science has made of some of Bentham's fictitious entities. In any case, theologians and all who would impose religious dogmas upon children can take no comfort in the discomfiture that a resurrected Bentham would have to endure.

When turning to criticisms of a psychological sort that can be lodged against Bentham for his attacks on Christianity in general and on Anglicanism in particular, a deep and profound irony appears. On his part, Bentham misunderstood the psychology of religion and therefore had little sympathy for it; or perhaps he had little sympathy for religion and therefore misunderstood its psychology. It hardly matters which. For their part, the practitioners of priestcraft (taken in the broadest sense) believe they speak the truths of another, higher world and attempt to show how the denizens and demands of that other world impinge on this world, but what they are really doing, to a large degree, is practicing personal (or individual) and social psychology. Moreover, in modern nations, they do so without being licensed. These practitioners are so focused on theology that they are largely blind to what they are doing psychologically. On the other hand, were they to perceive their religious activities for what they are, the practitioners thereof would probably lose much of their effectiveness. Effective or not, it is one thing to persist in manipulating people unwittingly; quite a different thing to do so consciously. Both types can be found in the clergy.[222]

Bentham's willing ignorance of the manifold roots of religion has been detailed in part 1 and needs no further elaboration. It is enough here to examine two instances of how psychological factors blunt his broadside against the Anglican Catechism. The reader will remember how unsparing he was in attacking the ritual practice of infant baptism. A moment of sympathetic reflection, however, would have revealed to him why contemporary Anglicans were eager to embrace the ritual in question, even though its practice was (and is) unsupported by Gospel teaching.

First, we begin with belief in a deity quite as dreadful as the one pictured in the AINR, especially when in wrathful moods. Then we insert ourselves imaginatively into the historical context in which Jesus made his appearance. In this context we find Jews blaming one another and themselves for the sins, corporate and individual, that presumably prompted the Bible-god to allow the heathen Romans to occupy the Promised Land. Into this context came prophets, now and again, predicting a purifying conflagration, from the ashes of which Israel would rise anew as a holy and liberated land. Such a one was John the Baptist who preached a baptism of repentance as a way to survive the wrath to come (Matt. 3:7–12). The Gospels give no hint that children were expected to repent to save themselves, much less infants who could not have repented. Into this situation came Jesus who, though he submitted to John's baptism, did so for a puzzling reason (Matt. 3:15). Needless to say, the adult Jews who submitted to John's baptism of repentance might as well have stayed at home. Israel did not rise anew, holy and liberated, after purging by any particular conflagration.

Despite bitter disappointment in the ill fortunes of Israel, Christian faith of a highly Jewish nature persisted intact until the self-appointed apostle to the Gentiles made his appearance and began to change the equation. Showing no interest in the salvation of the Jewish nation on earth, but focusing rather on the salvation of the individual (Jew and Gentile alike) in heaven, Paul preached a different baptism. Herein repentance is degraded in relation to beliefs, that is, to the beliefs that Jesus is Lord and that the Bible-god raised him from the dead (Rom. 10:9). Moreover, baptism as a ritual of purification is replaced by baptism as a ritual reenactment of Jesus' death, burial, and resurrection (Rom. 6:1–11). Those who have died to sin are buried in baptismal water even as he was buried in a sepulcher, and as he was resurrected from the dead so the redeemed rise into newness of life, here and hereafter in heaven.

Acts 16:25–34 confirms the contentions above. While Paul is imprisoned in Macedonia, an earthquake sets him loose, from walls and fetters alike. Though panic-stricken that his prisoner is free, the jailer is urged by Paul not to kill himself. The jailer then asks what he must do to be saved and is told that he should *believe* in the Lord Jesus. Here there is no mention of repentance nor of any connection with Israel's fortunes. In any case, the jailer is baptized forthwith, together with his whole family. Whether this is historically accurate or merely an edifying tale, the theological transition from John's baptism to Paul's is clear to see. Of only slightly less interest is whether or not the jailer's family included minor children or babes in arms. If so, then baptism had already become something quite different from what the Gospels had pictured it as being when John the Baptist burst upon the scene. Whatever the case, the practice of infant baptism has ancient roots in Christendom, its motivation being obvious.[223]

Given that heaven could not be heavenly, were one's beloved children not at hand, enjoying everlasting bliss; given that one could not forgive oneself for leaving any stone unturned that might guarantee redemption to one's children; given that children are born with original sin and are thus in mortal peril of falling prematurely into the hands of an "angry God"; and given that any of many vicissitudes might prevent one's children from reaching the age at which they could repent, confess their faith, and be baptized, what is to prevent good Christian parents from seizing the initiative? At the very least, what they do to save their infantile children can do no harm. With such dire prospects, what difference can it make that their efforts are unwarranted by the Gospels?

So, Christian parents of many stripes, together with pious godparents, present themselves at a church in the presence of its pastor (or other priest or preacher), solemnly make promissory oaths that they cannot keep, and suffer the newborn (who can in no way repent or confess its faith) to have some water dashed on its forehead. In these proceedings, the parents and godparents have done what they could, and, reassured, feel the better (i.e., less anxious) for it. In league with them, the pastor does his (rarely her) bit. Authoritative in clerical vestments, freighted with divine science, adept at performing magical rites such as baptism, and acting in blessed conformity with ancient tradition, this sanctified person reinforces the parents and godparents in the straws at which they grasp, and, withal, the child is loved. Only a scold would observe that the whole affair is highly suspect as far as the Gospels are concerned.

Bentham's attacks on the doctrine of the Trinity are no less savage than his attacks on infant baptism. Little or no appreciation is shown in *CECE* of how anybody could believe in the incomprehensibilities of Trinitarian dogma. The cost to Christian believers, however, is quite small in relation to the presumed payoff for such belief. Whatever else Christianity may be, it becomes intensely soteriological toward the end of believers' lives. They want forgiveness from the presumed sovereign of the world for failures in complying not only with his demands but also with societal demands, want assurance of safe passage to the supposed world to come, and want endless reunion with loved ones. Christians are not unique in these hopes. These are commonly held by the religious of the world. If the cost of these divine benisons is belief in various and sundry incomprehensibilities, well, then, the price is right.

The absurdities of Christian and other theologies are baffling only to finite minds, or so the argument goes. To the supposedly infinite mind of the so-called Divine Sovereign, they are eminently clear. To a greater or lesser degree, the adherents of Judaism, Christianity, and Islam are conditioned from infancy to denigrate their minds in this way. Hard upon the heels of Eve's original sin, together with Adam's thoughtless compliance (Gen. 3:1–6)[224] and the murder of Abel by Cain (Gen. 4:2–12), comes the story of the tower of Babel (Gen. 11:1–7). It shows divine intolerance for human prowess. The solution is to make wisdom and knowledge consist of the fear of YHWH (Prov. 1:7, 9:10; Ps. 111:10). However, it is to St. Paul that one must look to find the nadir in the degradation of human intelligence. In 1 Corinthians 3:18–20, he calls for nothing less than the stultification of human intellect. This gives Christians carte blanche to believe any number of absurdities and incomprehensibilities in their quest for salvation. Bentham should have known that when one's eternal weal and woe are believed to be at stake, intellect will be sacrificed gladly.

Muhammad, the founder of Islam, seems never to have encountered nor been bested by worldly philosophers, dialecticians, rhetoricians, and their learned ilk. Accordingly, his deity, Allah, felt no need to put such people down with revelations recommending stultification as a way of avoiding the wrath to come. Muhammad's fulminations were directed more toward idolaters, unbelievers, and apostates from scripture, Jewish and Christian alike, than toward those we would recognize as intellectuals, free from institutional religion. Nevertheless, the Koran abounds with reasons to fear Allah and his ghastly, everlasting punishments. The following quotations will give some of the flavor of Allah's revelations. First, in the segment of the Koran called "The Cow," we find,

> Allah: there is no god but He, the Living, the Eternal One. Neither slumber nor sleep overtakes Him. His is what the heavens and the earth contain. Who can intercede with him except by his permission? He knows what is before and behind men. They can grasp only that part of His knowledge which He wills.

From the segment called "The Imrans" comes,

> It is He who has revealed to you the Koran. Some of its verses are precise in meaning—others ambiguous. Those whose hearts are infected with disbelief follow the ambiguous part, so as to create dissension by seeking to

explain it. But no one knows its meaning except Allah. Those who are well-grounded in knowledge say: We believe in it: it is all from our Lord.

Finally, from "Cattle,"

> If We sent down to you a Book inscribed on real parchment and the unbelievers touched it with their own hands, they would still say: "This is nothing but plain magic." They ask: "Why has no angel been sent down to him?" If we had sent down an angel, We would have given him the semblance of a mortal, and would have thus confused them with that in which they are already confused.[225]

Philosophers such as Plato, Aristotle, Epicurus, and Zeno would have received very short shrift from Muhammad and his god. Islam, it must be remembered, means submission, and a Muslim is one who submits. Should submission to Allah require the stultification of intellect for entrance into Paradise, so be it. Islam is as adept as Christianity in creating in children and in adult converts the "prepared imbecility" necessary to maintain the faith.[226]

Finally, two closely related questions of psychological import remain to be asked: (1) is it not obvious that religious people are happier than those espousing no religion, and (2) since the moral object of Utilitarianism is to try to achieve the greatest happiness of (or for) the greatest number of people, should Bentham not have facilitated and promoted religion rather than attacking it? The answer to the first of these two questions is that it is not obvious that religion makes believers happier than the absence of religion makes unbelievers. Moreover, any attempt at finding the correct answer must be empirical rather than a priori or self-evidential.

Empirical attempts at finding a random, unbiased sample of religious people in America, for example, to compare with a random, unbiased sample of nonreligious people (as to degrees of happiness) are all but impossible. The second sample would clearly contain two subsets: those who are nonreligious because indifferent and those who are nonreligious because antireligious. Moreover, the second of these subsets would likely contain a larger proportion of highly educated people than the first subset and would thus be skewed. The first sample, without reference to any particular denomination, would likely have to contain two subsets composed of those who are less dependent on ecclesiastical control and of those who are more dependent.[227] The various subsets already mentioned are but the tip of a demographic iceberg. To complicate matters further, research instruments that might measure relative happiness (in relation to religion versus nonreligion) in scientifically advanced countries might not work well in third-world countries and even less well in pockets with populations characterized by widespread illiteracy, intense tribalism, or theocracy.

No valid study of religious satisfactions conducive to happiness can be undertaken nowadays in ignorance of research in neuropsychology and neurophysiology. Two articles in the *NYT*, written by the same author but separated by a span of five years, make this clear. The first was titled "Feeling Cheerful? Thank the Brain's Left Lobe"; the second, "Forget Money; Nothing Can Buy Happiness, Some Researchers Say." In the first of these articles, the author, Daniel Goleman, reported on the investigations of two researchers. They discovered independently that in people with happy, sunny dispositions there was a greater amount of activity in the left frontal cortex of the brain than in the right frontal cortex, whereas in people of a melancholy, anxious disposition there was greater activity in the right frontal cortex than in the left. One of these researchers, Richard Davidson, has since theorized that each of us is born with a set point for happiness, that is, "a genetically determined mood level that the vagaries of life may nudge upward or downward, but only for a while."[228] Although the percentage (if any) of mood control established genetically has yet to be discovered, it seems reasonable to expect that brain chemistry normally plays a part in happiness. The suspicion is that dopamine, a neurotransmitter (endemic to human brains) plays an important role in the set-point mechanism theorized. How, if at all, one's religion or lack thereof relates to dopamine levels remains to be seen.

Throughout the twentieth century, in the United States, for example, religion has presented a benign face. It has not always been so. Toward the end of the eighteenth century, America's founding fathers were at pains to deliver their new nation from the *evils* of religion. Whatever else religion is, it is a mode of partisanship that can range from a mild form of personal and social identification to a ferocious force dividing people into true believers and infidels. In a review of Walter Burkert's *Creation of the Sacred: Tracks of Biology in Early Religion*, Gustavo Benavides writes, "Burkert's work reminds us that through most of history, religion has had less to do with dismantling than with the erection of boundaries; less with peace than violence; less with spirituality than with efforts to manage physical reality. The wish of many in the industrial world that religion be essentially uplifting may be morally admirable, but that desire should not lead us to ignore the harsh realities with which religious practices and representations have been concerned."[229]

The repression, persecution, and torture of minorities by religious majorities; violent aggression designed not just to subdue but to exterminate unbelievers and false believers alike; the kidnapping and enslavement of individuals viewed as subhuman; and the subjection of women to lowly status (if not to the role of being mere chattel, including the fate of being treated as baby-making machines) have all been a monotonous and distressing feature of some religion or other throughout history.[230] Karl Marx

hit the bullseye when he wrote, "The social principles of Christianity justified the slavery of Antiquity, glorified the serfdom of the Middle Ages and
equally know, when necessary, how to defend the oppression of the prole-
tariat."[231] In a similar vein, but without promoting Marxism, I once wrote,
"Religion has, all too often, been hypostatized and subsequently perceived
as an intrepid pathfinder always moving ahead, ascending ever higher and
pausing only long enough for the vanguard of mankind to draw nigh
before faring forth again. Religion is, however, far more like a blind guide
than a pathfinder, more like a camp follower than a leader."[232] Religion, in
short, carries out the conservative function of sacralizing whatever social
system is established at a given time and in a given place, especially when
the system (as usual) benefits the reigning power structure, including the
higher priesthood. Historically, of course, the two have often been melded
into one, theocracies being commonplace. In this way, great evils can be
institutionalized. There is no slavery more complete than that in which the
slaves, along with the ruling classes, believe that they are all positioned as
they are because their god wills it. Put differently, a beloved tyranny is the
most effective tyranny.

To an infinity of instances of such religiously inspired cruelties as the
application of lethal violence, torture, persecution, slavery, repression,
degradation, and scapegoating (visited on minorities and unbelievers)
must be added an infinity of instances of ritual mutilation, self-inflicted
torture, and agonizing deprivation. Male and female circumcision and even
castration leap to mind in relation to ritual mutilation. Less well known
but grisly as well is the practice of finger sacrifice.[233] As for the innumerable
deprivations endured to please various deities, the reader can refer to the
latter half of my distillation of Bentham's *AINR*.[234] Espousing the dubious
notion that self-inflicted suffering now buys endless pleasure hereafter,
unnumbered millions, though not flagellants themselves, have nonetheless
deprived themselves the pleasures of this or that innocuous but taboo
object or activity.[235]

Typically, religions function in two ways that would clearly be contradictory, if not for the temporal separation of the functions at issue. They
routinely commence by debasing individuals, by lowering self-esteem, and
by increasing a person's sense of dependence while simultaneously minimizing that person's confidence in his personal control.[236] Rendered con-
trite and humble, the individual is finally told to buck up, that the deity
loves him, has sent grace (or its equivalent) and forgiveness, and that a glorious future beyond the grave awaits. So, at the end, religions become soteriological. In modern parlance, this is the bottom line of all religion. From
a psychological point of view, however, the problem is that many heed the
first part of the message, debase themselves satisfactorily, but never really
believe or fully accept the assurance of forgiveness and grace and, hence,

continue to live guiltily in more fear of future punishments and of death than might otherwise be the case, given different belief systems. In short, not everyone finds grace amazing!

Every experienced Christian pastor, ministering to the dying, encounters more apprehension among the "redeemed" than, theoretically, ought to be the case with those washed in the "Blood of the Lamb." How does one explain such unexpected frights and forebodings? However one goes about explaining it, the apprehensions of dying Christians over their fate, even when "saved," and fears at the end of mortal life must be factored into any attempt at deciding whether or not religion brings a greater balance of pain or pleasure. Bentham, on his deathbed, suffered no frights as to whether he had been redeemed or not.

When all the pains suffered by people resulting from all the evils or types of evil included above are computed, the question of whether or not Bentham ought to have promoted religion (as a good utilitarian) becomes a closer call than might have been expected. On a one-to-one basis, there are surely unbelievers who are as happy or happier than believers. The former, lacking religion, are not as constricted in their beliefs by myths and not as curtailed in their actions by taboos. They suffer no guilt over being human and do not fear posthumous pains. The latter, possessing religion, have the comfort of believing that "Someone" is in charge of the world, that prayer and ritual have an effect on the future, and that forgiveness is available. Since believers are so much more numerous than unbelievers, it can be argued that Bentham ought to have promoted the consolations and hopes religions offer their devotees.

Confronted thusly, one point is sure. He would not have given up his consequence-based ethics in favor of any alternative authority-based ethics, but he might have been willing to construe the Principle of Utility differently. In one final attempt at understanding Bentham, let us consider the following: suppose it were discovered that people, on the whole, were happier before Darwin confronted humankind with his claims of organic evolution, or suppose that people, on the whole, were very much happier before Copernicus confronted us all with the claim that the sun does not orbit our earthly home, but that we orbit it and moreover are not in the very center of the universe. In the former case, perhaps we should become as the "scientific creationists," denying science to Darwin and claiming it for Genesis, no matter the ensuing absurdity. In the latter case, perhaps we should become flat-earthers, denying science to Copernicus and claiming it for Ptolemy, no matter the ensuing absurdity. One is left to wonder how high a price ought to be paid for achieving the greatest happiness to the greatest number of people, should the ill-founded pleasures and illusory consolations of religion be factored into the equation.[237]

NOTES

173. George Albert Wells, *Religious Postures: Essays on Modern Christian Apologists and Religious Problems* (La Salle, IL: Open Court, 1988), pp. 57–63.

174. See *A Fragment on Ontology*, in *WJB*, 8:208. Those who wish to type Bentham as an atheist will have to deal with his assertion on this page that 'God', 'Author', and 'Creator' of nature are the names of "real entities: not names of fictitious entities."

175. There is also a conceptual difference between probity and perspicacity, but this difference is trivial when compared with the conceptual difference between temporality and gravity.

176. *A Fragment on Ontology*, in *WJB*, 8:199.

177. Genesis not only arranges for the male to be created first (2:23), but also arranges for sin to enter the world through the female (3:1–16). The extent to which female children are chattel in the ASS of the West can be seen in Exod. 21:7–8, wherein tips are given for selling a daughter into slavery. A son who curses his parents is to be executed (Exod. 21:17). Women who are regarded as the weaker sex in the New Testament (1 Pet. 3:7) are viewed as imperfect males by the medieval church and not of the right substance to handle holy objects. Hence, women are unfit for the priesthood.

178. *A Fragment on Ontology*, in *WJB*, 8:197.

179. This address was delivered to Division 24 of the American Psychological Association in 1968 and was first published in the *Journal of General Psychology* 82 (1970): 113–27, then reprinted in *Jeremy Bentham: Critical Assessments*, ed. Bhikhu Parekh, vol. 2 (London and New York: Routledge, 1993), 145–59. For the inconsistency noted in the text, see *Critical Assessments*, pp. 152–53.

180. *Essay on Language*, in *WJB* 8:327.

181. *A Fragment on Ontology*, in *WJB*, 8:196.

182. I know of no piece of theological writing (and doubt that any exists or has ever existed) in which the author distinguishes between the names imported from his or her theological WW as to whether they are, variously, the names of fabulous entities, of inferential entities, of fictitious entities, or of real entities. The presumption will be that all the theological names at issue are the names of real entities. When pressed on this point, some theologians will fall back upon metaphorical usage and claim that what is being referring to is real or true *spiritually*, even if not literally.

183. C. K. Ogden, introduction to *Bentham's Theory of Fictions* (London: Kegan Paul, Trench, Trubner, 1932), pp. ix, cvii.

184. William Van Orman Quine, *Ontological Relativity, and Other Essays* (New York: Columbia University Press, 1969), p. 72.

185. Ibid., p. 101. Bentham and Russell were both concerned with names and with the deceptions and illogicalities that could be foisted upon thought therewith. Bentham categorized the names in his philosophy of language according to the various entities, real, fictitious, fabulous, etc., expounded herein at great length. Russell (and others) learned how to dispense with names (implying entities) found in the primary (i.e., subject) position in assertions by using as needed for correct construal (1) a mathematized symbol system including the three basic terms of quantification

(i.e., everything, nothing, and something), which are meaningless in isolation from propositions; (2) variables (i.e., x, y, z, etc.) bound to these terms of quantification, equally meaningless in isolation; (3) the propositional functions of necessity, possibility, and impossibility; and (4) descriptions of the characteristics of entities or alleged entities in lieu of names. For those who wish to learn more about Russell's theory of descriptions and the symbolizing techniques of modern logic, the following should be helpful. The famous theory of descriptions was first expressed in Russell's article "On Denoting," *Mn*, n. s., no. 56 (October 1905): 479–83. See also Bertrand Russell, *Introduction to Mathematical Philosophy* (London: George Allen and Unwin, 1919), esp. chap. 16. More readily accessible physically than these sources, perhaps, is G. E. Moore, "Russell's 'Theory of Descriptions,'" in *The Philosophy of Bertrand Russell*, ed. Paul Arthur Schillp (New York: Tudor Publishing, 1944), pp. 177–225. Although this is a secondary source, it is so carefully expressed and was so agreeable to Russell that it can be depended on to express the latter's views on the subject accurately. This footnote and footnote 56 above have been difficult to present, because once one begins to show how modern symbolic logic has superseded Bentham's antiquated logic together with nearly the whole of Aristotelian logic, it is difficult to know when to quit. One point, however, is clear and can be put concisely: each is hard on metaphysics in general and on theology in particular.

186. For example, see *Chrestomathia*, in *WJB*, 8:120–21. The reason for needing a theory of language to bolster the still useful (to Bentham) aspects of Aristotelian logic can be illustrated with the following two syllogisms: (1) The person who coincidentally met his sister, Sacagawea (of the Lewis and Clark expedition), in the Bitterroot Mountains of North America was a Shoshone Indian. All Shoshone Indians were (or are) native Americans. Therefore, the person who met his sister, Sacagawea, was a native American; (2) The individual being called Gabriel, who addressed the Virgin Mary (at the time of the Annunciation), was an angel. All angels are members of the Heavenly Host. Therefore, the individual who addressed the Virgin Mary at the Annunciation was a member of the Heavenly Host. The parallelism and formal validity (in Aristotelian logic) of these two arguments should not deceive the reader into thinking that they are equally sound nor that they should be equally persuasive.

187. In his *Essay on Logic*, Bentham wrote, "In respect of miscarriage and success, the character and lot of the art of logic, as taught by Aristotle, may be considered as a sort of prototype of the art of alchemy, as taught by the searchers after the universal medicine, the universal solvent, and the philosopher's stone. In both instances, in respect of the ultimate object, a complete failure was the result; but, in both instances, in the course, and in consequence, of the inquiry, particular discoveries of no small use and importance were brought to light" (*WJB*, 8:238). So, Bentham saw heuristic value in Aristotelian logic. He also minted names for newly discovered (by him) informal fallacies (for a similar observation, see p. 234, and also *Chrestomathia*, in *WJB*, 8:120). Regarding Bentham's complaints, see *Essay on Logic*, in *WJB*, 8:217–20, and *Essay on Language*, in *WJB*, 8:338.

188. Bertrand Russell, *A History of Western Philosophy* (New York: Simon and Schuster, Touchstone Books, 1945), esp. chap. 22, pp. 195–202.

189. *DPR*, s. v. "Frege, Friedrich Ludwig Gottlob."

190. See John Wisdom, *Interpretation and Analysis* (London: Kegan Paul, Trench, Trubner, 1931). Although Wisdom was among the most trenchant critics of Bentham's logic (if not the most), his criticisms commence in an unsatisfactory way. He quotes Bentham (p. 32) as having said, "Propositions may be distinguished into purely real, purely verbal [i.e., tautological], [and] semi-real." It is unfortunate that Wisdom thought he was citing from Bentham's *Essay on Logic*, chap. 7, section 9, when he was actually citing from the *Essay on Language*, chap. 6, section 7, p. 333. He then attributes the following assertion to Bentham as an example of a purely real proposition: "Apples are nourishing." Bentham may well have said this, but not in Wisdom's mistaken citation above nor in my correction. In the *Essay on Language*, chap. 6, sect. 5, p. 330, Bentham wrote, "Apples are sweet." This is a better example than the one Wisdom attributes to him; nevertheless, let us examine Wisdom's selection concerning apples, first noting that in the context of different kinds of definitions, Wisdom calls Bentham's concept of a purely real proposition an interpretation. Whatever the assertion about apples may be called, *apples are nourishing* is unnecessarily misleading, and Wisdom ought to have noticed it. The properties of apples, as apples, are chemical, genetic, and morphological. It is incidental to apples, as such, that some organisms, including humans, can digest and metabolize them for energy. Apples remain apples even though they can, for example, never suffice for nourishing tigers. By the same token, grass, which nourishes cattle, remains grass, even though it does not nourish humans. One cannot assert truthfully that apples are nourishing (as though this were a universal property of apples) without specifying the contexts and conditions that would make it true. At best, apples are nourishing to some humans (but not to newborns) and, therefore, only sometimes and only to some organisms. Despite the confusion engendered by the muddle above, the point is that, on occasion, propositions attempt to describe objects by reference to one or more of their properties, while, on other occasions, propositions attempt to state the meaning of words using different but synonymous words or phrases. Bentham identifies such propositions as "purely verbal." Wisdom likes to see them as examples of what he calls analysis as opposed to mere interpretation. He quotes Bentham as saying, "A wight is a man." This definition of 'wight' by synonymy is found in the *Essay on Language*, chap. 6, section 7, p. 334. Wisdom then quotes Bentham again (from the source just cited), "A proposition is both really and verbally significant in so far as by the names given to the subject and the attribute, respectively, the nature of both or either of them is brought to view. Example: Wood anemones are plants; sea anemones are animals." Bentham took the two propositions about anemones to be mixed, partially about the relevant objects or kinds of objects, partially about the words used which include one set of things within a larger set. At best, these are propositions that attempt a sort of definition by classification. Citing Bentham correctly this time (*Essay on Logic*, chap. 7, section 2, footnote), Wisdom quotes him as saying, "A definition is either a definition of the word alone, or a definition by means of the word. A definition of the thing signified—meant to be expressed by it." Wisdom then accuses Bentham of failing to explicate the meaning of "definition [of an object or thing] by *means* of the word [or words being] used" (p. 36; emphasis added). The fundamental problem here consists in the difficulty of defining 'definition' to everyone's satisfac-

tion. For example, is the act of defining limited to words or symbols alone (resulting in analytical statements) or can objects (or things) also be defined? There is no doubt that they can be described or classified, but do these acts constitute definition? Wisdom writes, "Any analysis can be properly called a definition" (p. 60). Immediately thereafter, he gives as an example of definition by analysis the following: "'*x* is a granddaughter of *y*' can be analyzed 'There is a *z* (i.e., something or other) such that *y* is a parent of *z*, and *x* is a daughter of *z*.'"

191. Not everybody agrees with this criticism. Ogden, introduction to *Bentham's Theory of Fictions*, writes, "Thus when [Bentham] insists that fictions have a sort of verbal reality—i.e., we seem to be predicating something about them, though strictly the predicates are being applied only to names—he is readily misunderstood to be supposed to be asserting that the names stand for *nothing*; in which case he would appear to have been 'very much misled'" (p. lii). In any case, "a sort of verbal reality" does require as much clarification as possible. It is easy to predicate something or other about a word. For example, a given word may be of one syllable or more, may contain one vowel or more, may be derived from the Latin or from Anglo-Saxon, etc. When the word at issue is the name of a fictitious entity, however, the situation is different. Bentham wrote, "Of fictitious entities, whatsoever is predicated is not, consistently with strict truth, predicated (it then appears) of anything but their respective names" (*A Fragment on Ontology*, in *WJB*, 8:199). This raises the question of whether or not the name of a (or any) fictitious entity is susceptible to false predication or must always be predicated truthfully.

192. *Chrestomathia*, section 19, p. 121. To be a fabulous entity in Bentham's classification, the item in question must be visualizable and retrievable as a remembered image. It is hard to see how the set called 'plants' (past, present, or future) could be visualized, though easy to see how many of its members could be.

193. *A Fragment on Ontology*, in *WJB*, 8:196.

194. Ibid., p. 196.

195. *Chrestomathia*, in *WJB*, 8:84.

196. *Essay on Language*, in *WJB*, 8:328.

197. Ibid., p. 330.

198. Regarding point 2, instead of thinking of a ripe apple's mature seeds, Bentham probably had in mind the real psychical entities a ripe apple provides as opposed to those an unripe apple supplies. Even here paraphrasis can be used. For example, to the sense of touch (of fingers, teeth, and tongue) the unripe apple presents greater hardness than does the ripe apple. To the tongue, its chemical constituents provide more sourness than sweetness, and to the stomach of the eater, it is more liable to provide aches than is the ripe apple. It is incidental to the reproductive process of apples that the average person finds them at their optimum condition for eating at the very time their seeds become mature.

Regarding point 3, by being able to single out a process, I mean, for example, the ability to observe how the ripening of an apple differs from the ripening of a grapefruit. In a grapefruit, in the continuum from ripeness to overripeness, one can see (upon slicing open such a fruit) the seeds sprouting inside the grapefruit and growing, generally, toward the grapefruit's rind. Apple seeds do not behave in this way.

199. *A Fragment on Ontology*, in *WJB*, 8:211.

200. Ibid., p. 204.

201. Ibid., pp. 197, 204. Bentham refers to a moving body, having come to rest as being *at* rest and as being placed, as it were, on an imaginary pillar to which the body is anchored, as it were; see *Chrestomathia*, in *WJB*, 8:130.

202. *A Fragment on Ontology*, in *WJB*, 8:200.

203. See Ian R. Christie, *The Benthams in Russia, 1780–1791* (Oxford: Berg Publishers, 1993), esp. chaps. 3 and 4. Bentham took it for granted that the earth is a globe; see *Chrestomathia*, in *WJB*, 8:129.

204. The reader will probably have divined some of my annoyance with Wisdom. A word or two of explanation, though not in his defense, seems in order. *Interpretation and Analysis* is made more difficult to follow than necessary because more is going on therein than the criticism of Bentham's theory of fictions. In the 1920s and 1930s, there was a spirited debate, particularly in England, over some ramifications of Bertrand Russell's theory of descriptions (mentioned earlier). Throughout Wisdom's criticisms of Bentham, he is siding with G. E. Moore against some of Russell's positions. In 1905, Russell published a way of denoting nonexistent entities without tacitly presupposing their existence, then seeming to deny existence. His technique involved using variables having no meaning in isolation from the completed whole sentences in which they might appear. These and other symbols having no meaning outside the context of whole, completed assertions in which they appear came to be called incomplete symbols. Then, too, Russell concluded, for a time at least, that abstractions should be regarded as logical constructions. Accordingly, statements about the abstract term 'nation' (an example Wisdom uses) would be nothing over and above statements about all the doings of the members thereof. Thus, the doings of the English nation would be nothing but the doings of every Tom, Dick, and Harry constituting it as cocitizens, whereas the doings of the French nation would be nothing but the doings of every Pierre, Louis, and Marc constituting it as cocitizens. Wisdom remains oblivious throughout that this cannot be, for every (modern) nation also occupies a tract of land and has what we would now call an infrastructure. Thus, no nation can be reduced to its current members (and their doings) alone. Other examples of logical constructions will be found in the sources cited below. When one remembers paraphrasis (how Bentham insisted that sentences containing the names of fictitious entities ought to be translated into reconstituted sentences in which the only names appearing ought to be the names of real entities), one thinks of incomplete symbols. Are Bentham's fictitious entities anticipations of the incomplete symbols of modern logic or not? Likewise, when one realizes that the names of fictitious entities are also the names of abstractions, one is left to wonder whether or not they are logical constructions. On pp. 102–103, Wisdom lists five characteristics common to the two. Or was Bentham so muddled, using an outdated vocabulary, that one ought to use the modern understanding of incomplete symbols and logical constructions to dismantle his theory of fictions? Also, one must not neglect to ask after the relationship(s) of incomplete symbols and logical constructions to one another. However these questions are answered, *Interpretation and Analysis* bristles with references to incomplete symbols and logical constructions. Those with an appetite for more on these subjects should, of course, read this book in full, or failing that, from page 32 onward. The first half of the entry

on John Wisdom by Judith Jarvis Thompson in *EP* is as enlightening as it is easy. A splendid way to become thoroughly conversant with incomplete symbols and logical constructions is to look in the appendix of Schillp, *The Philosophy of Bertrand Russell*, for each relevant entry. Also see L. Susan Stebbing, *A Modern Introduction to Logic* (London: Methuen, 1930), esp. appendix B. She not only mentions Wisdom but sides with him and G. E. Moore in certain disputes with Russell.

205. *A Fragment on Ontology*, in *WJB*, 8:203.

206. Ibid., p. 201.

207. Ibid., p. 210.

208. *Chrestomathia*, in *WJB*, 8:129.

209. Ibid., pp. 129–31.

210. Ibid., pp. 132, 129.

211. Ibid., pp. 130–31; *A Fragment on Ontology*, in *WJB*, 8:200.

212. *Chrestomathia*, in *WJB*, 8:129; *A Fragment on Ontology*, in *WJB*, 8:200.

213. *A Fragment on Ontology*, in *WJB*, 8:207.

214. Ibid., pp. 207–208; *Chrestomathia*, in *WJB*, 8:130–31. For complicated reasons that do not require elucidation here, Bentham refused to consider the supreme inferential entity (i.e., God) to be the First Cause of the universe, contenting himself rather with the names 'Author' or 'Creator'.

215. *Chrestomathia*, in *WJB*, 8:129.

216. Ibid., p. 132; *A Fragment on Ontology*, in *WJB*, 8:208.

217. *Chrestomathia*, in *WJB*, 8:130; *A Fragment on Ontology*, in *WJB*, 8:200, 204.

218. *A Fragment on Ontology*, in *WJB*, 8:200, 203–204.

219. *Chrestomathia*, in *WJB*, 8:129–30, 132..

220. Ibid., p. 129.

221. One of the leading experts on time has defined it as follows: *"Time is the mode of activity, and without activity there can be no time."* This allows one to speak of time objectively without construing it as the name of a real entity in Bentham's terms; see Gerald J. Whitrow, *The Natural Philosophy of Time* (Oxford: Clarendon Press, 1980), p. 372. For an article that brings time into the closest association with gravity, see William Unruh, "Time, Gravity, and Quantum Mechanics," in *Time's Arrows Today*, ed. Steven F. Savitt (Cambridge: Cambridge University Press, 1995), pp. 23–65. For an extremely valuable book (esp. for the nonscientist) that touches on all the scientific topics that would confront a resurrected Bentham, see Stephen W. Hawking, *A Brief History of Time* (New York: Bantam Books, 1988).

222. I know whereof I speak, for in addition to having attended three theological schools, I was for nearly a decade an ordained, practicing clergyman.

223. Nobody knows the name of the first infant or minor child to be baptized nor when it occurred, but the practice is known to extend as far back as the third century and was commonplace until rejected by the Anabaptists in the sixteenth and following centuries; see *ODCC*, s. v. "Infant Baptism." Today's Southern Baptists, theological descendants of the Anabaptists, practice so-called adult baptism by immersion, but they extend adulthood to such a tender age that they are in effect baptizing children, if not infants.

224. Eve's original sin was disobedience, yet she was only seeking wisdom, which might have been thought praiseworthy but definitely was not, because it was sought rebelliously.

225. The Koran, trans. N. J. Dawood (London: Penguin Books, 1956), pp. 349, 395, 412.

226. Crimmins, "Bentham's Metaphysics and the Science of Divinity," *HTR* 79 (1986): 394–95, quotes the splendidly descriptive term 'prepared imbecility' from Bentham's unpublished works.

227. Steven Reiss, "Why People Turn to Religion," *JSSR* 39, no. 1 (March 2000), found that religiosity is associated "with a desire for low independence" (p. 51). If so, one would expect that those whose religious desires have been fulfilled (and are, therefore, happy) will be found in the more tightly controlled, dogmatic denominations.

228. Goleman's first article appeared in the *NYT* on February 12, 1991, the second on July 16, 1996. The articles refer to two scholarly journals that interested readers may wish to pursue.

229. Gustavo Benavides, review of *Creation of the Sacred: Tracks of Biology in Early Religion*, by Walter Burkert, *JSSR* 36, no. 3 (September 1997): 468–69.

230. Walter Burkert, *Creation of the Sacred: Tracks of Biology in Early Religion* (Cambridge: Harvard University Press, 1996), writes, "Religion can be deadly serious in the most direct way, sanctioning violence in a terrifying spectrum, ranging from human sacrifice to internecine wars, from witch-burning to an Ayatollah's *fatwa*—and no less shocking acts of self-sacrifice, down to mass suicide" (p. 8).

231. Karl Marx and Friedrich Engels, *Marx and Engels on Religion*, introduction by Reinhold Niebuhr (New York: Schocken Books, 1969), p. 83.

232. Delos McKown, "Religion as a Humanizing Force in Man's History: A Negative Response," *SHR* 4, no. 3 (summer 1970): 210.

233. Finger sacrifice is exactly what it appears to be. In various cultures such as the ones found on Tonga in the Friendly Islands and on Fiji, the cultures of the Hottentots and Bushmen in Africa, the Blackfeet Indians of North America, and various groups in India, the practice has been found. Walter Burkert, *Creation of the Sacred*, writes, "Worldwide, it seems, in situations of distress and illness or even in anticipation of disaster, people would cut off a finger or part of a finger" (pp. 38–39).

234. Also see *Principles of Morals and Legislation*, in *WJB*, 1:4, note.

235. Sexual "sins" come to mind at once when thinking of pleasurable activities that one ought to forego to please one's deity. For Bentham's liberal views on sexuality, including homosexuality, see chap. 9 in Crimmins, *Secular Utilitarianism*.

236. Christianity does this through the doctrines of original sin and total depravity (Gen. 3:17); through the notions that one is shaped in iniquity and born in sin (Ps. 51:5); that one's righteousness is as filthy rags (Isa. 64:6); and that all have sinned and fallen short of the glory of the Bible-god (Rom. 3:20–26). Here the heavy dependence on the Old Testament shows that the same indictment rests upon Jews as well as Christians.

237. Readers who would relish more of Bentham's attack on the Established Church of England are reminded that work on this very subject is now being undertaken by the Bentham Project, as noted in the preface and in the final note of part 2.

Afterword

In the Gospel of John 20:30–31, we find these words: "And many other signs truly did Jesus in the presence of his disciples, which are not written in this book: But these are written that ye might believe that Jesus is the Christ, the Son of God; and that believing ye might have life through his name." In close harmony with this, his Gospel ends with 21:25, which makes the following astonishing claim: "And there are also many other things which Jesus did, the which, if they should be written every one, I suppose that even the world itself could not contain the books that should be written. Amen."

Bentham, of course, performed neither signs nor wonders in the presence of his disciples and offered them neither a mystical identification with himself in this life nor postmortem consciousness in any future, ghostly state. He did, however, offer a kind of liberation—liberation from the morose notions that this life must be experienced as a vail of tears, a place of privation, and the mortification of the flesh in the illusory hope of gaining glory on some other shore. By emphasizing the idea of the greatest happiness to the greatest number of people, understood in terms of social policies and governmental actions, he liberated people to focus on lives more free from needless pains and more filled with innocuous pleasures than would otherwise have been the case.

As for books about Bentham and the room to house them, no problem ever arose, nor will arise, no matter how many volumes the Bentham Project may finally produce. Even if one were to add all of his unpublished writings to his many published writings, and even if he had had biographers cataloging his every thought and action, throughout his long life, only a modest amount of shelf space would have been (or would be) needed. And, of course, in this day and age of electronic storage, just a handful of compact discs could hold the whole of his life and works.

This book has been written that you, dear reader, might know a forgotten side of Bentham; that you might perceive with him the Pollyannaish nature of natural theology, even in its leanest deistical manifestations; that you might escape thralldom to St. Paul, who has exercised much too much influence on Western culture; and that you might loathe the evils of coerced oaths, especially when visited upon children in the service of deceitful religion, and, most especially, when such promissory vows call for belief in the gibberish of some religious word world or other.

Bibliography

Works by Jeremy Bentham

Philip Beauchamp [pseud.]. *An Analysis of the Influence of Natural Religion on the Temporal Happiness of Mankind.* Edited by George Grote. 1822. Reprint, London, 1866. Reprinted as Jeremy Bentham, *The Influence of Natural Religion on the Temporal Happiness of Mankind* (Amherst, NY: Prometheus Books, 2003).

Gamaliel Smith [pseud.]. *Not Paul, but Jesus.* London, 1823.

The Church-of-England Catechism Examined. 1824. 2nd ed., n.p.: Ramsgate, 1868.

The Works of Jeremy Bentham. 11 vols. New York: Russell and Russell, 1962. Reproduced from the Bowring edition of 1838–43 and containing the following works (with volume):

Anarchical Fallacies, vol. 2.

Bentham to His Fellow Citizens of France, vol. 4.

The Book of Fallacies, vol. 2.

Chrestomathia, vol. 8.

Complete Code of Laws, vol. 3.

The Constitutional Code, vol. 9.

Defence of Usury, vol. 3.

Essay on the Influence of Time and Place in Matters of Legislation, vol. 1.

Essay on Language, vol. 8.

Essay on Logic, vol. 8.

A Fragment on Government, vol. 1.

A Fragment on Ontology, vol. 8.

General View of a Complete Code of Laws, vol. 3.

An Introduction to the Principles of Morals and Legislation, vol. 1.

An Introductory View of the Rationale of Evidence, vol. 6.

Justice and Codification Petitions, vol. 5.

Letters to Count Toreno on the Proposed Penal Code, vol. 8.
Logical Arrangements, vol. 3.
Memoirs of Bentham and Correspondence, vol. 10.
Pannomial Fragments, vol. 3.
Principles of Penal Law, vol. 1.
Rationale of Judicial Evidence, vol. 6–7.
The Rationale of Reward, vol. 2.
Swear Not at All, vol. 5.
A Table of the Springs of Action, vol. 1.

The Correspondence of Jeremy Bentham. 11 vols. London: University of London and Athalone Press, 1968–.

Secondary Sources

Adam, Karl. *The Spirit of Catholicism*. Garden City, NY: Doubleday, 1954.
Allegro, John M. *The Sacred Mushroom and the Cross*. New York: Doubleday, 1970.
———. *The Dead Sea Scrolls and the Christian Myth*. Amherst, NY: Prometheus Books, 1984.
Andrews, Elias. *The Meaning of Christ for Paul*. New York: Abingdon-Cokesbury Press, 1949.
Andrews, Mary. "Paul, Philo, and the Intellectuals." *Journal of Biblical Literature* 53 (1934): 150–66.
Aquinas, Thomas. *Exposition of Boethius on the Trinity*. Edited by B. Decker. Leiden: Brill, 1955.
Archer, John Clark. *Faiths Men Live By*. Revised by Carl E. Purinton. New York: Ronald Press, 1958.
Aristotle. *Parts of Animals*. Translated by A. L. Peck. Loeb Classical Library. Cambridge, MA: Harvard University Press.
Atkins, Anselm. "From City of Man to City of God." *Humanist* 42 (1982): 26.
Augustine. *Enchiridion*. In *Basic Writings of Saint Augustine*, edited by Whitney J. Oates, translated by J. F. Shaw, 1:657–730. 2 vols. New York: Random House, 1948.
Ayer, A. J. *Language, Truth, and Logic*. 2nd ed. London: Victor Gollancz, 1946.
Baird, William. "Visions, Revelation, and Ministry: Reflections on 2 Corinthians 12:1–5 and Galatians 1:1–17." *Journal of Biblical Literature* 104 (1985): 651–62.
———. *The History of New Testament Research: From Deism to Tübingen*. 2 vols. Minneapolis: Fortress Press, 1992.
Barth, Karl. *Against the Stream: Shorter Post-War Writings*. Edited by Ronald G. Smith. New York: Philosophical Library, 1954.
BeDuhn, Jason David. "Because of the Angels: Unveiling Paul's Anthropology in I Corinthians 11." *Journal of Biblical Literature* 118 (1999): 295–320.
Beker, J. C. "Paul's Theology: Consistent or Inconsistent?" *New Testament Studies* 34 (1988): 364–77.
Belkin, Samuel. "The Problem of Paul's Background." *Journal of Biblical Literature* 54 (1935): 41–60.
Benavides, Gustavo. Review of *Creation of the Sacred*, by Walter Burkert. *Journal for the Scientific Study of Religion* 36 (1997): 468–69.

Benn, Alfred William. *The History of English Rationalism in the Nineteenth Century.* 2 vols. New York: Russell and Russell, 1962.

Benz, Hans-Dieter. "The Concept of the Inner Human Being (ὅ ἔσω ἄνθρωπος) in the Anthropology of Paul." *New Testament Studies* 46, no. 3 (2000): 315–41.

Bergson, Henri. *The Two Sources of Morality and Religion.* Translated by Ashley Audra and Cloudesly Brereton. London: Macmillan, 1935.

Berman, David. "Jeremy Bentham's Analysis of Religion." *Freethinker* (1982): 152–53.

———. *A History of Atheism in Britain: From Hobbes to Russell.* London: Croom Helm, 1988.

Best, Ernest. *A Commentary on the First and Second Epistles to the Thessalonians.* New York: Harper and Row, 1972.

Brandon, Samuel G. F. *The Fall of Jerusalem and the Christian Church.* London: S. P. C. K. [Society for Promoting Christian Knowledge], 1951.

———. "The Death of James the Just: A New Interpretation." In *Studies in Mysticism and Religion,* presented to Gershom Scholem by pupils, colleagues, and friends, pp. 57–69. Jerusalem: Magnes Press, 1967.

———. *Jesus and the Zealots: A Study of the Political Factor in Primitive Christianity.* Manchester, UK: University of Manchester Press, 1967.

Brodie, Fawn. *No Man Knows My History.* New York: AAK Fellowship, 1968.

Bronson, David B. "Paul and Apocalyptic Judaism." *Journal of Biblical Literature* 83 (1964): 287–92.

Bruce, E. F. *Paul: Apostle of the Heart Set Free.* Grand Rapids, MI: William B. Eerdmans, 1977.

———. "The Enigma of Paul." *Bible Review* 4 (1988): 32–33.

Brunner, Emil. *The Christian Doctrine of God.* Translated by Olive W. Lyon. Philadelphia: Westminster Press, 1950.

Brunt, J. "Rejected, Ignored, or Misunderstood? The Fate of Paul's Approach to the Problem of Food Offered to Idols in Early Christianity." *New Testament Studies* 31 (1985): 113–24.

Bultmann, Rudolf. *Jesus and the Word.* Translated by L. P. Smith and E. H. Lantero. New York: Charles Scribner's Sons, 1958.

———. *Kerygma and Myth: A Theological Debate.* Edited by Hans-Werner Bartsch. Translated by Reginald H. Fuller. London: S. P. C. K., 1972.

Burkert, Walter. *Creation of the Sacred: Tracks of Biology in Early Religions.* Cambridge, MA: Harvard University Press, 1996.

Burtt, Edwin A. *Man Seeks the Divine.* 2nd ed. New York: Harper and Row, 1957.

Cassirer, Ernst. *Language and Myth.* New York: Harper and Brothers, 1946.

"Catholic Sentenced to Die for Blaspheming in Pakistan." *Church and State* 46 (1993): 17.

Churchland, Patricia. *Neurophilosophy: Toward a Unified Science of Mind-Brain.* Rev. ed. Cambridge, MA: MIT Press, Bradford Books, 1986.

Churchland, Paul. *Matter and Consciousness: A Contemporary Philosophy of Mind.* Cambridge, MA: MIT Press, Bradford Books, 1988.

———. *The Engine of Reason, the Seat of the Soul.* Cambridge, MA: MIT Press, Bradford Books, 1995.

Coe, George A. "The Sources of Mystical Revelation." *Hibbert Journal* 6 (1907–1908): 367.

Collins, Adela Yarbro. "The Function of Excommunication in Paul." *Harvard Theological Review* 73 (1980): 251–63.

Copi, Irving M. *Introduction to Logic.* 7th ed. New York: Macmillan, 1986.

Cotton, Ian. "Dr. Persinger's God Machine." *Free Inquiry* 17 (1996–97): 47–51.

Crick, Francis. "The Recent Excitement about Neural Networks." *Nature* 337 (1989): 129–32.

Crimmins, James E. "Bentham on Religion: Atheism and the Secular Society." *Journal of the History of Ideas* 47 (1986): 95–110.

———. "Bentham's Metaphysics and the Science of Divinity." *Harvard Theological Review* 79 (1986): 387–411.

———. "Bentham's Unpublished Manuscripts on Subscription to Articles of Faith." *British Journal for Eighteenth-Century Studies* 9 (1986): 33–43.

———. *Secular Utilitarianism: Social Science and the Critique of Religion in the Thought of Jeremy Bentham.* Oxford: Clarendon Press, 1990.

Cullmann, Oscar. *Immortality of the Soul and Resurrection of the Dead.* London: Epworth Press / Macmillan, 1958.

Damascio, Antonio R. *Descartes' Error: Emotion, Reason, and the Human Brain.* New York: G. P. Putnam, 1994.

Davies, Stevan. *The New Testament: A Contemporary Introduction.* San Francisco: Harper and Row, 1988.

Davies, W. D., and D. Daube. *The Background of the New Testament and Its Eschatology.* Cambridge: Cambridge University Press, 1956.

Davis, Percival, and Dean H. Kenyon. *Of Pandas and People: The Central Question of Biological Origins.* Dallas: Haughton, 1989.

Dawsey, James M. "The Literary Unity of Luke-Acts: Questions of Style." *New Testament Studies* 35 (1989): 48–66.

Deismann, Adolph. *The Religion of Jesus and the Faith of Paul.* Translated by William E. Wilson. New York: George H. Doran, 1923.

Dennett, Daniel C. *Consciousness Explained.* Boston: Little, Brown, 1991.

Descartes, René. *The Passions of the Soul.* Translated by Stephen Voss. Indianapolis: Hackett, 1988.

Dewey, John. *A Common Faith.* New Haven, CT: Yale University Press, 1934.

Dodd, C. H. *The Meaning of Paul for Today.* London: George Allen and Unwin, 1949.

Donfried, Karl P., and I. Howard Marshall. *The Theology of the Shorter Pauline Letters.* Cambridge: Cambridge University Press, 1993.

Dressler, William W. *Stress and Adaptation in the Context of Culture: Depression in a Southern Black Community.* Albany: State University of New York Press, 1991.

Dunn, James G. D. "Mark 2:1–3:6: A Bridge between Jesus and Paul on the Question of the Law." *New Testament Studies* 30 (1984): 395–415.

———. "Works of the Law and the Curse of the Law (Galatians 3:10–14)." *New Testament Studies* 31 (1985): 523–42.

Durkheim, Emile. *The Elementary Forms of the Religious Life.* Translated by J. W. Swain. Glencoe, IL: Free Press, 1947.

Edelman, Gerald. *Bright Air, Brilliant Fire: On the Matter of the Mind.* New York: Basic Books, 1993.

Eisler, Robert. *The Messiah Jesus and John the Baptist.* Translated by A. H. Krappe. London: Methuen, 1931.

Ellis, E. Earle. "Dating the New Testament." *New Testament Studies* 26 (1980): 487–502.

Enslin, Morton Scott. *Christian Beginnings.* New York: Harper and Brothers, 1938.

Ephrem the Syrian, Saint. *Mary in the Documents of the Church.* Edited by Paul F. Palmer. Westminster, MD: Newman Press, 1952.

Epp, Eldon Jay, and George W. MacRae, eds. *The New Testament and Its Modern Interpreters.* Philadelphia: Fortress Press; Atlanta: Scholars Press, 1989.

Feuerbach, Ludwig. *The Essence of Christianity.* Translated by George Eliot. With an introduction by Karl Barth and a foreword by Richard Niebuhr. New York: Harper and Brothers, Torchbook, 1957.

Findlay, J. N. "Can God's Existence Be Disproved?" *Mind* (1948): 176–83.

Fletcher, Joseph. "An Odyssey: From Theology to Humanism." *Religious Humanism* 13 (1979): 146–57.

Forbes, Christopher. "Comparison, Self-Praise, and Irony: Paul's Boasting and the Conventions of Hellenistic Rhetoric." *New Testament Studies* 32 (1986): 1–30.

Fowlie, Wallace. "Rehabilitating Renan." *American Scholar* 57 (1989): 245–56.

Frame, J. E. "Paul's Idea of Deliverance." *Journal of Biblical Studies* 49 (1930): 1–12.

Freud, Sigmund. *The Future of an Illusion.* In *The Complete Psychological Works of Sigmund Freud,* edited by James Strachey, 21:5–56. 24 vols. London: Hogarth Press, 1961.

Furnish, Victor Paul. "The Paul-Jesus Debate: From Baur to Bultmann." In *Paul and Jesus: Collected Essays,* edited by A. J. M. Wedderburn, 17–49. Sheffield, UK: JSOT Press, 1989.

Gager, John G. "Some Notes on Paul's Conversion." *New Testament Studies* 27 (1981): 697–704.

———. "Jesus, Gentiles, and Synagogues in the Book of Acts." *Harvard Theological Review* 79 (1986): 91–99.

Gardner, Martin. *The Healing Revelations of Mary Baker Eddy.* Amherst, NY: Prometheus Books, 1993.

"Garland of Stalinisms." Soviet newspaper clipping cited by Howard Swearer. *Problems of Communism* 12 (1963): 87.

Gazzaniga, Michael. *The Social Brain: Discovering the Networks of the Mind.* New York: Basic Books, 1985.

Geertz, Clifford. *The Interpretation of Culture.* New York: Basic Books, 1973.

Gifford, William. "Jeremy Bentham's *Church-of-Englandism.*" *Quarterly Review* 21 (1819): 167–77.

Goodspeed, Edgar J. "The Editio Princeps of Paul." *Journal of Biblical Literature* 64 (1945): 193–204.

———. "Ephesians and the First Edition of Paul." *Journal of Biblical Literature* 70, pt. 4 (1951): 285–91.

Goulder, Michael D. "ΣΟΦΙΑ in I Corinthians." *New Testament Studies* 37 (1991): 516–34.

Grant, Michael. *Saint Paul.* New York: Charles Scribner's Sons, 1976.

Haenchen, Ernst. *The Acts of the Apostles: A Commentary.* Translated by Bernard Noble and Gerald Shinn. Philadelphia: Westminster Press, 1971.

Hagenbach, K. R. *A Text-Book of the History of Doctrines*. Translated by Henry B. Smith. 2 vols. New York: Sheldon, 1861.

Halévy, Elie. *The Growth of Philosophical Radicalism*. London: Faber and Faber, 1928.

Hammer, Paul L. "A Comparison of Kleronomia in Paul and Ephesians." *Journal of Biblical Literature* 79, pt. 3 (1960): 262–72.

Harrell, David Edwin, Jr. *Oral Roberts: An American Life*. San Francisco: Harper and Row, 1985.

Harshbarger, Luther H., and John A. Mourant. *Judaism and Christianity: Perspectives and Traditions*. Boston: Allyn and Bacon, 1968.

Hawking, Stephen W. *A Brief History of Time*. New York: Bantam Books, 1988.

Hay, David M. "Paul's Indifference to Authority." *Journal of Biblical Literature* 88, pt. 1 (1969): 36–44.

Hedrick, Charles W. "Paul's Conversion/Call: A Comparative Analysis of the Three Reports in Acts." *Journal of Biblical Literature* 100 (1981): 415–32.

Hengel, Martin. *The Pre-Christian Paul*. London: SCM Press, 1991.

Hopkins, E. Washburn. *Origin and Evolution of Religion*. New Haven, CT: Yale University Press, 1923.

Horgan, John. "Can Science Explain Consciousness?" *Scientific American* 271 (1994): 88–94.

Hultgren, Arland J. "Paul's Pre-Christian Persecutions of the Church: Their Purpose, Locale, and Nature." *Journal of Biblical Literature* 95 (1976): 97–111.

Hunter, Michael, and David Wooten. *Atheism from the Reformation to the Enlightenment*. Oxford: Clarendon Press, 1992.

Hutchison, John A. *Paths of Faith*. New York: McGraw-Hill, 1969.

Hutchison, John A., and James Alfred Martin Jr. *Ways of Faith*. New York: Ronald Press, 1960.

Huxley, Aldous. *'The Doors of Perception' and 'Heaven and Hell'*. New York: Harper and Row, 1954.

James, William. *The Varieties of Religious Experience: A Study in Human Nature*. New York: Modern Library, 1994.

Jaynes, Julian. *The Origin of Consciousness in the Breakdown of the Bicameral Mind*. Boston: Houghton Mifflin, 1976.

Jeffrey, Arthur, ed. *Islam: Muhammad and His Religion*. New York: Liberal Arts Press, 1958.

Josepheus, Flavius. *The Wars of the Jews*. In *The Works of Flavius Josephus*, translated by William Whiston, 1:3–52. 4 vols. Grand Rapids, MI: Baker Book House, 1974.

Judge, E. A. "Paul's Boasting in Relation to Contemporary Professional Practice." *Australian Biblical Review* (1968): 37–50.

Kaplan, Abraham. *The New World of Philosophy*. New York: Random House, 1961.

Kee, Howard C., and Franklin W. Young. *Understanding the New Testament*. Englewood Cliffs, NJ: Prentice-Hall, 1957.

Kennard, J. Spencer, Jr. *Politique et religion chez les juifs au temps de Jesus et dans l'église primitive* [Politics and religion among the Jews in the time of Jesus and in the primitive church]. Paris: n.p., 1927.

Kierkegaard, Søren. *Concluding Unscientific Postscript*. Translated by David F. Swenson, completed by Walter Lowrie. Princeton, NJ: Princeton University Press, 1941.

Kirk, G. S., and J. E. Raven. *The Presocratic Philosophers*. Cambridge: Cambridge University Press, 1962.

Klausner, Joseph. *From Jesus to Paul*. London: George Allen and Unwin, 1944.

Knifer, John. "Iran Obsessed with Martyrdom." *New York Times Magazine*, December 16, 1984, pp. 36ff.

Knox, John. "The Pauline Chronology." *Journal of Biblical Literature* 58 (1939): 15–29.

———. *Chapters in a Life of Paul*. Nashville, TN: Abingdon Press, 1950.

Kraabel, A. T. "The Disappearance of the 'God-Fearers.'" *Numen: International Review for the History of Religion* 28 (1981): 113–26.

Kümmel, Werner Georg. *The New Testament: The History of the Investigation of Its Problems*. Translated by S. McLean and Howard C. Kee. Nashville, TN: Abingdon Press, 1970.

Larssen, Edvin. "Paul: Law and Salvation." *New Testament Studies* 31 (1985): 425–36.

Leith, John, ed. *Creeds of the Churches: A Reader in Christian Doctrines from the Bible to the Present*. Garden City, NY: Doubleday, Anchor Books, 1963.

Lentz, John Clayton, Jr. *Luke's Portrait of Paul*. Cambridge: Cambridge University Press, 1993.

Leuba, James. *The Psychology of Religious Mysticism*. New York: Harcourt, Brace, 1929.

———. *A Psychological Study of Religion: Its Origin, Function, and Future*. New York: AMS Press, 1965.

Levy, Albert William. *Philosophy and the Modern World*. Bloomington: Indiana University Press, 1959.

Lohmeyer, Ernest. *The Lord of the Temple*. Translated by Stewart Todd. Richmond, VA: John Knox Press, 1962.

Loveday, Alexander. "Fact, Fiction, and the Genre of Acts." *New Testament Studies* 44 (1998): 380–99.

Lüdemann, Gerd. *Opposition to Paul in Jewish Christianity*. Translated by M. Eugene Boring. Minneapolis: Fortress Press, 1989.

Maccoby, Hyam. *The Mythmaker: Paul and the Invention of Christianity*. London: Weidenfeld and Nicholson, 1986.

———. *Revolution in Judaea: Jesus and the Jewish Resistance*. New York: Taplinger, 1980.

MacDonald, Dennis. "The Shipwrecks of Odysseus and Paul." *New Testament Studies* 45 (1999): 88–107.

Mack, Mary. *Jeremy Bentham: An Odyssey of Ideas*. London: Heinemann, 1962.

Macnicol, Nicol, ed. *Hindu Scriptures*. London: J. M. Dent and Sons, 1938.

Manchester, Paul T., and P. Thomas Manchester. "The Blindness of St. Paul." *Archives of Ophthalmology* 88 (1972): 316–21.

Martyn, J. Louis. "Apocalyptic Antinomies in Paul's Letter to the Galatians." *New Testament Studies* 31 (1985): 410–24.

Marx, Karl. *Writings of the Young Marx on Philosophy and Society*. Edited and translated by Loyd Easton and Kurt Guddat. Garden City, NY: Doubleday, Anchor Books, 1967.

Marx, Karl, and Friedrich Engels. *Marx and Engels on Religion*. With an introduction by Reinhold Niebuhr. New York: Schocken Books, 1969.

McCant, Jerry W. "Paul's Thorn of Rejected Apostleship." *New Testament Studies* 34 (1988): 550–72.

McCourt, Malachy. *A Monk Swimming.* New York: Hyperion, 1998.

McKown, Delos B. "Deception and Development in Plato's Theology." *Southern Journal of Philosophy* 5 (1967): 173–79.

———. "Religion as a Humanizing Force in Man's History: A Negative Response." *Southern Humanities Review* 4 (1970): 206–14.

———. *The Classical Marxist Critiques of Religion: Marx, Engels, Lenin, Kautsky.* The Hague: Martinus Nijhoff, 1975.

———. "A Theological Anomaly in Bentham's Ontology." *Mill Newsletter* 22 (1987): 2–8.

———. "What Does the Bible Say About Abortion?" *Free Inquiry* 11 (1991): 29–31.

———. *The Mythmaker's Magic: Behind the Illusion of "Creation Science."* Amherst, NY: Prometheus Books, 1993.

McLean, Bradley H. "The Absence of an Atoning Sacrifice in Paul's Soteriology." *New Testament Studies* 38 (1992): 531–53.

McReynolds, P. "Jeremy Bentham and the Nature of Psychological Concepts." In *Jeremy Bentham: Critical Assessments,* edited by Bhikhu Parekh, 2:145–59. 2 vols. London: Routledge, 1993. Also published in *Journal of General Psychology* 82 (1970): 113–27.

Mealand, David. "Positional Stylometry Reassessed: Testing a Seven-Epistle Theory of Pauline Authorship." *New Testament Studies* 35 (1989): 266–86.

Mearns, C. L. "Early Eschatological Development in Paul: The Evidence of I and II Thess." *New Testament Studies* 27, no. 2 (1981): 137–57.

Mills, Watson E. "Glossolalia: An Introduction." In *Speaking in Tongues: A Guide to Research on Glossolalia,* edited by Watson E. Mills. Grand Rapids, MI: William B. Eerdmans 1986.

———. "Glossolalia: A Survey of the Literature." In *Speaking in Tongues: Research on Glossolalia,* edited by Watson E. Mills. Grand Rapids, MI: William B. Eerdmans, 1986.

Monod, Jacques. *Chance and Necessity.* New York: Alfred A. Knopf, 1971.

Moore, G. E. "Russell's 'Theory of Descriptions.'" In *The Philosophy of Bertrand Russell,* edited by Paul Arthur Schillp, pp. 177–225. New York: Tudor, 1944.

Moorman, John R. H. *The Anglican Spiritual Tradition.* Springfield, IL: Templegate, 1983.

Morris, Desmond. *The Human Zoo.* New York: McGraw-Hill, 1965.

———. *The Naked Ape.* New York: McGraw-Hill, 1967.

———. *Manwatching: A Fieldguide to Human Behavior.* New York: Harry N. Abrams, 1977.

Mullins, Terrence. "Paul's Thorn in the Flesh." *Journal of Biblical Literature* 76 (1957): 299.

Munck, Johannes. *Paul and the Salvation of Mankind.* Translated by Frank Clerk. Richmond, VA: John Knox Press, 1955.

Murray, John. *The Epistle to the Romans.* Grand Rapids, MI: William B. Eerdmans, 1959.

Nagel, Thomas. Review of *The Rediscovery of Mind,* by John Searles. *New York Review of Books,* March 4, 1993, p. 37.

Neil, William. *The Epistle of Paul to the Thessalonians*. New York: Harper and Brothers, 1950.

Neill, Stephen, and Tom Wright. *The Interpretation of the New Testament, 1861–1986*. Oxford: Oxford University Press, 1988.

Nielsen, Kai. "Eschatological Verification." *Canadian Journal of Theology* 9 (1963): 271–81.

Nietzsche, Friedrich. *The Antichrist*. New York: Arno Press / New York Times, 1972.

Noss, John B. *Man's Religions*. 4th ed. London: Macmillan, 1969.

Ogden, C. K. *Bentham's Theory of Fictions*. London: Kegan Paul, Trench, Trubner, 1932.

Otten, Bernard J. *A Manual of the History of Dogmas*. 3rd ed. St. Louis: B. Herder, 1922.

Otto, Rudolf. *The Idea of the Holy*. Translated by John W. Harvey. 2nd ed. London: Oxford University Press, 1950.

Pagels, Elaine. *The Origin of Satan*. New York: Random House, 1995.

Pervo, Richard I. *Profit with Delight: The Literary Genre of the Acts of the Apostles*. Philadelphia: Fortress Press, 1987.

Peters, F. E. *Greek Philosophical Terms*. New York: New York University Press: 1967.

Pherigo, Lindsey P. "Paul and the Corinthian Church." *Journal of Biblical Literature* 68 (1949): 341–50.

Plato. *The Collected Dialogues of Plato*. Translated by A. E. Taylor. Edited by Edith Hamilton and Huntington Cairns. New York: Pantheon Books, 1961.

Preuss, Samuel J. *Explaining Religion: Criticism and Theory from Bodin to Freud*. New Haven, CT: Yale University Press, 1987.

Price, James L. *Interpreting the New Testament*. New York: Holt, Rinehart, and Winston, 1961.

Priest, Stephen. *Theories of the Mind*. Boston: Houghton Mifflin, 1992.

Quine, Willard Van Ormon. *From a Logical Point of View*. 2nd ed. New York: Harper Torchbooks, 1963.

———. *Ontological Relativity and Other Essays*. New York: Columbia University Press, 1969.

Radin, Paul. *Primitive Religion: Its Nature and Origin*. New York: Dover, 1957.

Räisänen, Heikki. *Paul and the Law*. Tübingen: Mohr, 1983.

———. "Galatians 2:16 and Paul's Break with Judaism." *New Testament Studies* 31 (1985): 543–53.

Rappaport, Roy A. "Ritual, Sanctity, and Cybernetics." *American Anthropologist* 73 (1971): 59–76.

———. "The Sacred in Human Evolution." In *Explorations in Anthropology: Readings in Culture, Man, and Nature*, edited by Morton H. Fried, pp. 403–20. New York: Thomas Y. Crowell, 1973.

———. *Ritual and Religion in the Making of Humanity*. Cambridge: Cambridge University Press, 1999.

Rea, Robert R. "The North Briton and the Courts of Law." *Alabama Lawyer* 12, no. 4 (1951): 415–21.

Reese, James M. *1 and 2 Thessalonians*. Dublin: Veritas, 1979.

Reicke, Bo. "The Law and This World According to Paul." *Journal of Biblical Literature* 70, pt. 4 (1951): 259–76.

Reiss, Steven. "Why People Turn to Religion." *Journal for the Scientific Study of Religion* 39 (2000): 47–52.

Rexine, John. *Religion in Plato and Cicero.* New York: Philosophical Library, 1959.

Reynolds, Vernon, and R. E. S. Tanner. *The Biology of Religion.* London: Longman, 1983.

Richardson, Peter. "Pauline Inconsistency: I Corinthians and Galatians 2:11–14." *New Testament Studies* 26 (1980): 347–62.

Riddle, Donald. "The Jewishness of Paul." *Journal of Religion* 23 (1943): 240–44.

Ridley, Mark. "Infected With Science." *New Scientist* 25 (1993–94): 22–24.

Roberts, Thomas. *A Practical List of Greek Word Roots.* New York: Abingdon Press, 1968.

Robertson, Archibald. *The Origin of Christianity.* Rev. ed. New York: International Publishers, 1962.

Robinson, H. Wheeler. *The Christian Experience of the Holy Spirit.* New York: Harper and Brothers, 1930.

Robinson, John Mansley. *An Introduction to Early Greek Philosophy.* Boston: Houghton Mifflin, 1968.

Rose, Hugh James. *A Critical Examination of Those Parts of Mr. Bentham's "Church-of-Englandism" Which Relate to the Sacraments and the Church Catechism.* 1818.

Rowlingson, Donald T. "The Jerusalem Conference and Jesus' Nazareth Visit." *Journal of Biblical Literature* 71, pt. 2 (1952): 69–74.

Rubenstein, Richard. *My Brother Paul.* New York: Harper and Row, 1972.

Russell, Bertrand. "On Denoting." *Mind*, n.s., 56 (1905): 479–83.

———. *Introduction to Mathematical Philosophy.* London: George Allen and Unwin, 1919.

———. *A History of Western Philosophy.* New York: Simon and Schuster, 1945.

Russell, Jeffrey Burton. *The Devil: Perceptions of Evil from Antiquity to Primitive Christianity.* Ithaca, NY: Cornell University Press, 1977.

Russell, Ronald. "The Idle in 2 Thess. 3.6-12: An Eschatological or a Social Problem?" *New Testament Studies* 34 (1988): 105–19.

Ryle, Gilbert. *The Concept of Mind.* London: Hutchison Publishing Group; New York: Barnes and Noble, 1949.

Sabatier, Auguste. *The Apostle Paul.* London: Hooder and Stroughton, 1903.

Sanders, E. P. *Paul, the Law, and the Jewish People.* Philadelphia: Fortress Press, 1983.

Sanders, Jack T. "Paul's 'Autobiographical' Statements in Galatians 1–2." *Journal of Biblical Literature* 85 (1966): 335–43.

———. "Who Is a Jew and Who Is a Gentile in the Book of Acts." *New Testament Studies* 37 (1991): 434–55.

"Saudis Behead Man Who Insulted Muhammed and Islam." *Church and State* 45 (1992): 3.

Schonfield, Hugh. *The Passover Plot.* New York: Bantam Books, 1967.

———. *Those Incredible Christians.* New York: Bantam Books, 1969.

Schweitzer, Albert. *The Mystery of the Kingdom of God.* Translated by Walter Lowrie. New York: Macmillan, 1954.

———. *The Mysticism of Paul the Apostle.* Translated by William Montgomery. New York: Macmillan, 1955.

Segal, Alan. *Paul the Convert: The Apostolate and Apostasy of Saul the Pharisee.* New Haven, CT: Yale University Press, 1990.

Selby, Donald J. *Introduction to the New Testament: The Word Became Flesh.* New York: Macmillan, 1971.

———. "Paul's Thinking about Resurrection in Its Jewish Context." *New Testament Studies* 44 (1998): 400–19.

Shepherd, Massey H., Jr. "Paul and the Double Resurrection Tradition." *Journal of Biblical Literature* 64 (1945): 227–39.

Smart, Ninian. *The Religious Experience of Mankind.* New York: Charles Scribner's Sons, 1969.

Smith, Morton. "What Is Implied By the Variety of Messianic Figures?" *Journal of Biblical Literature* 78, pt. 1 (1955): 66–72.

———. "Pauline Problems: Apropos of J. Munck, *Paulus und die Heilsgeschichte.*" *Harvard Theological Review* 50 (1957): 107–31.

———. "The Reason for the Persecution of Paul and the Obscurity of Acts." In *Studies in Mysticism and Religion,* pp. 261–68. Presented to Gershom Scholem by pupils, colleagues, and friends. Jerusalem: Magnes Press, 1967.

———. *The Secret Gospel.* New York: Harper and Row, 1973.

———. *Jesus the Magician.* New York: Harper and Row, 1978.

———. "Pauline Worship as Seen by Pagans." *Harvard Theological Review* 73 (1980): 241–49.

———. "Paul's Arguments as Evidence of the Christianity from Which He Diverged." *Harvard Theological Review* 79 (1986): 254–60.

Stace, Walter. *Mysticism and Philosophy.* Los Angeles: Jeremy P. Tarcher, 1960.

———. *The Teachings of the Mystics.* New York: New American Library, Mentor Books, 1960.

Stacy, Dennis. "Transcending Science." *Omni,* December 1988, pp. 55ff.

Stebbing, L. Susan. *A Modern Introduction to Logic.* London: Methuen, 1930.

Steintrager, James. "Morality and Belief: The Origin and Purpose of Bentham's Writings on Religion." *Mill Newsletter* 6 (1971): 3–15.

———. "Language and Politics: Bentham on Religion." *Bentham Newsletter* 4 (1980): 4–20.

Stendahl, Krister. "The Apostle Paul and the Introspective Conscience of the West." *Harvard Theological Review* 56 (1963): 199–215.

Stern, David. "What Are Spiritual Phenomena?" In *Proceedings and Addresses of the American Philosophical Association,* pp. 43–59. Yellow Springs, OH: Antioch Press, 1965–66.

Taylor, Richard. "Joseph Fletcher: Father of Biomedical Ethics." *Free Inquiry* 4, no. 2 (1984).

Thielman, Frank. "The Coherence of Paul's View of the Law: The Evidence of First Corinthians." *New Testament Studies* 38 (1992): 235–53.

Thiering, Barbara. *Jesus and the Riddle of the Dead Sea Scrolls: Unlocking the Secrets of His Life Story.* San Francisco: HarperSanFrancisco, 1992.

Tillich, Paul. *The Protestant Era.* Translated by James Luther Adams. Chicago: University of Chicago Press, 1948.

———. *The Courage to Be.* New Haven, CT: Yale University Press, 1952.

———. *Systematic Theology.* 3 vols. Chicago: University of Chicago Press, 1951.

Trasker, R. V. G. *The Second Epistle of Paul to the Corinthians.* Tyndale New Testament Commentaries. Leicester, UK, and Grand Rapids, MI: William B. Eerdmans, 1963.

Twain, Mark. *Mark Twain Laughing.* Edited by Paul M. Zall. Knoxville: University of Tennessee Press, 1958.

Unruh, William. "Time, Gravity, and Quantum Mechanics." In *Time's Arrows Today: Recent Physical and Philosophical Work on the Direction of Time,* edited by Steven F. Savitt, pp. 23–65. Cambridge: Cambridge University Press, 1995.

"Vatican Recants; Galileo Cleared." *Report of the National Center for Science Education* 12 (1992): 9.

Vernon, Thomas S. "An Omnipotent God." *American Rationalist* 34 (September–October 1989): 36–41.

Wallace, Anthony. *Religion: An Anthropological View.* New York: Random House, 1966.

Webb, R. K. "John Bowring and Unitarianism." *Utilitas* 4 (1992): 43–79.

Wedderburn, A. J. M. "Paul and Jesus: Similarities and Continuity." *New Testament Studies* 34 (1988): 161–82.

Welch, Holmes. *Taoism.* Rev. ed. Boston: Beacon Press, 1965.

Wells, George Albert. *Religious Postures: Essays on Modern Christian Apologists and Religious Problems.* La Salle, IL: Open Court, 1988.

———. *Who Was Jesus? A Critique of the New Testament Record.* La Salle, IL: Open Court, 1989.

Werkmeister, William. *Introduction to Critical Thinking.* Lincoln, NE: Johnsen, 1948.

Wernick, Robert. "Who the Devil Is the Devil?" *Smithsonian,* October 1999, pp. 113–23.

Wheelwright, Philip. *A Critical Introduction to Ethics.* Rev. ed. New York: Odyssey Press, 1949.

Whitehead, Alfred North. *Religion in the Making.* New York: Macmillan, 1927.

Whitrow, Gerald J. *The Natural Philosophy of Time.* Oxford: Clarendon Press, 1980.

Willey, Basil. *The Eighteenth Century Background: Studies on the Idea of Nature in the Thought of the Period.* New York: Columbia University Press, 1940.

Wilson, Edward O. *On Human Nature.* Cambridge, MA: Harvard University Press, 1978.

———. *Sociobiology: The New Synthesis.* Cambridge, MA: Harvard University Press, 1977.

———. "Biology's Spiritual Products." *Free Inquiry* 7 (1987): 13–15.

Wisdom, John. *Interpretation and Analysis.* London: Kegan Paul, Trench, Trubner, 1931.

Yinger, Milton J. *Religion, Society, and the Individual.* New York: Macmillan, 1957.

Zass, Peter S. "Catalogues [of Vice] and Context: I Corinthians 5 and 6:2." *New Testament Studies* 34 (1988): 622–29.

Index

church
  Jerusalem, 113n168, 174n41
  original or primitive, 166n30
Church, Holy Mother (as term), 332–33
Churchland, Patricia, 259n168
Churchland, Paul, 259n168
circumcision, 133–34, 144–45, 160n19,
    170n32, 174n41, 192, 225, 233, 243
circumcision party, 134–35
clairvoyance, 92
Clark, Albert C., 153n8
Clarke, Samuel, 53
classes (or sets), 223
Claudius (emperor), 279n227
clergy, 41–42, 66
Code of Hammurabi, 233
Code of Maimonides, 174n41
Coe, George, 109n151
cognitive dissonance, 110n162, 165n26
collection, of Paul, 176n48, 190
Collins, Adela, 162n21
Collins, Anthony, 53
Colls, John F., 354n161
Colossians (people), 257n157, 280n230
Colossians, Paul's letter to the, 263n196
Communion of Saints. See dogmas
compartmentalization, 102
composition fallacy, 223, 261n176
congregationalism, 168n30
Constantine (emperor), 180n57
Consubstantiation. See dogmas
contextual definition, 363. See also para-
    phrasis
Conversion story of Paul, 119–21
Conway, Stephen, 151n2, 194, 306n1
Copernicus, 377
Copi, Irving, 346
Corinth, 161n21, 193
Corinthians (people), 157n15
Corinthians, Paul's first letter to the, 195
Corinthians, Paul's second letter to the,
    195
Cornelius, 145
cosmogony, 212
cosmological. See arguments for the
    existence of a deity
cosmological argument. See arguments

cosmology, 212
cosmos, 55. See also universe
Cotton, Ian, 109n142
Council of Constantinople, 310n26
credulity, 40–41, 122
creed, 286
Crick, Francis, 259n168
Crimmins, James E., 15–16, 44nn4, 5,
    82n80, 103n81, 151n6, 189, 195,
    197–98, 239–46, 249–50n115,
    250–51n119, 253n144, 265n222,
    343–45
  as animistic, 202, 253n144
  as dualistic, 201
  as major Bentham scholar, 195
  naive criticisms of Bentham on reli-
    gion, 245
Cruden, Alexander, 194
Cullmann, Oscar, 113n168, 228, 230,
    259n167

daimonion, 230
D'Alembert, 348n71
Dalton, John, 359
Damascio, Antonio, 259n168
Damascus, 119–21, 125, 127–28, 130,
    156n14, 164n25
Damascus road, 127, 145, 155n11, 219,
    269
Darwin, Charles, 91, 377
Darwinism, 70
Daube, D., 181n59
David (king),163n22
Davidic kings,163n22
Davidic messiah, 215
Davidson, Richard, 375
Davies, Stevan, 189, 262n183
Davies W. D., 181n59
Davis, Percival, 82n77
Dawsey, James, 153n8
death
  as agent. See Paul
  as cessation of life, 228
Decalogue, 174n41. See also Ten Com-
    mandments
deep things of God. See Paul
de Félice, Philippe, 94